# Selected Letters of
# RAYMOND CHANDLER

books by Frank MacShane

THE LIFE OF RAYMOND CHANDLER
THE LIFE OF JOHN O'HARA

# Selected Letters of
# RAYMOND CHANDLER

EDITED BY
## Frank MacShane

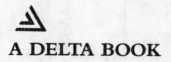

## A DELTA BOOK

A DELTA BOOK
Published by
Dell Publishing Co., Inc.
1 Dag Hammarskjold Plaza
New York, New York 10017

Delta® TM 755118, Dell Publishing Co., Inc.

ISBN: 0-385-29531-6

Reprinted by arrangement with Columbia University Press

Printed in the United States of America

February 1987

10 9 8 7 6 5 4 3 2 1

# Contents

# Chronology

| | |
|---|---|
| 1947 | Wrote original screenplay *Playback* for Universal. |
| 1949 | Publication of *The Little Sister* by Houghton Mifflin and by Hamish Hamilton. |
| 1950 | Publication of *The Simple Art of Murder* (early stories) by Houghton Mifflin and by Hamish Hamilton. Worked on screenplay of *Strangers on a Train* for Warner Brothers. |
| 1952 | Trip to England with Cissy. |
| 1953 | Publication of *The Long Goodbye* by Hamish Hamilton; published by Houghton Mifflin in 1954. |
| 1954 | Death of Cissy. |
| 1955 | Attempted suicide, trip to England. |
| 1956–1957 | Lived both in London and in La Jolla. |
| 1958 | Publication of *Playback* (novel) by Hamish Hamilton and by Houghton Mifflin. |
| 1959 | Died in La Jolla, March 26. |

# The Recipients

(The list does not include most editors of periodicals and correspondents personally unknown to Chandler.)

CLEVE ADAMS: Fellow detective writer and contributor to *Black Mask* magazine.

FREDERICK LEWIS ALLEN: Editor of *Harper's Magazine* and writer.

ALEX BARRIS: Canadian journalist and interviewer.

BERNICE BAUMGARTEN: Editor at Brandt and Brandt literary agency and wife of James Gould Cozzens. Miss Baumgarten handled booklength fiction at the agency.

JEAN BETHEL: Wife of Erle Stanley Gardner.

CARL BRANDT: Chandler's agent (1948–1952) and head of Brandt and Brandt literary agency. Brandt handled magazine publications for the agency.

PAUL BROOKS: President of Houghton Mifflin Company.

JAMES M. CAIN: American author of *Double Indemnity*, *The Postman Always Rings Twice*, and other novels.

ALAN K. CAMPBELL: Assistant Director of the Harvard Summer School.

ROBERT CAMPIGNY: French literary critic and reviewer.

EDGAR CARTER: Associate in H. N. Swanson literary agency, Hollywood.

GEORGE HARMON COXE: Fellow detective writer and contributor to *Black Mask* magazine.

FREDERICK DANNAY: With Manfred Lee, author of books published under the pseudonym of Ellery Queen.

JEAN DE LEON: Chandler's London secretary.

BERGEN EVANS: American language expert.

IAN FLEMING: English author of spy novels.

JAMES N. FOX: Dutch-born writer of adventure novels.

J. FRANCIS: Proprietor of Prince's Bookshop, Piccadilly, London.

ERLE STANLEY GARDNER:  Fellow detective novelist and contributor to *Black Mask*.

DOROTHY GARDINER:  Secretary of Mystery Writers of America and later co-editor of *Raymond Chandler Speaking*.

DEIRDRE GARTRELL:  Young Australian correspondent whom Chandler never met.

PHILIP GASKELL:  Bibliophile and librarian of King's College, Cambridge.

WILLIAM GAULT:  Detective writer and novelist, author of *Bloody Bokhara*, *Ring Around Rosa*, and many other books—living in California.

MICHAEL GILBERT:  English mystery writer and Chandler's solicitor in London.

HELGA GREENE:  Chandler's last literary agent and later his executrix and heir.

MAURICE GUINNESS:  English detective novelist, a cousin of Helga Greene.

HAMISH HAMILTON:  Chandler's English publisher.

JOHN HERSEY:  American novelist.

ALFRED HITCHCOCK:  English film director.

H. F. HOSE:  Chandler's contemporary and a master at Dulwich College.

JOHN HOUSEMAN:  Hollywood producer of *The Blue Dahlia* and many other films and plays.

JAMES HOWARD:  Official of Mystery Writers of America.

HOWARD HUNT:  Author and diplomat, later involved in Watergate scandals under President Nixon.

JAMES KEDDIE:  Sherlock Holmes enthusiast and book collector; member of the "Baker Street Irregulars."

ALFRED A. KNOPF:  Chandler's first American publisher.

BLANCHE KNOPF:  Wife of Alfred Knopf and his associate at the publishing house.

GENE LEVITT:  Adaptor of Chandler stories to radio.

LUCIANO LUCANIA:  Known as Lucky Luciano, a well-known Italian-American criminal.

ROGER MACHELL:  Director of Hamish Hamilton Ltd., Chandler's English publishers.

W. SOMERSET MAUGHAM:  English novelist and playwright.

FINLEY McDERMID:  Production head at M.G.M. studios, Hollywood.

JUANITA MESSICK:  Chandler's secretary in La Jolla for many years.

NEIL MORGAN:  Columnist for San Diego *Evening Tribune*.

CHARLES MORTON:  Associate Editor of *The Atlantic Monthly*.

HARDWICK MOSELEY:  Sales Manager at Houghton Mifflin Company.

E. JACK NEUMAN:  Writer and adaptor of Chandler's stories to television.

LUTHER NICHOLS:  Book editor of the San Francisco *Examiner*.

FRANK NORMAN:  English novelist and playwright. Chandler wrote the preface for his first book, *Bang to Rights*.

ERIC PARTRIDGE:  English literary critic and lexicographer, author of *A Dictionary of Slang and Unconventional English* in which he frequently cited Chandler.

S. J. PERELMAN:  American writer and humorist, frequent contributor to *The New Yorker*. He parodied Chandler in a story called "Farewell, My Lovely Appetizer."

J. B. PRIESTLEY:  English novelist and playwright, author of *Rain Upon Godshill*, *Let the People Sing* and many other books.

LEONARD RUSSELL:  English critic, literary editor of the *Sunday Times* of London.

JAMES SANDOE:  Librarian at the University of Colorado, critic and reviewer of detective fiction.

WILLIAM W. SEWARD:  Professor at Tift College, Forsyth, Georgia.

SOL SIEGEL:  Executive at Twentieth Century-Fox studio in Hollywood.

JOSEPH SISTROM:  Producer at Paramount studio, connected with various films Chandler worked on.

WILBUR SMITH:  Librarian and head of Special Collections at the University of California at Los Angeles. Chandler's papers are now collected there.

RAY STARK:  Hollywood agent representing clients of Carl Brandt, later a producer.

H. N. SWANSON:  Hollywood literary agent, known for representing such writers as Faulkner, Fitzgerald, O'Hara and Chandler.

WILLIAM TARG:  New York publisher, connected with various houses.

E. C. THIESSEN:  Assistant Treasurer, *The Atlantic Monthly*.

WILLIAM TOWNEND:  School friend of Chandler's from Dulwich College.

JESSICA TYNDALE:  Friend of Chandler's in New York and representative of Guinness Mahon bank in America.

DALE WARREN:  Publicity director of Houghton Mifflin Company.

EDWARD WEEKS:  Editor of *The Atlantic Monthly*.

LEROY WRIGHT:  Chandler's lawyer in San Diego.

# Introduction

"I have written letters that would have made Eros hysterical and I have also written long serious letters on literary technique as well as I understand it," wrote Raymond Chandler to his publisher. Chandler was not a vain man, but he understood his capabilities. "It is true," he said, "that in letters I sometimes seem to have been more penetrating than in any other kind of writing—at times—and that as I reread some of them, I am really astonished,—astonished at the facility of expression and the range of thought I seemed to show even when I was only a struggling beginner."

In an age when the telephone has gradually killed off correspondence, Chandler, the author of such internationally famous mystery novels as *The Big Sleep*, *Farewell, My Lovely*, and *The Long Goodbye*, was one of the greatest letter writers of his time. "I don't know why the hell I write so many letters," he noted. "I guess," he answered himself, "my mind is just too active for my own good."

Chandler began his literary career in London after leaving Dulwich College in 1905. Although born in the United States, in 1888, he had been educated in England. When his American father deserted the family, his Anglo-Irish mother took him to England to stay with her relatives in London. Chandler's pre-World War I schooling equipped him with a classical education and wistful sentiments. Like his contemporary, T. S. Eliot, he wrote melancholy romantic poems and sketches about shabby houses and empty streets. Chandler contributed to a number of literary weeklies in Bloomsbury but failed to make a go of it. He therefore returned to America and settled in Los Angeles. He learned accounting and became a bookkeeper in a number of banks, dairies, and other commercial establishments. After the war, in which he served in France with the Canadian army, he returned once more to California. He eventually became employed by the Dabney Oil Syndicate and rose to become office manager and director of several of its subsidiary companies.

For the ten years he worked in the oil business, Chandler seems to have been oblivious of literature, although he knew cultured and literary people in Los Angeles. He lived with his mother, and after she died, he married Cissy Pascal, an accomplished pianist who divorced her husband in order to marry him. She was seventeen years older than Chandler was, but when he married her he didn't know she was so much older nor did she look it. In time, however, Chandler seems to have grown discontented with his life. He started to drink, and finding himself often in the company of his younger contemporaries, he began to look for women younger and more exciting than Cissy was. By 1932, the situation had reached a crisis, and he was fired from his job for alcoholism. Despite the bad times, the jolt was sufficient to make him want to take up writing again. Although he had published nothing, he listed himself as a writer in the Los Angeles phone book and began his first serious apprenticeship as a fiction writer. He lived on savings and on money provided by his friends who had faith in his capacities.

Chandler wanted to be a "serious" writer and tried to imitate Hemingway and other prominent writers of the time, but his critical mind always interfered and made him feel inadequate. Then one day he came across some pulp magazines specializing in detective fiction. He decided to try his hand at this genre and soon found it congenial. Because no one took this kind of writing seriously, he did not feel inhibited by his own or anybody else's standards. He read and imitated the work of such established writers of the "tough guy" school of American detective fiction as Erle Stanley Gardner and Dashiell Hammett. By 1933, he published his first story in *Black Mask*, the most celebrated detective magazine of the period. Over the next five or six years, he continued to write stories and novellas, gradually developing his skill and extending his range. In 1939, he published his first novel, *The Big Sleep*. Although this book did not make his reputation overnight, among detective story enthusiasts it established him as one of the most brilliant new members of the "hard-boiled" school of crime fiction.

Over the next four years, he brought out *Farewell, My Lovely*, *The High Window*, and *The Lady in the Lake*. Together, they established Chandler's literary reputation, but they did not provide him the income he had expected. Paperback sales were then not so lucrative as they have since become for popular writers. He therefore began writing screenplays for Hollywood. His appearance at Paramount and other studios coincided with the growing popularity of such gangster and crime films as *The Maltese Falcon*. His first job was to collaborate with Billy Wilder on a screen version of James M. Cain's *Double Indemnity*. The film was a success and Chandler was given other assignments. But Chandler disliked working in the studios. As an artist, he was too independent to accept willingly the interference with and alteration of his work by other writers and by directors for whom he had little respect. When he had earned enough to live on, he withdrew from Hollywood and moved with Cissy to La Jolla where he lived for most of the rest of his life.

By this time, he had become world famous as a writer, and his next books, *The Little Sister* and *The Long Goodbye*, established him not simply as an American crime writer of the first rank, but as a novelist who rendered the actualities of American life as vividly and independently as any "straight" novelist. It was a triumph of style that he was able to transform a limited type of fiction into something having universal appeal. He virtually created Los Angeles as a literary entity, and this was the great achievement of the last decade of his life.

Despite the worldly qualities of his novels and the colorful life of his central character, Philip Marlowe, Chandler was himself a retiring person. Even in Hollywood, he had been a recluse. "I suppose in some ways I was a bit of a stinker in Hollywood," he wrote. "No swimming pool, no stone marten coats for a floozie in an apartment, no charge account at Romanoff's, no parties, no ranch with riding horses, none of the trimmings at all." Chandler found social activity difficult because he needed alcohol to relax. But if he drank, he tended to lose control of himself and to drink too much. It was safer to stay at home, especially as Cissy was now in her late seventies and tiring easily.

Driven more and more to depend on his own resources, Chandler turned to letter writing as a means of communicating with the outside world. He passed the long insomniac evenings after Cissy had gone to bed writing to correspondents from all over the world. Mostly he wrote to business associates—his publishers, agents, magazine editors, or professional critics of detective fiction. Rarely did he correspond with other writers or those whose letters might have nourished him as surely his delighted others. But his correspondence meant so much to him that he said, "all of my best friends I have never met."

For Chandler, letter writing was an emotional release from his isolation. Discussing his letters with his English publisher, he noted that "some are analytical, some are a bit poetical, some sad, and a good many caustic or even funny. They reveal, I suppose, a writer's reaction to his early struggles and later his attempts to ward off the numerous people who seek to exploit him in some way. There are also love letters and letters to an unknown girl in Australia which were merely a rather kind attempt to resolve her problems after she had given me more of her heart than (as she said) she had ever given to any of her family." These letters were also an important outlet for a writer who, in order to achieve success in fiction writing, had restricted himself to detective stories. There was so much left over, crying to get out. "A real writer," Chandler wrote, "and at times I think I am one, exists on many levels of thought. Perhaps as a result of my business training I always knew that a writer had to follow a line with which the public would become familiar. He had to 'type' himself to the extent that the public would associate his name (if they remembered it) with a certain kind of writing. But that would not be enough for him in his own mind. So I suppose in my letters I more or less revealed those facets of my mind which had to be obscured or distorted in what I wrote for publication."

Chandler dictated many of his letters onto discs while sitting in his study late at night, and the next day the secretary typed them up. Taken together, they are more like a writer's notebook than ordinary correspondence. A letter might begin with a business matter, but soon Chandler would move on to more enchanting subjects—his childhood in England, the position of the writer in Hollywood, his current reading, what it takes to be a novelist, or the mores of Southern California, where he lived like an alien in his own country, half-amused, half-outraged by the world around him.

Chandler never held back in his letters. He expressed his feelings and beliefs bluntly and honestly. He was a man of passion who could also express ideas in a rational and convincing way. His letters reveal the man behind Philip Marlowe as a writer who understands art and beauty but who has no patience with the pretentiousness that is so often a part of the literary life. His prose is forceful and vigorous, the product of a classical education that gave him a sense of form and structure. His feelings arise from his sensitivity to his surroundings, and he expresses them in metaphor, using a street vocabulary that keeps all phoniness at bay.

Many writers reserve their best energies for their own novels, short stories, or poems. Others reverse the process and waste their creative powers on correspondence. The peculiar circumstances of Chandler's life placed him in between these extremes. Chandler probably would not have written more fiction had he corresponded less. He took the detective story about as far as it could go in *The Long Goodbye.* Anything else would have been a repetition. Chandler's letters are long and generous because he had much more to say and because in his loneliness he wanted to express his thoughts and feelings to whoever would write him in return.

After his wife's death in 1954, Chandler began a slow decline. The last five years of his life were marked by frantic attempts to find a solution to loneliness, and his letters are filled with details of his domestic life as he moved back and forth from California to England in search of solace. As his life fell apart through drink and illness, his letters became less interesting and more verbose. Still, he knew he had made his mark. Swinburne once wrote that to publish an author's private letters was "to commit a despicable act of felony." But in his own lifetime Chandler had enough sense of his achievement to consider this possibility himself, even though he had doubts about the value of his letters to others: "Please believe I am not asking you to publish them at all," he wrote his English publisher, "merely wondering whether they could possibly be of enough interest to be worth publishing."

Over the years since his death on March 26, 1959 Chandler's letters have been frequently quoted in books and magazines. This testimony to their lasting power helps explain why they are gathered together here. They document a sad but decent life and also the achievement of one of the finest letter writers American literature has produced over the last two hundred years.

    •        •    

The texts of the letters are reproduced as Chandler wrote them, except for a few editorial changes. Chandler was often inconsistent in punctuation, spelling, and dating his letters, and for consistency I have italicized the names of books and films. I have also corrected obvious misspellings and typographical errors, and have supplied single words that were accidentally dropped. I have also changed Chandler's use of quotation marks, which was sometimes American, sometimes British, and sometimes a combination of the two, to standard American usage. I have not standardized Chandler's spellings, however, but have preserved the British and American variants, and I have left the dates of his letters as he had written them. The correspondents, for the most part, are identified in the list of recipients (see p. ix). Brief footnotes have been supplied within the letters where necessary.

The letters reproduced in this collection fall into different categories. The first are reproduced from signed original letters or photocopies of original letters. The second category consists of carbon copies of letters dictated or written by Chandler. These do not contain any emendations that might have been made on the original letters, nor are they signed. Therefore, they have been reproduced here without signatures. A few of the letters here reproduced have been taken from transcripts made of Chandler's correspondence by Dorothy Gardiner when she was preparing a collection of Chandler's writing called *Raymond Chandler Speaking*. I have indicated these by footnotes in the text. These transcripts are less reliable than original letters, since Miss Gardiner occasionally altered the word order or made cuts, without, however, changing the substance of a given letter. There are fewer than ten letters taken from transcripts; all the other letters in this collection are reproduced from the first two categories cited—original letters or carbon copies.

Wherever possible, I have reproduced the complete letter. On occasion, however, I have deleted material, and for any of three reasons: (1) the same information may have already appeared in another letter; (2) the material excised may be of no enduring interest (generally such omitted material relates to business matters Chandler has brought up with his agent or one of his publishers); (3) the material omitted may be private and perhaps hurtful to someone still living. All substantial excisions are indicated by three dots widely spaced between paragraphs.

Occasionally there are excisions within a sentence indicated by ellipses. These generally indicate that the material omitted is private and possibly damaging to a living individual. In the few letters reproduced by Dorothy Gardiner's transcripts, there are also ellipses, but I cannot explain the reason for the cuts she made. Sometimes an individual's name is indicated by a blank line, but as with other omissions, these are rare. Every effort has been made to keep the letters as complete as possible within the limits of taste and common sense.

.  .  .

Chandler's letters are found in three different types of collection. The first of these are university and public libraries. The largest of these is the Chandler collection in the Department of Special Collections at the library of the University of California at Los Angeles. Chandler himself helped establish this collection, and it contains, apart from books and manuscripts, original letters and photocopies of letters to many individuals such as James Sandoe and John Houseman. Dorothy Gardiner's transcripts have also been deposited in this collection. Other university libraries contain small collections: Boston University has Chandler's correspondence with Charles Morton of the *Atlantic Monthly*; Harvard has letters from Chandler to Dale Warren, Hardwick Moseley, and others at Houghton Mifflin Company; Indiana University owns Chandler's letters to Ian Fleming and Frank Norman; the Library of Congress has a letter to James Cain from Chandler; the University of Texas owns letters between Chandler and Erle Stanley Gardner, Somerset Maugham, and J. B. Priestley; Yale owns Chandler's letters to George Harmon Coxe.

The second category consists of large private collections. The most important of these is owned by Helga Greene, Chandler's agent and literary executor. This collection is in fact made up of Chandler's own private files, and it contains original letters as well as carbon copies and drafts of letters. Other large collections are those owned by Brandt & Brandt, Chandler's agents; Hamish Hamilton Ltd., his English publishers; and Alfred Knopf Inc., his first American publishers.

Smaller collections, which make up the third category, are owned by the *Atlantic Monthly*, Jean DeLeon, William Gault, James M. Fox, Juanita Messick, Neil Morgan, Dilys Powell, Jessica Tyndale, and Leroy Wright. I am grateful to all of these individuals and institutions for their help and kindness in making this correspondence available.

In addition, I should like to thank a number of individuals who have helped me in various ways. Some have called my attention to letters or have lent me those in their possession; others have gone out of their way to be helpful in other ways. I wish to record my thanks to all of them, and in particular Hilda Bohene, Carl Brandt, William Cagle, George Harmon Coxe, Bernard Crystal, Keith Deutsch, David Farmer, Donald Gallup, Deirdre Gartrell, Philip Gaskell, Howard Gotlieb, Hamish Hamilton, John Houseman, Howard Hunt, James Keddie, William Koshland, Elfrieda Lang, Gene Levitt, Kenneth Lohf, Roger Machell, James Mink, E. Jack Neuman, Frank Norman, Austin Olney, Robert S. Powell, Kathrine Sorley Walker, Edward Weeks, Stanley Wertheim, and Brooke Whiting. I hope I have not inadvertently omitted the name of anyone whose name should be here.

Above all, I am grateful to Helga Greene for her warm and consistent help to me with this project. Without her kindness and generosity, this book would never have been made possible.

Frank MacShane

# The Letters

## TO THE EDITOR OF
## *THE FORTNIGHTLY INTRUDER*[1]

June 15, 1937

Sirs:

Your essay on flower arrangement is priceless, as much so as the typography of your sheet, but to what audience in heaven's name do you address yourselves? You are precious, you write in a dead language, and in the delicate and occasionally sterile tones of the Eighteenth Century. You are of a pretty wit and a soothing yet deadly irony. Are there people who admire such fanciful tricks? I have lived in this city for some twenty-five years and now I find you, apparently also of its citizenry, dwelling with Chinese calm in a past that was even then as improbable as the novels of Richardson. Occasionally, also, as dull.

Your little paper one receives with pleasure, and yet with a certain discomfort, like a voice from an ancient chimney on a gusty October night. One hears death in it, and is tired of hearing death in so many things. You are decadent in an environment which, for all its fancy pants, is still provincial. You have the deadly smoothness of an old pistol grip.

It is only a few short years since I was told, with more emphasis than hope, that the American gentleman did not spit. Doth

---

1. A bibliophile's magazine, edited by William K. Etter, Jr. and published in Los Angeles. The text of the letter, including its omissions, is taken directly from the magazine.

he not so? I thought, then someday I shall meet him. Of course I did, but not so soon as I thought.

Who, except those by life already defeated and wasting in the twilight, has any taste for such writing as yours? I ask to know. Perhaps we are on the verge of a classic revival. God knows I am very tired of talking without moving my lips. But I'm a little afraid you are received too much with kindness, too little with understanding, that you come as a nostalgia for the Age of Culture (whatever that is, and may it rot, if it must be called by that odious word), and that you are accepted with that bewildered desperation which the Ladies of the Friday Morning Club reserved for the visiting English novelists of the tepid years before the War.

You too, Sirs, I should like to think of with gardenias in your morning coats, with grey-striped trousers of impeccable vicuna, with parted hair, and with the soft birdsong of the Oxford close in your gentle throats. But I'm afraid you wear corduroy pants and talk the flat language of the dehydrated New Englander. It is almost certain to be so. This American mind has its peculiar thinness. It acquires learning only by losing blood.

I wish you success—and can not, alas, predict it.

Sirs, Your Obedient Humble Servant,

R.C., Esqr.

## TO THE EDITOR OF
## *THE FORTNIGHTLY INTRUDER*

July 1, 1937

You do kid rather easily, don't you, pals? That I state a case against you is bosh. I pay you grave compliments and you mistake them for sneers. I call you precious, being precious myself. As to the corduroy pants, the remark was dated. It slipped out of my 1928 Anthology.

[2]

That you should have pride in your purer American heritage of language seems to me a slight thing. Latin became corrupt, but French is a sharper language than Latin ever was. The best writing in English today is done by Americans, but not in any purist tradition. They have roughed the language around as Shakespeare did and done it the violence of melodrama and the press box. They have knocked over tombs and sneered at the dead. Which is as it should be. There are too many dead men and there is too much talk about them.

But all this is beside the point, and still I lack the information for which I wrote to you the first time. It was kind of you to answer so soon, and at all. But who reads you? One knows, roughly, what sort of people read the *Post*, *Esquire*, *Terror Tales*, *New Republic*, *Mercury*, and the grand old man of Arlington Street, the *Atlantic*. But one suspects in the last case, where there is definite intention to preserve clarity of thought and expression and to exclude the sophisticated gimcracks of the cocktail mob, not only a paucity of support—which is a fact—, but a large element of snob readers whose minds are marionettes as completely as the fans of _____ or the followers of _____ .

You see, I have lived here so long. I have perhaps been unfortunate, but I have not met the people who would like your kind of writing, unless someone first told them they must like to be saved.

R.C., Esq.

# TO ALFRED A. KNOPF

Route 1, Box 421
Riverside, Calif
Feb. 19th. 1939

Dear Mr. Knopf:—
Please accept my thanks for your friendly letter and please believe that, whether you wrote to me or not, I should have written to thank you for the splendid send-off you are trying to give me.

[3]

Having been more or less in business a great part of my life, I have some appreciation of what this involves, even though I know nothing of the publishing business.

Mr. Conroy wrote to me twice that you had said something about my getting to work on another book and I answered him that I wanted to put it off until I had an idea what kind of reception this one would get. I have only seen four notices, but two of them seemed more occupied with the depravity and unpleasantness of the book than with anything else. In fact the notice from the *New York Times*, which a clipping agency sent me as a come-on, deflated me pretty thoroughly. I do not want to write depraved books. I was aware that this yarn had some fairly unpleasant citizens in it, but my fiction was learned in a rough school, and I probably didn't notice them much. I was more intrigued by a situation where the mystery is solved by the exposition and understanding of a single character, always well in evidence, rather than by the slow and sometimes long-winded concatenation of circumstances. That's a point which may not interest reviewers of first novels, but it interested me very much. However, there's a very good notice in today's *Los Angeles Times* and I don't feel quite such a connoisseur of moral decay as I did yesterday. They have Humphrey Bogart playing the lead, which I am in favor of also.[1] It only remains to convince Warner Brothers.

As to the next job of work for your consideration, I should like, if you approve, to try to jack it up a few more notches. It must be kept sharp, swift and racy, of course, but I think it could be a little less harsh—or do you not agree? I should like to do something which would not be automatically out for pictures and which yet would not let down whatever public I may acquire. *The Big Sleep* is very unequally written. There are scenes that are all right, but there are other scenes still much too pulpy. Insofar as I am able I want to develop an objective method—but slowly—to the point where I can carry an audience over into a genuine dramatic, even melodramatic, novel, written in a very vivid and pungent style, but not slangy or overly vernacular. I realize that this must be done cautiously and little by little, but I think it can be done. To acquire delicacy without losing power, that's the problem. But I should

1. In the film version of the novel, which was directed by Howard Hawks.

probably do a minimum of three mystery novels before I try anything else.

Thank you again and I do hope that when the returns are in, you will be not too disappointed.

Very sincerely,

Raymond Chandler

## TO GEORGE HARMON COXE

Route 1 Box 421 Riverside
April 9th. 1939

Dear George:—

Thanks for your letter, and I much appreciate your remarks about it and about the detective story business in general. I had a talk with Sanders[1] while he was out here, and after that I'm surprized that anyone writes or publishes the darn things at all. He told me about Simon and Schuster's Inner Sanctum mysteries, for instance. Yet about 150 mystery books are dished out every year. I suppose if you are good enough there is a bare living in it—very bare. However I'm used to that. I don't think I'd ever make the grade with slick magazines, unless in some kind of story quite different from anything I have attempted so far. I can't read their stuff for my own amusement, and that seems to be fatal. I should never have tried to work for *Black Mask*, if I hadn't, at one time, got a kick out of reading it.[2]

Knopf seems to think that if somebody comes along who can write as well as Hammett, he should have Hammett's success.[3] Knopf

---

1. Sydney Sanders, Chandler's first literary agent.
2. *Black Mask*, a famous magazine of hard-boiled detective stories, edited by Joseph T. Shaw.
3. Dashiell Hammett, founder of the hard-boiled school and author of such detective novels as *The Maltese Falcon* and *The Dain Curse*.

[5]

being a publisher should know his business, but my feeling is that somebody might come along who wrote a great deal better than Hammett and still not have anything like Hammett's success. But of course these things are quite unpredictable. In my opinion *Thieves Like Us* by Edward Anderson was an infinitely better and honester book than *Of Mice and Men*.[4] Did it get anywhere? I doubt it.

Your letter doesn't sound very happy somehow. I had the idea that you would do well in Hollywood for a long time, that you had enough facility, and that you had enough character not to be impressed by the phoney side. Of course I don't know you very well. Personally I think Hollywood is poison to any writer, the graveyard of talent. I have always thought so. But perhaps I have lived too close to it.

I'm terribly sorry about Shaw.[5] He never told me anything about his affairs, always had the attitude (that rather pathetic attitude of small men trying to maintain their pride) that his failures were his own choice. He had left the *Black Mask* on a matter of policy and he had left the agency he was with because too much was going on for a man to do his own thinking. That sort of attitude, not those words. I suppose it's natural enough. It's bad enough to be kicked in the seat of the pants without having to go around and show the bruise. But as to his success or lack of it as an agent I knew absolutely nothing, except what I might deduce from the fact that he had no secretary. I think it was natural for him to think an opportunity existed for a type of agent who might be more than a marketer of merchandise. In the long run, if he could stick it out, and if he was adaptable enough, there might have been. Unfortunately he is not very adaptable and he wants to run his writers. The only kind of writers you can run are the ones who are negative, and they're hardly worth running. It's too tough a racket for people who have to be propped up from behind. Yet Shaw has, strangely enough, a great insight into writing and he can give a man a buck up when he needs it as nobody else I know can, or does. That should be worth a lot somewhere. I agree with you that he ought to have a magazine. I'd like to see him have the magazine which for years I've wondered somebody did not think worth publishing, a high class pulp detective

4. Novel by John Steinbeck.
5. See note 2.

story magazine aimed at the rather large class of people who find the pulps mostly too juvenile and who don't like the big magazines because of their fundamental dishonesty in the matter of character and motivation. He himself thought the market existed, I know, but he was doubtful about the supply of material. In that I think he was wrong, because the magazine would in a short time create its own material. Sanders told me the big magazines are getting steadily more and more starved for material, largely because of the lowering of prices and standards in the pulps. New writers do not appear to replace the ones who go to Hollywood and either stay there or learn how not to write there and never get over it. And the new writers don't appear because there's nothing in the business anymore, no encouragement to do good work, and no recognition if, in spite of all practical considerations, you insist on trying to do it. I think the effect of this will be that some of the slick magazines will become more catholic in their tastes, more receptive to stories without Boy Meets Girl motivation, even to stories with unsatisfactory endings. Probably there will be some lowering of rates to balance some loss of cheap chic advertising. But in the long run there will be better and more readable magazines. I'm hoping.

If you come out to the Coast to live, you should look at La Jolla, before you decide where to live. I think it is a much better place than Laguna in every possible way. It is dear for a small town, but it has a perfect climate both winter and summer, the finest coastline on the Pacific side of the country, no billboards or concessions or beachfront shacks, an air of cool decency and good manners that is almost startling in California. It has a few writers, not too many, no Bohemian atmosphere (but they will let you take a drink). It has fine public tennis courts and a nice gang of people who play good, but not *too* good, tennis. It has good schools, including a very fine private girls school, a hospital, and is one of the most prosperous looking places you ever laid eyes on. I'm not being paid by the Chamber of Commerce either. I simply feel that La Jolla has that intangible air of good breeding, which one imagines may still exist in New England, but which certainly does not exist any more in or around Los Angeles. In theory one may not value very much that quality. One may like a free and easy neighborhood where they smash the empty bottles on the sidewalk on Saturday night. But in practice it's very comfortable. I expect to go back there in the fall, because

[7]

whatever is the matter with me, climate seems to make very little difference, and I hate these poor man's towns. My idea of perfection would be a home in La Jolla and a very good cabin at Big Bear Lake, not too close to Pine Knot. Maybe I'll have them before my joints begin to creak very badly.

Regards and best wishes. If you write again, send me news of Nebel.[6] I've never met him, but I have always thought a lot of him.

Ray

# TO ERLE STANLEY GARDNER

Route 1 Box 421
Riverside, California
May 5th 1939

Dear Erle,

When we were talking about the old *Action Detective* magazine I forgot to tell you that I learned to write a novelette on one of yours about a man named Rex Kane, who was an alter ego of Ed Jenkins and got mixed up with some flowery dame in a hilltop house in Hollywood who was running an anti-blackmail organization. You wouldn't remember. It's probably in your file No. 54276–84. The idea, probably not at all original to me, was so good that I tried to work it out on another tyro later on, but he couldn't see putting the effort into something he knew he couldn't sell, preferring to put the effort into nineteen things he thought he could sell and couldn't. I simply made an extremely detailed synopsis of your story and from that rewrote it and then compared what I had with yours, and then went back and rewrote it some more, and so on. It looked pretty good. Incidentally, I found out that the trickiest part of your technique was the ability to put over situations which verged on the

6. Frederick Nebel, fellow *Black Mask* writer.

[8]

implausible but which in the reading seemed quite real. I hope you understand that I mean this as a compliment. I have never come even near to doing it myself. Dumas had this quality in a very strong degree. Also Dickens. It's probably the fundamental of all rapid work, because naturally rapid work has a large measure of improvisation, and to make an improvised scene seem inevitable is quite a trick. At least I think so.

And here I am at 2.30 A.M. writing about technique, in spite of a strong conviction that the moment a man begins to talk about technique, that's proof he is fresh out of ideas.

Best wishes to you all,

Chandler

## TO BLANCHE KNOPF

Box 481 Big Bear Lake Calif<br>August 23rd. 1939

Dear Mrs. Knopf:

The effort to keep my mind off the war has reduced me to the mental age of seven. The things by which we live are the distant flashes of insect wings in a clouded sunlight. But——

I enjoyed meeting you so much. There is a touch of the desert about everything in California, and about the minds of the people who live here. During the years when I hated the place I couldn't get away, and now that I have grown to need the harsh smell of the sage I still feel rather out of place here. But my wife is a New Yorker, and that 95 with unlimited humidity doesn't appeal much either.

If I could write another 12,000 words I should have a draft of a book finished. I know what to write, but I have momentarily mislaid the urge. However by the end of September, as you said, there should be something for you to wrinkle your very polite nose at. It's rather a mixed up mess that will run 75,000 words but I'll likely cut it at least 5000 and perhaps more. It will take me a month to shape it up. The title, if you should happen to approve, is *The Second Murderer*.[1] Please refer to King Richard III, Act I, Scene IV.

Second Murderer:     What, shall we stab him when he sleeps?

First Murderer:     No; then he will say 'twas done cowardly
when he wakes . . . .
How dost thou feel thyself now?

Second Murderer:     'Faith, some certain dregs of conscience are yet within me.

However the joker is that the second murderer is———?

    Sanders has been impressing on me the dire necessity of so contriving a detective story that it might be serialized. This is only horse sense, even though good serials seldom make good novels. I do not think this particular opus is the one he is looking for. In fact, I'm very sure of it. I'm not sure anyone is looking for it, but there's a law against burning trash up here during the fire hazard.

        Yours very truly,

                Raymond Chandler


## TO GEORGE HARMON COXE

                      Box 481
                      Big Bear Lake Calif.
                      October 17th. 1939

Dear George:

I have never made any money out of writing. I work too slowly, throw away too much, and what I write that sells is not at all the sort of thing I really want to write. I often envy these lads whose minds

1.  Original title of Chandler's second novel, published as *Farewell, My Lovely*.

are tuned to the sort of story the slick magazines like—so that they really think it is good. I can't get around to that point of view. I sold a story to the *Post*[1] recently, but I wrote it principally because Sanders pestered me to try something for *Collier's*. I didn't think much of the story when I wrote it—I felt that it was artificial, untrue and emotionally dishonest like all slick fiction. Sanders didn't seem to think much of it either. However he sold it. I still don't know whether it is any good. When I read it in print I thought it was, but print can be so deceiving. On the other hand one of my oldest friends took the trouble to write me two pages telling me how lousy it was. I suppose you have had the same experience. Whatever you do you get smacked in the face and usually from an unprotected angle.

Is your house built and are you in it? How are you getting along? I suppose if I read the right magazines, I should know. I should like to come east very much and find somewhere to live there that is not too hot and full of mosquitos (or mosquitoes) in summer and not too damn cold in winter. Is there such a place, where a poor man can live? I'm sick of California and the kind of people it breeds. Of course I like La Jolla, but La Jolla is only a sort of escape from reality. It's not typical. Anyhow, it's not in the least a matter of how good California is or how intransigent I am. If after twenty years I still fail to like the place, it seems that the case is hopeless. My wife came from New York. She likes California except during the hot months, but I think she agrees with me that the percentage of phonies in the population is increasing. No doubt in years, or centuries to come, this will be the center of civilization, if there is any left, but the melting-pot stage bores me horribly. I like people with manners, grace, some social intuition, an education slightly above the Reader's Digest fan, people whose pride of living does not express itself in their kitchen gadgets and their automobiles. I distrust Jews, although I admit that the really nice Jew is probably the salt of the earth. I don't like people who can't sit for half an hour without a glass in their hands, although apart from that I think I should prefer an amiable drunk to Henry Ford. I like a conservative atmosphere, a sense of the past, I like everything that Americans of past generations used to go and look for in Europe, but at the same time I don't want to be bound by the rules. It all seems like asking a bit too much,

1. *Saturday Evening Post.*

now that I've written it. I like all the things about England which Margaret Halsey[2] liked and many of the things she didn't like, but that is largely because I was brought up there and English manners don't intimidate me. But I don't like Margaret Halsey, or any writer for whom a laborious and fizzled wisecrack is better than a simple truth.

.　　　　　.　　　　　.

Let's hear your news

Ray

## TO GEORGE HARMON COXE

1265 Park Row
La Jolla Calif.
Dec 19th. 1939

Dear George:
Thanks for your nice meaty letter of October 30th. which I hasten to answer with my usual headlong dash for the basket. Also for the photo of your house. It must be nice to have a home. We haven't had one in so long that I look back with a touch of nostalgia to any place we have stayed in as long as six months. I don't think we shall be here long either. Too dear, too damp, too elderly, a nice place, as a visitor remarked this afternoon, for old people and their parents.

If you still have that spare copy of your last book but one I'm hoping you are still feeling generous about it. The stock in the local library is all out anyway. You're not represented. But so are not a lot of other people who should be, and so *are* represented some mighty feeble gestures at detective fiction. What do you make of a place that has one book by Hemingway, nothing by Faulkner, or Hammett,

2. Margaret Halsey, *With Malice Towards Some*, 1938.

[12]

two pieces of oh-so-irritating wise guy crap by one Kurt Steel,[1] *everything* by one J. S. Fletcher a British brother who is far far duller than even a British brother has any right to be,[2] nothing by Coxe, Nebel, Whitfield,[3] or anybody you would think of as at all representative. And my god no Gardner, yet a book called *The Bigger They Come* by A. A. Fair which copies the Gardner technique exactly and even swiped Gardner's idea of how Ed Jenkins couldn't be extradited.[4]

I had to throw my second book away, so that leaves me with nothing to show for the last six months and possibly nothing to eat for the next six. But it also leaves the world a far far better place to live in than if I had not thrown it away.

The literary colony here has undergone a few modifications since we were here last year. That is, those of the boys who are making any money are now playing their tennis at the Beach Club. The old caste system at its dirty work again. I don't think the beach club is very expensive, but a few bucks off his whisky ration plays hell with a writer's inspiration. Max Miller[5] still frequents the public courts. He is a tall angular sourpuss with motheaten hair and very surly manners and a habit of swearing under his breath at himself and out loud at his partner. He is a splendid example of the good rule, Never Meet a Writer if You Liked his Book. There is also a dick pulp writer who writes under the name of Dale something or other—I daresay I could find out. Maybe it's Dale Carnegie.[6] This one has the shoulders of a weight-lifter and is very temperamental, throwing rackets and making tragic gestures at the sky, both arms extended and a look of agony on his face. Off hand I would say he is a lead nickel, but you never know. He might be The Shadow.[7]

.        .        .

RC

1.  Author of *Murder of a Dead Man* (1935) and other mystery stories.
2.  Author of *Mill House Murder* (1937), *And Sudden Death* (1938), and many other mystery novels.
3.  George Harmon Coxe, Frederick Nebel, and Raoul Whitfield were all members of the "tough guy" school of American detective fiction.
4.  A. A. Fair was, in fact, a psudonym used by Erle Stanley Gardner.
5.  Author of *I Cover the Waterfront* and a neighbor of Chandler's.
6.  Ronal Kaiser, who wrote under the name of Dale Clark.
7.  Hero of a popular radio series.

## TO BLANCHE KNOPF

818 West Duarte Road
Monrovia
California
January 17th. 1940

Dear Mrs. Knopf:

Terribly sorry to be so dilatory in getting out some work for you. I have had bad luck, bad health and a bad disposition for a long time. I finally did get a very rough draft done but was not at all pleased with it and had to put it aside for a while, in the hope of later discovering. whether it was just plain lousy or whether it was a distorted point of view that made me think so. However I am a bit cheered up about it (in absentia) as my researches have convinced me that just plain lousy is the normal temperature of the detective story.

The troubles of advancing age drove me away from La Jolla. I actually developed a rheumatic right arm. We have not yet found a place to live but hope to soon and when there is a little peace in a world which knows no peace—all I ask is a quiet corner and deaf and dumb neighbors—I'll get at this thing again. You couldn't do anything with it now anyway, I suppose.

With respectful greetings
Most sincerely

Raymond Chandler


## TO BLANCHE KNOPF

1155 Arcadia Avenue Arcadia Calif
June 14th. 1940

Dear Mrs. Knopf:

Sorry I haven't any snapshots to send you yet. I don't know how much time there is. My wife will try to take some, a very agonizing process for both of us, since she is very particular and I am very badly behaved. Commercial photos are no good. I am reaching the age where it takes an artistic touch to make anything of me. The fellows who have this want too much money, and I doubt the importance of the cause. While I am compelled by weight of opinion, some of it expert, some frankly prejudiced, to admit being one of the handsomest men of my generation, I also have to concede that this generation is now a little seedy, and I with it.

The last time no page proofs were sent me. Your Mr. Jacobs with whom I wrangled about this and that felt it was not necessary. I guess it wasn't. I never thought it was. As the book finally appeared there were, I think, two slight typographical errors, which should be a very low average for this kind of book. I certainly don't want to read two sets of proofs, if I don't have to. Nor do I want the set of galley proofs as finally corrected which they sent me. It seems to be a custom, but I regret to say I burned them. Too heavy to carry in my hip pocket.

One thing I should like and that is a few changes in the natty biographical sketch on the jacket, if it is to be repeated. I haven't a copy of the book here, having lent my last copy to a friend who has so far failed to return it. From memory I recall three things I didn't like, one of which was my own fault, the second a misunderstanding, the third a use of the expression "checkered career" which to me has a pejorative connotation. I used the phrase "tax expert." The word expert has become something rather trying. I'd rather omit that. The third point was that your promotion man seemed to get the impression that Dulwich College was a university. It is, in fact, one of the larger English Public Schools, not ranking with Eton, Harrow, Charterhouse, or Marlborough, but certainly ranking ahead of many of those which *Life* made a fuss over in its last issue. Incidentally the editors of *Life* seem entirely unaware that a School Tie and an Old School Tie are entirely different things. But I daresay these pathetic relics of a lost world are no longer worth accuracy.

Fourth point, and one I'm sensitive on, but one which is difficult to make other Americans understand. I am not an Irish-American in the sense commonly understood. I am of Quaker descent on both sides. The Irish family my mother belonged to had not a single Catholic relative or connection, even by marriage. Furthermore the professional classes in Southern Ireland are and always have been

[15]

largely non-Catholic. Those few Irish patriots who have had brains as
well as spite have also been non-Catholics. I should not like to say
that in Ireland Catholicism reached its all-time low of ignorance, dirt
and general degredation of the priesthood, but in my boyhood it
was bad enough. It does the Irish great credit that out of this flannel-
mouthed mob of petty liars and drunkards there has come no real
persecution of the non-Catholic elements.

Most cordially,

Raymond Chandler

## TO GEORGE HARMON COXE

1155 Arcadia Avenue
Arcadia Calif.
June 27th. 1940

Dear George:

On your recommendation and that alone I read Agatha
Christie's *And Then There Were None*, and after reading it I wrote an
analysis of it, because it was blurbed as the perfect crime story,
incapable of dishonesty by reason of the way it was constructed. As
entertainment I liked the first half and the opening, in particular.
The second half got pallid. But as an honest crime story, honest in the
sense that the reader is given a square deal and the motivation and
mechanisms of the murders are sound—it is bunk. The fundamental
conception of the book in particular annoyed me. Here is a judge,
a jurist, a man with a touch of sadism but withal a passion for exact
justice, and this man condemns to death and murders a group of
people on nothing but hearsay evidence. In no case did he have a
shred of actual proof that any one of them had actually committed
murder. In every case it was merely someone's opinion, or a possible,
even probable, inference from circumstances. But proof, even absolute
inner conviction, simply did not exist. Some of these people admit

their crimes, but this is all *after* the murders were planned, the judgment entered, the sentence pronounced. In other words it is as complete and shameless a bamboozling of the reader as ever was perpetrated. And I won't go into the mechanism of the crimes, most of which were predicated on pure chance, and some actually impossible. They also show an abysmal ignorance of lethal drugs and their action. But I'm very glad I read the book because it finally and for all time settled a question in my mind that had at least some lingering doubt attached to it. Whether it is possible to write a strictly honest mystery of the classic type. It isn't. To get the complication you fake the clues, the timing, the play of coincidence, assume certainties where only 50 per cent chances exist at most. To get the surprise murderer you fake character, which hits me hardest of all, because I have a sense of character. If people want to play this game, it's all right by me. But for Christ's sake let's not talk about honest mysteries. They don't exist.

Time out while I take a long breath.

The title of my book is not *The Second Murderer*, and that was not the title I had in mind when I was talking to you. I used that for a while as a working title, but I didn't like it, although Mrs. Knopf did. I didn't know it had been announced under that name. When I turned the manuscript in they howled like hell about the title, which is not at all a mystery title, but they gave in. We'll see. I think the title is an asset. They think it is a liability. One of us has to be wrong. I suppose, since they are in the business, it should be I. On the other hand I have never had any great respect for the ability of editors, publishers, play and picture producers to guess what the public will like. The record is all against them. I have always tried to put myself in the shoes of the ultimate consumer, the reader, and ignore the middleman. I have assumed that there exists in the country a fairly large group of intelligent people, some formally of good education and some educated by life, who like what I like. Of course the real trouble is that you can be read by an enormous number of people who don't buy any books. My book is supposed to come out in August. The proofs were a bloody mess. I've just finished them and don't feel at all that they are a clean job yet.

All the best,

Ray

[17]

## TO BLANCHE KNOPF

449 San Vicente Boulevard
Santa Monica, Oct. 9th. [1940]

Dear Mrs. Knopf:

The above address will be good for six months, I hope.

Thanks for yours of October 1st. which only just caught up with me. I am terribly sorry about the title and all that, and because the advance sales disappointed us, but you must remember that I didn't refuse to change the title, I just couldn't think of another one, you gave me no time at all, and although I said I liked the title, that should not have made you go against your business judgment.[1] Everyone I know likes the title very much, but of course they are not in the trade. And I still think '*Zounds, He Dies* was a good title.[2] If I had had some of the time the book was being prepared, I'm sure I could have come up with something that would have satisfied you. But you caught me off base and got me rattled.

Personally, and in this I am born out by one professional opinion, I think the handicap of the title will be only temporary and that if the sales do not do anything, it will really be for some other cause. For instance, the war. A woman out here who runs a string of rental libraries in and around Hollywood told a friend of mine that one of her branches had ten copies of the book out and that she hardly ever bought more than two copies of a mystery story. She said she thought this was in part due to a "very marvelous" review in the *Hollywood Citizen-News* of Sept 21st. I hope you have seen this. Evidently they jumped the gun on the publication date. Of course it would have only a local influence, but the mere fact that a critic who confessedly does not like mystery stories and thinks they are mostly tripe should take this book seriously as a piece of writing is worth an awful lot to me. Because I am not innately a hack writer.

Syd Sanders sent me a cut of your advertisement in the *New*

1. When Mrs. Knopf objected to *The Second Murderer*, Chandler suggested *Farewell, My Lovely*.
2. Another suggestion Chandler had made.

[18]

*York Times.* I don't see how you can afford it. If that doesn't start something, what's the use?

> With kindest regards,
>
> Raymond Chandler

## TO ERLE STANLEY GARDNER

> 857 Iliff Street
> Pacific Palisades, Calif.
> Feb 1st. 1941

Dear Erle:

Good God, we have moved again.

Thanks very much indeed for sending me that Brentano list, but who is this guy A. A. Fair who heads the list?[1] I got the book and read it and it held one of the three or four unmistakable techniques of detective story writing. And done to the nice crisp light brown that melts in your mouth. What goes on here? I suppose you know what I mean?

Living, if you call it that, in a big apartment house in Santa Monica, brand new and all that, I longed for your ranch. I longed for some place where I could go out at night and listen and hear the grass growing. But of course it wouldn't do for us, just the two of us, even if I had the price of a piece of virgin foothill. It's better over here, quiet and a house in a nice garden. But they are just beginning to build a house across the way. I shan't mind it as much as the good neighbors bouncing on the bed springs over at the apartment house.

Awfully sorry to hear you had been sick. I know what the streps can do to a person. Sulfanilimide seems to be able to cure anything but flat brain, which is what I suffer from.

Regards to your gang,

> Ray

1. Pseudonym used by Gardner.

[19]

# TO BLANCHE KNOPF

12216 Shetland Lane
Los Angeles, Calif.
March 15th. 1942

Dear Mrs. Knopf:

Your letter, kind and charming as always, reaches me at a very bad time. I'm afraid the book is not going to be any good to you.[1] No action, no likable characters, no nothing. The detective does nothing. I understand that it is being typed, which seems like a waste of money, and will be submitted to you, and I'm not sure that that is a good idea, but it is out of my hands. At least I felt that you should be relieved of any necessity of being kind to me in a situation where kindness is probably not of any use. About all I can say by way of extenuation is that I tried my best and seemed to have to get the thing out of my system. I suppose I would have kept tinkering at it indefinitely otherwise.

The thing that rather gets me down is that when I write something that is tough and fast and full of mayhem and murder, I get panned for being tough and fast and full of mayhem and murder, and then when I try to tone down a bit and develop the mental and emotional side of a situation, I get panned for leaving out what I was panned for putting in the first time. The reader expects thus and thus of Chandler because he did it before, but when he did it before he was informed that it might have been much better if he hadn't.

However all this is rather vain now. From now on, if I make mistakes, as no doubt I shall, they will not be made in a futile attempt to avoid making mistakes.

Most sincerely,

Raymond Chandler

1. *The High Window*.

[20]

# TO ALFRED KNOPF[1]

Idyllwild, Calif.
July 16, 1942

Dear Mr. Knopf:

I think the book is a very nice job indeed. I particularly like the type, which being smaller and yet very clear, keeps the page from looking crowded. The jacket also seems to be very effective. My wife does not like the photo on the back. All the photos I sent you were bad, and this is perhaps about the best, except the very first one, which no longer looks like me. I was reading in an English book the other day and noticed the remark, "the kind of squit who has his picture on the dust cover of his book," or something like that. I feel a good deal like that myself. It is the custom in this country, of course, but most writers are such horrible-looking people that their faces destroy something which perhaps wanted to like them. Perhaps I am oversensitive, but I have several times been so repelled by such faces that I have not been able to read the books without the face coming between. Especially these fat crowlike middle-aged women's faces.

# TO BLANCHE KNOPF

Cathedral City, California
October 22nd. 1942

Dear Mrs. Knopf:

Thank you very much for writing to me about the sales of my last story, and many thanks also for your kind invitation to lunch. But alas, I'm down here in the desert 130 miles from Beverly Hills and I'm afraid I simply can't make it this time. I'm trying to bake

1.  Letter reproduced from transcript.

out a sinus condition which has been weakening me for years. Don't expect any luck, but felt it had to be tried. I hope you and Mr. Knopf are well and are bearing up under the many cares of these times.

So sorry you are feeling badly about the sales of *The High Window*.[1] Last time you were out here you told me 4000 copies was the ceiling on a mystery. Either you were just saying that to comfort a broken heart or you are now repining for nothing at all. Why should it sell any more? And why should you spend so much advertising, and such very demanding advertising? I don't know anything about promotion, but when Mr. Knopf was out here he gave me the figures on what had been spent advertising *FML*, and to me they seemed very high.[2] I said: "Can you afford it?" He said: "No." But you keep on doing it. Why? *The High Window* was not the striking and original job of work that could be promoted into anything of consequence. Some people liked it better than my other efforts, some people liked it much less. But nobody went into any screaming fits either way. I'm not disappointed in the sales. I think it did well to get by at all. I am sure Sanders thinks so. I hope the next will be livelier and better and faster, because, as you know very well, it is the pace that counts, not the logic or the plausibility or the style. I have just been reading a book called *Phantom Lady*, by William Irish,[3] whoever that is. It has one of those artificial trick plots and is full of small but excessive demands on the Goddess of Chance, but it is a swell job of writing, one that gives everything to every character, every scene, and never, like so many of our overrated novelists, just flushes the highlights and then gets scared and runs. I happen to admire this kind of writing very much. I haven't seen the book advertised anywhere and such reviews as I have seen of it show a complete unawareness of the technical merits of the book. So what the hell.

But as I said I do hope the next one will be better and that one of these days I shall turn one out that will have that fresh and sudden touch that will click. Most of all perhaps, in my rather sensitive mind, I hope the day will come when I won't have to ride around on

1. Chandler's third novel.
2. *Farewell, My Lovely*.
3. Pseudonym used by Cornell Woolrich, mystery writer.

Hammett and James Cain, like an organ grinder's monkey. Hammett is all right. I give him everything. There were a lot of things he could not do, but what he did he did superbly. But James Cain—faugh! Everything he touches smells like a billygoat. He is every kind of writer I detest, a faux naif, a Proust in greasy overalls, a dirty little boy with a piece of chalk and a board fence and nobody looking. Such people are the offal of literature, not because they write about dirty things, but because they do it in a dirty way. Nothing hard and clean and cold and ventilated. A brothel with a smell of cheap scent in the front parlor and a bucket of slops at the back door. Do I, for God's sake, sound like that? Hemingway with his eternal sleeping bag got to be pretty damn tiresome, but at least Hemingway sees it all, not just the flies on the garbage can.

Heigho. I think I'll write an English detective story, one about Superientendent Jones and the two elderly sisters in the thatched cottage, something with Latin in it and music and period furniture and a gentleman's gentleman: above all one of those books where everybody goes for nice long walks.

Yours most sincerely,

Raymond Chandler

# TO ALFRED A. KNOPF

Cathedral City,
Calif.
February 8th. 1943

Dear Mr. Knopf:
Thanks for yours of Jan 14th. and it was friendly, understanding and welcome, as always. Thank you also for the two-bit edition of *The Big Sleep*. I looked into it and found it both

much better and much worse than I had expected—or than I remembered. I have been so belabored with tags like tough, hardboiled, etc., that it is almost a shock to discover occasional signs of almost normal sensitivity in the writing. On the other hand I sure did run the similes into the ground.

William Irish is a man named Cornell Woolrich, an author under his own name, and one of the oldest hands there are at the pulp detective business. He is known in the trade as an idea writer, liking the tour de force, and not much of a character man. I think his stuff is very readable, but leaves no warmth behind it.

No, I don't think the sinus condition is clearing up. This place bores me. But I've just about been talked into sticking out the mountains and the desert for another year. After that to hell with the climate, let's meet a few people. We have a one-store town here, and the meat situation would make you scream. On Wednesday morning the guy opens at 7 A.M. and all the desert rats are there waiting for him to give out numbered tickets.[1] Anybody who delays long enough to wash his face is automatically classed as parasitic and gets a high number, if he gets one at all. On Thursday at 10 the inhabitants bring their bronchitis and halitosis into the store and park in front of the meat counter and the numbers are coonshouted. When we, having a very late number, kick our way up to the collapsed hunk of hamburger we are greeted with a nervous smile that suggests a deacon caught with his hand in the collection plate, and we leave bearing off enough meat for the cat. This happens once a week and that is all that happens, in the way of meat.

Of course we go to Palm Springs. If we didn't, I should not be writing this letter. I should be out in the desert trying to dig up a dead gopher. We happened on a rib roast a couple of weeks back, just walked in and said hello, and there the damn thing was. We ate for six nights running, behind drawn curtains, chewing quietly, so the neighbors wouldn't hear.

There are a bunch of great guys in Washington, high-minded and pure, but once in a while I hunger for a touch of dirty Irish politics.

1. As part of meat rationing in wartime.

I hope to get a book out fairly soon. I am trying to think up a good title for you to want me to change.

Yours sincerely,

Raymond Chandler


# TO ALFRED A. KNOPF

Paramount Pictures Inc.
5451 Marathon Avenue
Hollywood, Calif.
November 13, 1943

Dear Alfred:

After I get through here, which should be about the end of this month, I'm going down to the desert and try to write at least the first draft of a book which presents a certain problem. I think perhaps you could help me on it. It is to be a story about a murder involving three men and two women, and practically nobody else. It is to take place in Bel-Air, and all these characters are wealthy people except the protagonist of the story. He is my problem. I should like to do a first person story about Philip Marlowe. I wouldn't have to develop him very much more than I have already because he is the sort of guy who behaves according to the company he is in. But the story is not going to be a mystery, and I hope to avoid its being tagged as a mystery novel. Is this possible if I use a character who is already established in mystery fiction?

There are probably things to be said for and against. I am strong for keeping Marlowe alive, and I feel that I may not write any more conventional mysteries. Also, the character will probably turn out to be Marlowe anyway, even if I give him another name. Would you please let me know what you think?

Kindest regards to yourself and Blanche,

Raymond Chandler

## TO JAMES SANDOE

Paramount Pictures Inc.
5451 Marathon Street
Hollywood 38, Calif.
January 26, 1944

Dear Mr. Sandoe:
Thank you for your very kind letter of January 12th. Somewhere put away with my papers in storage I have a complete list of all the stuff I have ever had published in this country. All the earlier stories were written for *Black Mask* when Joe Shaw was editor. The Avon Book Co. is bringing out a twenty-five cent edition in the spring sometime containing five of these novelettes. If they sell them they will probably publish others. As to your being able to obtain these old pulp magazines with stuff of mine in them, I doubt it very much. A friend of mine in Kansas City has been trying to build up a collection for years and has offered as much as two dollars a copy without any success.

What you say about me and Cain is very nice. It has always irritated me to be compared with Cain. My publisher thought it was a smart idea because he had a great success with *The Postman Always Rings Twice*, but whatever I have or lack as a writer I'm not in the least like Cain. Cain is a writer of the faux naif type, which I particularly dislike.

You are certainly not without company in your wish that "something could be done about the disadvantages of the redlight segregation of detective stories from 'novels' by the reviews." Once in a long while a detective story writer is treated as a writer, but very seldom. However, I think there are a few very good reasons why this

[26]

is so. For example: (a) Most detective stories are very badly written. (b) Their principal sale is to rental libraries which depend on a commercial reading service and pay no attention to reviews. (c) I believe the detective story is marketed wrong. It is absurd to expect people to pay any more for it than they would for a movie. (d) The detective or mystery story as an art form has been so thoroughly explored that the real problem for a writer now is to avoid writing a mystery story while appearing to do so. However, none of these reasons, valid or invalid as they may be, changes the essential irritation to the writer, which is the knowledge that however well and expertly he writes a mystery story, it will be treated in one paragraph while a column and a half of respectful attention will be given to any fourth-rate, ill-constructed, mock-serious account of the life of a bunch of cotton pickers in the deep south. The French are the only people I know of who think about writing as writing. The Anglo-Saxons think first of the subject matter, and second, if at all, of the quality.

Thank you again for your letter, and believe me

Yours very truly,
Ray Chandler

# TO JAMES M. CAIN

1040 Havenhurst Drive
Hollywood 46
March 20th. 1944

Dear Jim:

It was very kind of you to send me an inscribed copy of your book and I'm very grateful to you. We have been down in the desert for a month, with poor luck in weather. I don't offer that as an excuse for not writing before, the fact being that I was so completely pooped after nine months at Paramount that I couldn't even make myself write a letter. Just sat and stared morosely out of the window at the sand dunes.

[27]

Very glad to hear Warners bought *Mildred Pierce*.[1] It seems I may have a chance to work on it for them, but Paramount was not too keen about loaning me. Everybody who has seen *Double Indemnity*[2] likes it (everybody that has talked to me, at least). The feeling is that it is a pretty fine picture and for once an emotionally integrated story has got on the screen in the mood in which it was written. I don't think any of the changes we made were in conflict with your basic conception. In fact, you would have had to make them yourself. I do not doubt that some of them might have been made better, but they had to be made. The emotional integration is due to the fact that the three guys who worked on the job did not at any time disagree about what they wanted to achieve, but only on how to do it.

A curious matter I'd like to call to your attention—although you have probably been all through it with yourself—is your dialogue. Nothing could be more natural and easy and to the point on paper, and yet it doesn't quite play. We tried it out by having a couple of actors do a scene right out of the book. It had a sort of remote effect that I was at a loss to understand. It came to me then that the effect of your written dialogue is only partly sound and sense. The rest of the effect is the appearance on the page. These unevenly shaped hunks of quick-moving speech hit the eye with a sort of explosive effect. You read the stuff in batches, not in individual speech and counterspeech. On the screen this is all lost, and the essential mildness of the phrasing shows up as lacking in sharpness. They tell me that is the difference between photographic dialogue and written dialogue. For the screen everything has to be sharpened and pointed and wherever possible elided. But of course you know far more about it than I do.

I hope you get as good a script of *Mildred Pierce*. You don't need one quite so sharp. Are you working on it yourself?

All the best.

Ray

1. A novel by Cain, published in 1941.
2. Chandler and Billy Wilder wrote the screenplay for the film based on *Double Indemnity*.

[28]

# TO CHARLES MORTON

Paramount Pictures Inc.
5451 Marathon Street
Hollywood, Calif.
July 17, 1944

Dear Mr. Morton:

Sydney Sanders, my agent in New York, wrote to me some time ago saying that you might be interested in having me do a short article on the modern detective story for the *Atlantic*. Naturally I was both flattered and interested by the suggestion.

The last time I had an opportunity I tried to do a rough draft of such an article, only to discover that I hadn't the least idea how to go about it. The trouble seemed to be partly that I hadn't read enough detective stories to be able to indulge in the usual casual display of erudition, and partly that I really don't seem to take the mystery element in the detective story as seriously as I should. The main trouble with most detective stories, as I see it, is that the people who write them are bad writers. But this would not be a very interesting premise for an article. The detective story as I know and like it is a not too successful attempt to combine the attributes of two disparate types of minds; the mind which can produce a coolly thought-out puzzle can't, as a rule, develop the fire and dash necessary for vivid writing.

I am going to have some time off from motion picture work in the near future and I might have a fling at this article. If you have any ideas about what you would like to see me do, it would be a great pleasure to hear from you. I presume the matter of length is also important.

Yours very truly,

Raymond Chandler

# TO CHARLES MORTON

6520 Drexel Avenue
Los Angeles 36, Calif.
October 12th. 1944

Dear Charles Morton:

&bull;     &bull;

Thank you for two kind letters. I am sorry somebody has to lose a paragraph or two of marble prose to make way for such thoughts as mine, and sloppily tailored at that.[1] I could have procured you innumerable copies of _The Big Sleep_, had I known. The lunch money edition, that is. Last time I was in my agent's office (not Sanders' but the glittering palace on the Strip where my other agent parks his Daimler)[2] I noticed a whole row of them taking up shelf room and no longer of any use to anybody, since the thing is now sold to Warners and Howard Hawks is even now shooting a picture from it with Bogart and a new girl he has brought out in _To Have and Have Not_.[3] Bill Faulkner and a girl named Leigh Brackett wrote the script. 'Twill do. Hawks shoots from the cuff more or less, he tells me, merely using a rough script to try out his scenes and then rewriting them on the set. I could not have worked on it, since my contract with Paramount won't allow me to work for anyone else, even when I am not working for Paramount.

The article or diatribe or whatever on screen writing is just something I should like to do, but I cannot set a date for it at all. I am roughly halfway through a Marlowe book and may not get to the other for some time. I wish I could, but I am a fellow who writes 30,000 words to turn in five, and that is a lot of work. I do most certainly agree with you that it does even a writer no harm to use his stagnant brain once in a while in thought about something or other, and I am not deterred by any financial considerations at all. But I am getting old and my cerebrum squeaks against my cerebellum and I have to write some kind of a book before they forget me. A man of

1. "The Simple Art of Murder," an article Chandler wrote for _The Atlantic Monthly_, published December 1944.
2. Chandler's Hollywood agent was H. N. Swanson.
3. Lauren Bacall, who also starred in both films.

talent would write it in a month, a man of ability without talent in two months, and a genius would not write it at all. But it will take me about three more just to get a first draft.

The other day I thought of your suggestion for an article of studied insult about the Bay City (Santa Monica) police. A couple of D.A.'s investigators got a tip about a gambling hell in Ocean Park, a sleazy adjunct to Santa Monica. They went down there and picked up a couple of Santa Monica cops on the way, telling them they were going to kick in a box, but not telling them where it was. The cops went along with the natural reluctance of good cops to enforce the law against a paying customer, and when they found out where the place was, they mumbled brokenly: "We'd ought to talk to Captain Brown about this before we do it, boys, Captain Brown ain't going to like this." The D.A.'s men urged them heartlessly forward into the chip and bone parlor, several alleged gamblers were tossed into the sneezer and the equipment seized for evidence (a truckload of it) was stored in lockers at local police headquarters. When the D.A.'s boys came back next morning to go over it everything had disappeared but a few handfuls of white poker chips. The locks had not been tampered with, and no trace could be found of the truck or the driver. The flatfeet shook their grizzled polls in bewilderment and the investigators went back to town to hand the Jury the story. Nothing will come of it. Nothing ever does. Do you wonder I love Bay City? Alas that its gambling ships are no more. The present governor of California won his office by disposing of them. Others had tried (or pretended to) for years and years. But there was always the legal argument as to whether the 12-mile limit should be measured from this place or that. Warren solved it very simply, and no doubt quite illegally.[4] He commandeered enough boats and deputies to surround the ships and keep anyone from leaving them or reaching them. Then he just stayed there until they gave up.

A real clinical study of such a town would be fascinating reading.

Sincerely,

Raymond Chandler

4. Earl Warren, Governor of California and later Chief Justice of the United States.

[31]

# TO CHARLES MORTON

6520 Drexel Avenue
L.A. 36
Nov. 20th, 1944

Dear Charles:

Your letters have been weighing on me quite a bit, especially your wonderful letter about yourself. Perhaps I ought to live in Boston. The civilized intelligence is pretty rare out west. This sounds like a snobbish thing to say, but I have lived here a long time and met very few people who were not half-baked in one way or another. Hollywood is full of very clever people, some of them rather more than clever, but the hard, glossy patina of Hollywood and New York smartness depresses me. You meet the bright people who have written something successful and have arrived and are very damn conscious of the fact. You meet lively young men who are really keen on making good pictures, if it is at all possible. But you do not meet the quiet, restrained, well-bred and inconspicuously intelligent kind of mind that is fairly common in England and I imagine also in New England. At least I hope so.

One of these days I'll write you something about myself. In the meantime things are not going too well. P. Marlowe is acting up, I have had many interruptions, and also a long-drawn-out wrangle with Paramount about a contract. I wish I had one of these facile plotting brains, like Erle Gardner or somebody. I have good ideas for about four books, but the labor of shaping them into plots appals me. It would be much better if you do not expect anything from me until you get it. You don't have to like it then, but the feeling that the *Atlantic* needs encouragement from me is dreadful. I do, of course, recognize a certain duty, quite apart from any question of self-interest, to try and brighten your pages with a little arrogant nonsense here and there.

There was a time when I should have adored your kind of job, but would have been incapable of handling it. I never really had a great urge to write fiction, which is becoming more and more of a pseudo-art. (There's an article in that idea). But you guys have an obligation too. That is, to avoid pompously bad writing and the kind

[32]

of dulness that comes from letting flatulent asses pontificate about things they know no more about than the next man, if as much. There is a (to me) shocking example of this in the November *Harper's*, called "Salute to the Litterateurs."[1] Consider:

> "For writers are people of peculiar sensitivity to the winds of doctrine which blow with especial violence in a time of rapid change—some more so than others, but none, except the outright hacks, completely immune."

I regard that sentence as a disgrace to English prose. It says nothing and says it ponderously, in a cliched manner, and without syntax. The "some" obviously, by the sense, refers to writers, but just as obviously by the construction refers to "winds of doctrine." (Can't we leave phrases like that to Somerset Maugham?) How outright is a hack? And how completely immune is immune. Phooey. I continue:

> "They react this way and that; they resist the currents and run with them: and while some produce works of little value in literary or any other terms, others of greater ability and substance, and therefore of greater importance, exhibit the same tendencies in writings of a high degree of excellence."

Is there anything said here that could not be said better with a simple after-dinner belch? A little later he says:

> "When the present war was in the making the most indicative scratchings on the literary seismograph were in red."

When I showed that to my little seismograph he began to indicate four letter words in a very nasty shade of brownish-purple and had to be shut up in a dark room.

"Most indicative," "literature seismograph," "run with the current," two thousand years of Christianity and this is what we get in a literary magazine. Shame on you fellows!

I had an uncle in Omaha who was a minor politician—crooked, if I am any judge of character. I've been there a time or two. As a very small boy I used to be sent to spend part of the summer at Plattsmouth. I remember the oak trees and the high wooden sidewalks beside the dirt roads and the heat and the fireflies and

1. C. Hartley Grattan, "Salute to the Litterateurs," *Harper's Magazine*, November 1944.

walking-sticks and a lot of strange insects and the gathering of wild grapes in the fall to make wine and the dead cattle and once in a while a dead man floating down the muddy river and the dandy little three-hole privy behind the house. I remember Ak-Sar-Ben and the days when they were still trying to elect Bryan.[2] I remember the rocking chairs on the edge of the sidewoak in a solid row outside the hotel and the tobacco spit all over the place. And I remember a trial run on a mail car with a machine my uncle invented to take on mail without stopping, but somebody beat him out of it and he never got a dime.

After that I went to England and was raised on Latin and Greek, like yourself. I worked for the *Westminster Gazette* and the *Daily Express* and a very snooty weekly review called the *Academy*, owned by Oscar Wilde's fag, Lord Alfred Douglas and later by a man named Cowper, who claimed to be a direct descendant of the poet.[3] I wrote some of the nastiest book reviews ever written. I reviewed Farnol's *The Broad Highway* and predicted its tremendous success.[4] I reviewed Elinor Glyn, and how.[5] I don't think education ever did me any great harm.

Yours ever

Ray

## TO JAMES SANDOE

6520 Drexel Avenue
Los Angeles 36
Dec. 17th. 1944

Dear Sandoe:

Thanks for your card. I've been meaning to write you for some time, and to a lot of other people, but haven't done it. I'm not sure what you mean (in this context) by bowdlerlized. I didn't check, but I

2. Ak-Sar-Ben is Nebraska spelled backward. It was a social organization.
3. Cecil Cowper, editor of *The Academy*.
4. Jeffrey Farnol, popular English novelist.
5. Popular English novelist, born in Canada.

had a vague impression here and there that I had been ever so gently toned down. I know they had to cut, because the thing was too long, and is overlength as is. I had a very snazzy beginning which they cut out, because it didn't really have anything to do with detective stories. It was simply a general expression of contempt for what is known as significant writing. I only wrote this damn article after being hounded by Charles Morton. I had no desire to write it, particularly, and certainly it was a loss to me financially. Not that that matters; after a certain point money means nothing. I have no complaint; I could have done the cutting myself on the proof. I just didn't know how. As it is, I have enough material left over for another one. But I think most critical writing is drivel and half of it is dishonest (that is, conditioned by information about advance sales), and there is no point in my adding to it. It is a short cut to oblivion, anyway. Thinking in terms of ideas destroys the power to think in terms of emotions and sensations. I suppose, like other people, I have at times a futile urge to explain to whoever will listen why it is that the whole apparatus of intellectualism bores me. But you have to use the language of intellectualism to do it. Which is the bunk. The business of a fiction writer is to recreate the illusion of life. How he does it, if he can do it, it does not in the least help him to know.

Regards

Chandler

## TO CHARLES MORTON

6520 Drexel Avenue
Los Angeles 38
Dec 18th. 1944

Dear Charles:
    Yours of Dec. 14th. received and a Merry Christmas to you and the whole idea of Christmas this year has somehow taken on the utter vile commercial falsity of Mother's Day in Peoria.

I saw Mr. De Voto's remarks about Chandler and was of a mind to write to him and ask him to stop using words like "imperatives" and ideas like "functional style" but not to stop slamming people around. But this business of writing, writing to writers, is a career in itself. You end up by having personal thoughts about everyone and speaking your own mind about nothing.

Had a letter from an old unknown friend at the U. of Colorado Library who asks me if my piece in the *Atlantic* was bowdlerized.[1] Which I answered by saying that I had not checked, but had had a vague idea that it had been toned down with an ever so gentle hand here and there, and that of course it had been cut a little, which was my fault. But this just goes to show you that when a man starts to write about the apparatus of intellectualism he begins to use something that sounds like the language of intellectualism, which is a loathsome language. I re-read the *Atlantic* article and was startled to discover that in some thirty years of odd and even living I had learned nothing whatsoever about the English language. It still has me licked. I have old essays written for the *Academy* and sketches written for the *Westminster Gazette* away back when I was an elegant young thing with an Old Alleynian[2] hatband on a very natty basket weave strawhat; they show the same childish petulance and frustrated attempt to be brilliant about nothing.

I cannot complete my piece about screenwriters and screenwriting for the simple reason that I have no honesty about it. I may wake up with a different notion, but you cannot bully me into sending you something I am so deadly unsure about. There are points like these to make, but when you make them you get in a mess. E.g., 1. There is no mature art of the screenplay, and by mature I don't mean intellectual or postgraduate or intelligentsia–little magazine writing. I mean an art which knows what it is doing and has the techniques necessary to do it. 2. An adult, that is dirty or plain-spoken art of the screen, could exist at any moment the Hays Office (Title for an Essay on same: *Dirtymindedness As a Career*) and the local censorship boards would let it, but it would be no more *mature* than *Going My Way* is. 3. There is no available body of screenplay literature, because it belongs to the studios, not to the writers, and

---

1. James Sandoe.
2. Dulwich College was founded by Edward Alleyn in 1617.

they won't show it. For instance, I tried to borrow a script of *The Maltese Falcon* from Warners; they would not lend it to me. All the writer can do is look at pictures. If he is working in a studio, he can get the scripts of that studio, but his time is not his own. He can make no leisurely study and reconstruction of the problems. 4. There is no *teaching* in the art of the screenplay because there is nothing to teach; if you do not know how pictures are made, you cannot possibly know how to write them. No outsider knows that, and no writer would be bothered, unless he was an out-of-work or manqué writer. 5. The screenplay as it exists is the result of a bitter and prolonged struggle between the writer (or writers) and the people whose aim is to exploit his talent without giving it the freedom to be a talent. 6. It is only a little over 3 years since the major (and only this very year the minor) studios were forced after prolonged and bitter struggle to agree to treat the writer with a reasonable standard of business ethics. In this struggle the writers were not really fighting the motion picture industry at all; they were fighting those powerful elements in it that had hitherto glommed off all the glory and prestige and who could only continue to do so by selling themselves to the world as the makers of pictures. This struggle is still going on, and the writers are winning it, and they are winning it in the wrong way: by becoming producers and directors, that is, by becoming showmen instead of creative artists. This will do nothing for the art of the screenplay and will actually harm those writers who are temperamentally unfitted for showmanship (and this will include always the best of them). 7. The writer is still very far from winning the right to create a screenplay without interference from his studio. Why? Because he does not know how, and it is to the interest of the producers and directors to prevent him from learning how. If even a quarter of the *highly-paid* screenwriters of Hollywood (leaving out all the people who work on program pictures) could produce a completely integrated and thoroughly photographable screenplay, with only the amount of interference and discussion necessary to protect the studio's investment in actors and freedom from libel and censorship troubles, then the producer would become a business co-ordinator and the director would become the interpreter of a completed work, instead of, as at present, the maker of the picture. They will fight to the death against it.

I have a three year contract with Paramount, for 26 weeks

[37]

work a year, at a vast sum of money (by my standards). Nothing of the above would give particular offense to the studio, but much of it would be deeply resented by many individuals and would involve me in constant arguments which would wear me out. But there is still more to be said, and it is worse yet. A system like this, prolonged over a long period of time, produces a class of kept writers without initiative, independence or fighting spirit; they exist only by conforming to Hollywood standards, but they can produce art only by defying them. Few, very few, of them are capable of earning a living as independent writers, but you will always have to have them, because you will never find enough talent in all Hollywood to make more than one tenth of its pictures even fairly good. Granted that there are too many made; they are going to be made, or the theaters will be dark. Enormous vested interests and the livelihoods of countless thousands of people are involved. Granted again that ninety per cent of Hollywood's pictures are not really worth making; I say that ninety percent of the books and plays and short stories they were made from are not worth seeing or reading, by the same standards. And you and I know those standards are not going to change in our time.

Yet a writer, like me, who has little experience in Hollywood, and presumes to discuss the writers of Hollywood, must either lie, or say that they are largely over-dressed, overpaid, servile and incompetent hacks. All progress in the art of the screenplay depends on a very few people who are in a position (and have the temperament and toughness) to fight for excellence. Hollywood loves them for it and is only too anxious to reward them by making them something else than writers. Hollywood's attitude to writers is necessarily conditioned by the mass of its writers, not by the few who have what it calls integrity. It loves the word, having so little of the quality. Yet it is not fair for me to say in print that the writers of Hollywood are what they are; they have a guild and it may be that in so large an industry they must fight as a group; it is obvious that I have done nothing to help them achieve what they have achieved, and am not likely to, except indirectly, by helping to get out a few pictures a bit above the ruck. It is not even fair to call them overpaid; because other writers as a group are shockingly underpaid; Hollywood is the only industry in the world that pays its workers the kind of money only capitalists and big executives make in other industries. If

[38]

it is something less than ideal, it is the only industry that even tries for idealism; if it makes bad art, no other makes any art, except as a by-product of money-making. If it makes money out of poor pictures, it could make more money out of good ones, and it knows it and tries to make them. There is simply not enough talent in the world to do it with, on any such scale. Its pictures cost too much and therefore must be safe and bring in big returns; but why do they cost too much? Because it pays the people who do the work, not the people who cut coupons. If it drains off all the writing talent in the world and then proceeds to destroy it by the way it treats it, then why is it able to drain off that talent? Because it knows how to pay for talent. The man who publishes my books has made more out of me than I have out of him, and he has not made it by selling the books, but by cutting himself in on radio and motion picture and reprint rights, which did not cost him a cent. Did he venture anything on the books? Of course not, not a dime. He was insured against loss by the rental libraries. He does not even know how to sell my kind of books, or how to promote them or how to get them reviewed. He just sits there and waits for something to happen, and when it happens, he rubs his hands and cuts himself a nice fat slice of it. But Hollywood pays me a large salary merely to try to write something it can perhaps use. And when I write something that pays, then it tears up my contract and writes a better one. I cannot despise an industry that does this and I cannot say the men in it are bad artists because they do not produce better art. Yet, if I am honest about art, that is the only thing I can say. It is better to say nothing, is it not? At least, for the present.

Phew! I'm exhausted. And what do I know about art anyway? Thank heaven that when I tried to write fiction I had the sense to do it in a language that was not all steamed up with rhetoric. In spite of all your kindness and understanding I am beginning to hate you. It took me twenty years to get over writing this sort of twaddle and look at me now!

Ray

P.S. I clean forgot to thank you for the proof of Nabokov's fantasy.[3] I have a novel by him somewhere. It is exquisitely composed and

3. "Time and Ebb," published in *The Atlantic Monthly*, January 1945.

[39]

very charming. I have a strange feeling that I have met the beautiful closing simile before. It sounds like T. S. Eliot. I can't place it and therefore must assume that it is false memory (paramnesis to you). The tired brain is often thus afflicted.

R

## TO CHARLES MORTON

6520 Drexel Avenue
Los Angeles 36, Calif.
Jan 1st. 1945

Dear Charles:

A Happy New Year to you and the eggnog. And what horribly long letters this guy Chandler writes. Seeing the copy of it marked "excerpt" was like looking in an unexpected mirror just after falling downstairs. No, I don't keep carbons of them. I sometimes wish I did, but most of the time I am much happier not knowing. I didn't see the *New Yorker* for the day in question, but a man named McNulty whom Paramount has beguiled out here (he looks horrible already) is going to bring his copy down. He is a *New Yorker* man and has not yet bought a houndstooth sports coat.[1] I regret to say I have to go back to work tomorrow. The prospect makes me feel low enough to chin myself on the curbing. I worked all yesterday and today trying to get an article down on paper for you. You don't have to like it, because I would have written it anyway, if only to get rid of the subject. I see your point about Hollywood, and perhaps you are quite right. I guess I can get around to that after awhile.

It was very kind of you to send me Diarmuid Russell's piece, and very nice of him to write it.[2] I have known for some time that I was in a rut, but he, being an agent, should have known (as perhaps he does, privately) that the one you cash in on is not

1. John McNulty, author of *Third Avenue* (1936).
2. Son of the Irish poet A.E., and founder of Russell and Volkening, New York literary agency. He reviewed Chandler in the *New York Times Book Review*.

necessarily the one you did best; it may happen to be the one that arrives when the others have prepared the way. At any rate, sooner or later, I must do my obeisance before the trulls and pimps of Hollywood in a Marlowe story of no better or newer flavor. I have another story in mind which I hope to do before I die; it will have almost no surface toughness at all, but the go to hell attitude, which is no pose with me, is likely to appear in it all the same.

. . .

The only complaint I could make about Russell's remarks is that if you are going to take the trouble to say nice things about a man, and such very nice things, you should keep a few for the end and leave the reader with a slight taste of sugar in his mouth. I mean, I would myself have saved out a few kind words to close with, not in anyway modifying what was said in criticism, but merely arranging it a little differently. That, of course, is not at all my affair.

My doubtfully honest uncle's (by marriage only) name was Ernest Fitt, and he was a boiler inspector or something, at least in name. He is dead now. I remember him very well. He used to come home in the evening (in the Plattsmouth period) put the paper on the music rack and improvise while he read it. I have read somewhere that Harold Bauer used to play his programmes through while reading a paper, but I always thought him a dull pianist, so it didn't surprise me. My uncle had talent, but no musical education. He had a brother who was an amazing character. He had been a bank clerk or manager in a bank in Waterford, Ireland (where all my mother's people come from, but none of them were Catholics) and had embezzled money. He cleaned out the till one Saturday and, with the help of the Masons, escaped the police net to the continent of Europe. In some hotel in Germany his money was stolen, or most of it. When I knew him, long after, he was an extremely respectable old party, always immaculately dressed, and of an incredible parsimony. He once invited me to dinner and to the Ak-Sar-Ben festivities. After the dinner he leaned over and in a confidential whisper said: "We'll each pay for our own." Not a drop of Scotch blood anywhere either. Pure middle-class Protestant Irish. I have a great many Irish relatives, some poor, some not poor, and all Protestants and some of them Sinn Feiners and some entirely pro-British. The head of the family, if he is still living, is a very wealthy lawyer who hated the law, but

[41]

felt obliged to carry on his father's firm. He had a housekeeper who came of a county family and did not regard my uncle (the lawyer one) as quite a gentleman because he was a solicitor. She used to say: There are only four careers for a gentleman, the Army, the Navy, the Church and the Bar. A barrister was a gentleman, but not a solicitor. This in spite of the fact that his son was a lieutenant in the Royal Navy and another of his relatives was Adjutant-General of the Royal Marines. With her he never lived down being a solicitor. An amazing people, the Anglo-Irish. They never mixed with Catholics socially. I remember playing on a cricket team with some of the local snobs and one of the players was a Catholic boy who came to the game in an elaborate chariot with grooms in livery; but he was not asked to have tea with the rest after the game. He wouldn't have accepted, of course. People over here don't understand the Irish at all. A third of the population of Eire is Protestant, and it is by far the best educated and most influential third. Almost all the great Irish rebels were Protestants, and the whole tone of their present nation is Calvinistic rather than Catholic. I grew up with a terrible contempt for Catholics, and I have trouble with it even now. My uncle's snob housekeeper wouldn't have a Catholic servant in the house, although they were probably much better than the trash she did have. What a world! The rather amusing development in my uncle's case was that he took unto himself a Jewish mistress in London, raised her son, who was an illegitimate get of a couple of Sassoons, had two illegitimate children himself, and then married her. *But he never took her to Ireland!* I could make a book about these people, but I am too much of an Irishman myself ever to tell the truth about them.

Well, Hollywood is funny too. They had a contract with me and no story for me to work on. So I cooked up an idea and went in and told it to them and they rubbed their hands and said lovely, when do we start? But when my agent enquired what they proposed to pay for the idea, they tore their clothing into shreds and heaped ashes on their heads. It tooked several weeks of bitter wrangling to get them to see the light. I don't care anything about the money, I just like to fight. I'm a tired old man, but it takes more than a motion picture studio to push me around, it seems.

All the best,

Ray

[42]

# TO DALE WARREN

January 7th. 1945

Dear Warren:

    I finally unearthed your kind letter from a tangled mass of correspondence dating back to the Civil War, spurred on by your letter in the *Atlantic* about my little tirade. Do not think I have not meant to write to you. My wife regards you as a somewhat rare bird, since you wrote to me twice without mentioning the fact that you were connected with a publishing firm. The *Atlantic* article has got me into a lot of trouble. Mr. P. Marlowe, a simple alcoholic vulgarian who never sleeps with his clients while on duty, is trying to go refined on me. "What the hell," he says, "do you mean by keeping me in the basement all this time. Here you are unmasked as a guy who can write English—after a fashion—so get busy and write some about me." I can imagine the result. I suppose, if I write another article in the *Atlantic*, if there is one, he will demand spats and a monocle and start collecting old pewter.

    There are certain acute disadvantages in attracting attention, even the small amount that has come my way. People start telling you how you do things and then you start trying to do them that way. All I wanted when I began was to play with a fascinating new language, and trying, without anybody noticing it, to see what it would do as a means of expression which might remain on the level of unintellectual thinking and yet acquire the power to say things which are usually only said with a literary air. I didn't really care a hell of a lot what kind of story I wrote; I wrote melodrama because when I looked around me it was the only kind of writing I saw that was relatively honest and yet was not trying to put over somebody's party line. So now there are guys talking about prose and other guys telling me I have a social conscience. P. Marlowe has as much social conscience as a horse. He has a personal conscience, which is an entirely different matter. There are people who think I dwell on the ugly side of life. God help them! If they had any idea how little I have told them about it! P. Marlowe doesn't give a damn who is president; neither do I, because I know he will be a politician. There was even a bird who informed me I could write a good proletarian

[43]

novel; in my limited world there is no such animal, and if there were, I am the last mind in the world to like it, being by tradition and long study a complete snob. P. Marlowe and I do not despise the upper classes because they take baths and have money; we despise them because they are phoney. And so on. And now I see ahead of me either an acute self-consciousness about simple things which I never had any idea of explaining, or a need to explain them at length, and with fury, in the very lingo I had been trying to forget. Because that is the only lingo people who can understand explanations of the sort will accept them in.

I have a note from a friend of yours, Mary Lasswell.[1] Have to answer it, but have never read anything she wrote, which makes it embarrassing. I also have a letter from a lady in Caracas, Venezuela, who asks me if I would like to be her friend when she comes to New York. It has a faint suggestion about it of another letter I had once from a girl in Seattle who said that she was interested in music and sex, and gave me the impression that, if I was pressed for time, I need not even bother to bring my own pajamas. She probably had spots.

Raymond Chandler

## TO HAMISH HAMILTON

Paramount Pictures Inc.
5451 Marathon Street
Hollywood 38, Calif.
January 11, 1945

Dear Hamish Hamilton:

Blanche Knopf sent me a copy of your letter to her of December 5th, which was very kind of her. It points up for me how little nowadays a writer seems to have to do with his publisher. I suppose this is largely because of the agent. Once in a while I hear

1. Author of *Suds in Your Eyes*, 1943.

[44]

from Alfred or Blanche Knopf. Their letters are always friendly but there is a sort of remoteness about the whole thing. I seem to remember in the rather dim past having received one letter from you.

Another thing that strikes me is that one publisher calls the other publisher's attention to what you term "a magnificent boost in the Book Society News," and something by Desmond MacCarthy in the *Sunday Times*.[1] But nobody ever tells the writer anything about these matters. I wonder why. I have never even seen an English review of anything I wrote except once—something from the *Times*, I think.

You say also "I gather that he is a very big shot in Hollywood these days, and might resent advice, whoever the sender may be and however good his intentions." That really cuts me to the quick. I am not a big shot in Hollywood or anywhere else and have no desire to be. I am, on the contrary, extremely allergic to big shots of all types wherever found, and lose no opportunity to insult them whenever I get the chance. Furthermore, I love advice and if I very seldom take it, on the subject of writing, that is only because I have received practically none except from my agent, Sydney Sanders, and he has rather concentrated on trying to make me write stuff for what we call the slick magazines over here. That is, the big shiny paper national weeklies and monthlies which cater principally to the taste of women. I have always felt myself entirely unfitted for this kind of writing. I much prefer Hollywood, with all its disadvantages.

I should indeed like to write a more serious type of crime novel and have one firmly in mind. But as you very well know in this curious business, one has for a time at least, to follow a rather different trail. Probably by now I've gone about as far along that trail as it is worthwhile to go, but it has certainly been worthwhile to go thus far.

Why not try me with a little advice some time? I am sure I should treat yours with the greatest respect and should, in any case, like to hear from you.

Yours very sincerely,

Raymond Chandler

---

1. English biographer and man of letters, reviewer for *Sunday Times* of London.

# TO CHARLES MORTON

Paramount Pictures Inc.
5451 Marathon Street
Hollywood 38, Calif.
Jan. 15th. 1945

Dear Charles:

.        .        .

Yes, I know damn well that Harry Fitt was one of the clan of Limerick. I didn't know that he drank, but liquor was a family vice. Those who escaped it either turned religious or went in for white duck pants, like my Uncle Gus. Harry, your father's hired hand, must have been a cousin of my uncle. He was no near relation and I hardly know him, but when I read your letter I recalled that there was a Harry Fitt, that he lived in Omaha and that he worked in a hardware store. Since I was fresh out from England at the time and a hardware store was "trade" I could hardly be expected to get on terms of anything like familiarity with him. Boy! Two stengahs, chop chop!

I am back at the grind and you might as leave write me there for a while. It makes no difference. (Perhaps you won't be writing to me any more at all). In less than two weeks I wrote an original story of 90 pages like this. All dictated and never looked at until finished. It was an experiment and for a guy subject from early childhood to plot-constipation, it was rather a revelation. Some of the stuff is good, some very much not. But I don't see why the method could not be adapted to novel writing, at least by me. Improvise the story as well as you can, in as much detail or as little as the mood seems to suggest, write dialogue or leave it out, but cover the movement, the characters and bring the thing to life. I begin to realize the great number of stories that are lost by us rather meticulous boys simply because we permit our minds to freeze on the faults rather than let them work for a while without the critical overseer sniping at everything that is not perfect. I can see where a special vice might also come out of this kind of writing; in fact two: the strange delusion that something on paper has a meaning because it is written.

[46]

(My revered HJ rather went to pieces a bit when he began to dictate.)[1]
Also, the tendency to worship production for its own sake. (Gardner
suffers badly from this; but God never had any idea of making him a
writer anyway. Edgar Wallace ditto. But Dumas Père might really
have missed something by grinding the stuff out of the sausage
machine.)

Had a nice letter from Dale Warren, but I wish people would
stop writing letters about the neglected works of Raymond Chandler.
I am so little neglected that I am often actually embarrassed by too
much attention. Also, *The Big Sleep* and *Farewell My Murder My
Sweet* have between them, in some form or other, sold almost three
quarters of a million copies.[2]

All the best

Ray


# TO CHARLES MORTON


Jan. 21st. 1945

Dear Charles:

.        .        .

I have one complaint to make, and it is an old one—the cold
silence and the stalling that goes on when something comes in that is
not right or is not timely. This I resent and always shall. It does not
take weeks to tell a man (by pony express) that his piece is wrong
when he can be told in a matter of days that it is right. Editors do not
make enemies by rejecting manuscripts, but by the way they do it,
by the change of atmosphere, the delay, the impersonal note that
creeps in. I am a hater of power and of trading, and yet I live in a
world where I have to trade brutally and exploit every item of power
I may possess. But in dealing with the *Atlantic*, there is none of

1. Reference to Henry James.
2. The movie version of *Farewell, My Lovely* was called *Murder, My Sweet*.

this. I do not write for you for money or for prestige, but for love, the strange lingering love of a world wherein men may think in cool subtleties and talk in the language of almost forgotten cultures. There is little of this world; there is a pale imitation of it created by people like Barzun.[1] I like that world and I would on occasion sacrifice my sleep and my rest and quite a bit of money to enter it gracefully. That is not appreciated. It is something you cannot buy. It is something which, even when the gesture is imperfect, deserves respect. I can make $5000 in two days (sometimes), but I spend weeks trying to please the *Atlantic* for $250 or whatever it is. Do you think I want money? And as for prestige, what is it? What greater prestige can a man like me, (not too greatly gifted but understanding) have than to have taken a cheap, shoddy, and utterly lost kind of writing and have made of it something that intellectuals claw each other about? What more could I ask except the leisure and skill to write a couple of novels of the sort I want to write and to have waiting for them a public I have made myself? Certainly, the *Atlantic* cannot give that to me.

.         .         .

All the best,

Ray

## TO HAMISH HAMILTON

Paramount Pictures Inc.
5451 Marathon Street
Hollywood 38, Calif.
February 26, 1945

Dear Hamish Hamilton:

1. Jacques Barzun, historian and critic of detective fiction.

It is nice to hear from you and to be writing to you. I suppose agents are necessary to a writer because the writer, living a more or less secluded life as a rule, cannot possibly know what is going on in the literary world, what he ought to get for his material, and on what sort of conditions he should sell it. But I think the agent's function ends there. The moment he tries to influence a writer in his work, the agent just makes a nuisance of himself. I can assure you that no agent need come between us in any but the most routine financial matters.

I hope to meet you some day in London. It would probably come as a shock to some of my critics to know that I went to school at Dulwich and was raised on Latin and Greek.

Kindest regards and best wishes,

Yours sincerely,

Raymond Chandler

## TO CHARLES MORTON

Paramount Pictures Inc.
5451 Marathon Street
Hollywood 38, Calif.
March 19, 1945

Dear Charles:

A man named Inkstead[1] took some pictures of me for *Harper's Bazaar* a while ago (I never quite found out why) and one of me holding my secretary in my lap came out very well indeed. When I

1. Actually John Engstead.

get the dozen I have ordered I'll send you one. The secretary, I should perhaps add, is a black Persian cat, 14 years old, and I call her that because she has been around me ever since I began to write, usually sitting on the paper I wanted to use or the copy I wanted to revise, sometimes leaning up against the typewriter and sometimes just quietly gazing out of the window from a corner of the desk, as much as to say, "The stuff you're doing's a waste of my time, bud." Her name is Taki (it was originally Take, but we got tired of explaining that this was a Japanese word meaning bamboo and should be pronounced in two syllables), and she has a memory like no elephant ever even tried to have. She is usually politely remote, but once in a while will get an argumentative spell and talk back for ten minutes at a time. I wish I knew what she is trying to say then, but I suspect it all adds up to a very sarcastic version of "You can do better." I've been a cat lover all my life (have nothing against dogs except that they need such a lot of entertaining) and have never quite been able to understand them. Taki is a completely poised animal and always knows who likes cats, never goes near anybody that doesn't, always walks straight up to anyone, however lately arrived and completely unknown to her, who really does. She doesn't spend a great deal of time with them, however, just takes a moderate amount of petting and strolls off. She has another curious trick (which may or may not be rare) of never killing anything. She brings 'em back alive and lets you take them away from her. She has brought into the house at various times such things as a dove, a blue parakeet, and a large butterfly. The butterfly and the parakeet were entirely unharmed and carried on just as though nothing had happened. The dove gave her a little trouble, apparently not wanting to be carried around, and had a small spot of blood on its breast. But we took it to a bird man and it was all right very soon. Just a bit humiliated. Mice bore her, but she catches them if they insist and then I have to kill them. She has a sort of tired interest in gophers, and will watch a gopher hole with some attention, but gophers bite and after all who the hell wants a gopher anyway? So she just pretends she might catch one, if she felt like it.

She goes with us wherever we go journeying, remembers all the places she has been to before and is usually quite at home anywhere. One or two places have got her—I don't know why. She just wouldn't settle down in them. After a while we know enough to

[50]

take the hint. Chances are there was an axe murder there once and we're much better somewhere else. The guy might come back. Sometimes she looks at me with a rather peculiar expression (she is the only cat I know who will look you straight straight in the eye) and I have a suspicion that she is keeping a diary, because the expression seems to be saying: "Brother, you think you're pretty good most of the time, don't you? I wonder how you'd feel if I decided to publish some of the stuff *I've* been putting down at odd moments." At certain times she has a trick of holding one paw up loosely and looking at it in a speculative manner. My wife thinks she is suggesting we get her a wrist watch; she doesn't need it for any practical reason—she can tell the time better than I can—but after all you gotta have some jewelry.

I don't know why I'm writing all this. It must be I couldn't think of anything else, or—this is where it gets creepy—am I really writing it at all? Could it be that—no, it must be me. Say it's me. I'm scared.

Ray

## TO ALFRED A. KNOPF

Paramount Pictures Inc.
5451 Marathon Street
Hollywood 38, Calif.
March 24, 1945

Dear Alfred:

I don't quite know how to answer your letter of March 19th. Privately and verbally, I make no secret of my age, but printing it on the jacket of a book seems to me bad psychology. I don't think it's any of the public's business, and it can very easily give a false impression. My wife is very emphatic on this point, and I have never known her to be wrong in a matter of taste.

Certainly I should agree that if a writer is of any interest to the public at all, the things about him which made him a particular sort of writer are also of interest. I should agree, in my own case, it

[51]

might *possibly* be of interest that my education and social background are in almost violent contrast to my ideas about writing. I should agree that it might be of interest to know that a man who grew up in England is, in a literary sense, completely American; that a man who was at one time a classical scholar (of sorts) now chooses to write in the American vernacular. But I do not agree that my age, bathing habits, the color of my wife's eyes, or what time I get up in the morning, or, in fact, anything of a purely personal nature, is relevant. The intrusion of publicity-minded people into the private lives of writers seems to me an infinite vulgarity. It took lonely men whom I had never seen or heard of to find out that I could write with some distinction. All the blurb writers were able to see was thrill value.

A photographer for *Harper's Bazaar* made a picture of me and my cat which I think is just exactly the sort you should have for your purposes. If *Harper's Bazaar* uses it, it can't be used anywhere else. But it is one of several, and they may not use it; in which case I will send it to you.

Kindest regards to you and Blanche.

Yours,

Ray

## TO JAMES SANDOE

August 18th. 1945

Dear Sandoe:

I have *The Small Back Room* and in fact have bought several copies.[1] Even toyed with the idea of doing a picture from it, but it got away. It would have to be made in England. I thought it a great piece of writing, disfigured a little by the relationship of the man

1. By Nigel Balchin.

[52]

and his girl. I don't know on what grounds of logic it rests, if any, but I find it impossible to respect a woman who lives with a man. She can sleep with him all she blame pleases and with whomever else she pleases and in whatever place she pleases, but the tawdry imitation of domesticity gets me down.

.        .        .

Regards, R. C.

P.S. Am working on a screen treatment of *The Lady in the Lake* for MGM.[2] It bores me stiff. The last time I'll ever do a screenplay of a book I wrote myself. Just turning over dry bones.

# TO CHARLES MORTON

Big Bear Lake, Calif.
October 13th, 1945

Dear Charles:

.        .        .

As to talking about Hammett[1] In the past tense, I did myself in that essay. I hope he is not to be so spoken of. As far as I know he is alive and well, but he has gone so long without writing—unless you count a couple of screenplay jobs which, rumor says, La Hellman[2] really did for him, (I guess I needed that first comma after all)— that I wonder. He was one of the many guys who couldn't take Hollywood without trying to push God out of the high seat. I recall an incident reported to me when Hammett was occupying a suite at the Beverly-Wilshire. A party wished to make him a proposition and called late of a morning, was admitted by Hammett's house boy to a living room, and after a very long wait, an inner door

2. Chandler's fourth novel.

1. Detective novelist Dashiell Hammett died in 1961. His last novel, *The Thin Man*, was published in 1934.
2. Playwright Lillian Hellman, companion of Hammett for many years.

[53]

opened and the great man appeared in it, clad in an expensive lounging robe (no doubt with his initials on the pocket) with a scarf draped tastefully around his neck. He stood in silence as the man expounded. At the end he said politely: "No." He turned and withdrew, the door closed, the houseboy ushered the gent out, and the silence fell, interrupted only by the gurgling of Scotch from an inner room. If you ever saw Hammett, you will realize the dignity and pathos of this little scene. He is a very distinguished-looking guy, and I imagine he could say 'no' without perceptible trace of a Brooklyn accent. I liked him very much and he was an amazingly competent drunk, which, having a poor head for liquor, I seem always to admire. It was a great pity that he stopped writing. I've never known why. I suppose he may have come to the end of his resources in a certain style and have lacked the intellectual depth to compensate for that by trying something else. But I'm not sure. I think the man has been both overrated and underrated. Your friend Dale Warren recently read the *Falcon*,[3] for the first time too, and saw little in it. But I have read so much of this kind of writing that the gulf between Hammett and the merely tough boys seems to me vast. Old Joe Shaw may have put his finger on the trouble when he said Hammett never really cared for any of his characters.

I don't know whether this is a relaxed letter or not. I do begin to feel a little easing of the strain. This place is 7000 feet up, on the edge of a lake 20 miles long. It is no longer unspoiled nature, but it still has its points. The air is thin and dry like the desert (the Mojave is just down the hill to the east) and at this time of year it is very quiet, warm in the daytime and rather cold at night. We have had a fire before evening only once. There is nothing to do and I do it. We go out in the woods and I chop knots out of fallen trees and break up a few stumps of ironwood or mountain mahogany, a very hard reddish wood that burns like coal. I try to keep work out of my head, but can't quite do that. I had a bad time with MGM, very bad.[4] Not their fault, they were very nice to me. After the first two days I worked entirely at home, which is against their rules but they made an exception. The trouble was that I was already too fed up to do a good job on any script: that I did not like working on a story of my own, being stale on it long since; and that I assumed in the beginning

3. *The Maltese Falcon*, a novel by Hammett.
4. Chandler was working on the screenplay of his novel *The Lady in the Lake*.

that a preliminary script would be all they could expect, since they take a very long time making their pictures. I found out as I began to send it in that they were regarding it as a shooting script (subject to cutting) and didn't want any other writer on it. That put the heat on me and I began to get nervous. MGM never had a script in 13 weeks since the company was organized, and here they were talking about going into production in November. Towards the end when I realized that I was getting more mechanical every day I tried to explain to them that they were making a mistake, that this work was full of loose ends and tired attitudes, and that if they really wanted to start shooting that soon, they needed a writer with some enthusiasm. No soap. Of course these people never play straight with you. What will almost certainly happen, once they have milked me dry, will be that some executive above the producer will say, Look here, we got a lot of high-priced writers right here in the studio. For Chrissake put one on this and let him give it what he's got. The writer will then take good care, or as good care as they let him, to make enough changes to put his mark on the thing and get a credit. I don't grudge him the credit, but I do rather resent the waste of my own fading energies. On the other hand in all fairness I have to say that MGM would have kept me on the script indefinitely, had I wanted to stay. So I suppose it's all right, really.[5]

.        .        .

All the best

Ray

## TO CHARLES MORTON

6520 Drexel Ave.

Los Angeles 36, Calif.

Dec. 12th. 1945

Dear Charles:

I've owed you a letter for so damn long that I suppose you

5. The script was finished by Steve Fisher and Chandler refused any credit for the film.

wonder whether I am still alive. So do I, at times. Before I delve into your two letters to see if there are any questions you wanted replies to, let me report that my blast at Hollywood was received here in frozen silence.[1] I don't think any local paper or trade-paper even mentioned it (but can't be sure); Irving Hoffman did in his column, briefly, but he doesn't function here, although his stuff appears in the *Hollywood Reporter*. In view of the subject matter, and quite regardless of the reputation of the writer, and in view of the *Atlantic*, it seems to me reasonable to think there was a suppression of the subject by request of the studio publicity heads. I could be wrong, but that is what I'm inclined to think. In various roundabout ways I heard that the piece was not received with favor. My agent was told by the Paramount story editor that it had done me a lot of harm with the producers at Paramount. Charlie Brackett, that fading wit, said: "Chandler's books are not good enough, nor his pictures bad enough, to justify that article." I wasted a little time trying to figure out what that meant. It seems to mean that the only guy who can speak his mind about Hollywood is either (a) a failure in Hollywood, or (b) a celebrity somewhere else. I would reply to Mr. Brackett that if my books had been any worse, I should not have been invited to Hollywood, and that if they had been any better, I should not have come. Of course, as you and I know, the only kind of man qualified to deal with Hollywood in any such drastic fashion is one who has enough reputation to get a hearing, has not been in Hollywood long enough to lose his sense of proportion, but has been there long enough and has accomplished enough there so that it could not be said of him he was merely knocking a racket he couldn't lick.

I noticed that (unlike the *Post*) you did not open my fan mail. Too bad you didn't raise the point so that you could have. There wasn't much, but there was a very charming letter from Beirne Lay and also one from Studs Lonigan which I have still to answer.[2] He thinks I didn't go far enough, that I should have coordinated Hollywood with the social problems of the time. That's the worst of these deep thinkers. They can't let you speak your piece, then put

1. "Writers in Hollywood," *The Atlantic Monthly*, November 1945.
2. Beirne Lay, author of *Twelve O'Clock High*; Studs Lonigan is presumably James T. Farrell.

your hat on and go home. Everything to them is just a chapter in the unfolding of the human struggle for decent expression, or like another volume from Jules Romains.[3] Of course they're right in a way, more right than Wolcott Gibbs, for example, who seems to take the view, intellectually unsound, that an art which is practised badly is simply a bad art (I wonder if he ever read *Clarissa Harlowe*) and the view, socially and factually unsound, that a man is of necessity more intelligent than his cook.[4] I liked his piece because I like the way he says things; I like but do not crave to practise the somewhat arctic style of the *New Yorker*. It has made *New Yorker* writers out of too many people who might have been their own writers. But I should somehow like to ask Wolcott whether he really believes the medium which has produced *The Last Laugh, Variety, M., Mayerling, Night Must Fall, Intolerance, The Little Foxes* (screen version), *The More the Merrier*, etc. etc. is really inferior to the medium which has produced *Dear Ruth, The Voice of the Turtle, Mrs. Tanqueray's Past, The Lion and the Mouse, Oklahoma, Dear Brutus, Getting Married*, etc. etc. And if he agrees that it is not, I should further like to ask him whether criticism has any function whatsoever in the development and self-education of an art; because if it has, all he is really saying is that he does not want to review pictures because they are bad and bore him, whereas he does want to review plays because they are good and do not bore him. That may be his privilege, but it is certainly not a critical opinion.

In case you are still planning to use this article in your anthology, I should like, if there is time, to point out a few errors. They are not very important, but we might as well get the thing right. Whom do I address? Some of them are probably actual typographical errors of a sort. There is one I should like to mention, because it is the kind of thing I never can understand. It is the 9th. line from the end of the piece. It reads: "and not examine the artistic result too critically. The." What I wrote was; "and not too critically examine the artistic result." I believe, but am not certain, that it was this last way in the original proofs, perhaps not in the revised proof. It is obvious that somebody, for no reason save that he thought he

3. Author of a long series of novels called *Men of Good Will*.
4. Gibbs was drama critic of *The New Yorker*.

was improving the style, changed the order of the words. The length is the same, therefore that could not enter into it. I confess myself completely flabbergasted by the literary attitude this expresses. Because it is the attitude that gets me, the assumption on the part of some editorial hireling that he can write better than the man who sent the stuff in, that he knows more about phrase and cadence and the placing of words, and that he actually thinks that a clause with a strong (stressed) syllable at the end, which was put there because it was strong, is improved by changing the order so that the clause ends in a weak adverbial termination. I don't mind the guy being wrong about this. That's nothing. It could even, within limits, be a matter of opinion, although I do not agree. But here is somebody who apparently decided in his own mind that Chandler was using a rhetorical word order, which he was, and that he didn't know what the hell he was doing, didn't even know he was being rhetorical, and that he, Joe Doakes with the fat red pencil, is the boy to show him how wrong he is, by changing it back to the way the editor of the Weehawken County Gazeteer would have written it in his weekly editorial about the use of steel floss to clean chicken dirt off Grade AA eggs. Christ!

While still coughing hysterically into my kidney basin I thank you for your kind remarks from the wife of the Harvard Nieman Fellow, and I am still a bit dizzy from some remarks your pal Dale Warren made about *The Maltese Falcon*, which he apparently regards as quite inferior to *The Leavenworth Case* (Read it for laughs, if you haven't). I reread the *Falcon* not long ago, and I give up. Somebody in this room has lost a straitjacket. It must be me. Frankly, I can conceive of better writing than the *Falcon*, and a more tender and warm attitude to life, and a more flowery ending; but by God, if you can show me twenty books written approximately 20 years back that have as much guts and life now, I'll eat them between slices of Edmund Wilson's head.[5] Really I'm beginning to wonder quite seriously whether anybody knows what writing is anymore, whether they haven't got the whole bloody business so completely mixed up with subject matter and significance and who's going to win the

5. Edmund Wilson's article "Who Cares Who Killed Roger Ackroyd?" in *The New Yorker* was unfavorable to most detective writers. Chandler was excepted.

peace and what they gave him for the screen rights and if you're not a molecular physicist, you're illiterate, and so on, that there simply isn't anybody around who can read a book and say that the guy knew how to write or didn't. Even poor old Edmund Wilson, who writes as if he had a loose upper plate (was it DeVoto who said that?) dirtied his pants in the *New Yorker* a few short weeks ago in reviewing Marquand's[6] last book. He wrote: "A novel by Sinclair Lewis, however much it may be open to objection, is at least a book by a writer—that is, a work of the imagination that imposes its atmosphere, a creation that shows the color and modelling of a particular artist's hand." Is that all a good writer has to do? Hell, I always thought it was, but hell, I didn't know Wilson knew it.

Can I do a piece for you entitled *The Insignificance of Significance*, in which I will demonstrate in my usual whorehouse style that it doesn't matter a damn what a novel is about, that the only fiction of any moment in any age is that which does magic with words, and that the subject matter is merely the springboard for the writer's imagination; that the art of fiction, if it can any longer be called that, has grown from nothing to an artificial synthesis in a mere matter of 300 years, and has now reached such a degree of mechanical perfection that the only way you can tell the novelists apart is by whether they write about miners in Butte, coolies in China, Jews in the Bronx, or stockbrokers on Long Island, or whatever it is; that all the women and most of the men write exactly the same, or at least choose one of half a dozen thoroughly standardized procedures; and that in spite of certain inevitable slight differences (very slight indeed on the long view) the whole damn business could be turned out by a machine just as well, and will be almost any day now; and that the only writers left who have *anything* to say are those who write about practically nothing and monkey around with odd ways of doing it.

I think you're all crazy. I'm going into the motion picture business. I might even get to be a producer.

Ray

6. *Repent in Haste*, by John P. Marquand (1893–1960).

# TO HAMISH HAMILTON

6520 Drexel Ave.
Los Angeles 36 Calif.
Jan. 9, 1946

Dear Jamie:

I should have starved to death if I had been dependent on what Knopf paid me. I am quite sure he did his level best, but the tradition is all against any large sale of mysteries in their original edition. And the publishers have cooperated in the rental library swindle over a period of years with such infinite good humour that even I, who realise the poisition of the author and can afford to buy mysteries, very seldom do so, unless in cheap reprints. To say that a book which is not worth buying unless it is worth re-reading is no answer. Practically no fiction now being published is worth re-reading and damn little of it worth reading at all. Yet if a novel is well reviewed in *Time* or *The New Yorker* or *Newsweek*, etc. I am likely to order it sight unseen (often to be badly fooled of course). A mystery I do not buy unless I know what I am buying. There is something very wry about all this. I have a book called *Mr. Bowling Buys a Newspaper* which I have read half a dozen times and have bought right and left to give away.[1] I think it is one of the most fascinating books written in the last ten years and I know nobody in my limited circle who doesn't agree with me. Yet I doubt if it sold 5000 copies over here. There is something wrong with the book business. The publisher is probably far the best judge of books there is, but he simply cannot put them over. Either they sell themselves (in which case he can plunge on advertising and build them up very fast) or they do not sell. Of course we are all semi-literates over here and if a book is not 'significant,' we think it is trash. And by significant we mean that it does our thinking for us. God knows we can't do it ourselves. There is of course a leavening of superbly intelligent people, but the average

---

1. By Donald Henderson

'educated' American has the all round mental equipment of a fourth form boy in an English public school. Well—enough of the griping.

I am out on strike at Paramount—a one man strike. That is to say I refuse to perform under my contract and so far they refuse to cancel it. There is much talk of money, but that is a smoke screen. Beyond a certain point money merely means complication. You have the bother and expense of handling it and protecting it and you do not have the spending of it. Fundamentally the issue is freedom. I have only a limited number of useful years left and I do not want to use any of them up destroying what talent I have. It is possible to make good pictures—within limits—but to do it you have to work with good people. They exist in Hollywood, but they are scattered and at the moment none of them is available to me at Paramount. The studio is now under the control of a man whose attitude to picture-making is that if you own 1600 theatres, all you have to do is grind out the product as quickly and economically as possible. I cannot do anything in that atmosphere except spend time and collect a salary. It's not good enough. The last picture I did there nearly killed me. The producer was in the doghouse—he has since left—and the director was a stale old hack who had been directing for thiry years without once achieving any real distinction. Obviously he never could. So here was I a mere writer and a tired one at that screaming at the front office to protect the producer and actually going on the set to direct scenes—I know nothing about directing—in order that the whole project might be saved from going down the drain. Well, it was saved. As pictures go it is pretty lively. No classic, but no dud either.[2] But at what a price! And then I had to go to MGM to work on *The Lady in the Lake*, which bored me so enormously that I practically rewrote the story in order to have something fresh to look at. I didn't finish it, and it is probably all bitched up by now (or perhaps I bitched it up), but after that one was over I had to be hit on the head with a baseball bat to make me get out of a chair.

I am now doing a Marlowe story and frankly I wish it were better. In fact, except for practical reasons I'd like to forget all about Mr. Marlowe for several years. But I have to keep him alive somehow. There are radio programs in the offing and other low ways

2. *The Blue Dahlia.*

of making money. When and if this is done I have a novel in mind which (if I can write it) ought to be a step up. There is a murder in it, but it is not a mystery. The scene should properly be laid in England, since it is that sort of story, but I can't do it. It is too long since I left. Incidentally I still regard myself as an exile and want to come back. But I suppose it will be years before that is a reasonable thing to do.

Yours most sincerely

Raymond Chandler

## TO ALFRED KNOPF

6520 Drexel Ave.
Los Angeles 36, Calif.
Jan. 12th. 1946

Dear Alfred:

Good wishes to you and yours and many thanks for the Max Beerbohm book. I found it sad reading. It belongs to the age of taste, to which I once belonged. It took me back too far, to that first slim immortal volume which I still possess.[1] What a magnificent writer the old boy somehow did not become. Born half a century too late, I suppose.

I am enclosing a letter from a Jewish lady on a now familiar subject,[2] and my answer. This is the only one I have answered. Would you have the great kindness to send me a copy of my letter, in case I should want to use it again? That is, of course, if you agree with my writing it. If you do not, I should like to argue the point with you.

I no longer have a secretary since I no longer have a motion picture job. I am what is technically known as suspended. For refusing to perform under a contract which is not a proper expression of my standing in the motion picture business. I requested a

1. Max Beerbohm, *The Works of Max Beerbohm*, 1896.
2. See letter to Miss Aron, immediately following.

cancellation, but was denied that. There is no moral issue involved since the studios have destroyed the moral basis of contracts themselves. They tear them up whenever it suits them. In getting rid of a writer they use a term "adjusting the contract" which means paying him a few weeks salary under the threat of keeping his idea until his next option times comes up, with everyone knowing he has no assignment and that no producer on the lot wants him. This ought to work both ways. I have had no assistance worth mentioning in this controversy, since the Hollywood agent, however nice a fellow, is strictly a summer soldier. Syd wrote Mealand, Paramount's story editor, a very strong letter, and they were afraid to show it to Ginsberg, head of the studio.[3]

Paramount has raised the legal point that I cannot write for myself while suspended. This was all considered and thought out long ago. Their point has no validity, so far as I can determine, but they have the machinery to make trouble for me without cost to themselves, and I do not intend to spend my hard-earned (and God *was* it hard-earned) cash to defend law suits. Rather than do that I would go back and give them the two pictures I still owe.

One of the troubles is that it seems quite impossible to convince anyone that a man would turn his back on a whopping salary—whopping by the standards of normal living—for any reason but a tactical manoeuvre through which he hopes to acquire a still more whopping salary. What I want is something quite different: a freedom from datelines and unnatural pressures, and a right to find and work with those few people in Hollywood whose purpose is to make the best pictures possible within the limitations of a popular art, not merely to repeat the old and vulgar formulae. And only a little of that.

The ethics of this industry may be judged by the fact that late last night a very important independent producer called me up and asked me to do a screenplay of one of the most advertised projects of the year, do it on the quiet, secretly, with full knowledge that it would be a violation of my contract. That meant nothing to him; it never occurred to him that he was insulting me. Perhaps, in spite of my faults, I still have a sense of honor. I may quarrel, but at least I

---

3. Sydney Sanders was Chandler's agent, Richard Mealand was head of the story department, Henry Ginsberg was general manager of production.

[63]

put the point at issue down on the table in front of me. I am perfectly willing to let them examine my sleeves for hidden cards. But I don't think they really want to. They would be horrified to find them empty. They do not like to deal with honest men.

I am trying to finish up a Marlowe story. I am in a bit of a quandary about it. The practical need to keep the character alive is important for many reasons, among them the threat of a radio program which must eventually mature and which may go on for years. But I no longer have any passion for this stuff. I find myself kidding myself. I enjoy it and find it fun, but I have a suspicion that the quality that finally put these stories over was a sort of controlled half-poetical emotion. That for the story of blood and mystery I seem to have lost. Or rather I see so many other things I'd like to do. I have two novels in my head I want to write so much more. It is not that I have any ambition to become a writer of intellectual set pieces, because I know the audience I have to deal with and what they will not read is written in sand. From the beginning, from the first pulp story, it was always with me a question (first of course of how to write a story at all) of putting into the stuff something they would not shy off from, perhaps even not know was there as a conscious realization, but which would somehow distill through their minds and leave an afterglow. A man with a realistic habit of thought can no longer write for intellectuals. There are too few of them and they are too specious. Neither can he deliberately write for people he despises, or for the slick magazines (Hollywood is less degrading than that) or for money alone. There must be idealism but there must also be contempt. This kind of talk may seem a little ridiculous coming from me. It is possibly that like Max Beerbohm I was born half a century too late, and that I too belong to an age of grace. I could so easily have become everything our world has no use for. So I wrote for the *Black Mask*. What a wry joke.

No doubt I have learned a lot from Hollywood. Please do not think I completely despise it, because I don't. The best proof of that may be that every producer I have worked for I would work for again, and every one of them, in spite of my tantrums, would be glad to have me. But the overall picture, as the boys say, is of a degraded community whose idealism even is largely fake. The pretentiousness, the bogus enthusiasm, the constant drinking and drabbing, the incessant squabbling over money, the all-pervasive

[64]

agent, the strutting of the big shots (and their usually utter incompetence to achieve anything they start out to do), the constant fear of losing all this fairy gold and being the nothing they have really never ceased to be, the snide tricks, the whole damn mess is out of this world. It is a great subject for a novel—probably the greatest still untouched. But how to do it with a level mind, that's the thing that baffles me. It is like one of these South American palace revolutions conducted by officers in comic opera uniforms—only when the thing is over the ragged dead men lie in rows against the wall, and you suddenly know that this is not funny, this is the Roman circus, and damn near the end of a civilization.

Ray

## TO MISS ARON

6520 Drexel Ave.
Los Angeles 36, Calif.
Jan. 11, 1946

Dear Miss Aron:

I hope I address you correctly. I assume that you would have indicated, if it has been "Mrs." I thank you for your letter of November 30th and I quite agree that it deserves an answer. But I'm afraid I can't make a very good one, for the reason that I don't know what it is all about. I might say that I have received about a dozen letters on this subject, ranging from the pathological-vituperative to the courteous (of which yours is the only true example).

This book was published in 1942.[1] It has been for sale and in rental libraries for quite a long time. Apparently the outburst is due to the .25 edition. I had heard no previous whisper of complaint. I have many Jewish friends. I even have Jewish relatives. My publisher is a Jew. Are you one of those who object to that word? If so, what

1. *The High Window.*

[65]

would you like me to substitute? I am *not* being sarcastic. Also, *all* the letters have come from the east. Out here the Jews seem to be in a fair way to lose their inferiority complex. At least my doctor thinks so. He is a Jew also.

You say why don't I introduce a character as a "thin-blooded Roman Catholic or a rugged Episcopalian"? Simply, my dear, because religion has nothing to do with it. You may happen to be an orthodox Hebrew, but there are Roman Catholic Jews and Christian Scientist Jews and Jews with no religion at all, and Jews—very, very many—who are Hebrews just once a year, on the Day of Atonement. I call a character a Jew for purely intellectual reasons occasionally, since there is, except on the most exalted levels of personality a Jewish way of thought too.

The Jew is a type and I like types, that being as far as I have gone. He is of course many types, some recognizable a block away, some only on more intimate study, some hardly at all. I know there are Jewish people whom even Jews cannot pick out. I have had two secretaries who told me that, both being Jewish girls. There is a tone of voice, there is a certain eye, there is a coloring. It is not, dear lady, a matter of noses.

You are kind enough not to accuse me of anti-semitism. I am grateful for that since I am horribly tired of the whole subject. And at the same time I am terribly sorry for these tormented minds which cannot leave it alone, which worry it and keep it sore. A writer in the SRL lately said that what the Jews demand is not the right to have geniuses, but the right to have scoundrels.[2] I agree. And I demand the right to call a character named Weinstein a thief without being accused of calling all Jews thieves. That right, with certain people, I do not have.

Incidentally Dr. Carl Moss is a portrait of my publisher, Alfred Knopf. Not exact, but with the offhand respect which is all Philip Marlowe would have for anyone. And *I* am *not* Philip Marlowe.

Let me in all kindness say one final word. You are yourself not the type, but if among your friends there is an impulse to go on an anti-semitic witch hunt, let them look for their enemies not among those who call a Jew a Jew, who put Jewish characters in their books because there are many Jews in their lives and all interesting and all

2. *Saturday Review of Literature.*

different and some noble and some rather nasty—like other people—but let them look for their enemies among the brutes (whom they can easily recognize) and among the snobs who do not speak of Jews at all.

You are safe and more than safe with outspoken people like me.

Very sincerely,

Raymond Chandler

# TO ERLE STANLEY GARDNER

6520 Drexel Ave.
Los Angeles 36, Calif.
Jan. 29, 1946

Dear Erle:

Most of what you write is a complete surprise to me—including the idea that you are a lousy writer. I may later ask the privilege of addressing the Court on that point. I don't think I ever knew that Phil Cody had been editor of the BM[1] or that Hammett and you and others had been in the book for years. I didn't know the magazine until 1932 or 1933, although I later picked up a few older copies. In view of the fact that I was raised on Latin and Greek and once wrote essays and book reviews for a *very* highbrow English weekly, the story of how I became a multiple murderer may have a certain piquancy, but there's not time to go into it now. Nor did I know that Cody was the real discoverer of Hammett and his first strong encouragement. I think these things need airing. I have always received from Shaw the definite impression (borne out by his projected introduction to his projected anthology) that he invented the hardboiled dick story with a ready assist from Hammett.[2] Certainly

1. *Black Mask* magazine.
2. Joseph Shaw succeeded Cody as editor of *Black Mask*.

[67]

nothing of Shaw's own fiction that I have seen has any such germs in it. It's about the deadest writing I ever saw, on a supposedly professional level. I don't know what Hammett was writing before he and Shaw had the brainwave, but it is now obvious to me and would have been earlier if I had really done any serious thinking on the subject, that it did not happen all at once. There must have been experiments and discussions and a need to get an okay from the boss. Shaw's gifts as an editor seem to me now to be exactly what you rate them. He was a warm editor and always seemed to have time to write at length and to argue with you. To some of us I think he was indeed a genuine inspiration in that, just as you say, we wrote better for him than we could have written for anybody else. The proof of that is that some writers we both know have never reached the standard again that they attained in the *BM* under Shaw. I also agree with you that he was blind to any kind of writing he did not think the best at the moment. I don't believe Cornell Woolrich or Cleve Adams ever made the *BM* under his editorship, although both were probably far better men than some of his regulars. Norbert Davis also, who took his murders rather lightly when allowed, made the *BM* only two or three times.[3] He said Shaw was too fussy for him and took the whole thing too seriously. I'm quite sure Shaw would never have published a story I once wrote kidding the pants off the tough dick story, but Ken White did.[4]

.    .    .

I now address the Court, by permission, on the subject of one Gardner, an alleged writer of mysteries. As I speak I have two solid rows of Gardners in front of me, and am still trying to shop around to complete the collection. I probably know as much about the essential qualities of good writing as anybody now discussing it. I do not discuss these things professionally for the simple reason that I do not consider it worthwhile. I am not interested in pleasing the intellectuals by writing literary criticism, because literary criticism as an art has in these days too narrow a scope and too limited a public,

3.  Adams and Davis belonged to the hard-boiled school of detective novelists.
4.  "Pearls Are a Nuisance," originally published in *Dime Detective Magazine*, edited by White.

just as has poetry. I do not believe it is a writer's function to talk to a dead generation of leisured people who once had time to relish the niceties of critical thought. The critics of today are tired Bostonians like Van Wyck Brooks or smart-alecks like Fadiman or honest men confused by the futility of their job, like Edmund Wilson. The reading public is intellectually adolescent at best, and it is obvious that what is called "significant literature" will only be sold to this public by exactly the same methods as are used to sell it toothpaste, cathartics and automobiles. It is equally obvious that since this public has been taught to read by brute force it will, in between its bouts with the latest "significant" bestseller, want to read books that are fun and excitement. So like all half-educated publics in all ages it turns with relief to the man who tells a story and nothing else. To say that what this man writes is not literature is just like saying that a book can't be any good if it makes you want to read it. When a book, any sort of book, reaches a certain intensity of artistic performance, it becomes literature. That intensity may be a matter of style, situation, character, emotional tone, or idea, or half a dozen other things. It may also be a perfection of control over the movement of a story similar to the control a great pitcher has over the ball. That is to me what you have more than anything else and more than anyone else. Dumas Père had it. Dickens, allowing for his Victorian muddle, had it; begging your pardon I don't think Edgar Wallace approached it. His stories died all along the line and had to be revived. Yours don't. Every page throws the hook for the next. I call this a kind of genius. I regard myself as a pretty exacting reader; detective stories as such don't mean a thing to me. But it must be obvious that if I have half a dozen unread books beside my chair and one of them is a Perry Mason, and I reach for the Perry Mason and let the others wait, that book must have quality.

Strangely enough I didn't always feel this way, and I think for the same reason Shaw didn't. I was so steeped in the rugged stuff that I didn't realize how stupid it can be unless it is superbly well done. Today I could no more read a book by Coxe or Adams than I could eat a kangaroo. I think also that I do agree you didn't do your best work for *BM*. In fact you've only been doing it at the peak the last four or five years. It's pretty obvious to me why that is too. You never were a *Black Mask* writer in Shaw's meaning of the

[69]

term. You never really were tough. You owed nothing to Hammett or Hemingway. Your books have no brutality or sadism, very little sex, and the blood doesn't count. What counts, at least for me, is a supremely skilful combination of the mental quality of the detective story and the movement of the mystery-adventure story. I read the Doug Selby stories and like them and try to guess where the hell Madison City is (the nearest I can come is Riverside, and that isn't quite right) but there is something missing. I liked the A. A. Fair stories, especially the first ones, but they have in the end the same defect the Nero Wolfe stories have: an eccentric character wears out its welcome. The character that lasts is an ordinary guy with some extraordinary qualities. Perry Mason is the perfect detective because he has the intellectual approach of the juridical mind and at the same time the restless quality of the adventurer who won't stay put. I think he is just about perfect. So let's not have any more of that phooey about "as literature my stuff still stinks." Who says so— William Dean Howells?

As to me, I am not busy and I am not successful in any important way. I don't get written what I want to write and I get balled up in what I do write. I made a lot of money last year, but the government took half of it and expenses took half of the rest. I'm not poor, but neither am I in anything like your condition, or ever will be. My wife has been under the weather with the flu for ten days, but she wants to come down to your place as much as I do. I'm working at home because I refused to report to Paramount and took a suspension. They refused to tear up my contract. A writer has no real chance in pictures unless he is willing to become a producer, and that is too tough for me. The last picture I worked on was just one long row.[5] The producer was fine, but he was on the way out. The director has been thirty years in Hollywood without ever doing a first class job, or, I should add in fairness, a very bad one. But it was my picture, I wrote it from the ground up, and I hoped for a little more finesse than I got. However, they say it's good, and good original screenplays are almost as rare in Hollywood as virgins.

Ray

5. *The Blue Dahlia.*

# TO WILLIAM W. SEWARD

6520 Drexel Drive
Los Angeles, California
Mar 27 1946

Dear Professor Seward:

Some time ago, at your request, I sent you one of my books. I am wondering if you ever received it. It seems rather curious that you should not have acknowledged it, if it arrived.

I don't exactly know why I am writing this note. It is not a matter of great consequence either way. I suppose I find the incident rather shocking.

Yours very truly,

Raymond Chandler

# TO BLANCHE KNOPF

6520 Drexel Ave.
Los Angeles 36, Calif.
Mar 27 1946

Dear Blanche:

Thanks for your note, and it's always a pleasure to hear from you. I got pretty well into a Marlowe story but ran into a bad spell of flu and have been dragging myself around ever since. Also I am in trouble with Paramount and may have to go back and finish a couple of jobs for them. Short of an action to cancel the contract, there seems no other way to deal with the situation. And even an equity action takes time and money and is uncertain. I have developed a peculiar phobia about contracts, seem unable to function as a free man

[71]

when tied up in any way. All very silly, no doubt, but there it is. The mere fact that sometime I must go to a studio to do a job of work seems to prevent my doing anything valid for myself. Hollywood is a trying place in many ways, but at least they pay you for your work.

I don't understand this reprint situation at all. There is a body of opinion that seems to regard the royalities the Pocket Book people are paying as something like outright theft. I do not understand why a publisher should collect three times as much *in royalities* on a writer's books as the publisher pays the writer out in royalties on the original edition. I have a feeling that a situation has developed which needs airing. Why is it not explained? Is it right that a sale of a million copies of a two-bit reprint should bring the man who created the material sold a matter of $7500? This needs an answer. I do not think it *is* right. I think the author on *all* reprints should have a minimum royalty of ten percent of the retail price. Anything less has me wondering what goes on. No wonder writers accept the conditions of Hollywood and say to hell with bookwriting. Leave it to the women. It's all mechanics and promotion anyway. As I told my friend Morton of the *Atlantic* not long ago, the technique of marketable fiction has become almost entirely epicene. It won't be long now until somebody invents a machine to write novels. How often do I pick up a book and say, "This was written by an individual unlike any other individual, a unique person."? Practically never.

But don't take me too seriously. I am becoming a pretty sour kind of citizen. Even Hemingway has let me down. I've been rereading a lot of his stuff. I would have said here is one guy who writes like himself, and I would have been right, but not the way I meant it. Ninety per cent of it is the godddamndest self-imitation. He never really wrote but one story. All the rest is the same thing in different pants—or without different pants. And his eternal preoccupation with what goes on between the sheets becomes rather nauseating in the end. One reaches a time of life when limericks written on the walls of comfort stations are not just obscene, they are horribly dull. This man has only one subject and he makes that ridiculous. I suppose the man's epitaph, if he had the choosing of it, would be: Here Lies A Man Who Was Bloody Good in Bed. Too Bad He's Alone Here. But the point is I begin to doubt whether he ever

was. You don't have to work so hard at things you are really good
at—or do you?

I thank you.
Ray

# TO ERLE STANLEY GARDNER

6520 Drexel Ave.
Los Angeles 36 Calif.
April 4th. 1946

Dear Erle:

Thanks for your kind message. I don't think either my wife or
myself could hike or ride. She had an operation on her foot about
a year ago and it's still weak. We don't know how to ride. I am a
complete nervous wreck and theoretically could walk a few miles, but
probably not your kind of walking. Haven't the equipment anyhow.
What we hoped to do was just to get down to your place around
noon and spend a few hours with you. We have some business in
Riverside and were thinking of stopping over at the Mission Inn and
then driving to Temecula in the morning.

However, my war with Paramount has flared up again and I
am stuck here at any rate until next week, and then may have to go to
Santa Barbara. So we'll just have to let it ride for the time being. I
have been trying for six months to get my contract with Paramount
torn up. Have refused to go to work, they hurled threats, I responded
with a dignified silence (at times). We are now making an armistice to
be followed by a peace treaty. The great difficulty in dealing with
a studio is that the men you deal with are in their turn responsible to
a New York hierarchy which had no part in making pictures, but
only in exhibiting and promoting them. To them a picture is just as
much a manufactured product as a can of beans. They cannot allow

[73]

for the personal equation because they don't meet it. I believe I and my lawyer and agent have won a remarkable victory in fact, which can still by the studio's legal department be made to look like a practical victory for the company. And that of course is what they must have for face-saving purposes.

I was very eager to discuss the reprint situation with you. I understood that you did not agree with the position of Rex Stout's committee on reprint royalties, but I don't think I have heard why. I personally think that the royalty *to the author* on any reprint should not be less than 10 per cent of the retail price. It seems like pure theft that Pocket Books should shell out a measly fifteen grand on a million sale and that the publisher should get half of that. I may be all wet on this, but surely the publishers are getting an excessive share of the returns from markets which did not even exist when they made their contracts and which they have done almost nothing to create. Of course I admit you never get what you should. Nobody but the middleman ever does. In Hollywood it is now recognized that the screenplay cost should approximate ten per cent of the picture cost, but if a single writer does the whole job, he cannot get anything like that without going into a percentage deal. I am not talking about sales of screen rights, but of the cost of making the screenplay itself, the shooting script. The big money still goes to the wrong people. Nevertheless Hollywood does pay the writer pretty well if he is any good. The book trade pays him abominably unless he writes best sellers, and that means best sellers in the original edition. You and I may never write a best seller, even a moderate best seller, in that sense, and yet there is a better continuing sale for our kind of stuff than for any other kind. I think we are getting gyped on the reprints. A man whose book sells a quarter or half a million copies in any kind of edition ought to get a very substantial income out of it. We don't. You beat the racket by having so many books around. I can't beat it that way because I am a slow writer. Of course you don't beat it really. You simply make a lot of money, but that doesn't mean you shouldn't make five times as much for the same out put.

I refused to write an introduction for Shaw's anthology. Don't know whether he is hurt about it or not.

Ray

# TO HAMISH HAMILTON

Dear Jamie:

．　　　　．　　　　．

When and if you see *The Big Sleep* (the first half of it anyhow), you will realize what can be done with this sort of story by a director with the gift of atmosphere and the requisite touch of hidden sadism. Bogart, of course, is also so much better than any other tough-guy actor that he makes bums of the Ladds and the Powells. As we say here, Bogart can be tough without a gun. Also he has a sense of humor that contains that grating undertone of contempt. Ladd is hard, bitter and occasionally charming, but he is after all a small boy's idea of a tough guy, Bogart is the genuine article. Like Edward G. Robinson when he was younger all he has to do to dominate a scene is to enter it. *The Big Sleep* has had an unfortunate history. The girl who played the nymphy sister[1] was so good she shattered Miss Bacall completely. So they cut the picture in such a way that all her best scenes were left out except one. The result made nonsense and Howard Hawks threatened to sue to restrain Warners from releasing the picture. After long argument, as I hear it, he went back and did a lot of re-shooting. I have not seen the result of this. The picture has not even been trade-shown. But if Hawks got his way, the picture will be the best of its kind. Since I had nothing to do with it, I say this with some faint regret. Well, that's not exactly true because Hawks time after time got dissatisfied with his script and would go back to the book and shoot scenes straight out of it. There was also a wonderful scene he and I planned together in talk. At the end of the picture Bogart and Carmen were caught in Geiger's house by the Eddie Mars and his lifetakers. That is Bogart (Marlowe) was trapped there and the girl came along and they let her go in. Bogart knew she was a murderess and he also knew that the first person out of that door would walk into a hail of machine gun bullets. The girl didn't know this. Marlowe also knew that if he sent the girl out to be killed, the gang would take it on the lam, thus saving his own life for the time being. He didn't feel like

---

1. Martha Vickers.

playing God or saving his skin by letting Carmen leave. Neither did he feel like playing Sir Philip Sidney to save a worthless life. So he put it up to God by tossing a coin. Before he tossed the coin he prayed out loud, in a sort of way. The gist of his prayer was that he, Marlowe, had done the best he knew how and through no fault of his own was put in a position of making a decision God had no right to force him to make. He wanted that decision made by the authority who allowed all this mess to happen. If the coin came down heads, he would let the girl go. He tossed and it came down heads. The girl thought this was some kind of a game to hold her there for the police. She started to leave. At the last moment, as she had her hand on the doorknob, Marlowe weakened and started for her to stop her. She laughed in his face and pulled a gun on him. Then she opened the door an inch or two and you could see she was going to shoot and was thoroughly delighted with the situation. At that moment a burst of machine gun fire walked across the panel of the door and tore her to pieces. The gunmen outside had heard a siren in the distance and panicked and thrown a casual burst through the door just for a visiting card—without expecting to hit anyone. I don't know what happened to this scene. Perhaps the boys wouldn't write it or couldn't. Perhaps Mr. Bogart wouldn't play it. You never know in Hollywood. All I know is it would have been a hair-raising thing if well done. I think I'll try it myself sometime.

All the best,

Ray

## TO CHARLES MORTON

Paramount Pictures
5451 Marathon Street
Hollywood 38, Calif.
June 14, 1946

Dear Charles:

What Wolcott Gibbs has to say about it [*The Hucksters* by Frederic Wakeman] in *The New Yorker* doesn't mean a thing to me. The fact that Gibbs (together with other *New Yorker* critical minds) is gifted with a talent for derogatory criticism, doesn't necessarily make him a good critic. I remember, long ago, when I was doing book-reviews in London, that my first impulse always was to find something smart and nasty to say because that sort of writing is so much easier. In spite of its superficial sophistication, the whole attitude of the *New Yorker* seems to me to have that same touch of under-graduate sarcasm. I find this sort of thing rather juvenile. In fact, heretical as it may seem, I'm beginning to find the *New Yorker* a very dull periodical.

Kindest regards,<br>
Ray

## TO H. N. SWANSON

Sunday August 4th [1946]

Dear Swanie:

Thanks for yours of July 31st. I imagine everyone ought to meet Samuel Goldwyn this side of paradise, I've heard he feels so good when he stops. But since the whole thing is predicated on my working for him and I ain't gonna, is it worth while? I don't know. I don't know anything, except that the standard method of working with writers is not for me. I think it works for 80% of the writers in Hollywood, that through it the studios somehow get pictures they would never get and ought never to get, if they relied on the writers having any judgment of what is a picture. I don't think the system works for those writers who, whatever their faults, cannot work effectively unless they can somehow preserve the illusion that they are doing their own writing according to their own sense of what is right. If Paramount had had the sense to let me write my own idea of a rough screenplay on *Mrs. Duff*, without the interference of a producer's ideas, ambition, and eagerness to dominate a project to his own advantage, they would have got something in a comparatively

[77]

short time which would have shown them at a glance where the picture was.[1] It wouldn't have to be perfect, or even right. It would have been a screen treatment in screenplay form (with probably a lot of usable scenes) of the story as it interested me to write it. But no, they simply cannot realize that what they want from me is what I write in my own way; they think they can get that and at the same time control almost every move I make and every idea I have. It just can't be done. What I have to give them is not craftmanship but a certain quality. If they want that quality, they can't get it anywhere else. If they bring in the Steve Fishers to polish my work, they get something entirely different, so why bother with me at all?[2] I suppose you would regard Dudley Nichols as a great screenplay writer, and I shouldn't deny it. But what is there in his work that is Nichols? Is there anything in the *Bells of Saint Mary, Scarlet Street* and *Stagecoach* that belongs to one man and one man only? If there is, I can't see it. Perhaps to someone more expert in the business, it would be apparent. To me all three of these pictures, and any others of his you care to mention that I have seen, could have been written by different writers. As far as any individual style is concerned, they are completely anonymous. That is not the kind of work I want to do in pictures. If that is the only kind of work—or something much inferior, technically—I am allowed to do, then I have nothing to contribute. For this reason I will not work for dominating people like Selznick or Goldwyn. If you deprive me of the right to do my own kind of writing, there is almost nothing left.

We are going to La Jolla tomorrow for a few days.

What's holding me up on the book is that in the disgusted (and disgusting) state of mind I am in I wouldn't dare look at it.

Love

Ray

P.S. La Valencia Hotel, Glencoe 52175 (San Diego) in case of emergency. An emergency would to my mind be a lot of money for nothing.

R.

1. Chandler worked on the screenplay of *The Innocent Mrs. Duff,* a novel by Elisabeth Sanxay Holding.
2. Fisher completed the screenplay of *The Lady in the Lake.*

# TO DALE WARREN

6005 Camino de la Costa
La Jolla, California
October Second 1946

Dear Dale Warren:

 •          •          •

I suppose you read a bookseller out here was convicted of selling indecency in Edmund Wilson's *Memoirs of Hecate County*. Very discouraging. The book is indecent enough, of course, and in exactly the most offensive way—without passion, like a phallus made of dough. Now they are bootlegging the damn thing at $25 a copy. It isn't worth the original asking price. Being, like all those who have worked in Hollywood, somewhat of a connoisseur of the damp fart, I place Mr. Wilson high on the list. His careful and pedestrian and sometimes rather intelligent book reviews misguide one into thinking there is something in his head besides mucilage. There isn't.

Having started both the above paragraphs with I—I was taught not to as a schoolboy—let me add that I (we) have moved to La Jolla permanently, or as permanently as anything can be nowadays. If I do any more work for Hollywood, which I probably shall, I can do nine tenths of it here anyway. That is, if I can find a secretary. We live close beside the sounding sea—it's just across the street and down a low cliff—but the Pacific is usually very sedate. We have a much better home than an out-of-work pulp writer has any right to expect.

The story I am working on seems to me to lack some of the nobler qualities. In addition to which I find it dull. I wonder could I be washed up for good. It's possible. Better men than I have gone to grease in Hollywood.

 •          •

Sincerely,

Raymond Chandler

[79]

# TO HAMISH HAMILTON

Dear Jamie:

Your letter of September 30th. makes me rather uneasy. "A new Philip Marlowe story by Raymond Chandler, tentatively called *The Little Sister*, and dealing with some rather queer characters in Hollywood, not to mention an innocent little girl from Kansas, who may or may not be quite as innocent as she looks." That's about all I could tell you at the moment.

I have what you people called "a thing" about discussing or writing about anything I haven't licked. I'm never sure I shall lick it. I might blow up completely about page 250 (which means the silly little triple-spaced half pages I type on) and shelve the whole project.

Three years in Hollywood leaves its mark. My kind of writing takes a certain quality of high spirits and impudence. I'm a tired character, a battered pulp writer, an out of work hack. Also, as a mental hazard I might mention that although it seems to me almost mandatory as a business move that I should do a Marlowe story, I have a couple of other notions I'd much rather be trying to work out.

My title may not be very good. It's just the best I can think of without straining. I have peculiar ideas about titles. They should never be obviously provocative, nor say anything about murder. They should be rather indirect and neutral, but the form of words should be a little unusual. I haven't achieved this here. However, as some big publisher once remarked, a good title is the title of a successful book. Offhand, nobody would have thought *The Thin Man* a great title. *The Maltese Falcon* is, because it has rhyme and rhythm and makes the mind ask questions.

As to publishers, I wonder if they know anything about titles. Knopf made me change the title of *The High Window*, but I see Twentieth Century-Fox has restored the original title. Knopf objected strenuously to *Farewell, My Lovely*, and this, according to my Hollywood friends (who are a pretty good judge of these things) is one of the great titles of pure magic that rarely come along. Knopf still feels, I think, that the title hurt the sales of the book. Perhaps he is right. But Pocketbooks didn't find it any disadvantage.

Oh yes, the book will run in length, I hope, not more than 70,000 words, perhaps less.

I never really solved my agent problem. I still feel much about the same about agents as a class: that they are often a nuisance and sometimes do very stupid things. But living down here in La Jolla, and not being able to face a regular secretary around the house, I don't see how I could function without an agent. The thing about agents that really annoys me is not that they make mistakes, but that they never admit them.

All the best,

Ray

# TO WILLIAM TARG[1]

6005 Camino de la Costa
La Jolla, California
Nov. 14th. 1946

Dear Mr. Targ:

Thanks for yours of Nov. 12th. which I am sending to my Hollywood agent, Mr. H. N. Swanson, 8523 Sunset Boulevard, Hollywood 46, Calif. What New York representation he will arrange I do not know yet.

The terms on this deal I will leave to him. What I am concerned with is what goes into the book, and whether a somewhat intellectual article such as the *Atlantic* piece is an appropriate introduction to a collection of what are after all just old pulp novelettes. Frankly, I just don't know about the last point. The article rather takes the position, which I still think valid, that the old

1. Targ, then of World Publishing Company, had proposed an anthology of Chandler's *Black Mask* stories using Chandler's *Atlantic* article, "The Simple Art of Murder," as a preface.

fashioned body-in-the-library detection novel is a good deal of bunk a) because it can never be about anything real and b) because it doesn't stand up under its own rules. Then I say that the only thing that's any good is the realistic detective or mystery novel. And *then* I proceed to hand the public a bunch of stories which, whatever their merits or demerits, were certainly not what I was building up to in the essay. I could have written them much better even then, but the point is I wasn't allowed to. And I can't alibi on that score.

I can't avoid the thought that the use of the essay as a preface to my own early writings makes me look kind of silly. I presume you have considered that. I presume you have an argument against it.

As to the actual selection of the stories, since they have already been republished in both .49 and .25 editions, I suppose a larger book on the same reprint price scale is not going to do any harm. I know you want a fairly long book to justify your price. But there are a few of these stories I'd just as soon see go out of circulation, for various reasons. I'd like to discuss these reasons with my agent too. I'll be seeing him next week.

Sincerely yours,

Raymond Chandler

## TO H. N. SWANSON

6005 Camino de la Costa
La Jolla, California
December 20, 1946

Dear Swanie:

This is to thank you very, very much for your Christmas gift of the little radio.

From the shape of it, I gather that it was to be placed on a bookshelf. I have therefore placed it between Roget's *Thesaurus* and

Bartlett's *Quotations*, and the cretinous dialogue of "When a Girl Marries" coming out from between these two books certainly gives me a laugh.

My wife said (paraphrased slightly), "Why the hell should Swanson keep on giving you presents when you don't do a damned thing for him except cause him a lot of worry, and especially when you give him nothing in return?"

I am therefore going to look for a pair of twelve-hundred-year old Ming vases to present to you on your next birthday, and I hope they will be large enough to be used as receptacles for your discarded clients.

Kindest regards and best wishes to you and yours,


# TO MRS. ROBERT J. HOGAN[1]

December 27, 1946

Dear Mrs. Hogan:

My experience with trying to help people to write has been limited but extremely intensive. I have done everything from giving would-be writers money to live on to plotting and rewriting their stories for them, and so far I have found it to be all waste. The people whom God or nature intended to be writers find their own answers, and those who have to ask are impossible to help. They are merely people who want to be writers.

Yours very truly,

Raymond Chandler

1. A New Jersey teacher who had written asking for advice to give to the young.

# TO CHARLES MORTON

6005 Camino de la Costa
La Jolla, California
Sunday Jan. 5th. 1947

Dear Charles:

·        ·        ·

Have just finished reading *Command Decision*, not in the
*Atlantic*, the book.[1] I suppose some was omitted. I found it absolutely
(or almost) unputdownable and at the same time as complete a waste
of time in a sense as one of Gardner's Perry Mason stories, which I
also find unputdownable. *B.F.'s Daughter* is the same, but has a little
more penetration into character.[2] Books like this start me pondering
without getting very far on just what literature is turning into. I
wrote you once in a mood of rough sarcasm that the techniques of
fiction had become so highly standardized that one of these days a
machine would write novels. What bothers me about this book,
*Command Decision*, and others like it is that it has everything in the
way of skill and perception and wit and honesty a good novel ought
to have. It has a subject, something I never had yet; it has a sharp
immediate sense of life as it is right now. I'd be hard put to it to say
just what it does *not* have, but that thing, whatever it is, is more
important than what it does have. I'm absolutely sure of that,
although I don't expect to sell anyone else on the idea. Your Mr.
Weeks, who is a much more intelligent man than I am, thinks
Marquand is a serious writer.[3] I do not. I think he is a quick and
clever journalist. I think he will be utterly forgotten five years after he
dies, by all but a few. Is it that these books are written very quickly,
in a kind of heat? No answer; so was a lot of literature that has lasted
a long time. The time of composition has nothing to do with it;
some minds distill much faster than others. Is it that the writers of
these books are using completely borrowed techniques and
consequently do not convey the feeling that they have created, but

1. William Wister Haines, *Command Decision*, 1947.
2. By John P. Marquand.
3. Edward Weeks, editor of *The Atlantic Monthly*.

rather that they have reported? Closer, but still not quite the answer. Undoubtedly we are getting a lot of adept reportage which masquerades as fiction and will go on getting it, but essentially I believe that what is lacking is an emotional quality. Even when they deal with death, and they often do, they are not tragic. I suppose that is to be expected. An age which is incapable of poetry is incapable of any kind of literature except that cleverness of a decadence. The boys can say anything, their scenes are almost tiresomely neat, they have all the facts and all the answers, but they are little men who have forgotten how to pray. As the world grows smaller, so the minds of men grow smaller, more compact, and more empty. These are the machine-minders of literature.

Ray

## TO EDWARD WEEKS

6005 Camino de la Costa
La, Jolla, California
Jan. 18th, 1947

Dear Mr. Weeks:

I'm afraid you've thrown me for a loss. I thought "Juju Worship in Hollywood" was a perfectly good title.[1] I don't see why it has to be linked up with crime and mystery. But you're the Boss. When I wrote about writers this did not occur to you. I've thought of various titles such as *Bank Night in Hollywood, Sutter's Last Stand, The Golden Peepshow, All it Needs is Elephants, The Hot Shot Handicap, Where Vaudeville Went it Died*, and rot like that. But nothing that smacks you in the kisser. By the way, would you convey my compliments to the purist who reads your proofs and tell him or her that I write in a sort of broken-down patois which is something like the way a Swiss

1. Article on Hollywood Academy Awards. Published as "Oscar Night in Hollywood," *Atlantic Monthly*, March 1948.

[85]

waiter talks, and that when I split an infinitive, God damn it, I split it so it will stay split, and when I interrupt the velvety smoothness of my more or less literate syntax with a few sudden words of barroom vernacular, this is done with the eyes wide open and the mind relaxed but attentive. The method may not be perfect, but it is all I have. I think your proofreader is kindly attempting to steady me on my feet, but much as I appreciate the solicitude, I am really able to steer a fairly clear course, provided I get both sidewalks and the street between.

If I think of anything, I'll wire you.

Kindest regards,


## TO MRS. ROBERT HOGAN

March 8th. 1947

Dear Mrs. Hogan:
Thank you for your elegant letter. It was charming of you to write at such length. I'm pleased to find someone else than myself who writes long letters. A few notes on your questionnaire. I might say that my first piece of writing was a poem. I had extensive experience writing for daily papers and weekly reviews in England when quite young, but although I made as much at it as most people, I still did not make a decent living. So went into business when I came to this country. Started writing pulp during the depression as my highly paid executive job went by the board. Particular medium I picked was due to a belief on my part that (a) some of the pulps at that time had very honest and forthright stuff in them; (b) that the literary standard was flexible and there was a chance to get "paid while learning"; (c) that although the average story in the *Black Mask* was not too good, there was a possibility of writing them very much better without hurting their chances of being read.

I have never written but one story for a slick magazine. It was sold to the *Post* and they liked it and wanted more about the same character. But in spite of my agent's advice (later objurgation and finally almost fury) I had a conviction that the superficial neatness of slick writing was only natural when it was feminine, and that if I got good at it (which as I look back seems easy, but did not seem so then), I would eventually be damn sorry. Mine was of course a losing game, on the surface. I wrote pulp stories with as much care as slick stories. It was very poor pay for the work I put into them. I obeyed the formula because I honestly liked it, but I was always trying to stretch it, trying to get in bits of peripheral writing which were not necessary but which I felt would have a subconscious effect even on the semi–literate readers; I felt somehow that the thing to get in this kind of story was a kind of richness of texture, and that you couldn't get it in a slick story. Or at least I couldn't. In the end I did get it, and it is quite clear now that when men of the quality of, say Charles Morton of the *Atlantic* say they think any one of my novelettes is better than anything Hammett ever wrote, they are not talking about the quality of mystery or violence or plot, but about this richness of texture. I myself don't like the stories any more and am a bit apprehensive about their being published in a collected edition. But I do like what I was trying to do in them.

One of my peculiarities and difficulties as a writer is that I won't discard anything. I have heard this is unprofessional and that it is a weakness of the amateur not to be able to tell when his stuff is not coming off. I can tell that all right, as to the matter in hand, but I can't overlook the fact that I had a reason, a feeling, for starting to write it, and I'll be damned if I won't lick it. I have lost months of time because of this stubbornness. However, after working in Hollywood, where the analysis of plot and motivation is carried on daily with an utter ruthlessness, I realize that it was always a plot difficulty that held me up. I simply would not plot far enough ahead. I'd write something I liked and then I would have a hell of a time making it fit in to the structure. This resulted in some rather starting oddities of construction, about which I care nothing, being fundamentally rather uninterested in plot.

Another of my oddities (and this one I believe in absolutely) is that you never quite know where your story is until you have written the first draft of it. So I always regard the first draft as raw material. What seems to be alive in it is what belongs in the story. Even if the neatness has to be lost, I will still keep whatever has that effect of getting up on its own feet and marching. A good story cannot be devised; it has to be distilled. In the long run, however little you talk or even think about it, the most durable thing in writing is style, and style is the most valuable investment a writer can make with his time. It pays off slowly, your agent will sneer at it, your publisher will misunderstand it, and it will take people you never heard of to convince them by slow degrees that the writer who puts his individual mark on the way he writes will always pay off. He can't do it by trying, because the kind of style I am thinking about is a projection of personality and you have to have a personality before you can project it. But granted that you have one, you can only project it on paper by thinking of something else. This is ironical in a way; it is the reason, I suppose, why in a generation of "made" writers I still say you can't make a writer. Preoccupation with style will not produce it. No amount of editing and polishing will have any appreciable effect on the flavor of how a man writes. It is the product of the quality of his emotion and perception; it is the ability to transfer these to paper which makes him a writer, in contrast to the great number of people who have just as good emotions and just as keen perceptions, but cannot come within a googol of miles of putting them on paper. I know several made writers. Hollywood, of course, is full of them; their stuff often has an immediate impact of competence and sophistication, but it is hollow underneath, and you never go back to it. I don't, anyway.

If anyone asked me to give advice to beginning writers, I should probably say quite sincerely that I don't know enough to give advice of a general nature. You are largely preoccupied with the problem of showing people how to make their material marketable. You probably, or certainly, know a lot more about that than I do. Anyhow, I've never had any luck helping anyone to do it. Such wisdom as I may have acquired through my own struggles is only useful for the long pull, since it rather goes to the belief that too much preoccupation with the mechanics of writing is a sure sign of a weak talent or none at all.

Sincerely,

Raymond Chandler

[88]

# TO JAMES SANDOE

6005 Camino de la Costa
La Jolla, California
March 8th. 1947

Dear Sandoe:

Thanks for yours of 19th. Feb. Have had the flu and am just crawling out. Haven't sent *Blondes' Requiem* yet, but hope to Monday. No, I shouldn't take any action.[1] I am only one of several plagiarized writers and there is probably no measurable damage. I tried to get my publisher to write the publisher of *BR* telling him the facts, just in case he had a chance to put out a pocket book edition. Seems as if his lawyer was afraid to go even that far. I think he is wrong.

I dispute your point about *Pin to see Peepshow* connecting up with Hamlet, etc.[2] I think *Hamlet*, *Macbeth*, the great Greek tragedies, *Anna Karenina* and Dostoievsky etc. are quite another matter, not so much because they are better, as because they are not nervous-making in the same sense. There is a great difference (to me at least) between a tragic ending and a miserably unhappy ending. You cannot write tragedy on the level of the suburban novel; you just get misery without the purging of high emotions. And naturally the quality of the emotions is a matter of projection, how it is done, what the total effect of style is. It is not a matter of dealing with heroic-sized people.

I have not seen *Lady in the Lake*. It is only fair, I think. *The Brashear Doubloon*[3] is definitely bad: poor acting, poor direction, wretched scripting. It should have made the best picture of all of them. I messed up the story, but the story was there. I see where in his anthology Haycraft can't understand why you picked *The High Window* over *Farewell My Lovely*.[4] I felt in sympathy with you. *The High Window*, with its faults, was more than a tough stylized mystery.

No, I am not working on a story of murder without detection.

---

1. By Raymond Marshall, pseudonym for Rene Raymond, who also wrote under the name of James Hadley Chase. Chandler's publisher successfully pressed charges against this author for plagiarism of works by Chandler, Dashiell Hammett, and Jonathan Latimer.
2. F. Tennyson Jesse, *A Pin to See the Peepshow*, 1934.
3. Film version of *The High Window*.
4. Howard Haycraft, *Art of the Mystery Story*.

I have such a story in mind, but have not got down to it yet. I am working, or was, on another Marlowe, because for business or professional reasons I think the guy is too valuable to let die out. But I find myself spoofing more and more. My next job, however, is to do a job for Universal on one of the most unusual deals ever made in Hollywood, or so I am told.[5] They pay me a large sum of money and a percentage of the picture to write them a screenplay, and they only get the picture rights. The unusual feature, which may not seem striking to you but I can assure you it is, is that they do *not* employ me, but merely agree to buy the motion picture rights to something I write in my own way and without any supervision. Of course I can't control what they do to it in production. I tried to get that, but it was a little too rich for their blood. It is like a studio buying the rights to a screenplay a writer has turned out on his own time, with the difference that they gamble before I write a word.

.     .     .

I am a damn fool not to be writing novels. I'm still getting about $15,000 a year out of those I did write. If I turned out a really good one in the near future, I'd probably get a lot out of it. Curiously enough my best public, relatively, is in England where my publisher, in spite of the terrible shortage of paper, is re-issuing all my books. And over there the topflight critics, like Desmond MacCarthy and Elizabeth Bowen review them. MacCarthy panned me, said the toughness was largely bluff (which is true), but in view of the fact that he does only one article a week for the *Observer* or *Sunday Times*, I forget which, and devoted it all to one of mine, I am less concerned with his strictures than with what he did with his space.

Kindest regards,

RC

5. To write original screenplay of *Playback*.

# TO B. D. ZEVIN[1]

6005 Camino de la Costa
La Jolla, California
March 9th. 1947

Dear Mr. Zevin:

My only excuse for not writing to you before is that I have had a bad case of the flu, much more prolonged than usual, and am only now beginning to get sassy again.

Thank you very much indeed for the Sandburg book. These poems are curious reading now. When they were first published, apparently they were blunt and brutal as hell. Now they seem, if anything, restrained. They have a lot of Whitmanesque blether about man-child and woman-child etc. which seems curiously strained, like a pulp writer trying to achieve force by the use of harsh words instead of harsh things. The "he latchkeyed his way into the room" sort of style. Once in a while I find it in my old stories, but I don't think I put it there. Editors took a lot of liberties with me in those days. I have had a couple of letters from Sandburg, very nice ones and very kind. They are written in this same hopped-up lingo, which I suppose is natural to him by now, but I think originally it was just heavy breathing.

Regards and best wishes,

Raymond Chandler

1. Of World Publishing Company.

[91]

# TO THE EDITORS, HARPER'S MAGAZINE[1]

To the Editors:

It was kind of unfortunate that DeVoto's blast against professorial writing pretensions ["The Easy Chair," March 1947] should appear in the same number with Eric Bentley's elegant "Broadway and Its Intelligentsia," which is the only non-snotty piece of intelligent writing on the stage I have read for years. (I don't claim to have read them all.) Bentley is far too subtle for any point to be made in the way of generalization, but if a professor—*any* professor—can write as well as this, there is not much point in all this pseudo-elaborate differentiation between the professional and the amateur. No such difference exists, or ever did. DeVoto says that the difference "is not of degree but of kind. He (the professional) has a different nervous and muscular and psychological organization. The metabolism of his mind is different."

What kind of pretentious nonsense is this? Does DeVoto think before he writes, does he think *as* he writes, or does he let his rather muddy taste in language do his thinking for him? I suspect the last. I think he turns himself a neat bit of language and then thinks that way so he won't have to throw it away. It is, alas, a very common event with writers.

All this talk about "pros" is itself sheer amateurism. There is no such thing as professionalism in writing. Would DeVoto regard Miss Nancy Bruff and Miss Kathleen Winsor as more professional than the late Sir Walter Raleigh? Does DeVoto think he is a better writer than J. B. S. Haldane or Denis Brogan?[2] And if so, what do they have to do to get a union card—write a serial for *Collier's?*

Raymond Chandler

---

1. This letter was written in response to an article attacking the writing of English professors by Bernard DeVoto, in his column, "The Easy Chair," for March 1947. The text is reprinted from the magazine.
2. Kathleen Winsor and Nancy Bruff were popular novelists, Denis Brogan and J. B. S. Haldane professional historians whose books were widely read.

# TO EDGAR CARTER[1]

March 28, 1947

.        .        .

By the way, do you ever read the Bible? I suppose not very often, but I had occasion to the other night and believe me it is a lesson in how not to write for the movies. The worst kind of overwriting. Whole chapters that could have been said in one paragraph. And the dialogue! I bet you Macmillan's are sore as hell they didn't get to publish it. They could have made it a best-seller easy. And as for getting it banned in Boston I don't think they'd even have to grease the Watch and Ward Committee to put the red light on it.

Regards and wet fishes,

Ray

# TO JEAN BETHEL

6005 Camino de la Costa
La Jolla, California
April 20th, 1947

Dear Jean:

.        .        .

The really good mystery picture has not yet been made, unless by Hitchcock, and that is a rather different kind of picture. *The Maltese Falcon* came closest. The reason is that the detective in the picture always has to fall for some girl, whereas the real distinction of the detective's personality is that, as a detective, he falls for nobody. He is the avenging justice, the bringer of order out of chaos, and to make his doing this part of a trite boy-meets-girl story is to make

---

1. The text of this letter is taken from a transcript.

it silly. But in Hollywood you cannot make a picture which is not essentially a love story, that is to say, a story in which sex is paramount.

.        .        .

Ray


## TO DALE WARREN

6005 Camino de la Costa
La Jolla, California
2 June 1947

Dear Dale:

.        .        .

The status of my work of fiction is quo. I knocked off it, much to my regret, in order to do a screen play. I am supposed to finish this screen play about October, preferably 1947. After that, I will get back to work on the fiction, if by that time I am not in a strait-jacket.

.        .        .

I have always hated the book clubs, and I have always thought that the publisher grabbed far too much of the reprint and subsidiary rights to the books he published. The fact that he will occasionally make concessions to an established writer does not alter his practice towards unestablished writers. The publisher could justify himself perhaps, but he won't give any figures out. He won't tell you what his books cost him, he won't tell you what his overhead charge is, he won't tell you anything. He won't even give you decent, understandable, prompt, reports on your own books. The moment you try to talk business with him, he takes the attitude that he is a gentleman and a scholar, and the moment you try to approach him on the level of his moral integrity, he starts to talk business.

Kindest regards,

Ray

[94]

# TO ERLE STANLEY GARDNER

6005 Camino de la Costa
La Jolla, California
July 1, 1947

Dear Erle:

You didn't miss anything on last week's Philip Marlowe show.[1] It was thoroughly flat. Tonight, I hope, will be better.

Joe Sistrom (producer at U-I) was down over the week end and we tore the story to bits and remolded it slightly nearer to the heart's desire.[2] But I am going to have to go to Los Angeles next Monday and lay it out scene by scene, a job which may take all week. I am supposed to turn in a first draft screenplay August 1, but not a chance. My brain has been grinding along in low gear for quite a while.

I am without a secretary again. This last one was eager and willing and tried hard, but she simply had not the educational background to do the work, and being already in her forties would not be likely to learn anything. Everything she wrote had to be done over, and seldom was right even then. I sent out letters which contained gross errors of punctuation just from sheer boredom. In transcribing records she wrote stuff that was absolute nonsense, and was not aware that it was nonsense. She never came to me and said, This is what it sounds like to me, but it can't be right because it doesn't make sense. She just wrote it as she heard it and the hell with the sense. I can understand a girl not being able to spell "promissory" and spelling it "promisary," if she has no dictionary available. But I can't understand her not looking it up with a Webster's Unabridged a few feet away from her desk. It wasn't exactly carelessness; her knowledge of literate English contained such vast areas of desert that she took it for granted that half of what she wrote would be meaningless to her.

All the best,

Ray

---

1. Radio adaption of Chandler's stories.
2. Screenplay of *Playback*.

# TO JAMES SANDOE

6005 Camino de la Costa
La Jolla, California
August 10th 1947

Dear Sandoe:

 *The Partisan Review* arrived. I don't know why you should
take so much trouble. It is rather a good magazine of the sort. It has
no Cyril Connolly or Orwell, and certainly it is far below the old
*Dial*, for which I had a rather exacerbated devotion during the early
twenties. These clever-clever people are a useful catharsis to the
more practical minded writer who, whether he be commercial or not,
has usually lived long enough not to take any set of opinions too
seriously. As a very young man, when Shaw's beard was still red, I
heard him lecture in London on Art for Art's Sake, which seems
to have meant something then. It did not please Shaw of course; few
things did unless he thought of them first. But art for propaganda's
sake is even worse. And a critical magazine whose primary object is
not to think intelligently but to think in such a form as to exploit
a set of political ideas of whatsoever color always ends up by being
critical only in the colloquial sense and intelligent only in the sense of
a constant and rather labored effort to find different meanings for
things than other people have found. So after a while these magazines
all perish; they never achieve life, but only a distaste for other people's
views of it. They have the intolerence of the very young and the
anemia of closed rooms and too much midnight smoking. And God
help you if you have faith in them and then meet them in person. But
this last is a rather unfair jibe since it could be said of most writers. It
is an awful thing to admire a man's book and then meet him, and
have your entire pleasure in his work destroyed by a few egotistical
attitudes, so that not only do you dislike his personality, but you
can never again read anything he writes with an open mind. His nasty
little ego is always leering at you from behind the words.

.  .  .

Yours, Chandler

[96]

# TO JAMES SANDOE

6005 Camino de la Costa
La Jolla, California
October 2nd. 1947

Dear Jim:

The panning of *The Blue Dahlia* in *New Writing* is all right with
me. I agree with a lot of it. I have reached the happy state of being
thoroughly insensitive to adverse criticism while glowing with
pleasure at the other kind. If I were a letters-to-the-editor type guy, I
should put in a little time contesting a couple of points. E.g., it is
ludicrous to suggest that any writer in Hollywood, however
obstreperous, has a "free hand" with a script; he may have a free hand
with the first draft, but after that they start moving in on him. Also,
what happens on the set is beyond the writer's control. In this case I
threatened to walk off the picture, not yet finished, unless they
stopped the director putting in foolish dialogue out of his own head.
As to the scenes of violence, I did not write them that way at all.
Nor the massacre. The broken toe incident was an accident. The man
actually did break his toe, so the director immediately capitalized
on it.

The real point at issue here is whether physical violence is
worse than psychological violence. The element of burlesque is also
overlooked by this critic. But where he throws his hand in without
knowing it is in calling the cutting of the picture bad. What he really
means is that the directing was so bad that the cutting, which was
very expert, was not able to conceal it. Whenever you see a supremely
well cut picture, e.g. *Air Force*, *Murder My Sweet*, *The Big Sleep*,
you can be sure that either the director was once a cutter himself or
that a cutter was on the set and was consulted about the shots before
they were made. The best cutter in Hollywood cannot correct a
botched job of directing; he can't make scenes flow when they are
shot staccato, without reference to their movement on film together.
If the cutter wants to make a dissolve to cover an abrupt transition,
he can't do it unless he has the film to combine for the dissolve. If
every foot of film in a scene is needed for the essential action, there is

[97]

none over for a dissolve. The director has not contemplated the necessity for a dissolve (because he didn't know the scene right after the one he is doing might be left out), therefore he has not allowed film for it. Take a simple example. Two characters are discussing a letter which one of them expects. They are in an apartment, a man and a girl. The man says: He's writing to me General Delivery. The letter's probably there now. The girl says: Why don't you go down and get it? The guy says: Will you be here when I get back? The girl says: "Sure." and smiles enigmatically. The director, a bad director, holds on the enigmatic smile and holds long enough for a dissolve. He then shoots the exterior of the post office. Guy arrives in cab, pays cab, starts upstairs of post office. Close shoot of entrance doors, guy starts in, scene in lobby, guy moves across, close shot of General Delivery window, guy goes up to it and asks for letter. Clerk looks through letters and hands him one, etc. etc. Now the cutter knows that all this is bosh, dull, a holdover from the early days of the motion picture when movement itself was exciting. All you really want is the General Delivery window and the guy receiving a letter. But the director has failed to deliver this scene by dissolving on the girl's enigmatic smile and making the audience wonder what she has up her sleeve. So they have to have that wiped out by a totally unnecessary series of shots showing arrival at the post office. The director has tried to make a point of something which is not at this time a point at all, and thrown the cutting mechanism out of gear.

The point is whether a certain letter has come. A hand reaches across a counter and the guy takes the letter. That is all. But that is not what the preceding scene left you thinking about. You were thinking about what the girl would be up to while the guy went to the post office. And the poor cutter, to make his point, has to waste film to give the audience time to forget that. Not only that, but he has to make them look at dull film. Hitchcock, the only time I met him, gave me a lecture on this kind of waste. His point, which I have made above, was that Hollywood (and England too) was full of directors who had not learned to forget about the Biograph. They still thought that because a motion picture moved it interested people. In the early days of the pictures, he said, a man went to visit a woman at her home. They were old flames who had not seen each other for years. The bad director shot it this way. The man took a taxi, he was seen riding along in the taxi, there was a view of the

[98]

street and the house, the taxi stopped, the man got out and paid, he looked at the front steps, went up the steps rang the bell, the maid answered, he said, Is Mrs. Gilhooley in? The maid said, I'll see, sir. What name shall I say? The man said: Finnegan. The maid said: This way please. Inside house, hallway, open door, maid stands at open door, man goes in, maid starts upstairs, man in living room looks around, sits down lights a cigarette. Maid upstairs knocks on door, female voice calls Come in, she opens door. Inside maid says Mr. Finnegan to see you, ma'am. Mrs. Gilhooley says wonderingly, Mr. Finnegan? Then slowly. All right Ellen. I'll be right down. Goes to mirror, primps, enigmatic smile, starts out, shot of her descending stairs, entering living room after a slight embarrassed pause at door. Inside living room. She enters. Finnegan stands up. They look at each other in silence. Then they smile slowly. Man, huskily: Hello, Madge. You haven't changed a bit. Mrs. Gilhooley: It's been a long time, George. A long long time. And *then* the scene begins.

Every bit of this stuff is dead film, because every point, if there is a point, can be made inside the scene itself. The rest is just camera in love with mere movement. Cliché, flat, stale, and today meaningless. Well, I don't know why I run on about this. I suppose it's a sort of wonder at realizing that in spite of all the money, all the time, all the work, all the discussion and thought, there are still hardly any people who really know much about making pictures.

As to *Chimera*, if I haven't already written you about it, I enjoyed most of it very much.[1] This fellow Barzun always amuses me; he lives in a fool's paradise.[2] He thinks the detective story is dead because the kind of detective story he idolizes is dead. What he never suspects for a moment is that it never existed. What did exist was an elaborate scheme for gulling the public into thinking it was getting something it never really did get; and after awhile the fraud was found out. The tricks became known and there was nothing behind the tricks. They were fun for a while but human ingenuity could only go so far. The piece of broken watch spring that Dr. Thorndyke picked up from behind the sofa pillow meant a lot to Dr. Thorndyke, but the rest of us didn't have laboratories.[3] It meant nothing to us. And after

1.  Magazine edited by Barbara Howes.
2.  Jacques Barzun, Columbia University professor and critic of detective fiction.
3.  Dr. John Evelyn Thorndyke, hero of numerous mystery novels by R. Austin Freeman, 1862–1943.

a while we began to realise that the essential clue, openly planted apparently, was only a clue when fitted into a special background, and the reader was not given the background. Where the clue was not hidden behind a scientific or antiquarian screen it was messed up with so many other trivia that only a prodigious mnemonologist could hold on to it. Even the author had to keep looking back to make sure he didn't ball himself up. The real basis of the detection novel is that a problem exists which can be solved by close attention to physical clues and correct interpretation of them. My experience with reading them, and I have read as many as most people, is that the clues are only given in part. The physical clue a. has meaning only when added to the psychological clue b. And b. is always either misstated, or relies on hidden knowledge, or its importance is only revealed by a special interpretation. Otherwise the problem is transparent, and the interest, as in so many of Austin Freeman's stories, is not in the solution of the mystery, which is obvious, but in the exact reconstruction of the crime. All this type of fiction, therefore, presumes a point in time, a certain stage of knowledge, a certain freshness of routine which cannot be maintained, and a certain psychological falsity which can be manipulated only in the presence of the psychologically immature. The novel of detection little by little educates the public to its own weaknesses, which it cannot possibly remove, because they are inherent. It can flourish only until enough people know its vocabulary.

RC


# TO ERLE STANLEY GARDNER

6005 Camino de la Costa
La Jolla, California
October 23rd, 1947

Dear Erle:

[100]

Would you consider two objections I have to your writing, or would you be hurt? Both small things, but they bother me. One is where Mason says: "I don't know as I could do that." The other, he says: "Whom shall I ask for?" My contention is a) a night school lawyer might say the first, which is not just colloquial English but bad English. Perry wouldn't, I'm sure, b) and the man who says the first would not say the second, which is pedantic anyway by colloquial standards. For all I know your secretaries do this. I don't recall seeing the first in either of the last two books. Perhaps I am just crazy anyway. They always bring me up short. Also, there is carelessness in proof-checking once in a while. This sort of thing I've noticed more than once: track is lost of the speaker in quick dialogue. See p. 108 of *Lazy Lover*. Just below the single "Yes" halfway done. Mason says two speeches which are printed as though Drake had said one. "I know all about that" Mason. "Yes." Drake. "Then he must be familiar etc." Mason. "All right, cover every etc." Also Mason. I've caught this quite a few times in various books.

Love

Ray

## TO CHARLES MORTON

6005 Camino de la Costa
La Jolla, California
October 28th. 1947

Dear Charles:

· · ·

At the end of the week we have to go to Los Angeles and stay quite a long time—several weeks—while I polish my screenplay. This is a loathsome job, consisting of cutting out everything you like and then skimping on the rest, and beating the hell out of the poor tired lines and scenes until they have lost all meaning. I was talking to Joe Sistrom, my producer, about it last Sunday and demanding

[101]

plaintively why it was so impossible for a writer to have fun writing for the screen. Making pictures is a very interesting job, in spite of having to deal with actors, but the writing part of it is sheer drudgery. I still don't know why it has to be.

I had an idea for some time back that I should like to do an article on The Moral Status of the Writer, or more frivolously, The Hell With Posterity I Want Mine Now. Not a frivolous article really. It seems to me that in all this yapping about writers selling themselves to Hollywood or the slicks or some transient propaganda idea, instead of writing sincerely from the heart about what they see around them,—the people who make this kind of complaint, and that includes practically every critic who takes himself seriously, overlook the point (I don't see how they can, but they do) that no writer ever in any age got a blank check. He always had to accept some conditions imposed from without, respect certain taboos, try to please certain people. It might have been the Church, or a rich patron, or a generally accepted standard of elegance, or the commercial wisdom of a publisher or editor, or perhaps even a set of political theories. If he did not accept them, he revolted against them. In either case they conditioned his writing. No writer ever wrote exactly what he wanted to write, because there was never anything inside himself, anything purely individual that he did want to write. It's all reaction of one sort or another.

Oh the hell with it. Ideas are poison. The more you reason, the less you create.

Ray.

## TO CHARLES MORTON

6005 Camino de la Costa
La Jolla, California
January First 1948

Dear Charlie:
My first letter of the new year is to you. We are as it were old

02]

friends and have never enjoyed the privilege of disliking each other. *My* wife tells me I have a beautiful character. Have you a little liar in your home? I am one of those people who have to be known exactly the right amount to be liked. I am standoffish with strangers, a form of shyness which whiskey cured when I was still able to take it in the requisite quantities. I am terribly blunt, having been raised in that English tradition which permits a gentleman to be almost infinitely rude if he keeps his voice down. It depends on a complete assurance that a punch on the nose will not be the reply. Americans have no manners as such; they have the manners that arise from their natures, and so when their natures are sweet they have the best manners in the world, except those of the aristocrats, the real ones, now a dying race, of course. I always recall in this connection an incident that occurred to Logan Pearsall Smith. (I might even have read it in the *Atlantic*.) How by devious way he secured an invitation to a country home which had a very old library he wished to search; how the old gentleman, his host, would wander around and occasionally peer in at the library windows while Smith was browsing; how he never entered the room; how Smith sat at meat with the family day after day and none ever enquired of him what he sought in the library; and how he departed leaving them as ignorant as when he came, a tribute to their breeding that only a wise man could have thought of.

And then, as a comic reversal of this, I recall Train's visit to Bewly, or Beaulieu as the blighters spell it, and how an antique fly awaited him at the station to drive him to Beaulieu Castle, how charmingly and indifferently he was entertained, in such a way that he seemed to be obliging the people by being there; and how, at the moment of his departure, the butler, having received his tip, presented him with a bill for the rent of the fly.

And finally, from my own knowledge, the incident of the Scotch grouse moor invitation, at the end of which the guest, not used to such things or to the mixture of arrogance and geniality displayed by some upper crust people, tipped the head gamekeeper with a couple of shining golden sovereigns: tried to tip him, rather, and the Head Gamekeeper glancing down superciliously remarked, "I only accept paper," which in those days meant not less than a fivepunnote. And how, when the guest, outraged, refused to tip him at all, the H.G. refused to deliver the guest's guns; and how the titled host, being informed of this in a polite but chilly letter from London,

[103]

replied that he never interfered in such matters; and how it took a
solicitor to get the guns back to the now thoroughly-with-British-
hospitality-disgusted guest. I take it you agree with me that the
American gentleman would have been incapable of any one of these
attitudes. Interesting stuff, just the same.

So blessed be your days.

Ray

## TO E. C. THIESSEN

6005 Camino de la Costa
La Jolla, California
January 19, 1948

Dear Mr. Thiessen:
    I am in receipt through Mr. Weeks of your check in the
amount of $300 for a contribution to *The Atlantic Monthly*, not as yet
definitely titled but which you call "Crime Night" for convenience. I
understand that this article is to be featured in the March *Atlantic*
with a cover. I do not regard the amount of your payment as
adequate. For my last contribution I was paid $500. Would you be
kind enough to explain to me the basis on which you arrive at these
figures? Although I am of course aware that the decision is for Mr.
Weeks, it seems more graceful that I should approach the subject
through you.
    Lest there be any misunderstanding of my motives in raising
the question, let it be understood that the article is yours and that if
there were any necessity for it you could give me a token payment
of $10. I do not expect to make a living out of *The Atlantic Monthly*
and in fact I have indirectly done a great deal of work for its benefit
and my own without any remuneration whatsoever. I have thought
up ideas for articles and discussed them with Mr. Morton,

[104]

occasionally with the hope that if he liked them well enough he could get somebody else to do them when I was unable to do them myself. If this were an affair of friendship, I should want only such payment as would protect your proper legal rights; but if it is a business transaction, then I want the top price, as I am accustomed to getting the top price. Not everyone, I know, can write articles acceptable to the *Atlantic*; but of those who can and do, relatively few have any smash news value and any expert inner point of view on subjects of wide general interest. If the article is timely enough and good enough to excite your enthusiasm, then it should be paid for at the very highest rate your budget will permit. This is the only kind of business relationship that interests me, and business for the moment is what we are talking. I am well aware that magazine editors, like the Roman god Janus, must of necessity have two faces, one to smile benevolently on the literature contributor as writer and the other to regard more grimly the matter of his remuneration. That is part of his job, as it is also part of my job as a businessman not to let him do it too well.

Very truly yours,

Raymond Chandler

# TO JAMES SANDOE

6005 Camino de la Costa
La Jolla, California
January 27, 1948

Dear Jim:

.        .        .

I quite agree with you about the public's capacity and adaptability to a quality of entertainment which the yucks seem to be afraid to give them. I haven't seen a good detective story in ages,

[105]

have you? Yes, I'd like to read George Orwell's essay "The British People" very much. Orwell, like other clever people, probably including you and me, can be an ass on occasion. But that doesn't mean he is never interesting, perceptive, and very intelligent.

I've just read *The Iceman Cometh* and I wish somebody would tell me what is so wonderful about this guy O'Neill. Of course, I haven't seen the play. I've only read it. In fact the only play of his that I ever saw was *Strange Interlude*, and you can not only have that but, if necessary I will pay you to cart it away. An indelible characteristic of the second or third-rate talent is that it is only effective when dealing with something that borders on fantasy. When you have atmosphere you can get by without a deep perception of character. If O'Neill's purpose were not so grim and his thinking apparently so solemn, I should be inclined to say that as a dramatist he ranks beside Pinero and Henry Arthur Jones; that he is utterly artificial, and that nothing he writes has any very real context. I enjoyed *Ah, Wilderness* but it left me with no more enduring memory than, for example, *Kiss and Tell*. I am no fanatical admirer of Saroyan, but I think *The Time of Your Life* makes *The Iceman Cometh* look like a posey and laborious working over of trite materials. O'Neill is the sort of man who could spend a year in flophouses, researching flophouses, and write a play about flophouses that would be no more real than a play by a man who had never been in a flophouse, but had only read about them. If I am utterly wrong, please instruct me.

You asked my opinion about the Hollywood show in Washington. Well, I think it's pretty awful that an investigation of this sort should be conducted by a man who thinks *Abie's Irish Rose* is a novel.[1] Also, I do not think the Founding Fathers intended this sort of investigation to be conducted with microphones, flash bulbs, and moving picture cameras. Apart from that, until the Supreme Court defines the powers of Congressional committees and limits them (and our present Supreme Court is no bunch of legal masters) I cannot see where the committee exceeded its rights. If the Communist party in the United States is a legal organization, and if membership

1. Congressman J. Parnell Thomas, chairman of the Committee on Un-American Affairs of the U.S. House of Representatives, investigating Hollywood screenwriters.

in it is a matter of record available to a branch of the United States Government, then asking a man if he belongs to the Communist party or ever has belonged to it is not an invasion of his privacy. It is something like asking him if he ever was a registered Republican, which is not the same thing as asking if he voted Republican. I think the ten men who were cited had very bad legal advice. They were afraid to say they were Communists or to say that they were not Communists; therefore they tried to raise a false issue. If they had told the truth, they would have had a far better case before the courts than they have now, and they would certainly have had no worse a case as regards their bosses in Hollywood. If Jack Warner fires me because I admit to being a Communist, he's in a far more shaky legal position than if he does the same thing because, through refusing to answer the questions of the Congressional Committee, I have brought the moving picture industry into bad repute. And I guess we are all perfectly well aware, not being children, that if the Communist party is by legislative action outlawed in this country, the real practicing professional Communists will go right on doing what they are doing, only they will do it under another label and with a slightly different technique. As I understand it, there are only two grounds on which one may refuse to answer a question of a Congressional Committee. One is that to answer it would be to incriminate yourself, that is to say a truthful answer would be the confession of a crime; since membership in the Communist party is not a crime, that does not apply here. The other ground is that the question is not within the frame of the purpose for which the Committee was constituted. This is a deliberate test of the law and at least has the color of honesty. Even if a man were convicted of contempt on such refusal, it is unlikely that he would get more than a purely nominal sentence; because the courts would recognize that this man had raised a clear issue of fact and law, and had not sought to evade an issue by talking until he was thrown out of the witness chair. You call the defense forthright. What's forthright about it? It strikes me as a singularly incompetent attempt (partly unconscious, perhaps) to use the legalistic weaknesses of the democratic system in order to undermine or sabotage the functioning of that system. I don't mean that these ten men are all convinced and avowed Communists. I think about three of them are, that at least two definitely are not, and that the rest

[107]

don't know what the hell it's all about. But I ought to qualify my remarks about the boys by saying that, although I have no sympathy for them, and don't think anything very awful will happen to them, except that they will spend a lot of money on lawyers, and the worst kind of lawyers, I reserve my real contempt for the motion picture moguls who in conference decided to expel them from the industry. A business as big as the motion picture business ought to be run by men with a few guts, men with enough moral and intellectual integrity to say that while these matters are sub judice and while these men have not been declared guilty of any crime by the courts, the producers are not going to treat them as guilty. They don't have to hire them where they are not contract writers, and if they are contract writers, they can lay them off for twelve weeks a year and pay them their salary the rest of the time and not give them any work. They can do all this without public fanfare and striking poses of virtue. It might cost them a little money, but it would save them from an awful lot of real contempt. Sometimes I feel kind of sorry for the poor bastards. They are so damned scared they won't make their second or third million. In fact they are just so damned scared, period. What a wonderful thing it would have been if the Motion Pictures Producers Association had said to Mr. Thomas, "Sure, I guess we have Communists in Hollywood. We don't know who they are. How could you expect us to? We're not the F.B.I. But even if we did know, there's an Attorney General in this country. He hasn't accused these men of any crime. Congress hasn't legislated anything that would cause their present or future membership in the Communist party to be a crime, and until it does we propose to treat them just as exactly as we treat anyone else." You know what would happen if the producers had the guts to say a thing like that? They would start making good pictures, because that takes guts, too. Very much the same kind of guts.

I hope nothing in the above is annoying to you. If it is, if you are an extreme left-winger yourself, for example, we could have a lot of fun arguing about it. I've always wanted to know what made these fellows tick and if you happened to be one of them, I should get an intelligent answer.

With kindest regards,

[108]

# TO JAMES KEDDIE, JR.

6005 Camino de la Costa,
La Jolla, California
March 18, 1948

Dear Mr. Keddie:

Thank you for your letter of February 14. Offhand I can't recall how Frances Wallace got the idea that I preferred reading the English type of detective stories, because said so specifically it isn't true. As a matter of fact I don't read a great many detective stories of any sort. I do think that what might be called the second-grade English detective story is better reading than an equivalent accomplishment over here. But I think the best American mystery stories are ahead of the best English stories, for the reason that they recognize and accept the inherent fallacy of the form; whereas the English practitioners prefer to disregard it and go on talking about logic and deduction as if these words actually meant something in this connection. From the English point of view the mysteries of Freeman Wills Crofts and R. Austin Freeman, both of whom you mention, are rigidly honest simply because they don't tell lies or conceal material facts or, as Agatha Christie so often does, ring in violent reversals of character in order to justify an unexpected motivation. Yet no normal reader could solve a Crofts mystery, because no normal reader has that exact a memory for insignificant details. And no normal reader could solve an Austin Freeman mystery, because, although Freeman gives you the bare facts, he does not give you the esoteric scientific interpretation of these facts, and he has no right to impute it to you as a reader. As I see it, the truly honest detective story or novel of detection (a more respectable term perhaps) is one in which the reader is given all the material for solving the mystery, where nothing significant is under-emphasized and nothing insignificant over-emphasized, and where the facts themselves carry their own interpretation and do not have to be carried into a laboratory and analyzed under microscopes to disclose their meaning. In blunt words, the English novel of detection is either transparent or it is in some sense a psychological fraud. If you know of one which

[109]

isn't either I wish you'd tell me. I think it was the realization of these things that caused the development of the so-called "inverted detective story" in England, and in this country caused the emphasis to shift to character and action rather than a tabulation of clues.

As for the enjoyment of Sherlock Holmes, it appears to me at this date to rely partly on nostalgia and tradition and partly on qualities which did not originally make the principal interest of the Holmes stories. Doyle understood the uses of eccentricity, but to a person with any knowledge of the police and how they operate his policemen are utterly absurd. His scientific premises are very unreliable, and the element of mystery to a sophisticated mind frequently does not exist. Example: *The Red-Headed League*. Of course we do not have the privilege of reading Holmes fresh from the press.

With kindest regards,

Raymond Chandler

## TO JOSEPH SISTROM

March 23, 1948

Dear Joe:

I saw *Open City* again the other night.[1] You always see more the second time. I noticed, for example, that there is as much dialogue in the picture as in any of our more wordy specimens, but that this dialogue is so dynamically delivered that you don't get any impression of the action being slowed down. I am beginning to wonder whether the static quality of many pictures is not due simply to poor acting rather than overwriting or unimaginative directing. Or, if I may correct myself, I am not beginning to wonder; I am convinced.

Yours always

1. By Roberto Rossellini.

# TO JOHN HERSEY

6005 Camino de la Costa
La Jolla, California
March 29, 1948

Dear John Hersey:

What a charming, old-fashioned gesture, to write a man a letter entirely in your own handwriting. I wish I could return the compliment, but my writing is of the nervous, illegible, erratic type and I am afraid you would have a lot of misery trying to read it.

I haven't seen the magazine for a long time.[1] I was very, very *mildly* irritated that I was never asked to put any money into it in the beginning; but that is probably all for the best, since I am a very poor joiner. As for writing a five or six thousand word mystery short story for you, I simply don't have the short-story mind. From time to time I get letters from people like Ellery Queen and Rex Stout and sometimes from the big magazines asking me for stories or novelettes at various prices, all of them flatteringly high (I've been offered as much as a dollar a word); but it seems to me that either you are a short-story writer or you are not. Once in a while a writer gets what might be called a compulsive idea and I suppose I have had them, although not as many as a real short-story writer would have; but I find that I throw them off without any difficulty, or else they start to grow and grow and become confused in ramifications. The only short story I ever wrote of the type you mention was published in the *Saturday Evening Post* several years ago.[2] I guess I'm just not an idea man and a good short story does really need an idea.

This is not saying that I'll never try. It might be that one of these days, when no Hollywood producer is breathing down the back of my neck, I'll write a short story and then look at it and think it fairly good and decide it obviously is not formula, nor yet neurotic enough to appeal to the polite pickpockets of the "little" magazines. But why should I try? You are a writer and you will understand. The chances are I'll never get written half of what there is in my mind

1. It was called *Magazine*, with each number incorporated in the title (*Magazine* 1, *Magazine* 2, etc.). It was published in New York.
2. "I'll Be Waiting."

asking to be written at this moment. Money is no longer a compelling motive, unless I could make it by writing books. If I can't, I can always make it in the Hollywood slaughterhouse, ankle-deep in blood and screaming like a Saracen. As for prestige, the magazine which can confer it no longer exists. Prestige of a sort I already have, and however much more I might chance to acquire through luck or the stupidity of the public I should always have to say to myself privately: "Yes, that's all very well, but remember you didn't write *Hiroshima* and you never could." Of course I still have ambitions—subject to change without notice. I should like to write a book of fantastic stories. Not pseudo-scientific. Realistic stories in every sense, except that each one contains an impossibility. And I should like to write a good motion picture. The problem here is not writing but of somehow creating or contriving the circumstances in which it is possible to do the work. But the short mystery story—all I can say is why?

Yours very truly,

Raymond Chandler

## TO FREDERICK LEWIS ALLEN

May 7, 1948

Dear Mr. Allen:

Thanks for the kind words spoken in connection with your P. and O. notes on Eric Bentley. I did not rise to the occasion. I was afraid to try. This sort of thing can become a back-scratching routine of which the public tires very damn fast.

Just the same, I think Bentley's round-up of the plays was everything that anyone could desire. It would be invidious for me to remark (even if I knew what I was talking about) that Bentley is probably the best dramatic critic in the U.S. and, with the possible exception of Mary McCarthy, the *only* dramatic critic in the U.S.[1]

1. Eric Bentley.

[112]

The rest of the boys are just think-piece writers whose subject happens to be a play. They are interested in exploiting their own personal brand of verbal glitter. They are witty and readable and sometimes cute, but they tell you next to nothing about the dramatic art and the relationship of the play in question to that art.

It is not enough for a critic to be right, since he will occasionally be wrong. It is not enough for him to give colorable reasons. He must create a reasonable world into which his reader may enter blindfold and feel his way to the chair by the fire without barking his shins on the unexpected dust mop. The barbed phrase, the sedulously rare word, the highbrow affectation of style—these are amusing, but useless. They place nothing and reveal not the temper of the times. The great critics, of whom there are piteously few, build a home for the truth.

In his review of *The Iceman Cometh* that fading wit and tired needlepoint worker, George Jean Nathan says: "With the appearance of this long awaited work our theatre has become dramatically alive again. It makes most of the plays . . . produced during the more than twelve-year period of O'Neill's absence look comparatively like so much damp tissue paper." Cute and quite easy, and with two sentences the spuriousness of an entire career seems to stand revealed. A critic who could write that drivel about O'Neill's drivel is hors concours. It would be charitable to say he has lost contact with his brains; it would be far more accurate to say he has merely made public a truth which was privately known from the beginning: that George Jean Nathan's critical reputation is not founded on his knowing what he is talking about, since obviously he doesn't now and most probably never did, but on a certain personal dexterity with the choice and order of words.

This play, *The Iceman Cometh*, is a sort of touchstone. If that fools you, you are a knuckle-headed sucker for pretentiousness. That's all there is to say; it is quite simple, quite devastating, and there is no retrieving the position. I shall probably never read another line of Nathan. I know there is nothing there. I suspect there never was.

The current year's touchstone is *A Streetcar Named Desire*.[2] Bentley knocks it for a loop, so does McCarthy. O'Neill with a better shooting script. That's all. Zero in art, A or possibly A plus in

2. By Tennessee Williams.

[113]

adaptation to the circumstance that where there is no art, it is possible for an ingenious fellow to simulate it without losing money.

It is wrong to be harsh with the New York critics, unless one admits in the same breath that it is a condition of their existence that they should write entertainingly about something which is rarely worth writing about at all. This leads or forces them to develop a technique of pseudo-subtlety and abstruseness which, when acquired, permits them to deal with trivial things as though they were momentous. This is the basis of all successful advertising copy writing. Criticism is impossible in a world where the important thing is not to be right, or even to know the reasons for being right, but to write a column about a play—any damn play at all—which column however insignificant the ostensible subject, never lets down on the significance of the references to the subject. These people do not write about plays; they write about their neuroses. How else could they keep the ball in the air? Good critical writing is measured by the perception and evaluation of the subject; bad critical writing by the necessity of maintaining the professional standing of the critic.

I thought De Voto's piece about the drinking habits of the Great American Yahoo was quite wonderful.[3] So indirectly, and yet so devastatingly, he exposes that awful truth that where a civilization is in the process of going rotten, you will always find the symbols of this rottenness in the suburbs, in the lives and homes of supposedly rather ordinary decent people. When they begin to break up into devil worship, the disease is probably too far gone for a cure. Or would be, in any country but this.

Auden leaves me lost and groping. His piece about detective stories was brilliant in the clear cold classical manner. But why drag me in? I'm just a fellow who jacked up a few pulp novelettes into book form. How could I possibly care a button about the detective story as a form? All I'm looking for is an excuse for certain experiments in dramatic dialogue. To justify them I have to have plot and situation; but fundamentally I care almost nothing about either. All I really care about is what Errol Flynn calls "the music," the lines he has to speak. Here I am halfway through a Marlowe story and having a little fun (until I got stuck) and along comes this fellow Auden and tells me I am interested in writing serious studies of a

3. Bernard DeVoto, *Harper's* columnist.

criminal milieu. So now I look at everything I put down and say to myself, Remember, old boy, this has to be a serious study of a criminal milieu. Are you serious? No. Is this a criminal milieu? No, just average corrupt living with the melodramatic angle over-emphasized, not because I am crazy about melodrama for its own sake, but because I am realistic enough to know the rules of the game.

A long time ago whan I was writing for pulps I put into a story a line like "he got out of the car and walked across the sun-drenched sidewalk until the shadow of the awning over the entrance fell across his face like the touch of cool water." They took it out when they published the story. Their readers didn't appreciate this sort of thing: just held up the action. And I set out to prove them wrong. My theory was they just *thought* they cared nothing about anything but the action; that really, although they didn't know it, they cared very little about the action. The things they really cared about, and that I cared about, were the creation of emotion through dialogue and description; the things they remembered, that haunted them, were not for example that a man got killed, but that in the moment of his death he was trying to pick a paper clip up off the polished surface of a desk, and it kept slipping away from him, so that there was a look of strain on his face and his mouth was half open in a kind of tormented grin, and the last thing in the world he thought about was death. He didn't even hear death knock on the door. That damn little paper clip kept slipping away from his fingers and he just wouldn't push it to the edge of the desk and catch it as it fell.

With kindest regards,

## TO CHARLES MORTON

6005 Camino de la Costa,
La Jolla, California
May 7, 1948

Dear Charlie:

Your magnificent piece of prose about wedding presents was read at the last meeting of the La Jolla Hermosa Writers Club. For a

[115]

moment at the end there was a deathly silence, reminiscent of the silence that so discouraged Lincoln after his Gettysburg address. These hardened veterans of the rejection slip, the La Jolla writers, just sat stunned by your eloquence. Tears streamed down their worn faces and their toil-hardened hands tightened convulsively into knots of bone and sinew. Then, suddenly, with the crash of a giant comber on a reef the applause swelled up to thunder. They came to their feet as one man, although nine tenths of them were women, and screamed with enthusiasm. There were roars of Author! AUTHOR! A U T H O R ! and when the president restored order at last (by waving her hand-knitted bloomers) and it was explained that the Author was on the other side of the continent in a place called Boston (Laughter!) a resolution was passed that he be signed up for a series of lectures on *The American Home and How To Avoid It.*

Your health was then drunk in elderberry wine and a toast proposed by a recently exhumed member of the British colony, an Old Surbitonian complete with tie. There followed a rendering of several arias from *Madame Butterfly* by the Choir of Kept Women from the La Jolla Beach and Tennis Club, and the proceedings fittingly terminated by the entire company singing the Horst Wessel song in Yiddish, followed by the Palestinian National Anthem sung in Hebrew and the La Jolla Chamber of Commerce Glee Club leading the singing of the sacred Hymn to the Retail Credit Merchants Association of San Diego County. This was sung in what passes around here for English.

I think you would have been very pleased and proud and touched (for whatever you had on you—a lot of us don't eat regularly). The affair was quite orderly for La Jolla. Two stick pokings, one assault with pearl hatpin, a couple of fountain pen squirtings, and a few spitballs alone marred the perfect harmony of the occasion. There was a slight tendency to cluster at the end and one old lady was pushed a little by another old lady who told her to stick her ear trumpet in her own ear if she had to use it. For a moment it looked as if this disagreement might end in a spot of hair-pulling, but the president quickly began to read a short story of her own composition and the hall emptied in a flash.

Respectfully yours,

Raymond Chandler

[116]

# TO CARL BRANDT

6005 Camino de la Costa
La Jolla, California
May 11th. 1948

Dear Mr. Brandt:

Come Michaelmas, or thereabouts, I shall be in need of a literary agent. The purpose of this is to enquire whether your office would be interested.

At the moment there is nothing much to do. I would have a radio program, if I had had the right kind of people after it at the right time. But I don't think much could be done now. I have a mystery novel half finished. The writing is of an incomparable brilliance, but something has went wrong with the story. An old trouble with me. The brain is very very tired. I have lately finished a screenplay for Universal-International, want to finish this mystery and do another novel which has a murder in it but is not a mystery. Monday I am going north for a month.

What I want to do and what I do are not always of the same family. There is, of course, the usual collection of minor troubles, such as Portuguese rights, Italian rights, Penguin book rights to a bunch of novelettes not published in England (and perhaps not worth publishing.) These are annoying things, but not lucrative. I have no ambitions as a slick writer.

My references are poor. I was eight years with Sydney Sanders who would be delighted to warn you against me, unless be deemed it undiplomatic. After leaving Sanders I tried working through my Hollywood agent, H. N. Swanson, a good fellow and a nice fellow, with whom I am on excellent terms, but not quite in the right setting except for picture work, at which I have no doubt he is excellent.

You are a stranger to me and I can't very well let my hair down, but neither should I want you to be too much in the dark. I am not a completely amiable character any more than I am a facile and prolific writer. I do most things the hard way, and I suffer a good deal over it. There may not be a lot of mileage left in me. Five years of fighting Hollywood has not left me with many reserves of energy. Whether I have had any success your Hollywood representative will

[117]

be able to tell you, and if you should happen to ask him, I am hoping that for once he will (whoever he is, and I don't know) keep it to himself.

Yours very truly,

Raymond Chandler

## TO CARL BRANDT

6005 Camino de la Costa,
La Jolla, California
June 1, 1948

Dear Mr. Brandt:
Enclosed is approximately the first half of the mystery novel I was telling you about. It goes against all my principles to show it to you at this point, but I think in the circumstances you are entitled to see it if you want to. Please bear in mind that this material was all dictated to a dictaphone, an instrument which I have found very convenient for movie work, but I am not sure it is adapted to fiction writing. You will notice too many "he saids" and "she saids." Some of these were put in deliberately, so that my secretary, in transcribing the records, would know where a different speaker came on. I should probably omit a great many of these when I went over the draft. I think this batch of material runs to about 30,000 words.
It was very pleasant meeting you and talking to you. I hope we may be friends.

Yours very truly,

Raymond Chandler

[118]

# TO CARL BRANDT:

6005 Camino de la Costa
La Jolla, California
June 9, 1948

Dear Mr. Brandt:

I had a nice talk with Ray Stark last Sunday. He seems an extremely intelligent and lively young fellow and I can understand your enthusiasm for him. He seemed very frank and honest, also, even to the point of admitting that in Hollywood it is not always possible to be frank and honest, at any rate in his business.

I am sending you separately a couple of books of novelettes of mine. These were republished originally in Avon 25-cent books and then later in this World Publishing Company edition. Some time ago I raised the question with my English publisher, Hamish Hamilton, as to whether these novelettes or some of them could not be published in England, not necessarily under his imprint, but perhaps by the Penguin book people, who are bringing out some of my other books. I haven't had any reaction on them, but I know he has had two disastrous fires this year and probably has no time of anything but the most urgent matters. Do you think it would be worth while to send these on to your English representative, whoever he is? I have several more copies if you need them.

The four mystery novels which Knopf published were all handled in England by the Farquharson office for Sydney Sanders, and Innes Rose is, as I suppose you know, the successor to Farquharson, although he still uses Farquharson's name. Certain foreign translation rights have been sold, but I should have to draw up a schedule to be able to state definitely what: French, Swedish, Norwegian, Danish, Spanish, and some Italian rights I think. Innes Rose took the position that the agent in England who handled the original publication of the books was by English trade practice entitled to handle any and all publications, reprints, foreign language translations, and so on perpetually, regardless of any cessation of his agency representation. I took the position that this was a lot of bosh, that every right was a subdivision of the copyright and that he was only entitled to participate in contracts he had actually negotiated, and that his right to negotiate ceased when his agency ceased. He has conceded my point without abandoning the principle. I thought of taking this up with the Society of Authors in England, but so far have not done so. You will probably know far more about it than I do. The point is there are unsold rights, of what value I could not say. I assume you will eventually want to cover this field and see what has not been done.

When you were here we agreed in a general way that it was probably a mistake to quit a publisher without some definite reason, but I am wondering whether the mere fact that I have been ten years in some kind of an association with Knopf without ever having the slightest feeling of friendliness or warmth towards them isn't enough reason. . . . Knopf has made far more money out of his share of the reprint royalties than he has paid me on all of his own trade editions. I certainly don't owe him anything. I always thought their publicity, what there was of it, was miserable. It covered the ground all the way from irritating to down-right silly. Perhaps they sold as many of my books as the public would buy, but I've never really been convinced of it, when my English publisher, with only a third of the population to deal with, has sold just as many. I have a certain admiration for Alfred Knopf, because he has published a lot of books he couldn't possibly make any money on, and he has so far failed to publish one of those fat slabs of goosed history which almost dominate the best-seller lists these days. I have nothing positive against the house, but I think by this time I ought to have something positive in favor of it, and I haven't. It is a cold show. I have never been able to deal with people at arm's length.

With kindest regards,

Raymond Chandler

# TO CHARLES MORTON

6005 Camino de la Costa
La Jolla, California
July 28, 1948

Dear Charlie:

[120]

Your realization that I live far beyond any considerations of money is all wrong. My expenses are terrible and I am not even sure I can make a living writing fiction. I am pretty sure I can't unless I write a best seller (unlikely) or sell serial rights to one of the big magazines. I simply don't want to do any more work for Hollywood. There is nothing in it but grief and exhaustion and discontent. In no real sense is it writing at all. It carries with it none of the satisfactions of writing. None of the sense of power over your medium. None of the freedom, even to fail. I may have to do some more of it, but I'd rather not. And I shall do it more and more cynically if I do have to. As a practical editor as well as a rare and pawky mind, you know that the only way I can get by is to sell some stuff to the big, shiny-paper magazines. I have to have about $50,000 a year, and yet very little of that money goes for my personal expenses. If I worked for a salary, I could get along on half of that. But I have to pay for all sorts of things which are given to you as part of your job. This house has only three bedrooms, apart from the maid's room, and two of them are given over entirely to business, except that I sleep in one of them. If I can't make this kind of an income, I have to change my whole way of life. In some ways that would not be altogether unpleasant, and certainly would be nothing like what I went through after 1930. Between you and me the writing business has grown to be a hell of a bore. There is far too much office work involved in it, far too much filing, bookkeeping, making out tax returns of various sorts, far too much concern with detail. Sometimes it seems as if the only chance one has to write is when all these other things are taken care of; and by that time the edge is off.

Yours,

Ray

## TO HAMISH HAMILTON

6005 Camino de la Costa
La Jolla, California
August 10th. 1948

Dear Jamie:

Hardly necessary to tell you that I am typing this myself, no

[121]

longer have a secretary, just didn't have a full time job for one unless working in Hollywood. I shall probably be sorry, but can't help it. Have to retrench a bit anyhow. Things are awful over here as far as price is concerned.

The trouble with the Marlowe character is he has been written and talked about too much. He's getting self-conscious, trying to live up to his reputation among the quasi-intellectuals. The boy is bothered. He used to be able to spit and throw the ball hard and talk out of the corner of his mouth.

.           .           .

I am trying desperately to finish *The Little Sister*, and should have a rough draft done almost any day I can get up enough steam. The fact is, however, that there is nothing in it but style and dialogue and characters. The plot creaks like a broken shutter in an October wind.

.           .           .

Am reading *The Heart of the Matter*, a chapter at a time.[1] It has everything in it that makes literature except verve, wit, gusto, music and magic; a cool and elegant set-piece, embalmed by Whispering Glades. There is more life in the worst chapter Dickens or Thackeray ever wrote, and they wrote some pretty awful chapters.

All the best,

Ray

## TO DALE WARREN

6005 Camino de la Costa
La Jolla, California
August 18 1948

Dear Dale:

1. By Graham Greene.

The books arrived and so very many thanks for your kindness. The short stories were removed from my sight at once and I haven't had a chance to look at them. The anthology about writing I have dipped into, but found nothing except a remark of Gertrude Atherton's about Galsworthy. Like other puzzlers over literary matters I am often stumped to understand what it is that writers like Galsworthy and Cronin and Marquand have that makes them so readable and yet in a sense so negligible. A fellow named Nevil Shute has it too. Last night I sat up to two ack emma reading *No Highway*—just couldn't put it down. And yet I know it contains no real literary art, none of that peculiar magic which makes a piece of writing, regardless of its formula or purpose, seem to be a freshly minted coin that no one has yet touched. Gertrude thinks it is technique. I do not.

The Dorothy Baker book I shall inevitably like.[1] I did my darndest when I was at Paramount to get them to buy *Trio* for me to do a screenplay on it. I told them that the Lesbian angle could be so handled that the yucks wouldn't realize it was there, that it need not even be there. It could be the story of a nice young girl's attempt to escape from the dominance of a brilliant, charming and forceful woman who was so much what she would like to be herself and couldn't be that she was held in bond to her. That settled, all the other motivations fall into place. But the fact is these Hollywood people are so filthy-minded themselves that they smell dirt even where there is none. A fellow who read the script of *The Blue Dahlia* told me: "I loved the homosexual angle." I said, "What homosexual angle?" He said between the two guys that lived in the same apartment." I said: "Oh. They shared an apartment and ate meals together. That makes them homosexuals, does it?" Whereat he looked hurt.

. . .

Sure, I think you are good publishers. Trouble is to decide whether there is any valid reason to change publishers. I think there ought to be a very heavy one before it is done. So I thought I would

1. *Our Gifted Son.*

[123]

just keep my trap shut about it for the time being and let the wiser mouths speak. I know what my impulse is.

All the best,

Ray


# TO HAMISH HAMILTON

6005 Camino de la Costa
La Jolla, California
August 19th. 1948

Dear Jamie:

The end of Greene's book was great. It atoned for a lack I had felt before.

Yours of the 16th. crossed one of mine, so I leave the novelette question for later. The position as to *The Little Sister* is roughly that I have on paper in the rough about 85,000 words and lack two or three scenes at the end. Carl Brandt has seen half of the rough draft before I even read it over and he liked it. But I have a very, very tired mind. I can't judge the thing at all and I can't write with any regularity. I'm really exhausted with Hollywood rubbish. I do want to finish this thing so that I will have something to be published, and, although I don't expect any miracles from it, I don't want it to disappoint anyone too greatly.

The story has weaknesses. It is episodic and the emphasis shifts around from character to character and it is, as a mystery, overcomplicated, but as a story of people very simple. It has no violence in it at all; all the violence is off stage. If it has menace and suspense, they are in the writing. I think some of it is beautifully written, and my reactions to it are most unreliable. I write a scene and I read it over and think it stinks. Three days later (having done nothing in between but stew) I reread it and think it is great. So there you are. You can't bank on me. I may be all washed up.

Lately I have been trying to simplify my life so that I need not depend on Hollywood. I have no longer a business manager or a

[124]

secretary. But I am not happy. I need a rest badly and I cannot rest until this is done and I sometimes think that when it is done it will be as tired as I am and it will show.

Assuming, for the moment, that the thing is any good, I feel that you may rely on receiving some kind of a script in a month. It may need more work, but it will give you a chance to see whether I am crazy or not. I guess Carl Brandt would tell you, up to a point.

I hope this is some help.

Ray

P.S. It contains the nicest whore I ever didn't meet.


## TO CLEVE ADAMS

Sept 4th 1948

Dear Cleve:

It's nice to hear from you even in such queer circumstances. What is the source of your information? I may have an action for slander against someone.

I don't know Roy Huggins and have never laid eyes on him. He sent me an autographed copy of his book *Double Take* with his apologies and the dedication he says the publishers would not let him put in it. In writing to thank him I said his apologies were either unnecessary or inadequate and that I could name three or four writers who had gone as far as he had, without his frankness about it. I mentioned no names. If I had mentioned names (which, of course, I could) they would not have been the names of anyone with whom I am personally acquainted or who was writing for the pulps when I was.

I did not invent the hardboiled murder story and I have never made any secret of my opinion that Hammett deserves most or all of the credit. Everybody imitates in the beginning. What Stevenson called playing the "sedulous ape." I personally think that a deliberate attempt to lift a writer's personal tricks, his stock in trade, his

[125]

mannerisms, his approach to his material, can be carried too far—to the point where it is a kind of plagiarism, and a nasty kind because the law gives no protection. It is nasty for two main reasons. It makes the writer self-conscious about his own work; an example of this is a radio program which ran the use of extravagant similes (I think I rather invented this trick) into the ground, to the point where I am myself inhibited from writing the way I used to. The second reason is that it floods the market with bad money and that drives out the good. But none of these things can be helped. Even if I were granted the absolute power to stop such practices, I doubt that I would know where to draw the line. For one must bear in mind that they can't steal your style, if you have one. They can as a rule only steal your faults.

Since Hammett has not written for publication since 1932 I have been picked out by some people as a leading representative of the school. This is very likely due to the fact that *The Maltese Falcon* did not start the high budget mystery picture trend, although it ought to have. *Double Indemnity* and *Murder My Sweet* did, and I was associated with both of them. The result is that everybody who used to be accused of writing like Hammett may now be accused of trying to write like Chandler.

Somebody who read Huggins' book told me that it was full of scenes which were modeled in detail on scenes in my books, just moved over enough to get by. I didn't seem to notice it myself. Another party, whom I don't care to name on paper even writing to you, told me that when the script of *Double Take* was submitted, the publishers told Huggins, in effect, that it was bad enough for him to steal my approach and my method or whatever, but stealing my characters was going a little too far. I understand there was some rewriting, but cannot vouch for any of this. More power to Mr. Huggins. If he has been traveling on borrowed gas to any extent, the time will come when he will have to spew his guts into his own tank.

The law recognizes no plagiarism except that of basic plots. It is far behind the times in its concept of these things. My ideas have been plagiarized in Hollywood and I have been accused of plagiarism myself, by a guy who said *The Blue Dahlia* was lifted from an orginal of his. Luckily Paramount was in a position to show that his story never left the story department. Unconscious plagiarism is widespread and inevitable. Throughout the play *The Iceman Cometh* O'Neill

[126]

uses the expression "the big sleep" as a synonym for death. He is apparently under the impression that this is a current underworld or half-world usage, whereas it is a pure invention on my part. If I am remembered long enough, I shall probably be accused of stealing the phrase from O'Neill, since he is a big shot. A fellow over in England named James Hadley Chase, the distinguished author of *No Orchids for Miss Blandish* (which is half-cent pulp writing at its worst) made a practice in one of his books of lifting verbatim or almost verbatim passages from my books and from those of Jack Latimer and Hammett. He was eventually forced to make a public apology in the English equivalent of *Publisher's Weekly*.[1] And he also had to pay the legal costs of th..ee publishers incurred in forcing him to this apology. My American publisher's attorney would not even risk writing a letter to Chase's American publisher warning him about this. They still have some business honor left in England.

If I seem to write at too great length about all this, it is because I am very interested in the subject. Yet curiously enough, when I had a radio program last year, and when the only thing I had to sell was a character, it was found impossible to get a writer who could deliver that character or to write dialogue that sounded like him. As long as this is so, why should I worry?

As for you and Ballard, I wouldn't know what the idea was at all.[2] We all grew up together, so to speak, and we all wrote the same idiom, and we have all more or less grown out of it. A lot of *Black Mask* stories sounded alike, just as a lot of Elizabethan plays sound alike. Always when a group exploits a new technique this happens. But even when we all wrote for Joe Shaw, who thought everybody had to write just like Hammett, there were subtle and obvious differences, apparent to any writer, if not to non-writers. Your stuff could never have been mistaken for mine or mine for yours.

.        .        .

Yours always,

Ray

1. *Publishers Weekly* is the trade journal of the American book industry. The British equivalent is *The Bookseller*.
2. W. T. Ballard, prolific writer of westerns and detective novels.

# TO JAMES SANDOE

6005 Camino de la Costa
La Jolla, California
September 23, 1948

Dear Sandoe:

I shall order Shelley Smith's *The Woman in the Sea*. Sounds worth buying. But would very much like to see your copy of *Famous American Trials*. I did not care for *Wide Boys Never Work*,[1] but I could not tell you why, except that it belongs to the class of books I can't read because they make me nervous. They are grim and depressing without tragedy. Graham Greene's book has that quality too; very much overrated by my standards. The ending is very good, but the character of Scobie doesn't come off, largely because Greene is so utterly humorless. My reaction reminds me of a rather narrow-minded comment by an English friend on *Brief Encounter*.[2] "The point is that to people of that sort that sort of thing simply doesn't happen." He meant in England, of course. I couldn't go that far, although I am half British.

Your family sounds wonderful, including animals. Our cat is growing positively tyrannical. If she finds herself alone anywhere she emits blood curdling yells until somebody comes running. She sleeps on a table in the service porch and now demands to be lifted up and down from it. She gets warm milk about eight o'clock at night and starts yelling for it about 7.30. When she gets it she drinks a little, goes off and sits under a chair, then comes and yells all over again for someone to stand beside her while she has another go at the milk. When we have company she looks them over and decides almost instantly if she likes them. If she does she strolls over and plops down on the floor just far enough away to make it a chore to pet her. If she doesn't like them she sits in the middle of the living room, casts a contemptuous glance around, and proceeds to wash her backside.

1. By Robert Westerby.
2. By Noel Coward.

In the middle of this engaging performance she will stop dead, lift her head without any other change of position (one leg pointing straight at the ceiling) stares off into space while thinking out some abstruse problem, then resumes her rear-end-job. This work is always done in the most public manner. When she was younger she always celebrated the departure of visitors by tearing wildy through the house and ending up with a good claw on the davenport, the one that is covered with brocatelle and makes superb clawing, and it comes off in strips. But she is lazy now. Won't even play with her catnip mouse unless it is dangled in such a position that she can play with it lying down. I'm going to send you her picture. It has me in it, but you'll have to overlook that. I believe I told you how she used to catch all sorts of very breakable living things and bring them in the house quite unhurt as a rule. I'm sure she never hurt them intentionally. Cats are very interesting. They have a terrific sense of humor and, unlike dogs, cannot be embarrassed or humiliated by being laughed at. There is nothing in nature worse than seeing a cat trying to provoke a few more hopeless attempts to escape out of a half-dead mouse. My enormous respect for our cat is largely based on a complete lack in her of this diabolical sadism. When she used to catch mice—we haven't had any for years—she brought them alive and undamaged and let me take them out of her mouth. Her attitude seemed to be, "Well, here's this damn mouse. Had to catch it, but it's really your problem. Remove it at once." Periodically she goes through all the closets and cupboards on a regular mouse-inspection. Never finds any, but she realizes it's part of her job.

I sent my book off to Carl Brandt in New York yesterday. The only copy I had too.[3] A silly thing to do, but I couldn't find anyone to copy it quickly and I was beginning to chip at it too much. Never know when to let a thing alone. I begin at last to realize that I have a very unorthodox attitude to plots. Most writers think up a plot with an intriguing situation and then proceed to fit characters into it. With me a plot, if you could call it that, is an organic thing. It grows and often it overgrows. I am continually finding myself with scenes that I won't discard and that don't want to fit in. So that my plot problem invariably ends up as a desperate attempt to justify a lot of material that, for me at least, has come alive and insists on

3. *The Little Sister*, Chandler's fifth novel.

staying alive. It's probably a silly way to write, but I seem to know no other way. The mere idea of being committed in advance to a certain pattern appalls me.

The murder novel you mentioned ought to be written next, if I can write it. I'm not sure I can.

All the best,

Ray Chandler

## TO CHARLES MORTON

6005 Camino de la Costa
La Jolla, California
September 27, 1948

Dear Charlie:

An evening or two ago as I was toning up my intellect with Little Orphan Annie and our cat Taki was leafing through the last issue of *Time*, she let out a whimper of acute distress and slid to the floor and went under a chair. Picking up the rag, I saw before me, looking a little askance, as well he might, none other than short, dumpy, round-headed, balding, jug-eared, carnelian-nebbed, loud-bow-tied *Atlantic*-editor Morton. Well, strike me pink, lads, is this the face that launched a thousand japes and singed the snow-capped peaks of Henry Luce? It's a nice face, a nice honest, leprechaun of a face. It could be played by Barry Fitzgerald. It has character and good humor. The tie was a little careless, as though tied by one hand, while the other attended to the customary breakfast of tomato juice laced with Worcestershire sauce and a double old-fashioned, this being the regular Number Four on the bill of fare of our local hostelry, the Casa de Mañana, (clean beds.) But somehow it wasn't what I expected.

Where was the lean hawklike profile, the casual monocle balanced in the sardonic eye, the Balkan Sobranje held in the long shapely almost bloodless fingers, the cleft and bony chin, the dry

[130]

contemptuous and yet courtly smile? They just weren't there. Omaha, oh Omaha, what a spate of bourbon it took to tint that proboscis, or was it the sun on the icebergs, or the olfactory irritation of the unsolicited manuscript?[1] No use to speculate. There he is, a kind father and at times a virtuous husband, take him or leave him, give or take six points. Anyway, your piece on the fraternities was a joy. (Why did I say anyway?)

God help me I've been reading a book about the war by an English general named Fuller, who was, I believe, retired from the army while still in his prime, due to an incurable case of intelligence.[2] The book makes more sense of the war than anything I had read so far, and also of the double-cross at Versailles that we let Clemenceau put over on the Germans after they had surrendered on terms. Here is a man who has absolutely no prejudice in favor of his own countryman, who can even give Montgomery his due without gagging, who in a short brilliant chapter makes clear that MacArthur's island-hopping campaign in the South Pacific was as masterly a job of daring, imagination, and guts as the Italian campaign was a senseless and incredibly weak piece of strategic bungling. His disgust, both moral and practical and military, at so-called strategic bombing, is withering and precise. He thinks that in spite of our tactical brilliance we are a nation of military amateurs, and God knows history is proving him right. Even the English, who I am quite sure Fuller thinks incapable of all-out offensive war because there is always some muttonhead in a high place to kill a good idea or block a daring one,—even the English understood that if we did not end up in Berlin and Vienna, we had fought a war for nothing. I don't think he quite despises Eisenhower, although his temperament makes him go for men like Bradley and Patton, but it's clear he feels that Eisenhower was not a strong enough man for his job, and that at a crucial moment in September 1944 he threw away a quick victory because he couldn't stand up to either Montgomery or Bradley, but had to compromise with both. It's quite a book. The thing that stands out all through is Fuller's belief that an independent air force is a ghastly mistake, because it will insist on fighting with the most expensive, the least profitable and the most uselessly destructive weapon, the heavy

1. Morton was from Omaha, Nebraska.
2. Major General John Frederick Charles Fuller, author of *The Second World War*, 1948.

bomber, whereas its true function is ground support, interdiction of traffic and supplies, and logistics. When it was so used, usually unwillingly, the effect was immediate and startling; when it was used for saturation raids on cities like Hamburg, Berlin and Leipsig, it was militarily of small consequence and morally put us right beside the man who ran Belsen and Dachau.

Ray

## TO RAY STARK

October 1948

Dear Ray:

The point about Marlowe to remember is that he is a first person character, whether he shows up that way in a radio script or not. A first person character is under the disadvantage that he must be a better man to the reader than he is to himself. Too many first person characters give an offensively cocky impression. That's bad. To avoid that you must not always give him the punch line or the exit line. Not even often. Let the other characters have the toppers. Leave him without a gag. Insofar as it is possible. Howard Hawks, a very wise hombre, remarked to me when he was doing *The Big Sleep* that he thought one of Marlowe's most effective tricks was just giving the other man the trick and not saying anything at all. That puts the other man on the spot. A devastating crack loses a lot of its force when it doesn't provoke any answer, when the other man just rides with the punch. Then you either have to top it yourself or give ground.

Don't have Marlowe say things merely to score off the other characters. When he comes out with a smash wisecrack it should be jerked out of him emotionally, so that he is discharging an emotion and not even thinking about laying anyone out with a sharp retort. If you use similes, try and make them both extravagant and original.

And there is a question of how the retort discourteous is delivered. The sharper the wisecrack, the less forcible should be the way it is said. There should not be any effect of gloating. All this is a question of taste. If you haven't got it, you can't get it by rules. There are a lot of clever people in Hollywood who overreach themselves because they don't know where to stop. It's bad enough in pictures, but on the radio it is worse, because the voice is everything and you can't have an expression on the face that offsets the words. You can't really throw away a line as if it was something that tasted bad when you said it.

Oh well, I'm not so smart either.

Yours,

Ray

## TO H. N. SWANSON

6005 Camino de la Costa
October 15, 1948

Dear Swanie,

That was a very nice and very clever letter. Who the hell told you my name was Joe Ugly. I've been the most successful real-name-hider in the business. The Uglies (It should probably be Uglys in this case) are a small but persistent clan of hobnail-boot wearers well known and little liked for kissing their women to death of a Saturday night in small noisome alleys off the Mile End Road. Many a time as a kid sleeping in my old man's extra pair of hunting breeks have I seen Inspector Sir Marmaduke Fitzboodle (of the East Riding Fitzboodles) ease himself into the old man's pot of porter and ask a few searching questions about all that blood on the floor in the corner of the room. Once, I mind, they thought of digging up the floor, which was solid fish and chips twenty feet thick, but the old man just laughed and wiped his nose on the Inspector's knitted muffler. The Uglies never bothered about cops, except once in a while to kick one in a thick fog. Ah well, it's a long time since I put the boot to an underprivileged child.

Yes, I finished the book, if that'a a fair name for this ill-written and ill-constructed 75,000 words of nose thumbing.[1] What may happen to it I dunno. It's a mite fruity for the carriage trade and a little too literate for the Democrats, besides having only six murders in it. But I have not ripened into manhood. My five years in the salt mines left me a typical case of arrested development, and the more I stay away from the picture business, the better I like it. I suppose you know Joe Sistrom has left Universal and Paramount's top price for a property is five grand. Any moment now Henry the Gin will finalize a deal to a remake of The King of Kings, with Alan Ladd as Christ, Cecil B. de Mille as God, and Betty Hutton as the Virgin Mary. But I bet Bill Bendix steals the picture as Mary Magdalene. I will eat lunch with you only if my gun jams.

Ray

## TO JAMES SANDOE

Camino de la Costa
La Jolla, California
October 17, 1948

Dear Sandoe:

There is no top-drawer critical writing about the murder or mystery novel, factually based or otherwise. A book like Pritchett's *The Living Novel* would be very interesting, possibly not too remunerative in dollars, but well worthwhile from the prestige point of view.[1] Neither in this country nor in England has there been any critical recognition that far more art goes into these books at their best than into any number of fat volumes of goosed history or social-

1. *The Little Sister.*

_____

1. V. S. Pritchett, *The Living Novel*, 1946.

significance rubbish. The psychological foundation for the immense popularity with all sorts of people of the novel about murder or crime or mystery hasn't been scratched. A few superficial and a few frivolous attempts, but nothing careful and cool and leisurely. There is a lot more to this subject than most people realize, even those who are interested in it. The subject has usually been treated lightly because it seems to have been taken for granted, quite wrongly, that because murder novels are easy reading they are also light reading. They are no easier reading than *Hamlet, Lear* or *Macbeth*. They border on tragedy and never quite become tragic. Their form imposes a certain clarity of outline which is only found in the most accomplished "straight" novels. And incidentally—quite incidentally, of course, a very large proportion of the surviving literature of the world has been concerned with violent death in some form. And if you have to have significance (the demand for which is the inevitable mark of a half-baked culture), it is just possible that the tensions in a novel of murder are the simplest and yet most complete pattern of the tensions in which we live in this generation.

RC

## TO CARL BRANDT

6005 Camino de la Costa
La Jolla, California
November 12, 1948

Dear Carl:

We had lovely weather all the way to San Francisco and back. It rained the night we stayed at Carmel but was fine again in the morning. Carmel, which I suppose you know, is a very cute place, but has a slightly unreal look as though it had been constructed on MGM's back lot. It has been compared to La Jolla and does resemble it in the lack of billboards and other ugly things, but the resemblance stops there. I really think it is more attractive than La Jolla, and has

[135]

the advantage of not being near a large city. La Jolla is full of tired old men and tired old money; Carmel seems a more middle-class sort of place. If you ever go to Santa Barbara, stop at the Biltmore in Montecito. There is *really* a hotel. San Francisco I liked, but its hotels stink. The Fairmont has a magnificent lobby and that's all. The Mark [Hopkins] has a beautiful grill room (and the sky lounge, of course) but its food is exorbitant, its lobby has no trace of style, and the place is full of chisel-eyed characters who look as if they were afraid they might not smile at a producer. Next time we'll try the Clift, which we visited many times when Clift was alive, but not since. I regret to confess that I left the addresses home which Bernice sent me, but I probably should not have called them anyhow because we spent all our time shopping or trying to shop.[1] The thing I love about S.F. is its go to hell attitude. The narrow streets are lined with NO PARKING AT ANY TIME signs and also lined with parked automobiles which look as if they had been there all day. For the first time in my life I saw a lady traffic cop, a real cop too, complete with nickel star and whistle. I saw one other cop. He was driving around with a piece of chalk on the end of a long stick and about once a block he took a swipe at some rear tire, just to keep his hand in. The taxi drivers are wonderful too. They obey no laws but those of gravity and we even had one who passes street cars on the left, an offense for which you would probably get ninety days in Los Angeles. In case you should ever think I am too cynical about the police, it just isn't possible to be. A committee of Superior Court judges in L.A. has been going into the habeas corpus business which seemed to them to be flourishing too richly and taking up too much court time. The chairman just let loose with a statement in which he announced that he was fed up with the racket of arresting bookies or supposed bookies, then springing them on habeas corpus writs, at a cost of $500 in bail and anywhere from $200 to $500 legal fees. He said that the Vice squad boys seem to have perfected a system whereby they pull in supposed bookies and the moment the boys are booked along comes a lawyer and a bondsmen with a writ; when the case is called the cops have lost the evidence. Judge Ambrose said quite clearly and audibly that the Los Angeles police have developed a very slippery clutch on evidence. Five or six of these operations per night could be quite

1.  Bernice Baumgarten, of Brandt and Brandt agency.

lucrative over a period of time. The courts have to hear arguments on all these writs and they take up time. Anybody who is not a damn fool must know that this shakedown is all worked out in advance and is a substitute for the former method of having a "juicer" call around at the gambling houses for the rake-off. It has the advantage of looking legal too. The point is, of course, that each of these arrests and releases implies a crooked judge, a crooked lawyer, a crooked bondsman, and some crooked cops. No honest judge would set bail so high that the bond would cost $500. Last night a couple of the boys didn't get writs. They had to stay in jail, and were they sore! The judge got cold feet. The thing that gets me in our lovely civilization is the complete indifference with which the public greets these disclosures. We just don't expect anybody to be honest. A few weeks ago, for example, the *Times* caught a photo of an imcomplete forward pass on the goal line. It was incomplete because the end or back who was the receiver had his right arm locked tight between the left arm and body of the defending back. The whole dirty foul was as clear as daylight in the photo. THE PHOTO WAS PUBLISHED WITHOUT COMMENT as a photo of the play; there was simply no reaction to the foul at all. Well for Chrissake, if we teach the boys to be crooked in college, what can you expect? And they *are* taught to be crooked, coldly, deliberately and with malice.

All my best,

Ray

## TO HAMISH HAMILTON

6005 Camino de la Costa
La Jolla, California
November 20, 1948

Dear Jamie:

My punctuation is unorthodox at times, but I don't make any

[137]

mistakes of ignorance. They are deliberate violations of standard
practice. It's nice of Priestley to want to read my stuff.[1] Bless him! I
remember his saying of it, "They don't write like that at Dulwich."[2]
That may be, but if I hadn't grown up on Latin and Greek, I doubt if
I would know so well how to draw the very subtle line between what
I call a vernacular style and what I should call an illiterate or faux
naif style, There's a hell of a lot of difference, to my mind.

.        .        .

Yours,
Ray

## TO CARL BRANDT

6005 Camino de la Costa
La Jolla, California
November 26, 1948.

Dear Carl:

.        .        .

I worked at MGM once in that cold storage plant they call the
Thalberg Building, fourth floor. Had a nice producer, George Haight,
a fine fellow. About that time some potato-brain, probably Mannix.[1]
had decided that writers would do more work, if they had no couches
to lie on. So there was no couch in my office. Never a man to be
stopped by trifles, I got a streamer rug out of the car and spread it on
the floor and lay down on that. Haight coming in for a courtesy
call rushed to the phone and yelled down to the story editor (I forget
the name and never even met the man) that I was a horizontal writer
and for Chrissake send up a couch. However, the cold storage
atmosphere got me too quick, and the coteries at the writers table in
the commissary. I said I would work at home. They said Mannix
had issued orders no writers to work at home. I said a man as big as
Mannix ought to be allowed the privilege of changing his mind.

1. J. B. Priestley.
2. Chandler's English school.

---

1. Edgar J. Mannix, Thalberg's assistant, who later became General Manager of MGM
Studios.

So I worked at home, and only went over there three or four times to talk to Haight. I've only worked at three studios and Paramount was the only one I liked. They do somehow maintain the country club atmosphere there to an extent. At the writers table at Paramount I heard some of the best wit I've ever heard in my life. Some of the boys are at their best when not writing. I remember Harry Tugend's wonderful crack about _____, when Tugend was trying to be a producer and hating it. He said: "You know this is a lousy job. You got to sit and talk to that birdbrain seriously about whether or no this part is going to be good for her _____ career and at the same time you got to keep from being raped." Whereat a rather innocent young man piped up: "You mean to say she's a nymphomaniac?" Harry frowned off into the distance and sighed and said slowly, "Well, I gues she would be, if they could get her quieted down a little." The other was a contribution from a man named Seton Miller, a lousy writer but a very good brain in other ways. "Somebody was discussing the picture that introduced Miss Lauren Bacall to immortality, *To Have and Have Not*, and the singing she did in it. An innocent said, "I guess they probably dubbed that song in." Whereat Seton Miller screamed: "For Jesus Christ sake, you damn idiot, do you think somebody actually went out and *looked* for a voice like that?"

All the best,
Ray

# TO CARL BRANDT

6005 Camino de la Costa
La Jolla, California
December 5, 1948

Dear Carl:

As for Dore Schary, I'm sure he is an able man and a nice fellow, but like a great many intellectual Jews he is hipped on significance.[1] He believes in pictures that carry a message. I regard that

1. Motion picture producer and playwright.

as a facet of Hollywood's adult infantilism. I regard the whole matter of social significance in pictures as a bore. *Gentleman's Agreement* lasted twenty minutes with me before I walked out on it. I thought it one of the worst pictures I had ever tried to sit through, an insult to my intelligence, because its so-called message was pitched on a level I can only call grammar school. As a European by education, though not by birth, I share the European feeling that Hollywood's attempts to propound social and political ideas, claptrap about democracy and such, is an indication of a half-baked culture. "From the cinema one does not learn about politics; from films one can only learn about people."

Ray

## TO JAMES SANDOE

6005 Camino de la Costa
La Jolla, California
December 6, 1948

Dear Sandoe:

.       .       .

I knew a banker once from Aberdeen, Washington, who served two or three years in federal prison for making unsecured loans from the bank's funds to the ranchers on whom the bank's business was built. He was a perfectly honest man, he didn't make a cent out of what he did. It was during the depression and the ranchers had to have money or go broke. If they went broke, the bank went broke, because its mortgage loans would become worthless. With the bank's help the ranchers might weather the depression. If they did, they would repay the loans. This bank undoubtedly broke the banking laws. He admitted it. But who was he defrauding? The stockholders of the bank? He was one himself and the others were all men of property in the neighborhood. The stock was not traded in. He was

[140]

attempting by the only means he saw to keep the bank's source of income from collapsing. He was tried and convicted and the bank closed its doors. But up to that time the bank had withstood the depression, as very many other state banks had not. The chances are that it would have gone under anyway, because the whole area was directly or indirectly dependent on the lumber business, and the lumber business didn't recover until we started to rearm for World War II. But the man did his best. There is something tragically wrong with a system of justice which can and does make criminals of honest men and can only convict gangsters and racketeers when they don't pay their taxes. Of course to be fair I must also admit that there is something wrong with a financial system which insures that every corporation executive during a time of depression will risk going to jail a dozen times a month in his efforts to save his company. I personally believe, and I am not a socialist or anything of the sort, that there is a basic fallacy about our financial system. It simply implies a fundamental cheat, a dishonest profit, a non-existent value.

.        .        .

Ray


# TO MIKE GIBBUD, ESQ. FROM TAKI CHANDLER, ESQ.[1]


N.D. [Christmas 1948]

Dear Mike:

This is to thank you for your card and your good wishes, which I reciprocate, although I do not reciprocate the somewhat excessive familiarity of your mode of address since we have not, so far as I recall, been formally introduced. As to your suspicions of your "old lady" (do try to get rid of these palsy-walsy mannerisms) they are probably quite unfounded and due to an inferiority complex which

---

1. Chandler's cat. The text of the letter is taken from a transcript.

in turn is the product of your mixed blood. But don't worry about these things. This is an age of heraldic inferiority. A bend sinister is no more a disgrace today than it was in the Middle Ages. Your father may have been a gentleman, even if your mother was no lady. Your rat tail is all the fashion now. I prefer a bushy plume, carried straight up. You are Siamese and your ancestors lived in trees. Mine lived in palaces. It has been suggested to me that I am a bit of a snob. How true! I prefer to be.

Come around sometime when your face is clean and we shall discuss the state of the world, the foolishness of humans, the prevalence of horsemeat, although we prefer the tenderloin side of a porterhouse, and our common difficulty in getting doors opened at the right time and meals served at more frequent intervals. I have got my staff up to five a day, but there is still room for improvement.

As for your parting greeting: "Happy mouse hunting," you are, I trust, a little drunk. Cats of our lineage do not hunt mice.


## TO BERNICE BAUMGARTEN

6005 Camino de la Costa
La Jolla, California
December 29, 1948

Dear Bernice:

.          .          .

Of Jim's books I have *Guard of Honor*, *The Just and the Unjust*, *S.S. San Pedro*.[1] What others should I get? I mean, are there any that would be likely to disappoint me? If that is possible. I got *The Young Lions* for Christmas.[2] It looks as phony as hell in spots. And how do you do something "with careful deliberation." And, "But the girl's expression hadn't changed. She had broken off a twig from a

1. By James Gould Cozzens, Baumgarten's husband.
2. By Irwin Shaw.

[142]

bush and was absently running it along the stone fence, as though she were pondering what he had just said." The last clause and the 'absently' throw away the effect. You either describe an action and let the reader make the deduction of the inner reaction it expresses, or else you describe the inner reaction and view what she does from within. You don't do it both ways at the same time. A small thing, but it places the stuff for me. I guess I'm just being a stinker. And enjoying it.

Yours ever,

Ray

## TO CARL BRANDT

January 23rd. 1949

Dear Carl:

I've mislaid your last note, but I think you said you would be in LA about the middle of Feb. I think I can pop up and see you. Just came back from there and had a talk with Stark in so far as one can have a talk with a Hollywood agent in his lair at all. Not hopeful about any English deal. Looks like I'll have to pay my own way and I'd better get busy or I won't have a reservation. Stark came up with some brain wave about me writing a Marlowe story about he goes to London and Montgomery plays him and there he was (Stark) on the phone yelling for Montgomery that he don't get anywhere near at all. Having seen how the boys suffered with M over the script of *The Saxon Charm* (which may have been their fault, of course) I'm not keen except that he is a decent fellow for an actor. (My favorite producer once remarked in a tone of muted despair, just after an interview with one: "Of course, nobody can *really like* an actor!) What gets me about going to England is the awful mess of red tape, the reservations, the deadlines, the not knowing where to go. (Certainly not the Dorchester, might as well stay at that stinkhole the Beverly Hills Hotel.)

[143]

These Hollywood people are fantastic when you have been away for a while. In their presence any calm sensible remark sounds faked. Their conversation is a mess of shopworn superlatives interrupted by four telephone calls to the sentence. Stark is a nice chap. I like him. Everybody at his bagnio is nice. He has done a fine job with the radio show. It could have been on the air five years already, if I had had him in the first place. It has a better rating they tell me than some quite expensive shows. Just the same I came away depressed. I really don't know why. Perhaps it's just Beverly Hills. It was such a nice place before the Phoenicians took it over. Now it's just a setting for an enormous confidence racket.

Ray


## TO HAMISH HAMILTON

6005 Camino de la Costa
La Jolla, California
January 24th. 1949

Dear Jamie:

I'd want to go on one of the smaller Cunarders.[1] I'd not want to stop at the Dorchester and look at a lot of Phoenicians from Hollywood and New York. What is a good hotel where the food will keep one alive, where one can keep warm (it's going to seem awfully chilly to us after so many years of Southern California)? What clothes do I need of a special kind, if any? Do I need a dinner jacket etc? And might I use your house address for the no doubt unscrupulous purpose of telling the passport people where I am going? If so, what

1. For years Chandler had made plans to visit England, but did not go there until 1952.

[144]

is it? It seems they want to know. We live in the age of the Cads. You travel by air, but my wife won't, and I can't without her. I was thinking of having the food parcel man send me some food parcels. Much as I have read it is still a little hard for us to get a firm picture of what living is like in England. When would you suggest my coming? May or June or what?

Your remarks about red carpets, though ever so kindly meant, scare me a little. I'm strictly the background type, and my character is an unbecoming mixture of outer diffidence and inward arrogance. I don't do any of the things writers seem to do as a matter of course nowadays; I don't puff other writers' books and expect them to puff mine; I don't go to autograph parties or book marts or become a party to these cunning little interviews which are arranged by the promotion people to help their sales. In this country it is part of the racket; to me it's what makes it a racket. In England I have no doubt things are a little different. I do not come to England as a visiting author, God forbid, but as a man who loved England well when his heart was young and has never loved in the same way since, nor ever shall.

Of course I'll love the books. Brooding over the list I've been on the point of ordering a number of them. It's so very kind of you all to make so much of what to me is so simple a thing. After all what do I do? And if it were anything at all, which it is not, I have in my mind an unforgettable little story of some friends who visited Luxembourg a couple of years ago. They stayed at a very nice hotel where the food and wine were magnificent. The atmosphere was cheerful, people from all the countries of Europe, almost, were there, having their ease. At two tables were English people, only two. At one sat an elderly couple formerly well-to-do, now not so well-to-do. At the other a demobbed tank officer with his mother. On all the tables in the hotel dining room but these two were bottles of wine. This is a true story. The English could not afford wine. Those who had never surrendered drank water in order that those who had surrendered might drink wine. I think this story is wonderful. It is definitely and positively true, which makes it so much more wonderful.

Ray

[145]

# TO CARL BRANDT

6005 Camino de la Costa
La Jolla, California
(February 1949)

Dear Carl:

I am trying out a new Corona so my typing will be worse than usual. For years I used a noiseless portable and then I got a standard Remington and since then have been unable to use any noiseless machine. But I must have a portable I can take away from home.

Thanks for your letter of Jan. 26. Perhaps I had better not bother anybody about advice to a traveler to England until I'm sure I'm going there. I have some very difficult personal problems to solve, or they seem difficult to me, which is the same thing. There is first the question of the house. It is a nice house, one of the nicest in La Jolla, but it seems impossible to get any competent help here. Everybody has colored people and they are no damn good to us. My wife simply will not put up with their dirt. The house is too much for her, and even if it were not too much for her in a physical sense, taking care of it, going to market, cooking and cleaning up, would prevent her from doing anything else. I guess we all slow down and tire as we get older. I know I have. I am always tired. Also, apart from that, the house is too expensive. Disregarding the investment and taxes we find that in a La Jolla everything costs too much, every service is overpriced, everybody is on the chisel. Once the place was worth it. But we don't have the same seclusion any more. It is still far better than Los Angeles or that once charming and now ruined little city of Beverly Hills. Then it is too close to the ocean. I have a lot of trouble with my sinuses. Of course we don't know where to go yet. If it were not for the smog, we would have tried San Marino, the other side of Los Angeles. The San Fernando Valley has been corrupted by the Hollywood element. They spoil everything they touch. Reversing Johnson's epitaph on Goldsmith, one might say of the movie industry, NIHIL QUOD TETIGIT NON CORRUPIT. (It touched nothing which it did not corrupt.) The trouble with the valley is its heat in summer. On the other hand we want

[146]

to get a cabin at Big Bear Lake and want it not more than a couple of hours drive away. Altogether, quite a problem.

.　　　　.　　　　.

I have no idea what income I can count on. I am cutting my own throat by using up my time and energies doing things that have nothing to do with writing. But I can't make any stable arrangements until I know where and how I am going to live. I don't see how any writer except a writer of best-sellers, which I am not likely to be, can exist other than in the most modest way without either Hollywood money or a steady stream of serials in the big magazines. You can't depend on radio or selling motion picture rights. They are too chancy. If I write a book a year I can probably depend on an income of $25,000, but that wouldn't pay my way here. Gosh, when I think what that income would have bought when I was a schoolboy in England. A mansion standing in large grounds, three or four servants, a full time gardener and coachman, a couple of fine horses for the victoria and the brougham, and so on. High prices and heavy taxation will destroy a society just as effectively as war. Can you recall when amid howls of fury the English income tax reached a shilling in the pound?

I've got an article on writing in Hollywood for Charlie Morton. At least I have it on records, but it isn't typed. It's too long and may be repetitious, but I had to get it off my chest. If it seems too bitter, it need not be printed. (Also, he may not like it). But I had to write it. I don't believe in handling these birds with kid gloves. It's a disgraceful thing that no reputable writer can work for Hollywood without its ending in cynicism and disgust. But even at that I'd rather work in pictures than write these slick serials, even if I could.

I have a book in mind which I have only not started because it needs a third act, or rather a better third act. It has a good idea, was originally intended to have an English setting, but I couldn't do that now. Altogether I seem to be a bit mixed up, don't I?

.　　　　.　　　　.

God what a long and discontented letter. Sorry,

Ray

# TO BERNICE BAUMGARTEN

6005 Camino de la Costa
La Jolla, California
Feb. 13th 1949

Dear Bernice:

It is probably, in fact certainly, very inconsiderate of me to send you the enclosed in this form, but I have to get it away from me.[1] I can neither stop tinkering with it nor can I summon up the courage to throw it away. Someone is going to have to do that for me. If you approve of it, Charlie Morton has a moral option to see it and take it, if he wants it.[2]

This was something I had to get off my chest, be it ill-judged, undiplomatic and all the rest. It was something that preyed on me, but that does not mean it has to be published. I have a horror of pulling my punches for fear of offending Hollywood, for fear that that offense will hurt me in some indirect way, probably financial. If I write about it at all I will write what I think. I may be wrong but I am honest. But I do not have to write about it and I hope I shall never be betrayed into doing it again in any serious vein. Yet I did have to try to write this piece. I did have to justify to myself the conviction that the "professionalism" of the Hollywood film is killing it and that no amount of gloss, no amount of publicity build-up, no amount of Zanuckism, will save it in the long run if the imaginative basis of the film is destroyed.[3] And I have seen that happening all the time.

I am not at all sure that I approve of the fiction writer as a thinking animal. It's possible that he should do all his thinking with his solar plexus and leave the critical stuff to the boys who cannot write anything else. But there are two subjects which always seem to

1. Article entitled "The Film and the Writer." It disappeared and was subsequently replaced by "A Qualified Farewell," which was published as "Farewell, My Hollywood" in *Antaeus*, Spring/Summer 1976.
2. Editor at *The Atlantic Monthly*.
3. Reference to Darryl Zanuck at Twentieth Century-Fox Studio.

stir me up and make me want to rant and roar. One is the assumption
of such unshy pornographers as the gent who wrote about that
county[1] that the mystery novel is by definition inferior writing because
very many of the exhibits are inferior writing, that its particular
brand of fantasy is any less vital than that of the love story or the
novel of manners. They are all fantasy and scarcely anything in
literature is worth a damn except what is written between the lines.
The other subject is what I have written about in this piece. And
I don't really care what you do with it so long as you don't let me
tinker with it any more.

We are going to Riverside tommorrow Monday unless it pours
rain (which it is doing at this moment) and I assume Carl will be
out here by then.

Yours,

Ray

## TO JAMES SANDOE

La Jolla
February 25, 1949

.                                                            .

I know from my own knowledge that in the first world war, during
the final German retreat from the Hindenburg line the machine gun
crews left behind to hold up the advance as long as possible were
almost always bayoneted to the last man, even though they rose out
of the ground and tried to surrender. There is an element of hypocrisy
in these war trials that hurts. Hanging generals and politicians and
concentration camp people is fine, but when it comes to junior
officers and N.C.O.'s I'm not at all easy about it. Their freedom of
choice seems to me little more than freedom to prefer death to
dishonor, and that's asking too much of human nature.

1. Edmund Wilson, author of *The Memoirs of Hecate County*, 1949.

# TO BERNICE BAUMGARTEN

6005 Camino de la Costa
La Jolla, California
March 11th, 1949

Dear Bernice:

Every now and then I get a shock by seeing myself through
other eyes. In the current number of *Partisan Review* (which
incidentally has several very good things in it) a man writing about
*Our Mutual Friend* says: "It is possible that the question of true-to-life
did not arise, and that Dickens' contemporaries accepted his dark
vision of England and London . . . as readily as we today accept
Raymond Chandler's California with its brutal and neurotic crew of
killers and private eyes——" etc. Another writer in an avant garde
magazine referred to me as a "Cato of the Cruelties." Apart from the
obvious compliment of being noticed at all by the rarified intellectuals
who write for these publications—and I should understand them
well, because I was one of them for many years—I cannot grasp what
they do with their sense of humor. Or let me put it in a better way:
Why is it that the Americans—of all people the quickest to reverse
their moods—do not see the strong element of burlesque in my kind
of writing? Or is it only the intellectuals who miss that? It is as
though the public, most inconstant in its own emotions, expected a
writer to be utterly constant in his. And as for true-to-life I don't
think these cloud-dwellers can have much understanding of the kind
of world they live in and the kind of world Dickens lived in. There is
a strong element of fantasy in the mystery story; there is in any
kind of writing that moves within an accepted formula. The mystery
writer's material is melodrama, which is an exaggeration of violence
and fear beyond what one normally experiences in life. (I said
normally; no writer ever approximated the life of the Nazi
concentration camps). The means he uses are realistic in the sense that
such things happen to people like these and in places like these. But
this realism is superficial; the potential of emotion is overcharged, the
compression of time and event is a violation of probability, and
although such things happen, they do not happen so fast and in such a

[150]

tight frame of logic to so closely knit a group of people. I think there's an article in this.

Yours,

Ray

## TO HAMISH HAMILTON

6005 Camino de la Costa
La Jolla, California
March 12th. 1949

Dear Jamie:

.     .     .

I regret to say I find Elizabeth Bowen's last book entirely unreadable; in places an absolute parody of Henry James.[1] When you read HJ, however tenuous the web he spins, you do at last and at least realize that he is trying to say something precise, almost too exquisitely precise. But poor dear Elizabeth is falling into the sad error of thinking that the involution of the language necessarily conceals a subtlety of thought. It doesn't; it conceals a vacuum. I used to do this sort of thing myself in my thirties, but God gave me too much sense of humor to carry on with it. I'm awfully sorry for writers. They try so hard, they are so damn vulnerable, and they look so silly when they overextend themselves. I should be grateful that I went through the arty and intellectual phase so young and grew out of it so completely that it always seems a little juvenile in others, whatever their ages. I never took myself very seriously as a writer and always knew myself to be one of those people who can do fairly well at almost anything and therefore superbly well at nothing. And considering the vast amount of talent and intelligence there is in this country, not to mention England, I'm still a bit puzzled as to why no one has come along to make me look like thirty cents. But except for an occasional tour de force like *The Big Clock* or *Mr. Bowling Buys*

1.  Elizabeth Bowen's *The Heat of the Day*, 1948.

[151]

*a Newspaper* no one has.[2] There isn't a mystery writer on the horizon here that really has anything, or if there is, I have missed him. I thought Jack Iams might be going to amount to something, but his last book convinces me he is quite third-rate.[3] Gardner is of course tremendously saleable, but he is only by courtesy a writer at all, in a literary sense. Of course we haven't any really good fiction writers to speak of, in any field. The shoddiness of our educational system is beginning to show up in a terrible superficiality of mind. Compare the quality of the writing in the *Atlantic* and *Harper's* with the front article in the *Times Literary Supplement* and you see what has happened to us. And we don't know quality when we see it. Cozzens' *Guard of Honor* makes all the other war novels look like amateurish exercises in looking portentous, but none of the professional critics was able to evaluate it. They just don't know enough about writing.

Yours ever,

Ray

## TO ALEX BARRIS

6005 Camino de la Costa
La Jolla, California
March 18, 1949

Dear Mr. Barris:

I took some snapshots of this dump a few days ago and if they are any good I'll enclose a couple. I'm not any good with a camera, although I ought to be, with a Kodak reflex and a F 3.5 lens. We lived in a rather too large one-story house on a corner across the street from the ocean. La Jolla, as you might not know, is built on a point north of San Diego, and is never either hot or cold. So we get two seasons of tourists, one in winter, one in summer. Ten years ago the town was very quiet, exclusive, expensive, and almost as dull as Victoria, B.C. on a wet Sunday afternoon in February. Now it is just

2. *The Big Clock* by Kenneth Fearing; *Mr. Bowling Buys a Newspaper* by Donald Henderson.
3. Jack Iams' *The Body Missed the Boat*, 1947.

[152]

expensive. There is a lot of shingle here and lot of low soft sandstone cliff which the ocean has wrought into very strange shapes, but very little beach, except at the north end of the town where it is much more exposed than down where we live. Our living room has a picture window which looks south across the bay to Point Loma, the most westerly part of San Diego, and at night there is a long lighted coast line almost in our laps. A radio writer came down here to see me once and he sat down in front of this window and cried because it was so beautiful. But we live here, and the hell with it.

My wife desires no publicity, is pretty drastic about it. She doesn't paint or write. She does play a Steinway grand when she gets time. About half to two thirds of the time we are between cooks, and she does not have time. She is a New Yorker and connected with the family to which Clarence Day's mother belonged. My sister-in-law's name is Vinnie (for Lavinia) which was also Clarence's mother's name. I hasten to add that I never knew any of these people myself.

As you may know I am a half-breed. My father was an American of a Pennsylvania Quaker family originally and my mother was Anglo-Irish, also of a Quaker family. She was born in Waterford where there is still, I believe, a famous Quaker school—famous to Quakers anyhow. I grew up in England and I served with the 1st Canadian Division in the first war. As a boy I spent a lot of time in Ireland and I have no romantic ideas about the Irish.

I don't know any of these radio people, so they could tell you nothing about me whatsoever. I have nothing to do with the show except to pass along any ideas I might have through my Hollywood agent. They don't have to pay the slightest attention to them. If the show is any good, all the credit beongs to the writers, actors and producers. The character of Philip Marlowe, as I see him, doesn't show up very much in this program, but neither does it in any of the pictures made about him. That's hardly surprising.

What do I do with myself from day to day? I write when I can and I don't write when I can't; always in the morning or the early part of the day. You get very gaudy ideas at night but they don't stand up. I found this out long ago. I haven't been with Paramount for a couple of years and am not under contract to any studio, thank God. I feel about Hollywood just about as I did when I wrote that piece, and I don't see why any writer should feel any different,

[153]

although there could be more genial ways of expressing it. But the people who make pictures are not all idiots. They just behave as if they were.

It ought to be pretty obvious to you that I do my own typing. I'm not used to this Corona yet either. When I worked at screenplays I dictated to a secretary. A lot of screenwriters don't; it embarrasses them, but I could never do it any other way. And secretaries are about the nicest people in Hollywood. What those girls go through, what drivel they take down, what enthusiasm they engender for what lousy scripts! They are always on your side against the world and sometimes they are the only friend a writer in Hollywood has. And do they get any thanks for it? Hell, no. Most of these high-priced writers are too god damn cheap even to give their secretaries a little extra money on the side. And when the box office grosses begin to slide, it's always the secretaries that get laid off first.

When we came down here to live I got a dictaphone outfit and dictated script into that, but I never use if for fiction. I think you have to have that mechanical resistance to keep you from getting thin and prolix. Almost all the dictating writers suffer from logorrhea. When you have to use your energy to put those words down, you are more apt to make them count.

I'm always seeing little pieces by writers about how they don't ever wait for inspiration; they just sit down at their little desks every morning at eight, rain or shine, hangover and broken arm and all, and bang out their little stint. However blank their minds or dull their wits, no nonsense about inspiration from them. I offer them my admiration and take care to avoid their books. Me, I wait for inspiration, although I don't necessarily call it by that name. I believe that all writing that has any life in it is done with the solar plexus. It is hard work in the sense that it may leave you tired, even exhausted. In the sense of concious effort it is not work at all. The important thing is that there should be a space of time, say four hours a day at least, when a professional writer doesn't do anything else but write. He doesn't have to write, and if he doesn't feel like it, he shouldn't try. He can look out of the window or stand on his head or writhe on the floor. But he is not to do any other positive thing, not read, write letters, glance at magazines, or write checks. Either write or nothing. It's the same principle as keeping order in a school. If you make the pupils behave, they will learn something just to

[154]

keep from being bored. I find it works. Two very simple rules. a. you don't have to write. b. you can't do anything else. The rest comes of itself.

I hate publicity, quite sincerely. I've been through the interview mill and I regard it as a waste of time. The guy I meet in those interviews masquerading under my name is usually a heel I wouldn't even know. I'm an intellectual snob who happens to have a fondness for the American vernacular, largely because I grew up on Latin and Greek. I had to learn American just like a foreign language. To learn it I had to study and analyze it. As a result, when I use slang, solecisms, colloquialisms, snide talk or any kind of off beat language, I do it deliberately. The literary use of slang is a study in itself. I've found that there are only two kinds that are any good: slang that has established itself in the language and slang that you make up yourself. Everything else is apt to be passé before it gets into print. But I'd better not get off on this subject, or I'll be writing for a week.

Yours very truly,

Raymond Chandler

P.S. You asked how I got paid for this radio program. I get a royalty for the use of the character. That's all.
RC


## TO HAMISH HAMILTON

6005 Camino de la Costa
La Jolla, California
March 21st. 1949

Dear Jamie:

.          .          .

I remember several years ago when Howard Hawks was making *The Big Sleep*, the movie, he and Bogart got into an argument as to whether one of the characters was murdered or committed suicide. They sent me a wire (there's a joke about this too) asking me, and dammit I didn't know either. Of course I got hooted at. The joke was in connection with Jack Warner, the head of Warner Bros. Believe it or not he saw the wire, the wire cost the studio seventy cents, and he called Hawks up and asked him whether it was really necessary to send a telegram about a point like that.

That's one way to run a business.

Your letter just came in and I hasten to say that I was not in any worry about your possible failure to get things straight, because I know how careful English proof readers are. I do, however, remember in connection with *Farewell My Lovely* that the end of Chapter 34 a typographical error got into print, although there was clearly something wrong, since what was written made no sense. (On the other hand, of course, the printers might have assumed that it *must* make sense, even if not to them.) But a writer who deals in the vernacular and on occasion makes up his own language may find the printer making corrections of things he assumed to be errors, but which in fact were meant exactly as written. Knopf's printers once had the greatest difficulty in reconciling themselves to a sentence which read, "a guy's there and you see him and then he ain't there and you don't not see him," and which to them was clearly a double negative, but was to me a much more forcible way of saying, "don't miss him," obvious and conventional, but not alive.

.        .        .

All the best,

Ray

# TO BERNICE BAUMGARTEN

6005 Camino de la Costa
La Jolla, California
March 21st. 1949

Dear Bernice:

I finished *Point of No Return.*[1] Strange that such good writing should leave me with so little feeling of having read anything of the slightest importance. Apart from the constant backtracking and jumping about in time the story irritates by its very competence. A man has no right to write that well and in the end say so little. When all is said and done who the hell cares about the Charley Grays of this world? The people who always do, say, think and wear the right thing, and yet are vaguely and weakly conscious that it is only the right thing because it pays a little more money. So life got him over a barrel and that's a tragedy. My eye, it is. So he wanted the girl, but not enough to tell her father to go jump in a tub. And if he got her what difference would it make? What has this guy Marquand got that makes him so good? Well, whatever it is he has it. He writes the perfect Victorian novel, sad but not too sad, romantic in an epicene sort of way, beautiful detailed observation and the total effect of a steel engraving with no color at all. I guess God made Boston on a wet Sunday.

If I were not so pooped out, I think I should discharge my spleen by writing a Ballade of Lament for Assistant Vice Presidents, and the refrain could be: "I think I'll wear my herringbone today."

Sometimes I wonder how Marquand ever got a reputation as a satirist. I'm inclined to suspect that John O'Hara's remark about Sinclair Lewis is much more near the truth: "It always has seemed to me that Lewis woke up to find himself called a satirist, and became one by continuing to play straight. He is King of the Corn,—and by way of being the Sweetheart of it."

Compare this book with *Guard of Honor;*[2] it's the difference between a real artist and a clever suave hack who has so much on the ball in a technical sense that you are apt to forget he really hasn't any ball to be on.

I'm going down to Palm Springs for a week to try and shake this cough.

All the best,

Ray

1. By John P. Marquand.
2. By James Gould Cozzens.

# TO MRS. HOLTON[1]

6005 Camino de la Costa
La Jolla, California
March 26, 1949

Dear Mrs. Holton:

I'm sending my only copy of *LS* by air express today.[2] I guess Brandt and Brandt have a copy in their office. I certainly hope so. But Jamie Hamilton already has the book in page proofs.

No dedication. No front matter from me, unless you want to vary the usual protection clause on the back of the title page by saying that "The people and events in this book are not entirely fictional. Some of the events happened, although not in this precise time or place, and certain of the characters were suggested by real persons, both living and dead. The author regrets any resemblance to reality that may be found in the pages of his books, and he particularly regrets that he has on occasion made use of the names of real localities. He admits with shame that there actually is a place called Hollywood and a place called Los Angeles. It has streets and he has named some of them. It has a police department and he has referred to it. Los Angeles County has a District Attorney and said District Attorney has an office. To all of these matters the author has alluded. How careless of him! He should have called Los Angeles Smogville. He should have called its police department its Ministry of Corrections. Its District Attorney he might more admirably have referred to as the Master of the Rolls, and the office of this functionary might have been placed on an imaginary island somewhere off the coast of an imaginary state in an imaginary country. The characters in the story might, for additional security, have been referred to by letters of the Greek alphabet."

Yours very truly,

Raymond Chandler

1. Of Houghton Mifflin Company.
2. Chandler's fifth novel, *The Little Sister*.

## TO JAMES SANDOE

March 26, 1949

Dear Sandoe:

.                                           .

My wife thought Doyle an awfully dull man.[1] I thought him the sort
you would either like tremendously or writhe at. Found a two bit
edition of *Hound of the Baskervilles*. God, what tripe. It looks to me as
if Lincoln was wrong. You can fool all of the people all the time.

RC

## TO BERNICE BAUMGARTEN

6005 Camino de la Costa
La Jolla, California
March 31, 1949

Dear Bernice:

.                             .

    Red Barrow, my lawyer pal, and incidentally a terrific admirer
of the Cozzens talent, gave me the Francis Steegmuller stuff from
the *N.Y. Times*, which I never see. Mr. Steegmuller is quite a guy. He
not only quotes from me in quotes but without quotes. And where
did I ever say that only my type of detective story is serious literature?
My argument is and always has been merely that there is no such
thing as serious literature, that the survivals of Puritanism in the
American mind make all but the most literate people incapable of
thinking of literature without reference to what they call significance,
and that most of this so-called serious literature or fiction is the
most transient stuff in the world; the moment its message is dated,
damn quick, it is dead stuff.

1. Sir Arthur Conan Doyle.

It is one of the (few) charms of not being as young as you were that you can stick your neck out, because you don't give a damn. If a young writer knocks a reigning favorite, he can be accused of envy and malice, and it hurts him and makes him cautious. I get a lot of fun out of sticking pins in the popular balloons. The most fantastic pratfall of the moment is Elizabeth Bowen's last book, which in spots is a screaming parody of Henry James. Jamie Hamilton wrote me that the English critics are tying themselves in knots trying to be polite to it (because of course they know she is potentially a fine writer), knowing all the time that the poor girl is giving an exhibition of what happens when an over-earnest writer completely loses her sense of humor. I've felt fine ever since I went to Palm Springs. Wish I had a house there, but like everything else in California the place is overpriced.

                                                            Ray
P.S.

                .                .                .

        There's a lovely fight going on about the Academy. The boys were finally shamed into giving the award more or less on the basis of merit (except the musical award, which stank) and the five major companies which have been contributing to the cost of the show have withdrawn. "Look, fellows," they say without saying, "we want the Oscars to go to the best pictures all right, but we're not in business for our health. The best pictures from Hollywood, savvy." They don't care who is best as long as it's them.

                                                            Ray

# TO CARL BRANDT

                              6005 Camino de la Costa
                              La Jolla, California
                              April 3rd. 1949

Dear Carl:

The last actual research I did was in 1945 while writing *The Blue Dahlia*, the first story incidentally which betrayed to the public the fact that the head man of the Homicide Bureau, then a very nice guy called Thad Brown (Captain), did not even have a private office. His desk was set right next to that of a female secretary and his door was always open. Outside there was a bare largish room in which the dicks lounged about and quite literally did not have enough chairs to sit down in all at once. The entrance to this was a dutch door (which we didn't use in the film) and both of these rooms together would have fitted easily into our living room. This was positively all the boys had to work with and out of. This wasn't a top notch film by any means, largely because Veronica Lake couldn't play the love scenes and too much had to be discarded, but it did show the very meager accommodations the homicide boys have to make do with. They actually built the two rooms and the hall outside to scale, and some of the shots got a cluttered effect that was right. But of course nobody sees this stuff in films. A very good cop picture I saw recently called *He Walked by Night* shows some excellent technical stuff, but the shots inside Police Headquarters are much too spacious. You got the impression of a very complex and highly efficient organization staffed by innumerable men. As a matter of fact they are a pretty dumb bunch who operate about on the mental level of plumbers.

Yours,

Ray

## TO HAMISH HAMILTON

6005 Camino de la Costa
La Jolla, California
April 4 1949

Dear Jamie:

By the way, do you ever read Erle Gardner's stuff? Probably not,

[161]

since you have no professional reason for doing so. I know him very well and like him. He is a terrible talker, just wears you out, but he is not a dull talker. He just talks too loud and too much. Years of yapping into a dictaphone machine have destroyed the quality of his voice, which now has all the delicate chiaroscuro of a French taxi horn. His production methods amaze me (he can write a whole book in a week or ten days easily) and once in a while he does something pretty good. But his last Perry Mason really threw me. The first chapter is largely concerned with how much of a girl's legs Perry saw as she came down the fire escape. He discusses it with the lady and afterwards frisks her for a gun. This gives occasion for a few shady leers and the sexual implications are handled by Gardner with all the aplomb of a Classical form master paraphrasing some of the more outspoken portions of the Greek drama. Gardner is well aware that an appeal to the French postcard type of aficionado is not without a certain commercial value (a matter of which he is not apt to lose sight), and he tries to get in a little leg here and there without disturbing the suburban hypocrisy of the *Ladies Home Journal*. The result has all the naughty charm—for me at any rate—of an elderly pervert surprised while masturbating in a public toilet. The poor dear is just a bloody Victorian at heart. When he lets you get a glimpse of Della Street's well filled nylons as she slides gracefully out of a car, he seems to think the frantic reader is going to rush for a bottle of triple bromides as an alternative to raping the nearest char. Me, I find the excitement less than intense. Sex cannot be dealt with in this three-cushion style. You have to face it squarely or let it alone. Anything else is a little nauseating.

.        .        .

Frankly I have no idea why Houghton Mifflin are so slow getting out the proofs of the book. Perhaps they have been entangled in the massive job of publishing Churchill. Knopf used to send proofs rather quickly with an air of being in a furious rush, air mail special delivery and all that sort of thing, and when I rushed through them in a state of urgency and mailed them back absolutely nothing would happen for months and months. I never could discover why they had been in such a hurry nor what happened when they got the proofs back. You run into the same thing in Hollywood: wild rush for conferences over some deal, then an exhausted agreement as to terms,

[162]

and then a completely leisurely—in fact quite dilatory—writing of the contract. I remember once at Paramount, after a new contract had been negotiated to take the place of one I had grown to dislike, the legal department went for weeks without producing even a draft and during all that time of course I was not paid; they always hold your money up until the contract is signed. I then called the legal department and suggested politely that there was no need to write the new contract at all since they had breached the old one by not paying me any salary and there was now no agreement between us. It was fun while it lasted; their screams were audible for blocks. I always liked doing business with Jews. They are so excitable, so superficially sharp and tricky, but basically very reliable. They dramatise every business deal and act very tough and then suddenly give way in the most winning manner.

Ray

## TO JAMES SANDOE

6005 Camino de la Costa
La Jolla, California
April 14th. 1949

Dear Sandoe:

Have read *The Moving Target* by John Macdonald and am a good deal impressed by it, in a peculiar way.[1] In fact I could use it as a springboard for a sermon on How Not to be a Sophisticated Writer. What you say about pastiche is of course quite true, and the materials of the plot situations are borrowed here and there. E.g. the opening set up is lifted more or less from *The Big Sleep*, mother paralyzed instead of father, money from oil, atmosphere of corrupted wealth, and the lawyer-friend villain is lifted straight out of *The Thin Man*; but I personally am a bit Elizabethan about such things, do not think

1. John Ross Macdonald; he later dropped the first name to avoid confusions with John D. Macdonald, another mystery writer. The text is from a transcript.

[163]

they greatly matter, since all writers must imitate to begin with, and if you attempt to cast yourself in some accepted mould, it is natural to go to the examples that have attained some notice or success.

What strikes me about the book (and I guess I should not be writing about it if I didn't feel that the author had something) is first an effect that is rather repellant. There is nothing to hitch to; here is a man who wants the public for the mystery story in its primitive violence and also wants it to be clear that he, individually, is a highly literate and sophisticated character. A car is "acned with rust" not spotted. Scribblings on toilet walls are "graffiti" (we know Italian yet, it says); one refers to "podex osculation" (medical Latin too, ain't we hell?). "The seconds piled up precariously like a tower of poker chips," etc. The simile that does not quite come off because it doesn't understand what the purpose of the simile is.

The scenes are well handled, there is a lot of experience of some kind behind this writing, and I should not be surprised to find the name was a pseudonym for a novelist of some performance in another field. The thing that interests me is whether this pretentiousness in the phrasing and choice of words makes for better writing. It does not. You could only justify it if the story itself were devised on the same level of sophistication, and you wouldn't sell a thousand copies, if it was. When you say, "spotted with rust," (or pitted, and I'd almost but not quite go for "pimpled") you convey at once a simple visual image. But when you say, "acned with rust" the attention of the reader is instantly jerked away from the thing described to the pose of the writer. This is of course a very simple example of the stylistic misuse of language, and I think that certain writers are under a compulsion to write in recherché phrases as a compensation for a lack of some kind of natural animal emotion. They feel nothing, they are literary eunuchs, and therefore they fall back on an oblique terminology to prove their distinction. It is the sort of mind that keeps avant garde magazines alive, and it is quite interesting to see an attempt to apply it to the purposes of this kind of story.

R.C.

[164]

# TO ALEX BARRIS

April 16 1949

Dear Barris:

Excuse yellow paper, smeary ribbon etc. I'm doing this on a
Noiseless and something is awry.

I am an American citizen by birth. Educated in England,
Anglo-Irish mother. Strong pro-British feelings always and also pro-
Canadian, since I served in the CEF and spent months at Victoria
in Gordon Highlands of Canada long ago.[1] Don't know eastern
Canada at all, only Puget Sound area. If I called Victoria dull, it was
in my time dullish as an English town would be on a Sunday,
everything shut up, churchy atmosphere and so on. I did not mean to
call the people dull. Knew some very nice ones.

*Black Mask* pulp mag which in the thirties developed the
hardboiled mystery technique, famous by Hammett of course, but he
not only. Gardner wrote for it too, Coxe, and many who did better
work then than since. My *Atlantic* article "The Simple Art of Murder"
available in Pocket Books Anthology and Haycraft's *Art of Mystery
Story* covers subject. Mag still exists so far as I know but sold out to
Popular Publications, having lost circulation through too rigid
specialization, probably.

.　　　　　.　　　　　.

Marlowe development of character used in novelettes, first
named in *Big Sleep*. My views on Hammett expressed in article
referred to above. He was tops. Often wonder why he quit writing
after *The Thin Man*. Met him once only, very nice looking tall quiet
gray-haired fearful capacity for Scotch, seemed quite unspoiled to
me. (Time out for ribbon adjustment.)

.　　　　　.　　　　　.

I believe *Farewell My Lovely* would be called the best of my
books, *The High Window*, the worst. But I have known people who
would pick any of them as against the others. In some ways my

---

1. CEF is Canadian Expeditionary Force.

last, not yet published is the best.[2] But I'll never again equal *The Big Sleep* for pace nor *FML* for plot complication. I probably don't want to; the time comes when you have to choose between pace and depth of focus, between action and characters, between menace and wit. I now choose the second in each case.

Do I read my stuff when published? Yes, and at very great risk of being called an egotistical twerp, I find it damn hard to put down. Even me, that knows all about it. There must be some magic in writing after all, but I take no credit for it. It just happens, like red hair. But I find it rather humiliating to pick up a book of my own to glance at something and then find myself twenty minutes later still reading it as if someone else had written it.

The camera eye technique of *Lady in the Lake* is old stuff in Hollywood.[3] Every young writer or director has wanted to try it; it just so happened that Bob Montgomery was in a technical position where he could make them let him do it. I wrote about a sequence or part of a sequence in that manner in the first draft of the script (I refused screen credit on the final result) but it would be ridiculous for me to claim that as an inspiration to Montgomery. "Let's make the camera a character"; it's been said at every lunch table in Hollywood one time or another. I knew one fellow who wanted to make the camera the murderer; which wouldn't work without an awful lot of fraud. The camera is too honest.

Have I since "creating" Marlowe used any other central character outside screen plays? Yes, in several stories I wrote after *The Big Sleep*.

And do I think *Hamlet* was the best motion picture of 1948? Definitely not. Olivier was marvellous, Felix Aylmer was top notch, but the camera work was a pain in the neck and a lot of the acting barely acceptable. But I'm glad Hollywood was shamed into giving it [the Oscar] to a foreign picture for all that.

Yours, Chandler

---

2. *The Little Sister.*
3. In this film, Marlowe is the camera; everything is seen through his eyes.

# TO CARL BRANDT

6005 Camino de la Costa
La Jolla, California
April 18th. 1949

Dear Carl:

It was very kind of you indeed to send me a wire about
Norbert D.[1] However, right or wrong, I am sending him a couple of
hundred dollars. Who am I to judge another man's needs or deserts?
It's a pretty miserable thing to live off in the country and watch them
all come back and be scared. He says he has sold one out of fifteen
this last year. Say it's his fault, say he got big-headed or drunk and
lazy or what have you—what difference does it make? You suffer
just as much when you're wrong. More. Write it off, call it waste,
forget it, and hope the guy won't hate you for helping him, or
rather for having to ask you to help him. I cannot draw these hairline
distinctions. I only know that two hundred bucks won't buy me
the key to heaven, but there have been times when it would have
looked like it would, and I didn't have it, and nobody was around to
give it to me. I never slept in the park but I came damn close to it.
I went five days without anything to eat but soup once, and I had just
been sick at that. It didn't kill me, but neither did it increase my
love of humanity. The best way to find out if you have any friends is
to go broke. The ones that hang on longest are your friends. I don't
mean the ones that hang on forever. There aren't any of those.

Yours,

Ray

---

1. Chandler had asked Brandt's advice about lending $200 to Norbert Davis, a former
*Black Mask* writer.

# TO DALE WARREN

6005 Camino de la Costa
La Jolla, California
April 20 1949

Dear Dale:

.          .          .

. . . Priestley gave me a, for him, very elegant paragraph in his new column in the *New Statesman*.[1] His original comment on first looking into Chandler's abattoir was, "They don't write like that at Dulwich." How true.

I can't seem to get started doing anything. Always very tough for me to get started. The more things people say about you the more you feel as if you were writing in an examination room, that it didn't belong to you any more, that you had to protect critical reputations and not let them down. Writers even as cynical as I have to fight an impulse to live up to someone's else's idea of what they are. Story I've been fussing with really ought to have an English setting anyhow. Thought I could use Bel Air, but when you drag in the whole phoney Hollywood life, and everything becomes scenery, back projections, matt shots, miniatures, papier mache rocks, tubbed trees, deluges of tropical rain out of which the characters come in, having walked in it for hours, with one damp lapel and two curls out of place. Three feet of film later the suit's pressed and the guy has a fresh carnation in his buttonhole.

Well, it's not as bad as pinning a posthumous V.C. on the saddle blanket of a cavalry horse, which they did in *Lives of a Bengal Lancer*.

I see from the *Sunday Times* that your picture *He Walked by Night* didn't get much from Dilys Powell but a remark about the chase through the Sewers.[2] She's damn good too, and usually very fair about American pictures. What's the matter with the films? I rack

1. J. B. Priestley, the English novelist.
2. *He Walked by Night*, a 1949 film made in imitation of *Naked City*, was directed by Alfred Werker, produced by Brian Foy, and written by John C. Higgins and Crane Wilbur. Dilys Powell was film critic for the *Sunday Times* of London.

my brains for an answer, and I have a queer recurring thought that its isn't anything specific, the films aren't so bad, but they're simply no longer a novelty. The medium, the things it can do, have lost the sting. We're back where silent films were when Warners bought the Vitaphone. Except for forced focus there has hardly been a real technical advance in fifteen years, and you don't realize what forced focus does unless you look at a film made in the middle thirties and note that in a medium close shot everything more than ten feet from the camera is a blur.

.        .        .

Ray

## TO BERNICE BAUMGARTEN

6005 Camino de la Costa
La Jolla, California
April 21st 1949

Dear Bernice:
    Many thanks for answering me so promptly about the Mystery Guild.[1] I am dead against it and so far as I have any power I refuse to do it. . . . The economic squeeze has not got me yet although it may eventually. The money is not enough and the suggestion that these are not competitive with trade editions is to me so much baloney. I do realize that the sale of a mystery is apt to be over by, or very soon after, publication date. But it seems to me rather obvious that if my stuff has any real value, it is not as a mystery at all. Other writers do much better mysteries. Plot as such merely bores me. The people who really like my books are those who like them in spite of their being mysteries, not because of. Dorothy Sayers tried to make the jump from the mystery to the novel of manners and take the mystery along with her. She tried to move over, with all her baggage,

1.  Hardwick Moseley of Houghton Mifflin had proposed that Chandler accept the offer of the Mystery Guild to select *The Little Sister* as an offering for their members. See letter to Mosley, April 23, 1949.

[169]

from the people who can plot but can't write to the people who can write and, all too often, can't plot. She didn't really make it, because the novel of manners she aimed at was in itself too slight a thing to be important. It was just the substitution of one popular trivial kind of writing for another. I am not satisfied that the thing can't be done nor that sometime, somewhere, perhaps not now nor by me, a novel cannot be written which, ostensibly a mystery and keeping the spice of mystery, will actually be a novel of character and atmosphere with on overtone of violence and fear. If people call my book just another mystery I can't help it, but by God I'm not going to do the calling myself.

.        .        .

I found *Men and Brethren* and *Ask Me Tomorrow* in the public library here.[2] Not obtainable to buy. I had no card and when I asked for one, the elderly white haird prim-mouthed librarian said: "Oh, you're Raymond Chandler, the writer. I read one of your books when I was in the hospital last year." "I hope it didn't make you worse," said I. "I wanted to throw it across the room, it made me so mad," she said, then grudgingly, "But I didn't. There was something about the writing."

A perfect expression of the La Jolla mentality.

Ray

## TO HAMISH HAMILTON

6005 Camino de la Costa
La Jolla, California
April 22nd. 1949

Dear Jamie:
Thanks for a most delightful letter. I hope I may have a chance to insult this boor, Wilson, someday.[1] I have had at times a certain

2. Both by James Gould Cozzens, Bernice Baumgarten's husband.

---

1. Edmund Wilson.

modest success in this direction. As you (incidentally) mentioned
Spender[2] I happened to be reading four excerpts from an impending
autobiography, published here in *Partisan Review*, which is the nearest
thing we have to an intellectual magazine not edited in some
University English Course. I though it delightful writing all the way
through, clear and honest and beautifully yet not ostentatiously (as
Connolly is at times, I think) expressed. J. A. Spender, his uncle, was
the first editor who ever showed me any kindness. I got an
introduction to him from a wonderful old boy named Roland
Ponsonby Blennerhasset, a barrister with a House of Lords practice, a
wealthy Irish landowner (he owned some fabulous number of acres in
Kerry), a member, as I understood from my Uncle in Waterford,
of one of these very ancient untitled families that often make earls and
marquesses appear quite parvenu. Spender bought a lot of stuff from
me, verses, sketches, and unsigned things such as paragraphs lifted
from foreign publications. He got me into the National Liberal Club
for the run of the reading room; I was seconded by his political
cartoonist, a famous man in those days, but I have forgotten his
name. I never met him in the flesh. I got about three guineas a week
out of all these, but it wasn't enough. I also worked for a man
named Cowper who succeeded Lord Alfred Douglas in ownership of
the *Academy*, and did a lot of book reviewing for him, and some
essays which I still have; they are of an an intolerable preciousness of
style, but already quite nasty in tone. I seldom got the best books
to review, and in fact the only one of any importance I got my hands
on was *The Broad Highway*, for whose author, then unknown, I
am glad to say I predicted an enormous popularity.[3] Like all young
nincompoops I found it very easy to be clever and snotty, very
hard to praise without being ingenuous. I like this fellow Spender
very much. In fact I like him better than Auden, about whom I
have always had reservations. (I am also disturbed at your remark that
Connolly has no conscience.) His account of the silken barbarity of
Eton is wonderful, of course, and the way these fellows thought and
wrote and talked, at an age when Americans can hardly spell their
own names, is also most impressive. Nevertheless, there is something
about the literary life that repels me; all this desperate building of

2. Stephen Spender.
3. Novel by Jeffrey Farnol.

castles on cobwebs, the long-drawn acrimonious struggle to make something important which we all know will be gone forever in a few years, the miasma of failure which is to me almost as offensive as the cheap gaudiness of popular success. I believe the really good people would be reasonably successful in any circumstances; that to be very poor and very beautiful is most probably a moral failure much more than an artistic success. Shakespeare would have done well in any generation, because he would have refused to die in a corner; he would have taken the false gods and made them over, he would have taken the current formulae and forced them into something lesser men thought them incapable of. Alive today he would undoubtedly have written and directed motion pictures, plays, and God knows what. Instead of saying "This medium is not good," he would have used it and made it good. If some people had called some of his work cheap (which some of it is), he wouldn't have cared a rap, because he would know that without some vulgarity there is no complete man. He would have hated refinement, as such, because it is always a withdrawal, a shrinking, and he was much too tough to shrink from anything.

.           .           .

Ray

## TO HARDWICK MOSELEY

6005 Camino de la Costa
La Jolla, California
April 23, 1949

Dear Hardwick:

Many thanks for explaining your position about the Mystery Guild so gently. Bernice wrote to me too and I believe (she could tell you better herself) that her position is that she would not take the responsibility of turning down money for a writer in these times (or in any, perhaps) but that she would possibly like a little more time to observe the effects of such enterprises as Mystery Guild.

[172]

I regret to appear intransigent in any matter whatever in dealing with a publisher. I am hot-tempered but not vicious. I am against this thing—hard against it. In most respects it is a very bad thing for a writer to get in touch with real money, but it does help with decisions of this sort. $2500 just isn't important dough to me; not worth any kind of a sacrifice, any possible danger to a reputation that, after all, has grown up against all the rules. I have before me a list from PW[1] of the Mystery Guild selections up to and including September, which means that the selections are known when the books are put out by the publishers, I cannot see but that this is all wrong for me. One of these books (May to September selections) has a certain literary pretentiousness: *The Moving Target* by John MacDonald (Very likely a pseudonym).[2] One: *Port Afrique* is entirely strange to me.[3] The others are by people we know, and we know that whatever their smoothness and accomplishment in their field, they do not matter as writers, except in a purely commercial way. To put oneself in that company is to classify oneself, and the dough aint enough. Not nearly enough. I can get money from Hollywood, if I have to. I know the racket and I can take the lumps. I am engaged and have always from the very beginning been engaged in the effort to do something with the mystery story which has never quite been done. In one way Hammett came close; in another way Sayers came close. Neither was capable of imparting emotion to the right nerves. They didn't feel it. What I have tried to do (and if I fail, someone will succeed) is not at all to get to be a good enough writer to do a "straight novel"; I could have done that long ago, just as I could have trained myself to write slick serials, if I had really worked at it. The thing is to squeeze the last drop out of the medium you have learned to use. The aim is not essentially different from the aim of Greek tragedy, but we are dealing with a public that is only semi-literate and we have to make an art of a language they can understand.

In doing this I must accept certain handicaps. No snob appeal, no uplift, no apparent social significance. Very easy to deprecate, just another hardboiled mystery, and so on. But it's a funny thing, to get anywhere you have to interest the extreme intellectuals. Our

1. *Publishers Weekly.*
2. John Ross Macdonald; it is indeed a pseudonym. The author's real name is Kenneth Millar.
3. *Port Afrique*, 1949, by B. V. Dryer.

target is not the mystery addict. He knows nothing, remembers nothing. He buys books cheap or rents them. It all goes in one ear and crosses the vacuum to the other. Circumstances compel both of us to have an eye to the dollar; but only one eye.

This $2500 would help your promotional budget. Okay, forget the promotional budget. You don't need it. You can't make me into a smash best seller, and you would be wasting money to try. Just let me percolate. I'll find my public with almost no assistance from advertising. But do as little as possible to lump me in the public mind with the smooth and shallow operators like Marsh and Stout and Christie. Very likely they write better mysteries than I do, but their words don't get up and walk. Mine do, although it is embarrassing to have to announce it.

The real estate market is floperoo here. This house is valued at around $75,000, present worth, and that's too much money for all but the carriage trade. Sure, California is slipping. And thanks ever so much for your suggestion, about which there may well be serious thought. I want to go to England awfully badly, but I dread the scramble. You can't just get up and go anywhere anymore. You have to plan until you're sick of the whole project.

Yours ever,

Ray

## TO JAMES SANDOE

May 3, 1949

Dear Sandoe:

Houghton Mifflin seem to want to publish a trade edition collection of my old stories. I tried to argue that they had been around enough and were only pulp writing anyhow but they insist that they should be published and that "there is nothing like them anywhere." This I doubt very much.

[174]

I think I am going to have to do a little rewriting on *The Little Sister* and I dread it. In the end I was faced with the choice between a clear but boring explanation of who shot who, why and where etc., and more or less letting it hang in air on the theory that who cared anyway, it wasn't and couldn't pretend to be a proper mystery story. But the subconscious has been at work chiding me and I think I'm going to have to answer a few questions which the publisher's people (asked, for a gag) didn't seem at all clear about. As a constructionist I have a dreadful fault; I let characters run away with the scenes and then refuse to discard the scenes that don't fit. I end up usually with the bed of Procrustes. The system works if one is hitting on all twelve, but I've a few leaky sparkplugs now. But I do (since this damn letter is already impossibly egotistic) have one great advantage. I still regard myself as an amateur and insist on having some fun out of my work. I just can't take myself seriously enough to be otherwise.

## TO DALE WARREN

6005 Camino de la Costa
La Jolla, California
May 5, 1949

Dear Dale:

Sales of the *Cosmopolitan* in La Jolla are not sensational, which proves that competition of articles on impotence is not serious, as the incidence of this malady is probably higher in La Jolla than in any other locality or organization except the annual get-together of us Chickamauga veterans.

I withdraw recommendation of Pat Novack.[1] Had to turn it off last time I tried to give it my business. The affectation of the writing is just too much for me. The use of similes is unrestrained and was (admittedly, by the original writer of the show) copied from me, and has now been reduced to absurdity. The character can't even take

---

1.  Radio Show.

his hat off without saying the air striking his bald spot was as startling as a yes man saying no, or something just about that silly. Everything is like something else. You get to cringe when you feel one coming up. So ignore the whole business and tune in on the new Dick Powell show, which is swiped from Philip Marlowe which is swiped from Sam Spade which is swiped from Orson Welles's radio technique of the first person narration passing into direct dramatization. I don't know whether Welles invented it, but he certainly gets credit for adapting it to melodrama. The radio people are absolutely the most hidebound tradition-minded set in the world. They will never try anything new. I went down on my scarred knees to them to try doing a mystery show with sound effects instead of musical bridges. No soap. Their use of sound effect could be the most highly developed in the world, and should be, but they simply haven't the courage of their own craft. Norman Corwin used sound effects well, but he would insist on fouling everything up with significance. Gad, how I hate that word and all it implies.

STAY TUNED IN FOR THE DICK POWELL SHOW, STARRING (YOU GUESSED IT) DICK POWELL. THE GREATEST PRIVATE DETECTIVE OF THEM ALL (THAT SINGS TENOR).

If I wrote a non-fiction book, it would probably turn out to be the autobiography of a split personality. And speaking of Hitchcock, there is a good piece about him in the current issue of *Theatre Arts* (and hang the hanging participle.) But I don't think the man is quite fair to old Hitch. When you make a picture as good as *Shadow of a Doubt* and it flops, it takes the heart out of you. Same like *Night Must Fall* and *The Ox-Bow Incident*. . . . You mention Joan Fontaine as one of your pals. I met her once, at a lunch with John Houseman, but I know her husband, Bill Dozier, quite well. He hired me at Paramount, and gave my stoop of an agent a rooking on salary that was memorable, and remained an unhealed sore until I took Dozier for a hundred grand when he was a boss at U-I.[2] Paramount made a shocking mistake when they let him resign. At U-I it was understandable, because he was supposed to handle the contract producers while Bill Goetz handled the independent production units. These one by one folded and withdrew, leaving Goetz with nothing

2. Universal-International.

to do. Once looking out of Joe Sistrom's window on the U-I lot I happened to see the big boys strolling back from lunch in the exec dining room in a loose group. I was transfixed with a sinister delight. They looked so exactly like a bunch of topflight Chicago gangsters moving in to read the death sentence on a beaten competitor. It brought home to me in a flash the strange psychological and spiritual kinship between the operations of big money business and the rackets. Same faces, same expressions, same manners. Same way of dressing and same exaggerated leisure of movement.

.           .           .

Ray


## TO HAMISH HAMILTON

6005 Camino de la Costa
La Jolla, California
May 13, 1949

Dear Jamie:

.           .           .

I don't know what's happening to the writing racket in this country. I get an offer of $1200 a year for the use of my name on the title of a new mystery magazine. *Raymond Chandler's Mystery Magazine*. I have nothing to do with the magazine, no control over the contents and no contact whatever with the editorial policy. They are not even faintly aware that the offer is an insult and that for a writer to trade on his reputation without putting something into the pot is not permissible. You can sell your work any way you please, you can subdivide it and sell it in small pieces, but your standing with the public, high or low, you do not own—you hold it in trust. I'm aware that apparently reputable people do not agree with me. I am told they take money for puffing books (I have been offered some), and they go on autographing tours as a matter of course, they talk at book fairs, they are very occasionally photographed as Men of

[177]

Distinction holding a glass of blended whiskey that I should be almost afraid to pour down the drains, for fear of corroding the metal. Woollcott took money for writing personal letters to his friends recommending a certain brand of Scotch whisky.[1] I don't want to be revoltingly old-school-tie, but it does seem to me that a line has to be drawn, and I am even willing to argue that you can rule out ethics and you would still, if you had any vision, have to draw that line as a matter of policy. But such is the brutalization of commercial ethics in this country that no one can feel anything more delicate than the velvet touch of a soft buck.

. . .

Yours ever,

Ray

## TO BERNICE BAUMGARTEN

6005 Camino de la Costa
La Jolla, California
May 15, 1949

Dear Bernice:

. . .

I'm still boiling. If I were a commercially important writer, a big seller, which I know very well I am not, somebody's head would fall for this.[1] You just don't do this sort of thing and get away with it, because by doing it you proclaim your stupidity, carelessness or incompetence, your complete failure to understand what your job is all about. As it is, of course, all that will happen will be "A few copies got out before it was corrected," or some such soft soap which

---

1. Alexander Woollcott, theater critic.

---

1. Despite Chandler's refusal to sell *The Little Sister* to the Mystery Book Club, Houghton Mifflin announced that the book had been adopted by this book club.

[178]

I shan't believe, and which they, if they have any sense, will know I won't believe. A few copies my foot, how many booksellers do they suppose read the *Publisher's Weekly*—how many thousands of them? I've had a lot to do with publicity departments in Hollywood, and although they have intelligent individuals working for them, their total effort is bunk. They are the Great American Fake, that pseudo-religious belief that salesmanship is more important than quality and that you can sell anything if you make enough noise about it. Nothing you say need be right; it just has to be loud and incessantly repeated. When they are dealing with toothpaste or shaving lotion, articles of commerce that have absolutely no intrinsic value whatever, they are right. When they deal with books, God help us, they destroy the very basis on which the business rests. Ugh!

I'm still struggling with Charlie Morton about that Hollywood piece. I have explained to him carefully and patiently that it is now dated, and that by fall (when he says they plan publication) it will not be merely dated, it will be antique; that it is not right and so forth and so on, and that I simply do not want it published. I did not say, although it is obvious, that they have never accepted it formally, have never sent me a proof, have never given me the opportunity, which I asked and reserved, of declining publication, if I felt that the cut version misrepresented what I was trying to say.

I suppose all this makes me look like a very contentious person. I wish I could avoid that appearance. I am not really. I just don't tolerate fools gladly and I don't accept without protest the kicking around which writers get and usually take lying down. Hollywood taught me to fight and fight hard. It didn't teach me to fight clean, but I found that it respected clean fighting. The trouble is, you get so tired. The fight is never won. I was shockingly mishandled when I went to Hollywood and it took me two years of usually rather patient argument to convince Sydney Sanders, not an easy man to convince about anything, that this was so, but I don't think he ever accepted any responsibility about it in his own mind. This is a long story and I don't propose to bore you with it. Nothing like that could have happened with Carl or Ray Stark. I mention it only because in dealing with Houghton Mifflin I seem to have slipped back into a familiar atmosphere of casual and good-natured stupidity. Everybody makes mistakes and most people occasionally do stupid things, but there is a type of mistake which to me is like the red rag

to the bull, a type of mistake which only happens in bad
organizations. When it happens you sense that something is rotten.

Yours ever, and with apologies,

Ray

## TO HAMISH HAMILTON

6005 Camino de la Costa
La Jolla, California
June 17, 1949

Dear Jamie:

I am very uneasy in mind. I seem to have lost ambition and
have no ideas any more. I don't really want to do anything, or rather
one part of me does and the other doesn't. One of the penalties of
even a mild success is an indifference to it, and the effort to do
something that will attract interest and praise is really something it is
a pity to lose. I read these profound discussions, say in *The Partisan
Review*, about art, what it is, literature what it is, and the good life
and liberalism and what is the definitive position of Rilke or Kafka,
and the scrap about Ezra Pound getting the Bollingen award, and it all
seems so meaningless to me. Who cares? Too many good men have
been dead too long for it to matter what any of these people do or
don't do. What does a man work for? Money? Yes, but in a purely
negative way. Without some money nothing else is possible, but
once you have the money (and I don't mean a fortune, just a few
thousand quid a year) you don't sit and count it and gloat over it.
Everything you attain removes a reason for wanting to attain
anything. Do I wish to be a great writer? Do I wish to win the Nobel
Prize? Not, if it takes much hard work. What the hell, they give
the Nobel Prize to too many second-raters for me to get excited about

it. Besides, I'd have to go to Sweden and dress up and make a speech. Is the Nobel Prize worth all that? Hell, no. Or I read in some book like Haycraft's *Art of the Mystery Story* various so-called critical essays on the detective novel—and what second-rate stuff it all is! The whole business is on a plane of diminished values, there is a constant haste to deprecate the mystery story as literature for fear the writer of the piece should be assumed to think it important writing. This conditioned approach might well be the result of the decay of the classics, a sort of intellectual insularity which has no historical perspective. People are always suggesting to writers of my sort, "You write so well why don't you attempt a serious novel?" By which they mean something by Marquand or Betty Smith. They would probably be insulted if one suggested that the aesthetic gap, if any, between a good mystery and the best serious novel of the last ten years is hardly measurable on any scale that could measure the gap between the serious novel and any representative piece of Attic writing of the Fourth Century B.C., any ode of Pindar or Horace or Sappho, any chorus of Sophocles, and so on. You cannot have art without a public taste and you cannot have a public taste without a sense of style and quality throughout the social structure. Curiously enough this sense of style seems to have very little to do with refinement or even with humanity. It can exist in a savage and dirty age, but it cannot exist in the age of Milton Berle, Mary Margaret McBride,[1] the Book of the Month Club, the Hearst press, and the Coca-Cola machine. You can't produce art by trying, by setting up exacting standards, by talking about critical minutiae, by the Flaubert method. It is produced with great ease, in an almost offhand manner, and without self-consciousness. You can't write just because you have read all the books.

∙       ∙       ∙

All the best,

Ray

1. A radio personality.

# TO HAMISH HAMILTON

6005 Camino de la Costa
La Jolla, California
June 22, 1949

Dear Jamie:

My God, what a writer suffers with proofs. By the time he has
got the damn book written he hates it. And then proofs—oh my
God. In spite of this there were scenes here and there that stood up
wonderfully well. To say little and convey much, to break the mood
of the scene with some completely irrelevant wisecrack without
entirely losing the mood—these small things for me stand in lieu of
accomplishment. My theory of fiction writing (which is probably not
worth serious discussion) is that the objective method has hardly
been scratched, that if you know how to use it you can tell more in a
paragraph than the probing writers can tell in a chapter. Last night
I was reading at a hunk of pretentious twaddle called *Edge of Doom*,
by one Leo Brady, by Liam O'Flaherty out of Paddy's pig. You
say everything three times. You first state it as a more or less straight
fact. Then you probe into the underlying subtleties and restate it
as a psychic reaction. Then you express it in similes and metaphors.
It's the kind of thing that is considered very subtle writing by very
unsubtle people. The great Goldwyn paid a bag of sugar for this
psychothriller and it was sent to me to read with the idea of doing a
screenplay from it. Well, with patience and the destruction of several
sanities Goldwyn will undoubtedly get himself a sort of road show
*Informer* out of it. But not from this kid. According to my Hollywood
agent, Ray Stark, Goldwyn really does get off a Goldwynism now
and then. Talking about a script deal he pounded the desk and
shouted, "I'm getting sick and tired of writers chiseling on producers
in Hollywood. So here is the deal. You can either take it or like it."

I think my favorite Hollywood story is about the Warner
Brothers, Jack and Harry. The day after Hal Wallis (who had been
head of production at the studio) ankled and left them flat, there
was deep gloom and a horrid sense of catastrophe at the executive

[182]

lunch table. All the boys huddle down at the bottom of the table to get far away from Jack Warner when he came in. All but one, a pushing young producer named Jerry Wald (supposed by some to be the original of Sammy Glick in *What Makes Sammy Run*) who sits down near the head of the table. Jack and Harry Warner come in. Jack sits at the head of the table and Harry just around the corner. Jerry Wald is near and all the others as far away as possible. Jack looks at them with disgust and turns to Harry.

Jack:   That sonofabitch, Wallis.

Harry:  Yes, Jack.

Jack:   A lousy fifty dollar a week publicity man. We built him up from nothing. We made him one of the biggest men in Hollywood. And what does he do to us? He picks up his hat and walks out and leaves us cold.

Harry:  Yes, Jack.

Jack:   That's gratitude for you. And take that sonofabitch Zanuck. A lousy hundred a week writer and we took him in hand and built him up and made him one of the biggest men in Hollywood. And what did he do to us? Picked up his hat and walked out on us cold.

Harry:  Yes, Jack.

Jack:   That's gratitude for you. Why we could take any sonofabitch we liked and build him up from nothing and make him one of the biggest men in Hollywood.

Harry:  Yes, Jack.

Jack:   Anybody at all. (He turns and looks at Jerry Wald) What's your name?

Wald:   Jerry Wald, Mr. Warner.

Jack:   (to Harry) Jerry Wald. Why, Harry, we could take this fellow here, this Jerry Wald and build him up from nothing to be one of the biggest men in Hollywood, couldn't we, Harry?

Harry:  Yes, Jack, we certainly could.

Jack:   And what would it get us? We build him up to be a big man,

give him power and reputation, make him one of the biggest
names in Hollywood, and you know what would happen,
Harry? The sonofabitch would walk out on us and leave us flat.

Harry: Yes, Jack.

Jack: So why wait for that to happen, Harry? Let's fire the
sonofabitch right now.

Ray

## TO DALE WARREN

6005 Camino de la Costa
La Jolla, California
July Ninth 1949

Dear Dale:

For a long time I've owed you a letter and for a long time I've
found it very difficult to write letters. When my work is not moving I
seem to freeze up generally. I thought Laski's book had a great idea,
but she hasn't either the style or the comic invention to put it over.[1] If
Waugh had written it, it would have been really something. As for
*Stranger in the Land*[2] I thought it well-written in a negative
anonymous sort of way, but the subject repelled me. There ought to
be a good novel in homosexualism, but this isn't it. It is much
more honest than *Fall of Valor*[3] (which sounded faked to me) but I
don't seem to be much interested in the homo's problem in society.
What I think would be interesting would be a picture of the peculiar
mentality of the homosexualist, his sense of taste, his surface brilliance
often, his fundamental inability to finish anything. Connolly has
some good remarks on this in *Enemies of Promise*, but I forget just
what he says. I can't take the homo seriously as a moral outcast.

1. Marghanita Laski's *Little Boy Lost*, 1949.
2. By Ward Thomas.
3. By Charles Reginald Jackson, author of *The Lost Weekend*.

He's no more that than the other rebels against a sanctimonious and hypocritical society. There is no more disgusting spectacle on earth than the business man at a stag smoker, and this is just the type of man who would come down hardest on the abnormal. The difficulty of writing about a homo is the utter impossibility of getting inside his head unless you are one yourself, and then you can't get inside the head of a heterosexual man. If you ever read the cross examination of Wilde by Edward Carson in the suit against Queensberry, I think you are bound to admit that here were two people shouting across oceans of misunderstanding. The mob impulse to destroy the homo is like the impulse of the wolf pack to turn on the sick wolf and tear him to pieces, or the human impulse to run away from a hopeless disease. This is probably very old and very cruel, but at the bottom of it is a kind of horror, like a woman frightened by a scorpion. All cruelty is a kind of fear. Deep inside us we must realize what fragile bonds hold us to sanity and these bonds are threatened by repulsive insects and repulsive vices. And the vices are repulsive, not in themselves, but because of their effect on us. They threaten us because our own normal vices fill us at times with the same sort of repulsion.

God, why do I write stuff like this? Who wants to hear me gabble?

. . .

Speaking of Miss Laski, which I am not, I happened the other night to tune in on the Town Meeting programme, the one from London, about Liberty in the Socialist State, if any, and so forth. One of the speakers was Miss Laski's uncle, Professor Laski, a guy who on the strength of his voice, accent and platform manner, without further research, I should be happy to nominate as my choice for *the man you would most like to dunk in a sewer*. The forensic irony, the playing to the gallery, the professorial pompousness and tergiversation and circumlocution, all these imposed on a gutter accent from the slums of somewhere, made up a brew I found quite nauseous. I felt sorry for Max Lerner, an earnest and honest man, though mistaken I think, to be paired up with such a shoddy mountebank. They say this guy is the brains of the British Socialist party. That's silly. People like Attlee, Herbert Morrison, Bevin, and Cripps wouldn't use him to mop up the scullery floor. The only one in the gang I can see having any kinship with him is the rabble-rouser Nye Bevan who is a sort of leftwing Huey Long, but rather more of an emetic.[4]

Yours ever, RC

## TO PAUL BROOKS[1]

6005 Camino de la Costa
La Jolla, California
July 19, 1949

Dear Mr. Brooks:

In answer to yours of July 12th. let me say first of all that I personally see no good reason why these stories should be reprinted, but that I am told by other people with a more objective view that they should be. And, as I told Bernice Baumgarten, I imagined "Paul Brooks was tough enough to turn them down if they were not suitable." My English publisher didn't want to publish them; felt they were early work and might damage my reputation. I told him mystery writers didn't have reputations over here and it was anything for a smooth buck. So that clears that out of the air.

You realize probably that I am going to have to revise and edit this trash. There are crudities here and there which I can no longer tolerate. The worst thing about them, the vast number of murders, I cannot change. The total in all the stories must be something fantastic—close to a hundred. There are two other stories, called "Pick-Up on Noon Street" and "No Crime in the Mountains," which are also eligible. The first of these is in print in some form, but some damn editor made me whitewash four or five niggers in it and the

4. Clement Attlee was then Prime Minister; Morrison, Ernest Bevin, Sir Stafford Cripps, and Aneurin Bevan were members of his cabinet. Huey Long was Governor of and later Senator from Louisiana. He was assassinated in 1935.

1. Brooks had wanted to publish Chandler's early stories in book form.

original version was lost by the Avon people, on whom tears and entreaties are alike lost. The second has a nazi element in it which is of no importance to the plot and I should have to write it out, which would be a pleasure anyway.

Next point is that I object to the use of the *Atlantic* article (S.A.O.M.)[2] as an introduction, for the reason that the stories by no means live up to its promise, or hope. Rather put this at the end and let me do a new piece explaining in a more personal way how a high-strung sensitive lad like me came to get so nasty. About 3 or 4,000 words, or less, if necessary.

I quite agree with your remark that under ordinary circumstances a publisher who suggests a volume of short stories to an author ought to have his head examined. Have you had this done? And do you—I am sure you do—realize that in some form or other these stories have had a very wide circulation? By this I mean that a market for them would be without any appeal of novelty. It would simply be a question of whether enough people thought it worth while to have them all in one volume.

You say some of them I will doubtless want to omit. Or in other words they stink. Which? I doubt if I'm the best judge. Well, let's be bloody frank about this. If something dates or makes you cringe, out. If it is a small thing that can be fixed, I'll try to fix it. If it is inherent in the plot, I can't. Take the story called "Blackmailers Don't Shoot," the first I ever wrote. It took me five months to write this thing, it has enough action for five stories and the whole thing is a goddam pose. "Finger Man" was the first story I felt at home with. "Smart Aleck Kill" and "BDS" are pure pastiche. When I started out to write fiction I had the great disadvantage of having absolutely no talent for it. I couldn't get characters in and out of rooms. They lost their hats and so did I. If more than two people were on scene I couldn't keep one of them alive. This failing is still with me, of course, to some extent. Give me two people snotting each other across a desk and I am happy. A crowded canvas just bewilders me. (I could say the same of some rather distinguished writers, only they don't know it and I do.) I don't know who was the original idiot who advised a writer, "Don't bother about the public. Just write what

2. "Simple Art of Murder," published in *The Atlantic Monthly*, December 1944.

you want to write." No writer ever wants to write anything. He wants to reproduce or render certain effects and in the beginning he hasn't the faintest idea how to do it.

Yours,

Raymond Chandler

## TO JAMES SANDOE

6005 Camino de la Costa
La Jolla, California
August 15, 1949

Dear Sandoe:

You seem to have had a very fruity summer. Mine has been a total loss. Don't like the radio program and wish they would drop it. It could be good, but not with such routine writing and acting. Going to Lake Arrowhead (Arrowhead Lodge) tomorrow for as long as we can stand the local fauna. When I get back I'll send you a strange little brochure which came to me in the mail from one G. Legman, New York. Evidently privately printed and containing words which even I had not seen in print. It is substantially a bitter and possibly envious attack on all kinds of murder mystery, crime books, realistic sexy writing cum murder, on the theory that since we cannot in literature deal honestly with sex, the only adequate sublimation is sadism. A few years back this guy wrote to me and asked me some questions which I did not feel like answering, and he thereupon favored me with a nasty letter in which "on internal evidence" he called me a homosexualist. However, he lams into practically everybody and makes mincemeat of Hemingway en passant. The man is, like so many such soreheads, not without talent, but everything he says leaves a nasty taste in the mouth. And this has nothing to do with what he might happen to say about me. I am surely man of the world enough to expect a few gobs of nastiness here and there.

.        .        .

Read one rather good thriller, *Thin Edge of Violence*, by the author of *Repeat Performance*.[1] I think there is a picture in it, but Hollywood is so damn timid nowadays they would lose the picture while making it. My belief is, Hollywood will never find itself until it has the guts to tell the Catholics to go to hell.[2] I hope I am not being offensive, but I believe (and I believe they know it) that the political power of the Catholic Church is an evil thing, that it is used without scruple or fairness for only one purpose—to maintain that power, and that all the rest of the poppycock they talk is just for a smokescreen.

Yours,

RC

## TO JAMES SANDOE

6005 Camino de la Costa
La Jolla, California
Sept 14 1949

Dear Sandoe:

.        .        .

Sometimes I wonder what my politics would be if I lived in England. Can't imagine myself voting for socialism now that its nasty bureaucratic soul has been revealed. If you vote Conservative, what do you vote for? You don't, you just vote against. Very much like the last election here. All very well to talk about the patriotic duty of voting and so forth, but why should it be my duty to choose either of

1. William O'Farrell.
2. Reference to the Legion of Decency, a Roman Catholic organization that acted as unofficial censor of the arts.

[189]

two candidates when I don't believe either has any business in the White House? My English friends think the Labor Party will win the next election by a small majority and that by that time the country will be in such a mess that there will be a schism in the Labor Party between the moderates like Crossman and Attlee and the wild men like Nye Bevan. I wouldn't know. Eventually, I am afraid, even in England, the scoundrels will inherit the revolution. They always have where the revolution was real and internal, not a revolt against a foreign domination. And that, to dispose of the subject, is where I can't class the Catholic Church with the Communists. The Catholic church in spite of its sins and its hypocrisy and its politicking and its fascist tendencies and its nasty unprincipled use of the boycott is capable of internal dissension and growth without liquidation of its best elements. It can tolerate heresy and it is not afraid to go abroad among the heathen. (I've got Blanshard but haven't read a word of it yet.)[1] It proselytizes constantly, but it does not shoot people in the back of the head because they are forty-eight hours behind the party line.

.            .            .

How are you coming with your classification of mystery fiction? I regret to have to admit that I am becoming less and less interested in the standard apparatus and it's possible that the things you look for don't move me any more. Granted the presence of the livelier ingredients, a good mystery gives them a purpose and meaning, but it seems to me you just don't get it all in one package. Something has to give. I'd almost be willing to go along with Barzun in his conception of what a 'tec should be, if it ever was that. But it isn't. How long since you read one in which the prime matter was a really fascinating problem and a really compelling solution? And by the way what happened to [Josephine] Tey? Didn't you promise me another?

.            .            .

Yours,

RC

1. Paul Blanshard, *American Freedom and Catholic Power*, 1949.

[190]

# TO DALE WARREN

6005 Camino de la Costa
La Jolla, California
September 15, 1949

Dear Dale:

The news from here is rotten. Nervous, tired, discouraged, sick of the chauffeur-and-Cadillac atmosphere, bored to hell with the endless struggle to get help, disgusted with my lack of prescience in not seeing that this kind of life is unsuited to my temperament. Presumably my business is writing. Actually that is left to what meagre resources can survive the battle with the inessentials. Been sick too, and had a lot of trouble with my fingers coming apart. But that is going to get well with X-ray. Of course I ought to have a secretary to write letters and keep books and write checks and answer the damn telephone and kick the gardener in the fanny and so on. But somehow, although I can afford it all right, I can't seem to take myself seriously enough. To function with a secretary you have to believe that what you do is important, that your thoughts and words have an absolute validity, that your privacy is a vested interest. In short you have to be a bit of a conceited ass. In an office it's natural enough because you and the secretary are both part of the mechanism. In your own home you yourself are both the end and the means. My personality, always as sceptical of itself as of others, simply won't accept the part.

We have ideas of getting in a car and driving up to Canada pretty soon. I was thinking of doing a screenplay with my pal, John Houseman, but that's a lousy racket too. Can I write a book a year and make a living? I don't know. Depends on what you mean by a living. I suppose in some ways I was a bit of a stinker in Hollywood. I kept the money. No swimming pool, no stone marten coats for a floozie in an apartment, no charge account at Romanoff's, no parties, no ranch with riding horses, none of the trimmings at all. As a result of which I have fewer friends but a lot more money.

[191]

As to the comment you kindly quoted from me about the *LS*.[1]
I disagree that this story is much the best. I think *Farewell My Lovely*
is the top and that I shall never again achieve quite the same
combination of ingredients. The bony structure was much more solid,
the invention less forced and more fluent, and so on. Writers who
get written about become self-conscious. They develop a regrettable
habit of looking at themselves through the eyes of other people.
They are no longer alone, they have an investment in critical praise,
and they think they must protect it. This leads to a diffusion of effort.
The writer watches himself as he works. He grows more subtle and
he pays for it by a loss of organic dash. But since he often achieves a
real success in the commercial sense just about as he reaches this
stage of regrettable sophistication, he fools himself into thinking that
his last book is his best. It isn't. Its success is the result of a slow
accumulation. The book which is the occasion of success is more
often than not by no means the cause of it.

Ray

## TO JAMES SANDOE

6005 Camino de la Costa
La Jolla, California
Sept 20 1949

Dear Sandoe:

I have an unabridged Liddell and Scott, and in my old age I
propose to return to Classical Literature—no doubt in Loeb's Library
with parallel texts. I hate translations. Those into English from Greek
are usually made by classical professors who, I'm sure you'll pardon
me, are either pedants or pansies. Greek is a highly intricate language

1. *The Little Sister.*

with infinite shades of meaning and in translation about two thirds of it disappears. (Of course this is probably all a dream.)

.        .        .

I'm now reading Blanshard. Pretty deadly all right. As always I'd like to see a reasoned reply, but where would you get it? The Jesuits seem to have a monopoly on this sort of chore and their casuitical double talk would be disgusting if it were not so logically comical. Any time they get on dangerous ground they simply rule that its solidity is a matter of directed faith and not subject to question by the faithful. The rest are heretics who will burn in hell anyway.

I suppose I only concern myself with this because the closed mind is the worst enemy of freedom. The highbrows, fantastic as they sometimes are, seem to be about the only people we can rely on for a perpetual challenge to what passes for truth. That's why I read the *Partisan Review*. There's a lot of nonsense in it and some of the terminology used by these birds like Allen Tate nearly makes me throw my lunch. But at least they don't take things for granted. There's a beautifully written piece in the current number by William Barrett that warms my heart.

Like a lot of other people, I suppose, I have wondered persistently and even desperately why people who seem to be the kind of people I should be apt to like and admire become Catholic converts or Communists or Fellow Travelers. It is obviously neither viciousness nor stupidity. How after the Katyn Forest and the Moscow Treason Trials, the Ukraine famine, the Arctic prison camps, the utterly abominable rape of Berlin by the Mongolian divisions, any decent man can become a Communist is almost beyond understanding, *unless* it is the frame of mind that simply doesn't believe anything it doesn't like. How can the same decent man become a convert to a religious system that played ball with Franco in Spain, and still does, that never in the history of the world has refused to play ball with any scoundrel who was willing to protect and enrich the Church? Well, I guess nobody wants to hear from me about it.

Yours,

RC

[193]

# TO HAMISH HAMILTON

6005 Camino de la Costa
La Jolla, California
October 5th. 1949

Dear Jamie:

.        .        .

I think your sales of *LS* are quite wonderful considering the
sort of book it is.[1] Houghton Mifflin's advance sale was under 10,000
copies and that is not too good, since with mysteries the advance
sale is apt to be a large part of the whole thing, and there is also the
question of returns. One local bookseller bought 50 copies. I don't
think he can sell more than half. The American reviews that I have
seen or heard of are generally favorable. *Time* said I was in danger of
becoming a talented hack. That's not an unpleasant fate in times like
these. The *Atlantic* man reviewed the book at considerable length
on the announced basis that he felt about mysteries about as Edmund
Wilson did. I do not grudge reviewers their sad amusements, but
there is something rather comical in a man's starting out to review a
book by saying he doesn't like the kind of book it is and then
proceeding to deprecate it in a nice way for not being something it
never intended to be. He made one good point, though: that my
"virtues . . . are merely diversions thrown in to entertain and amuse.
They are embellishments; they are not intrinsic elements that
transform the genre." Rather, it is a good point to the extent that it
makes plain in simple language what I have suspected for a long time:
that the better you write a mystery, the more clearly you demonstrate
that the mystery is not really worth writing. The best mystery writers
are those whose perceptiveness does not out-range their material.
Christie and Gardner, for example, or your man John Dickson Carr,
whose literary performance is so dull that I can't read him in spite of
the ingenuity of his plots. If a man writes as well as I do (let's face
it honestly) he creates a schism between the melodramatic
exaggeration of his story and the way he writes about it. However,

1.  *The Little Sister.*

[194]

there is the point of view that the detective character in a mystery may acquire enough substance to compensate. Nobody rereading the Sherlock Holmes stories at this time can think anything about them except that *as stories* they are pretty thin milk. But that does nothing to diminish the character of Holmes himself. He rises above them and becomes a person people want to read about even when he is being silly. Unfortunately, this just bores the author. He finds that he is becoming weary of his character just about the time the public is becoming attached to him. And the intellectual type of critic is bound to be annoyed by a book like *LS*. The fact that he is reviewing it at all implies some unusual merit or reputation, yet he doesn't really like the book. If it is well written, it shouldn't be a mystery.

.        .        .

Yours ever,

Ray

## TO JAMES SANDOE

6005 Camino de la Costa
La Jolla, California
October 14, 1949

Dear Sandoe:

.        .        .

Am now reading Marquand's *So Little Time.* As I recall or seem to recall it was rather deprecated when it came out, but it seems to me full of good sharp wit and liveliness and altogether much more satisfying than *Point of No Return*, which I found boring in its total impact, although not boring as one read it. Have also started *A Sea Change* by Nigel Dennis which looks good. But I always like the wrong books anyhow. And the wrong pictures. And the wrong people. And I have a bad habit of starting a book and reading just far enough to make sure that I want to read it and look forward to reading it and then putting it to one side while I break the ice on a couple more. In that way when I feel dull and depressed which is too often I know I have something to read late at night when I do most of it and not that horrid blank feeling of not having anybody to talk or listen to. As for mysteries that's hopeless. There don't seem to be any worth the trouble. I picked up a thing called *Arm Chair in Hell* by Henry Kane which is so godawful tough and selfconscious that it becomes a burlesque and is not funny enough for a burlesque. It would be an excellent thing right now if someone would come along with a good cool analytical mystery, the hell with suspense and witty dialogue, and let us look at the fundamentals for fresh. The whole form has lost its way, the emphasis has gone to inessential matters. Why in God's name don't those idiots of publishers stop putting photos of writers on their dust jackets? I bought a perfectly good book, . . . , was prepared to like it, had read about it, and then I take a fast gander on the guy's picture and he is obviously an absolute jerk, a really appalling creep (photogenically speaking) and I can't read the damn book. The man's probably quite all right, but to me he is that photo, that oh so unposed-posed photo with the gaudy tie pulled askew, the man sitting on the edge of his desk with his feet in his chair (always sits there, thinks better). I've been through this photograph routine, know just what it does to you. But what it does to the sensitive reader!

RC

## TO JOHN HOUSEMAN[1]

[Circa October 1949]

Your article in *Vogue* was much admired here. I think it was

1. Reprinted from John Houseman, *Front and Center* (New York: Simon and Schuster, 1979), pp. 184–85. Used by permission.

beautifully written and had a lot of style. For me personally it had an effect (after-taste is a better word) of depression and it aroused my antagonism. It is artistically patronizing, intellectually dishonest and logically unsound. It is the last whimper of the Little Theatre mind in you. However, I'm all for your demand that pictures, even tough pictures, and especially tough pictures, have a moral content. (Because *The Big Sleep* had none I feel a little annoyed with you for not realizing that the book had a high moral content.) *Time* this week calls Philip Marlowe "amoral." This is pure nonsense. Assuming that his intelligence is as high as mine (it could hardly be higher), assuming his chances in life to promote his own interest are as numerous as they must be, why does he work for such pittance? For the answer to that is the whole story, the story that is always being written by indirection and yet never is written completely or even clearly. It is the struggle of all fundamentally honest men to make a decent living in a corrupt society. It is an impossible struggle; he can't win. He can be poor and bitter and take it out in wisecracks and casual amours, or he can be corrupt and amiable and rude like a Hollywood producer. Because the bitter fact is that outside of two or three technical professions which require long years of preparation, there is absolutely no way for a man of this age to acquire a decent affluence in life without to some degree corrupting himself, without accepting the cold, clear fact that success is always and everywhere a racket.

The stories I wrote were ostensibly mysteries. I did not write the stories behind those stories, because I was not a good enough writer. That does not alter the fact that Marlowe is a more honorable man than you or I. I don't mean Bogart playing Marlowe and I don't mean because I created him. I didn't create him at all; I've seen dozens like him in all essentials except the few colorful qualities he needed to be in a book. (A few even had those.) They were all poor; they will always be poor. How could they be anything else.

When you have answered that question, you can call him a zombie.

Love,

Ray

[197]

# TO BERNICE BAUMGARTEN

6005 Camino de la Costa
La Jolla, California
October 15th. 1949

Dear Bernice:

I cannot understand what is happening to my book, *LS*.[1]
There have been some wonderful reviews and Martindale's in Beverly
Hills my favorite booksellers write me that it is going great guns
and everybody loves it. Yet the two largest bookstores in San Diego
failed to show me a single copy. I didn't ask, being much too
diffident in that way, but I looked and couldn't find the damn thing.
I'm pretty sore about the *Newsweek* project—sore at myself really, not
at anyone else, because I let myself be taken for a ride again on that
tricky steed.[2] After getting the treatment from *Time* several years ago
I should have known better. But I was assured by the HM publicity
man that *Newsweek* was not like that. So you give them everything
they want, talking yourself silly and exhausting yourself with posing
for God knows how many pictures, get reproductions of older
pictures made for them, and in the end not only do they not give you
anything they promised, but they don't even review the book at
all. They absolutely ignore it. What hurts here is a sense of guilt
unrewarded, like the pickpocket who gets an empty wallet. When you
let yourself be persuaded into a deal like that you know in your
heart that it stinks, but you are just corrupt enough to gloss it over in
the hope that it will build up the sales. Then you get left and the
sense of humiliation is not pleasant. There is no halfway about
publicity. You either take it where and when you get it, in any form,
however vulgar, or you stick to your instincts and say, "I am not
interested in personal publicity of any kind, any time, any place, for
any purpose."

1. *The Little Sister.*
2. Chandler had been assured by the publicity department of Houghton Mifflin that
*Newsweek* magazine would do a cover story on him.

My fingers are well, thank God, but what a strange thing an allergy is. I am now told not to touch carbon paper or newsprint with my bare hands. So I have to read with gloves on, like a fading beauty of the stage.

Ray

## TO HAMISH HAMILTON

6005 Camino de la Costa<br>La Jolla, California<br>October 17, 1949

Dear Jamie:

The book business is really fantastic, as ridiculous in some ways as radio. Bill Townend, an English friend and a writer, tells me that *Dinner at Antoine's* sold 148,000 copies in England in a few weeks, so he got it to read and thought it the most utter trash, and he is a very tolerant guy. I haven't read it myself. And O'Hara's book *A Rage to Live*, which I have but haven't read, is the No. 1 best seller here with a perfectly appalling press. I am sorry about this because I am a great admirer of O'Hara. But it certainly begins to look as though one of the essentials is that a book should be long and crowded. I don't know why but almost all the successful books here have been long books. And offhand I don't think I could name one which is a first class piece of writing with the exception of Thornton Wilder's *Ides of March*. Marquand's *Point of No Return*, a smash hit, is a dull book, and the same old story as before, and far inferior in wit and sharpness to *So Little Time*, which got a rather poor press, comparatively.

Yours,

Ray

[199]

# TO BERNICE BAUMGARTEN

6005 Camino de la Costa
La Jolla California
Nov 8, 1949

Dear Bernice:

      &bull;      &bull;      &bull;

    I should admire to have your list of mysteries for that book.[1]
There is no one whose judgment I should respect more. You seem to
me to achieve what the best film producers achieve even when they
don't show it, the ability to be artistically intelligent and maintain a
sense of what is practical and possible at the same time. I am such
an extremist myself. I am at home with the avant garde magazines
and with the rough tough vernacular. The company I really cannot
get along with is the pseudo–literate pretentiousness of, let us say, the
*Saturday Review of Literature*. That sums up everything I despise in
our culture, including the out-at-elbows professors mewling
maliciously at everyone who has the brains and guts to make a dime.
But to be more specific to the subject in hand: I'd like to leave off
"The Bronze Door" because I'd like to do a group of fantastic stories
in which it would belong, if they ever got published (or written,
you will add). These stories, about ten of them, longish short stories,
would all be about murder in some sense, or the elimination of
some annoying person, all more or less fortuitously through the
happening on a magic means of doing it, all realistic in tone, with a
dash of humor, and all in the nature of a spoof on some type of
murder story. I am poking at one now which is a sort of reduction ad
absurdam of the locked-room puzzle.

      &bull;      &bull;      &bull;

                         Yours ever,

                            Ray

1. *The Simple Art of Murder*, 1950.

# TO HAMISH HAMILTON

6005 Camino de la Costa
La Jolla, California
November 11, 1949

Dear Jamie:

.     .     .

While reviewing generally is not very reliable anywhere, I really think that English reviewing is getting a bit absurd. There are far, far too many novelists reviewing other novelists. There is far too much consideration for books that are obviously going to get nowhere, and far too little understanding of what it is in books that make people read them. And there is a tight group of critics or reviewers who are monotonously willing to say something nice about almost any book at all. Your own ads show it. These names, supposedly of influence, really can't have any because they show no discrimination to speak of. . . . And at the other extreme is that ridiculous publication *The Times Literary Supplement*, which is apparently compiled from the blitherings of a group of aged dons, whose standards of comparisons, points of reference or what have you, seem to be stuck in the year when Jowett translated Plato. Fancy a so-called intelligent reviewer handling Faulkner's *Intruder in the Dust* as though it were just another thriller. You begin to wonder whether these people have any conception of what makes writing.

.     .     .

P.S. I suppose you know this, but I think it is wonderful, from *Fontemara*, by Ignazio Silone:

> At the head of all is God, lord of heaven.
> Then comes Prince Torlonia, lord of earth.
> Then comes the armed guard of Prince Torlonia.
> Then come the hounds of the armed guard of Prince Torlonia.
> Then nobody else.
> And still nobody else.
> And still again nobody else.
> Then come the farmers.

[201]

# TO BERNICE BAUMGARTEN

6005 Camino de la Costa
La Jolla, California
Nov 17th. 1949

Dear Bernice:

·       ·       ·

I have a letter inviting me to join the P.E.N. Club. I don't
know what to do about it. They evidently consider the invitation a
great honor, and I just don't give a damn. If they knew what a
bastard I was, they probably wouldn't want me. Their board of
directors contains the names of some people whom I regard as
blithering idiots, but not all, and I couldn't very well say that
anyhow.

Yours,

Ray

# TO HAMISH HAMILTON

6005 Camino de la Costa
La Jolla, California
Dec 4, 1949

Dear Jamie:

·       ·       ·

*Pride and Prejudice* arrived and bless you. I thank you in advance
for the "specially bound copy of the Little Sister"; god, what can
that be? I do not think my "works" are worth special binding, my
good Jamie, but the thought is damn kind. Your man Hodge is a
superb editor, the rarest kind of mind.[1] These trained–seal critics, even

---

1. Writer and co-editor, with Robert Graves, of *The Reader Over Your Shoulder*.

the best of them, bore me at least two thirds of the time. Give a
man a name of prestige and he is already a fair way to being an ass. I
do not suggest that Alan Hodge lacks prestige, but he is still in that
happy territory where the man's voice is more important than his
name. Surely no one could write better introductions. The Betjemans
(I may have spelled this wrong), the Quennels, the Mortimers, etc.
are always a little intent on making a good appearance before their
admiring public.[2] Hodge is concerned with the book and damn all
else.

.           .           .

I expressed myself badly about playwriting. Of course
Maugham is right, as he always is. It is more *difficult* to write plays,
harder work, I have no doubt, although I have never even tried to
write one. It is also very much more difficult to write screenplays
than novels. But it does *not*, in my opinion, take the same quality of
talent. It may take a more exacting use of the talent, a more beautiful
job of cabinet work, a finer or more apt ear for the current jargon
of a certain kind of people, but it is much more superficial all round.
Take any good, but not great, play and put it in fiction form and
you have a very slight matter. No richness, no vistas, no overtones,
no feeling of the country beyond the hill. It is all clear and literal
and immediate. The novelist, if he is any good, gives you a thousand
things that he never actually says. Incidentally, if I knew Maugham,
which I fear I never shall, I should ask him for an inscribed copy of
*Ashenden*. I've never asked a writer for an inscribed copy and as a
matter of fact I attach very little value to such things. (I wouldn't
mind having the prompt copy of *Hamlet*.) And I suppose it declares
my own limitations of taste to pick *Ashenden*. But I'm a bit of a
connoisseur of melodramatic effects, and *Ashenden* is so far ahead of
any other spy story ever written, while his novels, the best of them,
and good as they are, do not outclass the field. A classic in any
manner appeals to me more than the large canvas. *Carmen*, as
Merimée wrote it, "Herodias," "Un Coeur Simple," *The Captain's
Doll*, *The Spoils of Poynton*, *Madame Bovary*, *The Wings of the Dove*,
and so forth and so on (*A Christmas Holiday*, by God too), these are

2. John Betjeman, the poet; Peter Quennel, the historian; Raymond Mortimer, the critic.
All reviewed frequently for London papers.

all perfect.[3] Long or short, violent or still, they do something that never will be done as well again. The list, thank God, is long, and in many languages.

What a queer attitude the better minds have to mysteries. "Oh, it's just a mystery, a thriller, a 'tec. I read them in bed to put me to sleep. I read them when I am sick. I read them when I am too tired for serious reading." The deprecation is so obvious, but does anyone ever reply, "And what, my good sir, would you do if you were sick or tired or wakeful, and there *were* no mysteries?" The very people who declare they read them rapidly and forget them at once declare in the same breath that they cannot exist without them. And they know God damned well that they could exist indefinitely without the more massive classics.

Too bad you are such an old, old man of 50, or not quite. (Fiftieth year means past 49 over here.) Too bad. I have sympathy for you. It is a bad age. A man of 50 is not young, not old, not even middle-aged. His wind is gone and his dignity has not yet arrived. To the young he is already old and stodgy. To the really old he is fat and pompous and greedy. He is a mere convenience to bankers and tax collectors. Why not shoot yourself and be done with it? Think of the horrors that lie ahead. You might even get to be a whiskered bore like Shaw, a voluble cicada, an antediluvian scene-stealer.

Ray

# TO HAMISH HAMILTON

6005 Camino de la Costa
La Jolla, California
Jan 5, 1950

Dear Jamie:

3. "Herodias," "Un Coeur Simple," and *Madame Bovary* are by Gustave Flaubert; "The Captain's Doll" by D. H. Lawrence; *The Spoils of Poynton* and *The Wings of the Dove* by Henry James; *A Christmas Holiday* by W. Somerset Maugham.

*Ashenden* with very handsome dedication received safely.[1] Why in hell did you spend all that money on postage? It's a ridiculous extravagance, although extremely generous. Of course I'll write to the old boy, trying not to be too deferential on the one hand nor too clubby on the other. I have a feeling that fundamentally he is a pretty sad man, pretty lonely. His description of his seventieth birthday is pretty grim. I should guess that all in all he has had a lonely life, that his declared attitude of not caring much emotionally about people is a defense mechanism, that he lacks the kind of surface warmth that attracts people, and at the same time is such a wise man that he knows that however superficial and accidental most friendships are, life is a pretty gloomy affair without them. I don't mean that he has not friends, of course; I don't know enough about him to say anything like that. I get my feeling from his writing and that is all. In a conventional sense he probably has many friends. But I don't think they build much of a fire against the darkness for him. He's a lonely old eagle. I don't suppose any writer was ever more completely the professional. He has an accurate and fearless appraisal of his own gifts, the greatest of which is not literary at all, but is rather that neat and inexorable perception of character and motive which belongs to the great judge or the great diplomat. He has no magic and very little gusto. His style, which has been greatly praised, seems to me no more than a good competent mandarin English which often only narrowly escapes dulness. He can convey the setting for emotion but very little the emotion itself. His plots are cool and deadly and his timing is absolutely flawless. As a technician he is far ahead of the good second raters like Galsworthy and Bennett and J. P. Marquand. He can never make you catch your breath or lose your head, because he never loses his. I doubt that he ever wrote a line which seemed fresh from creation, and many lesser writers have. But he still outlasts them all with ease, because he is without folly or silliness. He would have made a great Roman.

.　　　.　　　.

Ray

1.  By W. Somerset Maugham.

# TO HAMISH HAMILTON

6005 Camino de la Costa
La Jolla, California
Jan 11, 1950

Dear Jamie:

    I often wonder why so many English intellectuals turn to
Catholicism, just as my schoolmaster friend often used to wonder
audibly why so many otherwise intelligent and normal people went to
Cambridge. (You'd love that.) But I wonder so many things and
as I grow older I have less and less respect for the human brain and
more and more respect for human courage. Over here the Catholics
are numerous, powerful and mostly quite genial, but the hierarchy is
overwhelmingly of Irish origin and the Irish Catholics, always
excepting the Jesuits of Maynooth, are pretty crude specimens of high
Catholic thinking, compared with the French, English, Scottish,
and Italian prelates. Of course I also wonder why people turn to
religion at all. As a young man I was very high-church and very
devout. But I was cursed with an analytical mind. It still worries me.
But this is a delicate subject unless you are sure you cannot offend.

    I need your comfort and guidance about some things over
there. You gave me the name of a hotel north of the Park and I must
look back and find it. Assuming that we should be over there for
about four months, do you think we must have hotel and travel
reservations all planned out? I'd hate it, but I'd better know. We don't
even know where we want to go. To Paris, I hope, and to other
places on the Continent, but which? A bit of England here and there
and even Scotland, but not by train. How does one do these things?
And what about food? After all you can't very well consume food
parcels in hotels. Laundry? Soap? Can one buy shirts and socks
and so on freely? This is a big thing to me; I don't want it to go sour.
I am not a very patient person, I've had a lot of illness, none serious,
and I haven't much stamina. Cissy, my wife, has more, but she is no
ironhorse either. Damn it, all this must sound very silly to you, but
we have lived a long time in a soft enervating climate. It's all so

[206]

difficult, perhaps I had better just go quietly back to bed. (I have a feeling amounting to a conviction that I am becoming a frightful bore.)

. . .

I don't think there is much chance of any motion picture outfit here buying the screen rights to LS.[1] They're tired of the private dick stories (having run them to death with a series of imitations) and the book is not too admiring of Hollywood. Fundamentally it is probably a question of money. Lots of stories are now sold for five or ten thousand dollars. I'm asking fifty. There was one producer at Warner's named Harry Kurnitz wanted to do it, but Jack Warner evidently said no. Nor do I think there is any feeling against me as an anti-Semitic. After all I dealt with dozens and dozens of Jews in Hollywood and was never accused by any of them of any such feeling. The people who do raise the point belong to that extreme fringe who resent anyone's using the word Jew at all. Some of my most stalwart supporters are Jewish. My favorite doctor is Jewish. He once said, "There's a bit of the anti-Semitic in all of us, Jews and Gentiles alike." What they seem to resent is the feeling that the Jew is a distinct racial type, that you can pick him out by his face, by the tone-quality of his voice, and far too often by his manners. In short, to some extent the Jews are still foreigners, especially the middle-Europeans. It was not so in England when I was a schoolboy. I must have known Jewish boys at school, but I can't remember which were which. One just didn't think about it. The only time I ever heard a man called a Jew in England was by one of his closest friends, and all he meant was that he was an orthodox Hebrew. Over here it is different. They are of all religions or no religion. When you call a man a Jew you are not thinking of his religion, but of certain personal characteristics of appearance or behaviour, and the Jews don't like that, because they know that is what you mean. They want to be like everyone else, indistinguishable from everyone else, except that they want to be Jews to themselves, and they want to be able to call non-Jews by the name of Gentiles. But even then they are not happy, because they know very well you can't insult a man by calling him a Gentile, whereas you *can* insult him by calling him a Jew. As long as

1. *The Little Sister.*

[207]

that is so I don't see how you can expect the Jews not to be oversensitive, but at the same time I don't see why I should be so unnaturally considerate of this oversensitiveness as never to use the word Jew. It's not so one-sided. I've lived in a Jewish neighbourhood, and I've watched one become Jewish, and it was pretty awful. I don't know the answer, and I'm pretty sure it will take a long time to find it. It really seems at times that the Jews ask too much of us. They are like a man who insists upon being nameless and without an address and yet insists on being invited to all the best parties.

Yours ever,

Ray

## TO SOMERSET MAUGHAM

6005 Camino de la Costa
La Jolla, California
Jan. 13, 1950

Dear Mr. Maugham:

In passing, but apparently not lightly enough, I mentioned to Jamie Hamilton that if I knew you, which was extremely unlikely, I should ask you for an autographed copy of *Ashenden*, and that this would be the only time I asked for or even desired such a thing from any author. But a suggestion to Jamie is as electric as a kick in the teeth to some people. The book now arrives with a very handsome inscription for which I can only wish in vain that I might thank you in words as graceful and unique as the person to whom they would be addressed. But, disdaining not to strike an attitude, I can only thank you quite simply and say that the nearness of your name to mine on the title page of a book is as near as I am likely to get to distinction, and a good deal nearer than I deserve.

Why *Ashenden* rather than something you probably value much more highly? Because I am a bit of a connoisseur of melodramatic effects and because *Ashenden* is unique. However great a novel you may claim, or others may claim for you, there are other great novels.

There are not other great spy stories—none at all. I have been searching and I know. It's a strange thing. The form does not appear so very difficult. Evidently it is impossible. There are a few good tales of adventure with a spying element or something of the sort, but they always overplay their hand. Too much bravura, the tenor sings too loud. They are as much like *Ashenden* as the opera *Carmen* is like the deadly little tale that Merimée wrote.

I think it's rather a pity that somewhere along the line, seeing you have had time for so many things, you did not write a detective story. Not only would it have given us something to shoot at, but it would have quieted my long annoyance with those who gabble about the "classic" detective story. We should have had at least one specimen to which the term might be applied without idiocy.

To the esteem in which you are held I can add nothing. But I can be grateful for the kindness which permits me to write to you.

Yours most sincerely,

Raymond Chandler

# TO DALE WARREN

6005 Camino de la Costa
La Jolla, California
Jan 15th. 1950

Dear Dale:

Bernice sent me the enclosed, which looks like an original, with no instructions about how to deal with it (mean keep it or return it). So I'm playing it safe.[1]

This is the sort of document that makes writers dog themselves out in a velveteen smoking jacket, a cap with a tassel, a pipe full of Craven Mixture, and lollygag around admiring themselves instead of putting out a little careful but uneven prose. The piece is a miracle

---

1. Presumably a biographical statement to be used on a dust jacket.

of overstatement. What about my classical profile, my head of wavy brown hair scarcely thinning at the temples, my erect bearing, and smiling Irish eyes and my unfailing courtesy to my social inferiors? What about those early days in the back of a Fifth Street bar, cleaning spittoons with the tail of my shirt, dining off the debris of the free lunch mixed with sawdust. A butt of bullies, a familiar of courtesans, a whipping boy for shamed alcoholics? What about the time I spent under the shadow of Saint Sulpice in that short but intoxicating affair with a demoiselle from Luxembourg—the one that afterwards became known the world over—but no, this is dangerous ground. Even in Luxembourg they have libel laws—in three languages as a matter of fact. And what about that lost six months I spent in the Höllenthal, trying to persuade a funicular railway to run on the level? You fellows leave so much out that happened and put so much in that didn't. What about those May mornings outside the Dôme—Garcon, deux Pernods, s'il vous plait, and ask that gentleman with the calvados to tuck his shirt in and stop flicking the muleta in my eyes. It wouldn't hurt him a lot to shave that grizzle off his muzzle either, and I see a spot for a hot bath if you can interest him at a very low price.

.　　　　.　　　　.

I should say that the fellow you write about appears to be knowable. When you are discussing writers that is a great deal. Most of them are what you said we had the biggest of in Washington.

Yours ever,

Ray

## TO SOMERSET MAUGHAM

6005 Camino de la Costa
La Jolla, California
Feb 15, 1950

Dear Mr. Maugham:
　　Herewith the tear sheets from a *Pocket Atlantic* with a

somewhat revised version of the article you desired.[1] I am delighted to send it and I have a number of other pieces which I should be glad to send you (if I may have them back) in case you had not seen them. I'd have to look them up to be sure what I have, but I know there are two pieces by Edmund Wilson from the *New Yorker*, a piece by Joseph Wood Krutch, one by Jacques Barzun from *SRL*[2] and a whole number of some avant-garde magazine called *Chimera* devoted to various praise and abuse. I have your own old piece from the *Post* and I've never forgotten the picture of Edith Wharton. Wouldn't she have been embarrassed if you had mentioned *The Turn of the Screw* to her? She would have *had* to like that, being a sort of road company Henry James herself. And if it isn't a thriller, I'd like to know what is.

I should have double-spaced this letter, but I'm a rotten typist and at the moment have no secretary.

Yours sincerely,

Raymond Chandler


## TO CARL BRANDT

6005 Camino de la Costa
La Jolla, California
Feb 26, 1950

Dear Carl:

.            .            .

Here are a couple of samples of unconscious humor that fascinated me. 1. Our cook lives at home and she has been taking the magazines home as we finish with them, mostly for a girl to read who is staying with her. She took home some *SRL's* along with

1. Maugham was preparing his essay "The Decline and Fall of the Detective Story," and he had asked Chandler for other writings on the subject.
2. *Saturday Review of Literature.*

[211]

others and I discovered there was missing a number in which Dale Warren had said he had a piece.[1] I asked her to bring it back. She brought it and several others and reported that her friend, on looking into the *SRL*, had remarked with a mixture of bewilderment and indignation: "There's nothing to read in here. It's all authors." 2. Somewhere in this town of La Jolla there dwell a couple of gnome-like females who always dress with large pulled down felt hats on their heads, bunchy shapeless garments under old raincoats and carry walking sticks. They walk past our house every single day and they never walk abreast, always one several paces behind the other as if they were not on speaking terms, but were held together by some unbreakable tie. They look like something out of Grimm's Fairy Tales. One day as they passed a real estate man who was here to size up the house happened to glance out of the window and see them. He stared open-mouthed for a couple of seconds and then said suddenly: "What country are we in?"

Ray

## TO DALE WARREN

6005 Camino de la Costa
La Jolla, California
April 4, 1950

Dear Dale:

.          .          .

It's a good thing I did catch your piece because I'm discontinuing my subscription to the *Saturday Review*.[1] It bores me further and further.

1. *Saturday Review of Literature.*

---

1. Warren had written an article on masters of ceremony.

[212]

The reviews are absolutely no good. Their editorials I skip. Some of the letters are amusing and some of Cerf's stuff too.[2] But that's hardly enough reason to bring another magazine into a house already overloaded with them. I guess they do a great job in selling what looks like the intellectual point of view to people who think they are intellectuals. But I must be one of the few living Americans who do not crave to have their minds improved. I know too much already. I would be happier knowing less. What decided me to drop this roadshow version of the cultured mind from my mailing list was a debate between Mr. Eric Johnston and Mr. Norman Cousins on the subject of the movies.[3] This item was strictly an affair of a couple of four-round prelim fighters accidentally boosted into the main event. Mr. Cousins has some fine qualities, including the courage to get up at that red symposium in New York and tell the Communists where to get off. Believe me, that takes courage. But he has such an extreme case of social consciousness that he is, and cannot help being, a good deal of a bore to my type of mind. As for Mr. Eric Johnston, Hollywood's ambassador-at-large, I think he does a terrific job of making the motion picture business look just exactly as silly as its worst enemies call it. I remember a few years back, at an Academy Award's affair, he glued himself to a microphone and announced in clear, ringing accents that the motion picture was the greatest art form since the Greek drama. You could have knocked me down with a baby Austin. I was inspired to write an unpaid contribution to the *Screen Writer*, now defunct alas, recommending that this statement not be allowed to die but that it be engraved on an old bottle cap and handed for safekeeping to one of the monkeys in Griffith Park zoo.

Yours ever,

Ray

2. Bennett Cerf, publisher, had a column in *The Saturday Review*.
3. Eric Johnston, director of the Motion Picture Association, whose Production Code governed the sexual and moral content of Hollywood films. Norman Cousins was editor of *The Saturday Review*.

# TO MORRY RABIN[1]

6005 Camino de la Costa
La Jolla, California
April 11, 1950

Dear Mr. Rabin:

Thanks for your letter and I'm damned if I see any reason why I should be on your sucker list. No thanks to whoever put me there. I was never a working newspaper man. I was once a free lance journalist and a book reviewer for a literary weekly in London.

With the greatest possible reluctance I am enclosing a check for twenty-five dollars ($25.00). The amount is large enough to annoy me and too small to make you hysterical. The only reason I send it is that if I spent this much taking some one to dinner at Romanoff's (deductible, naturally) I shouldn't think very hard about it. Why should you be less expensive?

Do you want any copy? From time to time, especially around the time the bills come in, I have projected an essay on La Jolla entitled *A Sweet Little Town and You Can Have It*. But as long as I live here, wiser not. I have a silly piece called *Advice to a Young Critic* knocking around in my files somewhere. I thought of fixing it up for the *Atlantic* but I never got it to jell just right. But as the farm boy said when he brought the bucket of thin milk over to the neighbor, "Maw says it's only skim, but it's good enough to give away."

I should add that I want no publicity of any kind. "Before you clicked and became a name," quoted from your letter, meaning me. If I ever clicked, I never heard it. If I became a name, that is one mistake I should have liked to rectify. I always despised pseudonyms, and I found out too late that I was wrong.

Yours,

Raymond Chandler

---

1. President of the San Diego Newspaper Guild. This letter probably was never sent.

# TO LEROY WRIGHT

6005 Camino de la Costa
La Jolla, California
April 12, 1950

Dear Mr. Wright:

In common with a lot of other people I find that I quite often don't know what I am talking about. After writing stories for years about the Los Angeles Police Department, Homicide Bureau, etc., I did some actual research and found out how it really operated. I was somewhat surprised at the modesty of the facilities. Same with private dicks. I want to check up. Some time when you are not to busy or when someone in your office is not too busy, would you be good enough to let me know the present status of the licensed private operative. Specifically (but not all inclusively):

What authority licenses him? How must he qualify? What are his rights, privileges and duties? What information does he give, and what shows on the license? Must it be in plain view on the wall of his office? How much is his bond? Are his fingerprints on record locally and in the FBI files? Has he automatically a right to carry weapons or must he qualify like anyone else? Is this within the discretion of the Sheriff or whom? Are his weapons registered and testfired? By whom?

How is a complaint made against him (a) by a private citizen, (b) by a police authority? What is the procedure in hearing such a complaint (assuming the matter to be short of a criminal charge)? On what grounds may his license be canceled? If it is for a specific period (what is the fee?) is it automatically renewed, or must he re-qualify?

To what extent is information given him by a client a privileged communication? (A lot of stories turn on this.) Has he any greater power of arrest than the ordinary citizen? Can he be held without bond as a material witness at the discretion of the D.A.? Has he any kind of badge (not being a uniformed special officer such as the men who patrol baseball parks, movie lots and so on)? What identification, etc. is he *required* to carry?

The private detective of fiction is, of course, pure imagination.

[215]

He does not and could not exist. He is the personification of an attitude, the exaggeration of a possibility. But that is no reason why he should not know the rules under which he operates. (The real life private dick is often quite vague on the subject, incidentally.)

Yours

Raymond Chandler

## TO HAMISH HAMILTON

6005 Camino de la Costa
La Jolla, California
May 18, 1950

Dear Jamie:

I have to thank you for the Turgenev in your Novel Library and for Eric Partridge's *Here There and Everywhere*. By the way where does this spelling of Turgenev come from? Why is the "i" dropped after the "n"? In Russian there is a letter which is pronounced like "ny," like Spanish "n" with a tilde or Portuguese "nh." I wonder who started this crackpot modern custom of transliterating foreign names with no regard to the fact that the foreign letters, although the apparent equivalent of the English, do not correspond in sound.

Partridge is interesting but makes me uneasy. These scholars of the vernacular, cant, slang, etc. cover an awful lot of ground and one wonders how accurately they do it, if one happens to have any special knowledge of a small part of their field and find their report on that shading a little off the exact. Take p 104 1.16 "chiv": This does not mean a razor. Chiv, or more commonly shiv means a knife, a stabbing or cutting weapon, perhaps (but I don't think so) including a razor; but that is not the meaning. P. 105 1.15 "flop" means to go to bed and perhaps includes the idea of sleep, but doesn't mean sleep. Flophouse is a cheap transient hotel where a lot of men sleep in large rooms. I also question the translation of "gay-cat" as "look-out man or finder." A gaycat is a young punk who runs with an older

[216]

tramp and there is always a connotation of homosexuality. Again he could be a "look-out" (outside man) or a "finder" (finger or finger man), but that is a derived or occasional meaning and not exact. On the same page "piped" does not mean "found" but saw or spotted (with the eyes). Flivvers are not "cheap cars;" they are Fords and only Fords, at least in my part of the country. I never heard the word applied to any other make. Of course when this piece was written, 1926, there were no other cars as cheap. The nearest was a Chevrolet, always "chevvy." (A couple of flivvers and a chevvy.) Page 107 1.18 "case dough." This means the same as nest egg really, not money for a trial which would be only one of many, many uses. It is the theoretically untouchable reserve for emergencies—that and nothing more. ("I'm down to case dough" means I've spent all my spare money and have nothing left but a getaway stake, etc.) In his analysis of "queer" Partridge is no doubt historically correct and all that, but it has only two meanings in modern American slang: counterfeit and sexually abnormal. Somewhere along in here he uses or quotes "beak" several times as meaning judge. In England, yes, but not in America. Anyone who has looked at an elderly judge with his wig on knows why he might be called a beak. There is no point in it here. Also, Walla Walla (page 106) is *not* a penitentiary for women. It is the Washington state penitentiary, just like Sing Sing or San Quentin. In his chapter on soldiers' slang he covers a lot of ground that I don't know. But some of his remarks don't click with me. P.B.I. (page 64) he says "a term rarely used by the 'poor bloody infantry' themselves." It was constantly used in my unit. And doesn't he overlook some of the most constantly used words? E.g. "bomb-proofer," "cushy job," "bivvy;" and above all, "napoo," "strafe's long's," for bombardment (The morning strafe), "street cars" or "tram cars" for heavy long range shells, "whizbangs" for rapid small shells, and the inimitable American "goldbrick" which is as superior to English "lead-swinger," as "milk run" (from the last war) is to "piece of cake."

What always gets me about these scholarly excursions into the language of the underworld, so to speak, is how they smell of the dictionary. The so-called experts in this line have their ear to the library, very seldom to the ground. They do not realize what a large proportion of these cant terms (using cant a bit too broadly) is of literary origin, how many of them crooks and cops use *after* writers

[217]

have invented them. It is very difficult for the literary man to distinguish between a genuine crook term (like "back-door parole," prison slang for dying in prison) and an invented one (like "Chicago overcoat" for coffin). How do you tell a man to go away in hard language? Scram, beat it, take off, take the air, on your way, dangle, hit the road, and so forth. All good enough. But give me the classic expression actually used by Spike O'Donnell (of the O'Donnell brothers of Chicago, the only small outfit to tell the Capone mob to go to hell and live): What he said was "Be missing." The restraint of it is deadly.

Throughout his play *The Iceman Cometh* O'Neill used "the big sleep" as a synonym for death. He used it, so far as one can judge from the context, as a matter of course, apparently in the belief that it was an accepted underworld expression. If so, I'd like to see whence it comes, because I invented the expression. It is quite possible that I re-invented it, but I never saw it in print before I used it, and until I get the evidence, I shall continue to believe that O'Neill took it from me, directly or indirectly, and thought I was using a standard term. The whole tenor of his writing in this play shows that he knows very little about his subject.

.    .    .

My apologies to Mr. Partridge, but if he enters the field he must expect to get mixed up with people like me.

.    .    .

## TO DALE WARREN

6005 Camino de la Costa
La Jolla, California
June 14, 1950

Dear Dale:

[218]

It must be about twenty years since I stopped wearing a hat. I remember that for years after I did people were always asking me if I hadn't forgotten my hat. And why does a man who hasn't worn a hat for years always look like a clown in one? Or did he always look that way?. . . . Strange things the eyes. Consider the question of the cat. The cat has nothing to express emotion with but a pair of eyes and some slight assistance from the ears. Yet consider the wide range of expression a cat is capable of with such small means. And then consider the enormous number of human faces you must have looked at that had no more expression than a peeled potato. What a waste of material is here.

I have a publisher in my new book, of which I have written the first chapter and I am inclined to think the first chapter will also be the last. It never occurred to me that you would want me to send you a copy of my novelette. Anyhow, I don't think I have a copy to send you. The *Cosmopolitan* has just rejected it, so I feel rather deflated. It appears they are having some kind of change in trend or tone, or whatever they call these things in a magazine. Why the hell can't they once in a while reject something just because it stinks?

"Dear Sir: Your story *Midnight at Dawn* has been carefully read by our editorial staff. We are returning it herewith and suggest you use it to line a bureau drawer."

Very disconnected letter. Sorry.

Yours, Ray

## TO HAMISH HAMILTON

6005 Camino de la Costa
La Jolla, California
June 23, 1950

Dear Jamie:
Your Paris trip sounds like a typical publisher's jaunt, every

meal an interview, and authors crawling in and out of your pockets from morning till night. I don't know how publishers stand these trips. One writer would exhaust me for a week. And you get one with every meal. There are things about the publishing business that I should like, but dealing with writers would not be one of them. Their egos require too much petting. They live over-strained lives in which far too much humanity is sacrificed to far too little art. I think that's why I decided years ago that I should never be anything but an amateur. If I had the talent to be first-class, I would still lack the hard core of selfishness which is necessary to exploit that talent to the full. The creative artist seems to be almost the only kind of man that you could never meet on neutral ground. You can only meet him as an artist. He sees nothing objectively because his own ego is always in the foreground of every picture. Even when he is not talking about his art, which is seldom, he is still thinking about it. If he is a writer, he tends to associate only with other writers and with the various parasitic growths which batten on writing. To all these people literature is more or less the central fact of existence. Whereas, to vast numbers of reasonably intelligent people it is an unimportant sideline, a relaxation, an escape, a source of information, and sometimes an inspiration. But they could do without it far more easily than they could do without coffee or whiskey.

.        .        .

Yours ever,

Ray

## TO JAMES KEDDIE

6005 Camino de la Costa
La Jolla, California
August 15, 1950

Dear Mr. Keddie:

[220]

Thank you also for the report of the proceedings of *The Speckled Band*. No, I don't think you could convert me. This is not due to any superciliousness on my part towards the faithful, nor towards the great Sherlock. It is just that I do not seem to find any hollow place in my life which the cult of the master alone could fill. If I were drawn into any esoteric activity of this sort, I think it would probably be a group devoted to the desperate analysis of certain actual crimes which have never been satisfactorily explained and of course never will be. For example, the Maybrick case, the Julia Wallace case, the disappearance of Judge Crater, and so forth and so on. Or to put it another way, an examination into how and by what grotesque process of legalistic reasoning the best legal minds in England (with one exception) were able to convince themselves that the late William Joyce, Lord Haw Haw, owed allegiance to his sovereign majesty the King, and so thinking were able to convict him of the crime of bearing aid and comfort to the King's enemies on the testimony (and this was the only evidence adduced in the trial) of one detective inspector, who had once heard William Joyce speak at a meeting in England and had once heard a broadcast of Lord Haw Haw's and said it was the same man.[1] The history of actual trials is so full of these beautiful and impossible tangles that a devotion to the minutiae of the life of Sherlock Holmes seems to me rather a waste of energy— nothing against it of course. I should say it was comparable with the composition of Sapphic odes or a study of Provençal French.

With kindest regards,

Raymond Chandler

---

1. Joyce was convicted for having broadcast propaganda for Germany during World War II.

## TO BERNICE BAUMGARTEN

6005 Camino de la Costa
La Jolla, California
September 13, 1950

Dear Bernice:

I'm still slaving away for Warner Brothers on this Hitchcock thing, which you may or may not have heard about.[1] Some days I think it is fun and other days I think it is damn foolishness. The money looks good, but as a matter of fact it isn't. I'm too conscientious and, although I do not work nearly as fast as I would have worked twenty years ago, I still work a good deal faster than the job requires or has any right to expect. For the most part the work is boring, unreal, and I have no feeling that it is the kind of thing I can do better than anybody else. Suspense as an absolute quality has never seemed to me very important. At best it is a secondary growth, and at worst an attempt to make something out of nothing.

With kindest regards,

Ray

## TO HAMISH HAMILTON

6005 Camino de la Costa
La Jolla, California
September 28, 1950

Dear Jamie:

1. The screenplay for *Strangers on a Train*, to be directed by Alfred Hitchcock.

[222]

Well, here we are (as the debonair character in the operetta said) back on the scene of our former triumphs. I sent in the last of my movie script Tuesday night.[1] It arrived at Warner Bros Wednesday morning—apparently about 8.30 A.M. At nine I received a wire from my agent telling me I was off salary. Just imagine the frantic speed these boys moved at and so early in the morning too, to avoid having to pay me for an extra half day or so! The bastards, no wonder nobody ever, or hardly ever, tries to deal ethically with them. One week I got a touch of food poisoning and didn't do much work, so I refused to accept any pay. Nevertheless to meet a deadline I knew nothing about when I took the job I worked Saturdays and Sundays to clean it up. I could just as easily have held on to the final pages to the end of this week. But I said to myself, I'm not dealing with pikers. I was wrong. They're all pikers. They hire writers as a necessary evil because all the brilliant second guessers, who can tell you what is wrong with what you do, can't do anything themselves. They hire writers, I said, and sometimes at a high salary (mine is very high for present conditions in Hollywood) but they hate them every minute. They would rather save a thousand bucks by cutting off a writer before he has time to catch his breath than save fifty thousand by using their brains during production.

The picture will hardly be any better than *Stage Fright*, which was not rated very highly here. There seems to be a general feeling about Hitchcock that he has shot his wad, but that is always a dangerous assumption with a man of any talent. He is definitely a man of talent, but he belongs to the type which is rather dull outside its particular skill. Some movie makers, like some writers, seem to do their work without committing more than a small part of their real abilities. These belong to the class I call the amateurs; when they are big enough, they are geniuses. Others can do some particular thing extremely well, but you would never think they had it in them merely by meeting them. These are the technicians. I'd say Hitch belongs to this group, but of course I don't really know the man. I had a few discussions with him and then he went blank on me. It's very unusual for a writer to do an entire screenplay without one single conference with the producer. He may have decided this was the best way to handle me. In one sense he was clever about it. I

1. Screenplay for *Strangers on a Train*.

[223]

worked very fast for me. Even if my script was not as perfect as it might have been with more discussion of knotty points, he got it pretty cheap, considering how little there was to go on. The book had one idea, and that was all. But I didn't work fast just to please Hitchcock or Warners. I worked fast because of a feeling about 10 or 12 weeks was the most I could give to a film job. After all I'm drawing on capital now. The job's not worth any more time. Most of the boys have the attitude that as long as they are working they are being paid, so let's make it last, fellows. I have the attitude that film work is too valuable a connection to discard completely but not valuable enough to let it dominate your life. Hack work is all right in small doses, but they must be kept small. I know that mystery writers are regarded as hacks in certain quarters simply because they are mystery writers. This is a confusion of thought, to my mind.

A writer who accepts a certain formula and works within it is no more a hack than Shakespeare was because to hold his audience he had to include a certain amount of violence and a certain amount of low comedy, no more a hack than the Renaissance painters were because they had to exploit the religious motives which were pleasing to the church. My definition of a hack is a man who lets someone else tell him how and what to write, who writes, if he is a writer, not to an accepted formula, but to some editor's definition of it. But the frontier is always vague.

.         .         .

Yours ever,

Ray

## TO JAMES KEDDIE

6005 Camino de la Costa
La Jolla, California
September 29, 1950

Dear Mr. Keddie:

Yes, I know the books of Austin Freeman and Freeman Wills Crofts very well. I think my favorite Freemans are *Mr. Pottermack's Oversight* and *The Stoneware Monkey*. Freemans are very hard to get hold of. I haven't been able to get *The Stoneware Monkey* at all since I first read it. *Pontifex, Son and Thorndike* is also very good. The hansom cab era appeals to me very much. And I always enjoy the long walks across London which Thorndike and Jervis seem to take as a matter of course. Their legs never become tired apparently. As a matter of fact, Freeman is rather a poor writer compared with Conan Doyle. If you read him out loud he makes you laugh, he's so stilted. And Thorndike at times is a bit of a bore, especially when explaining to Jervis that he now has all the facts and that if he sits down and studies them, he should come up with a few ideas. Can it be possible that the acute Dr. Thorndike would ever think Jervis would ever come up with an idea? Dr. Watson, though no mental giant, was on occasion capable of a moderately sensible remark. But not Dr. Jervis. His mind is a complete blank. Some of the most delicious moments in Freeman to me are when Thorndike politely inquires of Jervis whether he will be free from engagements on the following date to accompany him on some expedition. Jervis is always free of course. He will always be free. One can hardly imagine anybody employing him to do anything more exacting than copying out a laundry list. Whether or not Freeman writes really good detective stories is quite another matter. In cases where, as in the example of *The Mystery of 31 New Inn*, there is no analysis of scientific evidence, in spots they are extremely transparent. And where the solution of a mystery turns on the correct analysis of scientific evidence, there arises a question of honesty. I realize that this is a big problem in detective stories—just what honesty is. But if you accept the basic premise, as I do, that in a novel of detection the reader should have been able to solve the problem, if he had paid proper attention to all the clues as they were presented and drawn the right deductions from them, then I say that he had no such opportunity if, to evaluate said clues, he is required to have an expert knowledge of archaeology, physics, chemistry, microscopy, pathology, metallurgy, and various other sciences. If, in order to know where a man was drowned, I have to identify the fish scales found in his lungs, then I, as a reader, cannot be expected to tell you where he was drowned. I should not be expected to. And if to solve the mystery I must be able to solve this point, then so far as I am concerned the clue is suppressed just as effectively as though it had never been given. In spite of all this, I have a very high regard for Freeman. His writing is stilted, but it is never dull in the sense that Crofts's writing is dull. That is to say, it is never flat. It is merely old-fashioned. His problems are always interesting in themselves, and the expositions at the end are master-pieces of lucid analysis. Thorndike is a far more accurate thinker than Sherlock Holmes. He is the only expert in fiction who would have been a match, and I think rather more than a match, for the real experts such as Sir Bernard Spillsbury.

With kindest regards,

Raymond Chandler

## TO DALE WARREN

6005 Camino de la Costa
La Jolla, California
October 4, 1950

Dear Dale:

I get it from a pal back East that I got a stinking bad review in the *New York Times* from one John Dickson Carr, about as stinking as the one I got from Anthony Boucher. *Time* speaks of his taking "deadly aim" at me. I have not seen the review. Obviously people like Boucher and Carr are committed in advance to disliking me, because they are well aware that I regard their kind of detective story as apt to be a crashing bore, even when it is a good deal better written than they could ever write it. The only thing deadly is the assumption that the proper man to review a book is somebody who is drooling for a chance to get his knife into the writer, a snide theory

[226]

of criticism, which can taste nothing but its own bile. If they don't like my opinions, why don't they sit down and refute them on the same level instead of waiting until I write something else and then take their spleen out on that? I could write a better defense of the deductive mystery than they could.

.        .        .

There ought to be a few ethics in this reviewing business. If I were offered a book by Mr. John Dickson Carr—supposing I reviewed books at all—would I jump at the chance because I knew I was going to dislike it and would have a field day being nasty about it? I'd say no thanks, I'm not the man for this job. I'm prejudiced. A reviewer need not perhaps be as just as Aristides, but he should at least be able to see the good in books he may not personally care for. If the editor if the book section of the *Times* knows the facts and offers the assignment deliberately to somebody who has just got a sharp knife waiting for the author, then the editor of the book section of the *Times* is not an honorable man. Of course that's a silly way to put it. He's most probably some frightened hack who won't have a job if he doesn't pull in enough full-page ads. And of course you publishers back him up. You think space is all that counts. You'd rather have a good review, but a bad one is better than none. A bad one that takes a column is better than a good one that takes a quarter of a column. And for all I know, you may be right. I don't know how much space the *Times* gave to this last job. I think they gave a column to *The Little Sister*. But what I'm wondering is, did they give the space to Mr. John Dickson Carr, or did they give it to me, or did they give it to your full-page ad. Interesting thought, isn't it? God, what a sleazy business newspaper and magazine criticism has become. How many critics could you name whose opinions have any validity above the level of a fireside chat, or a tout for the lending libraries? How many who really know anything about writing beyond the fact that they pooped out at it themselves? How many could you name who could read a page of a man's book and know for sure whether he's a real writer, regardless of his opinions on the current social and political scene? Not very many I'm sure. Look what they've done to the old war horse, Hemingway, and what they've been doing to him for a good many years for that matter. He'd have quit writing a long

[227]

time ago if he had the faintest suspicion that any of them knew what they were talking about, that they had no spite in their systems, and that they were not sniping at him just because he had made good. Let's face it. One of the penalties of any kind of success is to have the jackals snapping at your heels. They don't hate you because you're bad. They say you're bad because they want to hate you.

Yours always,

Ray

## TO CHARLES MORTON

6005 Camino de la Costa
La Jolla, California
October 9, 1950

Dear Charlie:

Quite a lapse in our once interesting correspondence, don't you think? Of course it's my fault because the last letter was from you. And you are most correct in saying in it that I owe you a letter. For quite a long time, I have owed practically everybody a letter. Why? Apparently it is what the years do to you. The horse which once had to be driven with a tight rein now has to be flicked with a whip in order to make him do much more than amble. Instead of being ready to slug it out with all comers, you find yourself having to give yourself pep talks before you can get a glove up. "Come on, you dumb loafer, start hittin' them typewriter keys." So much energy is wasted in winding the clock, so little is left to make the clock run. We still have dreams, but we know now that most of them will come to nothing. And we also most fortunately know that it really doesn't matter. Walter Bagehot once wrote, (I am quoting from an increasingly unreliable memory) "In my youth, I hoped to do great things. Now, I shall be satisfied to get through without scandal." In a sense, I am much better off than he was because I never expected to do great things; and in fact have done much better than I ever hoped to do. But as your energies shrink, you become rather niggardly in spending them. Normally a man should do his day's work, whatever it is, and then write a couple of letters to keep in touch with people that he likes and doesn't see in person. But I find that when I have done what passes for a day's work, I am sucked dry. I have nothing to say in the damn letters. I start them but don't finish them. I have a box file stuffed solid with carbon copies of letters that I wrote to just one man somewhere around fifteen years ago. Gosh, what a lot I had to say, and on the whole how well I said it. Now, it is becoming a bit of an effort to say anything. I am only too well aware that I have said it all before, and said it better.

My compliments to Mr. Weeks on belonging to that very small minority of critics who did not find in necessary to put Hemingway in his place over his last book.[1] Just what do the boys resent so much? Do they sense that the old wolf has been wounded and that this is a good time to pull him down? I have been reading the book. Candidly, it's not the best thing he's done, but it's still a hell of a sight better than anything his detractors could do. There's not much story in it, not much happens, hardly any scenes. And just for that reason, I suppose, the mannerisms sort of stick out. You can't expect charity from knife throwers naturally; knife throwing is their business. But you would think some of them might have asked themselves just what he was trying to do. Obviously he was not trying to write a masterpiece; but in a character not too unlike his own, trying to sum up the attitude of a man who is finished and knows it, and is bitter and angry about it. Apparently Hemingway had been very sick and he was not sure that he was going to get well, and he put down on paper in a rather cursory way how that made him feel to the things in life he had most valued. I suppose these primping second-guessers who call themselves critics think he shouldn't have written the book at all. Most men wouldn't have. Feeling the way that he felt, they wouldn't have had the guts to write anything. I'm damn sure I wouldn't. That's the difference between a champ and a knife thrower. The champ may have lost his stuff temporarily or permanently, he can't be sure. But when he can no

1. Edward Weeks, editor of *The Atlantic Monthly*, had reviewed Ernest Hemingway's *Across the River and into the Trees*.

[229]

longer throw the high hard one, he throws his heart instead. He throws something. He doesn't just walk off the mound and weep. Mr. Cyril Connolly, in a rather smoother piece of knife throwing than most of the second-guessers are capable of, suggests that Mr. Hemingway should take six months off and take stock of himself. The implication here apparently is that Hemingway has fully exploited the adolescent attitude which so many are pleased to attribute to him, and should now grow up intellectually and become an adult. But why? In the sense in which Connolly would define the word, Hemingway has never had any desire to be an adult. Some writers like some painters are born primitives. A nose full of Kafka is not at all their idea of happiness. I suppose the weakness, even the tragedy, of writers like Hemingway is that their sort of stuff demands an immense vitality; and a man outgrows his vitality without unfortunately outgrowing his furious concern with it. The kind of thing Hemingway writes cannot be written by an emotional corpse. The kind of thing Connolly writes can and is. It has its points. Some of it is very good, but you don't have to be alive to write it.

With kindest regards,

R.C.

# TO HAMISH HAMILTON

6005 Camino de la Costa
La Jolla, California
October 13, 1950

Dear Jamie:

No, I don't despise Hollywood. Why should I? They're tough

and hard-boiled about money matters, but they take an awful gouging themselves from agents, from the unions, for the exhibitors. Their manners are bad. As a friend of mine put it, "They are arrogant when they should be humble and timid when they should be bold." They are extremely friendly when they want something and brutally indifferent when they don't. After all I wrote a treatment and a screenplay on a story, with nothing usable except an idea, in a matter of ten weeks. I was told at the beginning there was no hurry at all; and halfway through the job I found out that there had been a deadline for commencing shooting. I worked some nights, Saturdays and Sundays in order to get the thing out on time. I refused salary for a week when I was partly incapacitated by a little food poisoning and didn't do a full week's work, although I did some work. I wrote this screenplay to the best of my ability exactly as Hitchcock wanted it as to story line, etc., and I didn't get a single word of appreciation or acknowledgement of any kind from Hitchcock or from anybody else at Warner. Perhaps they didn't like the script. But if they didn't, they could see it as it came in bit by bit, and they didn't have to keep me on it since I was on a week to week basis. I just don't think this is the way to treat people, and from a purely practical point of view, I don't think it's the way to treat people. You don't get the best out of them that way. But all this doesn't mean that I am lacking in respect for a lot of the people who do very good work in Hollywood, and try to do good work even when they can't do the best. After all, the intrigue and backbiting are no worse than they would be in most big corporations or in the higher echelons of the civil service. A couple of non-Semitic writers and myself were once discussing what a bunch of bastards they are, and one of them remarked cogently, "Well, after all, the Jews know how to pay for what they get. If a bunch of Irish Catholics were running the motion picture business, we'd be working for fifty dollars a week."

.        .        .

Yours ever,

Ray.

[231]

# TO BERNICE BAUMGARTEN

6005 Camino de la Costa
La Jolla, California
October 16, 1950

Dear Bernice:

.       .       .

I gather from your note that this is a poor book season. According to
Mr. Maugham (Somerset Maugham) the American public has ceased
to read and now spends its time looking at television. Well, I've spent
a little time lately looking at television for the first time, and my
opinion is that the people who look at television for any length of
time and with any regularity have not ceased to read. They never
began. It's a great deal like the chimpanzee who played the violin. He
didn't play it in tune; he didn't play anything recognizable as a
melody; he didn't hold the bow right; he didn't finger correctly. But,
Jesus, wasn't it wonderful that he could play the violin at all?

.       .       .

Yours always,

Ray

# TO FINLAY McDERMID

6005 Camino de la Costa
La Jolla, California
Nov. 2, 1950

Dear Mr. McDermid:

I am a cad not sooner to have made acknowledgment of your
two letters dated July 7 and August 22. I remember very well the
time when you (at the ungodly hour of 9:30 in the morning)
conducted me to a projection room where I sat alone and watched

[232]

*The Big Sleep*. I was trying to do a script on *The Lady in the Lake* for M.G.M. then, and we were very anxious to be sure that we did not imitate any effect which Warners had got in the Howard Hawks' picture.

As to the week for which I did not receive payment working on *Strangers on a Train*, was I a damn fool about that! I had had a touch of food poisoning, incurred in the course of duty at a lunch with Hitchcock; and for three days I just sat around and gloomed, although I did work the rest of the week including Saturday and Sunday. In fact I worked Saturdays and Sundays all the time I was on this assignment. What strange delicacy of conscience induced me to give any weight to this, I wonder. It must have been that I thought I was dealing with people as precise as myself in these matters.

When I took this assignment, I was told by Mr. Hitchcock that there was no hurry—no hurry at all; no pressure—no pressure at all. About halfway through it I heard from his factotum that there was a shooting date of October 1, because Mr. Hitchcock had to go East before the leaves fall and he would have to have, or at least very greatly desired, the completed script some little time before that; and that there was even the possibility (although this may have been just talk) that if a page marked "The End" was not received by the studio before October 1, then Mr. Hitchcock might not be allowed to begin shooting. So I, as the phrase is, exerted myself to the full and perhaps a little more than to the full. I completed the script on the evening of Tuesday, September 26, mailed it to you special delivery, and it must have been in your hands early the next day, because early the next day I had a wire from Ray Stark that I was off salary as of Monday night. Incidentally, or perhaps not incidentally, I was not paid for Tuesday, September 26. I have raised this point in several places and at several times, and still I am not paid for Tuesday, September 26.

Of course my thought had been that I would be paid for the whole week. In the circumstances surely this would have been only a minimum of decency. I could very easily have kept the work going until the end of the week. Almost any writer you would deal with would have done so. And in view of the way Hollywood treats writers, I think he would have been justified in so doing. I am aggrieved about this, Mr. McDermid. I am not particularly greedy for money, but I am greedy for fair treatment.

Are you aware that this screenplay was written without one single consultation with Mr. Hitchcock after the writing of the screenplay began? Not even a telephone call. Not one word of criticism or appreciation. Silence. Blank silence then and since. You are much too clever a man to believe that any writer will do his best in conditions like this. There are always things that need to be discussed. There are always places where a writer goes wrong, not being himself a master of the camera. There are always difficult little points which require the meeting of minds, the accommodation of points of view. I had none of this. I find it rather strange. I find it rather ruthless. I find it almost incomparably rude. And I think in your heart of hearts you would be very apt to agree with me.

Yours very sincerely,

Raymond Chandler

## TO FLEUR COWLES[1]

Nov. 7, 1950

Dear Mrs. Cowles:

Thank you for your very handsome letter of October 21 and for taking the time to write. I have to admit that I have never seen a copy of *Flair*, and I suppose politeness suggests that I should add "to my shame." I had an idea that it was almost fantastically smart, clever, and sophisticated, and I make claim to none of these qualities. Of course I am going to get a copy, as I see I have been missing things, especially such items as "The New Expense Account Society" by John O'Hara, and "The New Society in Crime" by Robin Harris. As for trying to do a piece for you, I suppose you wouldn't suggest it if you didn't think I could do it, but I am very easily intimidated by cleverness. In the days when I read *Esquire*, I was rather appalled by the bright and brittle quality, especially of the letters in the "Sound

1. Editor of *Flair* magazine. The text of this letter is taken from a transcript.

[234]

and Fury" department. My God, I thought, if they can be as clever as that for nothing, what would they be like if they got paid. I had to give it up. First thing you know I'd have been demanding champagne with my bread and cheese and Caesar salads for breakfast.

I am sending a copy of your letter on to Carl Brandt in New York. It always pays to let your agent know that you have high-class friends.

## TO HAMISH HAMILTON

6005 Camino de la Costa
La Jolla, California
November 10, 1950

Dear Jamie:

·       ·       ·

Why do people want biographical material? Why does it matter? And why does a writer have to talk about himself as a person? It's all such a bore. I was born in Chicago, Illinois, so damned long ago that I wish I had never told anybody when. Both my parents were of Quaker descent. Neither was a practicing Quaker. My mother was born in Waterford, Ireland, where there was a very famous Quaker school, and perhaps still is. My father came of a Pennsylvania farming family, probably one of the batch that settled with William Penn. At the age of seven I had scarlet fever in a hotel, and I understand this is a very rare accomplishment. I remember principally the ice cream and the pleasure of pulling the loose skin off during convalescence. I spent five years in Dulwich and thereafter lived in France and Germany for a couple more years. At that time I was thought to be a British subject, since my mother had regained her British nationality while I was still a minor. So that when I returned to the United States, the record shows that I was admitted as a British subject. It took a long, long struggle, and finally a law suit against the Attorney General of the United States to get it changed. The point

[235]

of law was that a minor cannot be expatriated, and I don't know why they found it so hard to accept this. It cost me quite a lot of money to force it on them. I had done several years free lancing in London in a rather undistinguished way. I did book reviews, essays, etc., for the old *Academy*, sketches and verses for the *Westminster Gazette*, odd paragraphs here and there, etc. I served in the First Division of the Canadian Expeditionary Force in what used to be called the Great War, and was later attached to the R.A.F., but had not completed flight training when the Armistice came. So far I had shown very little talent for writing, and that little was riddled with intellectual snobbery. I arrived in California with a beautiful wardrobe, a public school accent, no practical gifts for earning a living, and a contempt for the natives which, I am sorry to say, has in some measure persisted to this day. I had a pretty hard time trying to make a living. Once I worked on an apricot ranch ten hours a day, twenty cents an hour. Another time I worked for a sporting goods house, stringing tennis rackets for $12.50 a week, 54 hours a week. I taught myself bookkeeping and from there on my rise was as rapid as the growth of a sequoia. I detested business life, but in spite of that I finally became an officer or director of half a dozen independent oil corporations. The depression finished that. I was much too expensive a luxury for those days. Wandering up and down the Pacific Coast in an automobile, I began to read pulp magazines, because they were cheap enough to throw away and because I never had any taste at any time for the kind of thing which is known as women's magazines. This was in the great days of the *Black Mask* (if I may call them great days) and it struck me that some of the writing was pretty forceful and honest, even though it had its crude aspect. I decided that this might be a good way to try to learn to write fiction and get paid a small amount of money at the same time. I spent five months over an 18,000 word novelette and sold it for $180. After that I never looked back, although I had a good many uneasy periods looking forward. I wrote *The Big Sleep* in three months, but a lot of the material in it was revamped from a couple of novelettes. This gave it body but didn't make it any easier to write. I was always a slow worker. In the best month I ever had, I wrote two 18,000 word novelettes and a short story which was sold to the *Post*. For Gardner this would be the work of a couple of days, but for me it

[236]

was a terrific production and I have never approached it since. I went to Hollywood in 1943 to work with Billy Wilder on *Double Indemnity*. This was an agonizing experience and has probably shortened my life; but I learned from it as much about screen writing as I am capable of learning, which is not very much. I was under contract to Paramount after that and did several pictures for them, including one original screen play, *The Blue Dahlia*, which was written from scratch (that is without any basic story) and shot complete in twenty weeks. I was told at the time that this was some sort of a record for a high budget picture. All my books, except *The Little Sister*, have been made into pictures, two of them twice. Like every writer, or almost every writer, who goes to Hollywood, I was convinced in the beginning that there must be some discoverable method of working in pictures which would not be completely stultifying to whatever creative talent one might happen to possess. But like others before me I discovered that this was a dream. It's nobody's fault; it's part of the structure of the industry. Too many people have too much to say about a writer's work. It ceases to be his own. And after a while he ceases to care about it. He has brief enthusiasms, but they are destroyed before they can flower. People who can't write tell him how to write. He meets clever and interesting people and may even form lasting friendships, but all this is incidental to his proper business of writing. The wise screen writer is he who wears his second-best suit, artistically speaking, and doesn't take things too much to heart. He should have a touch of cynicism, but only a touch. The complete cynic is as useless to Hollywood as he is to himself. He should do the best he can without straining at it. He should be scrupulously honest about his work, but he should not expect scrupulous honesty in return. He won't get it. And when he has had enough, he should say good-bye with a smile, because for all he knows he may want to go back.

By the end of 1946 I had had enough. I moved to La Jolla. Since then I have written two screen plays, one of them with only occasional visits to a studio to talk over the story, and one without any visits to the studio at all. I shall probably do others, and if so I shall do them as well as I know how; but I shall keep my heart to myself.

I have been married since 1924 and have no children. I am

supposed to be a hard-boiled writer, but that means nothing. It is merely a method of projection. Personally I am sensitive and even diffident. At times I am extremely caustic and pugnacious; at other times very sentimental. I am not a good mixer because I am very easily bored, and to me the average never seems good enough, in people or in anything else. I am a spasmodic worker with no regular hours, which is to say I only write when I feel like it. I am always surprised at how very easy it seems at the time, and at how very tired one feels afterwards. As a mystery writer, I think I am a bit of an anomaly, since most mystery writers of the American school are only semi-literate; and I am not only literate but intellectual, much as I dislike the term. It would seem that a classical education might be rather a poor basis for writing novels in a hard-boiled vernacular. I happen to think otherwise. A classical education saves you from being fooled by pretentiousness, which is what most current fiction is too full of. In this country the mystery writer is looked down on as sub-literary merely because he is a mystery writer, rather than for instance a writer of social significance twaddle. To a classicist— even a very rusty one—such an attitude is merely a parvenu insecurity. When people ask me, as occasionally they do, why I don't try my hand at a serious novel, I don't argue with them; I don't even ask them what they mean by a serious novel. It would be useless. They wouldn't know. The question is parrot-talk. The problem of what is significant literature I leave to fat bores like Edmund Wilson—a man of many distinctions—among which personally I revere most highly (in the *Chronicles of Hecate County*) that of having made fornication as dull as a railroad time table.

Reading over some of the above, I seem to detect a rather supercilious tone here and there. I am afraid this is not altogether admirable, but unfortunately it is true. It belongs. I am, as a matter of fact, rather a supercilious person in many ways. I shouldn't be at all surprised if it shows in what I write. And it may well be this which arouses such flailing anger in pip-squeaks like John Dickson Carr and Anthony Boucher.

.        .        .

Yours ever,

Ray

[238]

# TO DALE WARREN

6005 Camino de la Costa
La Jolla, California
November 13, 1950

Dear Dale:

.           .           .

You don't sound completely satisfied with the Fitzgerald book.[1] I'm sad about that, because Fitzgerald is a subject no one has a right to mess up. Nothing but the best will do for him. I think he just missed being a great writer, and the reason is pretty obvious. If the poor guy was already an alcoholic in his college days, it's a marvel that he did as well as he did. He had one of the rarest qualities in all literature, and it's a great shame that the word for it has been thoroughly debased by the cosmetic racketeers, so that one is almost ashamed to use it to describe a real distinction. Nevertheless, the word is charm—charm as Keats would have used it. Who has it today? It's not a matter of pretty writing or clear style. It's a kind of subdued magic, controlled and exquisite, the sort of thing you get from good string quartettes. Yes, where would you find it today?

.           .           .

Yours ever,

Ray

# TO EDGAR CARTER

6005 Camino de la Costa
La Jolla, California
Nov 15, 1950

Dear Eddie:

.           .           .

I am having a feud with Warners. I am having a feud with the

---

1. Probably a reference to Budd Schulberg's novel *The Disenchanted*, which was based on an episode in Fitzgerald's life.

[239]

gardener. I am having a feud with a man who came to assemble a Garrard changer and ruined two LP records. I had several feuds with the TV people. Let's see who else—oh, skip it. You know Chandler. Always griping about something.

Yours ever,

Ray

## TO CHARLES MORTON

6005 Camino de la Costa
La Jolla, California
November 22, 1950

Dear Charlie:

•     •     •

Perhaps in some way the worse television is, the better. A lot of people are looking at it, I hear, who had long since given up listening to radio. Perhaps enough of these people will realize after awhile that what they're really looking at is themselves. Television is really what we've been looking for all our lives. It took a certain amount of effort to go to the movies. Somebody had to stay with the kids. You had to get the car out of the garage. That was hard work. And you had to drive and park. Sometimes you had to walk as much as half a block to the theater. Then people with big fat heads would sit in front of you and make you nervous. Reading took less physical effort, but you had to concentrate a little, even when you were reading a mystery or a western or one of those historical novels, so-called. And every once in awhile you were apt to trip over a three-syllable word. That was pretty hard on the brain. Radio was a lot better, but there wasn't anything to look at. Your gaze wandered around the room and you might start thinking of other things—things you didn't want to think about. You had to use a little imagination to build yourself a picture of what was going on just by the sound. But television's perfect. You turn a few knobs, a few of those

mechanical adjustments at which the higher apes are so proficient, and
lean back and drain your mind of all thought. And there you are
watching the bubbles in the primeval ooze. You don't have to
concentrate. You don't have to react. You don't have to remember.
You don't miss your brain because you don't need it. Your heart and
liver and lungs continue to function normally. Apart from that, all
is peace and quiet. You are in the poor man's nirvana. And if some
nasty-minded person comes along and says you look more like a
fly on a can of garbage, pay him no mind. He probably hasn't got the
price of a television set.

Yours ever,

Ray

# TO GENE LEVITT

6005 Camino de la Costa
La Jolla, California
November 22, 1950

Dear Gene:

.        .        .

I'd like to have a television show, but I don't suppose I'll get it. A
television contract was actually sent to me at one time from Century
Artists. It was a new low, or high, in unmitigated gall. I am only
a very recent possessor of a television set. It is a very dangerous
medium. Radio was bad enough, but at least you didn't have to look
at it. You didn't have to watch the kind of direction and camera
work that would have been considered ridiculously incompetent in the
movies twenty-five years ago. And as for the commercials—well, I
understand that the concoction of these is a business in itself, a
business that makes prostitution or the drug traffic seem quite
respectable. It was bad enough to have the sub-human hucksters
controlling radio, but television does something to you which radio
never did. It prevents you from forming any kind of a mental picture

[241]

and forces you to look at a caricature instead. There's no escape. Take the show that Ralph Bellamy is doing. "Man Against Crime" I think it's called. The writing, I suppose, is no worse than it was in lots of radio shows, but by being more intrusive it *seems* worse. It's no more good enough for television than it would be for any but the cheapest movies, the kind of thing PRC[1] makes, or the type of western movie turned out wholesale by Republic and never shown in neighborhood theaters. If you have spent fifteen years building up a character, a fairly complicated character, you can't deliver him to the sort of people that do these shows. I don't think the plots are terribly important. But I think the actor and the dialogue are very important—so much so that if I were offered a television show (which I have not been) I would have to demand approval of the actor playing Philip Marlowe and also script approval. I simply can't afford to have this character murdered by a bunch of yucks. A voice like Gerald Mohr's gave you a personality which you could fill out according to your fancy. But television shoves the whole thing right down your throat. And if the actor says one flat, stupid, trashy line, it sticks out like a lighthouse in a storm.

.　　　.　　　.

With kindest regards to you both,

Yours ever,

Ray


## TO ALFRED HITCHCOCK

6005 Camino de la Costa
La Jolla, California
December 6, 1950

Dear Hitch:
    In spite of your wide and generous disregard of my

1.  Producers Releasing Corporation, or PRC pictures, which released such films as *Swamp Woman, Wife of Monte Cristo,* and *Why Girls Leave Home.*

communications on the subject of the script of *Strangers On a Train*[1] and your failure to make any comment on it, and in spite of not having heard a word from you since I began the writing of the actual screenplay—for all of which I might say I bear no malice, since this sort of procedure seems to be part of the standard Hollywood depravity—in spite of this and in spite of this extremely cumbersome sentence, I feel that I should, just for the record, pass you a few comments on what is termed the final script. I could understand your finding fault with my script in this or that way, thinking that such and such a scene was too long or such and such a mechanism was too awkward. I could understand you changing your mind about the things that you specifically wanted, because some of such changes might have been imposed on you from without. What I cannot understand is your permitting a script which after all had some life and vitality to be reduced to such a flabby mass of clichés, a group of faceless characters, and the kind of dialogue every screen writer is taught not to write—the kind that says everything twice and leaves nothing to be implied by the actor or the camera. Of course you must have had your reasons but, to use a phrase once coined by Max Beerbohm, it would take a "far less brilliant mind than mine" to guess what they were.

Regardless of whether or no my name appears on the screen among the credits, I'm not afraid that anybody will think I wrote this stuff. They'll know damn well I didn't. I shouldn't have minded in the least if you had produced a better script—believe me, I shouldn't. But if you wanted something written in skim milk, why on earth did you bother to come to me in the first place? What a waste of money! What a waste of time! It's no answer to say that I was well paid. Nobody can be adequately paid for wasting his time.

There are minor changes in this construction, or plot order or whatever, which don't bother me at all, such as the drunken professor on the train, although the notion is not original and I simply do not believe for a moment that the professor sober would not even remember the existence of the song he sang when drunk. The idea of having more things happen on trains is all right too. But I certainly thought I had you talked out of this Hennessy nonsense, the idea that the Washington police, or any police, would put a twenty-four hour

1. Chandler was sent the final script of *Strangers on a Train*. This letter was never sent.

watch on a man against whom there was no evidence except motive, and do it for no apparent purpose except that if Guy had committed one murder and they watched him closely enough, they might catch him committing another. The ease with which he evades this watch reduces the whole procedure to absurdity. Also, I think there is a serious mistake in your reversal of the scenes between Guy and Bruno and between Guy and the Burton family immediately after Miriam's murder. The great difficulty of the story always was to make it credible to an audience that Guy should behave in the damn-fool way in which he did behave. Even to approach a solution it was necessary to have the scene with the Burton family first, and to realize what kind of people they are and what their relationship is to Guy and to one another; so that when Guy finds out that Bruno is the murderer, the audience will realize he is not stopped from going to the police solely by fear for himself. I might add that the expressed realization by Guy and Anne, that now that Miriam has been murdered there is nothing to prevent them from being married, will probably be hooted at. Also, take such items as scene 134 on page 47. This is after the scene between Guy and Bruno. Consider the effect of Guy saying on the telephone to Anne, "But you sound upset. Is anything wrong?" You better take that out fast, Hitch. You really better.

Another thing which seems to me dramatically wrong is the failure to have Bruno state specifically why he's going back to Metcalf. You deduce and expect the audience to deduce it from the fact that he says he has a date with the moon—an idea so crazy that only Bruno would think of it. However, these things often look less irrational on the screen than when you are reading the script. I think you may be the sort of director who thinks that camera angles, stage business, and interesting bits of byplay will make up for any amount of implausibility in a basic story. And I think you are quite wrong. I also think that the fact that you may get away with it doesn't prove you are right, because there is a feeling about a picture that is solidly based which cannot be produced in any other way than by having it solidly based. A sow's ear will look like a sow's ear even if one hangs it on a wall in a frame and calls it a French modern. As a friend and well-wisher, I urge you just once during your long and distinguished career—or perhaps I should say just once again—to get a sound and sinewy story into the script and to sacrifice no part of its soundness for an interesting camera shot. Sacrifice a camera

[244]

shot if necessary. There's always another camera shot just as good. There is never another motivation just as good.

The characters have had things happen to them. Anne was always a bit of a stick, but now she's a piece of spaghetti. Mrs. Antony is nothing. Mr. Antony hardly exists. And I do think it's a pity to have removed the tennis motivation from Senator Burton—the idea that he was a sort of frustrated champion who wanted someone else to win the title he could never win. I guess this is about all. The final shot was in my notes, but I didn't put it in my script. I talked it over with my secretary, and we sort of agreed that this was a pretty grim story and should be kept pretty grim and that you couldn't end it with a joke. In any case, I wish you all good luck. No one can predict the fate of a picture, since it often depends on some gimmick which seemed relatively insignificant while the picture was being made. Good pictures fail and bad ones succeed. The shrewdest minds are never quite sure why. Sometimes it seems that a good picture has to fail (example *Night Must Fall*) in order that a whole trend of pictures later on may succeed by the same formula of making a heel or a murderer out of what was formerly a glamour star. After all, a Hitchcock picture always has something.

Yours very truly,

Raymond Chandler

# TO JAMES SANDOE

6005 Camino de la Costa
La Jolla, California
December 7, 1950

Dear Jim:

.        .        .

You should by all means catch *The Bicycle Thief,* and if possible an English picture called *I Know Where I'm Going,* shot largely on the

[245]

west coast of Scotland—the coast that faces the Hebrides. I've never seen a picture which smelled of the wind and rain in quite this way, nor one which so beautifully exploited the kind of scenery people actually live with, rather than the kind which is commercialized as a show place. The shots of Corryvreckan alone are enough to make your hair stand on end. (Corryvreckan, in case you don't know, is a whirlpool which, in certain conditions of the tide, is formed between two of the islands of the Hebrides.) But you'd better forget about the Hitchcock film, because I have seen the final script made up from what I wrote, but a good deal changed and castrated. It is, in fact, so bad that I am debating whether to refuse screen credit. I don't know what's happened to Hitchcock. You call him flabby. I'd be inclined to call him idiotic, because if he wanted the kind of script this thing has turned into, why one earth did he go to the expense of hiring me to write a script for him? The sort of stuff he is presumably shooting he could have got for one-fifth or less of the money Warners paid me.

.                 .                 .

I have just been reading a book called *The Beast Must Die*, by Nicholas Blake, the pseudonym of Cecil Day Lewis. Once again I am struck, you might even say shattered, by the devastating effect on the story of the entrance of the detective, Nigel Strangeways, an amateur with wife tagging along—this wife is one of the world's three greatest female explorers, which puts her in the same distinguished, and to me utterly silly, class as the artist wife of Ngaio Marsh's Roderick Alleyn. Up to that point the story is damn good and extremely well written, but the amateur detective just won't do. He wouldn't do even when his brother was a duke and he had a title and was a classical scholar of considerable attainments, and he won't do as Nigel Strangeways any better, or as well.[1] The private eye admittedly is an exaggeration—a fantasy. But at least he's an exaggeration of the possible. The amateur gentleman who outthinks Scotland Yard is just plain silly. From a plot point of view I think Blake made a bad mistake in allowing his protagonist, the author of the diary, to find his hit-and-run murderer so soon. It should have been a long hard job with many frustrations and should have taken up

1. Reference to Lord Peter Wimsey, the detective in the novels by Dorothy Sayers.

about two-thirds of the book, or anyway half. It's not only that it's absurd that an amateur should so easily find someone the police could not find, because I could swallow that if necessary; it's that the search itself always has a built-in suspense, and not to prolong it to the limit is simply throwing away good material. However, in the matter of plotting I have to confess that every man is entitled to proceed according to his own taste.

Yours ever,

Ray


# TO CARL BRANDT

6005 Camino de la Costa
La Jolla, California
December 11, 1950

Dear Carl:

. . .

I'm not going to discuss the credits on the screenplay, because the only point here was whether I should refuse any credit on the ground that the final script was so poor a job that I didn't want my name on it.[1] I may still do it or, for all I know, one of the other writers may be dissatisfied with the allocation of credits and ask for an arbitration. The fallacy of this operation was my being involved in it at all, because it is obvious to me now, and must have been obvious to many people long since, that a Hitchcock picture has to be all Hitchcock. A script which shows any sign of a positive style must be obliterated or changed until it is quite innocuous, even if that means making it quite silly. What Hitchcock does with his camera, his actors, and his stage business is quite all right. I haven't a thing against it. And I'm not going to suggest that he would do better if he

1. Screenplay for *Strangers on a Train*. Chandler wrote the first screenplay and then was replaced on the job by Czenzi Ormonde, with whom he eventually shared credit for the film.

had a little more sense of dramatic plausibility, because maybe he wouldn't do better. Maybe he'd do worse. Stark seemed to enjoy suggesting that my script was bad.[2] But it wasn't bad. It was far better than what they finished with. It just had too much Chandler in it and not enough Hitchcock. That is my considered opinion, and not mine alone. I feel annoyed that the lady who did the rewriting behind my back, and who is probably little more than a note-taker for Hitchcock, should have been supplied by Stark's office. It's bad enough to be stabbed in the back without having your agent supply the knife. But of course I admit this could happen with any agency.

.　　　　.　　　　.

With kindest regards,

Ray

## TO HAMISH HAMILTON

6005 Camino de la Costa
La Jolla, California
December 11, 1950

Dear Jamie:

.　　　　.　　　　.

J. A. Spender was editing the *Westminster Gazette* in the days when I worked for it. I got an introduction to him from a very charming old boy named Blennerhassett, a landed proprietor in Ireland, a barrister with, I think, a House of Lords' practice. It seems to me that I have written to you about him before. He was the sort of man who could make a frightened young nobody feel at ease in the company of the cream of patrician society. Spender put me up for the National Liberal Club in order that I might have the use of its reading room, and I used to browse through the French and

2. Ray Stark, Chandler's Hollywood agent, assigned him by Carl Brandt, his literary agent.

[248]

German papers looking for odd paragraphs and news items which could be translated and adapted for a column the *Westminster Gazette* ran. Spender thought I could make six guineas a week out of this, but I don't think I ever made more than about three. I wrote quite a lot of verses for him also, most of which now seem to me deplorable, but not all, and a good many sketches, mostly of a satirical nature— the sort of thing that Saki did so infinitely better. I still have a couple of them somewhere, and they now seem to me very precious in tone. But I suppose they weren't so bad, considering how little valid experience I had to back them up. Of course Naomi Royde-Smith may have been connected with the *Westminster* at that time, but I never personally came into contact with her. As a matter of fact, I had only the most limited personal contact with Spender. I would send the stuff in, and they would either send it back or send me proof. I never corrected the proof, didn't even know whether I was expected to. I simply took it as a convenient form of acceptance. I never waited for them to send me the money but appeared regularly on a certain day each week at their cashier's office and received payment in gold and silver, being required to affix a penny stamp in a large book and sign my name across it by way of receipt. What a strange world it seems now! I suppose I have told you of the time I wrote to Sir George Newnes and offered to buy a piece of his trashy but successful weekly magazine called *Tit-Bits*. I was received most courteously by a secretary, definitely public school, who regretted that the publication was not in need of capital, but said that my approach had at least the merit of originality. By the same device I did actually make a connection with *The Academy*, then edited and owned by a man named Cowper, who had bought it from Lord Alfred Douglas. He was not disposed to sell an interest in his magazine, but pointed to a large shelf of books in his office and said they were review copies and would I care to take a few home to review. I wonder why he did not rather have me thrown down his murky stairs; perhaps because there was no one in the office who could do it since his entire editorial staff seemed to consist of one placid middle-aged lady and a mousy little man, named Vizetelly, who was (I believe) the brother of another and more famous Vizetelly—the one who was arrested in New York in connection with an obscenity complaint over the American publication of the translation of *Madame Bovary*. I met there also a tall, bearded, and sad-eyed man called Richard Middleton, of whom I think you may have heard. Shortly afterwards he committed suicide in Antwerp, a suicide of despair, I should say. The incident made a great impression on me, because Middleton struck me as having far more talent than I was ever likely to possess; and if he couldn't make a go of it, it wasn't very likely that I could. Of course in those days as now there were popular and successful writers, and there were clever young men who made a decent living as free lances for the numerous literary weeklies and in the more literary departments of the daily papers. But most of the people who did this work either had private incomes or jobs, especially in the civil service. And I was distinctly not a clever young man. Nor was I at all a happy young man. I had very little money, although there was a great deal of it in my family. I had grown up in England and all my relatives were either English or Colonial. And yet I was not English. I had no feeling of identity with the United States, and yet I resented the kind of ignorant and snobbish criticism of Americans that was current at that time. During my year in Paris I had run across a good many Americans, and most of them seemed to have a lot of bounce and liveliness and to be thoroughly enjoying themselves in situations where the average Englishman of the same class would be stuffy or completely bored. But I wasn't one of them. I didn't even speak their language. I was, in effect, a man without a country. Having passed third (and first on the classical list) in an open civil service examination, I could have had a life-long and perfectly safe job with six weeks' vacation every year and ridiculously easy hours. And yet I thoroughly detested the civil service. I had too much Irish in my blood to stand being pushed around by suburban nobodies. The idea of being expected to tip my hat to the head of the department struck me as verging on the obscene. All in all, perhaps I ought to have stayed in Paris, although I never really liked the French. But you didn't exactly have to like the French to be at home in Paris. And you could always like some of them. On the other hand, I did like the Germans very much, that is the South Germans. But there wasn't much sense living in Germany, since it was an open secret, openly discussed, that we would be at war with them almost any time now. I suppose it was the most inevitable of all wars. There was never any question about whether it would happen. The only question was when.

I have just received my copy of the Old Alleynian Yearbook, and although Dulwich is not, I suppose, quite out of the top drawer as public schools go, there is an astonishing number of quite distinguished old boys with enormous strings of letters after their names, titles, peerages, etc. I notice that two of us, though quite undistinguished, have addresses in La Jolla. Apparently there is only one more in all of California, a fellow named Gropius, who seems to have had the same address in San Francisco for the past thirty years, and probably went to school sometime during the reign of William IV.

Yours ever,

Ray

## TO H. N. SWANSON and EDGAR CARTER

6005 Camino de la Costa
La Jolla, California
Dec. 15th. 1950

Dear Swanie and Eddie:

Our little black cat had to be put to sleep yesterday morning. We feel pretty broken up about it. She was almost 20 years old. We saw it coming, of course, but we hoped she might pick up strength. But when she got too weak to stand up and practically stopped eating, there was nothing else to do. They have a wonderful way of doing it now. They inject nembutal into a vein of the foreleg and the animal just isn't there anymore. She falls asleep in two seconds. Then, after a few minutes, just to make certain, they inject it into the heart directly. Pity they can't do it to people. I watched my mother die under morphine and it took almost ten hours. She was

[251]

completely unconscious, of course, but how much better if it took two seconds—if it had to be anyhow.

All the best,

Ray

## TO BERNICE BAUMGARTEN

6005 Camino de la Costa
La Jolla, California
December 19, 1950

Dear Bernice:

I have just received a copy of the Italian translation of *The Little Sister* published by Mondadori. I hope you have a copy in your office to glance at. It looks to me like a rotten job. According to the contract, Paragraph 2, the publishers agree to publish a "faithful and accurate Italian translation." My Italian is admittedly very sketchy, but I can spot eight or ten mistakes on the first page—the sort of mistakes which suggest that the translator may know schoolbook English but doesn't know the language I write at all. They appear to be mistakes of understanding. Also, the entire first paragraph of the book is omitted, and there are other omissions in the first chapter. In the cast of characters, for example, I think it's idiotic for them to put down that Mavis Weld is the sister of the Quests. This is something that should not be disclosed until it's disclosed in the story. They have Dr. Lagardie down as a functionary of the police along with the two detectives. This must be a complete misunderstanding. They have Ballou down as a producer instead of an agent. The description of the bluebottle fly is all fouled up; there isn't even an attempt to translate what I wrote. A "bar" is not a drugstore. To say the elevator "functions" is not to say it is free. After the line "Better try the University Club" on page 3 of my book here is what the translator puts instead of what I wrote: "I know that there are a pair of detectives there, but I do not think you would succeed in persuading them to work for you." This, if you please,

[252]

is supposed to be an Italian translation of "I heard they had a couple left over there," (gentlemen, that is) "but I'm not sure they'll let you handle them." At the end of this chapter they put "shut the door" instead of "lock the door." The whole thing is simply ridiculous. And all this in a column and a half on one page. God knows what it's like to go on with it.

I'm sure your agent on the spot, or Heath's agent on the spot, will confirm what I say here about the translation.[1] Most likely the translator did not understand what I wrote. If he did, he made no attempt to render it in Italian. I'm going to send my copy to Jamie Hamilton, whose wife is an Italian, and ask what they think of it. I certainly wouldn't want to have any more to do with this publishing house. There is too little money at stake to make it worthwhile to put up with this sort of thing. As for anything else being at stake, such as literary reputation, it is obvious that a translation of a book of mine into the same sort of Italian as the English used by Wilkie Collins is throwing away everything in it of any stylistic value. If the French can find translators who know the American language and can render it into idiomatic French—and they can and do—I should say that the Italians are capable of the same thing. If Mondadori can't or won't find the people to do it, then I should not have anything to do with Mondadori.

Yours ever,

Ray

## TO CARL BRANDT

6005 Camino de la Costa
La Jolla, California
December 21, 1950

Dear Carl:

•     •     •

Your Night Letter just received shows that you are aware of

1. A. M. Heath and Company, Chandler's London agent.

the problem. I don't specifically dislike Ziff or Queen and I don't turn down five or six hundred dollars just to be cute, as you know.[1] What I see in this situation is purely and simply a question of the commercial value of prestige. In the literary market as in Hollywood it seems to me that a man's going price is largely determined by the kind of company he keeps. If you publish in cheap magazines, you are inevitably labelled for the qualities in your writing which coincide with cheap fiction. But it is precisely the qualities which do not belong to cheap fiction, which are overlooked or ignored by magazine and publisher alike, but not by the intelligent public, which finally make your reputation. Knopf did not realize this, neither does Houghton Mifflin, at least for promotion purposes. That is one reason why Jamie Hamilton consistently outsells them; to Jamie Hamilton I am not just a tough writer; I am the best there is in my line and the best there has ever been; I am tough only incidentally; substantially I am an original stylist with a very daring kind of imagination. To Jamie it is ludicrous that the *New York Times* should allow John Dickson Carr to sneer at me for not being able to handle the English language; he knows I can not only handle it in any style but that I am helping to make it. If I write an offbeat story like "Bingo," which admittedly may be good or bad, I do not think it is good business to accept a last chance publication when the better magazines turn it down. When this story comes out in a book, as it will with half a dozen others, I want no credits to pulp magazines on the back of the title page. I don't want the thought slid into the mind of the reviewer or reader that this is pulp material. I want him to take it on its merits as serious writing in a very difficult medium. And I want this, not because I am proud, but because in the long run I believe it pays. I am just as mercenary as you are—or as you pretend to be. It is rather that I have strong feelings about how best to be mercenary.

From now on I am going to write what I want to write as I want to write it. Some of it may flop. There are always going to be people who will say I have lost the pace I had once, that I take too long to say things now, and don't care enough about tight active plots. But I'm not writing for those people now. I'm writing for the people who understand about writing as an art and are able to separate what a man does with words and ideas from what he thinks about

1. Referring to offers to publish his work by Ziff-Davis and the *Ellery Queen* detective story magazine.

Truman or the United Nations. (I have a low opinion of both.) If I feel like writing a fast tough story, I'll write it, but not because there is a market for it and because I've done it before. If I feel like writing a poetic or ironic fantasy, I'll write that. You have to get some fun out of this job and you can't get it by filling orders. You can't get it by forcing yourself to do something you have lost interest in doing. At least I don't think you can. Obviously I don't think very much of even the big magazines, since I never read their fiction. But they pay the kind of money you can't refuse.

Yours ever,

Ray

## TO SOMERSET MAUGHAM

6005 Camino de la Costa
La Jolla, California
January 5, 1951

Dear Mr. Maugham:

Herewith a few tear sheets of articles about the detective story which I promised to send you and which you are now ready to receive.[1] My file is not as complete as I thought it was, a couple of items apparently having gone astray. One of these was an article by Joseph Wood Krutch, but I find that it is included in a book called *The Art of the Mystery Story* edited by Howard Haycraft, published by Simon & Schuster in 1946. This book, in case you don't know it—and I don't think you do or you would have some of the material you wanted from me—contains a great many articles in various moods about mystery stories. If you have any difficulty in getting a copy, I should be only too glad to lend you mine. But your New York agent can probably dig one up and get it to you much more quickly than I could. If not, please drop me a line.

1. Maugham had asked Chandler for help on his article about detective fiction called "The Decline and Fall of the Detective Story."

I have seen a number of the television films of your stories and, admirable as the material is, I cannot help feeling a dissatisfaction with the way in which it is presented. There is something wrong with this medium as it is now used. For one thing the acting is not casual enough. The emphasis of stage acting (one might even call it over-emphasis) had to be enormously reduced for films, and it seems to me that it must be still further reduced for television. The slightest artifice glares. The feeling of a restricted space is so intense that one almost expects the dialogue to be carried on in whispers as by a couple of people hiding in the clothes closet. The camera work seems to me to be pretty bad, as bad as the camera work in those English films of the '30's of which we see so many on television now. The settings are so poor that one feels it might be better to do without them altogether and play against a back drop. But the worst thing to me is that the actors, instead of interpreting the story and making it come alive, seem to bulk right between the story and the audience. Their physical presence is overpowering. Their slightest motion distracts the eye. It strikes me that good acting is very much like style in a novel. You should not be too conscious of it. Its effect should be peripheral rather than central. But in television you can hardly be conscious of anything else.

With kindest regards,

Yours very truly,

Raymond Chandler

## TO HAMISH HAMILTON

6005 Camino de la Costa
La Jolla, California
January 9, 1951

Dear Jamie:

.        .        .

All my life I have had cats and I have found that they differ almost as much as people, and that, like children, they are largely the way

[256]

you treat them except there are a few here and there who cannot be spoiled. But perhaps that is true of children also. Taki had absolute poise, which is a rare quality in animals as well as in human beings. And she had no cruelty, which is a still rarer quality in cats. She caught birds and mice without hurting them, and had no objection whatever to having them taken away from her and released. She even caught a butterfly once. In a group of people she would march straight up to the one cat lover in the room, and she would ignore absolutely the occasional individual who was pronouncedly anti-cat. I have never liked anyone who disliked cats, because I've always found an element of acute selfishness in their dispositions. Admittedly, a cat doesn't give you the kind of affection a dog gives you. A cat never behaves as if you were the only bright spot in an otherwise clouded existence. But this is only another way of saying that a cat is not a sentimentalist, which does not mean that it has no affection.

Yours ever,

Ray

## TO EDGAR CARTER

February 5, 1951

Dear Eddie:

*The Picture Post* is for people who move their lips when they read. Surely they can get anything they want from my English publisher, Hamish Hamilton, Ltd., 90 Great Russell Street, London, W.C. 1. The questions you quote would seem to me to indicate the intellectual level of the editorial department of the *Picture Post*. Yes, I am exactly like the characters in my books. I am very tough and have been known to break a Vienna roll with my bare hands. I am very handsome, have a powerful physique, and change my shirt regularly every Monday morning. When resting between assignments I live in a French Provincial chateau of Mulholland Drive. It is a fairly small place of forty-eight rooms and fifty-nine baths. I dine off gold plate and prefer to be waited on by naked dancing girls. But

[257]

of course there are times when I have to grow a beard and hole up in a Main Street flophouse, and there are other times when I am, although not by request, entertained in the drunk tank in the city jail. I have friends from all walks of life. Some are highly educated and some talk like Darryl Zanuck.[1] I have fourteen telephones on my desk, including direct lines to New York, London, Paris, Rome, and Santa Rosa. My filing case opens out into a very convenient portable bar, and the bartender, who lives in the bottom drawer, is a midget named Harry Cohn.[2] I am a heavy smoker and according to my mood I smoke tobacco, marijuana, corn silk, and dried tea leaves. I do a great deal of research, especially in the apartments of tall blondes. I get my material in various ways, but my favorite procedure (sometimes known as the Jerry Wald system) consists of going through the desks of other writers after hours.[3] I am thirty-eight years old and have been for the last twenty years. I do not regard myself as a dead shot, but I am a pretty dangerous man with a wet towel. But all in all I think my favorite weapon is a twenty dollar bill. In my spare time I collect elephants.

> Yours respectfully,

## TO CARL BRANDT

> 6005 Camino de la Costa
> La Jolla, California
> February 13, 1951

Dear Carl:

. . .

I've known a number of these not-quite writers. No doubt you have also. But in your profession you would get away from them as fast as possible; whereas I've known several of them quite well. I have spent time and money on them and it's always wasted, because even if they make an occasional sale it turns out that they have been traveling on somebody else's gas. I guess these are the hardest cases,

1. Head of Twentieth Century-Fox Studio.
2. Head of Columbia Pictures.
3. Of Warner Brothers Studio.

because they want so hard to be professionals that it doesn't take very much encouragement to make them think they are. I knew one who sold a short story (most of which, incidentally, I had written for him) to that semi-slick MacFadden publication that Fulton Oursler used to edit—I forget the name of it.[1] Some cheap outfit bought the picture rights for five hundred bucks and made a very bad B picture with Sally Rand in it. This fellow thereupon got drunk and went around snooting all his writer friends because they were working for the pulps. A couple of years later he sold a short story to a pulp magazine, and I think that is the total of his contribution to literature in a commercial sense. To hear this fellow and his wife discussing and analyzing stories was a revelation in how much it is possible to know about technique without being able to use any. If you have enough talent, you can get by after a fashion without guts; and if you have enough guts, you can also get by, after a fashion, without talent. But you certainly can't get by without either. These not-quite writers are very tragic people and the more intelligent they are, the more tragic, because the step they can't take seems to them such a very small step, which in fact it is. And every successful or fairly successful writer knows, or should know, by what a narrow margin he himself was able to take that step. But if you can't take it, you can't. That's all there is to it.

.            .            .

Yours,

Ray

## TO HAMISH HAMILTON

6005 Camino de la Costa
La Jolla, California
February 14, 1951

Dear Jamie:

.            .            .

Priestley descended on me out of the skies yesterday without

1. Fulton Oursler (1893–1952) was editor of *Liberty* and vice-president of MacFadden publications.

[259]

warning, except a telegram from Guadalajara just before he came, and at a damned inconvenient time, because my wife is not well and unable to entertain him.[1] However I have done the best I could. I drove down to Tijuana and picked him up, a damned long unpleasant drive, if there ever was one, and have installed him in our best hotel since we have no spare room. He is a likable, genial guy; fortunately a great talker, so about all I had to do was click my tongue against my teeth. He was not entirely satisfied with my company, for which I do not at all blame him, and suggested gently as I departed from him late last night at the door of his hotel that tonight possibly we might meet some of the fellows. So this morning I burst into tears and threw myself at the feet of Jonathan Latimer, who knows everybody and likes everybody (whereas I am just the opposite); so tonight I am going to take him over to Latimer's house, where will be gathered a reasonable selection of what passes for intelligent humanity in our city.[2]

> Yours ever,
>
> Ray

## TO H. F. HOSE

[February 1951]

Dear Hose:

It is most unlikely that I should quarrel with your reading tastes or habits. If I didn't write detective stories, I should probably not read them. And I don't recall offhand that I ever read more than three or four before I began to write them. As you remark, most of them are very badly written and even those which have, at least in an academic sense, a certain purity of style are usually ridiculous in other ways. I agree with you that most contemporary writing is

1. J. B. Priestley, the English novelist.
2. Jonathan Latimer, a mystery writer, also lived in La Jolla.

rubbish. But hasn't that always been true? The situation is no different over here, except that hardly anyone pays much attention to Latin and Greek any more. I think the English writers generally speaking are apt to be much more leisurely and urbane than ours, but these qualities do not seem to carry them very far. I suppose a generation gets the literature it deserves, just as it is said to get the government it deserves.

Most of us become impatient with the messiness that is around us and are inclined to attribute to the past a purity of line which was not apparent to the contemporaries of that past. The past after all has been sifted and strained. The present has not. The literature of the past has survived and it has prestige on that account, apart from its other prestige. The reasons for its survival are complex. The past is our university; it gives us our taste and our habits of thought, and we are resentful when we cannot find a basis for them in the present. It is just possible that they are there just the same. You can't build a Gothic cathedral by assembly line methods; you can't get artistic stone masons from the union. For myself, I am convinced that if there is any virtue in our art, and there may be none at all, it does not lie in its resemblance to something that is now traditional, but which was not traditional when it was first produced. If we have stylists, they are not people like Osbert Sitwell—Edwardians who stayed up too late; nor are they pseudo-poetic dramatists like T. S. Eliot and Christopher Fry; nor bloodless intellectuals who sit just at the edge of the lamplight and dissect everything to nothing in dry little voices that convey little more than the accents of boredom and extreme disillusion. It seems to me that there have been damn few periods in the history of civilization that a man living in one of them could have recognized as definitely great. If you had been a contemporary of Sophocles, I think you might have thought of him almost as highly as you do now. But I think you might have thought Euripides a little vulgar. And if you had been an Elizabethan, I am quite sure you would have thought Shakespeare largely a purveyor of stale plots and over-elaborate rhetoric. I don't know why I'm saying this. I'm not trying to defend anything, and I certainly would not wish to diminish your pleasure in that which gives you pleasure, even if I could.

Yours ever

[261]

# TO JAMES SANDOE

6005 Camino de la Costa
La Jolla, California
February 20, 1951

Dear Sandoe:

For once I don't know whether I owe you a letter or you owe me a letter, or whether it is a Mexican stand-off. I am not even sure that I have been polite enough to thank you for sending me that book. I am still a little dizzy from the descent on me of the English novelist, playwright, etc., J. B. Priestley. He cost me a good deal of time and a good deal of money, and I'm not quite sure what I got out of it if anything, except the satisfaction of having been as polite as possible to a friend of my English publisher. He likes my books, says he smiling politely in order to get the subject out of the way and forget it, then he wishes I would write something without murders in it. Now isn't that a typical attitude? You slam murder mysteries a la Edmund Wilson, because they are usually written, you say, by people who can't write well. And the moment you find someone who you are willing to admit can write well, you tell him he should not be writing murder mysteries. Meantime, have you been reading any good trash lately?

I have been having another look at the Adelaide Bartlett case, God knows why.[1] I think one of its most confusing elements is that Sir Edward Clarke's defense was so brilliant in contrast to the rather uninspired defense of Maybrick and Wallace that you are almost fooled into ignoring the facts. But the facts, if you look them straight in the eye, are pretty damning. For example:

Edwin Bartlett died of drinking liquid chloroform. Adelaide, his wife, had liquid chloroform procured for her surreptitiously by Dyson, the clergyman, who, if not actually her lover in a technical sense, was certainly doing some very high-powered necking. Her stated reason for wanting the chloroform is nonsense. Edwin was an

1. Adelaide Bartlett was brought to trial at the Central Criminal Court in London in 1886 for murdering her husband. The case was known popularly as the Pimlico Poisoning case.

[262]

unattractive and unnecessary husband and was a dope as well. If he died she got Dyson and Edwin's money. Edwin's health was excellent in spite of his constant complaining. It was more than usually good the night before he died. His insomnia seems to have been severe, but is not consistent with his hearty appetite. Morphia and chloral hydrate had both been tried on him without effect. He was obviously a hard person to drug. See about the gas at the dentist's. The wine glass which was found smelled of chloroform behind brandy. The chloroform bottle was not found. According to Adelaide it had been on the mantel earlier. The house was not searched, and Adelaide was not searched. Adelaide had opportunity to hide what remained of the chloroform. She admitted to disposing of it later. There are three principal arguments against her guilt: (1) her nursing care seemed genuine and fairly self-sacrificing; (2) she urged a quick post mortem and herself scouted the chance of his having taken the chloroform himself; (3) the difficulty of poisoning Edwin by this method was enormous according to medical testimony, and there was no previous record of murder by this means. But assuming her guilt, the first argument is meaningless. What else would you expect? How else has any poisoner ever acted? As to the second argument, there is no reason to assume, as the judge did, that she *knew* a delay in the post mortem would be in her favor. How about the theory of "methinks thou dost protest too much"? He didn't die of jugged hare. There was bound to be an investigation. If you know that and if you have murdered him, how best can you look innocent? The way she did. The judge disposed of the third argument. If she murdered him, it was by a method which had one chance in twenty of succeeding. But she didn't know that. To her it may have looked easy.

The insomnia makes me laugh. I have had insomnia—quite severe insomnia. I did not want a big meal of jugged hare. I did not want a supper of oysters and cake. I did not want a haddock for breakfast—a large haddock—so badly that I would have been willing to get up an hour earlier in order to start eating. I think this guy was a neurotic insomniac. That is to say, if he didn't feel as fresh as a daisy in the morning, he said he hadn't slept more than twenty minutes the night before. But if I don't believe his insomnia was severe, I can't believe he would be desperate enough to take the chloroform himself, even though the unpleasantness of it is not a

[263]

conclusive argument because people used to take castor oil. If you hold your nose, you can swallow almost anything without tasting it. But you do have to believe that this guy was desperate from insomnia and yet had a very fine appetite for his food. It is quite true that the stuff burns. But if you have sniffed enough of it to make you woozy, it might be that your senses would be blunted. Apart from murder, this seems to be the only possiblity. And it is not a very convincing one.

Assuming Adelaide's guilt, her behavior with the bottle must have been entirely to protect Dyson, because if she admits possession of the chloroform, she has to tell how she got it. If she is willing to do that, her best bet is to leave the bottle where it was and stand on the insomnia and Edwin's desperate attempt to overcome it. Dr. Leach, the dope, will certainly back her up. Some of the medical history is in favor of it (but not the jugged hare). It makes a neat little problem all right. If she makes him sniff enough chloroform to put him almost under but not quite, and then gives him a nice fat drink of it in circumstances where he doesn't exactly know what he is drinking, just takes things on trust, then he swallows the chloroform and it kills him. The doctors say that if he had been quite unconscious, he wouldn't have swallowed it, that his swallowing would not be working. But they also seem to think that if he had swallowed it while he was conscious, he would have thrown it up. What they really mean is that they would, or you would, or I would. Edwin is a little bit different from us. You can feed anything to Edwin, and all he wants is to get up an hour early the next morning and start eating more. I think the man had a stomach like a goat. I think he could digest sawdust, old tin cans, iron filings, and shoe leather. I think he could drink chloroform just like you and I could drink orange juice. Anyhow, any argument against his being able to retain it in his stomach is nonsense, because he did retain it in his stomach; so the only real argument is against the difficulty of getting it down his throat. And in Edwin's case that doesn't seem to me a very strong argument. He probably thought he was drinking ginger wine.

Yours ever,

R.C.

[264]

# TO HAMISH HAMILTON

6005 Camino de la Costa
La Jolla, California
February 27, 1951

Dear Jamie:

.　　　.　　.

I wouldn't say that I found Priestley tactless, and I certainly haven't any quarrel with him. He plays the part of the blunt-spoken Yorkshireman very well. He was very pleasant to me and went out of his way to be complimentary. He is rugged, energetic, versatile, and in a way very professional; that is, everything that comes his way will be material and most of the material will be used rather quickly and superficially. His social philosophy is a little too rigid for my taste and a little too much conditioned by the fact that he finds it impossible to see much good in anyone who has made a lot of money (except by writing of course), anyone who has a public school accent or a military bearing, anyone in short who has speech or mannerisms above the level of the lower middle class. I think this must be a great handicap to him, because in his world a gentleman of property is automatically a villain. That's a rather limiting viewpoint, and I would say that Priestley is a rather limited man, and that his point of view as a writer does not arise from any artistic perception, but that his artistic perception, such as it is, is strictly limited by a point of view he already had. Of course I don't like socialism, although a modified form of it is inevitable everywhere. I think a bunch of bureaucrats can abuse the power of money just as ruthlessly as a bunch of Wall Street bankers, and far less competently. Socialism so far has existed largely on the fat of the class it is trying to impoverish. What happens when the fat is all used up? What happens when economic prosperity depends on the profits of industries run by bureaucrats, and when those industries don't show a profit but more likely a deficit? What happens when what Roosevelt called the "wukkahs" find out that there's no one left to pay for their luxuries but themselves and that they're paying the kind of income taxes the

[265]

rich used to pay? Well, I don't know and I don't think Priestley knows.

. . .

Yours ever,

Ray

## TO JAMES SANDOE

6005 Camino de la Costa
La Jolla, California
March 6, 1951

Dear Sandoe:

. . .

  I don't know whether you have a television set, or whether having one you could have seen films of the Kefauver committee hearings.[1] I saw part of those held in Los Angeles and found them fascinating. Obviously nothing that a mystery writer could dream up could be more fantastic than what actually goes on in the hoodlum empire which infests this country. Kefauver himself is worth the price of admission any day—a big powerful guy with absolute poise of manner and unfailing politeness to the witnesses, no trace of Southern accent whatever. He was hardly ever even sarcastic. Nevertheless, he made these racketeer witnesses very nervous, much more nervous I think than if he had been really tough with them. Even when he produced a piece of documentary evidence which made nonsense of what they had been saying, he didn't do it with any air of pouncing but in an offhand, casual manner as if it didn't really matter what they said, because it had all been decided somewhere else what was going to happen to them. I hope it has, although it is pretty obvious that under our present laws only income tax evasion could ever really be proved against these fellows. There was one fascinating little session in which an ex-sheriff of San Bernardino county described

1. Senator Estes Kefauver (Democrat of Tennessee) was chairman of a Senate committee investigating the influence of organized crime.

a visit to Big Bear Lake up in the mountains, where he heard two women mourning over some gambling losses their husbands had sustained locally and he found out where the gambling house was and went there. He said there were about a hundred and fifty people in the place, two roulette wheels were operating, at least one crap table, and numerous slot machines. He circulated around, determined who the managers and gamblers were, then talked to them and found out that the house was owned by a man named Gentry, who was the foreman of the grand jury. He then arrested all the gamblers, confiscated all the gambling equipment apparently with no opposition at all, although he was alone and not young, took the gamblers down to the justice of the peace, where they pleaded guilty and paid fines. Thereafter he was approached by emissaries of Mr. Gentry offering him money to get the gambling equipment back. Kefauver then put Mr. Gentry on the stand, the former foreman of the grand jury. Mr. Gentry said: (a) that he had never owned any gambling equipment and therefore had never sent anybody to try and buy it back from the sheriff; (b) that he had never owned this house in Big Bear Valley, although he had once had a twenty-six hundred dollar mortgage on it; (c) that he had never lived in it; (d) that the house consisted of a rather small living room, a bedroom, a small kitchen and a bathroom, and that if you could get fifteen people into it, the walls would bulge. Senator Kefauver smiled politely, thanked him, and left it at that.

Yours ever,

Raymond Chandler

## TO HAMISH HAMILTON

6005 Camino de la Costa<br>
La Jolla, California<br>
March 19, 1951

Dear Jamie:

.        .        .

I had a friendly note from Priestley, flawlessly typed on Gracie Fields' stationery.[1] I hear she is giving up California and going to live in Capri. She seems to feel about Los Angeles very much as I do: that it has become a grotesque and impossible place for a human being to live in. Priestley left me with one uncomfortable and probably exaggerated idea, but it is one in which he seems to believe implicitly. He thinks the entertainment world in England and the literary world for that matter, at least from the critical side (stage, films, radios, television, reviewing, etc.) is completely dominated by homosexuals, and that a good fifty per cent of the people active in these things are homosexuals; including, he says, practically all the literary crtitics. . . . He also mentioned several rather distinguished writers as pansies, whom I had never thought of in that way. And when I said, "Well, if there are so many of them, why doesn't somebody write a really good novel about it?" he mentioned the name of a *very* distinguished novelist, a notorious case according to him, and said that he had retired from publication for several years and written a long novel about homosexualism from the inside by an expert, but that nobody would publish it. Well, well. These are dangerous thoughts to implant in a young and impressionable mind like mine. Now, every time I read one of these flossy and perceptive book reviewers, I say to myself, "Well, is he, or isn't he?" And by God, about three-quarters of the time I am beginning to think he is. *The Saturday Review of Literature* published an article a couple of weeks ago about twelve new and presumably promising novelists of 1950, together with their photographs. There were only three whom, on their physiognomy, I would definitely pass as male. From now on I'll be looking for them under the bed like an old maid looking for burglars. Maybe I ought to try an article for *The Atlantic* on the subject. I could call it, "You Too Could Be A Pansy"; or perhaps simply, "Homo Sapiens."

.           .           .

Yours ever,

Ray

1. English comedienne and motion picture actress.

# TO BERNICE BAUMGARTEN

[April 1951]

Dear Bernice:

　　Your reaction to Eric Ambler's book is extremely interesting
to me, because of your great professional gift for judging a piece
of writing within a narrow context, and yet not losing sight of the
fact that that narrow context is far from all there is.[1] It would seem to
me that Ambler has fallen between two stools and that he has
succumbed to a danger which afflicts all intellectuals who attempt to
deal with thriller material. I know I have to fight it all the time.
It is no easy trick to keep your characters and your story operating on
a level which is understandable to the semi-literate public and at the
same time give them some intellectual and artistic overtones which
that public does not seek or demand or in effect recognize, but which
somehow subconsciously it accepts and likes. My theory has always
been that the public will accept style provided you do not call it style
either in words or by, as it were, standing off and admiring it. There
seems to me to be a vast difference between writing down to the
public (something which always flops in the end) and doing what you
want to do in a form which the public has learned to accept. It's
not so much that Ambler let himself get too intellectual in this story
as that he let it become apparent that he was being intellectual. That
seems to be the fatal mistake, although I myself liked the book, just as
I did not particularly like Helen MacInness' book *Neither Five nor
Three*. She offends me by dealing with very complicated issues in a
sort of half-baked manner like a school girl analyzing Proust. You
can't laugh Communism off just as a dirty conspiracy. You have to
justify its intellectual appeal to some very brilliant minds and destroy
it nevertheless. I guess the lucky writers are those who can outwrite
their readers without out thinking them.

1. *Judgment on Deltchev.*

# TO D. J. IBBERSON[1]

April 19, 1951

Dear Mr. Ibberson:

It is very kind of you to take such an interest in the facts of Philip Marlowe's life. The date of his birth is uncertain. I think he said somewhere that he was thirty-eight years old, but that was quite awhile ago and he is no older today. This is just something you will have to face. He was not born in a Midwestern town but in a small California town called Santa Rosa, which your map will show you to be about fifty miles north of San Francisco. Santa Rosa is famous as the home of Luther Burbank, a fruit and vegetable horticulturist, once of considerable renown. It is perhaps less widely known as the background of Hitchcock's picture *Shadow of a Doubt*, most of which was shot right in Santa Rosa. Marlowe has never spoken of his parents, and apparently he has no living relatives. This could be remedied if necessary. He had a couple of years of college, either at the University of Oregon at Eugene, or Oregon State University at Corvallis, Oregon. I don't know why he came to Southern California, except that eventually most people do, although not all of them remain. He seems to have had some experience as an investigator for an insurance company and later as investigator for the district attorney of Los Angeles county. This would not necessarily make him a police officer nor give him the right to make an arrest. The circumstances in which he lost that job are well known to me but I cannot be very specific about them. You'll have to be satisfied with the information that he got a little too efficient at a time and in a place where efficiency was the last thing desired by the persons in charge. He is slightly over six feet tall and weighs about thirteen stone eight. He has dark brown hair, brown eyes, and the expression "passably good looking" would not satisfy him in the least. I don't think he looks tough. He can be tough. If I had ever had an opportunity of selecting the movie actor who could best represent him to my mind, I think it would have been Cary Grant. I think he dresses as well as can be expected. Obviously he hasn't very much

1.  An English correspondent.

[270]

money to spend on clothes, or on anything else for that matter. The horn-rimmed sunglasses do not make him distinctive. Practically everyone in Southern California wears sunglasses at some time or other. When you say he wears 'pyjamas' even in summer, I don't know what you mean. Who doesn't? Were you under the impression that he wore a nightshirt? Or did you mean that he might sleep raw in hot weather? The last is possible, although our weather here is very seldom hot at night. You are quite right about his smoking habits, although I don't think he insists on Camels. Almost any sort of cigarette will satisfy him. The use of cigarette cases is not as common here as in England. He definitely does not use bookmatches which are always safety matches. He uses either large wooden matches, which we call kitchen matches, or a smaller match of the same type which comes in small boxes and can be struck anywhere, including on the thumbnail if the weather is dry enough. In the desert or in the mountains it is quite easy to strike a match on your thumbnail, but the humidity around Los Angeles is pretty high. Marlowe's drinking habits are much as you state. I don't think he prefers rye to bourbon, however, He will drink practically anything that is not sweet. Certain drinks, such as Pink Ladies, Honolulu cocktails and crème de menthe highballs, he would regard as an insult. Yes, he makes good coffee. Anyone can make good coffee in this country, although it seems quite impossible in England. He takes cream, and sugar with his coffee, not milk. He will also drink it black without sugar. He cooks his own breakfast, which is a simple matter, but not any other meal. He is a late riser by inclination, but occasionally an early riser by necessity. Aren't we all? I would not say that his chess comes up to tournament standard. I don't know where he got the little paper-bound book of tournament games published in Leipzig, but he likes it because he prefers the continental method of designating the squares on the chess board. Nor do I know that he is something of a card player. This has slipped my mind. What do you mean he is "moderately fond of animals"? If you live in an apartment house, moderately is about as fond of them as you can get. It seems to me that you have an inclination to interpret any chance remark as an indication of a fixed taste. As to his interest in women as "frankly carnal", these are your words, not mine.

·     ·     ·

Marlowe cannot recognize a Bryn Mawr accent, because there is no such thing. All he implies by that expression is a toplofty way of speaking. I doubt very much that he can tell genuine old furniture from fakes. And I also beg leave to doubt that many experts can do it either, if the fakes are good enough. I pass the Edwardian furniture and pre-Raphaelite art. I just don't recall where you get your facts. I would not say that Marlowe's knowledge of perfume stops at Chanel Number 5. That again is merely a symbol of someting that is expensive and at the same time reasonably restrained. He likes all the slightly acrid perfumes, but not the cloying or overspiced type. He is, as you may have noticed, a slightly acrid person. Of course he knows what the Sorbonne is, and he also knows where it is. Of course he knows the difference between a tango and a rumba, and also between a conga and a samba, and he knows the difference between a samba and a mamba, although he does not believe that the mamba can overtake a galloping horse. I doubt if he knows the new dance called a mambo, because it seems to be only recently discovered or developed.

Now let's see, how far does that take us? Fairly regular film-goer, you say, dislikes musicals. Check. May be an admirer of Orson Welles. Possibly, especially when Orson is directed by someone other than himself. Marlowe's reading habits and musical tastes are just as much a mystery to me as they are to you, and if I tried to improvise, I'm afraid I would get him confused with my own tastes. If you ask me why he is a private detective, I can't answer you. Obviously there are times when he wishes he were not, just as there are times when I would rather be almost anything than a writer. The private detective of fiction is a fantastic creation who acts and speaks like a real man. He can be completely realistic in every sense but one, that one sense being that in life as we know it such a man would not be a private detective. The things which happen to him might still happen to him, but they would happen as the result of a peculiar set of chances. By making him a private detective, you skip the necessity for justifying his adventures.

Where he lives: in *The Big Sleep* and some earlier stories he apparently lived in a single apartment with a pull-down bed, a bed that folds up into the wall and it has a mirror on the under side of it. Then he moved into an apartment similar to that occupied by a character named Joe Brody in *The Big Sleep*. It may have been the same apartment, he may have got it cheap because a murder had

[272]

taken place in it. I think, but I'm not sure, that this apartment is on the fourth floor. It contains a living room which you enter directly from the hallway, and opposite are French windows opening on an ornamental balcony, which is just something to look at, certainly not anything to sit out on. Against the right-hand wall as you stand in the doorway is a davenport. In the left-hand wall, nearest to the hallway of the apartment house, there is a door that leads to an interior hall. Beyond that, against the left-hand wall, there is this oak drop leaf desk, an easy chair, etc; beyond that, an archway entrance to the dinette and kitchen. The dinette, as known in American apartment houses or at any rate in California apartment houses, is simply a space divided off from the kitchen proper by an archway or a built-in china closet. It would be very small, and the kitchen would also be very small. As you enter the hallway from the living room (the interior hallway) you would come on your right to the bathroom door and continuing straight on you would come to the bedroom. The bedroom would contain a walk-in closet. The bathroom in a building of this type would contain a shower in the tub and a shower curtain. None of the rooms is very large. The rent of the apartment, furnished, would have been about sixty dollars a month when Marlowe moved into it. God knows what it would be now. I shudder to think. I should guess not less than ninety dollars a month, probably more.

As to Marlowe's office, I'll have to take another look at it sometime to refresh my memory. It seems to me it's on the sixth floor in a building which faces north, and that his office window faces east. But I'm not certain about this. As you say, there is a reception room which is a half-office, perhaps half the space of a corner office, converted into two reception rooms with separate entrances and communicating doors right and left respectively. Marlowe has a private office which communicates with his reception room, and there is a connection which causes a buzzer to ring in his private office when the door of the reception room is opened. But this buzzer can be switched off by a toggle switch. He has not, and never has had, a secretary. He could very easily subscribe to a telephone answering service, but I don't recall mentioning that anywhere. And I do not recall that his desk has a glass top, but I may have said so. The office bottle is kept in the filing drawer of the desk,—a drawer, standard in American office desks (perhaps also in England) which is the depth of two ordinary drawers, and is intended to contain file folders, but very seldom does, since most people keep their file folders in filing cases. It seems to me that some of these details flit about a good deal. His guns have also been rather various. He started out with a German Luger automatic pistol. He seems to have had Colt automatics of various calibers, but not larger than .38, and when last I heard he has a Smith & Wesson .38 special, probably with a four-inch barrel. This is a very powerful gun, although not the most powerful made, and has the advantage over an automatic of using a lead cartridge. It will not jam or discharge accidentally, even if dropped on a hard surface, and is probably just as effective a weapon at short range as a .45 caliber automatic. It would be better with a six-inch barrel, but that would make it much more awkward to carry. Even a four-inch barrel is not too convenient, and the detective branch of the police usually carries a gun with only a two and a half-inch barrel. This is about all I have for you now, but if there is anything else you want to know, please write to me again. The trouble is, you really seem to know a good deal more about Philip Marlowe than I do, and perhaps I shall have to ask you questions instead of your asking me.

With kindest regards,

Yours ever,

## TO JUANITA MESSICK

[Easter week-end 1951]

Memo to J.M.

Office will be closed Thursday and Friday. On Friday you should go to church for three hours. On Thursday you will have to be guided by your conscience, if any. Leona[1] won't be here from Wednesday night until the following Monday but she doesn't get paid this time. Some damn nonsense about the child getting married. I suppose the nuns have told her she is to become the bride of Christ. Do Catholics get confirmed at the age of 8? I thought you had to

---

·1.  Leona was the maid.

have some idea what it was all about. I was confirmed by the Bishop of Worcester. He had a beard.

RC

## TO JUANITA MESSICK

n.d. [1951]

This is a completely useless uncommercial story but I had fun writing it and you may as well copy it off and I'll annoy Carl Brandt with it.[1] It might make the *New Yorker* or one of the monthlies.

I estimate it runs about 6000 words. Make three carbons, please.

RC

## TO SOL SIEGEL

April 27, 1951

Dear Sol:

•          •          •

I'd like to submit a couple of thoughts to you, although they are probably both present in your mind already. The first is that there are basically two kinds of screen writers that the industry can use (leaving out the hacks). There are the adept technicians, who know how to work with the medium and how to subordinate themselves to the use of the camera and the actors by the director. Their work is polished, effective, and entirely anonymous. Nothing they do bears any stamp of individuality. Then there is the writer whose personal touch must be allowed to come through, because his personal touch is what makes him a writer. Obviously a writer of this kind should never

1. "A Couple of Writers."

work for a director like Hitchock, because there must be nothing in a Hitchcock picture which Hitchcock himself might not have written. It is not merely a question of how Hitchcock uses his camera and his actors; the point is that there must be nothing in his pictures which is outside of his range. Eventually there will be a type of director who realizes that what is said and how it is said is more important than shooting it upside down through a glass of champagne.

The second thought I would like to express is that the public is getting increasingly tired of the kind of film which explores the technical resources of the medium with relentless cleverness, but contains nothing which could be acted out on a bare stage and still make its effect. There was a time when all the tricks were interesting in themselves, just as there was a time when the mere fact of movement was fascinating. The chase through the sewers or up the steel girders of a bridge or in the depths of Boulder Dam or what have you, all this is getting old hat. What remains is characters and their relationships to one another and what they have to say. And you will never get this from the technicians. There is a fade in *Sunset Boulevard* where the camera moves in close on a window, and then a hand reaches up and pulls the blind down over the window and the blind fills the screen and is dark, and that is the fade out. To the people in the business that's a clever fade. To the public it means absolutely nothing. What they want to know is what's going to happen next. And the only camera angle they care a nickel about is that which lets them see what's going on without fuss or calling attention to itself. Writers—whatever they cost, however much they are overpaid—are still the cheapest element in picture making. But of course it is not the business of story editors to admit that.

Best of luck and kindest regards.

# TO SOMERSET MAUGHAM

6005 Camino de la Costa
La Jolla, California
May 4, 1951

Dear Somerset Maugham:

[276]

Thank you for returning the material about detective fiction. By all means use any quotes from my stuff you find useful. But I think most of it has already been quoted all over the place.

Priestley was in La Jolla a couple of months ago, and was kind enough to tell me that I wrote well and that I should write a straight novel. Of course I have heard this before in other connections. If you write well, you should not be writing a mystery. Mysteries should only be written by people who can't write. I regard this as vicious propaganda from the Edmund Wilson crowd. Obviously you can't expect detective fiction to be anything but sub-literary, to use Edmund Wilson's word, if you insist on weeding out from that field anyone who shows any pretensions to skill or imagination in the use of words.

With kindest regards,

Yours,

Raymond Chandler

## TO HAMISH HAMILTON

6005 Camino de la Costa
La Jolla, California
May 9, 1951

Dear Jamie:

.        .        .        '

I suppose you have been hearing a lot about the big fuss over MacArthur.[1] In some ways he reminds me of a story I used to hear in Hollywood about Cecil B. DeMille. It seems that DeMille died and went up to heaven and St. Peter met him at the gates with a beaming smile and outstretched hand. "I can't tell you how glad we are to see you up here, Mr. DeMille," said St. Peter. "Your organizing ability has been admired by us for a very long time, and I think you

1. General MacArthur had recently been relieved of his Korean War command by President Truman.

will find heaven just the field your talents can do the most with. We really do need a bit of reorganizing after all this time." "Well, I'll be delighted," DeMille says to St. Peter, "and I'll get to work right away. You can expect a detailed report from me within a few weeks. I'm a very fast worker when I'm interested, but I warn you I'm also very meticulous." "Just what we want," says St. Peter. So DeMille goes to work and about six weeks later he seeks out St. Peter. He is carrying under his arm, neatly bound in a blue cover, a thorough analysis of conditions in heaven and a blueprint of a proposed reorganization. St. Peter is delighted, takes the report and promises to read it that very night. The next morning he seeks DeMille out. "This is wonderful, Mr. DeMille. Wonderful," he says enthusiastically. "Such a gift for analysis. Such clear thinking. And such a wonderful talent for design." DeMille is very pleased. St. Peter adds in a slightly altered voice, "But there's just one small thing, Mr. DeMille, just one small thing. I don't really think God is going to like being vice-president."

. . .

Yours ever,

Ray

## TO H. R. HARWOOD[1]

July 2, 1951

Dear Mr. Harwood:

I could not advise any man either to become a writer or not to become one. Contrary to popular belief, it is a very arduous profession and only a small fraction of those who attempt it ever succeed in making any kind of a decent income. The decline of the pulp magazines makes it more difficult for beginners even than it used to be, and it was never anything but difficult. I gather, however, that your special circumstances are such that this writing trade is

1. A correspondent from Missouri.

[278]

physically within your means, and I am hoping that you do not have to make a living out of writing at least for a long time to come, since the chances that you will are very, very slight. You say you are arranging "for immediate schooling in the fundamental principles of the narrative technique that any beginner should have." Let me warn you out of such experience as I have that any writer who cannot teach himself cannot be taught by others, and apart from the extension courses of reputable universities, I take a very dim view of writing instruction in general, above all the sort that is advertised in the so-called writers' magazines. They will teach you nothing that you cannot find out by studying and analyzing the published work of other writers. Analyze and imitate; no other school is necessary. I admit that criticism from others is helpful and sometimes even necessary, but when you have to pay for it, it is usually suspect. Since you are a grown man, you ought to be able to figure out why.

As to methods of plotting and plot outlines, I am afraid I cannot help you at all, since I have never plotted anything on paper. I do my plotting in my head as I go along, and usually I do it wrong and have to do it all over again. I know there are writers who plot their stories in great detail before they begin to write them, but I am not one of that group. With me plots are not made; they grow. And if they refuse to grow, you throw the stuff away and start over again. Perhaps you will get more helpful advice from someone who works for a blueprint. I hope so.

Yours sincerely,

# TO CHARLES MORTON

6005 Camino de la Costa
La Jolla, California
July 5, 1951

Dear Charlie:

.        .        .

Now as to this business of pre-publication plugs on book

[279]

jackets, where do you get this bittersweet stuff? I wasn't writing to you but to a man named Dana at Lippincott's.[1] Evidently somebody with an important name dropped dead or got jailed for mopery at the last moment, so he had to root around in the weeds for a substitute; so I just had a little fun with him, meaning no harm to anyone. Secretly of course I was delighted that he hit me when I didn't have time to think, because I hate the whole lousy racket. The proper time to praise a writer is after his book has been published, and the proper place to praise him is in something else that is published. You must be well aware that there is practically a stable of puff merchants back in your territory who will go on record over practically anything including the World Almanac, provided they get their names featured. A few names occur with such monotonous regularity that only the fact of their known success as writers keeps one from thinking this is the way they earn their groceries. As a matter of fact I know that payment is sometimes made, because my Hollywood agent once called me up from New York and carefully propositioned me on the subject. My personal reaction to complimentary remarks on dust jackets, other than those quoted from reviews, is to refuse to have anything to do with the book enclosed in the jacket. But that's only personal, and of course I don't claim to be the most amiable character in the world. Over in England they carry this quote business, though not pre-publication so much, to the point where it is absolutely meaningless. The currency of praise has been so depreciated that there is nothing to say about a really good book. It has all been said already about the second, third, and fourth rate stuff which appears, circulates briefly, and then is forgotten. Anyhow if some thing comes along that you feel a sort of moral compulsion to praise to all the world if you have the opportunity, are you going to do it through the medium of a promotion department? I should hope to kiss a duck you're not.

.        .        .

Yours always,

Ray

1.  Chandler had written Morton's publisher a somewhat begrudging blurb for his latest book.

# TO LEROY WRIGHT

6005 Camino de la Costa
La Jolla, California
July 6, 1951

Dear Leroy:

Referring again to the 1945 income tax refund claim recently disallowed, I have dug up some 1939 diary entries which have a bearing on the case. I have no good explanation as to why I did not dig them up before, except that I seem somehow to have derived the impression that since the book *The Lady in the Lake* was published in 1943, we were only concerned with the two years prior to that, that is to say an attempt to establish that during the three years ending with 1943 I was working on the book.

.　　　　　.　　　　　.

Now the novel *The Lady in the Lake* was based on two novelettes called "Bay City Blues," published in June, 1938, and *The Lady in the Lake*, published January 1939. But in order to demonstrate method, I think it might be necessary to go beyond this. *The Big Sleep* was written in the spring of 1938 and was based on two novelettes called "Killer in the Rain," published January, 1935, and "The Curtain," published September, 1936. Included in this book also was a fairly long sequence taken from a novelette called "The Man who Liked Dogs," published March, 1936. *Farewell, My Lovely* was based on two novelettes called "Try the Girl," published January, 1937, and "Mandarin's Jade," published November, 1937. In the early part of 1939, that is to say up to April 12, I seem except for fumbling around with plots to have been writing novelettes and short stories. There is evidence of about four of them, not involved in this case, being written or partly written in that time. On April 12 I have an entry "Page 10—'The Girl from Brunette's'" with a question mark after it. This is evidently *Farewell, My Lovely*, because almost immediately the title was changed to "The Girl from Florian's" on April 18, when I'd reached page 52. Florian's is the Negro dive on Central Avenue involved in the beginning of the book. There is on March 31 an entry called "Page 14—'Law is Where You Buy It.'"

That apparently died right there and frankly I'm not sure what it refers to, since later in the year in the diary there is some evidence that I switched the titles around and applied this particular title to more than one book, although the idea of the title evidently derives from the story "Bay City Blues." That is a story which happens in a town so corrupt from the law enforcement point of view that the law is where you buy it and what you pay for it. To resume, on April 23 I am at page 100 with the notation "First lap—'The Girl From Florian's.'" On April 29 I am at page 127 and there is a reference to a girl named Anne Riordan who appears as a character in *Farewell, My Lovely*. This sort of thing goes on intermittently to May 22, when I'm at page 233, with a notation, "This story is a flop. It smells to high heaven. Think I'll have to scrap it and try something new." After that for several days I seem to have been toying with a story called "Tony Gets Out." I think this eventually developed into the short story called "I'll Be Waiting." On May 29 there is a notation "Tomorrow get out draft of 'The Girl From Florian's.'" On May 30 I evidently did this because I am checking the draft up to page 87, but that's as far as it goes. I didn't like it. Now come the entries, although this foregoing explanation is going to be necessary later on. On June 1, "Page 4—'Murder Is a Nuisance.'" This in itself means nothing except there is a mention of a character named Adrian Fromsett who is a character in *The Lady in the Lake* book and nowhere else. Next day, June 2, I'm at page 10 and I'm calling it *The Lady in the Lake*. This apparently died on me, because on June 5 I wrote 18 pages of a novelette called "Goldfish," but immediately dropped that for the time being. There are many notations that show that I didn't feel well. On June 12 I'm up to page 30; June 13, page 50; June 14, Page 60, and here is a notation "Leave photo of Fromsett," which seems to indicate what I am writing; June 15, page 71; June 16, page 127; June 17, page 148; June 18, page 169; June 19, page 191, and the damned thing is now called "The Golden Anklet." Now this ties it clearly to *The Lady in the Lake* because on the chapter headings of *The Lady in the Lake* novelette, inserted by the magazine editor, (I never used chapter headings myself) was "The Golden Anklet," and a golden anklet does figure in the story. June 20 I am at page 203, I'm now calling it "Deep and Dark Waters." That title is self explanatory. On June 28 I'm up to page

337. On June 29 there is this notation, "Tragic realization that there is another dead cat under the house. More than three-quarters done and no good." This certainly refers to the draft of *The Lady in the Lake* by whatever provisional title I might happen to have been calling it at the time. Now I write on half sheets of paper, turned endwise, and they figure out about six to a thousand words. Therefore 337 of these pages would make about 55,000 words of rough script, which is a very substantial hunk even though all done within a month.

.        .        .

The year 1940, partly from reasons of health and still more from the state of the world, seems to have contained an abnormal amount of vacillation. By the end of November I had made less real progress than I sometimes would make in a week. I also puttered with at least three other stories, only one of which was ever finished. The end of the year finds me having written 157 pages of the novelette "No Crime in the Mountains." I bring all these matters up just to show that I never worked on just one thing at a time for very long. *But* eventually somehow I would finish practically all these projects, no matter how long it took nor how many things I did in the meantime.

Mostly, but not without interruption, I worked on *The Lady in the Lake* for the rest of that year 1942, but not until April 4, 1943, is there any indication that I finished it. From the foregoing it is clear that from 1929, specifically the month of June, to April, 1943, I had this story in hand and worked on it intermittently, except possibly in 1940. It may be that I did no work on it in 1940. However, I certainly did do work on it in 1939, 1941, 1942, and 1943, and it seems almost certain that during the year 1940 I at least took it out and looked at it and thought about it. On the evidence of these entries and taking into account the method of work—a very bad method one must admit—although in my case it has proved successful—the job of writing the book *The Lady in the Lake* was definitely in hand from 1939 to 1943, that a very substantial amount of writing was done on it as early as 1939 (excluding the novelettes entirely), and that insofar

[283]

as the denial of the refund claim was based on lack of proof of facts, this deficiency can now be repaired.

. . .

Yours very truly,

Ray

## TO FREDERIC DANNAY

July 10, 1951

Dear Frederic Dannay:

No, I would not care to nominate the ten best living detective-story writers. I don't mind sticking my neck out, but the point is, one has to agree on a few fundamentals before one starts picking lists of ten bests. For instance, does the category include writers of suspense stories in which there is little mystery, or none at all? If it does not, you eliminate some of the best performers, such as Elisabeth Sanxay Holding, certainly one of my favorites. And if it does, why call them detective stories? Charlotte Armstrong's *Mischief* contains no puzzle element whatever. On the other hand, some puzzle merchants, the people who have timetables and ground plans and pay the most meticulous attention to details, can't write a lick. There is a saying that a good plot will make a good detective story, but I personally question whether you can have a good plot if you can't create any believable characters or situations. My list, if I made it, would probably leave out some of those names which will inevitably appear on your ten best list. I just don't think they're any good, because by my standards they can't write. And it may also happen that single book, such as *The 31st of February* by Julian Symons, or *Walk the Dark Streets* by William Krasner, or the aforesaid *Mischief*, or *Mr. Bowling Buys a Newspaper* by Donald Henderson, will immediately put the writer above and beyond a whole host of writers who have written twenty or thirty books and are extremely well known and

[284]

successful, and from a literary point of view entirely negligible. I don't particularly care for the hard-boiled babies, because most of them are traveling on borrowed gas, and I don't think you have any right to do that unless you can travel a little farther than the man from whom you borrowed the gas. I don't care about the had-I-but-known girls, because I don't care whether dear little Lucille gets her neck stretched or not. But that's not quite honest. If I had a choice, I'd prefer that she did get it stretched. I don't care for the week-end chichi either here or in England. I don't seem to care who conked Sir Mortimer with the poker, nor why, nor who set the grandfather's clock twenty minutes slow. How did Frank Fustian come to be eating fly agaric in the locked room? I couldn't care less. It isn't that I don't like puzzles, because I like, for example, Austin Freeman. I like him very much. There is probably not one of his books that I haven't read at least twice, yet he bores a lot of people stiff. I even like his Victorian love scenes. And I have liked some very pedestrian stories, because they were unpretentious and because their mysteries were rooted in hard facts and not in false motivations cooked up for the purpose of mystifying a reader. I suppose the attraction of the pedestrian books is their documentary quality and this, if at all authentic, is pretty rare, and any attempt to dish it up with chichi and glamour turns my stomach immediately. I think you are up against a difficult problem, because I think we may take it as granted that a mystery fan would rather read a bad mystery than none at all. You are bound to give some weight to volume of production, and strictly speaking volume of production means absolutely nothing. A writer discloses himself on a single page, sometimes in a single paragraph. An un-writer may fill a whole shelf, he may achieve fame of a sort and fortune of a sort, he may occasionally concoct a plot which will make him seem to be a little better than he really is, but in the end he fades away and is nothing. All good writers have a touch of magic. And unless we are to agree with Edmund Wilson that detective fiction is on the sub-literary level, and I personally do not agree with this, we demand that touch of magic; at least I do, although I am well aware that the public does not.

Yours very truly,

# TO JOSEPH HINES[1]

August 13, 1951

Dear Mr. Hines:

Once in awhile I get a special delivery letter. Sometimes they are put into my box, since that is my official address, and sometimes they are delivered to the house. Whoever does this lately seems to have developed a habit of arriving at 7:30 in the morning and trying to batter the front door down, thus arousing my wife from sleep which she badly needs. I don't criticize the man at all, since he is probably impelled by a strong sense of duty. But may I, in all courtesy and friendliness, point out: first, that a special delivery letter is hardly that urgent, as anything really urgent would come by wire or telephone; and second, that there is a mail slot in the side door of our house at ground level, and that simply dropping the letter in that slot would be my idea of a beautiful job accomplished with tact and consideration. If this should prove impossible to accomplish or should be in violation of any postoffice rule, then may I request that special delivery mail be deposited in my box, No. 128, just like any other first-class mail. In my case at least it does not really require the red light and siren treatment. When this house was built the mail slot was put in the side door deliberately so that the mail man would not have to climb any steps. Usually whoever delivers special delivery mail does not know this, so he climbs to the front door, finds no mail slot and is thereby stung to fury.

Yours very sincerely,

# TO S. J. PERELMAN

September 4, 1951

Dear Sid:

If you are still interested in Rancho Santa Fe and haven't forgotten all about it by this time, there is no objection there to your keeping tropical birds and a few tropical animals, provided you keep them off the main street and out of the dining room at the

---

1. Superintendent of the US. Post Office in La Jolla.

Rancho Santa Fe Inn. Rancho Santa Fe is part of the San Dieguito high school district, the school being located back of Encinitas, which you passed on the Coast Highway not very far north of Del Mar. And there is a school bus from Rancho Santa Fe. I don't know anything about the scholastic standing of this school, if any. I have heard the California high schools range from putrid to rotten, and I have one relative, fortunately distant, who graduated from the Fairfax high school in Los Angeles while still struggling with the alphabet. As to the La Jolla schools, which might be representative of this part of the state, the only authentic comment I have heard is from a party living across the street from my sister-in-law. This party has four children and is thinking of moving back to Kansas where there is a possibility of their being educated. It seems that they all get "A's" out here, although they know nothing and do no work. She regards this as very suspicious, inasmuch as before coming to California they did some work and got nowhere near any "A's" at all. I don't know much about this personally, and I resent the suggestion that we who live in California are cultural imbeciles.

.        .        .

    I am still reading your brutal account of your family's efforts to keep you from being certified as a lunatic, and by God there are times when you don't speak of them at all nicely. Needless to say I enjoyed seeing you tremendously, although I realize that the gibbons will always come first.

                                                    Yours ever,


## TO HAMISH HAMILTON

                                    6005 Camino de la Costa
                                    La Jolla, California
                                    September 19, 1951

Dear Jamie:

.        .        .

    I don't know if you have ever been to a dude ranch. I had

[287]

never been to one before. This one is called the Alisal, which in Spanish means a grove of sycamores, according to the publicity. It is a small part of a 10,500 acre cattle ranch, which is one of the few intact Spanish land grants of California and was originally made to the Carrillo family. It has a lovely climate, at least at this time of year. It is situated in an inland valley, the Santa Ynez valley just north of Santa Barbara, and is almost as dry as a desert, very hot in the daytime, very cool in the mornings, in the evenings and at night. I should think it must be pretty awful in the summer. We found the place both very amusing and intensely boring, expensive, badly run but nicely laid out with the usual swimming pool, tennis courts, etc. The kind of place where the people who work in the office wear riding boots, where the lady guests appear for breakfast in levis riveted with copper, for lunch in jodhpurs with gaudy shirts and scarfs and in the evening either in cocktail gowns or in more jodhpurs and more gaudy shirts and scarfs. The ideal scarf seems to be very narrow, not much wider than a boot lace, and run through a ring in front and then hangs down one side of the shirt. I didn't ask why; I didn't get to know anybody well enough. The men also wear gaudy shirts, which they change constantly for other patterns, all except the real horsemen, who wear rather heavy wool or nylon and wool shirts with long sleeves, yoked in the back, the kind of thing that can only be bought in a horsy town. I imagine the place is a lot of fun for the right sort of people, the kind who go riding in the morning, swimming or tennising in the afternoon, then have two or three drinks at the bar, and by the time they arrive for dinner are able to be quite enthusiastic over the rather inferior and much too greasy cooking. For us who were rather tired and out of sorts and consequently much too finicky, the place was a trial. But it was fun to see a whole army of quail strolling unconcernedly past the bungalows in the evening and to see birds that looked like jackdaws, which we never see anywhere else, not even in the mountains. While I was there I read three of the Hornblower novels by C. S. Forester, bound in one large pocketsize book. I had never read any of his stuff before and I don't think I could read it here at home. The detail of the handling of the ships, the maneuvers for battle and all that sort of thing seems to me quite fascinating and wonderfully exact. I don't suppose I had ever before realized the immense amount of skill that goes into the handling of a sailing ship. Apart from that the stuff is appallingly dull to my mind. The emotions are about on the level with G. A. Henty.[1] He has no conception of character, and I say this with the full knowledge that Captain Horatio Hornblower is probably thought to be quite an achievement in character drawing. To me he is nothing of the sort. Except for his seamanship Forester never gets above the level of slick magazine writing, which I have always detested. But I know Forester must be a publisher's delight, and I may be a little unfair to him, even in a literary sense. If so, it was probably because I had just read Popski's *Private Army*.[2]

I suppose you have by now seen the *New Yorker's* profile of your boy, John Dickson Carr. They seem to have done him rather well, at least without condescension, very much in the way in which they handled Rex Stout some time ago. He sounds like a fellow for whom one could have a certain remote admiration without much affection. One sentence I found illuminating. After describing his fondness for the macabre and his ingenuity in plot making, the writer said in effect, I can't quote the exact words, "He hates the actual writing." This explains to me in a flash why I can't read the man, because a writer who hates the acutal writing is as impossible as a lawyer who hates the law, or a doctor who hates medicine. Plotting may be a bore even if you are good at it. At least it is something that has to be done so that you can get on with the real business. But a writer who hates the actual writing, who gets no joy out of the creation of magic by words, to me is simply not a writer at all. The actual writing is what you live for. The rest is something you have to get through in order to arrive at the point. How can you hate the actual writing? What is there to hate about it? You might as well say that a man likes to chop wood or clean house and hates the sunshine or the night breeze or the nodding of flowers or the dew on the grass or the songs of birds. How can you hate the magic which makes of a paragraph or a sentence or a line of dialogue or a description something in the nature of a new creation? Well, apparently you

1. British author (1832–1902) known for boys' adventure tales.
2. Popski is a pseudonym of Vladimir Peniakoff.

can and be successful in spite of it. But it certainly depresses me to
feel that this is possible.

.         .         .

With all my best,

Yours ever,

Ray

## TO JAMES SANDOE

6005 Camino de la Costa
La Jolla, California
September 25, 1951

Dear Sandoe:

.         .         .

I am glad to hear that you are going back to reviewing again,
although I don't exactly envy you the job of reading the stuff. I
guess my tastes must be changing because I find it very difficult to get
any fun out of most of them. I have neither your tolerance nor your
catholicity of taste. If the stuff doesn't vibrate, the hell with it. I don't
care how ingenious the plot is, it seems to me to mean nothing
unless the prose has that glimmer of magic. Well, you can't often
expect that. Why should you? And frankly the general run of serious
fiction leaves me just as flat, if not flatter. Since I have now arrived at
an age where I should normally be a laudator temporis acti, and in
fact in most things I am, I am pleased to declare that this does not
apply to mystery stories. The good ones are far better than they
ever were. They have more atmosphere, more character, more style,
more wit, more color, more sense of detail, more background. But
the good ones are extremely rare. Many is the time I've come home
from the rental library with three or four books and returned them all
unread. You are going to have to help me out if you find anything
good. If you can't, no one can. Anyhow this is one metier in which
the so-called giants of the past look pretty puny to me, and not only

the giants of the remoter past but the giants of the immediate past. Not long ago I made an effort to reread Dorothy Sayers's *Gaudy Night*. God, what sycophantic drivel. A whole clutch of lady dons at an Oxford college all in a flutter to know about Lord Peter Wimsey and to know about the plot of Harriett Vane's latest mystery story. How silly can you get? And yet this is far from being a silly woman.

With kindest regards,

Yours ever,

Ray

## TO HAMISH HAMILTON

6005 Camino de la Costa
La Jolla, California
October 5th. 1951

Dear Jamie:

. . .

I do hope to have a book in 1952, I hope very hard. But dammit I have a great deal of trouble getting on with it. The old zest is not there. I am worn down by worry over my wife, and that is why I am writing this myself and keeping no copy. We have a big house, rather, hard to take care of, and the help situation is damn near hopeless. For months after we lost our last cook, Cissy wore herself out trying to get someone, to endure what we got, to give up and start again. We cannot live here without help. Cissy can do very very little, she has lost a lot of ground in the last two years. She is a superb cook herself and we are both pretty much overfastidious, but we can't help it. I have thought that the sensible thing might be to get a small house and do for ourselves, but I'm afraid she is no longer capable even of that. When I get into work I am already tired and dispirited. I wake in the night with dreadful thoughts. Cissy has a constant cough which can only be kept down by drugs and the drugs destroy her vitality. It is not TB nor is it anything cancerous, but

I am afraid it is chronic and may get worse instead of better. She has no strength and being of a buoyant disposition and a hard fighter, she fights herself to the point of exhaustion. I dread, and I am sure she does, although we try not to talk about it, a slow decline into invalidism. And what happens then I frankly do not know. There are people who enjoy being invalids, being unable to do anything, but not she. She hates hospitals, she hates nurses, and she does not greatly love doctors. In bad moods, which are not too infrequent, I feel the icy touch of despair. It is no mood in which to produce writing with any lift and vitality.

You say nice things about what I write and I know you mean them, but I have never felt important as a writer. In every generation there are incomplete writers, people who never seem to get much of themselves down on paper, men whose accomplishment seems always rather incidental. Often, but not always, they have begun too late and have an overdeveloped critical sense. Sometimes they just lack the necessary ruthlessness and think other people's lives as important as their own, other people's happiness more essential than the expression of their own personalities, if any. I guess maybe I belong in there. I have enough material success to see through it, and not enough sense of destiny to feel that what I do matters a great deal.

Don't think I worry about money, because I don't. There are always ways to make money if you really need it. I rather envy people who think art and literature worth any sacrifice, but I don't seem to feel that way. My salute to posterity is a thumb to the end of the nose and the fingers outspread. Publishers read too many critics, in the course of business, naturally. And just who are the critics after all? People of small accomplishment, mostly, whose dignity in life depends on the perpetuating of a set of artificial values conceived by other critics who were also people of small accomplishment. My standards are too high for me to admire the successful hacks very much, and too unorthodox for me to care what the pundits say. Also, I have blind spots. I admit it. I think your Nancy Mitford is probably a charming and clever woman but the stuff means nothing to me. The wit is not real, the satire is not of the vintage year, the whole performance tries to be something it is not capable of being. An absolutely trivial writer, but you don't agree and you shouldn't. This is strange (that I feel that way) because as a rule I admire the good second-raters, like Marquand and Irwin Shaw and Herman Wouk, etc.

[292]

I like to read them and *while* I read them they seem very good. It is only afterwards that the quality fades. Same for Nicholas Montserrat. Or Priestley. Essentially one good chunk of Flaubert or Hemingway at their best is worth the whole pack of them. I had almost said Faulkner, but I think he is overrated. Well, all this matters nothing, except that a writer to be happy should be a good second-rater, not a starved genius like Laforgue. Not a sad lonely man like Heine, not a lunatic like Dostoevski. He should definitely not be a mystery writer with a touch of magic and a bad feeling about plots.

We still hope for "Europe in the spring," but is it more than hope now? Anyhow, Churchill will be in and I hope he doesn't make an ass of himself. These great men can be awfully silly in their dotage. It doesn't show in the rest of us. Nobody is looking.

I look upon you as a dear friend, Jamie. I am sorry to be such a depressing bore.

Ray


## TO MR. INGLIS

[October 1951]

Dear Mr. Inglis:

I practically always answer letters eventually, but in your case I'm afraid the eventually is the key word. Anyhow thank you for yours of July 12th and for taking the trouble to cover so much paper at a time when you had a stiff wrist.

I'm afraid I can't give you much of an argument about your concept of what you call maturity, just as I cannot recall having used the expression or in fact the idea behind the expression in that essay of mine to which you refer. It may be that your "advanced psychology student" friend was pulling your leg a little, or it may be that the advanced psychology itself has got him into a state of confusion in which he will probably remain for the rest of his life. We seem to be somewhat over supplied with psychologists nowadays, but I suppose that is natural enough, since their jargon, tiresome as it is to me personally, seems to have the same attraction for muddled minds that theological hair-splitting had for people of a former age. I don't think my friend Philip Marlowe is very much concerned about whether or no he has a mature mind. I will admit to an equal lack of concern about myself. But it is very natural that you, being what you term a "shabby twenty-three," and having had apparently a fairly hard time of it should be more concerned than I am with what the boys in their sweet lingo call the social orientation of the individual. Don't take it too hard. Very few people are capable of straight thinking on any subject. If being in revolt against a corrupt society constitutes being immature, then Philip Marlowe is extremely immature. If seeing dirt where there is dirt constitutes an inadequate social adjustment, then Philip Marlowe has an inadequate social adjustment. Of course Marlowe is a failure and he knows it. He is a failure because he hasn't any money. A man who without physical handicaps cannot make a decent living is always a failure and usually a moral failure. But a lot of very good men have been failures because their particular talents did not suit their time and place. In the long run I guess we are all failures or we wouldn't have the kind of world we have. But you must remember that Marlowe is not a real person. He is a creature of fantasy. He is in a false position because I have put him there. In real life a man of his type would no more be a private detective than he would be a university don. Your private detective in real life is usually either an ex-policeman with a lot of hard practical experience and the brains of a turtle or else a shabby little hack who runs around trying to find out where people have moved to. It is obvious that the more highly organized police work becomes, the leaner are the pickings left for the private operator. I think I resent your suggestion that Philip Marlowe has contempt for other people's physical weakness. I don't know where you get the idea, and I don't think it's so. I am also a little tired of the numerous suggestions that have been made that he is always full of whiskey. The only point I can see in justification of that is that when he wants a drink he takes it openly and doesn't hesitate to remark on it. I don't know how it is in your part of the country, but compared with the country-club set in my part of the country he is as sober as a deacon. As for your questions, and I hope you kept a copy of them, the answer to Number One is: Yes. I wanted to be a barrister, but I didn't have enough money. The answer to Two is: So far as I know the cops read my stories and don't resent them in the least. Question Three: My comments on the film production of my work are that it was probably as good as could be expected. My stories are about a man, and no one can satisfactorily recreate another man's character. I worked on *The Lady in the Lake* myself, although I refused screen credit because I didn't like the final script, but curiously enough I found that in writing the screen play I was almost entirely indifferent to the story I was supposed to be working from, and it was the producer of the picture who kept telling me, and not me him, "Look, stick to the book a little more." Question Four: Practically all the screen work I've done has been for other films. I always use my own name, but you don't always get your name on the picture and you don't always want your name on the picture. I have never been in police business properly speaking, although at one time I worked with a district attorney's investigator on an embezzlement case. It is true that Dashiell Hammett was once a Pinkerton agent, and I certainly owe a good deal to him, which I have admitted very publicly. Yes, I have met him, but I can't say that I'm a friend of his. I only met him once. He had at that time a shocking capacity for liquor, which I am frank to say I envied as I was never much of a drinker myself. Question Eight: You are not annoying me or I would not be writing to you.

Yours very sincerely,

## TO CARL BRANDT

6005 Camino de la Costa
La Jolla, California
October 27 1951

Dear Carl:

.      .      .

I am having a hard time with the book.[1] Have enough paper

---

1. *The Long Goodbye*.

[295]

written to make it complete, but must do all over again. I just didn't
know where I was going and when I got there I saw that I had come
to the wrong place. That's the hell of being the kind of writer who
cannot plan anything, but has to make it up as he goes along and then
try to make sense out of it. If you gave me the best plot in the world
all worked out I could not write it. It would be dead for me. Perhaps
a year later I might tackle it, but no sooner.

All the best to you.

Ray

# TO JAMES SANDOE

6005 Camino de la Costa
La Jolla, California
October 31, 1951

Dear Sandoe:

I gather that you didn't think much of the Bingo story, and
you could be right.[1] But I'm not going to allow myself to worry
about it. I think possibly it was a little too grim for a fantastic story
and a little too fantastic for a grim story. But when you say why
in hell would Joe bother, I don't get the point. Why wouldn't he?
Anyhow I had fun writing the story, although it didn't turn out
quite the way I expected. I started out to do a burlesque on the locked
room mystery and somewhere along the line I lost interest in the
burlesque angle and became preoccupied with the thought that a
miracle is always a trap. As you know, good fantastic stories are
extremely rare, and they are rare for a rather obvious reason, that in
them it is almost impossible to turn the corner. Once you have
exposed the situation, you have nowhere to go.

1. "Professor Bingo's Snuff."

[296]

I don't deny the mystery writer the privilege of making his detective any sort of a person he wants to make him—a poet, philosopher, student of ceramics or Egyptology, or a master of all the sciences like Dr. Thorndike. What I don't seem to cotton to is the affectation of gentility which does not belong to the job and which is in effect a subconscious expression of snobbery, the kind of thing that reached its high-water mark in Dorothy Sayers. Perhaps the trouble is that I'm an English Public School man myself and knew these birds inside out. And the only kind of Public School man who could make a real detective would be the Public School man in revolt, like George Orwell. But if English people and others like this sort of thing, there is no reason why they shouldn't have it.

Dale Warren, one of Houghton Mifflin's editors, writes me that you are doing a fine job for the *Herald Tribune*. And how are all your cats? We have a new black Persian who looks exactly like our last one, so exactly that we have to call him by the same name, Taki. He is going to be a very large fellow I think when he gets his full growth, as he weighs eight pounds at seven months. I had a Siamese kitten for awhile, but he chewed everything to pieces and was so much trouble to handle that I had to give him back to the breeder. I felt rather bad about it, because he was an affectionate little devil and full of life. But he chewed up blankets, chewed up my clothes, and he would have chewed up all the furniture. We just couldn't let him run loose, and a cat who can't run loose in our house has no business in it. We never let them run loose in the street, but in the house they own everything.

Yours ever,

R.C.

## TO DALE WARREN

6005 Camino de la Costa
La Jolla, California
November 7, 1951

Dear Dale:
You asked me how anyone can survive Hollywood? Well, I

must say that I personally had a lot of fun there. But how long you can survive depends a great deal on what sort of people you get to work with. You meet a lot of bastards, but they usually have some saving grace. If you are a writer, most of your work is wasted it is true. And when it isn't, somebody else grabs most of the credit. A writer who can get teamed up with a director or producer who will give him a square deal, a really square deal, can get a lot of satisfaction out of his work. Unfortunately that doesn't happen too often. A really creative writer ought to become a director, which means that in addition to being creative he must also be very tough physically and morally. Otherwise by the time he has been kicked around enough to have learned to write a script that can be shot, that is camera-wise and not just writing, he has probably lost all his bounce. If you go to Hollywood just to make money, you have to be pretty cynical about it and not care too much what you do. And if you really believe in the art of the film, it's a long term job and you ought to forget all about any other kind of writing. A preoccupation with words for their own sake is fatal to good film making. It's not what films are for. It's not my cup of tea, but it could have been if I'd started it twenty years earlier. But twenty years earlier of course I never could have got there, and that is true of a great many people. They don't want you until you have made a name, and by the time you have made a name, you have developed some kind of talent which they can't use. All they will do is spoil it, if you let them. The best scenes I ever wrote were practically monosyllabic. And the best short scene I ever wrote, by my own judgment, was one in which a girl said "uh-huh" three times with three different intonations, and that's all there was to it. The hell of good film writing is that the most important part is what is left out. It's left out because the camera and the actors can do it better and quicker, above all quicker. But it had to be there in the beginning.

I should say these thoughts ought to be rambling enough to suit you.


Yours ever,


Ray

[298]

# TO JUANITA MESSICK

November 15 [1951]

•     •     •

Messick—I forgot—the Community Chest. This bothers the hell out of me. I don't feel the slightest desire to contribute to it. I don't like their method of coming around and handing you a numbered pledge with your name on it. The organization is not what it was supposed to be in the beginning, and more and more drives outside the Community Chest are accumulating. Also, they say openly that 90% of the money collected by the Community Chest goes in one way or another for the care of children, which seems to me entirely out of balance. What is the reaction among your friends and acquaintances to the Community Chest? And what is the cause of this latent hostility that one meets here and there. I often wonder and I shall probably end by sending them a token contribution of not more than $25, but I'd really like to tell them to take the whole thing and shove it.

# TO JUANITA MESSICK[1]

[1951]

We are going to cut out afternoon tea for a while and see how we manage without it. It often interrupts Cissy in a nap. She doesn't particularly care about it. Neither do I, and it is one more chore in a day already overloaded with them so far as I'm concerned. I'm sure you won't mind making youself a cup with tea bags if you want it. . . . There seems to be no immediate prospect of our getting our help. The one we had coming in the morning and in the evening was a rotten cook, in fact to call her rotten is flattery. So we had to cut out the evening and that discouraged her and now she won't come in the morning. . . . There just doesn't seem to be the kind of help we want, the only kind we can tolerate. And it looks to me as if until my wife gets better, I'm going to have to do most of the cooking.

1. The ellipses in this communication appear in a transcript made by Dorothy Gardiner. The original note has disappeared.

[299]

I'm a pretty good short order cook. I can cook steak, chops and vegetables far better than the restaurants can . . . and I rather like the idea of learning to be a little more of an accomplished cook, though I prefer to stop short of the elaborate stage. But it's a grind and there's no doubt about that. . . . I get up at 8 o'clock in the morning. . . . It takes me until 10 o'clock to get the two breakfasts and tidy. That gives me until one o'clock to try to do a little writing. That's not very much but it's probably as much as I'm good for the way things are. Then I have to go uptown and market, which doesn't matter because I was never any good at working in the afternoon, even as a schoolboy I was always dead in the afternoon. Then I come back and the minute I'm inside the house, there's this damn tea. . . .

By 5 o'clock, even on the short order basis, I have to get busy in the kitchen preparing the vegetables and so on. Then after dinner there are the dishes. If we had somebody really good to come in the morning, I think I might leave the dinner dishes—stick them down in the dishwasher, something of that sort. But it's almost as much trouble to do that and tidy up and wash off the stove and sink and drainboard as to do the whole job. . . . I've got to face the fact that Cissy hasn't got any stamina. . . . she's never going to get back to where she once was. And I dare say she knows it, although we don't talk about it. There's no sense in our relying on getting good help or on relying on keeping one if you did happen to get a good one. There's always something the matter with them. If they can cook, they're crotchety and spoiled, and very few of them can cook even moderately well. . . . So I guess it's up to this tired character as long as he holds out. Of course these things are not so hard when you get into a routine. You learn not to waste motion and not to do unnecessary things and not to walk your legs off.

## TO JUANITA MESSICK

[1951]

JM

.      .      .

The use of present participles to avoid relative clauses should be very

[300]

cautiously approached. "A man wearing a green hat came up the steps." This is fine because a lot simpler and less cumbrous and doesn't make too much of the green hat. "A man who was wearing a green hat came up the steps." Seems to hit it too hard. It seems that Tidwell's trouble is not poor syntax (what he writes is correct enough) but lack of feeling for the weight of words.[1] A statement as portentous should not be made with such a light and passing construction. It's getting towards a thing like: "De Musset was thirty three years old that day, being guillotined at two in the afternoon." Obviously what is wrong with that is the style, not the grammar. His age is made more important than the fact that he had his head chopped off. I should say—correct me if I am wrong—that this, next to the cliché, is the greatest fault of writing, important enough in its content, which is turned out by scientists, some scholars, and technical writers generally, and is the result of the separation of the Humanities from the special departments of knowledge. Not true of the best, of course. A really first class mind can always express itself. Why do we go on wasting our school years the only years we have in which to learn how to use our brains and minds and tongues? Why? Is it a question of money, of politics in the schools, or are we really intellectually a second-class people? And if so, do we want to be? Do we think it more manly to stumble over simple syntax provided we can reassemble a Ford or throw a football 45 yards?

RC

Why don't I shut up!

## TO PAUL McCLUNG[1]

December 11, 1951

Dear Mr. McClung:
    It may be better for me to answer your letter by mail rather

1. This communication arose through Chandler's query to Juanita Messick raised in a newspaper column entitled "Take My Word" by Frank Colby. In this column James Tidwell, a contributor to a publication of the American Dialect Society, was criticized for infelicitous phrasing and misplaced emphasis.

---

1. Of the Dell Publishing Company.

than wire. The doctor on whose point of view I founded the opinion you quote has been dead for several years. In any case I doubt very much whether he would have appreciated my revealing his identity to a magazine or a newspaper in connection with an opinion which his profession as a group would probably consider defeatist and most improper. I remember his saying to me in effect: "The toughest thing about trying to cure an alcoholic or a user of dope is that you have absolutely nothing to offer him in the long run. He feels awful at the moment no doubt; he feels shamed and humiliated; he would like to be cured if it is not too painful, and sometimes even if it is, and it always is. In a purely physical sense you maybe say he is cured when his withdrawal symptoms have passed, and they can be pretty awful. But we forget pain, and to a certain extent we even forget humiliation. So your alcoholic cured or your former dope addict looks around him, and what has he achieved? A flat landscape through which there is no road more interesting than another. His reward is negative. He doesn't suffer physically, and he is not humiliated or shamed mentally. He is merely damned dull." Obviously such a point of view is inconsistent with the Pollyanna attitude we impose on the medical profession. They know better, but they have to live too, although there are times when in particular cases one doesn't quite see why.

I put my opinion, which you seem to have taken rather seriously, in the mouth of a crook. In times like these only a crook may safely express opinions of this sort. Any medical man of standing would have to add something like: "Of course with proper psychiatric treatment, blah, blah, blah—" He would have to leave you on the up-beat. And by mentioning psychiatry he would, for me at least, instantly destroy the entire effect of any frank statement into which he may have ventured, since I regard psychiatry as fifty per cent bunk, thirty per cent fraud, ten per cent parrot talk, and the remaining ten per cent just a fancy lingo for the common sense we have had for hundreds and perhaps thousands of years, if we ever had the guts to use it.

.           .           .

Yours very truly,

[302]

# TO EDGAR CARTER

December 13, 1951

Dear Eddie:

I think a man ought to get drunk at least twice a year just on
principle, so he won't let himself get snotty about it. But I don't seem
to want to. When Priestley was here I threw a party for him at the
Marine Room, the guests being mostly Annie Oakleys invited by Jack
Latimer and his wife, people I had never seen before with one
exception, and have never seen since and don't care if I never see
again. I think I had about eight Scotches that night, which was well
below the average of the participants, but this was purely self-
protection on my part. If I hadn't had them, I would probably have
wanted to call the cops to throw the bastards out. It just goes to
show, but I'm not sure what, because I've forgotten what I was
talking about.

Yours ever,

# TO HAMISH HAMILTON

6005 Camino de la Costa
La Jolla, California
December 21, 1951

Dear Jamie:

Well, Christmas with all its ancient horrors is on us again. The
stores are full of fantastic junk and everything you want is out of
stock. People with strained, agonized expressions are poring over

[303]

pieces of distorted glass and pottery, and being waited on, if that is the correct expression, by specially recruited morons on temporary parole from mental institutions, some of whom by determined effort can tell a teapot from a pickaxe.

My love and best wishes to you and yours.

Yours ever,


## TO BERNICE BAUMGARTEN

6005 Camino de la Costa
La Jolla, California
December 21, 1951

Dear Bernice:

.   .   .

I finally the other day made it through Irwin Shaw's book, *The Young Lions*. The first time I tried it a couple of years back, I floundered and gave it up. It's a powerful and effective book, and I must say that I thought that most of it was damnably well done. But I do admit to a certain weariness with the sensitive young Jewish boy who gets kicked all over the lot by crude and brutal people. Couldn't we just once have one who does not get into a company of Georgia Crackers with an uncouth C.O., who does not have to get battered to pieces by a half dozen men twice his size in order to prove his manhood, who is not called a kike by anyone, and who does not have to carry the two thousand years of Jewish martyrdom on his shoulders every time he crosses the street?

.   .   .

Yours ever,

Ray

[304]

# TO JAMES SANDOE

6005 Camino de la Costa
La Jolla, California
Dec 27 1951

Dear Sandoe:

Many thanks for letter and books. The one on Gertie seemed to me as subtle as all hell, a bit over my head, in fact.[1] Frankly I don't think the old girl was worth the effort but I can see that an English prof who has to dish out a book now and again is wise to champion a cause that is not too lost and not too won. My own views of Gertie come closer to those of Mrs. Porter. She talked a great game, but if she ever cracked ninety, she moved her ball. She has the sort of reputation that depends less on what she did than on what the intellectuals said about her. When I read Eliot's play *The Cocktail Party* I wondered what all the fuss was about. But of course I knew. There are always enough sterile critics looping around hunting for a piece of stale cake they can wrap up in a distinguished name and sell to the host of snob-fakers that infest all semi-literate societies.

Happy New Year

RC

# TO CARL BRANDT

6005 Camino de la Costa
La Jolla, California
Dec 27, 1951

Dear Carl:

Secretary on vacation, the typing will be very bad. Excuse

1. By Donald Sutherland, *Gertrude Stein: A Biography of Her Work*, 1951.

please. So sorry. We had a lousy Christmas, thanks. The cook took sick, and the turkey didn't get cooked, and my wife is either in bed or lying down most of the time, trying to slough an obstinate bronchitis. Swanie sent me a tie for Christmas.[1] It is all covered with Sherlock Holmeses and bloody footprints. I wish Hollywood agents didn't feel they had to give Xmas presents to clients— especially as the presents are a far too accurate register of client's standing. A guy who worked up to a wrist watch and then slid back to a tie knows exactly what his rating is; he ought to be working for Republic. (By the way, do you know anybody dopey enough to wear a tie all covered with S.H.'s and bloody footprints. Be so happy to unload it. I wouldn't wear the thing to a post mortem on an Ozark sharecropper.)

·     ·     ·

Cheerio,

Ray

## TO WILLIAM TOWNEND

January 3, 1952

Dear Bill:

·     ·     ·

Your publishers are probably quite right to ask you to cut your book. I think we all grow a little more prolix as we grow older. Our memories are so packed with experiences and emotions that all our perceptions are overlaid by a patina of memory. We lose interest in plot which is kindergarten stuff mostly, and we forget that the public has interest in very little else. I hope you will always go on believing that your next book is going to be a big success. Even a hundred thousand words seems to me too long; eighty thousand

1. H. N. Swanson, Chandler's Hollywood agent.

ought to be the limit. Only a very rich writer, rich that is in style and illusion, should go beyond eighty thousand words. As for Priestley's book, *Festival*, I confess that I did not read it nor did I want to read it. He wrote it very quickly and was very proud of having written so long a book in such a short time—I think about three months. I think there is a good deal to be said for his point of view that a man should write a great deal in volume and variety, and write fast. Certainly some of the best writers have done just that. But you have to be a genius to do it consistently well, and I do not think Priestley is a genius or anywhere near a genius. I quite agree with Wodehouse that most novels would benefit by being cut; and yet there is a sort of writing, which one might call peripheral writing, which cannot be cut without destroying the whole effect of a book. You couldn't cut Proust or Henry James for example, because the things you would be apt to cut would be the very things that make these men worth reading.

I also agree that it is perfectly absurd that Wodehouse cannot go back to England.[1] Surely a Conservative Government makes some difference. After all Churchill was one of the men who boosted the fund for the defense of von Manstein.[2] And plenty of people both in England and in America are beginning to think that the War Crimes Trials were a bad mistake regardless of whether the people who were tried deserved hanging, which of course most of them did. They were bad because they assumed the Germans were bound by laws which did not exist and do not exist now; they were bad because they removed the defense of obedience to superior orders, and in effect made a soldier decide whether an order was proper to be obeyed even though refusal to obey it might result in his being summarily shot. Even if the Hitler government was vicious, it was still a government legally constituted in its own country, and we recognized it as such. Yet in these trials we now say that generals who had sworn an oath of allegiance to their government had no right to be bound by an oath of allegiance. Also, the trials were in effect drumhead court-martials by the victors. An American general writing in the *Saturday Evening Post* about the Battle of the Bulge told how

1. P. G. Wodehouse, English humorist, also a schoolboy at Dulwich. During World War II, while a captive of the Germans, he made five radio broadcasts for them.
2. Field Marshal Erich von Manstein served on the Russian front until he was discharged by Hitler during the retreat.

[307]

after a bunch of American prisoners had been murdered in cold blood by German tank crews, various American units were taken to see their bodies laid out in the field. He went on to say that thereafter we, that is the Americans, took the two prisoners a day required by Intelligence and no more. That's just another way of saying that we shot every other German who tried to surrender. That in any fair view of the matter is just as much an atrocity as many of the things the Germans did. And if the Germans had won the war, they could just as easily have tried our generals for crimes against international law. Men attacking under fire often shoot prisoners, or rather men who try to make themselves prisoners, for the simple reason that they cannot let the surrendered men get behind them and that they have no way to handle them. Also, under the Charter of the United Nations most of these war trials would now be impossible, because the evidence under which a great many of the convictions were obtained would be inadmissible in any real international court of justice. So it is all the more absurd that a man like Wodehouse should be tried for a few unwise remarks, probably distorted at that. I can't even agree that a man like [William] Joyce, Lord Haw Haw, was legally convicted. I think he was judicially murdered, because he could only be convicted by a declaration of law to the effect that a man on a falsely obtained British passport owes allegiance to the British crown. Joyce was convicted of giving aid and comfort to the enemy at a time when he was an American citizen and when America was not in the war. This was held to be treason because he held a British passport, which he was not entitled to hold and which he had obtained by a false declaration. That of course was a crime, but it was not a capital crime. In this country it would mean five years penal servitude in a federal prison at most, and actually that would probably mean about two and a half years. But the British had to hang Joyce, and in order to hang him they had to accuse him of treason. And in order to accuse him and convict him of treason they had to put forward the fantastic legal fiction that the possession of a British passport wrongfully acquired put him in exactly the same position as though it had been legally acquired, and although he was not a British subject he was still capable of treason towards a country of which he was not a citizen. I don't think they would try Wodehouse. And if they did, I think they would just make themselves look silly and the whole thing would blow up in their faces. But that doesn't

[308]

solve his problem. And you could hardly expect the authorities to give him an assurance in advance that if he went back to England he would not be tried.

.        .        .

Yours ever,

# TO S. J. PERELMAN

January 9, 1952

Dear Sid:

A fellow I know has a theory that if you delay long enough in answering somebody's letter, the guy will ultimately write to you again and apologize for not writing before. I've known it to work once or twice, but you can't rely on it. Anyhow, I do owe you a letter in answer to yours from Key West, Florida, dated October 24, 1951. And you shouldn't give the stuff away like that when you can sell it, unless of course your letters are just rough notes for articles. I guess you've lost interest in Rancho Santa Fe and so have I, but only because in their efforts to keep the place from getting cluttered up with the conveniences of life, the property owners have gone so far in the other direction that there is only one store for food, and that not much of a store, no drugstore, no movie theater (this probably would not be a blow to you, but your children might dislike it) and the essential technicians of life, such as plumbers, electricians and carpenters, are probably so scarce that one would find the aristocratic hauteur of their manners even more trying than the union scale for tramping dirt into the best carpets. I do think Rancho Santa Fe would be a pretty ideal place in which to bring up children, not that I regard that as one of the essential occupations. As for Florida, there must be some attractive spots in it but evidently not those you visited. Why is your wife so mad at Hollywood? After all there are lots of nice people in Hollywood, far more than there are in La Jolla. The picture business can be a little trying at times, but I don't suppose working for General Motors is all sheer delight, and working for Henry Ford, if one can believe any of Harry Bennett's

book, must have been just about as restful as being a bodyguard for
Dutch Schultz.[1]

.     .     .

     I am frankly not interested in your Florida sex hunger. Nobody
made you go to Florida. And don't tell me you have to earn a living,
because your children are certainly old enough and smart enough to
support you by now, even if your wife won't work. And I rather
gathered from your writings that about all she does is put perfume in
her hair and loaf around in a mink coat and slacks. And in the
meantime may I remind you of your promise to lend me that book of
Nathanael West's, which seems to be unobtainable here.

     With kindest regards,

Yours ever,

## TO DALE WARREN

6005 Camino de la Costa<br>
La Jolla, California<br>
January 11, 1952

Dear Dale:

.     .     .

Your advance notice on the novel in which the frustrated lady school
teacher jumps down the well after certain adventures with a Negro
janitor prompts me to implore you not to send me the book when
you publish it. I don't say it would not be successful; the taste of
the public is as mysterious as the taste of critics. Look at the success a
fellow called Mickey Spillane is having, a success comparable to
that in England of James Hadley Chase, the distinguished author of
*No Orchids for Miss Blandish.* Mickey Spillane is just about on the
same low level of phoniness, and as far as I'm concerned just as
unreadable. I did honestly try to read one just to see what made them
click, but I couldn't make it. Pulp writing at its worst was never
as bad as this stuff. It isn't so very long since no decent publisher

---

1.  Harry Bennett, *We Never Called Him Henry*, New York, 1951. Dutch Schultz was a
famous gangster during the Prohibition years of the 1920s and early 1930s.

would have touched it. I suppose it won't be long until the Book of the Month Club selects a handsomely produced volume of French postcards as its contribution to the national culture. This Spillane stuff, so far as I can see, is nothing but a mixture of violence and outright pornography. He and his publishers have had the courage, if that is the correct word, to carry these a little further than anyone else without interference from the police. I can't see anything else in it. This sort of thing makes the home boys with their libraries of elegant erotica seem rather nice people.

Last night inveigled by the critics and the ballyhoo, although I should now know better, we went to see *A Place in the Sun*.[1] This morning, looking through the *Variety* anniversary number, I see it is listed as the number 8 top grosser for 1951, three and a half million dollars domestic gross, which is very high for these times. So for once the New York critics and the public are agreed. My sister-in-law, who likes practically any kind of picture except slapstick, hated it. And I despised it. It's as slick a piece of bogus self-importance as you'll ever see. And to mention it in same breath with *A Streetcar Named Desire* seems to me an insult.[2] *Streetcar* is by no means a perfect picture, but it does have a lot of drive, a tremendous performance by Marlon Brando, and a skillful if occasionally rather wearisome one by Miss Vivien Leigh. It does get under your skin, whereas *A Place in the Sun* never touches your emotions once. Everything is held too long; every scene is milked ruthlessly. I got so sick of starry-eyed close-ups of Elizabeth Taylor that I could have gagged. The chi-chi was laid-on not with a trowel, not even with a shovel, but with a dragline. And the portrayal of how the lower classes think the upper classes live is about as ridiculous as could be imagined. They ought to have called it "Speedboats for Breakfast." And my God, that scene at the end where the girl visits him in the condemned cell a few hours before he gets the hot squat! My God, my God! The whole thing is beautifully done technically, and it reeks of calculation and contrivance emotionally. Mr. Montgomery Clift gives the performance of his career, which is not saying a great deal, since he had already demonstrated in *The Heiress* that he didn't

1. Film based on Theodore Dreiser's *An American Tragedy*. It was produced by George Stevens and starred Montgomery Clift and Elizabeth Taylor.
2. Film based on the Tennessee Williams play, directed by Elia Kazan and starring Vivien Leigh and Marlon Brando.

belong on the same screen with first-class actors.[3] The picture was
made by a guy who has seen everything and has never had a creative
idea of his own. Not once but twice in the picture he uses that great
trick which Chaplin used in *Monsieur Verdoux*, where instead of a
fadeout to close an act he shoots out of a window and watches the
darkness turn to daylight. But this slab of unreal hokum makes three
and a half million dollars and *Monsieur Verdoux* was a flop. My God,
My God! And let me say it just once more. My God!

.　　　.　　　.

Yours ever,

Ray

## TO THE EDITOR OF *SEQUENCE*[1]

February 15, 1952

Dear Sir:

　　I have *Sequence* 7, 13 and 14, and if you have any copies of 4, 8
and 11 remaining in stock, I should be glad to receive them. I think
you owe me two issues on my subscription, but that is not important.
I'll be glad to pay for any copies you send me if you need the money.

　　I hate to see the magazine fold. There is so little intelligent
writing about films, so little that walks delicately but surely between
the avant garde type, which is largely a reflection of neuroticism,
and the deadly commercial stuff. I think you have been a little too
hard at times on English films, which even when not top-notch
do give you the feeling of moving around in a civilized world—
something which the Hollywood product fails pretty short of as a
rule. Even if you had been less intelligent, I should be sorry to see
you go. *Sight and Sound* is all very well so far as it goes. I suppose it
is subsidized, and everything that is subsidized compromises, and
everything that compromises ends up by being pretty negative.

Yours with admiration and regret,

3.　Based on Henry James's *Washington Square*, this film was directed by William Wyler
and starred Olivia de Havilland and Ralph Richardson.

---

1.　A film magazine.

## TO H. N. SWANSON

March 10, 1952

Dear Swanie:

What do you mean do a trailer plugging a picture named *The Ragged Edge*? You want I should be a man of indistinction or something sitting behind a borrowed desk, looking straight into the camera and giving a spiel? Or is it that I should write the stuff for fifty dollars a week maybe, like a publicity man? I think that Sherlock Holmes tie you sent me has gone to your head. Seriously, the only thing about this proposition, if you could call it a proposition, that interests me is the fact that anybody would want me to do it. They're crazy anyhow. I have about as much publicity value as a fuzzy caterpillar. After five and a half years in La Jolla I don't think I even got my name in the local paper.

Yours disgustedly,

## TO DALE WARREN

6005 Camino de la Costa
La Jolla, California
April 25, 1952

Dear Dale:

As for a cook book, for God's sake if you wanted a La Jolla cookbook, why didn't you apply to me? Except for my wife and one or two others, I am probably the best cook in La Jolla.

Kidding aside, somebody really ought to write a cookbook and put in all the things that the regular cookbooks leave out, the things which, if you're a beginner, the cookbooks don't tell you. They take too much for granted. Also, any decent cookbook should have a few special recipes, a touch of the unique. And this I could easily supply. My Swordfish Mascagni is famous for all of three blocks, and

[313]

that just in a light breeze. With a good stiff one off the ocean practically the whole of La Jolla is reeling. And my apples baked in cider are vociferously admired by practically everyone who owes me money. How do you make soup without a can opener? Well, that's a mystery of the trade to which very few people know the answer. But it can be done. Just as it is possible to bake a cake out of plain ordinary flour if you have a little cornstarch around the house. You don't really have to buy the cake half baked in a cellophane bag at the A & P. Most people think you do, but it's an error. Why, in my cookbook I could even tell people how to poach an egg in open water. And if you think that's easy, we've had fifty or sixty cooks who couldn't do it. Most of them couldn't even poach an egg in an egg poacher, which doesn't really poach an egg at all.

.        .        .

## TO BERNICE BAUMGARTEN

> 6005 Camino de la Costa
> La Jolla, California
> May 14 1952

Dear Bernice:

I'm sending you today, probably by air express, a draft of a story which I have called *The Long Goodbye*. It runs 92,000 words. I'd be happy to have your comments and objections and so on. I haven't even read the thing, except to make a few corrections and check a number of details that my secretary queried. So I am not sending you any opinion on the opus. You may find it slow going.

It has been clear to me for some time that what is largely boring about mystery stories, at least on a literate plane, is that the characters get lost about a third of the way through. Often the opening, the mis en scene, the establishment of the background, is very good. Then the plot thickens and the people become mere names. A very good example of this is a current work called *Reclining Figure* by my friend Harry Kurnitz, (Marco Page.) It begins so well, but in the end it is the same old hash. Well, what can you do to avoid this? You can write constant action and that is fine if you really enjoy it. But alas, one grows up, one becomes complicated and unsure, one becomes interested in moral dilemmas, rather than who cracked who on the head. And at that point perhaps one should retire and leave the field to younger and more simple men. I don't necessarily mean writers of comic books like Mickey Spillane.

Anyhow I wrote this as I wanted to because I can do that now. I didn't care whether the mystery was fairly obvious, but I cared about the people, about this strange corrupt world we live in, and how any man who tried to be honest looks in the end either sentimental or plain foolish. Enough of that. There are more practical reasons. You write in a style that has been imitated, even plagiarized, to the point where you begin to look as if you were imitating your imitators. So you have to go where they can't follow you. The danger is that the reader won't either.

.    .    .

Yours ever,

Ray

# TO BERNICE BAUMGARTEN

6005 Camino de la Costa<br>La Jolla, California<br>Sunday May 25, 1952

Dear Bernice:

You will have received my wire by now and I hope it has been in time to stop the script from being copied and to withhold same from Jamie.[1] I thank you for your letter and needless to say I regret having sent the script out when I did. I was just too impatient to get rid of it. I knew the character of Marlowe had changed, and I thought it had to because the hardboiled stuff was too much of a pose after all this time. But I did not realize that it had become Christlike, and sentimental, and that he ought to be deriding his own emotions. It may be that I am no good any more. God knows, I've had enough worry to drive me off the beam. Being old-fashioned

1. Bernice Baumgarten and Carl Brandt had written Chandler making numerous suggestions for changes in *The Long Goodbye*.

[315]

enough to be deeply in love with my wife after twenty-eight years of marriage I feel the possibility that I have let emotion enter my life in a manner not suitable to the marts of commerce, as the cliché has it. Of course there is also the possibility—faint as it is, I admit—that you could be a little wrong.

I'll take a quick trip through the script when I get it back and then lay it aside for long enough to get perspective. I've always wanted to do that. I was never able to. I was always afraid that if I did I would junk the whole thing when I came back to it. I'm not afraid of that now. I know that whatever errors of emphasis or plot and so on the story contains it is fundamentally all right for me. I've never ridden with a loose rein before. That may be more of a trick than I know.

I am dropping a note to Jamie because he cabled me. If by any chance you have sent him a script, I shall ask him to return it to me direct.

Curiously enough I seem to have far fewer doubts about this story than I had about *The Little Sister*. Why that is I haven't the remotest idea. It has been said, I think, that writers always like the wrong things in their own work.

My thanks again and my apologies for putting you through it.

Yours ever,

Ray

# TO HAMISH HAMILTON

6005 Camino de la Costa
La Jolla, California
May 25, 1952

Dear Jamie:

I am withdrawing the script of my book for revision. I have wired Bernice to return all copies to me and not to show it to anyone. I'm sorry and it's a damn nuisance. But Houghton Mifflin could not (apparently) have published this year anyhow. If a script should have been sent to you, please disregard it, and send back to me just any old way. No hurry.

[316]

This happens as the result of criticisms made by Bernice and concurred in by Carl Brandt. Some of these comments, if correct, are devastating, and if incorrect, are intolerable. Surely they are more likely to be the former than the latter. The character of Marlowe has become "Christlike" and sentimental, and he should be deriding his own emotions all through the book, or words to that effect. There are also detailed criticisms of no particular importance.

It's all my fault, of course. I should have put the damn thing to one side and let it simmer on the stove for awhile. Instead of that I hurry it out in an unregenerate condition and get slapped in the face for being so careless. It happened to me once before with Sydney Sanders, and much more brutally. It was over the book called *The High Window*, original and proper title *The Brashear Doubloon*, and changed as an effort of superb idiocy on the part of Knopf who thought my title sounded like a boy's story. That book is usually considered my weakest effort to date (I will no doubt surpass it and may have already—in weakness), although there are people who think it the best. It is still selling here and there, but you know how ignorant the public is. Compared with an agent the public knows nothing.

Another talent in which agents are greatly gifted is imploring you to let them see work in progress or unfinished or unedited, and when you succumb to their pleadings, hitting you in the face with it. And all for so modest a fee.

Yours ever

Ray

## TO ERIC PARTRIDGE

May 29, 1952

Dear Eric:

Incidentally, it doesn't follow that a man who has been in stir writes

[317]

the best prison lingo any more than it follows that a man who has been a police officer writes the best detective stories. My experience is to the contrary. As you say, the lingo varies from place to place, and it also varies from year to year. And there is no doubt that a large part of it is of literary origin, literary here being used in a very generous sense. Cops and crooks are readers of crime literature, and I have no doubt that many a Western sheriff has ornamented his language and perhaps even his costume from a study of six-gun literature.

Yours ever,

## TO CARL BRANDT

6005 Camino de la Costa
La Jolla, California
June 11, 1952

Dear Carl:

I am doing a good deal of revising on my book, especially toward the end, which I think I shall change. But I probably do not have the same confidence that I had before I received Bernice's remarks. Some of the things she said are matters which I would automatically have taken care of on revision. Some seem to me quite without point. As to the character of Marlowe, I may be all wrong but I was trying to write the book the way I wanted to write it and not the way somebody else thinks I ought to write it. The irony of a writer's career—I suppose most writers are confronted with it in some form—is that he may write a couple of books which pass with little notice at the time of their publication, and then as time goes by they slowly build up a reputation and in the end are used as yardsticks by which to measure his later work, sometimes by the very people who were quite unable to discuss any merit in the early performance at the time. A writer of my type should never show

[318]

unfinished work to anyone. He should wait until he is sure that he has what he wanted, or as near to it as he is capable of producing.

With kindest regards,

Yours ever,

Ray

## TO BERNICE BAUMGARTEN

6005 Camino de la Costa
La Jolla, California
July 20th. 1952

Dear Bernice:

Thanks for note, but I see no reason why you should, even as a matter of form, apologize for speaking what was in your mind. You were probably, almost certainly, quite right. One never knows what sort of impact a letter will make, since one never knows the mood or very much of the circumstances in which it will be read. Complete tact requires more knowledge than is given to us. It was all my fault anyhow, as I've said. My present trouble is that I don't know where I am at, don't know whether there is anything in all this mess worth salvaging, or whether it would be cleverer to throw it away and start fresh. I am not much good at tinkering or revising. I lose interest, lose perspective, and whatever critical sense I have is dissipated in trivialities such as whether it is better to put in "he said" or let the speech stand alone.

My kind of writing demands a certain amount of dash and high spirits—the word is gusto, a quality lacking in modern writing—and you could not know the bitter struggle I have had the past year even to achieve enough cheerfulness to live on, much less to put into a book. So let's face it: I didn't get it into the book. I didn't have it to give.

.          .          .

All the best,

Ray

[319]

# TO PAUL BROOKS

The Connaught Hotel
Carlos Place, London W.1.[1]
September 28, 1952

Dear Paul Brooks:

Thanks for your letter which was forwarded to me here. Today is an English Sunday and by God it's gloomy enough for a crossing of the Styx. I thought England was broke but the whole damn city is crawling with Rolls Royces, Bentleys, Daimlers and expensive blondes.

Never thought I'd get sick of the sight of a grouse on toast or a partidge, but by God I am.

On my return Oct. 7 via *Mauretania* shall be at the Hampshire House for a few days and will call up to say hello, if you are available. The book (seen from here in perspective) is all right. It had a few changes here though. Bernice is an idiot (I hope).

In England I am an author. In the USA just a mystery writer. Can't tell you why. God knows I don't care one way or the other. I have met:

(1) An Oxford don who writes bad Westerns under a pen name.
(2) A secretary who lunches on bread and butter and straight gin.
(3) A valet who enters without knocking while my wife is having a bath.
(4) A publisher who makes the world's worst martinis.
    And so on.

Yours ever

Raymond Chandler

---

1. Chandler and his wife Cissy visited England for a month in the autumn of 1952. They sailed from Los Angeles on a Swedish motor ship via the Panama Canal and returned on the *Mauretania* of the Cunard line. It was Chandler's first visit to England since 1918.

# TO LEONARD RUSSELL

6005 Camino de la Costa
La Jolla, California
October 29, 1952

Dear Leonard:

I hope I am not too forward in so addressing you.

Herewith the story about which we spoke briefly the night before my wife and I left the Connaught Hotel for Southampton. You expressed a desire to see it. I warned you that it had not been received with the slightest trace of enthusiasm on this side of the Atlantic. So if you don't like it, I shall not be in the least chagrined; I shall simply feel that there is something in the story which I did not succeed in getting on paper. To me it seems in some vague way one of the best things I ever wrote, but an author is a very poor judge of his own stuff.

I can't tell you how much I enjoyed meeting you and Dilys Powell.[1] The reason I can't tell you is that I feel it requires a much more ample expression than I am capable of at the moment. Today the style is not worthy of the subject; perhaps later on it will be, and you will hear from me again. My wife and I both feel that the evening we spent at your house, alcoholic as it was, was one of the high spots of our visit to London. And nothing would give us greater pleasure or joy than to repeat it at least twice a week for the rest of our lives.

Yours ever,

Ray

---

1. Russell's wife and film critic for the *Sunday Times*.

# TO J. FRANCIS

6005 Camino de la Costa
La Jolla, California
October 30, 1952

Dear Frank:

    As to Maugham's remarks about the decline and fall of the
detective story, in spite of his flattering references to me, I do not
agree with his thesis.[1] People have been burying the detective story
for at least two generations, and it is still very much alive, although I
do admit that the term "detective story" hardly covers the field any
more, since a great deal of the best stuff written nowadays is only
slightly if at all concerned with the elucidation of the mystery. What
we have is more in the nature of the novel of suspense. I'm going
to write him a long letter one of these days and take up the argument
with him. I may even write an article in reply if anybody wants to
print it. I should have valued his references to Philip Marlowe even
more if he had remembered to spell Marlowe's name correctly. Some
of this stuff of Maugham's was published a long time ago. The
fascinating and acid little vignette of Edith Wharton for example was
published in the *Saturday Evening Post*, and I still have the tear sheets
(I think) from the issue. And I seem to recall that Edmund Wilson
took rather nasty issue with Maugham about Maugham's claim that
the writers of straight novels had largely forgotten how to tell a story.
I hate to agree with such an ill-natured and bad mannered person as
Edmund Wilson, but I think he was right on this point. I don't think
the quality in the detective or mystery story which appeals to people
has very much to do with the story a particular book has to tell. I
think what draws people is a certain emotional tension which takes
you out of yourself without draining you too much. They allow
you to live dangerously without any real risk. They are something
like those elaborate machines which they used to use and probably
still do use to accustom student pilots to the sensation of aerial

---

1. Published in *The Vagrant Mood*, 1953.

[322]

acrobatics. You can do anything from a wing over to an Immelmann in them without any danger of going into a flat spin out of control. Well, enough of that for now.

.            .            .

Kindest regards to everyone,

Yours ever,

Ray Chandler

## TO HAMISH HAMILTON

6005 Camino de la Costa
La Jolla, California
November 5, 1952

Dear Jamie:

You people over there write one another so many little polite notes on all sorts of occasions that I suppose I was very stupid not to realize that I should not have waited until I had time to do a more substantial kind of letter. I am extremely sorry to have hurt your feelings inadvertently. There have been certain excuses but not any complete excuse. I could have written to you on the *Mauretania*, illegible as my writing is. I could have written to you from New York. I could have written to you on the train coming across the country. As soon as I got back here I wrote a couple of duty notes: one to Francis, who made me a present of a book just before I left and I had not time to thank him for it in person, the other to Leonard Russell. But these were short and not at all the kind of letter I should have liked to write to you. I think letter writing is more of a chore to me than it is to you, because I cannot write longhand so that anyone can read it. I don't like typing letters myself, because I don't type well enough, although I type rapidly, and I have fallen into the habit of dictating. But none of this is any adequate excuse for me to have been so neglectful that your feelings were hurt. And I do apologize

[323]

most sincerely. As for my being offended about anything, you cannot use that word to me with impunity. *I just simply am not the type that gets offended*, even when there might be thought to be some justification and certainly there could never be from you. You were kindness itself, and I'm sure you spent far more hours worrying about me than you should have. I have had my feelings hurt, sometimes intentionally. Like most writers I have occasionally been sneered at and maligned. I don't say I have never been hurt and never discouraged, but I have never felt it a personal matter. I never sulk. I am never huffy. Sometimes, I admit, I can be pretty irritable, but this is perhaps more the fault of a nervous temperament than of any innate vice.

It seemed natural for Cissy to write to Roger, because he sent flowers to the boat and she certainly had to thank him, though if they had been sent to me, I might well have waited until I got home to do it. I can see now that that would have been wrong. So please, dear Jamie, try to understand that I think you and yours were all utterly kind and charming to us, and that even though certain things about our stay in London were a little annoying at the time, they are all very pleasant in retrospect. The annoying things were mostly things that could not be avoided. There was the desperate struggle on Cissy's part (when she was in no fit condition to do it) to find something to wear, and not merely something to wear to a dinner party but things which she badly needed and things which she simply could not find in the West End of London. She couldn't even find a decent pair of shoes to put on. At fantastic prices they were selling what we should over here regard as quite second-rate English goods. Of course I do understand why, but it was annoying just the same. I couldn't find a decent pair of woolen socks. The only things I found were fit for lumberjacks. I thought the hotel charges were pretty outrageous for a not too comfortable room. But all that is to be expected and I am sure as things go it is a pretty damn good hotel. Next time, however, I should like to try another, possibly Claridge's. And compared with New York, which is an abominable place in far too many ways, I think London is a paradise of charm and good manners. Soon after we reached London, although we said very little about it at the time, Cissy hurt herself getting into a taxi, just because the damn doorman wouldn't take the trouble to get the taxi up to the curb, and the strap on one of her shoes slipped. She

[324]

developed a very serious bruise which should have been bandaged at once if we had realized how serious it was. But as a matter of fact it was not bandaged until she got on the *Mauretania*. She has been wearing bandages ever since. Evidently a large vein was broken and there was a great deal of subcutaneous hemorrhage which refused to absorb. On the way back on the train she developed some kind of infection, probably due to the use of harsh towels washed in detergent and insufficiently rinsed. I should say it was allergic in origin, but just the same it was bad and still is bad, very hard to shake off. I have been under the weather myself, but I'm all right now. And we were in such appalling difficulties from a domestic point of view that we had to ask Cissy's unfortunate sister to come right back and help us out, when she had been away from her own home for two months and was pretty fed up with being here. Also, I have been deeply depressed about my book. I felt, and I still feel, that Bernice was wrong in all but a few rather insignificant details. But there was always the chance that I was wrong and she was right. And when you're not feeling well, these things are apt to loom very large. After all I'm not getting any younger and I haven't turned out a book for quite a while and this sort of thing can't go on indefinitely. But I think I see now the answer to what problems there are, and that if we can have some peace in our home, things will start to move.

I didn't like the *Mauretania*. It wasn't a ship at all. It was just a damned floating hotel. I didn't like the hotel we stayed at in New York, and Cissy disliked it even more than I did. I suppose there is an amiable and pleasant side to New York we just didn't happen to see, except that I have one very good friend who took the trouble to come down from Old Chatham and meet us and stay several days with us. But frankly it seems to me a dirty, lawless, rude, hard-boiled place. It makes even Los Angeles seem fairly civilized. The New York taxi drivers were a bunch of hard-boiled, dirty-looking Jews except for an occasional grizzled and civilized Irishman. And most of them are crooks into the bargain. I have never been in any place that gave me such an acute feeling that no one had the time or inclination for even a modicum of good manners unless there was a quick buck in it for him. Oh yes, I will make one exception in favor of the customs inspectors. They are supposed to be tough. I found them charming and extremely clever. The one we got (after waiting an hour and a half because the Cunard people lost one of our suitcases and didn't even take the trouble to apologize when they finally found it) made a great to-do about the Berenson book, which I think was the only thing in our ten pieces of luggage he even looked at. But I had a very strong impression that his looking at it and talking about it and asking questions about it was simply a device for sizing up his customer, and that after a few moments of this he made up his mind what sort of people he was dealing with, and from then on he didn't want to see or know anything at all. He didn't even ask us to open our bags. I had declared this book on the customs declaration as a gift and put an estimated value on it, because it was the sort of expensive thing that I didn't want them to find without being told. But at the same time I wouldn't try to fool with these people. They caught a slick-looking Jew with a fine batch of very expensive looking French costume jewelry wrapped up in an old shirt. And they took no time at all in marching him off to a senior officer, the Jew remarking plaintively as he departed that he wasn't trying to get away with anything. Famous last words.

Well, Jamie, let's face it. We loved London and we had a lovely time there. What little inconveniences we happened to have suffered were all due to our own inexperience and probably would not happen again. All your people were wonderful to me. It was really extremely touching. I am just not used to being treated with that much consideration. There are things I regret, such as losing several days over my vaccination, such as not going to any of the picture galleries, such as only seeing one rather poor play, such as not having dinner at your home. I spent too much time talking about myself, which I don't enjoy, and too little time listening to other people talk about themselves, which I do enjoy. I missed seeing something of the English countryside. And childish as it may sound, I missed very much not having hired a Rolls Royce and a driver for a day and driven to Oxford or Cambridge or some place like that. But all in all there was a hell of a lot I did not miss, and all of it good. And for that you above all others are to be thanked. I'll be writing you again soon. In the meantime my best love to you and Yvonne, and that goes for Cissy too. I think the trip did her a lot of good. She had bad luck, but psychologically she was buoyed up no end.

Yours ever,

Ray

[326]

P.S. The Maugham book just came, and thanks ever so much for sending it. Francis had sent me a bound copy of the proof. I wish Maugham had taken the trouble to spell Marlowe's name right, and I don't agree with his thesis that the detective story is dying. That's just an elderly gentleman's point of view. Such predictions have been made periodically ever since one can remember. I'm sure I did thank you for the Berenson book, which I shall have a hard time getting away from Cissy, and for the *Journal* of Delacroix. But what's this about a Partridge book? You didn't send me a Partridge book, or if you did, I haven't received it.

R.

## TO W. TOWNEND

November 11, 1952

Dear Bill:

　　The London of 1952 probably struck me as a much more amiable and attractive place than you found it, because I probably never saw it at its best, at least not since I was a very young man. The present generation of English people impressed me very well. There is a touch of aggressiveness about the working classes and the non-Public School types which I think is something new and which I personally do not find at all unpleasant, since it is even more emphatic in this country. And the real Public School types, or many of them, with their bird-like chirpings are becoming a little ridiculous, I thought. I grant you that English food is pretty dreary. There was no shortage of anything at the hotel, but we did find the menu pretty monotonous and the cooking not too good. We thought at the time this was probably due to the shortage of some of the necessary cooking materials and ingredients, the little things that give flavor. But on the *Mauretania* where there is no shortage of anything, in fact where there is far too much food and far too great a variety, we

[327]

found the same sort of dullness in the cooking, so I am driven to the conclusion that it is just English. Compared with the Swedes, even on a modest ship like a passenger-freighter, the English are no cooks at all. For instance, at the Café Royale we had pork chops, pork apparently being the only unrationed fresh meat. Now pork chops are not particularly difficult to cook. I can cook them myself. You cook them in their own fat, they bring with them everything that is necessary except salt and pepper. Yet these pork chops were badly cooked and were messed up with some kind of sauce, which added nothing to their flavor and probably took away what little they had left. It's this sort of bastard imitation of French cooking, a fussiness without the skill or the grace, which I found so trying at the hotel and in London generally. I don't suggest that there are no good English cooks. Far from it. But in a general way it seems to me they cannot take a piece of perfectly good meat or fish or fowl and cook it simply and properly so as to bring out its natural flavor and let it go at that. All in all I think the best thing that they cook is oysters on the half-shell. Whitstable oysters are very good indeed, every bit as good as Blue Points or Cape Cod oysters back East in the U.S.A.

Yes, I met a few of the literary and theatrical people who are big names in London. We had lunch with Priestley, and a very good lunch it was. We had dinner with Leonard Russell, and his wife, Dilys Powell. It wasn't much of a dinner, but it was elegantly served by a butler, and the company was very nice indeed. Dilys Powell I found charming; Leonard Russell, Cissy found charming. Not that I didn't like him, but I didn't go overboard for him the way she did. Also present were Val Gielgud, who is head of dramatic productions for BBC; Nicolas Bentley, the son of the fellow who wrote *Trent's Last Case*,[1] his wife, who is the daughter of Sir Patrick Hastings; one of the daughters-in-law of H. J. Massingham, who used to edit the great liberal weekly, *The Saturday Review*; Campbell Dixon, who is some kind of a film reviewer and has been a foreign correspondent and a special feature writer in many places, and his wife, who also works for the BBC and has some connections with Korda.[2] I had lunch with Eric Partridge, and we did happen to miss a dinner at

1. E. C. Bentley.
2. Sir Alexander Korda.

which Cyril Connolly and Peter Ustinov[3] were to have been present. I can't say I met all the bigwigs, even very many of them. But those I did meet were all very nice people and made an unnecessary amount of fuss over me. No, I haven't read Cary's book, *Prisoner of Grace*, and don't think I shall; so if that makes me a nitwit, I'll be one right along with you.

.      .      .

Of all the people we met in London, that is those we had not known before, I think we liked best Roger Machell, a director of Hamish Hamilton, a cheerful, rather pudgy, light-hearted character, with a droll sense of humor and the sort of off-hand good manners which you rarely find except in a genuine aristocrat. This fellow is an old Etonian, which of course is not conclusive. He is a great grand-nephew of Queen Victoria, he is the grandson of Prince Hohenlohe, and his mother, Lady Something or Other Machell, lives in St. James Palace. Just why, I don't know, because none of this information came from Machell himself. He was badly wounded in the war and made a joke of it. He seemed to think it was characteristic that he should have been wounded while telephoning London from a French pub. A bomb dropped on it and blew a piece of a wall through his chest. It just missed killing him, but he seems to show no ill effects now. He said he got a commission as a major in some guard's regiment, but he didn't know how, probably pure luck or else someone made a bad mistake. When he reported one morning to a barracks in London in uniform he found them in the act of the changing of the guard. He said he didn't know whether he was supposed to salute the guard or if the guard was supposed to salute him, so he just sat in his car outside until it was all over. He has the sort of humorous, self-deprecating manner which by sheer magic of personality is never overdone or posey or artificial. He lives handsomely in chambers in the Old Albany, drives a ramshackle old car, mixes perfectly awful Martinis in a two-quart water pitcher (two of them would knock you out for a week) and took us on a wonderful tour of London, including the East End bombed-out district, making all the time such comments as, "Well, let's run down and take a look at the Tower, supposing I can find it," and "over

3. Cyril Connolly, critic and author; Peter Ustinov, writer and actor.

[329]

there is St. Paul's or something of that sort." He had us in giggles the whole time, yet he is in no sense of the word an intentional comedian. I claim that a man who can get away with this sort of thing and be perfectly natural about it is a bit of a genius.

　　With much love from both of us to both of you,

Ever yours,

## TO DALE WARREN

November 13, 1952

Dear Dale:

.　　　　　.　　　　　.

　　I owe an apology to Paul Brooks for failing to call in at your New York office as he asked me to and meet a couple of people there. This is going to sound rather corny, but the simple fact is I forgot all about it. I don't know why, and I have no excuse. It simply happened. I think possibly I developed a certain amount of subconscious reluctance to have anything to do with New York taxi drivers. Those that don't whine or bluster want to make a travelogue out of a ten-block ride. I suppose New Yorkers get used to them, just as hotel doormen get used to standing out in the middle of the street, blowing whistles all day long; just as you get used to seeing cars double and triple parked all over the place and the police taking no notice; and just as you get used, or do you, to going out into the middle of the street to get into a taxi and never by any chance getting one at the curb. I see in the current *New Yorker* that Sacheverell Sitwell, that visiting virtuoso of the quill pen, remarks that New York traffic is better managed than that in London, about as idiotic a remark as I have ever heard or read. New York traffic isn't managed at all. It is absolute chaos. London traffic, generally speaking and considering the fantastic pattern of the streets, is superbly managed. Of course the system wouldn't work in New York because it depends on a certain element of decency and obedience to the law. The only real fault I found with the London traffic system was their

[330]

allowing left turns from places like Oxford Circus during rush hours.
With which gripe I conclude.

Yours ever,

# TO MR. SHEPPARD[1]

November 14, 1952

Dear Mr. Sheppard:

Whatever happened to my photographs, those that were taken
on October 6th last by the Russian–Armenian lady in the smock
and the Apache style coiffure? You remember the proofs were to have
been sent to you by the following Friday, which would have been
October 10th; and unless they were on the face of it quite impossible,
were to have been sent to me. It was agreed, you remember, when I
submitted myself to this degrading ordeal that I should have the
privilege of passing on the proofs and that nothing should be used
which I did not like. Experience has taught me to be very sensitive
about photographs. I am no fuzzy chicken and I can be made to
look pretty ghastly, as was well demonstrated by the *Sunday Times*.
All questions of personal vanity apart (and I do not consider them
very much, although I do not say I don't consider them at all) I am
convinced as a member of the reading public myself that bad
photographs are bad business. I have been put off reading books,
which otherwise looked rather attractive, by the puss of the author
printed on the back of the dust cover. It is not a question of making
you handsome when you are not, or of making you young when
you are not. It is a question of not presenting the reader with an
image which will turn his stomach at the worst, and at the best haunt
him with just enough distaste for the personality of the author to
give him a bias against the author's writing. I don't think publishers
pay enough attention to this sort of thing. I do think, and positively,
that a poor photograph is worse than none at all. In his writing,
if he is going to get anywhere, an author has to present the public
with an attractive personality. It may be and often is an artificial

1. Publicity director of Hamish Hamilton, Chandler's London publishers.

[331]

personality, something the author as a human specimen cannot live up to. But time and time again publishers will destroy the effect the author has managed to achieve in his writing by presenting a photographic study of him as a conceited ape or a flat-faced homunculus whom you would not on his looks think capable of a BBC talk about the sex life of a caterpillar.

It is obvious from this letter that a mere discussion of the disastrous effects of photographing authors can bring out the worst in at least one of them. Anyhow, it was delightful to meet you. It was very kind of you to trundle me down the street to the sordid neighborhood of the Garrick Club and to suffer with me in that bleak little studio. But I would like to know what happened—that is if anything happened.

With kindest regards,

Yours ever,

## TO HOWARD HUNT[1]

November 16, 1952

Dear Mr. Hunt:

Your letter to the editors of Pocket Books, accusing me of self-plagiarism, was sent on to me by them without comment. Since the letter was not addressed to me, there is no real reason why I should answer it, but I will take up a couple of points. First, as to *The Hard-Boiled Omnibus*, you were perfectly right. As a matter of fact I suggested the idea of this anthology to Joe Shaw, a former editor of the *Black Mask* and a long-time friend of mine, and I signed a permission to him for this story when I was very busy at Paramount and not paying any particular attention to it. That is to say, I relied on his good faith. Later I read the story and immediately raised a howl and secured his undertaking in writing not to use it but to substitute something else which had not been, as I term it, "cannibalized."

1. At the time, attached to the American Embassy in Mexico City. Later, as an aide to President Nixon, he was embroiled in the Watergate scandal.

When the book came out he explained somewhat lamely that the editors of Simon & Schuster had overruled him. Legally of course I had no remedy, although I spent several hundred dollars in lawyers fees trying to find one. I had signed the permission. The most I achieved was to prevent the inclusion of this story in the English edition of that anthology.

You should not blame the editors of Pocket Books, because the volume of their business is so great that they naturally take these things on trust from the publishers from whom as a rule they secure the reprint rights. I consider that my confidence was abused, but that is just my personal opinion.

As to your broader charge of self-plagiarism, based on the use by me of scenes, characters, incidents, background, color, etc., from old *Black Mask* novelettes: first of all, let me say that I have a perfect right to use them; I am the copyright owner, I can use my material in any way I see fit. There have been many instances of short stories being expanded into books which were published, and then being dramatized into plays which were published, and so on. Where the novel takes over the essential plot and story line of the briefer story, I would say that the reader should be put upon notice of this, particularly if the title is changed. Where the material used is merely character and incident, there is no fraud on the public because the thing is re-created in another form. Even if occasional lines of dialogue are used, there is no fraud. There is no moral or ethical issue involved. You may dislike the procedure, but that's as far as you can go.

There is another consideration which may have escaped your attention. That is that these old stories of mine were written for the most ephemeral possible kind of publication, one which had a life of thirty days and then was as dead as Caesar. At the time it would never have occurred to me that any of these stories would ever be resurrected, remembered, republished again in any form. I am not sure that they ever should have been republished in their original form, but I took a wide selection of opinions on the subject before I consented. It was brought home to me that a whole generation had grown up that had never known the *Black Mask*, and that that generation might just possibly want to read these stories, and certainly would not be able to read them unless they were republished. There might happen to be a few odd copies of the magazine obtainable in

[333]

some secondhand magazine store, but who would be likely to look for them except a fanatic. I was even assured by a somewhat austere critic of this type of fiction, James Sandoe by name, that even people who knew the stories and had perhaps kept them in some other form would still be very likely to want them in hard covers.

I have a further remark. As you may know, writers like Dashiell Hammett and myself have been widely and ruthlessly imitated, so closely as to amount to a moral plagiarism, even though the law does not recognize anything but the substantial taking of a plot. I have had stories taken scene by scene and just lightly changed here and there. I have had lines of dialogue taken intact, bits of description also word for word. I have no recourse. The law doesn't call it plagiarism. Against this background you must pardon me if I find it just a little ludicrous that you should object to my using what is mine in the way that seems to me most suitable and most convenient. If my early stories had been published in a magazine of prestige and significance, the situation would have been rather different, and I would have been much more reluctant to do what you complain of. But as it is, I wish I had carried the process much further and used more of my old novelettes as material instead of republishing them with all their crudities, some of which crudities I now find almost unbearable.

I think my principal reason for writing this letter is that in all these years you are the only person who has ever raised this objection, that is to say, the only person other than myself. I have a file of pretty bitter correspondence on the subject of the first paragraph of your letter.

Yours very truly,

## TO LEONARD RUSSELL

6005 Camino de la Costa
La Jolla, California
December 11, 1952

Dear Leonard Russell:

[334]

Remember me? Chandler? We met once briefly in London. We had dinner at your house, and very charming it was. And you had a couple of pink gins at my hotel, and very charming that was, except that it led me to send you a story called "A Couple of Writers," which was dispatched by airmail on October 29, 1952. And the rest is silence. Don't think I'm anxious. Don't think I'm disheartened. I told you the worst about the story. And after all, you asked me to send it to you. I think some brief acknowledgement might be in order, if the story ever reached you. I'm beginning to wonder if it did.

My wife has been very ill. She is back home from the hospital, but still very frail and still in bed. Mostly on that account we have decided to forget all about Christmas this year, cards included. So may I now wish you and Dilys Powell whatever in this sad world remains of peace and happiness, such as red sunsets, the smell of roses after a summer rain, soft carpets in quiet rooms, firelight, and old friends.

Yours ever,

Ray

## TO ERIC PARTRIDGE

January 19, 1953

Dear Eric:

.　　　　.　　　　.

The best shaggy dog story I know, it tops them all I think, was published a long time ago in *Collier's*, but it was published in a way that suggested that it was not original but that somebody had heard it from somebody else who had heard it, etc. It seems that on a very hot summer afternoon a couple of hippopotamuses, or hippopotami if you want to be a purist, were basking in the muddy water of the Nile with their noses just showing above. They appeared very contented and even a little drowsy. Finally one of the hippopotamuses raised his snout out of the water enough so that he

[335]

could open his mouth. He said dreamily, "Somehow you know, I can't help thinking this is Thursday." End of story.

I know a wonderful story which probably doesn't quite qualify as a shaggy dog story. As a matter of fact, the definition of a shaggy dog story is pretty vague to me, except that it's supposed to be pure nonsense and yet somehow funny. It seems that a Polish farmer had murdered his wife and her lover. He had been tried, convicted, and the judge before sentencing him asked him if he had anything to say. The Polish farmer had quite a lot to say, but I will not attempt to reproduce his dialect, nor do I know what dialect a Polish farmer uses. He said in effect, "Your Honor, I'm a hard working man. I work hard in the fields all day. I come home six o'clock. I wash my hands and face at the pump. I go in house. Dinner on table. I sit down with wife. Eat dinner. Look at the paper a little while. I go to bed. I sleep. Get up at five o'clock. Work hard in the fields all day. Well, one night I come home. Wash face and hands at the pump. Go in house. Dinner on table. It six o'clock. No wife. Go upstairs. Wife in bed with lover. Go downstairs. Eat dinner. Look at paper. Lover go way. I go to bed. Get up at five o'clock in the morning. Work hard in the fields all day. I get home six o'clock. Wash hands and face at the pump. Go in house. No dinner on table. Go upstairs. Wife in bed with lover. I kill wife and lover." Then he raised his voice to a shout, pounded his fist in his palm and said, "Dinner must be on the table at six o'clock!"

.          .          .

With all best wishes for the New Year to you and yours,

Sincerely,

# TO AN UNKNOWN CORRESPONDENT[1]

March 13, 1953

Thank you so much for sending me *The Mind of the Maker* by

1. Unidentified carbon in Chandler's files.

[336]

Dorothy Sayers. I must say that I find it pretty damned dull. Either my mind is completely vitiated, or this is a pretty fair example of the oversubtilized kind of thinking that really is a neurosis of the intellectual. Take an example at random: "The criterion is, not whether the associations are called up, but whether the spirits invoked by this kind of verbal incantation are charged with personal power by the magician who speeds them about their new business." Or to put it more simply: does it contain irium. She is talking about people like T. S. Eliot who use a great deal of classic and other quotation and allusion in their poems. I once had a radio program, a summer replacement for thirteen weeks, which was sponsored by the Pepsodent people. I tried very hard to find out what irium was. I don't think they know because I don't think it exists. It's just another name for the ineffable. So the criterion, as Miss Sayers puts it, seems to be not whether the ingredients in the poems of T. S. Eliot (or in Pepsodent toothpaste perhaps) are good in themselves but whether when they are put together there is something there that wasn't there before. It hardly seems to me worth arguing about. The answer always has to be yes. I long ago made up my mind that subtlety was not a dimension of thinking but merely a technique, and not a particularly difficult technique at that.

Thank you so very much anyhow.

## TO H. N. SWANSON

6005 Camino de la Costa
La Jolla, California
Mar 14 1953

Dear Swanie:

. . .

*Playback* is getting a bit tired.[1] I have 36,000 words of doodling and not yet a stiff. That is terrible. I am suffering from a very

---

1. Chandler's last novel, not published until 1958.

uncommon disease called (by me) atrophy of the inventive powers. I can write like a streak but I bore myself. That being so, I could hardly fail to bore others worse. I can't help thinking of that beautiful piece of Sid Perelman's entitled "I'm Sorry I Made Me Cry."

Did you ever read what they call Science Fiction. It's a scream. It is written like this: "I checked out with K 19 on Aldabaran III, and stepped out through the crummalite hatch on my 22 Model Sirus Hardtop. I cocked the timejector in secondary and waded through the bright blue manda grass. My breath froze into pink pretzels. I flicked on the heat bars and the Brylls ran swiftly on five legs using their other two to send out crylon vibrations. The pressure was almost unbearable, but I caught the range on my wrist computer through the transparent cysicites. I pressed the trigger. The thin violet glow was icecold against the rust-colored mountains. The Brylls shrank to half an inch long and I worked fast stepping on them with the poltex. But it wasn't enough. The sudden brightness swung me around and the Fourth Moon had already risen. I had exactly four seconds to hot up the disintegrator and Google had told me it wasn't enough. He was right."

They pay brisk money for this crap?

Ray

## TO ROGER MACHELL

6005 Camino de la Costa
La Jolla, California
Sunday March 15th [1953]

Dear Roger:
          This is going to be awful because I'm balling the jack myself and on a Corona yet. On Sunday nobody works but Chandler and he breaks his heart seven days a week and without no music.

.          .          .          .

          Please thank Jamie for sending me *The Big Change* and tell him I shall be writing to him anon. And thank you for the stuff from

[338]

*John O'London's* and the piece from the Westminster Bank.[1] In most ways I liked that better. As to Peter Forster, every interview makes a different man, and that is one reason why I don't like them. The photo is rather ugly. The hands are obviously those of a strangler. But Ida has rather cleverly minimised the hump on my back. The physical description of Chandler is unrecognizable by anyone who knows him. He calls me small. What is his standard? I have hardly ever weighed less than twelve stone—is that small in England? I have often weighed almost 13 stone. Attired for the street I am an inch short of six feet. My nose is not sharp but blunt, the result of trying to tackle a man as he was kicking a ball. For an English nose it would hardly be called prominent. Wispy hair like steel wool? Nuts. It is limp. Walks with a forward-leaning lope, huh? Chandler cantered gaily into the cocktail lounge, rapidly consumed three double gimlets and fell flat on his kisser, his steel wool hair curling gracefully against the pattern of the carpet. No wonder this man Forster thinks me observant. By his standards anyone who noticed how many walls the room had would be observant.

Yours ever,

Ray

# TO JUANITA MESSICK[1]

[1953]

That is a lot of bunk—removing the grid while preheating. Because why? The grid gets hot very quickly during cooking. The meat splatters grease all over it. The meat has to be turned and

1.  Interviews. The one by Peter Forster is called "Gentle Tough Guy," *John O'London's Weekly*, March 6, 1953.

1.  In answer to a note from Juanita Messick on cleaning the stove.

therefore does not always lie in the same place. What drivel sales people do talk! Take cigarette advertising. Every favorite brand is milder and less irritating than every other. The ideal cigarette has no taste at all. Therefore why smoke? What we need for broiling is a non-spattering steak, a steak containing no grease, fat, or other injurious ingredients, and incidentally, no flavor. What we need is a steakless steak to be broiled on a heatless broiler in a non-existent oven and eaten by a toothless ghost.

## TO JUANITA MESSICK

[1953]

Did you find "neg-otiator"[1] somewhere? It looks all wrong to me. Some words are very hard to split and probably should not be split at all unless there is an obvious place. You can split a word after a prefix or before a suffix, you can split it after a root, but how else? There must be some rule about it.

The "neg" in negotiate has nothing to do with the neg in negative. The big Webster gives the syllable split on all words, some in four or five places, but they don't all look right when you put them down on paper. It seems to me that the first part of the split word, that at the end of the line, should at least suggest a meaning of some sort, or a word association which could become a meaning. The mind rejects a meaningless syllable, like the first two letters ("ne-") although this might be technically right. There should be enough of the word to show its probable shape. Somehow it seems better for the split-off part to suggest the wrong meaning than no meaning at all.

RC

1. Webster's Second and Third New International Dictionaries both divide the word as ne-go-ti-a-tor.

# TO ALAN K. CAMPBELL

April 22, 1953

Dear Mr. Campbell:

I am replying to your kind letter of April 1st, inviting me to
have something to say at a conference of the Harvard Summer School.
Naturally I am grateful and flattered that you should think of me,
and I am regretful that largely for personal reasons I cannot be in
Boston in August. I say largely for personal reasons, and these reasons
are compelling. But I do not say entirely, since it is not within my
scheme of living, and I don't see how it ever could be, to get up on a
platform and tell anyone about anything. Perhaps I am trying to
make a virtue out of diffidence. I hope that is not entirely true, but it
may be. I am not a lecturer nor have I any qualifications to be one.
Too bad. It would be a nice one to drop into the still pool of
respectful attention, "You know I lectured at Harvard last summer. It
was rather fun." Thank you again, and believe me

Yours most respectfully,

# TO HAMISH HAMILTON

Box One Twenty Eight
La Jolla, California
May 11, 1953

Dear Jamie:

Two things I am annoyed about in *The Journal of Eugene
Delacroix*: one is the India paper, which of course I like very much in
some ways but when the tops of the pages are painted they are so
hard to turn; the other is reading a book as fine as this is in English
when I might just as well be reading it in French. I suppose that
this is an excellent translation, but the style seems to me a bit stuffy
compared with the French. Take any sentence at random. Take the
second one in the book: "My keenest wish is to remember that I am
writing only for myself." What a heavy lump of suet that is compared

[341]

with the lightness and ease of the French, the casual arrangement of the words and so on. Damn translations anyway. We have to have them because there are so many languages we don't know, but they're never the real thing, not even the best of them. Thank you so much for Eric Partridge's book on punctuation just received. What a frightfully industrious old bird he is! Makes me nervous just to think of him spending day after day, month after month in the British Museum with mountains of books stacked all around him.

. . .

As to my own efforts, I should say I am about four-fifths of the way through *Summer in Idle Valley*, which I no longer like as a title, almost completely rewritten because of my unfortunate inability to edit anything except changing a word here or there.[1] If it isn't right, I always have to start all over again and rewrite it. It seems easier to me; it isn't easier I know, it just seems easier. Every now and again I get stuck on a chapter, and then I wonder why. But there's always a reason, and I have to wait for the reason to come to me. I got about halfway through the other book before I decided that that needed a very drastic revision also. This one is no longer any fun; I've been too close to it too long, and it may turn out not to be any good.

. . .

Yours ever,

## TO ALFRED KNOPF

Box One Twenty Eight
La Jolla, California
July 16, 1953

Dear Alfred:

.

No, I am not on strike against publishing methods. I'd be

1. The title was later abandoned, and the book was published as *The Long Goodbye*.

foolish to criticize them too much, since I don't know the problems behind them well enough. I don't agree and I never have agreed that a publisher is entitled to collect more money in reprint rights than he pays out in royalties on his trade editions. He probably wouldn't be doing it, or not in all cases, if the silly old Authors League hadn't put everybody's back up by delivering ultimata with nothing to back them up but screams of anguish. Nor do I agree that a book is in print within the meaning of the terms of a publisher's contract when it is only in print in some paper-back edition which the publisher did not publish. But these may well be matters of opinion. I have just finished a book, as a matter of fact. I was never very productive, and I am not as productive as I used to be. I am much harder to satisfy than I used to be, also more easily tired. I am no longer with Brandt & Brandt, and in a way I regret that I was ever persuaded to leave you, although I realize I was no great financial asset to your publishing house. But I did, and a man can't keep jumping about from publisher to publisher. Anyhow, you have your hard-boiled writer now, and for a house of your standing one is enough.[1] I'm a little tired of the kick-'em-in-the-teeth stuff myself. I hope I have developed, but perhaps I have only grown tired and soft, but certainly not mellow. After all, I have fifty per cent Irish blood.

    Yours with best wishes and kindest regards,

                        Ray


## TO ROGER MACHELL

Box One Twenty Eight
La Jolla, California
July 17, 1953

Dear Roger:

       ·       ·       ·

I should especially like you to check me on two points that are outside

1.  Probable reference to Ross Macdonald.

my territory: one, that it is neither quick nor easy for an enlisted man on active service to get permission to get married; and two, what is the procedure for getting married at the Caxton Hall Registry Office?[1] I am assuming that it is still in business. If it isn't, please suggest another that would be suitable. I have assumed that although a person making a false declaration is liable for perjury, it would not be very difficult to get married under a false name if you weren't afraid of being hooked for perjury. If there's anything else I should know that would involve any alterations in the script, would you please tell me. And remember that this is in war time. To cut it short, all I want to know is that what I said happened could have happened, because if it couldn't have happened, then I have to think of something else. It's always like this. You state one fact, but you have to have twenty other facts that you don't state to back it up.

Yours ever,

Ray

## TO PHILIP GASKELL

Box One Twenty Eight<br>
La Jolla, California<br>
July 17, 1953

Dear Mr. Gaskell:

.            .            .

I will send you the information about the films as soon as I can. I don't suppose you are in any hurry for it. It's amusing that you should have mentioned Montgomery's version of *The Lady in the Lake* having nothing much to do with the book of that name.[1] I wrote the first script for this, but as I was under contract to Paramount

---

1. The questions relate to the typescript of *The Long Goodbye*.

1. Robert Montgomery, director and star of the film version of *The Lady in the Lake*.

[344]

and was only permitted thirteen weeks' work for another studio, this was not long enough for me to do the second and final shooting script. I didn't like the way that was done and refused to have my name on it. The amusing part is this—when I was working on the script I kept forgetting all about the book, because it was so much easier to do it ab initio. And it was the producer who kept saying to me, "Let's stick to the book a little here and there." This is the only published fiction of mine which I have tried to adapt for films. And it would take a lot of money to make me try it again, and I don't think that kind of money would be paid me now from Hollywood. When a man has written a book and rewritten it and rewritten it, he has had enough of it.

Yours very truly,

Raymond Chandler

## TO JUANITA MESSICK

August 8 1953

Nita: I have a rather sad message for you. I'm afraid that the end of this month you and I are going to have to part company on the present basis, but I sincerely hope are not going to have to part company completely. The simple fact of the matter is that I cannot, as things now are, afford the luxury of a secretary who costs me nearly 2000 dollars a year. I just can't do it and that's all there is to it. You know my circumstances perfectly well and you know that except for windfalls on which no one can count, I can hardly look forward to an income of more than 10 or 12 thousand dollars a year, gross. You know that I'm getting older and more tired, and that I have many worries. It is just not in the picture that I should be able to spend a fifth or a sixth of my gross income for a secretary. I should go it alone—entirely alone—for a month and see what kind of help, the extent of the help I most urgently need and should have. And I should then like, if possible and convenient to make some kind of an arrangement with you. Of course if I had a script to be copied, I'd

[345]

need somebody to copy it. I mean even want, say a day a week from you for letters. But I think I write many unnecessary letters and many unnecessarily long letters. And I think these letters consume a great deal of your time. The keeping of the books and the writing of the checks is nothing to me. The files are something else. They will probably be neglected unless you help with them. The same with the royalty statements. But after all, I'm pretty well on the downgrade and does it really matter so seriously? I am a worn, tired, man. I have lost my appetite and I have lost so much weight that I've had to punch two fresh holes in my belts. My clothes don't fit me any more. I'm depressed often and sleep badly. I have a sick wife who is not getting any better. I hope she will, and above all I hope that by the spring of this next year she will be well enough to go away somewhere for a long time. I'd like to go to Europe for a year. The cost of living in this country is so outrageous that when you begin to get old and have a little money saved up, it seems ridiculous not to go somewhere where life is a little cheaper. We have no very binding ties. I have found out that in my need nobody helps me. I'm not complaining. Nobody has that obligation.

.        .        .

I don't want to have to work in Hollywood or in television, nor in fact in any way at all except the writing of fiction. And I don't want to be driven in that. Well, if that is the situation, there is only one answer. You have to cut down on your expenses if you're going to cut down your output. Cissy has been going through a very bad time. And nobody helps her either, least of all the doctors. Perhaps they can't. They're not miracle workers. The fact is they don't. And I don't think any L.J. doctor will.[1] And I'm not sure that any doctor anywhere will.

I was 65 years old on my last birthday. As things go nowadays that's not old age exactly, but it does mean that you slow down, that you tire more quickly, that you have less ambition, that you are more easily irritated by business matters. And above all, you would occasionally like to sit in the sun and do nothing. Getting the breakfast, then driving myself to the typewriter for 3 or 4 hours, then almost at once going out to do the marketing, coming back and

1. La Jolla.

[346]

immediately starting to prepare the dinner, cooking it, washing the dishes, cleaning up afterward—this is not easy for me. It's not easy at all. I do it willingly, for I'd rather do it than have the kind of tramps in the house that we've had for the most part. But it's not easy. It takes its toll.

## TO JUANITA MESSICK

August 12, 1953

Dear Nita:
    Thank you for your note and all the rest of it, and I'm sure that we shall be able to work something out which won't interfere too much with what you are doing, and will not be unnecessarily elaborate from my point of view.
    Please don't drive yourself too hard. If you are not comfortable, don't come. Don't be too conscientious about anything. It's always easy to overdo it. A certain amount of selfishness is necessary to the business of living. This is difficult for unselfish people to achieve, but it is very necessary, believe me.
    By clearing out the files I meant mostly getting rid of the purely formal letters, etc., which contain no substantial material of any kind. I would not of course expect you to destroy any masterpieces of letter writing. Once in a while I run across one myself in the files, and I'm a little staggered if I happen to be the author of it to think I could have been so brilliant for no money. What a pity it is that there is nothing in essay writing. I could have been a very fine essayist, and should thoroughly have enjoyed that. Much more so than murder stories, which part of my mind always looks on with a certain condescension.

.        .        .

    As to when you take a week off to take a trip, I should say you should take it when you can get something out of it. I may need a little help around Christmas time—that is the week before Christmas, but it isn't anything that couldn't be done the week before that if

[347]

that should happen to be the week you want to take—I mean that if the week before Christmas should happen to be the week you want to take. I don't see that it really matters very much. We don't have to file another income tax estimate until the 15th of January and that one should be practically final. That is to say, the books should be posted and balanced up to the end of the year, the allocations of expense distributed, etc.; the depreciation schedules worked out.

As to your being a bore—or rather as to its being a bore to have somebody here all the time, that depends on the person. I did find it so with Mildred Onstine, because although she was an extremely likeable and efficient person, she had a sort of officy personality. I kept wondering if I was doing her justice and realizing that I was not. Your being here doesn't bore me; it doesn't bore my wife; and it doesn't bore Leona; and I'm quite sure it doesn't bore Taki.[1] But if in a tactfully indirect way you happen to be nudging at the suggestion that there are some things that you want to do or some activities that you want to follow which you find yourself cramped in attending, then I say you know how to arrange your work. Go ahead and do what you want to do and take the time you need to do it. This is not a factory. As you have probably realized by now, my greatest problem in life is to do any work. More and more, as the years go by, I am distracted and irritated by gardeners, plumbers, electricians, painters, carpenters, insurance men, and all the types that you have to have to do things for you, and that a man who is really a business man (which I am not) should be able to take in stride and then put them out of his mind. To me, each of these things is an operation. I get tired much more easily than I used to. Unfortunately I have a rather pugnacious temperament and I lack the stamina that ought to go with it to make it effective. I was once a main eventer, but I'm strictly a four-round prelim boy now. So the more of this stuff you can accustom yourself to handle, the more happy I shall be and the more productive my life would be. It costs a lot of money to live in La Jolla; it costs a lot of money to live the way we live, although I don't think we live extravagantly. And I can't make that money wrangling with technicians. I don't know why the hell I write so many letters, and I don't know why the hell when I do write letters, I have to write such long letters. I guess my mind

1. Leona the cook; Taki the cat.

is just too active for my own good. I have too much in me that never gets a chance to get said. It's probably not worth saying, but then that doesn't help me to realize that.

There is another thing you are probably well aware of, although I'm a little reluctant to mention it. And that is that my wife is not able to do what she did only a few years ago. When we came down here in 1946, sometimes she did all the housework, or almost all of it, with some daily help. She cooked the meals; she did the marketing; she dealt with painters and people of that sort; and she liked doing it. And I know that secretly she feels a little bit depressed that she can't do it now, and I wouldn't even talk to her about it. Won't mention it to her. But the fact is, she can't. For instance, she would say to me "Well you forget about the gardener. I'll get a gardener and handle him and attend to him. Just put it out of your mind." Then she'd get busy on the telephone and wear herself out talking to various people and finally get a gardener and he'd come and she'd follow around with him and spend a lot of time with him. And I could see it was tiring her too much. And then I'd gradually edge in and take over, and I wouldn't like it. I mean I wouldn't like to have to do it. I'm a man who takes very little lightly.

Now a secretary in the home is in an awkward position, that is an awkward position for most people. I don't think it is so for you, because it's not only the place where the man works. It's also his wife's home, and she doesn't like to take on herself things which she may not think are her business. So I should suggest to you that if the thought occurs to you "Well I could do that if he'd let me or he wants me to," or "I could do that for Mrs. Chandler, if she wants me to." Then I suggest that you say so right off, and that you ask my wife if she wouldn't like you to do so and so. But never hint to her that you don't think she's able to do it. And if you see me starting to do something which you know is going to end in my getting mad at somebody, why come right out and say, "You'd better leave me to do that. I think I can handle it. And if I can't I'll tell you." Or something to that effect. You can be even blunter. You don't have to be so damn polite. And as for being bored, again, with having somebody around all the time, I'm not bored, and I shan't be bored. But I'm perfectly well aware that there are times when it would be very natural for you to be bored. And when those times come, I suggest you simply get up and say "Well, I'm going out for awhile."

[349]

Or, "I'm going to San Diego this afternoon, and if you don't like it, to hell with you." Of course I shan't mind in the least, because you'll know better than I do whether it is going to be difficult or inconvenient.

Ten years ago I could have looked after this garden all by myself and enjoyed it. I'd have put in three or four hours a day on it probably. And though there would have been times when it would have bored me a little, on the whole I should have got a lot of fun and satisfaction out of it. I don't think I could do it now. One of the penalties of having enough money—and you never realize it until you have enough money—is that you don't get any satisfaction out of doing the things that save money. I admire the man who can paint his own house and roof and get a lot of healthy exercise and save himself a good big painter's bill. But saving that painter's bill probably means a lot to him—a lot more than it could possibly mean to me. That's something people don't think about. In my business it's a great deal easier to make money than it is to save it. But for some reason, or set of reasons I don't quite understand, I haven't lately been very successful in getting myself in the right mood to make money. It's my own fault. I shall never be able to change my temperament now. The most I can hope for is to outfox it occasionally.

Message ends.

# TO H. F. HOSE

Box One Twenty Eight
La Jolla, California
Sept. 16 1953

Dear Hose:

I should write to you oftener. I have lost weight lately and I tire easily. I do a little work, then business letters, and after that no energy. No doubt you know the feeling. After sixty a man should not worry about trifles, but I do. (I don't mean that writing you is a trifle, but rather that worrying about trifles saps one's energies.) The best doctor I know has told me that I shall probably die of exhaustion, as there is nothing else to kill me, no deterioration. I don't remember as well as I did. I have to make notes and lists. Sometimes quite familiar names slip off the edge of memory and hang out of sight, then pop back grinning.

When I was in London Slacker[1] told me that they retired masters at 60 (I believe that is the ridiculous age) because it was so much cheaper to employ a young man. That struck me as a ridiculous way of looking at things. He also said men of that age were out of touch with the boys. I should reply that in most cases any adult is out of touch with the average or even rather better than average boy. One of the weird problems of our time is the juvenile delinquent. Gangs of young crooks pop up in the most exclusive neighborhoods. Atlanta, Georgia, had a wave of burglaries and vandalism and it was traced to the young of some of the wealthiest families in the city. Our local high school (realschule or grammar school) had a Thieves Club among the children of the best families. Those who have much to do with the young tell me the delinquents come from the very poor and the rich, seldom from the ordinary middle class people. I happen to know it is not true. They come from any level of income. The wars have had a lot to do with it, no doubt, but much of it would have happened anyhow. There is no discipline in the schools because there is no means of enforcing it. And in the home parents argue with their children, they don't tell them. If I had children, and thank God I never had any, I should send them abroad to school. American schools are rotten, especially in California. If your boy won't behave himself, you can try a military school where he will be taught to behave himself (or expelled), but he won't learn anything else. You can send him to one of the New England snob schools like Groton, if you can afford it but unless you are well off it is not a kind thing to do. He will meet boys who drive Jaguars and Rileys and have too much spending money and he will feel inferior. Or you can send him to a Jesuit school, regardless of religion. The public schools are trash. About all they learn there is the increasingly simple art of seduction. The state universities have laughable standards of scholarship as a rule. One of my wife's nephews graduated (they say 'was graduated' over here, but I dislike the locution intensely) from high-school with the mental equipment of the Lower Fourth, say the

1. A mutual friend from Chandler's Dulwich days.

[351]

middle third of that form. But he has turned out very well. He couldn't have got into a state university, much less a place like Stanford or Pomona, but he faced the problem of earning a living without any trouble at all. I find that curious, and very American. He did fourteen months in Korea without any trace of old soldier nonsense about him, he is married, and he is very scrupulous about money. But you couldn't talk to him for five minutes about anything which assumed a knowledge of history or literature or even an awareness that such things exist.

      •      •      •

No. I have never published anything under a pseudonym. I'm sure I don't know how the rumor you heard came about. I'd like to know. I have been ruthlessly imitated and even plagiarized of course, but there is nothing one can do about it. A few years ago a man wrote a story which was a scene by scene steal from one of mine. He changed names and incidents just enough to stay inside the law, which is not difficult as the courts have a very primitive attitude on plagiarism. The publisher to whom the book was sent demanded indignantly of the agent submitting it how he dared send them a book by Chandler under a pseudonym without saying so. When he learned that I had not had anything to do with the book he demanded certain changes to tone down the blatancy of the imitation and then published it. It did very well too. Someday an enlightened jurist of the type of Curtis Bok or Learned Hand may announce that the plagiarism of style is the most nefarious of all forms of plagiarism and the shabbiest. But it would be very difficult to draw the line between the natural imitativeness of a writer influenced by another and the deliberate attempt to steal his characteristic mise en scene. After all if another writer can really steal your style, it can't be very important. The answer is that he can't, he can only produce some of the superficial characteristics.

      •      •      •

And so to bed, but without any particular content of mind.

Yours ever,

Ray

[352]

# TO J. B. PRIESTLEY

Box One Twenty Eight
La Jolla, California
December 10, 1953

Dear Priestley:

Many thanks for yours of November 25th and the comments therein. In thinking I should write a Marlowe story without a murder or any violence in it you are one with my wife who thinks exactly the same thing. Would it be all right if he got conked on the head with a Scotch bottle just once? On the other hand, the whole business of writing demands a lot of verve, and I just don't have it any more. It doesn't seem to matter.

I never did thank you for arranging that showing of *Last Holiday*, to which we were conducted by a furious character named Peters, coldly furious I should add, who would make a perfect superintendent of police at Scotland Yard. His manner was impeccable, but the whole deal was obviously a crashing bore to him and he could hardly wait for it to be over. We enjoyed the picture immensely, but I had some qualms about the ending. I don't mean that it was wrong, and I'm quite sure you gave it plenty of thought. But the irony did seem a little factitious. The picture hasn't shown up out here, although it is playing in New York, but when and if it does, I'd like very much to see it again. It has some lovely scenes.

My wife remembers the luncheon with you with a great deal of pleasure. I regret to say that she is not at all well, as she was not when you were here. I am hoping but rather against hope that we shall be able to make to Europe again next spring. She felt very badly all the time we were in London but tried hard not to show it.

With kindest regards,

Yours ever,

Ray

[353]

# TO HAMISH HAMILTON

Box One Twenty Eight
La Jolla, California
Jan 16, 1954

Dear Jamie:

Thank you so much for the bound copy (I should have said specially bound) of *LG*.[1] I don't really think my books are worth so handsome a binding and I have moments when I feel like hiding them—except that it would look rather ungrateful to you. I have visions as it were of some snooty character looking over my bookshelves and saying to himself: "Does this type really think his books belong in calf with gold edges and gold tooling?" However, what is a man to do?

· · ·

Los Angeles has nothing for me anymore. It's only a question of time until a Gentile has to wear an armband there. The story I am fitfully working on at the moment is laid in La Jolla and will be much shorter and more light-hearted than *LG*. But I'm fed up with the California locale.

I don't know whether this true story will have any meaning for you, but it amused me no end. A woman and her small boy were in the local bookshop and the woman was browsing and the kid was trying to tell her about a dog that was hurt by a car. She was giving him the usual absent, "Yes, darling," while really thinking of something else. "The poor little dog was hurt awful bad, Mummy," the kid said. "He was hurt awful bad." "Was he, dear?" "Yes, Mummy, he was hurt awful bad but he dragged hisself all the way home, Mummy. He was hurt so bad but he dragged hisself all the way home, Mummy." "Did he, dear? Well, that's nice." The kid looked up at her sadly, then said, "He got home all right Mummy. But he passed on."

· · ·

When duller letters are written, Chandler will write them.

Ray

1. *The Long Goodbye.*

[354]

P.S. Your letter with clippings arrived just as I was about to post this, so I have opened it to add a little. I don't begin to understand this reference to Henry James (of whom once I was a desperately ardent admirer). Over here I have never been treated otherwise than as a rather good second-rate thriller writer and I thought the same was the attitude in England and I assumed that these desires for interviews were more the result of your kindly machinations than any spontaneous wishes on the part of newspapers, etc. It has always been clear to me that if the good Lord had intended me to be an important writer, he would not have allowed me to waste twenty years of my life in offices, almost ten of them as the factotum of a corrupt multi-millionaire. (Anyone who thinks I don't understand rich people of a certain type is wrong.) There are things about writing that I love, but it is a lonely and ungrateful profession and personally I'd much rather have been a barrister, or even an actor. It is always a misfortune to be taken seriously in a field of writing where quality is not expected nor desired. The highbrows find it hard enough to forgive popularity, even moderate popularity such as mine, but popularity plus pretentions to any kind of literary distinction—that is too, too much. How they must have suffered over Maugham!


## TO MR. LOVELL[1]

Box One Twenty Eight
La Jolla, California
Feb 9, 1954

Dear Mr. Lovell:

.        .        .

 I suppose in the history of writing there must have been quite a few one book writers. *Delay in the Sun* by Anthony Thorne (he has written other books but ng.) The most impressive examples I recall are *The Unbearable Bassington* by Saki (of course he wrote a lot of

1. A book collector

[355]

short pieces but I think no other novel) and a book you probably never heard of called *The Great Humpty-Dumpty* by Daniel Chaucer.[2] When one is young one has love affairs with books as with girls. I recall this book with delight but should be afraid to read it now, just as I should be afraid to reread another early darling of mine called *The Loves of Edwy* by Rose Ceil O'Neill. (She was really a gifted illustrator, but this book got to me when I was at the impressionable age.) Chaucer's book was to have been called *The Dark Forest* but he found out Hugh Walpole had published a book with that title. Hence the regrettable substitution.

A la recherche du temps perdu—that way lies disillusion. Like the fellow who wanted to take his bride to see the little lake near Saint Cloud with the swans on it that he remembered so vividly from a childhood in France. It was to be one of the high lights of their honeymoon. When they arrived there and established the location—no lake, no swans. There never had been a lake there and there never had been any swans.

The swans of our childhood were probably just pigeons.

Yours,

Raymond Chandler

# TO JAMES M. FOX[1]

Box One Twenty Eight
La Jolla, California
February 16, 1954

Dear Fox:

I don't know why I should write an autobiography. My English publisher said once I should, but I fail to agree with him. If I

2. Pseudonym used by Ford Madox Ford for this book *The New Humpty-Dumpty*.

1. Author of *Dark Crusade* and other books.

did it, it would be full of lies. I don't think anyone else could do it, though, and I shouldn't care for the idea. What your arguments are I have no idea, but they will almost certainly not convince me. There is no reason why a man should not write his autobiography if he can make it interesting enough. He doesn't have to be a person of any vast distinction. The only point is, is it a book? Like Neville Cardus (not sure of the way he spells his first name).[2] You don't read it because you are curious about him, but because he makes his life interesting. It is quite another matter for a man to assume that he is so much of a personality that a biography is a matter of public interest, regardless of who writes it.

.     .     .

As to the ending or denouement not being a surprise, what ending is to someone in the trade? You are opening up a large box of crackers here. I could exhaust myself discussing it because it is one of my favorite beefs. I claim that no "honest" mystery plot will fool the aficionado. The operative word here is "honest" and I mean it in a very rigorous sense. You don't write for just one kind of people. A mystery subtle enough to come near fooling the analytical mind will make no sense to the ordinary rental library ghoul. So you have a choice. Either assume that your denouement is going to be transparent to some people or else cheat. Very often you do both without realizing it. The cheat may be merely a matter of over or under-emphasis, the burying of the essential clue in a mass of trivia, the revelation early in a book of a certain abnormal facet of character which is then immediately dropped until the end. The first person story is assumed to tell all but it doesn't. There is always a point at which the hero stops taking the reader into his confidence. There is the solution which turns on a recondite piece of knowledge, as in Austin Freeman. There is the solution which depends on something not disclosed to the reader until almost the end, such as in Sayers's *Have His Carcase*. That is a cheat for two reasons; one, because it was withheld too long, the other because the police surgeon, unless he was an idiot, would have known the dead man was a hemophiliac. I don't want to labor the point. I never bother about who bumped off Sir Montague Core-Cavendish in the gun room with the doors

2. Music critic, journalist, and author of books on cricket.

and windows all locked. Very often just for the fun of it I look at the
end and then amuse myself with watching the author trying to
smudge his fingerprints. And a surprise ending is no good if you
don't believe it. If the reader doesn't think he *should* have known, he
has been had. And what doesn't fool you will fool all sorts of other
people, including reviewers. The typical mystery novel is like that
thing on Studio One last night. An obvious suspect is presented and
played up and you immediately eliminate her just because she has
been played up. An old man in a wheel chair can get out of it to
snitch a drink at the sideboard. Another red herring. The old
housekeeper is obviously just what she pretends to be. The youngest
sister is in love with the doctor who is going to solve the mystery. So
who is left? The sister who got the poison pen letters. So she wrote
them to herself. Why? No reason that makes sense. So she did it
without knowing what she was doing. At that point I didn't give a
damn and was far more interested in speculating why the doctor went
out of the room leaving his medical bag open in the presence of a
loony and what drug he would have with him that worked almost as
fast as cyanide and yet gave the dear girl time to use her exit line.
I had to give up on that one.

So long,

R.C.

## TO HARDWICK MOSELEY

Box One Twenty Eight
La Jolla, California
March 23rd, 1954

Dear Hardwick:

I'm sick as a dog, thank you, with one of these lousy virus
infections the doctors have invented to cover up their ignorance. But I
know you want an answer. I missed seeing Paul Brooks two weeks
ago and I'm still rocking. I also missed a *Time* photog but they
intrinsically lied. He was from the San Diego *Union-Tribune* and there

is no worse murderer than a newspaper flash gun artist. They did one of me in London that made me look like Grandma Moses and I swore I'd never have another. (By the way where did you get that beastly thing you put in your spring list?) Of course *Time* doesn't matter because the fact that they interview you or photograph you is no guarantee. Imagine those lice in *Newsweek* not even paying for the photographs they ordered![1]

You better do a damn sight better with *The Long Goodbye* than you did with *Little Sister*. I realize the appalling situation but I also realize that the publishers are not indefinitely going to be able to make their profits if any by their share of the reprints. Writers of forgettable fiction will simply be forced into the paperback market. How the hell can you expect anyone to pay dollars three for a mystery novel? I might be the best writer in this country, and with two exceptions I very likely am, but I'm still a mystery writer. For the first time in my life I was reviewed as a Novelist in the London *Sunday Times* (but Leonard Russell is a friend of mine and may have leaned a little out of kindness). I was discussed on the BBC by as addled a group of so-called intellectuals (among whom Dilys Powell hardly got a word in) as ever had soup on their vests. But over here? *The New York Times* which surely should know what it is doing if any newspaper does has twice given books of mine for review to mystery writers who had been waiting for years for the chance to knife me because I have ridiculed the sort of thing they write themselves (not mentioning them by name in any sense nor even by suggestion). Neither had either the guts or the ability to make a reply on the same level as the original article. It could be that the *Times* has it in for me because I have persistently refused to review books for them; on the other hand they change personnel so often that they probably don't even know I refused. But what I'm getting at is that if a paper of that quality can't judge a book by its quality as a piece of writing rather than by its news value or subject matter, how in hell can one expect a semi-literate public to do anything more intelligent?

.    .    .

We are still trying to sell this house, much as we like it. My wife is far from well, domestic help is unobtainable unless you have,

1.  Chandler had been promised a *Newsweek* cover story, but it was never published.

as we have, a treasure. But we have her only five days a week, she is not too well herself, and she has troubles which may end her for us at almost any time. If I get sick over a week end, it is a catastrophe. My wife almost fainted two or three times last weekend trying to take care of me. We can't live here indefinitely. We are thinking of the south of France. The climate would be good for Cissy. But it's a pretty risky adventure all the same. I have an operative working on it. What acquaintances tell you is no good unless you know their own standards. I'm not terribly fond of French people but I know the language and they at least do their own thinking and can express it in language. A stevedore on the docks is more articulate in France than most senators and Congressmen are here. And McCarthy would last over there about the length of time necessary to uncover the cesspool.[2]

I salute you finally with two animal stories, one true, one not. A family on the street behind us has a black French poodle, small, toy size, I guess. The animal is taking piano lessons, $35 a month. As of now he can play Peter, Peter, Pumpkin Eater, not technically very exacting, but one has to begin, n'est-ce pas? Little steps for little feet. Later one hopes he will make his debut in Carnegie Hall. The people can afford it and that's all it takes. One looks forward, perhaps a little hesitantly, to his scintillating performance of Chopin's Barcarolle, a difficult piece seldom played and never played really well since de Pachmann.[3] Rubinstein is supposed to be a Chopin virtuoso, but to me he is very in and out. The poodle has a pretty clear field there. It's nice to have ambitious neighbors, and to live in a milieu where money is spent on Art, not just on Cadillacs, Jaguars, and colored butlers. This is true. $35 a month for lessons. Black toy French poodle.

The other one is about a guy who went to the *Cinema* (English accent please) and was annoyed by a large, tall and far too wide fur coat in front of him. Leaning over he perceived that the fur coat was a bear. He tapped the man beside the bear on the shoulder.

"I say, old man, is that your bear?"

"He's with me."

"Well get him out of here right away, old man. This is no place to bring a bear."

2. Senator Joseph McCarthy.
3. Vladimir de Pachmann (1848–1933), eccentric Russian pianist and champion of Chopin.

"I shall do nothing of the sort. He's paid for his ticket and he's enjoying himself."

Man subsides, very annoyed. Picture ends finally, lights go up, man with bear seems about to leave. Objecting man has a change of heart.

"I say, old man, sorry I spoke like that about your bear. Seems dashed well behaved. But why bring him to the pictures, old man?"

"Oh, he's very fond of the *cinema*, very fond indeed. And he particularly wanted to see this film. He liked the book so much."

Ray

## TO ROGER MACHELL

Box One Twenty Eight
La Jolla, California
March 24th. 1954

Dear Roger:

There's quite a bit to answer in your good letter but before I get on to it, two or three items I'm afraid of forgetting. 1. For God's sake save your people the anguish and expense of sending me 8 copies of Finnish translations. Four would be more than enough. My wife keeps one (she has a new issue of everything of mine ever published, even pulp magazines), I keep a so-called file copy and it's always possible in this polyglot country that I may run across someone who would like a book in Finnish. They do a nice job on them, but Jesus what a language! Everything is backwards. I once hoped to be a comparative philologist (just a boyhood fancy no doubt) and dabbled in such strange lingos as Modern Greek (there's a debased language for you—it just *looks* like Greek, all the richness and variety is gone, all the subtlety, all the charm), Armenian, Hungarian, besides the simpler and more obvious Romance tongues and the Germanic group. I slept with a chart of the 214 key ideographs of the Chinese Mandarin language pinned to the wall at the head of my bed in the Pension Narjollet, 27 Boulevard St. Michel, au cinquième. But Finnish, hell it's worse than Turkish.

[361]

As for Commercial TV, here is a small true story of the kind of atmosphere the domination of the big advertising agencies can create. A few years back the Pepsodent Company took over sponsorship of a radio series on Philip Marlowe as a summer replacement. Their agency was a big firm which also at the time handled Chesterfield cigarettes. The producer of the show is the brother of a very well-known actor. He told me the story. A company big shot (partner) visited the L.A. office on business, a severe and elegant gentleman immaculate and grey, one of these extraordinary people of our time who seem to be able to reconcile wealth, position, blameless private lives and perfect manners with an idiotic devotion to the latest brand of skin-poisoning detergent or face cream (if the manufacturer is their account, natch). This geek happened to see a junior executive entering the premises that morning smoking a Philip Morris cigarette. He stopped him and said: "I observe, Mr. Jones, that you do not care for the product of our sponsor." Mr. Jones flushed and looked at the cigarette he was holding. Oh, I'm extremely sorry, Mr. Blank. I was rather in a hurry this morning and instead of my own Chesterfields I must have grabbed up one of my wife's cigarettes." Mr. Blank stared at him in silence for a long moment, then, as he turned away, he remarked icily: "I presume that your wife has an income of her own."

You know, that sort of thing makes a cold shiver run down my spine.

Ray

## TO DOROTHY GARDINER[1]

April, 1954

As a writer of 20 years' professional experience I have met all kinds of people. Those who know most about writing are those who can't write. The less attention you pay to them the better. They

---

1. Former secretary of the Mystery Writers of America. This statement was written for *The Third Degree*, the bulletin of that organization.

[362]

are on the outside looking in and what they see is no good to the man inside; it is in a different category of mind. So I have made three rules of writing for myself that are absolutes: Never take advice. Never show or discuss work in progress. Never answer a critic.

## TO HARDWICK MOSELEY

Box One Hundred Twenty Eight
La Jolla, California
May 6, 1954

Dear Hardwick:

    •      •      •

No one has ever attacked me so far and yet in every book I have written there is what is described by more perceptive friends as a "thinly disguised portrait" of some notorious local character. In every case, the thinly disguised etc. has been a portrait of someone I didn't even know existed. In *The High Window* I had an Italian mortician on Bunker Hill who was a political boss on the side. Well, whaddaya know, there actually was an Italian mortician on Bunker Hill who was a political boss, and a pretty crooked one, on the side. But I never heard of him. I invented him. I suppose it's an old story. And yet when you do use some really notorious person as a model nobody spots it.

    •      •      •

Some crazy idiot at Little Brown sent me a book called *Freak Show*.[1] I haven't the slightest intention of reading it nor have I the faintest idea why they published it. So it may easily be a bestseller. I would say the guy might be a road show James Cain except that James Cain is a road show James Cain himself.

With malice towards all,

Yours always,

Ray

1. *Freakshow*, by Jacquin Sanders.

[363]

# TO ROGER MACHELL

Box One Twenty Eight
La Jolla, California
May 25, 1954

Dear Roger:

Thanks for your letter and statements and for the remittance which the Canadian Bank of Commerce has duly confirmed. I'm enclosing a letter from a Portuguese agent in Lisbon which will possibly be of no interest to you. The only point that stuck me, if it is valid, was his statement that Portuguese readers do not like Brazilian translations. I'm sure this is very likely since the South American languages must have departed considerably from the standard of the mother country.

I see that Cassells had an ad in the *Sunday Times* which quoted part of Mr. Iles' gratuitously offensive remarks ("snide" is our word for that sort of thing) but did leave out the slur about nymphomaniacs.[1] Somebody ought to tell these dessicated creeps what a nymphomaniac is. They apparently seem to think the word is synonymous with promiscuity, or even with a mild fling at adultery. Of course I ought not to pay any attention to them and usually I just take the bad with the good and realize that I have probably had more than my share of the good. But if I were somewhat younger and heartier, I might take a fling at it anyhow, realising the weakness of the legal position (it would be far weaker here) but also realising that it is one thing to slam a book when it has been handed to you for review and quite another to keep sniping at a writer under cover of reviewing somebody else. There is a certain class of 'tec writer or ex-'tec writer who will never forgive me for having blown up their pretense of writing deduction. In this class are Anthony Boucher over here, John Dickson Carr, Lenore Glen Offord, Anthony Berkeley and so on. There are no doubt many others, but I mention those who review books. "Oh that mine enemy would write a book!" I've often been asked to review books that seemed more or less up my alley but I have always declined—The *N.Y. Times* was especially

1. Francis Iles and Anthony Berkeley are pseudonyms for Anthony Berkeley Cox, a reviewer and critic.

[364]

persistent—because I am aware of having prejudices and I don't think I have any right to exploit them at the expense of some struggling writer.

The practical effect of all this sneering at me is to make me self-conscious to the point where it is difficult for me to write anything in my somewhat bravura manner without wondering whether I am not just making an ass of myself. That is the writer's cross and few bear it without getting weary. Theoretically he should be as hard as nails, as insensitive as the pavement. If he were, he would have no magic, and without some magic there is nothing. He does not expect everyone to like him and, in fact, he is often enough surprised that anyone likes him. No matter how successful he has been, he always starts from scratch on the next job. The public or whatever small fraction of it reads him expects from him always much the same thing. He is supposed to deliver a staple article. But the critics expect him to break new ground with every new effort. Of course if he did, they would be most happy to announce that he would have been wiser to stay within the established formula.

Yours ever,

Ray

## TO ROGER MACHELL

Box One Twenty Eight
La Jolla, California
Sunday July 11, 1954
Tuesday July 13, 1954

Dear Rog:
This is what they would call you if you lived over here. We are so goddam busy watching TV that we don't have the time to speak anyone's full name.

.        .        .

THE UCLA Library (University of California at Los Angeles)

[365]

has asked for the typescript of any of my books, but I never have kept it. However they got *The Long Goodbye* from Houghton Mifflin. What on earth they want it for I can't imagine. They also wanted to purchase a first edition of *Farewell My Lovely*. I didn't have one but offered them the first English edition of which I had a copy, and they accepted it with an ornate scroll. By the way this title, which I thought entirely original, turned up as the title of a piece by E. B. White (under a pseudonym—Lee Strout White) about the Model T Ford. This was, I think, originally published in the *New Yorker*, but long before I ever looked at the magazine. It wasn't until I went to work in Hollywood that I knew the magazine existed and I have never really liked it. There is an undertone of spitefulness about too much of its writing—not all, of course—that is quite missing from *Punch*. *Punch* you have to read; the *New Yorker* you just glance through. I don't know how these things happen. One would think I had seen the magazine in a doctor's office but no. My memory for that sort of material is much too good. It happens just as people happen to steal your story ideas before you even use them. Certain things are in the air.

Leave us all go home.

Yours ever,

Ray

## TO HAMISH HAMILTON

July 15th, 1954

Dear Jamie:

Thank you so much for sending me the books; *Pompadour*, *The Long Beat Home*, *The Woman with No Past*, and the pseudo-Victorian novel which Cissy has and I forget the title.[1] *The Long Beat Home* looks like a nice try, but it doesn't seem to me to have that crisp something that gets you by the throat and holds on. I don't know whether we Americans (I always feel like a phoney when I say 'we

1. *Madame de Pompadour*, by Nancy Mitford; *The Long Bear Home* by Peter Gladwin; *The Woman with No Past*, by Serge Groussard.

Americans' because basically I never have and never will feel quite a native) are more mentally lazy than you English; I rather think we are, but I'm not sure; but I do think we are more resentful of having to do the donkey work of getting interested in something—unless we know in advance that is worth the effort. For instance *The Go-Between* was a very highly praised book, but I started it and dropped it and went back half a dozen times before I got far enough into it to give a damn about anyone.[2] And even then I did a lot of skipping. And I never quite believed the book. I tried to see the world through the eyes of this boy, but I was a twelve year old myself and in much the same period and it just didn't look that way to me. Somehow for me the novel lacks a dimension. Or I lack one. I've read Maugham's articles in the *Sunday Times* as far as they have come this way.[3] Maugham would have done that story to perfection, but he wouldn't have written it through the eyes of a 12 year old boy. He would have known damn well that it is not possible and he is much too acute to attempt the impossible. Sometimes one thinks that is rather a pity. So long and distinguished a career deserves at least one magnificent failure.

*Pompadour* is a lot of fun. What a woman, what a world, what a waste! But the world I grew up in is almost as remote. A wonderful world if you were born into exactly the right family, a blasted cold hypocritical cruel world if you were not. Still, at least part of the population had a good time. No one has nowadays except the crooks and the oil millionaires (there may be a slight distinction here but I was in the oil business for about ten years and the distinction is very fine), and perhaps some of the higher civil servants, but they are usually too stupid to know it. What a strange sense of values we had. What godawful snobs! My grandmother referred to one of the nicest families we knew as "very respectable people" because there were two sons, five golden haired but unmarriagable daughters and no servant. They were driven to the utter humiliation of opening their own front door. The father painted, sang tenor, built beautiful model yachts and sailed a small yawl all over the place. My grandmother was the widow of an Irish solicitor. Her son, very wealthy later on, was also a solicitor and had a housekeeper named Miss Groome who sneered at him behind his back because he wasn't a barrister. The

2. By L. P. Hartley
3. A series on the authors and their novels.

Church, the Navy, the Army, the Bar. There was nothing else. Outside Waterford in a big house with gardens and gardens lived a Miss Paul who occasionally, *very* occasionally invited Miss Groome to tea on account of her father had been a canon. Miss Groome regarded this as the supreme accolade because Miss Paul was County. It didn't seem to bother Miss Paul but it sure as hell made a wreck of Miss Groome. It would be some comfort to add that she was a capable housekeeper, but she was not. My uncle had a succession of awful Irish Protestant maids and cooks and so on—always Protestants, as they and the Catholics had little or nothing to do with one another on any level. I remember playing a cricket match with one of my cousins and one of the boys was a Catholic from some probably rather important family. Anyhow he came in a carriage with a coachman and footman and after the game immediately departed without even having tea with the teams. My uncle was a man of rather evil temper on occasion. Sometimes when the dinner did not suit him he would order it removed and we would sit in stony silence for three quarters of an hour while the frantic Miss Groome browbeat the domestics below stairs and finally another meal was delivered to the master, probably much worse than the one he had refused; but I can still feel that silence.

A strange and puzzling thing, the English snobbishness. I was a poor relation and one of my cousins had a short job as some kind of companion to a very well-to-do family living in a suburb not very far away. Later on when I was about seventeen, I think, I was invited over to their house to play tennis. They were rather gaudy people, except the father. A number of the guests were very young girls and young men, all expensively dressed, and several rather drunk. I was in no way expensively dressed, but far from feeling inferior I realized at once that these people were not at all up to the standard even of Dulwich, and heaven knows what Eton or Rugby would have thought about them. The boys and girls had gone to private schools, but not the right kind. There was a little something about their accents, and more than a little about their manners. (One sicked up in the drawing room.) During the course of an afternoon of rather studied courtesy on my part the family dog chewed up my straw hat with the school ribbon on it. When I left, the head of the family, a very nice little man in some kind of "trade" in the City, insisted on paying for the hat. I coldly refused to accept his money, although in those times it was quite usual for the host to tip a schoolboy at the end of a visit. But this seemed to me different. This was taking money from a social inferior: not to be thought of. Yet they were kind people and full of fun and very tolerant and, as I look back on it now, probably much more worth knowing than my stupid and arrogant grandmother. Of course the genuine top drawer people were quite different, insofar as I ever got close to them for a few brief moments.

Yours ever,

Ray

What a lot of drivel!

## TO EDGAR CARTER

September 21, 1954

Dear Eddie:

Herewith the CBS contract, signed, and signed also the declaration that I am not, have not ever been, and do not intend ever to be a hole in a piece of Swiss cheese.[1] My God, what is this country coming to? What are we afraid of? As a charter member of the C.B.S.A. (Colored Baby Sitters of America, Inc.) I resent the suggestion that I am not a four hundred per cent loyal American and that I must sign a document of this type in order that something which I once wrote may be transmuted into something that somebody else has since rewritten, and no doubt abominably, for the purposes of television, which has, by a far less brilliant mind than mine, been described as "infinite boredom in a little room." Nevertheless, the soft buck is paramount; nothing must be allowed to interfere with its oleaginous progress into the bank account. However, for the moment I think we are fairly safe. Of the seventeen decorations I received from Stalin, fifteen are buried in an old salmon can under the third

1. Anti-Communist loyalty oath.

juniper tree to the left, and the other two are buried in the back of my neck. And after all, the stuff I stole wasn't very important really. I think the best find the FBI made was that scribbled greeting, "Good morning, chief," which I had rather inefficiently concealed behind the lining of my second-best silk hat. But I don't think they ever would have found that if they hadn't happened on an agent with two heads who insisted upon wearing two silk hats all the time. Something besides his ears must have rustled in one of them.

Yours ever,

## TO H. N. SWANSON

Box One Twenty Eight
La Jolla, California
September 22, 1954

Dear Swanie:

I know that you can make a lot of money out of the big magazines if you have the right approach and the temperament to accept their suggestions and fit yourself into their ideas of what makes good fiction. Half a dozen third-rate mystery writers are getting their stories serialized in the slicks regularly, and more power to them. You spent about three months trying to get some bid for the serial rights of *The Long Goodbye*, whereas you ought to have known in the beginning it never would be serialized. Or perhaps you did know and didn't want to trust your own judgment. I don't know what the difference is; I don't know just what it is that I haven't got, but it is something. I guess maybe there are two kinds of writers; writers who write stories and writers who write writing. There are a hundred clever plot architects for every writer who can do you a paragraph of prose with a touch of magic to it on whatever level, in whatever vein you happen to be interested in. Perhaps some of the better magazine editors know the difference, but I'm damned sure the critics

don't. . . . You're a sweet guy, Swanie, one of the nicest I ever
met. In fact, until I met you I didn't think it was possible for an agent
to be a nice guy, and in that I should like to include Eddie.[1] But
don't believe very much the magazine editors tell you. Some day you
might do me a favor, if you felt inclined. Get some of these fiction
writers to write me a letter direct and tell me, if they have happened
to have read anything I have written, just what I would have to
do to please them. I don't know, and I don't think you do either.

Yours ever,

Ray

## TO HAMISH HAMILTON

Box One Twenty Eight
La Jolla, California
September 27, 1954

Dear Jamie:

Yours of September 13th contains a word which I had to look
up in the dictionary, "inspissate."[1] This annoyed me very much,
as although there are many words in fairly common use which I
probably do not know accurately, having but a cloudy idea of their
exact meaning, it isn't often that I come across a word that I don't
know at all. It was some relief to find that Webster's Unabridged marks
the adjectival form, which you used, as obsolete. Please don't think
that I grudge you the word; you probably picked it up from some
antique and over erudite pansy decomposing in an Italian villa amid a
welter of fake masterpieces.

• • •

When I write to Roger [Machell] I shall have the pleasure of
giving him a detailed account of how I broke my toe, because he, as a
victim of gout, would probably have some small sympathy for me.

1. Edgar Carter, Swanson's associate.

1. It means to thicken, usually by evaporation.

I've got nowhere with the recital over here. Some little time ago I was
in the garage where we send our cars to be serviced and having about
fifteen minutes of spare time on my hands to converse with the
assistant manager, I thought this might be a good opportunity to tell
him all about my toe. But I didn't even get a complete sentence
out. As soon as he realized what I was leading up to he started on a
long and detailed account of how he dislocated his thumb. I think the
foundations for the accident went back to his childhood and to a
time when he was about five years old, and from then on the detail
was copious. I left him with many expressions of sympathy and
by this time I don't think he even knew I had broken my toe. It's
been the same everywhere. Nobody wants to hear about my toe.

.           .           .

As to writing my memoirs, Jamie, and you are not the only
one who has suggested it to me nor is this the first time you have
suggested it, I can only say that I don't think I could face it. It seems
to me there are people who can write their memoirs with a reasonable
amount of honesty, and there are people who simply cannot take
themselves seriously enough. I think I might be the first to admit that
the sort of reticence which prevents a man from exploiting his own
personality is really an inverted sort of egotism.

.           .           .

If you really want to know what I should really like to write, it
would be fantastic stories, and I don't mean science fiction. A dozen
or so of them have been rattling around in my head for a great many
years, pleading to be put down on paper. But they wouldn't make
a thin worn dime. That would just be a wonderful way to become a
Neglected Author. God, what a fascinating document could be put
together about these same Neglected Authors and also the one book
writers: fellows like Edward Anderson who long ago wrote a book
called *Thieves Like Us*, one of the best crook stories ever written.
John Houseman made a picture from it for Howard Hughes and
Anderson wrote to Houseman and said that he was trying to build
himself a house somewhere down in Texas and could they possibly
give him another hundred dollars! Then there is James Ross who
wrote a novel published by Houghton Mifflin, called *They Don't
Dance Much*, a sleazy, corrupt but completely believable story of a

North Carolina town about the size of Raleigh. I've read the book several times and I've never heard that he ever wrote anything else. When I was a boy a man named Daniel Chaucer wrote a book called *The Dark Forest*, and then found out that there was a novel of the same name by Hugh Walpole and had to change the title to *The New Humpty-Dumpty*.[2] It was a better book than Walpole could ever hope to write, and I don't think Chaucer ever wrote anything else. And there's Aaron Klopstein. Who ever heard of him? I don't suppose you have. He committed suicide at the age of 33 in Greenwich Village by shooting himself with an Amazonian blow gun, having published two novels entitled *Once More The Cicatrice* and *The Sea Gull Has No Friends*, two volumes of poetry, *The Hydraulic Face Lift* and *Cat Hairs in the Custard*, one book of short stories called *Twenty Inches of Monkey*, and a book of critical essays entitled *Shakespeare in Baby Talk*.

Well, I guess that's enough for now, Jamie. All the best to you.

Yours ever,

Ray

## TO LEONARD RUSSELL

December 29, 1954

Dear Leonard:

Your letter of December 15th has just reached me, the mails being what they are around Christmas time. I have received much sympathy and kindness and many letters, but yours is somehow unique in that it speaks of the beauty that is lost rather than condoling with the comparatively useless life that continues on.[1] She was everything you say, and more. She was the beat of my heart for thirty years. She was the music heard faintly at the edge of sound. It was my great and now useless regret that I never wrote anything really

2. Chaucer was Ford Madox Ford.

---

1. Chandler's wife Cissy died on December 12, 1954.

worth her attention, no book that I could dedicate to her. I planned it. I thought of it, but I never wrote it. Perhaps I couldn't have written it.

She died hard. Her body fought a hundred lost battles, any one of which would have been enough to finish most of us. Twice I brought her home from the hospital because she hated hospitals, and had her in her own bed in her own room with nurses around the clock. But she had to go back. And I suppose she never quite forgave me for that. But when at the end I closed her eyes she looked very young. Perhaps by now she realizes that I tried, and that I regarded the sacrifice of several years of a rather insignificant literary career as a small price to pay, if I could make her smile a few times more.

No doubt you realize that this was no sudden thing, that it had been going on for a long time, and that I have said goodbye to my Cissy in the middle of the night in the dark cold hours many, many times. She admired and liked you very much. I'm not sure that she liked Dilys as much as I did, because possibly she suspected that I liked her too much. And it is just possible that I thought she liked *you* a little too much.

I hope that you are both well and prosperous and that I may have the privilege of seeing you again in the not too distant future, with or without the butler from the Ritz. And I hope I am not being too sentimental if I sign myself,

Yours affectionately,

## TO HAMISH HAMILTON

Box One Twenty Eight
La Jolla, California
January 5, 1955

Dear Jamie:

It was nice to talk to you on the telephone. It was the first and probably the only time I shall ever permit myself the luxury of a trans-Atlantic telephone call. The occasion seemed somehow to justify it, and it did not cost as much as I expected. Thank you for your several kind letters and also for the books you sent. Please don't send me any more books, as they will only have to go into storage. I don't recall whether I told you that I have sold the house, but I have, and I will be out of here about March 15th or before. I don't think I can make it to New York early in February. In fact, I don't think that the trip would be worthwhile, because I am planning to take a Swedish boat through the Canal about the first or second week in April. The dates of sailings are not fixed yet so I can't be absolute. I'll let you know as soon as I know myself about when I shall be in London. I gather from your letter that you would like me to stay with you at your house for a little while. But if I may say so without sounding ungrateful, I should rather be on my own. I'd like to be at a hotel—any good hotel, even the Connaught—until you can help me find a service flat. And I don't want to spend a fortune. I should like to stay in Europe about six months, and spend as much time in England as I can without incurring the risk of being called a resident. I should also like to go to Paris, and perhaps though not certainly, to the South of France for part of the time. I don't want to be a burden or a nuisance to anyone. I am pretty badly broken up, and for me it may last a long time, as my emotions are not superficial. I have friends with me, and they are going to Europe with me, although I do not think that in the beginning they will go to England. We hope to come on one of the new Swedish cargo boats, which are about fifty per cent more expensive than the other ships of the type, and for that reason it is easier to get reservations on them. They probably go to Antwerp, Rotterdam and London, but God knows where in London, very likely the East India docks.

I hope the answer to your cable about *The Big Sleep* was satisfactory. I don't really care what they do with it. I assume the *Daily Sketch* is the type of paper you and I don't read.[1]

Leonard Russell sent me a very touching letter which I have already answered. If it is convenient, you might telephone Eric Partridge and tell him that I know I owe him a letter, and tell him why I have not so far been able to write to him. You probably realized when we were in London that Cissy was in rather frail health. When we got back she looked and felt better than she had in a couple

1. Proposal to serialize the book.

of years, but it didn't last. She got weaker and weaker and more and more tired. She tried to drive herself, and there were a few occasions when she actually drove her car out, and on several others I drove her somewhere she wanted to go, or just out of doors for the air, or to do some shopping for clothes she badly needed. But even that ceased. Usually, until about a month before she died, she was able to get up part of the day and to dinner. She had an obscure and rather rare ailment, I am told, called fibrosis of the lungs. I don't think they know very much about it or what causes it. It's a slow hardening of the lung tissue, starting at the bottom of the lungs and progressing upwards. The part that is fibrosed returns no oxygen to the blood, which of course puts more strain on the heart and the breathing. As far back as 1948 her X-rays showed the condition as existing, but it was quite a long time before I realized that it could only have one ending. I don't think that she herself ever quite gave up hope, or if so during the last weeks, she didn't let anyone else know that she had given up hope. We tried a number of doctors. Mostly they just gave up without saying why. Late in October we tried a Dr. Neber, whom we had known when we first came to La Jolla but had given up because his medicine had never seemed to agree with Cissy, and he started her on cortisone. We tried him principally because he had three or four cases of fibrosis of the lungs, which is unusual for one doctor to have in a small place like La Jolla. With his other patients he had had great success with cortisone. A couple of them that had been bedridden had been able to get up and go about their business almost normally. But it is a very strong medicine, and Cissy was always peculiar about drugs. It affected her brain, and especially it affected her memory and made her very uncomfortable. She couldn't remember anything for five or ten minutes. I had to measure out all her medicines, or else she would take them twice or three times over without realizing she had already taken them. The cortisone didn't work, so at the end of the first week in November he took her off that and started her on ACTH, and this, after the first shots, I was able to give her myself hypodermically, as I had been used for several years to give her hypodermic shots of various vitamins. This didn't do very much good either. She got lower and lower and more and more depressed, and she was not an easily depressed person. On November 30 she developed pneumonia and had to be taken to the hospital in an ambulance. Early the next morning she was clamoring

[376]

to be taken home in an absolute fury of indignation. From seven o'clock on she called repeatedly or had her nurse call. I managed to persuade her to stay there that day and until the following morning, and then her temperature being normal and the penicillin having apparently aborted the pneumonia, the doctor reluctantly allowed me to bring her home, which made her very happy. But the next day she had already forgotten about the horrors of the hospital—and no one ever hated hospitals more—and was wanting to go back again. The doctor furthermore wanted to try a medicine called ruwaulfia, or African snake root, which apparently has the property of inducing a condition of euphoria without any damage and can be taken indefinitely. He told me at the time that she would have to spend the rest of her life in a sanitarium and that he was hoping the ruwaulfia would put her in such a complaisant mood that she would accept that. The next morning again she called up early and demanded to be taken home. So I got in touch with the doctor and I said I couldn't stand her mental suffering, and he again reluctantly allowed me to bring her home. By this time she was very ill and very weak, had to be helped to the bathroom, had to have someone stay there with her. Her sister Vinnie and I were just about done in, especially Vinnie, because we got very little sleep. I then managed to get nurses around the clock to take care of her, but she was very miserable, gasped all the time, coughed violently, and said she was in great pain. By December 7th I realized she was dying. In the middle of the night she suddenly appeared in my room in her pajamas looking like a ghost, having evaded the nurse somehow. We got her back to bed and she tried it once more, but this time the nurse was watching. At three A.M. on the morning of December 8th her temperature was so low that the nurse got frightened and called the doctor, and once more the ambulance came and took her off to the hospital. She couldn't sleep and I knew it took a lot of stuff to put her under, so I would take her sleeping pills and she would tie them in the corner of her handkerchief so that she could swallow them surreptitiously when the nurse was out of the room. She was in an oxygen tent all the time, but she kept pulling it away so that she could hold my hand. She was quite vague in her mind about some things, but almost too desperately clear about other. Once she asked me where we lived, what town we lived in, and then asked me to describe the house. She didn't seem to know what it looked like. Then she would turn her head away and when I

[377]

was no longer in her line of vision, she seemed to forget all about me. Whenever I went to see her she would reach her handkerchief out under the edge of the oxygen tent for me to give her the sleeping pills. I began to be worried about this and confessed to the doctor, and he said she was getting much stronger medicine than any sleeping pills. On the 11th when I went to see her I had none and she reached out under the edge of the oxygen tent with the handkerchief, and when I had nothing to give her she turned her head away and said, "Is this the way you wanted it?" About noon that day the doctor called me up and said I had better come over and talk to her as it might be the last chance I would have. When I got over there he was trying to find veins in her feet to inject *demerol*. What an irony that I should have written about *demerol* in my last book! He managed to get her asleep, but she was wide awake again that night. That is she seemed to be wide awake, but I'm not even sure that she knew me. She went to sleep again while I was there. A little after noon on December 12th, which was a Sunday, the nurse called up and said she was very low, which is about as drastic a statement as a nurse ever makes. Vinnie's son was here then with Vinnie, and he drove me over to the hospital at fifty miles an hour, breaking all the traffic regulations, which I told him to ignore as the La Jolla cops were friends of mine. When I got there they had taken the oxygen tent away and she was lying with her eyes half open. I think she was already dead. Another doctor had his stethoscope over her heart and was listening. After a while he stepped back and nodded. I closed her eyes and kissed her and went away.

Of course in a sense I had said goodbye to her long ago. In fact, many times during the past two years in the middle of the night I had realized that it was only a question of time until I lost her. But that is not the same thing as having it happen. Saying goodbye to your loved one in your mind is not the same thing as closing her eyes and knowing they will never open again. But I was glad that she died. To think of this proud, fearless bird caged in a room in some rotten sanitarium for the rest of her days was such an unbearable thought that I could hardly face it at all. I didn't really break until after the funeral, partly because I was in shock and partly because I had to hold her sister together. I am sleeping in her room. I thought I couldn't face that, and then I thought that if the room were empty it would just be haunted, and every time I went past the door I would

[378]

have the horrors, and that the only thing was for me to come in here and fill it up with my junk and make it look the kind of mess I'm used to living in. It was the right decision. Her clothes are all around me, but they are in closets or hidden away in drawers. I have a couple of very old friends staying with me, and they are patient and kind beyond any expectation. But the horrors are all mine just the same. For thirty years, ten months and four days, she was the light of my life, my whole ambition. Anything else I did was just the fire for her to warm her hands at. That is all there is to say.

I'm afraid my Christmas orders were put in a little late, but I hope they arrived in time to cheer you all up a little. I don't know how things are over there now, but I gather from Roger that they are a lot better than they used to be.

Love to all,

Yours ever,

Ray

## TO HAMISH HAMILTON

6005 Camino de la Costa
La Jolla, California
Jan 22 1955

Dear Jamie:

.          .          .

I try not to think too much about Cissy. Late at night when people have gone to bed and the house is still and it is difficult to read I hear light steps rustling on the carpet and I see a gentle smile hovering at the edge of the lamplight and I hear a voice calling me by a pet name. Then I go out to the pantry and mix a stiff brandy and soda and try to think of something else. Unfortunately I cannot read poetry except by daylight. Poetry is too sad. You are always running across lines like:

Or shredded perfume, like a cloud
From closet long to quiet vowed,

[379]

With mothed and dropping arras hung,
Mouldering her lute and books among.
As when a queen, long dead, was young.

I dug out some of my own old poetry and was rather startled to find
some of it not too bad. It lacks the acerbity and I-dare-you-to-
understand-what-I'm-talking-about of the modern stuff. It is, I
suppose, Grade B Georgian. I'll send you a couple one of these days. I
never regarded myself as a publishable poet, of course, although a
certain amount of it was published a long time ago in the *Westminster
Gazette*, etc.

As to the service flat I'd rather go to a hotel for a time and get
a chance to look around. The location of the flat is important to
me and I am not sure just what is meant by service flat. How far does
the service go? Do they come in and make your bed and wash dishes
in the morning? Is there a restaurant in the building? That sort of
thing.

.        .        .

That should be enough for now.

With love to all

Ray


# TO ROGER MACHELL

6005 Camino de la Costa
La Jolla, California
Jan 28, 1955

Dear Roger:
Just a quick chit to let you know that I'm changing my ideas
about going through the Canal in spite of my fondness for Swedish
cooking. I have something the matter with one of my sinuses and half
the time I have no voice. I think the natural venom of my disposition
is slipping down on to my vocal chords at night and making me

cough and get hoarse. I could be dying, but I think not. Anyhow I may need attention from a nose wrecker for some time and better not get holed up on a 12 passenger ship. They might even refuse to take me. The captain probably has a supply of narcotics on board but might be stingy with them. He also, no doubt, has a set of carpenter's tools for setting broken bones, and a bottle of aspirin. Apart from all that the idea of going through the Canal without Cissy has a certain sadness. So I'm going east in late March and I have a single cabin on the Hotel Cecil (*Mauretania* to you) sailing April 12th. She should get to Southampton some time on April 18th unless we meet a large iceberg. You will know all about that as I shall myself a little later. Anyhow I shall confirm it to you when the ticket is in my possession.

I had a charming letter from Jamie. He should be in New York by next Wednesday, but if my voice is not better than it is now, I shan't be able to talk to him by telephone with much success. I hope he can bring back some good books with him. Things are really weird over here in the publishing racket. A friend of mine had two books turned down because they were submitted to the paperback people before the publisher would take them on, and the paperback people are being very cagey just now. Bankruptcies and mergers are imminent. Prostitution, flagellation and the dope racket seem quite sound still, but trade editions of books—ye gods, look at the current bestseller list. It is headed by an item called *Love Is Eternal* by one Irving Stone. No doubt as a business venture you would be glad to publish it, I know the man and I read one of his early books, the one about Van Gogh. Since then I have given him none of my business. Not that he needs it. However, bestsellers at their worst are not as asinine as English critical writing. That seems to be done entirely by exhumed corpses suspected of containing arsenic.

You can see that I am coming along pretty well. I still sleep badly but the old spirit is returning slowly. Seldom a day without its reasonably well-phrased insult.

Yours ever

Ray

[381]

# TO ROGER MACHELL

Feb 7 1955

Dear Roger:

       •       •       •

The *Mauretania* takes six days, so I should arrive in England on the 18th. of April, but at what hour of the day I have no idea. Could you contrive a hotel room and bath for me for about a week from then on? I think I'd like the old Connaught well enough. The only thing I really had against them was that I paid a service charge on the bill including the bar bill (which was quite large) whereas the bar people get nothing from it, since they are a concession. This hardly seems quite fair. Also in spite of the fact that this service charge was supposed to take the place of tipping, I couldn't make myself let it go at that and actually I tipped everyone I had any dealings with, and even gave five quid to the dining room staff without so much as an acknowledgement from the maitre d'hotel. I rather resent that. Maybe the black tie character I gave it to pinched the lot. I need some advice on this point. Tipping is really the horror of travel. I never know how much to give and I always for that reason give too much. Of course I do that here also. I always overtip. I like to think of it as generosity, but it is probably exhibitionism.

Then comes the problem of a service flat. Just what the hell *is* a serivce flat? How much service do you get, what do they do for you, how much does it cost and so on. Jamie says you are an expert in these matters. Frank Francis wrote to me that the Whitehall Court expects about 30 guineas a week. That is a bit steep even if they supply naked dancing girls. And do these places have dining rooms? And can you make as much noise as you like? For instance I sit up half the night playing records when I have the blues and can't get drunk enough to feel sleepy. My nights are pretty awful. And they don't get any better. I've been alone since Saturday morning when Vinnie went home. Alone except for Mable the Marble, my Pennsylvania Dutch cook and housekeeper. She has a lot of fine qualities, but she is not much company. She is not even beautiful. She's as fat as a porpoise and when she bends over you see a pair of gams that an all-in wrestler would envy. For size, if not for shape.

I'd like to go to Paris for two or three weeks at a good time of year and possibly also to Nürnberg. But by that time Europe will be so loused up with Americans that it will be impossible to get a flea in with a shoehorn. I don't want any Georges Cinq stuff, but a decent hotel where I can have a room and bath, assuming such luxury is possible for a struggling writer who owns no oil wells in Texas. What I particularly do not crave is a load of American tourists all over the place. Je m'en foute pas mal des touristes Américains. I understand the current phrase is: Sortez les, sortez les, sortez les!

Perhaps when I get away from this house and all its memories I can settle down to do some writing. And then again I may just be homesick and to be homesick for a home you haven't got is rather poignant.

Tomorrow is or would have been our thirty-first wedding anniversary. I'm going to fill the house with red roses and have a friend in to drink champagne, which we always did. A useless and probably a foolish gesture because my lost love is so utterly lost and I have no belief in any after life. But just the same I shall do it. All us tough guys are hopeless sentimentalists at heart.

All the best,

Ray

## TO ROGER MACHELL

Box One Twenty Eight
La Jolla, California
March 5th 1955

Dear Roger:

.     .     .

I got off a short airmail letter to Jamie which should have reached him before he left for home. If it did not, it wasn't too important, just a few lines to tell him everything was all right with

[383]

me, or as near as one could hope for.[1] I couldn't for the life of me tell you whether I really intended to go through with it or whether my subconscious was putting on a cheap dramatic performance. The first shot went off without my intending it to. I had never fired the gun and the trigger pull was so light that I barely touched it to get my hand in position when off she went and the bullet ricocheted around the tile walls of the shower and went up through the ceiling. It could just as easily have ricocheted into my stomach. The charge seemed to me to be very weak. This was borne out when the second shot (the business) didn't fire at all. The cartridges were about five years old and in this climate I guess the charge had decomposed. At that point I blacked out. The police officer who came in then told me later that I was sitting on the floor of the shower trying to get the gun into my mouth, and then when he asked me to give him the gun I just laughed and handed it to him. I haven't the slightest recollection of this. And I don't know whether or no it is an emotional defect that I have absolutely no sense of guilt nor any embarrassment at meeting people in La Jolla who all knew what happened. It was on the radio here, on the wire services, in papers all over the country, and I had piles of letters from all over the place, some kind and sympathetic, some scolding, some silly beyond belief. I had letters from police officers, active and retired, from two Intelligence officers, one in Tokyo and one in March Field, Riverside, and a letter from an active professional private eye in San Francisco. These letters all said two things: 1, they should have written to me long before because perhaps I hadn't known what my books meant to people, and 2, How in the name of wonder did a writer who had never been a cop come to know them so precisely and portray them so accurately. One man who said he had served 23 years on the Los Angeles Police said he could put an actual name to practically any cop I put in any of my stories. He seemed to think I must actually have known all these men. This sort of thing staggered me a little because I had always supposed that if a real live police officer or detective read a mystery, it would be just to sneer at it. Who was it— Stevenson possibly—who said, Experience is largely a matter of intuition?

1. Chandler had attempted to commit suicide on February 22, 1955, by shooting himself in the bathroom of his house in La Jolla. He was in despair over his wife's death.

In England, I believe, and in some other places, including New York State, attempted suicide, or what looks like it, is a crime. In California it is not, but you have to go through the observation ward at the County Hospital. With a more than able assist from a friend of mine who does a column in the San Diego paper, I talked myself out of it the next noon but on condition I went to a private sanitarium.[2] This I did. I had more trouble talking myself out of that. I stuck it for six days and then got a feeling I was being strung along with half promises. At that point I announced that I was going to discharge myself. Upheaval. This simply wasn't done. All right, I said, Tell me the law that keeps me here. There wasn't any and he knew it. So finally he conceded that I could leave any time I wished, but would I come to his office and talk to him. I said I would, not because I expected any good from it, but because it would make his case record look better, and in addition, if he was perfectly frank with me, I might be able to help him.

So I came home and since then nothing has mattered to me about the whole business except that they shot me so full of dope to keep me tractable that I still have a little hangover from it. Isn't it amazing that people should sit around depressed and bored and miserable in those places, worried about their jobs and their families, longing to go home, subjected every other day to Electrical Shock Treatments (they didn't dare try that on me) and in between insulin shock, worrying about the cost of it all and the feeling of being a prisoner, and yet not have the guts to get up and walk out? I suppose it is part of what's the matter with them. If they had more guts, they wouldn't be there in the first place. But that's hardly an answer. If I had had more guts I shouldn't have let despair and grief get me so far down that I did what I did. But when I found myself dealing with people and with a lot of psychiatric claptrap and with a non-existent authority that tried to make me think it had power, I didn't find that it took any special amount of daring to tell them all what I was going to do and to do it. And in the end strangely enough they almost seemed to like it. The head nurse kissed me and said I was the politest, the most considerate and cooperative and the most resilient patient they had ever had there, and God help any

2. Neil Morgan was the person who arranged for Chandler's release.

doctor who tried to make me do anything I wasn't convinced I ought to do. And so much for that.

Love

Ray

## TO WILLIAM GAULT

Hotel Del Charro<br>2380 Torrey Pines Road<br>La Jolla, California<br>[n.d. April 1955]

Dear Bill Gault:

I'm answering your letter on the hop, not because it is kind, which of course it is, and I have had a hundred kind letters from all parts of the world (nothing in this is deprecating), but because of your idea that I look down on the mystery story. I don't know how this notion came to you. I can't recall ever having written or said anything of the sort. It's possible that had I been a little younger when I started to write fiction, had I been a better observer and a better rememberer, I might have made a reputation as a straight novelist. It never occurred to me to try. I thought I was extremely lucky to get as far as I did in our field, and believe me when I say lucky I am not talking to the birds. Talent is never enough. The history of literature is strewn with the corpses of writers who through no fault of their own missed out on the timing or were just a little too far ahead of their generation. An old and wise friend of mine once said the world never hears of its greatest men; the men it calls great are just enough ahead of the average to stand out, but not far enough ahead to be remote.

I believe there is a peculiar kind of satisfaction in taking a type of literature which the pundits regard as below the salt and making of it something which the fair-minded among them are forced to treat with a little respect. You must never admit to yourself that the kind of writing you and I do is by definition inferior. It is as good as the

[386]

man who writes it and the record proves it will outlast 99.44 per cent of the touted best sellers.

Yesterday I finished the rather agonizing business of getting the furniture out of my house and closing it up for the new buyer. When I walked through the empty rooms checking the windows and so on I felt a little like the last man on a dead world. But it will pass. On Wednesday I leave for Old Chatham, New York to stay with my best friend and on April 12th I sail on the *Mauretania*. I expect to be back about the end of October and to find a house in La Jolla—much smaller of course—because it is an easy place to live in and everybody knows me here.

Thank you for writing to me and for what you say and I hope you are not exaggerating too much, unconsciously. It would not matter so much to me, since I am a naturally modest fellow, but it would not be good for you. Because you have it in you to be as good as the best. Don't ever write anything you don't like yourself and if you do like it, don't take anyone else's advice about changing it. They just don't know. All the best

Ray

## TO HARDWICK MOSELEY

The Connaught Hotel,
Carlos Place, London, W.1.
April 24, 1955

Dear Hardwick:
Thank you for your kind wire. I am here at least until May the 8th. after which I may have to sleep in Green Park. I am not happy and I am terribly hoarse from laryngitis. The racket here is just too intense also; you go to a luncheon with eight people and next day five of them invite you to a dinner party. So dine, drink and drab is about all you do. I love this hotel, though, but I do not love being stared at and being pointed out to people, and I do not love newspaper interviews.

[387]

It seems quite likely now that I shall never accomplish anything here and that I shall come back, if I can arrange it, early in June. I am already quite homesick.

Yoursever,

Ray

PS This is a new Olivetti and I haven't quite mastered it. It's a beautiful piece of work.

## TO HAMISH HAMILTON

The Connaught Hotel
Carlos Place
London, W.1.
27.4.1955

Dear Jamie:

Would you please have someone tell the *Daily Sketch* that not only would I not do a piece of writing for them but that I wouldn't use their rotten rag even to stuff up a rat hole. Our press is no bargain, but your gutter press is fantastically bad. You might also call that nice Mr. Harris of the *Standard* and tell him I'm sorry but cannot now put my mind to what he wants, don't feel well enough and simply cannot get my private letters written. I'll write him a note and send him back his tear sheets because I liked him personally more than anyone in his peculiar profession that I happened to meet.

The whole thing last night was rather weird. Natasha Spender is a charming and devoted hostess and served up a magnificent meal and everybody got tight. They poured it on me a little too thick, I imagine. A Sonia[1] somebody . . . said that I was the darling of the British intellectuals and all the poets raved about me and that Edith Sitwell sat up in bed (probably looking like Henry the IVth, Part 3) and read my stuff with passion. They said [Cyril] Connolly had

1. Sonia Orwell.

[388]

written a piece about me which was considered a classic. The funny part of it was that they seemed quite sincere. I tried to explain to them that I was just a beat-up pulp writer and that in the USA I ranked slightly above a mulatto.

Well anyhow it was a lot of fun.

This morning the BBC, always a little slow, called up. I'm not talking to anyone I don't know anymore until they write and explain what they want and I get a chance to check with you.

Yours,

Ray

This typewriter is much better but still a bit strange to me.

## TO NEIL MORGAN

116, Eaton Square
London S.W.1.
June 3rd. 1955.

Dear Neil,

I tried for almost three days to get you on the telephone, and then became so disgusted that I cancelled the call. I know I have owed you a letter for a long time, as I owe you for other things, which I shall never forget.

I don't think you would recognise me if you saw me now. I have become so damned refined that at times I loathe myself. I still don't sleep well and often get up at 4 or 5 in the morning, and lately have been indulging in a form of polite pornography, which would probably interest you mildly and I am, therefore enclosing a couple of samples.[1] You should understand that the basic motif behind this is an attempt to spoof the upper-middle class sort of talk. There can be no greater mistake than to think that we and the English people speak the same language.

1. These sketches were called "Routines to Shock the Neighbors," and were written to help prepare Chandler to write for the English stage. Two are printed in *The Notebooks of Raymond Chandler*, 1976.

[389]

Mostly I run around with the St. John's Wood–Chelsea literary, artistic crowd, and perhaps they are a little special. Of course I know some cockneys too, but the people that I do run around with have expressions of their own which need translating. For instance: "I simple adore her" means "I'd stick a knife in her back if she had a back." "They are absolutely and utterly precious" means "What rubbish, but that woman never did have any taste." "I rather care for that" means "Give it to me quick." And "I'm simply impossibly in love with him" means "He has enough money to pay for the drinks."

It has been a wonderful spring, the squares flaming with the most gorgeous tulips three and even four feet high. Kew Gardens is a paradise of green and color, rhododendrons, azaleas, amaryllis, flowering trees of every kind. It catches you by the throat after the hard dusty green of California. The shops are beautifully dressed and full of all kinds of wonderful things. Harrods is easily the finest department store in the world. Nothing in New York or Los Angeles can equal it. The traffic control system here is superb. The one thing lacking is tender meat. They simply haven't got the storage to age it. You get it at very good hotels like the Connaught, the Savoy or Claridge's, but almost nowhere else. What they call a filet in most places eats like round steak.

But the women! If they ever had buck teeth I don't see them now. I've seen glamour girls at parties that would stun Hollywood. And they are so damn honest they won't even let you pay their taxi fares. If you know them well enough you can give them the money privately, but you can't give it to the driver. If you want them to go to bed with you, you have to say "please" five times. A CIC officer I know was a bit worried about this.[2] He was asking me how to get a really topdrawer, refined English girl—no G.I. bait—into bed. So I told him what I just wrote. "But what if she refuses?" he asked. "Brother, if you can't tell in advance by her eyes, the way she moves and looks at you or doesn't look at you, by the tone of her voice, you're lost." He was rather depressed. Americans are not as a rule successful with the best type of English girls and women. They move too fast and too roughly. There is far too much of this "Come on, baby, let's hit the hay" motif. They don't like it. They expect

2. Probably Counterintelligence Corps.

to be treated as ladies. They are perfectly willing to sleep with you if they like you and if you treat them with deference, because in a country where women outnumber the men so excessively that is almost inevitable, but they don't want to be treated as easy lays. They want you to work up to it slowly and fastidiously, and I certainly think they are right.

.            .            .

Ray


# TO THE EDITOR OF *THE EVENING STANDARD*

June 30, 1955

Dear Sir:

As a part-time resident and full-time friend and admirer of England, I have always, until now, respected its legal system—as has most of the world. But there is at times a vein of savagery that repels me.

I have been tormented for a week at the idea that a highly civilized people should put a rope around the neck of Ruth Ellis[1] and drop her through a trap and break her neck. I could understand perhaps the hanging of a woman for bestial crime like a multiple poisoning, and axe murder (à la Lizzie Borden) or a baby-farm operator killing her charges, but this was a crime of passion under considerable provocation. No other country in the world would hang this woman.

In France she would get off with light sentence or none. In America it would be first or second degree manslaughter and she would be out of prison in anywhere from three to seven years.

This thing haunts me and, so far as I may say it, disgusts me as something obscene. I am not referring to the trial, of course, but to the medieval savagery of the law.

Raymond Chandler

1. Ruth Ellis, a convicted murderer, was condemned to be hanged. Chandler's letter contributed to a public outcry over her punishment and questions were raised in Parliament. Nevertheless, the sentence was carried out in July.

[391]

# TO JESSICA TYNDALE

116 Eaton Square
London, S.W.1.
SLO 3691
Sept. 17th., 1955

Jessica, darling, you worry about me far too much. Your letter of Sept. 13th. just came and the conclusions you draw are really quite exaggerated. I'll come to Helga later, but first let me say that I have written things to you I would not have written to any other human being, because I could feel in you absolute sincerity and trust.[1] You know, you never really saw me sober and I have been sober now for some weeks—absolutely bone-dry sober. Dull as it may be I intend to remain that way. Something in my chemistry will no longer accept alcohol. There is some sort of chain reaction. I start off with a drink of white wine and end up drinking two bottles of Scotch a day. Then I stop eating. After four or five days of that I am ill. I have to quit and the withdrawal symptoms are simply awful. I shake so that I can't hold a glass of water. I can't stand up or walk without help. One day I vomited eighteen times. I wasn't sick at all, but something kept dropping down at the back of my throat from inflamed sinuses and every time that happened I gagged my life out. For three days I could drink nothing but sips of ice water. Well, that's thirty for me. My father was an alcoholic and I have lived all my life in the fear of becoming one but until my wife died I could always quit drinking on my own power when I felt there was a real need for it. For three years before she died I was as dry as a bone. The funny thing is I don't mind in the least. It's other people who mind, some even resent it a little. But they will just have to take it. I suspect that all people who drink more than the odd cocktail are secretly a little aware of weakness and resent anyone who doesn't share that weakness. Certainly it has nothing to do with morality. I know men who can drink enormous quantities of liquor without any apparent damage.

1.  Helga Greene, a friend of Jessica Tyndale's, who later became Chandler's literary agent.

They will probably all die of cirrhosis of the liver, but one has to die of something.

. . .

With much love and please stop worrying,

Ray

## TO JESSICA TYNDALE

c/o Barrow
Old Chatham, N.Y.
10/21/55

Dearest Jessica:

. . .

Any one who can drink a great deal steadily over a long period of time is apt to think of himself as an alcoholic, because liquor is part of his life and he is terribly let down without it. Yet he is not an alcoholic, because he is the same guy even with a load on. . . . The problem comes when our physical systems can't oxydize the stuff fast enough and we have to cut down or stop. If we stop, we feel awful, because our emotional systems are tuned to the stimulation and the sedative effect of alcohol. Yet, if we can, we stop altogether for a while (hating it every minute) until we are completely free of it and then we try to learn to drink. How much can we absorb without either feeling high at the time or let down the next day? That is what we have to find out and we have to be rather cautious about it. If we don't get enough to feel cheered up, it's a waste. It seems to me that there is a certain level to find, and if you find it, you are all right, even if you sometimes slop over a little. If I had found out all about this when I was twenty years old (I did almost no drinking then) I think I should have cut it out absolutely and I shouldn't have felt any the worse, because of the resilience one has at that time. But at my age, that no longer makes sense. At my age, there is

[393]

nothing to replace it. . . . Drinking, after all, except when it is a social ritual, is rather a negative business.

.             .             .

Much, much love,

Ray

## TO HELGA GREENE

Box 958
La Jolla, California
November 13th. 1955

Dear Helga:

It seems funny to be writing a businessy letter to you. I am sitting on two bed pillows at the writing desk in my room at the Del Charro Hotel (but address me only at the above), I am smoking a Craven A cigarette which is no match for the Benson and Hedges Superfine but imported cigarettes here are just a little too steep. Am I comfortable? No. Am I happy? No. Am I weak, depressed, no good, and of no social value to the community? Yes. Outside my window is an illuminated swimming pool. Phooey on it! The service here is excellent, the food fair, the price of my room slightly above what I paid at the Connaught, but an infinitely better room. Light wood furniture, two wide couch beds set in a right angle triangle with the heads against a roomy built-in stand with two of those focussed reading lights. There is a chest of six drawers (not enough), three closets, a dressing room with side lights at the table, and a beautiful bathroom, bathtub with sliding glass doors for the shower. There is a built-in electric heater in the bathroom and a built in gas heater in the bedroom, which is really a bed-sit. It is cheap compared with New York.

.             .             .

Much love,

Ray

[394]

# TO NEIL MORGAN

Nov 18 1955

Dear Neil:

On the eve of my departure into regions where Eskimos starve and the polar bears wear mittens and goloshes and are still dissatisfied (Anybody ever see a polar bear that liked anybody?),[1] and on the eve of your dive into marriage with a lovely girl—I'm not sure that dive was the word I wanted—may I wish for you the kind of magic that Maeterlinck's donkey could hear: the roses opening, the grass growing and the day after tomorrow coming. May I wish for you the kind of magic vision that birds have, such as on a morning after rain seeing a worm make love to its other end. (This joke was stolen from me and somehow finally got to Groucho.)[2] May I wish for you the knowledge (I'm getting a little heavy-handed here) that Marriages do not Take Place, they are made by hand; that there is always an element of discipline involved; that however perfect the honeymoon, the time will come, however brief it is, when you will wish she would fall downstairs and break a leg. That goes for her too. But the mood will pass, if you give it time. Here are a few words of sound advice. I know.

1. Ride her on a short rein and never let her think she is riding you.
2. If the coffee is lousy, don't say so. Just throw it on the floor.
3. Don't let her change the arrangement of the furniture more than once a year.
4. Don't have any joint back accounts unless she puts in the money.
5. In case of a quarrel, remember it is always your fault.
6. Keep her away from antique shops.
7. Never praise her girl friends very much.
8. Above all never forget that a marriage is in one way very much

1. Chandler was taking a polar flight to England. Although he had just returned from London, he felt he had to return almost immediately, because of his concern for Natasha Spender's health.
2. Groucho Marx

like a newspaper. It has to be made fresh every damn day of every damn year.

I'll be at the Connaught Hotel, Carlos Place, London W.1. in case I didn't tell you. For a while that is.

Love,

Ray

## TO IAN FLEMING

49 Carlton Hill
London N.W.8.
11th April 1956

Dear Ian,

Thank you so much for your letter of Wednesday and if the payment for my outstanding review had been received a little earlier I should have been able to eat three meals a day.[1]

I thought my review was no more than you deserved and I tried to write it in such a way that the good part could be quoted and the bad parts left out. After all, old boy, there had to be some bad parts. I think you will have to make up your mind what kind of a writer you are going to be. You could be almost anything except that I think you are a bit of a sadist!

I am not in any Hampstead hospital.[2] I am at home and if they ever put me in a hospital again I shall walk out leaving corpses strewn behind me, except pretty nurses.

As for having lunch with you, with or without butler, I can't do it yet—because even if I were much better than I am I should be having lunch with ladies.

Yours affectionately,

Ray

1. Chandler had reviewed Fleming's *Moonraker* for the *Sunday Times*.
2. Chandler had been hospitalized for excessive drinking.

## TO PAUL BROOKS

49 Carlton Hill
London N.W.8.
April 30, 1956

Dear Paul;

I'm sorry but our lunch date will have to be changed because my dentist, whom I need very badly, wants to push the appointment up an hour, which cuts it much too fine.

I also had the idea that Etoile is pretty stale to me and might be to you. Unless you have seen enough of the Garrick Club, we might have lunch there. The food is the best English food in London. They don't eat until 1.30. Up to that time they drink.

Then there is a rather little used place in Greek Street called Le Jardin des Gourmets. it has a very nice corner on the 1st floor (Anglicé).

I have no dates on the 5th. or the 7th. nor the following week. Since I am half-dead most of the time, I probably should not have any at all, but you can't get out of them in London.

Do you remember Mae Murray? I had a note from her asking me to lunch. I can't imagine why. I never met her.

With apologies profuse,

Ray

## TO IAN FLEMING

The Grosvenor
35 Fifth Avenue
New York
June 9th. 1956

Dear Ian:

I didn't like leaving England without saying good-bye to the few friends I knew well enough to care about, but then I don't like saying good-bye at all, especially when it may be quite a long time before I come back. As you probably know, I long overstayed the

six months allowed, but I had a compelling reason, even if I get
hooked for British income tax. I am also likely to lose half my
European royalties, which isn't funny. It's all a little obscure to me,
but there it is. And it doesn't matter whether your stay in England is
broken half a dozen times. If the time adds up to over six months
within the fiscal year, you are it.[1]

I am looking forward to your next book. I am also looking
forward to my next book.

I rather liked New York this time, having heretofore loathed
its harshness and rudeness. For one thing the weather has been
wonderful, only one hot day so far and that not unbearable. I have
friends here, but not many. Come to think of it I haven't many
anywhere. Monday night I am flying back to California and this time
I hope to stick it out and make some kind of modest but convenient
home there.

I am wondering what happened to all the chic pretty women
who are supposed to be typical of New York. Damned if I've seen
any of them. Perhaps I've looked in the wrong places, but I do have a
feeling that New York is being slowly downgraded.

Please remember me to Mrs. Fleming if you see her and if she
remembers me (doubtful). And how is His Grace and Duke of
Westminster these days?[2] Painting lots of houses, I hope.

With love

Yours ever,

Ray

## TO HELGA GREENE

Hotel Grosvenor
Fifth Avenue at Tenth Street
New York 3, N.Y.
June 10th. 1956

Dearest Helga:

1. Chandler had overstayed his permit because of his concern for Natasha Spender's health.
2. Fleming lived in Victoria Square in property owned by the Duke of Westminster.

I bet you haven't many boy friends who write you two letters in two days. And perhaps it bores you, but since Friday noon I haven't a damn thing to do but write letters, read, take a taxi or bus uptown and potter about a bit, or just go for a walk through the Village, which always fascinates me with its quaint houses, little culs-de-sac, iron railings painted in odd colors, innumerable hidden restaurants, and the people themselves, the way they dress and the look they have of belonging to another world from uptown New York.

.          .          .

Ray


# TO HAMISH HAMILTON

Hotel Grosvenor
Fifth Avenue at Tenth Street
New York 3, N.Y.
June 10th. 1956

Dear Jamie:
My deepest thanks to all for the very kind farewell telegram. I didn't see as much of the boys and girls this time as I should like to have (done, as the English say, a disgusting locution to me).
I've been in New York all this time. . . . When I first landed after a rotten twenty four hour flight via Iceland and Gander, on account of storms in mid-Atlantic—I always thought the BOAC prided itself on flying right through them—and an hour wait in the customs and the usual barbaric treatment, a sort of studied insolence (but not on the part of my particular inspector when I finally got him) I was willing to expatriate myself permanently. Surely no other country in the world makes you feel like a dirty immigrant from Central Europe. Not even the Spaniards and they are high-handed enough. I bought a copy of *Newsweek* and started to read the letters in the front. One of them went over to another page and believe me there were four solid pages of advertising before I got to the

conclusion of the letter. I knew where I was all right, but this country reeks of wealth. It is so different from England where almost everything is touched by a faint air of squalor. Not your house, of course, nor Roger's nor Helga Greene's, but I have been into many lavatories where a single dirty towel was thrown on the floor; grimy little kitchens such as I had in Carlton Hill, bath tubs that needed scrubbing and had needed it for quite a while, people dripping with amusing or intellectual small talk who don't wash their hands when they go to the bathroom. All this is bearable, and you would get it anywhere but in this country, if only the talk were not so malicious, if only there were not so goddam many queers all around you.

.          .          .

Yours ever,

Ray

## TO HELGA GREENE

Hotel Del Charro
2380 Torrey Pines Road
La Jolla, California
June 14, 1956

Dear Helga:

.          .          .

I went to dinner with some friends last night and it was a little trying to see them have three or four drinks and I nothing but tonic water with a little fresh lime in it. It wasn't that I wanted the alcohol—I didn't at all—but it kept them gingered up while I had nothing to support me but my beautiful if slightly tarnished character. That has always been the trouble with me during the many periods of my life when I was not drinking. The people who do outlast me and I get very tired and rather irritable. But there is no help for it.

[400]

I'm convinced that it has to be a permanent thing, and that for some strange reason alcohol is poison to me.

Love,

Ray

## TO HELGA GREENE

June 19, 1956

My Sweet Helga:

I love fantastic stories and have sketches of perhaps a dozen that I should love to see in print. They are not science fiction. My idea of the fantastic story—possibly a little out of date—is that everything is completely realistic except for the basic impossible premise. Both those I have mentioned are concerned with vanishing or invisibility. I have one about a man who got into fairyland but they wouldn't let him stay. Another about a princess who traded her tongue for a ruby and then was sorry and it had to be retrieved. One about a young society novelist whose father was a magician and kept making a duke disappear so his son could make love to the duchess. I may add that the duke took it with good grace (a joke) although he was rather annoyed. That sort of thing. Quite rare nowadays.

I met Marcel Duhamel (of Gallimard's Série Noire) in New York and took them and Jessica to lunch at the Pierre. Lunch just average. Duhamel has a perfect command of English and is so energetic he tires me out. His wife is charming. I'd like to sleep with her. Right now I'd like to sleep with almost any pretty soft gentle woman, but of course I shan't do it (even if I had the chance) because there has to be love. Without that it is nothing.

[401]

Can a man not be genuinely in love with two women—especially a man who expects nothing but the privelege of loving them? And caring for them when he can, and always being devoted and kind? I am not an average man. There is nothing predatory in me. I am much more of a giver than a receiver. I don't think the sexual act is in itself so terribly important, but I do think compassion and tenderness are vastly important. My sister-in-law says I was the most wonderful husband a woman ever had. But isn't it easy to be a wonderful husband if you have a wonderful wife? And isn't it just because I loved her so much that now that she is gone I love all gracious and tender women. . . .

 Goodnight, darling. Perhaps I have talked too much. I signed the lease today. Now, out of furniture for a house with a huge living room, a fancy powder room, a solarium (with rattan furniture) four bedrooms and four and a half baths, I have to select what I can use in two bedrooms, a reasonable but not large living room with a dining alcove, and one bathroom. Not so easy. And the books! Dear God, what on earth shall I do with books that overflowed a large house? I guess you have to be ruthless about possessions.

 I love you dearly,

       Ray

## TO HARDWICK MOSELEY

       Hotel Del Charro
       2380 Torrey Pines Road
       La Jolla, California
       June 20, 1956

Dear Hardwick:

 This place really has a climate. You have to go through an

English winter to appreciate it. Very seldom hot and very seldom cold, built on a point of land with the Pacific on three sides, with hills behind it, no railroad and only two roads of ingress. I have tried to use it as the setting for a story I am trying to write;[1] I have changed the topography a little and changed the name, and in doing this I have to accept the handicap of all English mystery writers: I can't make heavies of the cops, because they are nice cops and most of them are friends of mine. I call them "the boys with the beautiful shirts" because their tan shirts and slacks are always immaculately creased military style. The captain in charge is a grizzled veteran of long service and he told me he had never fired his Smith and Wesson .38 except to qualify on the police target range, as per the standing orders. Sometime last year a man shot his wife in a store here and the cop who came rushing in—too late—was so nervous that he shot a bystander by mistake. (He didn't kill him.)

Yours ever,

Ray

# TO JESSICA TYNDALE

July 3rd. [1956]

Darling Jessica:

No one but you could have sent me the books and I thank you, thank you. *The Talking Bug* is neat, concise and to the point, an expert job without a trace of anything memorable. That's the nice thing about a good thriller. You can read it once a year. Mr. Bagby I have reservations about. I really don't care much for these chaps who try to use a European background without having absorbed it. I don't want to be too bitter, because some of the many mistakes in his very first chapter may be the fault of the publisher or printer. (One moment, please. There is a girl outside my window in a two-

1. *Playback.*

piece swimsuit. The bra is about two inches wide and if her pants shrink any more, I'll probably go right through the glass with a brush and comb).

No, she saved me by putting a loose white shirt on. The difference in types is very striking. When I first came here they were all sunburned coarse Californians. Now we are getting the hot weather refugees from Texas and the East and they not only have more delicate skins, but are more gracfully built. (Do you think I pay too much attention to such things? Possibly.)

Have you read *Bhowani Junction*?[1] I think you should. It's a damn good job and there are several effing scenes in it that I should have been proud to write, but God knows much prouder to have lived them. But I'm afraid I'm not that good any more.

.            .            .

Yours lovingly,

Ray


# TO JESSICA TYNDALE

July 12th. 1956

Dearest Jessica:

If I sound a little as if I had been smoking reefers, I had a tooth out this afternoon and am still a little on the goof side. No pain at all, but beginning to feel feverish. I was pretty indignant about the whole thing because I have never lost a tooth but once, as a schoolboy with a tooth growing in behind two others. Also I felt that if the dentist had taken X-rays oftener, he could have stopped the decay before it reached a nerve. Wonderful how they do it though. I never knew it was out until he showed it to me. I supposed they had to strap you down and pull like hell. It was a molar too.

1. By John Masters.

This place is an unfurnished apartment on the ocean front. That is, it was unfurnished. It now has so damn much furniture in it that only a steeple-chaser would feel at home in it. But in spite of having all this lovely (and to me now detestable) furniture, a fine electric stove, a Frigidaire and some curtains, in spite of being full of nice yellow cartons which keep me from putting my shirts and underclothes away, in spite of having a small private patio and a large private storeroom, all I have to eat off of is one cup, one saucer, one plate, all borrowed. But a full set of sterling silver, oh my yes.

. . .

I know now what is the matter with my writing or not writing. I've lost any affinity for my background. Los Angeles is no longer my city, and La Jolla is nothing but a climate and a lot of meaningless chi-chi. I went to a cocktail party a week or two ago and my God there was a man there in a checked dinner jacket and another in a rose moiré dinner jacket. And today in Dutch Smiths shop I saw one in puce. This country is riding the crest of a boom, everybody is making fine wages and everybody is in debt to the ears from instalment buying. God help them if rearmament slows down. As far as I'm concerned the country is overpriced. I just can't afford to live here. There's nothing for me to write about. To write about a place you have to love it or hate it or do both by turns, which is usually the way you love a woman. But a sense of vacuity and boredom—that is fatal.

. . .

I send you large amounts of love and I know damn well I sound like a bitter and disappointed man. I guess I am at that. I was the first writer to write about Southern California at all realistically, as the UCLA Librarian admitted when asking for my original manuscripts for the Special Collections of their library. Now half the writers in the country piddle around in the smog.

. . .

With lots and lots of love,

Ray

[405]

# TO HELGA GREENE

La Jolla
July 13th, 1956

Helga Darling:

. . .

One thing I regret is never having based a story on the Palm Springs, Cathedral City desert locale. It is unique. Perhaps I may still do it from memory. At any rate my book about La Jolla is going to be much more brutal if I am safely in Europe.[1] There is really nothing here but a climate (wonderful, I admit, but I'd take the worst of London gladly in exchange) and a lot of very stupid chi-chi. How did the French expression chi-chi which means fuss come to have its American meaning of silly elegance? After all, puce dinner jackets! Or am I just getting too old? I am already sick to death of skins like burnt orange and smiles like gashes. I am sick of people who never put a glass down and cocktail parties where no one (but me) can sit down. Alas, not all my country is hopelessly vulgar, but this part of it certainly is.

Materially we have everything, and an English person would for a time be fascinated by our gleaming kitchens and bathrooms, by our beautifully designed houses, by the wonderful work of our decorators (if you can afford them). After a few weeks' visit they would return to their gloomy houses with glowing accounts. But this is all on the surface. Underneath is vacuity and boredom. TV, cocktails, bad cooking, and what do we do next except buy another and more garish car, go to some idiotic and exorbitant hotel in a resort, read the *Post*, *Time*, and *Ladies Home Journal*, and if one is exceptionally intellectual, one might even rise to the *New Yorker*. We are a very clean people. We take showers every day, which only rare people like yourself do in England. Our best restaurants are appallingly dull and expensive, not in the least equal either in menu or service to La Speranza, which I suppose is only second class in London. . . .

1. *Playback*.

I am really terrified of trying to live in France. I shall be most awfully lost. When I was a young man and very innocent I lived in a pension on the Boule Miche and was very happy wandering around, with very little money, but a sort of starry-eyed love of everything I saw. The only thing that upset me was the whores at the door of the apartment building if I happened to be out a little late. And I so innocent that I didn't realize that there were two girls at the pension that couldn't keep their feet off mine and were offering themselves to my innocence and I never even knew it. I knew so little about women then, I know almost too much now. And yet I have never become cynical about them, never ceased to respect them, never for a moment failed to realise that they face hazards in life which a man does not face, and therefore should be given a special tenderness and consideration. I have never seduced a virgin nor intruded upon a valid marriage. I think this feeling which I have about women, and which women obviously do not feel about themselves. . . . was the basis for my fury about the Ruth Ellis case. There is nothing to argue about here, so far as I am concerned. If a woman gives herself to me, for one night or for much longer, I regard the gift as a delicate and almost a sacred thing, and although I am, I suppose, subconsciously aware that she gets something out of it too, I always think of myself as the recipient of a royal favour. Women are so damned vulnerable to all sorts of hurts.

.        .        .

Terribly much love,

Ray

## TO JESSICA TYNDALE

6925 Neptune Place
La Jolla
August 20th. 1956

My Darling Jessica:
I have been neglecting you shockingly but not only you. I

don't think I've written a letter in three weeks until yesterday, when I wrote several business letters. I have just come back from the Las Encinas Sanitarium in Pasadena, a very wonderful place but frightfully expensive. Cost me over $1400. But hold your hat, I was *not* drunk and have two witnesses to prove it. It was much more serious really (if anything can be more serious). Twice in the past two years my world has crumbled to pieces around me. It was more than I could take. . . . After a little while I stopped caring about my meals, and then I stopped eating altogether, but I ask you to believe me—it was not drink. I was drinking very little and some days not at all. And if finally occurred to me: Boy, you may not know it in your conscious mind, but you've got a death wish. You're too proud to do it openly and directly again, but you are starving yourself to death because you want to die. Well, it was like a voice speaking softly in the night but it threw me. I had to find out if I was off my rocker and didn't know it. And Las Encinas is the place to find out. They have a psychiatrist there that an intelligent man can really respect. They treat all kinds of people, senile old people (with money, natch), incurable alcoholics, guys on benders . . . a few psychotics who have to be kept in a special locked bungalow, depressed people, etc. It's a beautiful place, carefully landscaped, all bungalows, and the atmosphere is absolutely uncritical. The doctors are very attentive, the food magnificent. They kept me in a state of semi-somnolence for several days until I started to eat, and God, how I did eat then. I had some of the best food I've ever had in my life. Then they went through the usual boring program of tests, and after that they went to work on me. I told them the whole truth very frankly. I said that I had been married so long and so happily that after the slow torture of my wife's death it seemed at first treason to look at another woman, and then suddenly I seemed to be in love with all women. I had no idea what I had to give them that they gave so much to me, that the most strict and puritantical woman I had ever met had been in bed with me a week after I met her. That the strange thing was that such affairs as I had had never ended. There was never any bitterness or boredom. I loved them all still and they seemed to love me. But I could not live alone. It destroyed me. Therefore I could not be completely faithful to any woman who could not share my life, but that I didn't regard this as infidelity, because after all sex is only a rather minor part of love, delicious as it is when it is right. I said I really didn't want to

[408]

get married again because my heart was in too many places and a wife would never have more than a part of me.

.　　　　.　　　　.

They gave me tests, apperception tests, Rorschack tests, wood block tests. I haven't had the lowdown on them yet, but I think I was pretty brilliant except on the drawing. I never could draw, couldn't even learn under a drawing teacher at school.

Finally the head guy said: "You think you are depressed, but you are quite wrong. You are a fully integrated personality and I wouldn't dream of trying to intefere with it by psycho-analysis or anything of that sort. All that's the matter with you is loneliness. You simply cannot and must not live alone. If you do, you will inevitably drink and that will make you sick. I detect no signs in you of a suicidal impulse. You seem to me to be vibrant and full of ambition, but something has got in your way, and that something to my mind is that you can't live alone. After all it takes a long time for a man who has lived your life, always with a woman close to him, to get used to being a loner. And if you could make it, you would probably dry up in the process." I said: "Doctor, am I an alcoholic? They told me I was in New York." He said: "In the first place I have been studying alcoholics for twenty years, I have read all there is written on the subject, and discussed it with everyone who is preoccupied with the problem. There is no definition of an alcoholic. Nobody, but nobody, knows what an alcoholic is, except by a pragmatic definition. An alcoholic is a man who can't take the second drink because he can't take the first. One incontrovertible fact is that no alcoholic can ever become a controlled drinker. If you can become a controlled drinker, and personally I think you can with the right sort of life, you are not an alcoholic." "The right sort of life," I said. "But I don't want to get married." "Marriage is a religious and civil institution of great importance," he said. "People in love with each other should be married and should stay married. But morals are not my business. I am concerned with your mental health and stability, as I said. From that point of view, and especially at your age, I don't care whether you live with one woman or twenty, as long as you live with someone. That in my opinion is an absolute."

I thought he was damned clever to take me to pieces so

[409]

smoothly. I hadn't expected anything so penetrating. Well, you know
Chandler.

.        .        .

Ray


## TO MICHAEL GILBERT

6925 Neptune Place
La Jolla, California
Sept. 6th. 1956

Dear Michael:

.        .        .

La Jolla is no place in which to live. The climate is all right
(although lately we have had a lot of thin fog) and the shops are
wonderful. The place has style—no billboards or advertising signs are
permitted. But it's too dear and too dull. There is no one to talk
to. All the well-to-do and almost well-to-do crowd accomplish in
their lives is an overdecorated home—the house beautiful for gracious
living—a wife who, if she is young, plays tennis at the Beach Club,
lies on the beach until her visible skin looks like brown sandpaper and
feels the same, I have no doubt, swills several cocktails before dinner
(almost always in company with friends), several highballs after
dinner and ends up either being pawed by some other girl's husband
or shrieking with laughter at some joke which hardly merits more
than a mild "huh." If she is verging on middle age, she is very chic in
a tasteless way, talks a great deal about how she is going to have
the guest room done over by some jerk with long sideburns, has her
husband so tamed that he is afraid to sit down in some of the chairs,
and however tired he may be, he must shower and shave and put on
his white dinner jacket (in summer) because Mr. and Mrs. Whoosis
are coming over to play bridge, which he hates almost as much as he
hates Mr. and Mrs. Whoosis. While waiting for dinner, cooked
with much supervision by the lady of the house, but all the coolie

[410]

labor done by some sulky coloured girl, he is compelled to read the funny paper to his brats, although they have read it four times already and made a crumpled mess of the part *he* wants to read. Then there are the quite elderly, quite rich retired people. They dress immaculately, are helped into Cadillacs by coloured butler-drivers and are driven to the Beach Club, where they sit in perfect silence, or converse in low monosyllabic voices with others of their kind.

There are also the working people, but most of them are, in any real sense, illiterates also.

The hell with me!

all the best to you,<br>Ray

## TO WILLIAM GAULT

6925 Neptune Place<br>La Jolla, California<br>Sep 7 1956

Dear Bill:

I am feeling rather disgusted with life at the moment. One of my girl friends just got herself married to a lunkhead whom I found quite repulsive, and I'm afraid the poor girl has made a mistake. . . . I guess she is just damn well fed up with living alone.

So am I. If there is anything in life I hate it is going out to dinner alone. I could cook it, but that would be worse. Four days a week I have someone to go with, but the other three are hell. I feel like chucking the whole thing and going back to England to come a resident and pay their bloody taxes. The cost of living is so much lower there (except in the four or five best hotels) that the difference in that might easily equal the difference in tax, or even go beyond it. Also my secretary has abandoned me for schoolteaching, a pretty sensible idea or her part, but it involves her dumping files, contracts, books of account, cash journals, bills to pay, letters to write—all

[411]

bang in my lap and in an apartment where I have hardly enough room to be halfway comfortable without all that. In London I had a hell of a good secretary who cost me .70 an hour (five shillings) on a half day job. She had more brains in one finger than most girls in that line have in both legs.

Yours despondently,

Ray

## TO ROGER MACHELL

6925 Neptune Place

La Jolla, California

Sep 12 1956

Dear Roger:

. . .

Jamie wrote me a long and pleasant letter about covers and misprints and some great artist (for covers) whom many had tried to bribe away from him. This incorruptible genius designed the cover for *The Long Goodbye*. Jamie said that the booksellers liked pictures on the covers of my sort of book. I still don't like it. I don't like the blood, the arm and hand seem to me out of proportion (she has a hand like a first baseman), the spray of roses that tall would not stand up in a shallow dish, but these are not the point. My point was and remains that the effect on me and on others I know was cheap. Houghton Mifflin's covers tend to an extravagance of design which is supposed to suggest something rather than hit you on the nose with it.

. . .

A working man [in La Jolla] lives far better than most white collar people in England—that is if you don't examine what is in his brain. He has all the gadgets, a new car every year or so, and he is buying his house on a government loan that he will pay off in twenty years, maybe. He has TV, an automatic stove that does everything but sing Tristan and Isolde, a garbage disposal thing in the sink, a dishwasher which only nicks or cracks about fifteen dishes a month, a clothes washer, a dryer, an ironer, a deep freeze unit in his garage where he keeps enough food for six months, (he buys that on time too) and most of the other food he eats comes ready prepared and half-chewed. Unless his wife really wants to cook well, and I'm told by an authority that a great many of them really do want to cook well, all his wife has to do to make dinner and dessert could be done in ten or fifteen minutes. All our clocks are electric, all our heating is automatic, and in fact I sometimes wonder what the hell we are here for. Certainly not to use our minds.

Yours lovingly,

Ray

# TO HAMISH HAMILTON

6925 Neptune Place
La Jolla, California
Oct. 26, 1956

Dear Jamie:

.　　　　.　　　　.

Roger and I had some amiable growling about your covers, but it was all amiable—how could anything be otherwise with Roger—and I haven't changed my opinion in the least. Have you ever looked at the dust jacket of *The Little Sister*, for example? It portrays a desiccated schoolteacher or librarian of some 38 to 40 years of age, about as sexy as a rat-trap. Yet this little girl was young, and without her glasses or with smarter ones, looked good enough to fumble with. Some day, just for the hell of it, a dust jacket artist ought to submit to the excruciating agony of reading the damn book.

.　　　　.　　　　.

Much love to all,

Ray

[413]

## TO HELGA GREENE

6925 Neptune Place<br>
La Jolla, California<br>
Nov. 20, 1956

Helga Darling:

They won't give you two bedrooms and a communicating bath in this damn hypocritical country. They don't refuse outright everywhere, they just don't have the vacancy. They will give you a suite with a sitting room, but when you arrive you are apt to find that what you have is two separate rooms with a sitting room in one, but no connection. Of course at a place like the —————— in Los Angeles it doesn't matter. They have a bordello wing, well away from the main building, in which no questions are asked. I was there once in an emergency and next door to me were two couples, obviously unmarried, all four union organisers, all four drunk and dirty and profane. First of all there was a loud and clear discussion as to which girl should sleep with which man. Then it appeared that both wanted the same man. Then there was a fight, at first with words, but in the end with more than words. The fight ended in tears and a reconciliation, after which the two couples obviously paired off and fornicated in the twin beds side by side. I heard all this, not because I tried to, but because I couldn't help it. Don't ever talk to me about union organizers.

I think of you constantly, and always with love<br>
Ray

## TO HARDWICK MOSELEY

6925 Neptune Place<br>
La Jolla, California<br>
Jan 5, 1957

Dear Hardwick:

[414]

How *are* you? I am very fit and have gained about ten pounds and have survived any and every kind of test. My doctor here regards me as some kind of freak and says he can't see any possible thing I could die of, except exhaustion. He says it is very unusual to give an exhaustive examination to a man of my age and not detect some clue as to what may eventually take him off. But enough of bragging.

Spent the time since December sixth until the last week taking an English friend all over Arizona and part of Nevada and then Palm Springs. Arizona never had such a going over; perhaps, since this friend is an incorrigible and insatiable sightseer, which I am not. Friend was entranced with the wild mountain scenery, which is unlike anything in Europe or California. The Dolomites are rugged enough, but the cypresses grow halfway up their sides, whereas everything in Arizona is barren, as though God had quit with the job unfinished.

Am going to Palm Springs again on Monday for three weeks. Address there General Delivery. Your two year-end remittances of royalties touched me deeply: one direct and one through Brandt and Brandt. They totaled forty some dollars. Almost at the same time I had a check from England for over $5000 net after commissions. No wonder the boys are selling direct to paperbacks. What in the world can be the matter? You put out a beautiful book on good paper and meticulously proofread. But who will pay the price? People can rent the damn book to read it and if they want it again later, they can get it in Pocket Books. An English publisher puts out a rather cheap book, not on very good paper, not well proofread, and sells 40,000 copies. Later he puts out a cheaper edition from the same plates and later still a paperback (my publisher does, anyhow) and also an English language Continental edition, like the old Tauchnitz books. I believe I could write a bestseller, American style, if I wanted to badly enough. I seems to me that all it takes is a gimmick. But I shouldn't have the reputation I have, especially in England, Germany and Scandinavia—it can't be any news to you that the Swedes buy more books, proportionately, than any other people. Somehow, if you write something deliberately aimed at the wide public, it always shows. I don't suppose that any mystery writer since Conan Doyle and perhaps Willard Huntington Wright (and what drivel *he* wrote) was ever a bestseller in a large way.[1] But I don't complain. Quite the

1. Wright wrote the Philo Vance detective stories under the pseudonym of S. S. Van Dine.

contrary, I think I have been very lucky, but not in trade editions, except that without them I could never have been paid $2500 a week in Hollywood or $100,000 for a screenplay. I've turned down quite a few movie offers lately because I didn't feel that I could take the beating.

．　　　　　．　　　　　．

Yours,

Ray

## TO JESSICA TYNDALE

General Delivery
Palm Springs
Jan 18 57

Darling Jessica:

．　　　　　．　　　　　．

I have a couple of good friends in La Jolla (by good friends I mean people who take the trouble to keep in touch with you), and of course dozens and dozens of acquaintances. But the place is a desert intellectually. I met [Christopher] Isherwood in Santa Monica and liked him. I think he is the only queer I have felt entirely at ease with. I also met Gerald Heard (he wrote a very clever thriller called *A Taste For Honey*) and found him amusing and very learned, but much too pontifical. Americans generally seem to be quite content to be lectured at for a whole evening. I resent it, no matter how clever the talk is. N. [Natasha Spender] said I was very hostile to him, but her social standards and mine are quite different. *She* thinks I am rude when I am just blunt or sarcastic. *I* think people are extremely rude when they carry on a very private and intimate conversation (I call it "The Derek-Peter-Nigel Routine") which excludes another guest who may also, and it has happened to me, be the guest of honor. You can't interrupt these people, because they constantly interrupt one another and someone is always talking. You *could* interrupt them but it would take violence. Really one should, since once they realize

[416]

they are cornering the conversation they become apologetic. I am quite happy in a company of two or three or even four (including myself) but beyond that I tend to clam up.

Much love,

Ray

## TO MICHAEL GILBERT

Palm Springs, California

Jan 26, 1957

Dear Michael,

    Last night, since it was the last night, we went to the Starlite Room of the Chi-Chi Restaurant here. The technique is absolute, although rather demeaning. You make a booking in advance and say what sort of table you want. Since this place is on two levels, the back part just a matter of four or five feet above the front part, the ideal position is in the middle of the first row of the back section, from which you have an uninterrupted view of the stage and floorshow. The decor is rather magnificent in its way, with a semicircular curtain around the stage. Having booked the table you arrive and your car is taken by an attendant in uniform. You enter and are greeted by the maitre d'hotel (they have half a dozen captains) and you say, "Good Evening, I believe I had a reservation, but possibly you could not manage to give me the table I rather wanted." At the same time you slip a folded five-dollar bill into his hand. Now, in this part of the country very few people do that. They demand, they do not politely ask, and above all they do not themselves provide the maitre d'hotel in advance with a situation for which he may only have to offer the mildest apology. As a result of this approach (and the five bucks) you get the best table in the house, and the captains won't even let the waiters wait on you, or pour the wine. You can't light your own cigarette. The lighter is already there as you put it in your mouth. It simply amazes me how few Americans understand the art combining generosity in tipping with demanding very little. But that is the whole point. These headwaiters are tough, callous and cynical, but they must behave with deference to the most impossible people. Then someone comes along who treats them with deference, and they simply can't do enough for you. I suppose my own approach is a bit calculated, but my manners are not, and when you are with a lady for whom you have a very high regard, you are not thinking in the least of yourself; you are trying to create around her an atmosphere of ease and graciousness. So that even in America you can achieve something that here is very rare: an attentiveness that will not allow a lady to unfold her own napkin, a realisation that her chair must be held by her escort and not by a waiter, so that a captain will deliberately stand back and wait for you to seat your guest, instead of, as is usual here even in the best places, holding her chair himself. He will not attempt to help her off with her coat or wrap, but when you have done it, he will be at your elbow to take it and put it in the cloakroom, and when the wine is brought, a Pontet Canet 1928 (I was a bit afraid of it, because we get all the bad years here, since we don't know the difference) no one is allowed to touch the bottle except the captain who originally conducted you to your table. Rather a farce in a way, but an English lady probably doesn't realise what a rare thing it is in America—or perhaps I should say, most of America—for this sort of thing to happen.

Unfortunately, the Pontet Canet 1928 costs just about as much as Krug Champagne costs at Boulestin's.

• • •

Yours always,

## TO HELGA GREENE

6925 Neptune Place<br>La Jolla, California<br>Feb 11 1957

Helga Darling:

[418]

It's difficult enough to accept that your wife, or mine, had two other husbands, one of whom at least must have been a better lover than I. But to accept infidelity when one is totally committed is very very difficult. That is, if one regards marriage as a serious business. I personally, and am probably quite wrong, don't think infidelity is a matter of much importance if one has a casual view of marriage. But if you find an ideal and an inspiration, you don't cheapen it. It's not so much that an individual is hurt, but that one's whole level of being is hurt.

Much love, darling

Ray

## TO JEAN DE LEON

6925 Neptune Place
La Jolla, California
Feb 11 1957

Jean Darling:

It was very sweet of you to send me some of your poems. Little as I am qualified, I should like to discuss them with you, but not without your permission. I shall say only that the one you wrote for me seems better than any of them. I think it is a very dangerous thing to criticize poetry, because a poet is so easily discouraged. As an offering to make myself vulnerable I am sending you three things I wrote myself. I never claimed to be a poet, although as a young man I wrote quite a lot of verse which was published in various English papers and magazines. I haven't any of it now, which might indicate a certain modesty. I don't even remember much of it. I suppose it was fair or it would not have been published, but that is as far as I could go.

I am very glad that you can accept your father's death without too much grief. But of course I know from my own experience

[419]

that it takes time, quite a lot of time, to reconcile oneself, and that so far you are being brave. I am one of those who do not believe in personal immortality, since I see no reason for it. God probably finds something to preserve, but what, I don't know. He might find even in me, a sensual, sardonic, cynical man, some essence worth preserving, but I don't really think it is anything I could recognize. So much of us is external, environmental, caused by our experiences here on earth, so little of us is pure and undiluted. God knows, but I don't. I share your antipathy to dogmas, but more than that I will just not surrender my right to examine, to dissect, to question. Creo quia impossibile seems to me just one of those devices the Catholic hierarchy is too clever at, and yet, taking it broadly and admitting the many corruptions, the Catholic religion is the only one in our world (I'm not considering the religions of the East) which really lives. The Church of England and our Episcopalian church here live in individual priests, but not as a faith. Its services have beautiful words (which it didn't write) and many of its priests are fine people; but the faith itself is barren and tired. (I ought to apologize for my typing, but I have three fingers bandaged, and that makes me clumsy.)

.          .          .

Your theory of poetry may be right; I don't know. I have no theories about writing; I just write. If it doesn't seem to me to be good, I throw it away. There is a certain quality indispensable to writing, from my point of view, which I call magic, but which could be called by other names. It is a sort of vital force. So I hate studied writing, the kind of thing that stands off and admires itself. I suppose I am a born improviser, I calculate nothing in advance, and I believe that whatever one may have done in the past, one always starts from scratch. Damn, I said this before.

I don't deny you your right to be tolerant of homosexuality; one more or less has to in England. But I do think that homosexuals (not bi-sexuals, that is a matter of time and custom), however artistic and full of taste they may seem to be, always lack any deep emotional feeling. They are wonderful with surfaces. I simply could not read Angus Wilson's novel, his last, because it seemed to me that he described his characters and did not create them. I just found the book dull.[1] ——— is always trying to write fiction, but he can't do it,

1. *Anglo-Saxon Attitudes*, 1956.

because people of his kind have no real emotional life. They see life through mirrors. As for their having a better understanding of women, be off with you. I know more about women than any of them will ever know, and yet I don't know very much. They like women who are sympathetic to them, because they are always afraid, even if they act arrogantly. Their physical bravery was proved in the war, but they are still essentially the dilettante type. Some of them, like Isherwood, are very likable, some of them are repulsive. My wife hated them and she could spot one just by walking into a roomful of people.

．　　　．　　　．

But I am not ashamed to be a lover of women. The difficult thing to make another person understand is that I have a code, that I adhere to it, that I have always adhered to it. There was a time in my life as a young man when I could have picked up any pretty girl on the street and slept with her that night. (Bragging again, but it is true.) I didn't do it because there has to be something else and a man like me has to be sure he is not hurting anyone, and he can't know that until he knows more about her. There are lots of cheap women, of course, but they never interested me. There are women who are inaccessible, and I can tell that in five minutes. I always could. There are women who could be had tomorrow night but not tonight. That I know also. There are women who for one reason or another would give themselves wrongly, and who would feel awful about it the next morning. That also I had to know. Because one doesn't love in order to hurt or destroy. There were girls who could have been scarred for life by giving way to a normal human impulse, but not by me. If by someone else, I expect I couldn't help it. There were girls who didn't care, but for them I didn't care either. I don't know whether it is a talent or a curse, but I always know. I don't know how I know, but I could give you specific instances in which, against all the outward appearances, I knew. Sometimes this haunts me. I feel as though I must be an evil man, that this intuition is given to me only to destroy me. But I guess I don't mind being destroyed very much any more. After all, I was a loving and faithful husband for almost thirty-one years, and I watched by wife die by half-inches and I wrote my best book in the agony of that knowledge, and yet I wrote it. I don't know how. I used to shut myself in my

[421]

study and think myself into another world. It usually took an hour, at least. And then I went to work. But I always listened. And late at night I would lie on the eight-foot couch reading because I knew that round midnight she would come quietly in and that she would want a cup of tea, but would never ask for it. I always had to talk her into it. But I had to be there, since if I had been asleep, she wouldn't have wakened me, and wouldn't have had her tea.

Do you think I regret any of this? I'm proud of it. It was the supreme time of my life.

Ray


## TO EDWARD WEEKS

6925 Neptune Place
La Jolla, California
27-2-1957

Dear Mr. Weeks:

I expect to go back to London in a few months. I have had a few ideas for articles which you might have liked, but I don't know— I could be all wrong. You know I don't write articles for money but to express something which to me needs saying. When I wrote a couple of rather caustic things about Hollywood writers warned me that I had destroyed myself; but I never had a word of criticism from any important executive. In fact, it was after you published these things that I had the most lucrative assignments. I think Hollywood people are much underrated; they think, many of them, what I think, but they just don't dare say it, and they are really rather grateful to anyone who does. I always knew there was only one way to deal with them. In any negotiation you must be prepared to lay your head on the block. A writer never has anything to fight with but whatever guts the Lord gave him. He is always up against business organizations that have enough power to destroy him in an hour. So all he can do is try to make them understand that destroying him would be a mistake, because he may have something to give them.

[422]

I found it quite wonderful to deal with the Moguls. They seemed so ruthless, they conceded nothing, they knew they could throw me out, that in a sense I was nobody, that I said things to them that a writer in Hollywood simply does not say to the big bosses. But somehow or other they were too clever to resent it. And in the end I almost think they liked me for it. At any rate, they never tried to hurt me. And some of them are very clever people. I wish I could write the Hollywood novel that has never been written, but it takes a more photographic memory than I have. The whole scene is too complex and all of it would have to be in, or the thing would be just another distortion.

Well, I suppose all this is a bit boring and too long-winded. I'm not young any more and I am afraid of no one. I have been through hell and I still exist. I had a long and happy married life and I watched my wife die by half-inches and while she was dying, and I knew she was dying, I wrote my best book. I wrote it in agony but I wrote it. I suppose that is some sort of accomplishment. No doubt, other men have gone through the same ordeal. I'm not bragging at all (I hope). I am simply trying to say that all in all I have been a very lucky man, but that I have paid for that luck in the only way I knew how.

I'm afraid this letter may seem to you too personal. If so, may you forgive me? Sometimes I feel terribly alone.

Yours with kindest regards,

Ray Chandler

## TO DEIRDRE GARTRELL

6925 Neptune Place
La Jolla, California
2nd March 1957

Dearest Deirdre:

.            .            .

Courage is a strange thing: one can never be sure of it. As a platoon commander very many years ago I never seemed to be afraid, and yet I have been afraid of the most insignificant risks. If you had to go over the top somehow all you seemed to think of was trying to keep the men spaced, in order to reduce casualties. It was always very difficult, especially if you had replacements or men who had been wounded. It's only human to want to bunch for companionship in face of heavy fire. Nowadays war is very different. In some ways it's much worse, but the casualties don't compare with those in trench warfare. My battalion (Canadian) had a normal strength of 1200 men and it had over 14,000 casualties.

.        .        .

Ray

## TO PAUL BROOKS

6925 Neptune Place
La Jolla, California
March 10, 1957

Dear Paul:

.        .        .

As to the doctor book idea, it may be a little while before I can send you samples of the material, or at least samples of the sort of thing it would be.[1] The book would not be liked by the bigwigs in the medical profession, by the surgeons who perform all sorts of unnecessary operations to get the money, by the hospitals who charge patients for all sorts of unnecessary tests, by the "operators" who, although often very competent, put every patient they get into a long and expensive routine, no matter how simple his ailment may be to diagnose. Nor by the "come back boys" (I'd like to see you again on Friday) when there is nothing to come back about. Nor by the sort of doctor who wants to get you into a hospital so that he can pop

1. For a brief time, Chandler considered writing a nonfiction book on the medical profession.

in two or three times a day and say a few pleasant words and stick you ten bucks for every time he drops in. Nor by certain types who want to give every medicine by hypodermic and charge you for giving it to you and charge you for the material at (they say what it costs them) but at four or five times what it costs them. I know them all; I've had dealings with them all. There are many things people don't know about such practises, nor how to beat overcharges. They don't even know the various county medical associations have scales of fees. They don't know that no doctor has a right to make an unrequested call, unless he does not charge for it. They don't know how to beat an overcharge. Suppose you receive what you think is an exorbitant bill—it happened to me when my wife was ill, and she was ill many times—and I wrote that I considered it exorbitant and explained why. The next thing I knew I was served by a collection agency. Well, it so happened that one of the lawyers we used at that time (I was in the oil business then) volunteered to represent me and my wife, and refused any fee. So we went to court and the doctor sent one of his juniors to testify. On the stand he had to admit that he had not rendered any of the services involved and did not of his own personal knowledge know anything about them. The attorney immediately moved for a dismissal and he got it. He might not have got it from every judge—some of them almost automatically give judgment for a collection agency—but he got it this time. So I called the doctor and told him what I thought I should pay and he accepted gladly, although he had already lost half of it to the collection agency. I might add that he was personally a very charming man.

But my technique was all wrong. I should have called him up at once when I got the bill and told him I thought it was exorbitant, that he had made many unnecessary calls and done nothing when he made them, and that I proposed to file a complaint with the Los Angeles County Medical Association. He would almost certainly have said: "Oh, I'm very sorry, there must have been some mistake in the office. I'll be glad to send you a corrected bill for whatever amount you think fair."

There is the sort of doctor—I know one in New York—to whom you go for perhaps a sinus condition that you know is chronic, but is a little worse than usual, and he puts you in a hospital for a general check-up (although he knows very well from what you tell him that what you have is a chronic allergic rhinitis), gets another

[425]

doctor, an internist to supervise an exhaustive and very expensive series of tests, all most competently done, but all leading to nothing but a big bill. And every day you are there this ear, nose and throat man pops in pleasantly, although he has absolutely no responsibility for the check-up, and later sends you a bill for fifteen or perhaps even twenty dollars for every time he popped in.

The country is full of all these types, mostly in rather well-to-do (exclusive is the word they use) communities or in large cities. And then of course there is the driven, overworked honest doctor who makes at the most a very modest living, who never gets enough sleep, and never collects all or nearly all of his bills. And of course there are the "doctor's patients," mostly neurotic or elderly people, especially women, who just love to have doctor come and see them three times a week, even though there isn't a damn thing the matter with them that a kick in the pants might not help. These people pose a dilemma to the most honest doctor, is he really doing any good? If so, perhaps he is justified in making the calls, but if he does, in the end, he will find himself giving the patient the medicine she wants, and not anything he knows to be necessary.

My own doctor is too damned honest. After he had seen my wife a few times, and seen her X-Rays and knew she had advanced fibrosis of the lungs and that there was very little hope, he said: "I'm very sorry, Mrs. Chandler, I wish I knew how to help you, but I don't. If I were in New York, I could send you to a specialist who knows everything there is to know about cases like yours. But here I simply don't know of anyone to send you to, and it wouldn't be right for me to let you keep coming to see me when I know I can't help you." Well, she was mad at him. Of course he knew she was going to die, but he couldn't know how long it would take—perhaps years. If an honest doctor is certain that you are going to die in three or six months, say of an advanced inoperable cancer, he will think it his duty to tell you. But with a very slowly progressive but incurable disease such as my wife had, he doesn't know how long it will take, and it would be cruel for him to tell the patient or the patient's husband that there was no cure.

And there is the doctor I went to in La Jolla when I had about my fourth attack of angioneurotic edema, which is an inflamation of the skin of the neck (probably allergic in origin) with redness, swelling and the most unbearable itching. Sometimes it spreads up

[426]

onto your face and sometimes the itching is so unbearable that you have to have morphine. Well, I knew how it had to be treated from previous experience, but this doctor didn't and said so. I told him I had to have injections of certain drugs. So he thought a moment and asked me if I was sure. "You can call a doctor in Los Angeles who has treated me and he will confirm it." "Well they are not drugs that could hurt anyone," he said. So he called the drugstore and made them send the stuff over and gave me the shots. Then he gave me back the two or three bottles, and what he charged me was, I think, about three dollars for an office visit and for the drugs, not what they would have cost me, but what they cost him.

Sorry to write at such length. I wanted to give you an idea of what it was all about. Later I'll send some actual and rather dramatic cases.

With kindest regards, and apologies too,

Yours always,

Ray

P.S. I'll finish the damn Marlowe novel one of these days.[2] I just got fed up with it.

## TO JESSICA TYNDALE

6925 Neptune Place
La Jolla, California
March 14, 1957

Jessica Darling:

I promised to tell you about my struggles with the Alien Registration people in England. When I went to Italy I was due to

2. *Playback.*

[427]

report, and I tried the night I was leaving, but I couldn't get the damn passport pictures in time. When I came back I asked my solicitor what I should do. He told me to hurry over to the principal police station of the Westminster district—it was such an obscure place that the taxi driver had a hell of a time finding it. I went and the sergeant said, "Oh no, you don't report here. You have to go to the Alien Registration office in Piccadilly Place." I'd never heard of that either, but I finally found out that the building was the old Vine Street police station. An amiable young man looked at my passport and said, "Oh, you don't have to report. You've broken your residence." A couple of days later I received a stern letter from the Commissioner of the Metropolitan Police ordering me to report at once at the Alien Registration office with two passport photos, all my travel documents, and five shillings. So over I buzzed and the same amiable man introduced me in the office of, I suppose, the head guy, who shook hands with smiles all over him and said he was very pleased to make my acquaintance. Then the other chap came in with a day book that looked about three hundred years old and wrote something in and stamped my passport. They wouldn't look at the passport photos or the five bob.

The next time I had to report, early in 1956, I got the refugee treatment. Lots of questions, quite polite but quite firm, the passport photos and the five bob taken from me. The next day I had to go back again and was given a permit which I was required to show to any police officer who asked to see it. Naturally they never did. The whole thing is such a farce, because there is no liaison. The Home Secretary says one thing, the solicitor says another, the Alien Registration Office pays no attention whatsoever to any of them.

.        .        .

Ray


## TO HELGA GREENE

6925 Neptune Place
La Jolla, California
March 19th. 1957

Helga Darling:

[428]

I agree with you about the word "affair," but what else can you say? The obvious word is not to be used except on very intimate occasions. I remember a hardboiled RAF chap in the war who said, "I don't fool around. If I see a nice dame (he was an American) I walk up to her and say, 'Madam, do you f–ck?'" Someone asked him if he didn't get an awful lot of ballings out. He said, "Sure, but I get a lot of the other thing too."

Personally, I am completely amoral, if it is possible to be that and at the same time to have a very exacting code about women. Women understand it, but most men wouldn't. Jessica [Tyndale] called me a "passionate moralist." But bourgeois morality is too hypocritical for my taste. I wasn't faithful to my wife out of principle, but because she was completely adorable and the urge to stray which afflicts many men at a certain age, because they think they have been missing a lot of beautiful girls, never touched me. I already had perfection. When she was younger she used to have sudden and very short-lived tempers, in which she would throw pillows at me. I just laughed. I liked her spirit. She was a terrific fighter. If an awkward or unpleasant scene faced her, and at times we all face that, she would march right in, and never hesitate a moment to think it over. And she always won, not because she deliberately put on the charm at the tactical moment, but because she was irresistible without even knowing or caring about it. So she had to die by half-inches. I suppose everything has to be paid for in some manner.

Much, much love,

Ray

## TO DEIRDRE GARTRELL

6925 Neptune Place
La Jolla, California
March 20, 1957

Darling Deirdre:

Love is a strange thing. I smoked a pipe from morning to night when

[429]

my wife was alive and I loved it. I can't smoke cigarettes at the typewriter. I'm not much of a smoker anyhow. I used to drink a great deal of tea, and my wife loved that, just as she loved to see me smoking a pipe. I have a large collection of them, all English. Since she died I don't smoke a pipe or drink tea; I suppose it may be wrong, but everything intimately connected with her likes has died in me when she died. I don't mean I am unhappy—not at all. I was for a long time, but not now. The irrevocable can finally be endured. It would in a way be far worse if she had divorced me (this is just an example, we adored each other) and had married some other man and I had to think of her living with and loving that man, and saying to him the same tender things she said to me.

.           .           .

You pay me a great compliment in feeling sure and happy when you put your thoughts and feelings in my hands, but you are quite right. I do have a strange sort of instinct for understanding people, especially women. And I can always be trusted, although by bourgeois standards I am no moralist. I am more than twice your age and it may be out of place for me to be saying these things to you, but it is nevertheless a simple fact that I could never hurt, cheapen or demean a woman, and often, when I was young and unmarried, I had to think for the girl too, to prevent her sometimes from doing something which I knew would shame her later. I always seemed to know. I don't have any idea why. I don't go too far with this, because after all I am writing to a well-bred young lady, and I don't want to offend her. I could go much farther, but would it be right?

Surely you realize, that when you write so frankly to me, it is because I am far away and because we may never meet. I rather hope we shall, unless it destroys an illusion. You need the illusion. And it might be that if we did meet, and even if I didn't too much disappoint you, you would never again be able to open your heart to me. As for your being born too late or I too early, I shouldn't have had the marriage I had, if it had been otherwise. Do you understand what it is to love a woman so deeply and be so deeply loved that no day in thirty years was not in its way a courtship? I always held her chair for her at the dinner table—until she couldn't come to it any more. I always opened the car door for her and helped her in. I never

[430]

let her bring me anything. I always brought things to her. I never went out of a door or into a door before her. I never went into her bedroom without knocking. I suppose these are small things—like constantly sending her flowers, and always having seven presents for her birthday, and always having champagne on our anniversaries. They are small in a way, but women have to be treated with great tenderness and consideration—because they are women.

.     .     .

Ray

## TO MICHAEL GILBERT

March 25, 1957

Dear Michael:

I always feel like a beginner when I start a new job. Of course I have been successful and of course I have made a lot of money, but these things may be largely luck. I don't feel any more important than when I was writing for the pulps. Why should I? Also, there is the background that I was a successful business executive, managed eight corporations, had perhaps the best office staff in Los Angeles, because I knew how to treat them and how to pay them. I don't think these are important talents, but they do make me realize that for a writer or author to be self-centred or arrogant, is just a sign of stupidity. What have we to be arrogant about? One does the best he can at the time, sometimes in very torturing circumstances. Perhaps it is good, perhaps it is bad. But he does his best, and if he has a big success, that doesn't make him anything he wasn't before. He still has his neck on the block. He can still flop or lose his touch. I am the same man I was when I was a struggling nobody. I feel the same. I know more, it is true, I break all the rules and get away with it, but that doesn't make me important. I may have written the most beautiful American vernacular that has ever been written (some people think I have),

[431]

but if it is so, I am still a writer trying to find his way through a maze. Should I be anything else? I can't see it.

## TO JAMES HOWARD

6925 Neptune Place
La Jolla, California
March 26, 1957

Dear Mr. Howard:

.　　　　.　　　　.

Of course I was fortunate. I was in the oil business as an executive for years, and when I decided to give it up, I wasn't broke. I had written very highbrow stuff in London as a young man—my mother was British, but I was an American by birth—and I went to school in England, France and Germany. In 1931 my wife and I used to cruise up and down the Pacific Coast, in a very leisurely way, and at night, just to have something to read, I would pick a pulp magazine off a rack. It suddenly struck me that I might be able to write this stuff and get paid while I was learning. I spent five months on my first novelette, but I did something I have never been able to persuade any other writer to do. Writers who asked me for help or advice later on. I made a detailed synopsis of some story—say by Gardner, he was one of them, and he is a good friend of mine—and then tried to write the story. Then I compared it with professional work and saw where I had failed to make an effect, or had the pace wrong, or some other mistake. Then I did it over and over again. But the boys who want you to show them how to write won't do that. Everything they do has to be, they hope, for publication. They won't sacrifice anything to learn their trade. They never get it into their heads that what a man wants to do and what he can do are entirely separate things, that no writer worth the powder to blow him through a barbed wire fence into hell is ever in his own mind anything but starting from scratch. No matter what he may have done in the past, what he is trying to do now makes him a boy again, that however much skill in routine technical things he may have

[432]

acquired, nothing will help him now but passion and humility. They read some story in a magazine and get a lift out of it and start banging the typewriter on borrowed energy. They get a certain distance and then they fade. They don't know why, so they come to someone like me, or perhaps someone like you, and ask what is wrong. You try to tell them, but you never get it home. They think all they need is some little twist; they never get it into their heads that writing is like an iceberg, for every foot that shows above water there are eight below.

Yours very truly,

Raymond Chandler

## TO WILLIAM GAULT

6925 Neptune Place
La Jolla, California
March 31st. 1957

Dear Bill:

I am ashamed to confess that I haven't yet read the book you so kindly sent me. I hope you will forgive me. I want to read it, but I can't seem to catch up. I have had an awful mass of letters to write, I am in a tax hassle with the British government which has involved a lot of correspondence with the British Consulate and with my lawyer in London. Also, I have three very badly inflamed fingers—must be some kind of allergy—all the outer skin is gone and I have to bandage them rather heavily. Otherwise I couldn't type at all, and I can't type without making a lot of mistakes.

By evening I get so tired that I don't even want to read. I just lie on my back and look at TV until one or two A.M. Sometimes I go to sleep on the couch and sleep through a whole film. But I study the thing, because I believe it is worth it. A lot of programs are junk, but there is some very good writing. If I were a young man

[433]

I think I'd go into it seriously, but the pressure would be too much for me now. I loathe some of the commercials, but don't have to listen to them, because I have a blab-off, had one in 1950 before they were even on the market.

Your attitude to writing is probably right for you, but it wouldn't have been right for me. Once, because my agent worried me about it so long, I wrote a slick story.[1] It has been anthologized to death, and I lately re-read it in this paperback anthology, and I didn't like it very much. It was too studied, too careful. I just don't take to that sort of writing. The story was all right, but I could have written it much better in my own way, without trying to be smooth and polished, because that is not my talent. I'm an improviser, and perhaps at times an innovator. Some slick writing is very good, on the surface, but it seems to lack something for me. Also, it's dangerous. You can adapt yourself to a certain magazine and then the editor changes, the policy changes, and they don't want your stuff any more. And much to your surprise you find that you have lost your individuality, given away too much. Or, as has happened recently, the damn rag folds up. The angle boys may have a temporary success, but they spend so much time and effort pleasing editors that they never have a chance to find out what they can do best. But perhaps I have a different idea about writing and shouldn't be saying this.

I want to go to England to see if I can learn to write plays. London is the best place in the world to do it, they have so many active theatres, and they are not overawed by the critics. I need a change; I've probably written the best story of the kind that I could ever write. The thing becomes a routine in the end. The Gardners and the Christies can go on forever, but Chandler has to believe in something. To me writing is not a business or a racket, it is an art. Perhaps I talk too big. If so, I'm sorry. I know writers have to live and that it is not easy for them to make enough to live on, and I don't blame them for making concessions, but it's not for me. Screen writing is different, you're not even the author of what you write, and things are changed on you without your knowledge. It's not exactly hack work, because there are a lot of clever people in Hollywood, as well as some awful idiots, and sometimes you can do

1. "I'll Be Waiting," *Saturday Evening Post*, October 14, 1939.

something good, and if you have the right producer, it may even be kept that way. But however much money you get, and I got a hell of a lot, nothing you do ever really belongs to you. I once wrote an original screenplay in about three weeks, because the studio had three actors they had to pay and no film for them.[2] It was written, shot, cut and in the can in, I think some 41 days, and it was not a cheap picture at all. One of the actors was supposed to be called up and it had to be done quick. It was no wonderful job, but it had its points, and it made a lot of money. But I don't call that sort of thing writing. You do it for the money, and you do it in a constant struggle to keep some top heavy director from messing it up. If I could, I'd far rather write for the stage. A writer has some authority there; he may have to change lines because some temperamental actor or actress doesn't like them (and often they are right), but you have something to say about the casting and the direction. You are not a hired hand.

.         .         .

I've often tried to figure out what makes these teenagers what they often are. Do they think they live in a lost world? Even here in La Jolla, after a very nice party down somewhere at La Jolla Shores, the boys and girls amused themselves by slashing tires on the way home. Why? Why do highschool kids of decent families get fun out of destroying things belonging, for all they know, to people who may having a hard time getting by? Is it a sort of revolt against a world they don't believe in? Is it the result of the war? I don't know, but it is not just us. In London they have the Teddyboys, so called because they affect clothes of the Edwardian era. They are plenty tough and their girl friends too, but so far they stay out of the good residential districts, but for how long? I have a girl friend in London who likes to go walking late at night. She used to come to see me when I lived in Eaton Square, not far away from where she lived, and I was always afraid something might happen to her. It never did, but I thought it a bit dangerous all the same. She is my English agent, the daughter of an immensely rich man, but she works hard at being an agent and lives quite simply.[3] I used to have to go down and open

2. *The Blue Dahlia*, 1945. Produced by Joseph Sistrom and John Houseman, the film starred Veronica Lake and Alan Ladd, who was about to be drafted into the army.
3. Helga Greene.

the front door for her—it was always locked at ten P.M.—and I would see this lonely distant figure coming towards me along the deserted street, and I'd know damn well that couple of tough kids with knieves would be more than I could handle. But she was never afraid. We would sit and have a drink or two and talk about all sorts of things, and then she would go home the same way. I couldn't do a thing about it. A foreigner (and very few Englishmen) can't get a permit to carry or even own a gun in England, except a sporting gun, and even if you shoot a burglar in your own home, you have a tough time proving it was in self defense. So if I had walked her home, I should have been just an added attraction. They would have knocked me out or knifed me, taken my money, and she would have been worse off, because she was a witness. Finally I moved to where she would have to come to see me in her car. But you can't do much with English people of the sort I know. You can't scare them. Even during the worst part of the Blitz in the last war none of them ever went to air raid shelters. More likely, at a dinner party, if the bombs got too close and too loud, they would say in that offhand way they have: "A bit noisy tonight, isn't it?" And that's not affectation, that's the way they are. Sometimes I think they carry this stiff-upper-lip attitude a little too far, but they don't do it to show off; it's natural to them.

All this doesn't settle the problem of the juvenile hoodlums. I don't know the answer. Do You?

One of these days or weeks I have to go to the British Consulate in Los Angeles. When I do, I hope we shall get together.

Yours always,

Ray

# TO LEROY WRIGHT

6925 Neptune Place
La Jolla, California
March 31, 1957

Dear Leroy:

I have gone as far as I can with the mystery story. I may have written the best one of its type ever written. Many people think so. The thing becomes routine; a man gets tired of producing the same sort of scenes and the same sort of effects. He begins to wonder if he is only imitating himself. But to attack a new and difficult kind of writing would do wonders for me, even if I failed. After all, I am a good dialogue writer.[1] Beyond that I should like to write an English novel, not as an American attempting a tour de force, but as a writer perfectly at home with the nuances of British English and yet ambitious to make it become a little more alive. For months I have been writing sketches in various kinds of stylized English (they are mildly pornographic, but that was only to make them fun to write). Some were exaggerated spoofs, some were self-conscious and off the beam, but the last I did has passed the criticism of one of the best writers I know in England. Not a word or an expression wrong, she says. If you think we and the upper-middle and upper-class English speak the same language, you couldn't be more wrong. The affectations, especially of some women, are very funny. Samples:

| | | |
|---|---|---|
| I rather care for that. | Meaning: | I'm crazy about it. |
| I'm madly in love with him. | " | He has enough money to take me to nice places |
| I simply adore your house. | " | The woman hasn't a shred of taste. A perfectly awful place. |
| Darling, it was absolutely sublime. Call me again soon, won't you? | " | Well, that's the end of that, Thank God. |
| Would you adore to have dinner with me on Friday? And so on. | " | She has lost a lover and is scouting for a new one. |

With kindest regards,

Ray

1. Chandler had hopes of writing for the London stage.

6925 Neptune Place
La Jolla, California
April 16th, 1957

Helga Darling:

I remember my first love, but that was a different world. When we met my throat choked up and I could hardly get a word out. To have held her hand would have been ecstasy, to have kissed her would have been unthinkable. But I don't think at that point one is really in love with a particular girl; one is in love with love. Of course one never finds out, because when one meets her later on, if one does, she has long since been married, and usually to some dullard one considers quite unsuitable. Did you ever read a novel by Leonard Merrick called *Conrad in Quest of His Youth*? Probably not too good by our standards, but I liked it. The moral is, Never go Back.

love, love, love

Ray

## TO JEAN DE LEON

6925 Neptune Place
La Jolla, California
April 18th. 1957

Dearest Jean:

·               ·               ·

No, I haven't read *The Light of Asia*.[1] I really feel that formal

1.  A life of Gautama Buddha by Sir Edwin Arnold, 1879.

religions, however liberal in thought, are a little too late for me now. And perhaps—I hope so—I am not the type who runs crying to an Unknown God when he feels, alone, desperate, or facing death. I think I shall take it as calmly as I took the dangers in my war so long ago. But one never knows. Anyone can be broken by suffering. Perhaps, in a way, I am lucky to have reached the decision to take my own life and to have failed, since in a sense I have already known what it is to look death in the eye. Neither prayers nor religion could have helped me then. It was between me and myself, so to speak. Of course, torture is something else. I doubt very much that I could have put on as good a show as so many did.

Why would I not like your love poem? You and I might disagree about certain aspects of love, surely that could not affect what I thought about your poem. Poems are not sermons or thesis plays, at least, I hope not.

I don't know what I think of Billy Graham. I saw him once on TV and he seemed a well-dressed, pleasant sort of chap, young, good-looking, and so on. But in America we are inclined to regard all such people as "on the make," I suppose. There have been too many of them over here and they have made too much money. The flagrant cases seem to me Aimee Semple MacPherson and Father Divine.

.     .     .

Not long ago I wrote a column for a friend, Neil Morgan, who does a regular daily column for the *San Diego Tribune*, not much of a paper, but San Diego is still a hick town, even though the population is almost half a million. In the column I expressed my views about La Jolla (calling it a reluctant suburb of San Diego) and about the emptiness of life among the retired rich, but I also said nice things. The column made quite a stir and someone put up a painted sign at the southern limit of La Jolla—there is a permanent sign there too—and the sign read: YOU ARE NOW ENTERING RAYMOND CHANDLER'S RELUCTANT SUBURB OF SAN DIEGO. It was probably taken down by the first police car that passed, but not until someone photographed it and sent the photograph to Neil Morgan, who promptly printed an item in his column. I didn't think my column very good; it was hastily and easily written, and for nothing, of course. Morgan had the flu at the time (this was stated at the head of my column) and he

[439]

says that since then people have been asking him, "Why don't you get sick more often?"

Ray

# TO DEIRDRE GARTRELL

6925 Neptune Place
La Jolla, California
April 23, 1957

Deirdre Darling:

Most people make do with what is available and seemingly appropriate to their condition. Ferocious romantics of my sort never make do with anything. They demand the impossible and on very rare occasions they achieve it, much to their surprise. I was one of those, one of the perhaps two per cent, who are blessed with a marriage which is forever a courtship. I can't, as I think back, find any reason why I should have been so favoured. Above all, since as a young man I was anything but virginal.

You will never lose dignity with me, since it is obviously a part of you. To answer one question, I never proposed marriage formally to anyone. My wife and I just seemed to melt into each other's hearts without the need of words.

With much love,

Ray

[440]

# TO HELGA GREENE

6925 Neptune Place
La Jolla, California
Easter Sunday, April 28th.
[1957]

Darling Helga:

.        .        .

When I was about sixteen I had an infatuation for a girl, but was too
shy even to speak to her about it. I used to write letters to her. It
would have been an ecstasy to hold her hand. A kiss would have been
almost unthinkable. Not that I was so damned pure. Very young I
belonged to a neighbourhood gang (not criminal in any way) and
found myself paired up with a nice little girl, whom I used to undress
up to a point, purely out of curiosity, and she rather expected it. I
also used to take down the drawers of a cousin of mine in Nebraska,
about my age, and since her four year old brother was with us, we
used to take down his pants just to get him into the act and make him
feel he was not excluded. The curious thing, as it seems to me now,
was that I wasn't in the least interested (so far as I knew) in her
genital organs, but only in her nice firm round backside. I suppose it
was a dawning sex feeling in a way, but it never appeared to me
as anything but naughty and rather nice. I think I was a strange boy
in some ways, because I had an enormous personal pride. I never
masturbated, thinking it dirty. (I had plenty of wet dreams however.)
The headmaster, who ran the pre-confirmation interviews, clearly,
to me, never believed that I had never masturbated, because
practically all boys did. I got hold somehow of a curious idea, must
have read or heard it somewhere. "When you do that, you think you
are holding in your arms a beautiful and unattainable woman. When
you get one really, you will find it very disappointing." Well I didn't,
perhaps partly because I had not filled myself with sexual fantasies
and partly because I was a rather intelligent boy. I have never known
a woman or girl who in any way disgusted me or made me feel
cheap, just as I never to my knowledge made a girl feel cheap.
Sometimes, afterwards, they would burst into sobs and tears, and that

[441]

would frighten me terribly, until they told me it was purely an emotional reaction, and not in the least because they were ashamed. God, how little any man can know about women.

Ray

## TO HELGA GREENE

6925 Neptune Place
La Jolla, California
April 30, 1957

Helga Darling,

I hate to go against your advice, but I have fought many hard battles in my life, and I never found that there was any way to fight them except directly, accepting the risks, knowing that all I had to fight with was my brain and my courage, and that I could easily lose against much more powerful people than myself. But I did not become one of the three or four highest paid writers in Hollywood by letting anyone walk over me. I wasn't really ever a very good film writer, but I must have had something or other. I think today there are much better film writers than I could ever be, because I never quite saw things in the terms of the camera, but always as dramatic scenes between people. I suppose you know the famous story of the writer who racked his brains how to show, very shortly, that a middle-aged man and his wife were no longer in love with each other. Finally he licked it. The man and his wife got into a lift and he kept his hat on. At the next stop a lady got into the lift and he immediately removed his hat. That is proper film writing. Me, I'd have done a four page scene about it. What this chap did took a few seconds. It isn't a question of whether I might have written a good scene— taken as a scene—but whether I was really thinking for the camera. Somehow I don't think I ever was. Good film writers should become

[442]

directors, as they do more and more. But in a sense they cease to be writers, because a writer creates his own world on his own terms, in his own way.

.        .        .

A schoolmaster of mine long ago said, "You can only learn from the second-raters. The first-raters are out of range; you can't see how they get their effects." There is a lot of truth in this. While I dislike calling myself anything more than I am, even to make a point, a fellow mystery writer quite a while ago told me that he had read my stories over and over again, line by line, and almost word by word, and he still didn't grasp how I achieved certain effects. I didn't either, to be honest. Nor did I know that I had achieved them. All I really know, and I'm sure I've said it before, is that for all of fifteen years a lot of quite good writers have been almost desperately trying to imitate me, and that not one of them has even come close. It's a sort of mystery. There are much better plotters than I am, and much better idea men, but it doesn't seem to matter. When they write the scene, there is no magic. Why?

.        .        .

All my love,

Ray

## TO HELGA GREENE

6925 Neptune Place
La Jolla, California
May 5th, 1957

Darling Helga:

.        .        .

I was an executive in the oil business once, a director of eight companies and a president of three, although actually I was simply a high-priced employé. They were small companies, but very rich.

[443]

I had the best office staff in Los Angeles and I paid them higher salaries than they could have got anywhere else, and they knew it. My office door was never closed, everyone called me by my Christian name, and there was never any dissension, because I made it my business to see that there was no cause for it. Once in a while, not often, I had to fire someone—not someone I had picked myself, but someone who had been imposed upon me by the big man—and that I hated terribly, because one never knows what hardship it may mean to the individual. I had a talent for picking out the capabilities of people. There was one man, I remember, who had a genius for filing. Others were good at routine jobs but had no initiative. There were secretaries who could remember everything and secretaries who were wonderful at dictation and typing, but whose minds were really elsewhere. I had to understand them all and use them according to what they were. There was one girl, not pretty and not too bright, who could have been given a million dollars in cash, and a month later, without being asked, she would have known the number of every bill and listed it, and would have, at her own expense, taken a safe deposit box to keep the money in. There was a lawyer on salary in our office (I didn't approve of the idea, but was overruled by the Board) who was very acute but also very unreliable, because he drank too much. I found out just how to use his brain, and he said often and publicly that I was the best office manager in Los Angeles, and probably one of the best in the world. (Eventually, he crashed a police car and I had to get him out of jail.) When I hadn't been long with the firms we had an embezzler. His method would only be possible in a badly organized office. But I found him out and at his trial I had to sit beside the Assistant D.A. and tell him what questions to ask. The damn fool didn't know his own case.

.            .            .

My only excuse for what I wrote of my business career was a hope of convincing you that I am not exactly a baby in these matters. I always somehow seemed to have a fight on my hands. At one time I employed six lawyers; some were good at one thing, some at another. Their bills always exasperated the Chairman; he said they were too high. I always paid them as rendered because they were not too high, in the circumstances. Business is very tough and I hate it. But whatever you set out to do, you have to do as well as you know how.

[444]

I remember one time when we had a truck carrying pipe in Signal Hill (just north of Long Beach) and the pipe stuck out quite a long way, but there was a red lantern on it, according to law. A car with two drunken sailors and two girls crashed into it and filed actions for $1000 apiece. They waited almost a year, which is the deadline here for filing a personal injury action. The insurance company said, "Oh well, it costs a lot of money to defend these suits, and we'd rather settle." I said, "That's all very well. It doesn't cost you anything to settle. You simply put the rates up. If you don't want to fight this case, and fight it competently, my company will fight it." "At your own expense?" "Of course not. We'll sue you for what it costs us, unless you pay without that necessity." He walked out of the office. We defended the action, with the best lawyer we knew, and he proved that the pipe truck had been properly lighted and then we brought in various bar men from Long Beach (it took money to find them, but it was worth it) and that they had been thrown out of three bars. We won hands down, and the insurance company paid up immediately about a third of what they would have settled for, and as soon as they did this I cancelled the policy, and had it rewritten with another company.

Perhaps all this sounds a little hard-boiled. But I wasn't like that really at all. I was just doing what I thought was my job. It's always been a fight, hasn't it? Everywhere you go, everything you do—it all takes it out of you. It takes more out of me than it did once, but still I have the same feeling.

.       .       .

Love, love, love,

Ray

6925 Neptune Place
La Jolla, California
May 7th., 1957

Darling Helga:
I am sending you my story "English Summer" herewith. It is

[445]

about 8500 words long, not the best length commercially. It may not be commercial at all, but I enjoyed writing it and rewriting it very much. It might be a little over-written, but I think I'd rather have it that way.

.            .            .

If you go somewhere to study new surroundings, absorb new atmospheres, meet different types of people, you always have at the back of your mind at least a hope of getting some use from it all. I have lost Los Angeles as a locale. It is no longer the part of me it once was, although I was the first to write about it in a realistic way. Now half the writers in America live in or near it, the war has made it an industrial city, and the climate has been ruined partly by this and partly by too much vegetation, too many lawns to be watered, and in a place nature intended to be a semi-desert. It was hot and dry when I first went there, with tropical rains in winter, and sunshine at least nine-tenths of the year. Now it is humid, hot, sticky, and when the smog comes down into the bowl between mountains which is Los Angeles, it is damn near intolerable.

So naturally I look around for something else to write about. I can't write about England until I feel England in my bones. Love is not enough.

.            .            .

Ray


# TO DEIRDRE GARTRELL

May 8th 1957

Deirdre Darling:

.            .            .

May I comment on the fact that in none of your letters to me have you ever told me about anything external to your own thoughts? You have never described your room, your university, the buildings,

[446]

the place, the atmosphere, the climate, what sort of place Armidale is. You may think this unimportant, but to me it indicates a state of mind; a state of mind which must be unhappy. I am interested in Australia, in everything about it, what it looks like, what its houses are like, how many rooms they have and what sort, what flowers grow there, what animals and birds are there, what the seasons are, what the ordinary life of people of your sort consists of. You tell me a great deal about your thoughts, but nothing about the life around you. Do you suppose I became one of the most successful mystery story writers of any age by thinking about me—about my personal torments and triumphs, about an unending analysis of my personal emotions? I did not. And you should know that very well. But from you all I hear is about you. This is not said to blame you or accuse you of being egocentric at all.

With much love and some hope,

Ray

## TO HAMISH HAMILTON

6925 Neptune Place
La Jolla, California
May 16th., 1957

Dear Jamie:
First, greetings, salutations and love to all who might be interested in any of these, especially to yourself and Roger.

Next, I have a faint—really quite faint—recollection that at one time you thought my letters might be worth publishing. I raise the subject now only because I have such an accumulation of them that I must destroy them unless my recollection was right. A friend of yours called me a "flaming egotist." For a long time I thought myself

[447]

to be a rather modest man, but I am beginning to believe this friend was right, that all writers are bound to be egotists since they drain their hearts and souls to write at all, and therefore become introspective. I think I have lately become worse, because I have been praised too much, because I live a lonely life and have no hope of anything else from now on.

As to the letters, some are analytical, some are a bit poetical, some sad, and a good many caustic or even funny. They reveal, I suppose, a writer's reaction to his early struggles and later his attempts to ward off the numerous people who seek to exploit him in some way. There are also love letters and letters to an unknown girl in Australia which were merely a rather kind attempt to resolve her problems after she had given me more of her heart than (as she said) she had ever given to any of her family. Naturally, many of them could not be to a name, and many of them would require a note of explanation about the circumstances which caused them to be written. A good many were to you.

It would be quite a job to sort them out and select those which might be worth while any one's attention. One editor of Houghton Mifflin wrote that I had revived the lost art of letter-writing. I make no comment on this, but it is true that in letters I sometimes seem to have been more penetrating than in any other kind of writing—at times—and that as I reread some of them, I am really astonished— astonished at the facility of expression and the range of thought I seemed to show even when I was only a struggling beginner. Please believe that I am not asking you to publish them at all, merely wondering whether they could possibly be of enough interest to be worth publishing. A real writer, and at times I think I am one, exists on many levels of thought. Perhaps as a result of my business training I always knew that a writer had to follow a line with which the public would become familiar. He had to "type" himself to the extent that the public would associate his name (if they remembered it) with a certain kind of writing. But that would not be enough for him in his own mind. So I suppose in my letters I more or less revealed those facets of my mind which had to be obscured or distorted in what I wrote for publication.

This may sound to you a little silly, but I hardly think so. For instance lately I sold a serious poem to the *Atlantic* and I have just written a longish short story with an English setting (but told by an

[448]

American). And I am now back on the Marlowe thing which I hope
to finish soon.[1]

I ask you about the letters because it will be quite a lot of work
to go through hundreds of them and pick out those which seem to
have something and then have them copied and make the necessary
notes. I don't want to do it, if it is of no interest. You must over
the years have received enough letters from me to get some idea
whether the project is worth the time and expense, although I should
never expect a publisher to commit himself in advance except in
general terms.

I'll send the carbon of this to Helga and then, dammit, I'll
probably forget what I wrote.

Love,
Ray

# TO THE EDITOR OF THE *DAILY EXPRESS*

May 21, 1957

Dear Sir:

I have read in the Los Angeles *Times* Mr. Rene MacColl's
remarks on certain things which he does not seem to like about my
country, and with many of them I am forced to agree. There is
another side to America which Mr. MacColl seems to have
overlooked. We became too rich and too powerful through a sort of
genius of production technique, and as a result I think we placed
ourselves in a position to dominate the world before we had any real
knowledge of how to do it or any real desire to do it. We were just
stuck in the Number One spot. For 100 years, as you may remember,

1. The poem is called "Requiem" and the story is "An English Summer." The Marlowe
novel is *Playback*.

[449]

England dominated the world and was rather cordially detested by everyone else. That seems to be the price of power, however unwanted or undesired. The position we find ourselves in is almost impossible to maintain either gracefully or cleverly.

I admit that most of our values are quite wrong, but they result from something which we did not intend to be wrong. I admit that our motor cars tend to be absurd in their design, but we live in an economy of overproduction and fantastic advertising campaigns are waged to make us think that anything six months old belongs with the Pharaohs. I admit that the cost of living here has reached absurd levels, but at least we have clean kitchens and clean bathrooms— and we bathe. I admit our manners are not always what they should be, but with us a cab-driver has as much right to punch you in the nose as a marquess would in England. I admit that our grocery-store bread is tasteless, but what could be more awful than your coffee or your bacon? I admit that tea bags are offensive, but there is tea to be obtained in this country without bags and of a far better quality than anything you have.

Ours is a young, large, and variegated country. We don't know everything. Do you? We try, and have tried very hard, to do what we think we should do in the world, and our workmen occasionally do a day's work, which is more than yours do so far as I have observed. Once on Wimpole Street while waiting for a friend in a doctor's office, I watched two men moving those light-weight fireproof bricks which are extensively used in construction in England. It took two of them to move two of them across the pavement and drop them into a chute—and that seemed to make them very tired. We should have devised a machine to do it in twenty minutes. They were probably at it for two days.

Not everything about us is right, of course; but is everything about England right? It is so easy to write a newspaper article sneering at some other country; but it is not easy to create a civilization in that country, however many men of good will and great ability may try.

If Mr. Rene MacColl would like me to write a few comments on England as disparaging as his about America, I should not do it, although I could. It would be too cheap a victory over a friend.

Yours respectfully,

[450]

# TO HELGA GREENE

6925 Neptune Place
La Jolla, California
May 25th. 1957

Darling Helga:

"Non-U Author desires the services of a private secretary (very private) who can cook, wash dishes, make beds, tidy flat, and do some secretarial work. Hours long (sometimes all night), seven days a week, salary liberal, employer American, fairly good manners, but not too reliable. Works like hell when he feels like it, but occasionally has other interests. Applicant, if interested, should be unmarried, reasonably pretty, approachable. Please send photograph, preferably in the nude. Lunches and dinners at good restaurants would be provided, and occasional trips abroad. Applicant should be university-educated and very refined, but not too damned refined. Should be adept at shorthand, a fast and accurate typist, have knowledge of filing (not on the floor). Good quality lingerie essential, and not too much of it. Working conditions will be pleasant, but not conservative. If interested, please apply in writing stating salary expected, height, weight, age and colour of mink stole. This is an exceptional opportunity. Don't miss it. Box Z-2098, *The Times*."

Helga, darling: I'd better start all over again. Your cut from the *Times* threw me. Your letter arrived at 7.30 A.M. I had been up until 3. But reading your letters was worth it. I think I have to agree that "English Summer" won't make a play, because by the time I had licked the difficulties, I'd have another story entirely. I really sent you the story to make you understand how difficult it is going to be for me, since plays, I think, need tight construction and a clear, not too complicated line. But I am by nature, so far, a rather discursive writer who falls in love with a scene or a character or a background or an atmosphere. Once, in a book that was not too good as a whole, although it had some cunning scenes, I wrote a description as an attempt to find out whether purely through the tone of the description I could render a state of mind.

. . .

Ray

[451]

# TO EDGAR CARTER

June 3, 1957

Dear Eddie:

.                    .                    .

    I think you have the job of convincing these lunatics that if a show is to last, it must cost not too much and must have some sort of special quality, and that quality must be on terms the public can understand and appreciate.[1] I may be wrong, but to me Marlowe is a character of some nobility, of scorching wit, sad but not defeated, lonely but never really sure of himself. He will at any time, because he is that sort of a man, meet any danger, since he thinks that is what he was created for, and because he knows the corruption of his country can only be cured by men who are determined if necessary to sacrifice themselves to cure it. He doesn't talk or behave like an idealist, but I think he is one at heart; and I think that he rather hates to admit it, even to himself. I have written practically nothing about his sex life because I thought it was his own business, but I did in my last book break down a little. It is impossible to think that such a man would not have a sex life, but so many writers of this sort of story have made it too blatant and too vulgar. Since I am just about finished with the mystery story, I think I may confess that Philip Marlowe, unlike myself (he is not me, of course), would get almost any woman into bed with him by a certain obscure technique which depends almost entirely on making a woman feel that you respect her, that you never make any cheap gestures or suggestions, that you never—or almost never—touch her until you know. Ask your wife if I am right. Women always know so much more about these things than men.

    I suppose that a man who was married for almost 31 years to a woman he adored becomes in a sense a lover of all women, and is forever seeking, even though he does not know it, for something he has lost. You can never cheapen a woman. No man of my sort thinks of her exactly as she thinks of herself. After all, her body is to

---

1. Reference is to television adaptation of Marlowe material.

her a familiar thing; but to some men it is always a sort of shrine. Women are very subtle in these things. For hundreds and hundreds of years, they had to please men with their looks, their charm, etc. Inevitably it must have left somewhere in their minds a deep intelligence about sex, because once that was all they had.

Some of this had to go into Philip Marlowe if he is to be any good. Otherwise, he would be just another sharp-talking nobody. If it is not possible to achieve this, I think we should forget the whole thing. After all, a great many writers have been trying to steal him from me for 15 years or more, and they have never made it yet. I suppose all writers are crazy, but if they are any good, I believe they have a terrible honesty.

Yours,


## TO MRS. DOROTHY BEACH[1]

6925 Neptune Place
La Jolla, California
June 3, 1957

Dear Mrs. Beach:

Thank you for your letter. I have no quarrel with Mr. Rene MacColl personally, but if he is pro-American, I am a two-headed chimpanzee. I was interviewed by him in the spring of 1955, and I think I am entitled to my personal impression of him. I am not a "great gentleman," kind as you are to say so. I am merely an ordinary American. If you count me on a par with Erle Stanley Gardner and Rex Stout, I am very sorry. I count myself far above them. This will prove to you that I am not a gentleman at all.

I entirely agree with you that understanding between Britain and America is vastly important to the future of the world, but of

1. A correspondent replying to Chandler's public letter on Rene MacColl.

course as one man I cannot achieve it. I can only resent things that seem to me to damage it.

Yours very truly,

Raymond Chandler

## TO HELGA GREENE

6925 Neptune Place
July 11th. 1957

Darling Helga:

.      .      .

I think it would be impossible for me to live here. I am not surrounded by old friends, because in order to have friends you have to cultivate them and for years I almost never went out at night and never had anyone to the house. Also the sort of people one would expect to know are a stupid lot whose lives centre around the Beach and Tennis Club. You probably have exactly the same sort of people in England, but in London you can find others. Here there are no others. The furniture is a nightmare. The only thing to do with it is for me to get out and let someone sell it piece by piece on commission. I have over fifty cartons and a dozen barrels. I have so many clothes that the closets in both bedrooms won't hold them, nor all the drawers in all the chests. I have suits that I had forgotten, shirts beyond any possible need, underwear for all seasons, and about 18 pairs of shoes. Good God!

.      .      .

Love, love, love

Ray

[454]

# TO DEIRDRE GARTRELL

6925 Neptune Place
La Jolla, California
July 25, 1957

Darling Deirdre:

It seems that I have a serious anaemic condition. Not fatal, but quite serious. These diagnoses never make much impression on me, since I have lived my whole life on the edge of nothing. Once you have had to lead a platoon into direct machine-gun fire, nothing is ever the same again.

I don't quite know why you are so close to my heart, but you are. In some mysterious way you have put me inside of you, so that I have to lie awake at night and worry about you—you a girl I have not even seen. It must sound ridiculous to you. All I can say is that in some strange way you have become a part of me, so that I wake in the night and wonder what is Deirdre thinking or doing, is she making a fool of herself with some nice but stupid man, and if she is what can I do about it? All very silly, but there is a certain devotion in it also, entirely because of your letters. I have had thousands of letters, and I suppose I have written thousands. A collection of my letters is to be published when I can weed them out. But that is not the point. Why should I take Deirdre into my heart when hundreds of charming people made no impression on me at all deeply?

The older you get, the less you know.

With all my love,

Ray

[455]

# TO HELGA GREENE

6925 Neptune Place
La Jolla, California
Sept. 20, 1957

Helga Darling:

.           .           .

    I haven't seen the *New Yorker* for months, just got tired of it. So I did not see the Angus Wilson story. I tried to read his fairly recent novel, but it didn't hold me. Like all people of his sort, however clever, he doesn't create his characters, he describes them. But I think I may have become a bit crotchety from loneliness, worry, illness and physical suffering. My ideas of what constitutes good writing are increasingly rebellious. I may even end up echoing Henry Ford's verdict on history, and saying to unlistening ears: "Literature is bunk." In the meantime, I don't think I should passionately care for either *The Last Angry Man*[1] or the one on the other side of the sheet you so kindly sent me. You are an agent, you have to keep abreast. I may satisfy myself with *Richard II* or a crime novel and tell all the fancy boys to go to hell, all the subtle-subtle ones that they did us a service by exposing the truth that subtlety is only a technique, and a weak technique at that; all the stream-of-consciousness ladies and gents, mostly the former, that you can split a hair fourteen ways from the deuce, but what you've got left isn't even a hair; all the editorial novelists that they should go back to school and stay there until they can make a story come alive with nothing but dialogue and concrete description: oh, we'll allow them one chapter of set-piece writing per book, even two, but no more; and finally all the clever-clever darlings with the fluty voices that cleverness, like perhaps strawberries, is a perishable commodity. The things that last—or should—I admit they sometimes miss—come from deeper levels of a writer's being, and the particular form used to frame them has very little to do with their value. The test of a writer

---

1. By Gerald Green, 1957

is whether you want to read him again years after he should by the rules be dated.

Much, much love,

Ray

6926 Neptune Place
La Jolla, California
Oct. 20th. 1957

Helga Darling:

I don't know how many times I have taken the Marlowe story out and looked at it and put it away again with a sigh, knowing all too well that my heart was too sad to let me capture the mood and gusto and impudence which is essential to that sort of writing.[1] Perhaps you can help me out of it. It seems that I cannot learn to stand loneliness, and that is another reason why I dread Paris.[2] But perhaps we can talk of these things when you are here.

With all my love,

Ray

# TO WESLEY HARTLEY[1]

Dec 3rd., 1957

Dear Mr. Hartley,

My most humble apologies for not answering your letter much

1. *Playback*.
2. Chandler was thinking of living in France for tax reasons.

---

1. California schoolmaster who had sent questions to Chandler.

[457]

sooner. I had a rather bad virus sore throat, and on November 20th. I came down to Palm Springs with an English lady who is my agent for everything but Motion Picture stuff, if any (I don't much want to work in Hollywood), and TV.[2] This needs an American specialist. I've had three American agents, not counting Hollywood and the good ones do a good job in America, and their English opposite numbers are all right, except that they are careless about translation rights, don't really know who the best foreign language publishers are, and practically always use a local agent. Also they are careless about watching performance dates and payment dates. My agent, who speaks three languages fluently, can make deals directly on a ten percent to me instead of the usual 20 per cent. She is also brilliant and beautiful.

I was educated at Dulwich College, an English Public School, not quite on a level with Eton and Harrow from a social point of view, but very good educationally. In my time they had two "sides," a Modern Side intended mostly for boys who expected to go into some sort of business, and a Classical Side for those who took Latin and Greek and expected to go to Oxford or Cambridge. I went up the Modern Side to the top and then switched down to the lowest form (class) in the senior school on the Classical side. I went up that to the form next to the Sixth, the top form. You usually stay in the Remove, as they call it, for a year before being sent on to the Sixth. I left school at seventeen—the usual leaving age then was before one's twentieth birthday, which was compulsory, I mean one had to leave before the 20th. birthday.

After this I had six months each in Paris and Germany. In Paris at school and in Germany with a private tutor. I could speak German well enough then to be taken for a German, but not now, alas, and the language has changed a lot (but I don't think the Germans will ever change). French one never speaks well enough to satisfy a Frenchman. Il sait se faire comprendre is about as far as they will go. Or Il parle très bien le français, mais (a shrug) l'accent—horrible!

Now to answer your questions. College or university education is definitely not necessary, provided one learns anything in high school and only real students do. I have a nephew, really my dead wife's nephew, who was graduated from Fairfax High in L.A., and he

2. Helga Greene.

didn't know a bloody thing. In his last year he took an elective course in music appreciation and he knows as much about music and has as little interest in it as a horned toad. He said the seniors he knew talked of nothing much but sports and dates and girls, that some of them were secretly married, and many were having affairs all over the place. The same went for the girls, except that they substituted primping for sports.

You could tell your lively students, and I realize they must be of a very different type, that although I did a lot of writing as a young man in London (some publicity or jacket blurb writers have called me English, but I was born in Chicago of a British mother and an American father from a Pennsylvania Quaker family), but I couldn't write fiction to save my life. I couldn't get a character in or out of a room, I couldn't even get his hat off. I learned to write fiction by a method which I have recommended to other young struggling writers I tried to help, but no soap. Everything they did had to be for sale. What I did was take a novelette, I think it was by Gardner, and make a detailed synopsis of it. From this synopsis I wrote the story, then compared it with the original to see where he, Gardner, had got an effect and I had got nothing. I did this over and over again with the same story. I think I did learn a great deal that way. My first novelette for the *Black Mask* took me five months to write, and I got $180 for it. Another device I used, especially for the pulp field, was to write a straight story and then rewrite so that it *seemed*, just seemed, like something else. I concentrated on the detective story because it was a popular form and I thought the right and lucky man might finally make it into literature. My books are so considered in England and most of Europe. The Germans and Italians are a little inclined to look down their noses at this sort of fiction. The Germans are a rather stupid type of intellectual snobs, in spite of their language having a magnificent slang. Only the French and ourselves equal or surpass it. The Italians seem to want either tragic stories in which everyone is dirty, never has any decent clothes or money, and every one is rude to every one else; or else novels in which the hero spends practically all of his time in bed with some woman. Some years ago some girl wrote for *Esquire* an article called "Latins Are Lousy Lovers." It gave great offense and the issue was even banned in Cuba. But I happen to know that she was absolutely right. Latins talk a great game and make a rather dignified parade of love-making, but in the actual result the Northern nations and ourselves have them beat to a frazzle.

At the moment I can't think of much else to tell you. I am finishing up my seventh Marlowe story. It is not a very big production for a mystery writer, of course, but I take a great deal of trouble and am not naturally prolific. I do very little pencil or pen revising. If a scene seems wrong to me, I throw it away. I know that what was good in it, if anything, will stay with me when I rewrite it. I probably write ten thousand words for every thousand that get published. Early in 1958 I am going to England to try to write plays. There are forty active theatres in London and if the producers like a play, they will keep it on until the public has a chance to react. The critics in England are far less influential than the New York critics. The English are an old and wise and well-balanced people, and they don't seem to care a hoot in hell that some high-powered reviewer, so he thinks, doesn't get hysterical with delight over something the public comes to regard favorably. Often it takes a little time, and the English producers will as a rule give it time. Also, scalping is illegal in England. All an agency may charge is a quite reasonable service charge. In addition to all this, the Continent of Europe with its hundreds and hundreds of state-supported theatres, is always screaming for new plays.

That doesn't mean I'm giving up Marlowe. I'm far too fond of him. Apart from Marlowe, I have turned to poetry again. The *Atlantic* took a thing called "Requiem" from me—it hasn't yet appeared— and I have just finished a sequence of three sonnets in the classical manner which my agent thinks are very good. I wrote two devastating articles about Hollywood in the *Atlantic* and the writers, not the best of them told me I was through, and one of the trade papers which is dishonest (its reviews can be bought) printed that "Chandler was on a slow march to the guillotine." As a matter of fact, I made far more money after these articles than before. I also took the agents to pieces in an essay called "Ten Per Cent of Your Life." And I took the formal English detective story to pieces in another essay called "The Simple Art of Murder." My first agent was very annoyed with me because I didn't become "his top slick writer" to use his own phrase. I told him that a slick writer might die overnight because a magazine changed its policy, or changed editors and the new one didn't like some types of stories, or BECAUSE

A MAGAZINE, AS HAS ACTUALLY HAPPENED, PRINTS FEWER STORIES AND MORE NON-FIction. (Sorry, the capitals were not intended. I had the wrong key). I said it was my belief that a writer should create his own public, if he could, even though for a time he made far less money than he would get from the big slicks. However, to be nice, I did write one story for the *Saturday Evening Post* to please my agent.[3] They were very doubtful about it at first—it got one NO, which rejects a story or did then, but the Editor took it anyhow. They demanded extensive changes of all sorts. I was still being nice so I made the changes. Then they printed the story exactly as I had first written it, and for years they asked me for more stories about the same character and simply could not get it through their heads that he was a one-shot character, as he was. Some of the best fun I had was writing a novelette which lampooned my own kind of fiction.[4]

The great and difficult problem of the writer in our day—if he wants to make a living—is to write something acceptable to the public and yet at the same time write what he thinks is good writing. A lot of big best sellers are very badly written. I am still getting royalties on things written 25 years ago, so I do think I chose the right way. Very few slick writers ever become good novelists. Marquand did, although he has become a bit of a bore lately. I finished *Yours Sincerely, Willis Wayde* by main force.[5] I think it is one of the dullest books ever written.

If you have any questions, I'll try to answer them. I hope I have not been boring or too egotistical. All successful writers, even though they try to fight against it, inevitably become a little egotistical. It is a lonely and uncertain life and however such success you have had, you always start from scratch. So, I guess when you achieve a certain amount of world-wide recognition, you inevitably feel, "Well, I must be pretty good after all. It was a tough road, and I haven't come to the end of it. But I've come a good long way and perhaps I am entitled to give myself a pat on the back once in a while."

Yours very truly,

3. "I'll Be Waiting."
4. "Pearls Are a Nuisance."
5. Title is actually *Sincerely, Willis Wayde*.

# TO HELGA GREENE

6925 Neptune Place
La Jolla, California
Dec 4th. 1957

My Beloved Helga:

. . .

I thought Dwight Macdonald's piece on James Agee was piffling compared with his slow and patient liquidation of *The Outsider*.[1] I could only get half way through it. Perhaps I missed the best part. (Why don't we do a book called A Child's Garden of Curses?) He says: "Why are our (American) writers so much more at home with children than with adults?" They're not. Very very few writers can write effectively about children. Salinger, for example, can. Irwin Shaw is not bad, but he doesn't quite get it. "The stained glass of the L. and N. depot smoldered like an exhausted butterfly"[2] This is Agee. He tried too hard and stuck his foot in his mouth. Anybody seen an exhausted butterfly smoldering lately? The bit about the street car, too long to quote, much admired by Macdonald, was a perfect piece of pretentious and overstrained writing. "big drops, silent as a held breath, and the only noise the flattering noise on leaves and the slapped grass at the fall of each drop." More Agee. Macdonald thinks this is magic. Make up your mind, Agee; was it silent as a held breath or wasn't it? "All right, Mary I hate to go, but it can't be avoided." Agee. "The last sentence, in rhythm and word choice, seems to me perfect." Macdonald. What's the matter with the man? About as perfect as, for example: "Why isn't dinner ready, Susan? I'm so hungry I could eat the hind leg of a goat." It says what it says, of course, but why rave about it? Would you rave about a sentence like: "If we hurry, we may catch the next bus."?

Well, he read the book which is probably more than I could

---

1. Reviews in *The New Yorker* for November 16, 1957, and October 13, 1956. *The Outsider* is by Colin Wilson.
2. Quotation from James Agee, *A Death in the Family*.

have done, because I loathe pretentious writing, and, after all, he got paid for it. Peace be unto him—and may he recover his mind.

.        .        .

I love you very dearly.

Ray

## TO E. JACK NEUMAN

Harlow Haven
Palm Springs
Dec 9, 1957

Dear Jack:

.        .        .

To fill up the space a few of what I call my morning limericks, usually indecent.

A charming young lady of France
Had scorned my most careful advance
Till a sunny day
Made her feel very gay,
And I found she was wearing no pance.

A certain young charmer of Ghent
Was rather too clearly enceinte
When her father yelled: "Who??"
She replied with a coo:
"I don't know. He just came—and he went."

There once was a lady of Spain
Who regarded my love with disdain,
Till one night on champagne
She was feeling no pain,
And we did it again and again.

[463]

A lovely young charmer named Jean
Was dainty and tender and clean.
Her legs I adored,
But I always deplored
That I never could get in between.

Rather a single track mind, wouldn't you say. I make these up in a few seconds. I also write serious poetry at times.

R.

## TO JESSICA TYNDALE

December 23rd., 1957

Darling Jessica:

. . .

Helga and I get along so perfectly that I am amazed. She seemed so aloof when I first knew her. We never quarrel, she takes everything in stride, and all is peace and happiness between us, as it never was with you know who. For reasons of her own life and temperament she doesn't want to get married again, and this is all right with me, as long as I can live close to her and go away with her.

. . .

I am flying to Palm Springs today to attend a very fancy party at the home of a rich woman to whom my doctor gave me an introduction. She begged me so hard to come that I finally gave in. She is a redhead (with assistance), about fifty, very easy to get along with and a fine dancer. I want to use her house in my next Marlowe story, which I plan to lay in Palm Springs, with Marlowe married to the 8 million dollar girl from *The Long Goodbye*. I think the struggle between them as to whether he is going to live her kind of life or his own might make a good sub-plot. Either she will give in, or the marriage will bust up. I don't know. But I do know that nobody, but nobody, is going to keep Marlowe from his shabby office and his unremunerative practice, his endurance, determination and his

[464]

sarcastic pity. She'll probably want to redo his office, but she won't get to first base with that either.

## TO PAUL BROOKS

Harlow Haven
Palm Springs, California
Dec 28th 1957

Dear Paul:

　　·　　　　·　　　　·

By getting up at 6 A.M. and working 10 hours straight with no food but coffee and Scotch I finished the Marlowe book.[1] Haven't been over it yet but I think it will stand up. I plan to dictate the whole thing—as an experiment—from my rough draft. Helga should have it within a month unless I have made a mess of it somewhere. I don't really think so. I'll probably bring you a copy or two, but Helga is the boss.[2]

Love,

Ray

## TO HELGA GREENE

6925 Neptune Place
La Jolla, California
January 7th. 1958

My Beloved One:

　　·　　　　·　　　　·

It was just like me to lose that piece that Robert Campigny (?)

1. *Playback.*
2. Helga Greene.

wrote in the Paris *Revue-Critique*, and also to lose the reply I had
made to him, in the rough. I think I left them at the Ranch Club on
Saturday night. On Friday night Jessie took me there and we had
a very pleasant time. On Saturday I had a date with a tall and rather
exquisite girl who is a waitress at the Doll House, but I don't think
you ever saw her. I had noticed her several times, not so much for her
looks, but for the way she carried herself and her swift exact
movements. I knew at once that she must be a wonderful dancer, and
I found out (through careful investigations) that she was. So one
morning, when she happened to wait on me—her hours were very
irregular—I asked her whether she would consider dining and dancing
with me, and made it clear that I had no other intentions. She finally
said she would think it over. This was very funny to me, as she
obviously did not believe what I said. One night I was having dinner
there alone and she ignored me completely until a certain man left,
and then she came over to my table and was very nice, and slipped
me her telephone number on a folded piece of paper. She said she
was going to Las Vegas over the week-end, but would I call her when
she returned. She didn't seem like a pickup at all, but I hardly
expected her to be a virgin. She was very frank and told me that men
made her all kinds of propositions and it was not easy for her to
tell which were on the level and which were not. I said I had the same
trouble with girls. They didn't seem to be able to believe that all I
wanted was a dancing partner, and only a good one. I could tell she
was very good indeed, just by watching her move.

So on Saturday last she was "available" and asked me to call
for her at 8.30 P.M. This I did and found her dressed in a stunning
white dress with plenty of cleavage. She put on a white fur wrap,
which she certainly had not acquired as a waitress. Unfortunately,
when we arrived at the Ranch Club, the joint was packed. I hadn't
made a reservation because it had been so easy the night before.
They offered me a table halfway into the kitchen which I promptly
refused. We sat in the bar for a while, and then the hostess came
and said they now had a good table for me. It proved to be quite a
distance from the dance floor. I said I was used to a table at the
edge of the dance floor, but I couldn't make it this time. I then said I
should very much like to have the members of the band drop over to
my table when they had time, as I had had a very pleasant experience
with them the night before. They never came. The girl had a large

and healthy appetite and she told me a good deal about herself, more, really, than I wanted to know. She also called me "dear," which I didn't like too well, because it rather placed her. But she behaved very nicely, held her liquor well, and looked really gorgeous. We tried one dance, but it was impossible. No room to move. All one could do was shuffle. At midnight we had enough and when they came with the bill there was a further bill for drinks for the band. I said: "What's this? I asked the boys over here for a drink of champagne. As you can see, there is almost a full bottle left." "The band had the drinks in the other room." I took the bill and tore it up. "I'm sorry," I said, "But when I want to entertain my guests by long distance, I'll let you know." They went away and after a moment or two the head man of the band appeared and was very apologetic and said there had been a mistake, and he was sorry, and there would be no charge. The girl was quite amused. She said they tried that sort of thing all the time, but very few people ever called their hand. So we went back to her apartment. By this time I think, but of course can't be sure, that she expected me to spend the night with her. But I had no such intention and I rather think she would have been a rather too practiced sleeping companion. At any rate, she didn't let on, and we parted in front of her apartment with excellent manners on both sides. It's rather sad about these girls, although few of them have the looks and the style this one had. They are so insecure and so vulnerable. She was 27 years old, had been married and divorced, and with her looks, why was she still a waitress? I suppose the only answer is that a girl in that position thinks she is one day going to meet the right sort of man, but she never does, because the right sort of man would never think of her as anything but a waitress, unless, like me, he wanted to dance with her and no more. And there are so few serious dancers.

But I have to admit that she never made the slightest attempt to involve me in any way in anything I didn't want. The next morning I called her up and asked her what colour roses she preferred. She said: "Why should you send me roses?" I said: "When a lady does me the honour to dine with me, I usually send her roses." "Well, if you must—I like red ones," she said, and then she burst into tears. "What's the matter? Have I offended you?" There was a silence for a little while and then she said, "I guess, I'm just not used to being treated this way. Usually—oh, the hell with it. What can I say except thanks very much. Will I see you again?" "I'm afraid not. I'm going back to La Jolla today, and in a little while to London. I'm sorry about last night. I managed badly. I wanted very much to dance with you, but I took you to the wrong place. So I guess this is goodbye." Then she said a very strange thing. "I'm sorry we didn't dance. But what can you do more for a girl than what you did?"

I'd better stop now, or I'll be writing another lousy sonnet, and with 16 lines yet.

Ray

## TO BERGEN EVANS

January 18th 1958

Dear Sir:

I happened (and by this I don't imply that I feel superior to TV, but only that the time is unusual for me, as I am usually working then) to see part of your programme today.[1] I was particularly interested because I am an admirer of Mr. Peter Ustinov, and we have mutual friends in London. I barely missed a dinner party at the house of my publisher, Hamish Hamilton, at which Mr. Ustinov was to be present.

If my memory is not at fault, and if there are no technical reasons which I do not understand, then I confess to being puzzled by your panel's attitude to the phrase, which I hope I quote correctly, "All and everyone of the Persians drank their sherbet."

As I remember it, the discussion, rather brief, turned on sherbet. Sherbet can be a fairly solid thing which one eats with a spoon, or in other parts of the world a liquid. No one, so far as I remember, made what seemed to me the two essential points. The use of "everyone" is quite incorrect, and "each and everyone," even *if*

1. The linguist conducted a television show called *The Last Word*.

[468]

correct, does not make a plural phrase. I know that it is far too easy to become puristic, or even pedantic, in these manners, and I, as an experimenter in the American vernacular, am perhaps not supposed to know anything about literary language. It so happens that I know a very great deal.

If the sentence had read: "Each and all of the Persians, etc." the sentence should have continued, "drank his or her sherbet." This assumes that the context does not make it clear that all were men. The sentence could also have read: "Each and every Persian," and would still have taken a singular verb. Mr. Ustinov made an amiable attempt to indicate that this was a compound phrase, but others of your panel were so busy showing off their learning, that he received little attention.

As for "He didn't go to the ball game on account of he was in bed with a virus sore throat,"—I'm making this up, but the point is not altered, this is an outright vulgarism.

I can't say that our language will not tolerate such locutions in the end. Once you let the bars down, you may as well forget that rules exist. But rules are not made by grammarians; they are recognized by grammarians. During the depression of the thirties, when Will Rogers was writing a daily column, it seems that some Bostonian type objected to his use of "ain't." His answer was, "A lot of people that ain't sayin' ain't, ain't eatin'."

If that's how you make a language which can be accurate, vital, elegant, colorful and imaginative, I quit. If a lot of moronic halfwits are to decide what is right or wrong (I'm not thinking of Rogers, who was a charming man), I quit twice. We have an educational system which is the laughing stock of the world. It will remain so as long as it is under the control of political appointees. We are nice people, but in some ways insufferably stupid. Of course the boy or girl who really wants an education will get it under any system. And there will always be those who cannot be educated, because (or on account of) there is no foundation on which to build. These exist everywhere, but however meaningless the pass degree at Oxford or Cambridge, at least a certain standard of polite behavior seems to go with it.

I don't really know why I am writing this. I have a hundred things to do which are more important to me personally. Perhaps I have more love for our superb language than I could ever possibly

[469]

express. Perhaps I don't like fools. Perhaps I don't like the theory that anything may become correct if enough halfwits insist on making it current. Much of our slang comes from such people; they do have their moments. But I hardly think that gives them the right to be arbiters.

There is an old story about us Americans which, to the right mind, tells a great deal. At a fork in the road there are two signs. One said, TO A CONCERT OF THE MUSIC OF BACH. The other said, TO A LECTURE ON THE MUSIC OF BACH. Guess which way the Americans went.

Sincerely,


# TO JESSICA TYNDALE

6925 Neptune Place
La Jolla, California
February 3rd. 1958

My Sweet and Adorable Jessica:
Please pardon the effusiveness, but since I finished the goddam book I have been a little nutty. Tomorrow my copyist will go to work on the final copy. You know, if it hadn't been for Helga, I'd never have finished the damn book. She arouses my mind and my ambition by some strange quality in her own mind. She makes me want to conquer the earth, which of course I shan't do, but wanting do it is a lot different from my lackadaisical attitude of the past few years. There are many sweet and adorable women in the world, and you are one of the sweetest and most adorable, but there is some sort of chemistry between Helga and me that gives me a driving impulse. With Helga around I feel as though I could write anything— sonnets, love poems, idiocies, plays, novels, even cookbooks. What on earth happened between this rather cool, aloof woman and me? Something very strange. She has built for herself an oasis into which no one may intrude. I don't know why—whether it is an escape from a too domineering father, or a refuge from the pain of a lost

[470]

marriage. But I'd never intrude upon it; it's something she has to have, and I think she knows I would never try to intrude upon it, and that this knowledge brings us closer together, rather than creating a barrier. I don't believe in this day and age that any man should have the right to invade the privacy of a woman, however fond of her he may be. With me Helga will always be safe; she will never for an instant have to fear that I should try to take from her anything that belongs to her. But that is not exactly why I am writing in this fashion. It is what she does to me as a writer that I find so amazing. And I don't know how she does it, nor even that she makes the slightest attempt to do it. In fact, I am sure she does not. But somehow, just by the way she talks and acts, by her simplicity, her lack of pettiness, the keenness of her mind, she inspires me. And she does it without trying to. She is much more valuable to me as an agent and a friend than I could possibly be to her as a client.

.       .       .

With much love to both

Ray


# TO ROBERT CAMPIGNY

February 7th. 1958

Cher Robert Campigny:

La Pièce que vous avez dernièrement écrit dans La *Revue-Critique*, sous la titre 'Raymond Chandler et le Roman Policier' m'a parvenu de la part de mon éditeur a Londres, and mon ami depuis longtemps, M. Hamish Hamilton, and aussi de la part de Mme. Helga Greene, qui est ce qu'en anglais on appelle 'my literary agent'. Je ne suis pas trop sûr du mot précis en francais.

Il va sans dire que j'ai eu grand plaisir en lisant ce que vous avez écrit, et je vous remercie plus que beaucoup pour l'honneur que vous m'avez fait en écrivant avec tant de soin sur une espèce de literature qui is souvent regardé comme peu de chose. Naturellement,

[471]

je ne sais pas écrire en francais avec la netteté de style que vous possédez. Mais ce que dis, c'est moi tout seul qui le dit.

Il n'est guère probable ni même à désirer que l'écrivain de romans soit toujours d'accord avec les opinions exprimées par l'écrivain-critique. Ce dernier doit créer quelque chose qui lui appartient, qui a une valeur unique, qui possède une vrai raison d'être. Au même temps je me trouve forcé de vous agréer sans reculement que le roman policier américain du genre 'hardboiled' peut bien devenir un cliché de style aussi ennuyant que ces petits tours de force anglais, sur lesquels j'ai écrit des mots pas trop pleins d'admiration.

Je trouve votre louange de Agatha Christie un peu difficile à engloutir. Sans principe sérieux, it est très mauvais goût de déprécier ses livres seulement parceque je les trouve sans intérêt pour moi, mais l'idée que Madame Christie dejoue ses lecteurs sans farce me parait presque impossible à croire. N'est ce pas qu'elle fait ses surprises en détruisant le portrait d'une caractère ou d'un personnage de roman qu'elle a jusque qu'à ce moment peintu en couleurs complétement opposées au portrait fini? Tout cela est sans aucune vrai importance, sans doute, et les lecteurs qui a besoin d'être taquinés par cette espèce de mystère ne se donnent la peine d'être faché si le mystère existe seulement parceque ces autres sont trop paresseux de faire l'effort de penser.

Tout ce que j'ai écrit ici n'est guère autre chose qu'une manière de vous rendre mes égards. Rien de cela nous vous échappe—j'en suis bien sûr. L'écrivain de métier a du apprendre depuis longtemps que les jugements de l'écrivain-critique—souvent, sinon toujours tres justes—ne sont pas le témoignage décisif. C'est plutôt l'espace qu'une publication d'importance a donné au critique pour presenter ses idées au grand public.

Agréez, mon cher M. Campigny,
mes salutations les plus amicales.

Raymond Chandler[1]

1. Translation:

Dear Robert Campigny:
    The piece you wrote recently in the "Revue Critique," entitled "Raymond Chandler and the Detective Novel," reached me from the office of my London publisher, my longtime friend, Mr. Hamish Hamilton, and also from Mrs. Helga Greene, who is what is called in English "my literary agent." I am not quite sure of the correct word in French.

# TO MAURICE GUINNESS

February 10th., 1958

Dear Maurice:

Your letter charmed me completely and I should not have been
so slow in answering it, but I really have had a rather stringent life
lately. Finally, mostly due to Helga, I finished a book, and mostly due
to you I left Marlowe in a situation where he could be married—
but it was not certain. I hope I picked the right woman. It seems to
me, from my point of view as a writer, that there would be nothing
in his marrying just a nice girl. But if he married, or almost married,
a woman whose ideas about how to live were completely antagonistic
to his, even though in shall we say, the boudoir, they met on very
equal and satisfactory terms, there would be a struggle of personalities
and ideas of life which would make a good sub-plot. I plan my next
Marlowe story with a background of Palm Springs, *Poodle Springs* I
call it, because every third elegant creature you see has at least one
poodle. I have the very house in which Linda Loring might care to

It goes without saying that I took great pleasure in reading your work and I thank
you very much indeed for the honor you have given me in writing with such care on a
kind of literature which is often considered insignificant. Of course, I cannot write in
French with your precision of style, but what I say is said by me alone.

It is scarcely probable nor even desirable that the novelist should always agree with
the critic. The latter must create something that belongs to him alone, that has a unique
value, and that possesses a true *raison d'être*. At the same time, I am forced to agree with
you without much reservation that the American detective novel of the "hard-boiled" type
can certainly become a stylistic cliché as boring as those little English *tours de force*, about
which I have written unadmiringly.

I find your praise of Agatha Christie a little hard to swallow. Without serious
consideration, it is in bad taste to denigrate her books simply because I find them without
interest, but the idea that Mrs. Christie baffles her readers without trickery seems almost
impossible for me to believe. Isn't it true that she creates her surprises by destroying the
portrait of a character or of a person in a novel whom she has up to this point depicted
in colors completely opposed to the finished portrait? All this is doubtlessly without great
importance, and readers who need to be teased by this sort of mystery do not take the
trouble to become angry if the mystery exists only because others are too lazy to make
the effort to think.

All that I have written here is merely a way of sending you my regards. None of
this will escape you, I am certain. The professional writer has had to learn early on that
the judgments of the critic—often, if not always, correct—are not the definitive word: It
is rather the space that an important publication grants a critic to present his ideas to the
public.

Sincerely yours

[473]

live. The house is in La Jolla. It has the sort of offhand elegance and virtuosity which was once fairly usual in England among the upper classes. The people who live in it are clearly rich, but their enormous drawing room, or living room as we call it, escapes that air of having been done by an expensive decorator. It is full of things which I feel sure are priceless, but are treated in the most casual way. It has the largest oriental rug on the floor that I have ever seen. It has space and warmth. You sit in the room and you know that everything in it cost the earth, and you feel perfectly comfortable and at ease. I haven't known many genuine aristocrats in my life, naturally, but the real ones all have a certain way, not only of behaving with perfect ease in any situation, but of being able to impart this ease to others.

.        .        .

In most of the activities by which a man or woman makes money, there is a loser. I don't say this is wrong—living at all is a pretty competitive affair. But when a writer writes a book, he takes nothing from anyone. He adds to what exists, he does not deprive anyone for his own sake. There are writers, of course, and I have known them, who say to me: "Why do you help him? Are you creating competition for yourself?" I think this is a very narrow view. It is quite possible, of course, that if the *Saturday Evening Post* could publish four stories and yours or my story was the cause of their rejecting another, we might *appear* to be in competition with the other writer. But actually we are only in competition with a standard. If his story had been very good, instead of merely acceptable, the magazine would have taken it, and found a place for it. There is never enough good writing to go around.

.        .        .

You make light of your accident in rock-climbing, but it must have been rather awful just the same. And I do realise how depressing it must be to find oneself on retirement from a position of responsibility, importance, and affection. Retiring is a kind of dying. The best way to revive is certainly what you have in mind. Work like hell at something just a little creative. No man grows old as long as he can create. You may die in the midst of it—so may I, who am older than you are—but you don't die of lethargy. I hesitate even to suggest that I might be of any help to you other than as a man who has faced the same problems and understands them, but if it should ever occur to you that I could be of help, surely you would not hesitate to allow me that honour.

.           .           .

Ray


# TO LUCIANO LUCANIA[1]

21st March, 1958

Caro Signor Lucania,

I am an American author, not a journalist, not connected with any newspaper. I shall be in Naples shortly and should greatly appreciate the favour of an interview with you and the purpose of this interview would be solely the attempt one man to understand another and would be in no way under any circumstances to smear you.

I suppose we are both sinners in the sight of the Lord and it is quite possible that you have not been represented to the public in my country as you really are. I am aware that it is not what a man does, but what it is made to appear in court which decides.

I myself run a certain danger in this because a sympathetic interview with you might possibly make trouble for me, but I am willing to face this danger because the object of my life is to understand people, their motives, their origins, how they become what they are and not ever to judge them.

Some of my questions to you may be rather brutal, but if you decline to answer them, there will be no record that they have been asked. There will be nothing published by me which you do not say, but of course, I cannot be responsible for editorial comment.

I am sincere and I would like you to believe so, but I imagine

1. Lucania, known as "Lucky Luciano" was living in Naples, having been deported from the United States for criminal activities. Chandler interviewed Lucania and wrote a sympathetic article called "My Friend Luco" for the *Sunday Times* of London, but it was never published.

[475]

that it is now very difficult to believe that anyone would approach you sincerely.

If you are receptible to my request, would you kindly reply on this prepaid telegram, to the Ritz Hotel, since I do not yet know at which hotel in Naples I shall be staying.

Raymond Chandler


## TO LUTHER NICHOLS

[September 1958]

Answers.[1]

1. Yes, I think the hardboiled dick is still the reigning hero, but there is getting to be rather too many of him. The principal challenger is, I think, the novel of pure suspense. The best of these seem to be written by women. There is an occasional very good detective story written almost in classic form, such as *Last Seen Wearing* by Hillary Waugh, but there are not enough of these to be a threat.

2. I wouldn't call any writer psychoneurotic. We're all crazy to some extent. It's a hard lonely life in which you are never sure of anything. Spillane is perhaps an extreme example of the sadistic writer, but I may be wrong. I can't read him.

3. My best offer [to explain its popularity] is that the detective story (I prefer the term mystery story myself—detective story suggests a type to me) is a completely integrated thing if it is any good; most novels are sloppy by comparison. It has the elements of tragedy without being tragic, and the elements of heroism without being heroic. It is a dream world which may be entered and left at will, and it leaves no scars.

4. No effect whatsoever [on actual crime] except that a man contemplating murder might pick up an idea of how to do it and escape afterwards. But the crime was already there.

---

1. Answers to questions from Nichols and written on form provided. Most of the questions are self-explanatory. The nature of others is indicated in brackets.

5. A decline of the hardboiled story on the basis of Gresham's law [is the trend]. They are too numerous, too violent, and too sexy in too blatant a way. Not one in fifty is written with any sense of style or economy. They are supposed to be what the reader wants. Good writers write what *they* want and make the reader like it. The hard-hitting story will not die completely but it will have to become more civilized. The mystery story in some form will never die in the foreseeable future.

6. I don't worry about reviewers. I've had it both ways, and that is how it should be. Some are stupid, even vicious, but so are some writers. My comment on mystery fiction in general is that I wish more people could write it as well as it can be written. It *can* be literature, you know. In Europe, especially in England, they recognize that.


## TO HELGA GREENE

824 Prospect Street
La Jolla, California
October 1, 1958

Helga My Sweet One:

· · ·

My short story, if you tell me to write it (I'll probably write it anyhow, because the problem is attractive) is about a man who tried to get out of the Syndicate organization, but he knew too much, and he got a tip that a couple of pros were being sent to wipe him out.[1] He has no one to turn to for help, so he goes to Marlowe. The problem is what can Marlowe do without getting in front of the guns himself. I have some ideas and I think the story would be fun to write. Needless to say, if the killers fail, others will take care of them. You don't fail the syndicate and go on living. The discipline is strict and severe, and mistakes are simply not tolerated. The only syndicate boss who was ever convicted of murder was Lepke

1. The story was called "The Pencil" and was actually written.

[477]

Buchhalter, at one time head of Murder Inc. in Brooklyn and head of a 'protection' racket in New York. I don't know how they got him, but he and one of his top men did finally go to the chair. They put [Frank] Costello in prison for a while and they may still be after him, but they won't get far, I should think. These boys all have good business fronts and very clever, although crooked, lawyers. Stop the lawyers and you stop the Syndicate, but the Bar Associations are simply not interested.

Ray

## TO ROGER MACHELL

824 Prospect
La Jolla, California
October 14th. 1958

My Dear Roger:

My next book is to be laid in Palm Springs with Marlowe having a rather tough time getting along with his wife's ideas of how to live. He loves her and they are beautifully matched in bed, but there is trouble looming. She won't like it that he insists on sticking to his own business and modest way of life, and she fills an overdecorated and rather chi-chi house with freeloaders, even if the damn house (of which I have a detailed description) is only rented for the Palm Springs winter season. I don't know whether the marriage will last or whether he will walk out of it or get bounced. Of course I have to have a murder and some violence and some trouble with the cops. Marlowe wouldn't be Marlowe, if he could really get along with policemen.

Love,

Ray

[478]

## TO WILBUR SMITH

824 Prospect
La Jolla
October 16th. 1958

Dear Mr. Smith:

You are quite wrong. Marriage will not be the end of Marlowe, but will in fact provide a sub-plot.[1] It will be a running fight interspersed with amorous interludes. Marlowe, a poor but sincere man, in spite of his tendency to crack wise, will hate Linda's style of living, he will hate the house she has rented for the season in Palm Springs, an over-decorated job of which I have an exact description. He will detest the bunch of freeloaders who are about all you can find for party guests. She on her side will never understand why he insists on sticking to a dangerous and poorly-paid profession. I think they will only completely agree in bed.

I haven't the main, or murder, plot yet. *Playback* was fifth on the bestseller list in England, the last I heard—it's probably off by now, but I doubt that it will make any best seller lists in this country.

Yours sincerely,

Raymond Chandler

## TO FRANK NORMAN

824 Prospect
La Jolla, California
October 16th. 1958

Dear Frank:

.        .        .

I haven't finished *Bang To Rights*[1] yet, but it stands up

---

1. Chandler envisioned Marlowe as being married to Linda Loring, a character from *The Long Goodbye*.

---

1. Norman's book was about prison life in England and was derived from the author's own experience.

[479]

well. . . . A real life story may easily lack the dramatic climax one
has to contrive in fiction. The quality called suspense has to be in all
fiction, although it may be got in various ways. The reader has to
be made to want to know what is going to happen next. Life doesn't
always give you this.

Helga has written to me that you had a story in *Vogue* and an
article on slang somewhere. I am so glad to hear about it. How
is the book going—what are the sales, as far as you know? Don't
hesitate to demand the information from the publishers, since it is
vitally important to you. I think your description of the attitude of a
man in prison, forbidden to be himself, deprived of his own
personality on the surface and condemned to a continuous false
facade—I think you do all this very well, and it is remarkable that
you kept a sense of humour. Very much to be admired. There is good
sound sense about the effect or non-effect of prisons in the book too.

I'll write to you again after a while. Please let me know how
things go with you. I know Helga is very anxious to help you in any
way she can. No one who knows you would think of you as a
natural wrongo, but a man can be driven to desperate things by
persecution or hopelessness.

Yours always,

Ray


## TO HELGA GREENE


October 22nd. 1958

Helga My Darling:

.　　　　.　　　　.

Don't mess around with writers as clients who don't sell anything to
make it worth your while. I've always had a sneaking idea that a
professional failure was always a moral failure. There are writers who
look the situation squarely in the face and decide that they are willing
to be poor if they can write well enough to satisfy their souls. I

[480]

respect them, but a lack of appreciation is narrowing. Henry James felt it. It tends to make a writer exaggerate the very things that keep the public away from him. I am not a mercenary writer, but I do feel that in this tangled generation a writer who cannot face the rather cynical realities of his trade is lacking in more than popularity.

As for your Angry Young Men, it's natural in every generation to have them. But if they don't grow out of it they are immature. Shaw said, as you will remember, "If a man is not a Socialist at twenty, he is lacking in heart. If he is one after thirty, he is lacking in brains." Rather extreme, like so many of his statements, but it has a point.

.    .    .

Ray

## TO CATHERINE BARTH[1]

524 Prospect St.
La Jolla, California
February 7, 1959

Dear Miss Barth:

I spoke to you on the telephone to thank you for the great honor the Mystery Writers of America have done me; but that does not seem quite enough—especially as the real work has to be done by the Executive Vice-President, Herbert Brean, and the Executive Committee, who seem to do all the work and get none of the praise.

I am sure you realize that I take this honor as a token of a long career, and that I do not take it very personally. I wish it could mean more to the Mystery Writers of America. I feel very humble about this, but I suppose there must be reasons why I have been chosen, even if these reasons are obscure to me. After all, most of my life has been spent in trying to make something out of the mystery

1. Barth was Executive Secretary of the Mystery Writers of America; Chandler was elected President of the organization.

[481]

story—perhaps a little more than it was intended to be—but I am not at all sure that I have succeeded.

I am enclosing a couple of pieces which might possibly be of interest to you; if they are not, I shall not be in the least hurt if you deposit them in the wastepaper basket. I do not feel that we have made enough progress in promoting the dignity of the mystery story. I am sure every effort has been made, but somehow it seems always to end in frustration. This may be due to the fact that the organization does not have enough money at its disposal. My experiences in Hollywood proved to me that you have to be very tough to get anywhere, that this toughness may be resented at first, but that in the end it will be accepted if it is backed up by a logical attitude.

Now of course we face television, which is sometimes good but always poisoned by bad commercials. Therefore, I feel that as the titular head of an incomparable organization, I should make some effort to make our mutual endeavor seem as important as it really is. How to go about this requires assistance of other brains than mine. Mine, such as they are, are always at your disposal; but mine alone are not enough.

I have reached a stage in my career where I have nothing to fear. Probably I shall get worse; possibly I shall get better. I have a feeling that hard-cover publication has become in this country rather silly; that you give too much away, and that the question of prestige is no longer important, since one already has it.

I feel that any sort of discussion on these subjects would be something in which I should be vitally interested, and in which I should if possible desire to be of assistance.

Yours cordially,

# TO MAURICE GUINNESS[1]

Feb. 21, 1959

. . .

I think I may have misunderstood your desire that Marlowe

1. Reprinted from a transcript.

should get married. I think I may have picked the wrong girl. But as a matter of fact, a fellow of Marlowe's type shouldn't get married, because he is a lonely man, a poor man, a dangerous man, and yet a sympathetic man, and somehow none of this goes with marriage. I think he will always have a fairly shabby office, a lonely house, a number of affairs, but no permanent connection. I think he will always be awakened at some inconvenient hour by some inconvenient person to do some inconvenient job. It seems to me that that is his destiny—possibly not the best destiny in the world, but it belongs to him. No one will ever beat him, because by his nature he is unbeatable. No one will ever make him rich, because he is destined to be poor. But somehow, I think he would not have it otherwise, and therefore I feel that your idea that he should be married, even to a very nice girl, is quite out of character. I see him always in a lonely street, in lonely rooms, puzzled but never quite defeated.

# Index

Chandler, Raymond (*continued*)
Messick, Juanita; writing for *Black Mask*, 64, 127, 459; denies Marlowe is himself, 66; royalties, 72, 74, 415, 461; refused to write introduction for Shaw's anthology, 74; on *New Yorker*, 77, 366; as screenwriter, 77–78, 89, 90, 94, 95, 97, 101–2, 121, 138, 179, 222–24, 231, 233–34, 237, 295, 298, 344–45, 435, 442–43; advice/help to writers, 83, 88, 166, 258–59, 278–79, 306–7, 432–33, 458–59, 474, as screen writer: suspended, 62–63; on Marquand, 84, 157; on writers, 88, 123, 148, 164, 220, 261, 289, 292–93, 370, 476, 480–81; on first drafts, 87–88; on tragedy, 89; reading public of, 90; on Sandburg, 91; on Bible, 93; on detectives, 93–94; on films, 93–94, 97–99, 110, 139–40, 148, 168–69, 276, 311–12; on book clubs, 94; on reprint and subsidiary rights, 94; radio program, 95, 117, 127, 132–33, 144, 153, 155, 175–76, 188, 337, 362; on critical magazines, 96; on cleverness, 96, 234–35; on criticism of his works, 97; on Barzun, 99; personal characteristics, 103, 238, 324; on manners, 103–4, 418; on O'Neill, 106; on Orwell, 106; on Committee on Un-American Activities, 106–8; on Doyle, 110, 159; does not want to write short stories, 111–12; prestige, 112; writing ambitions, 112; on translations, 119–20, 192, 341–42; on plots, 122, 246–47; changes publishers, 123–24, 343; depression, fatigue, 125, 146, 292, 300, 315, 319, 325, 345–46, 348, 350–51, 394, 405, 408–9, 411, 457; on plagiarism, 125–27, 332–34, 352; on World War II, 131–32; on U.S. justice and financial systems, 140–41; on Cozzens, 142; projected trips to Europe, 143, 144–45, 146, 206–7, 293, 375, 380–81, 382–83, 387; personal life and problems, 146–47, 291–92, 299–300, 359–60; on mystery story as literature, 149, 181, 386–87; on War Crime Trials, 149, 307–8; on mystery writers, 152, 224, 238, 364; method of learning to work, working, 154–55, 459; dislikes publicity, 155, 214; rejects Mystery

Guild offer, 169, 172–74; on Sayers, 169–70; value in his works not as mysteries, 169–70; something in his literary life repels him, 171–72; financial and tax matters, 173, 233–34, 281–84, 292, 345, 348, 350, 416, 433, 460; use of the mystery medium, 173–74; ethics, 177–78; refuses Mystery Book Club offer, 178–79; book promotion, 179, 198, 257–58; loses ambition and ideas, 180–81; rejects screenplay offer, 182; on homosexuality, 184–85, 420–21; on English politics, 185–86, 189–90, 307; literary reputation, 186, 254, 318, 320, 355, 359, 388–89, 415–16; on his short stories, 187; on Greek language, 192–93; on Communists, 193; on mystery story, 194, 196, 204, 277, 290, 314–15, 472, 473n1; on writing mystery story, 194–95; *Newsweek* cover story project, 198, 359; on successful books, 199; on British reviewing, 201; reaction to invitation to join P.E.N., 202; on playwriting, 203–4; on Maugham, 205; receives inscribed copy of *Ashenden*, 208–9; on *Saturday Review of Literature*, 212–13; on unsolved crimes, 221; on A. Freeman, 225–26; on reviewers, reviewing, 226–28; on his slowing down with age, 228–30; on television, 232, 240–41, 256, 433–34; is asked to write article by *Flair*, 234–35; on Fitzgerald, 239; on radio, 240–41; screen credits, 243, 246, 247, 345; on amateur detective character, 246–47; entertains Priestley in California, 259–60, 262, 303; on Priestley, 265–66; on Adelaide Bartlett case, 262–64; on socialism, 265–66; on Kefauver committee hearings, 266–67; should write straight novel, 277, 353; diary entries on works in progress, 281–84; on schools, 287, 351–52; at dude ranch, 287–88; never feels important as a writer, 292; on character of fictional detective, 297; on style, 300–1; on alcoholism, 302, 393–94; drinking, sober, 303, 392–94, 396n2, 400–1, 408, 409; on length of books, 306–7; rejects request to do film publicity, 313; on his cooking, 313–14; self-doubt, 315–16;

[489]

194, 198; screen rights, 207; Italian translation, 252–53
*Lives of a Bengal Lancer* (film), 168
*Living Novel, The* (Pritchett), 134
London, 320, 324, 326, 327, 330–31
Long, Huey, 186
*Long Beat Home, The* (Gladwin), 366
*Long Goodbye, The* (RC), 129–30, 295–96, 314–16, 318–19, 320, 325, 342n1, 344n1, 354, 359, 366, 370, 412, 464, 479n1
Loring, Linda (character, RC), 473–74, 479n1
Los Angeles, Calif., 215, 268, 354, 405. *See also* Hollywood
*Los Angeles Times*, 4, 449
*Lost Weekend, The* (Jackson), 184n3
*Love Is Eternity* (Stone), 381
Lovell (Mr.): letter to, 355–56
*Loves of Edwy* (O'Neill), 356
Lucania, Luciano (Lucky Luciano): letter to, 475–76

*M.*, 57
MacArthur, Gen. Douglas, 131, 277
*Macbeth*, 89, 135
McBride, Mary Margaret, 181
MacCarthy, Desmond, 45, 90
McCarthy, Joseph, 360
McCarthy, Mary, 112, 113
McClung, Paul: letter to, 301–2
MacColl, Rene, 449–50, 453
McDermid, Finlay: letter to, 232–34
Macdonald, Dwight, 462
Macdonald, John D., 163n1
MacDonald, John Ross; *see* Millar, Kenneth
Macdonald, Ross; *see* Millar, Kenneth
Machell, Roger, 329–30, 371, 400, 447; letters to, 338–39, 343–44, 361–62, 364–66, 380–81, 382–86, 412–13, 478
McInness, Helen, 269
McNulty, John, 40
MacPherson, Aimee Semple, 439
*Madame Bovary* (Flaubert), 203, 204n3, 249
*Madame de Pompadour* (Mitford), 366, 367
*Magazine*, 111
Magazines, 7; slicks, 45, 86–87, 370–71, 460–61
*Maltese Falcon, The* (Hammett), 5n3, 54, 58, 80; film, 37, 93, 126

"Man Against Crime" (television program), 242
"Mandarin's Jade" (RC), 281
Mannix, Edgar J., 138
Manstein, Erich von, 307
"Man Who Liked Dogs, The" (RC), 281
Marlowe, Philip (character, RC), 25–26, 30, 32, 41, 43–44, 61–62, 64, 66, 71, 75–76, 80, 90, 122, 153, 165, 166, 242, 322, 327, 353, 427, 449, 457, 460, 477; radio series, 95, 117, 127, 132–33, 144, 153, 155, 175–76, 188, 337, 362; character of, 197, 294, 452, 478, 483; RC gives "facts" about, 270–74; change in character of, 315, 317, 318; adaptation for television, 452–53; marriage (proposed), 464–65, 473, 478, 479, 483
Marquand, John P., 59, 84n2, 123, 157n1, 181, 195, 199, 205, 292, 461
Marsh, Ngaio, 174, 246
Marshall, Raymond. *See* Raymond, Rene
Marx, Groucho, 395
Mason, Perry (character, Gardner), 69, 70, 84, 101, 162
Massingham, H. J., 328
Masters, John, 404n1
Maugham, Somerset, 33, 203, 204n3, 232, 322, 327, 355, 367; RC on, 205; letters to, 208–9, 210–11, 255–56, 276–77
*Mauretania* (ship), 320, 323, 325, 327–28, 381, 382, 387
*Mayerling*, 57
Mealand, Richard, 63
*Memoirs of Hecate County* (Wilson), 79, 238
*Men and Brethren* (Cozzens), 170
*Men of Good Will* (Romains), 57n3
*Mercury, see American Mercury, The*
Merimée, Prosper, 203, 209
Merrick, Leonard, 438
Messick, Juanita: letters to, 274–75, 299–301, 339–40, 345–50
MGM, 53, 54–55, 61, 138, 139n1, 233
Middleton, Richard, 249–50
*Mildred Pierce* (Cain), 28
*Mill House Murder* (Fletcher), 13n2
Millar, Kenneth, 163, 173n2, 343n1
Miller, Max, 13
Miller, Seton, 139
*Mind of the Maker, The* (Sayers), 336–37
*Mischief* (Armstrong), 284
Mitford, Nancy, 292, 366n1

[495]

Mohr, Gerald, 242
Mondadori (publisher), 252–53
*Monsieur Verdoux* (film), 312
Montgomery, Field Marshal Sir Bernard, 131
Montgomery, Robert, 143, 166, 344
Montserrat, Nicholas, 293
*Moonraker* (Fleming), 396n1
*More the Merrier, The,* 57
Morgan, Neil, 385n2, 439–40; letters to, 389–91, 395–96
Morrison, Herbert, 185, 186n4
Mortimer, Raymond, 203
Morton, Charles, 35, 72, 87, 104–5, 147, 148, 179; letters to, 29–34, 35–42, 46–48, 49–51, 53–59, 76–77, 84–85, 101–2, 102–4, 115–16, 120–21, 130–32, 228–30, 240–41, 279–80
Moseley, Hardwick, 169n1; letters to, 172–74, 358–61, 363, 387–88, 402–3, 414–16
Moss, Dr. Carl (character, RC), 66
Motion Picture Producers Association, 108, 213n3; production code, 108
*Moving Target, The* (Macdonald), 163–64, 173
*Mr. Bowling Buys a Newspaper* (Henderson), 60, 151–52, 284
*Mr. Pottermack's Oversight* (Freeman), 225
*Mrs. Tanqueray's Past,* 57
Munro, Hector Hugh (Saki), 249, 355–56
Murder Inc., 478
*Murder My Sweet* (film), 97, 126; *see also Farewell, My Lovely*
*Murder of a Dead Man* (Steel), 13n1
Murray, Mae, 397
"My Friend Luco" (RC), 475n1
Mystery Book Club, 178n1
*Mystery of 31 New Inn, The* (Freeman), 225
Mystery story, 93–94, 196, 204, 238, 277, 290, 314–15; sales, 60; critical writing re, 134–35; literary value of, 134–35, 149, 181, 386–87, 477; fantastic element in, 150; hard-boiled, 165; RC looked on with part of his mind with condescension, 347; honesty in, 357–58; *see also* Detective story
Mystery-adventure story, 70
Mystery Guild, 169, 172–73
Mystery writers, writing, 152, 194–95.

*See also* Writers
Mystery Writers of America, 362n1, 481–82

Nabokov, Vladimir, 39–40
*Naked City* (film), 168n2
Nathan, George Jean, 113
Nebel, Frederick, 8, 13
Neber, Dr., 376
*Neither Five nor Three* (MacInness), 269
*New Humpty-Dumpty, The* (Chaucer), 356, 373
Newman, E. Jack: letter to, 463–64
Newnes, Sir George, 249
*New Republic, The,* 3
*New Statesman, The,* 168
*Newsweek,* 60, 198, 399; cover story, 198, 359
*New Writing,* 97
New York City, 32, 324, 325, 330, 398, 399
*New York Times, The* 18–19, 159, 226, 227, 254, 359; RC asked to review for, 364–65; review of RC books in, 4
*New Yorker, The* 40, 57, 58n5, 59, 60, 77, 211, 289, 330, 366, 406, 456, 462n1
Nichols, Dudley, 78
Nichols, Luther: letter to, 476–77
*Night Must Fall,* 57; film, 176, 245
Nobel Prize, 180–81
"No Crime in the Mountains" (RC), 186–87, 283
*No Highway* (Shute), 123
*No Orchids for Miss Blandish* (Chase), 127, 310
Norman, Frank: letter to, 479–80
*Notebooks of Raymond Chandler, The* 389n1
Novack, Pat, 175

*Observer* (London), 90
O'Donnell, Spike, 218
O'Farrell, William, 189n1
Offord, Lenore Glen, 364
O'Hara, John, 157, 199, 234
*Of Mice and Men* (Steinbeck), 6
*Oklahoma,* 57
Olivier, Lord Laurence, 166
O'Neill, Eugene, 106, 113, 126–27; used RC's term "the big sleep," 218
O'Neill, Rose Ceil, 356

Frank MacShane, the editor of these letters, is a literary biographer whose works include *The Life of Raymond Chandler* and *The Life of John O'Hara*. He has long had a special interest in encouraging the development of young writers and is a professor in the Writing Division at the School of the Arts, Columbia University.

**Audrey kiss ...**

Brian froze. Her soft, warm lips pressed against his and short-circuited his brain, sending an electric charge through his skin. He wanted more, he wanted all of her, with an urgency that stole his breath, but he also recognized the kiss for what it was.

A gesture of gratitude and relief.

And he would have had to be the worst kind of bastard to take advantage of it. Brian pulled back and saw surprise flicker in her eyes before he looked away. Surprise at her own spontaneous gesture or at his reaction.

It didn't matter. He wasn't going there.

He couldn't.

# DANA MARTON
# CAMOUFLAGE HEART

TORONTO • NEW YORK • LONDON
AMSTERDAM • PARIS • SYDNEY • HAMBURG
STOCKHOLM • ATHENS • TOKYO • MILAN • MADRID
PRAGUE • WARSAW • BUDAPEST • AUCKLAND

To Kim Nadelson, a wonderful editor and dear friend.

Acknowledgments:

With many thanks to Allison Lyons, Jenel Looney
and Anita Staley for their help and support.
And with much appreciation to my family and friends
for not minding that writing is all I talk about and
for cheering me on. Pat and Ariff, thank you for sharing
your vast knowledge of Malaysia. All mistakes are my own.

ISBN 0-373-22875-9

CAMOUFLAGE HEART

www.eHarlequin.com

**Printed in U.S.A.**

## ABOUT THE AUTHOR

Dana Marton lives near Wilmington, Delaware. She has been an avid reader since childhood and has a master's degree in writing popular fiction. When not writing, she can be found either in her garden or her home library. For more information on the author and her other novels, please visit her Web site at www.danamarton.com.

She would love to hear from her readers via e-mail: DanaMarton@yahoo.com.

## Books by Dana Marton

### HARLEQUIN INTRIGUE
806—SHADOW SOLDIER
821—SECRET SOLDIER
859—THE SHEIK'S SAFETY
875—CAMOUFLAGE HEART

# CAST OF CHARACTERS

**Audrey Benedict**—When her sister is kidnapped by Malaysian guerillas, she rushes to pay the ransom money, but is captured.

**Brian Welkins**—Member of a top secret military group (SDDU). Four years ago, he was captured by the guerillas and kept in a cage since. All he wanted was to escape and get as far from the jungle as possible. And then Audrey came along.

**Nicky Benedict-Sawyer**—She came to Malaysia on an adoption trip to provide moral support to her sister, Audrey. But a simple sightseeing excursion to the island of Borneo ended in disaster.

**Jamil**—Once a true freedom fighter, now he leads a small guerilla group that's becoming increasingly difficult to control.

**Omar**—Jamil's younger brother who thinks it's past time he took charge and led the group to fight.

**Hamid**—Head of the group that took twelve Western hostages. But the kidnappings are not his worst crime. He has plans for the ransom money that will send shockwaves through the region.

**SDDU**—Special Designation Defense Unit. A top secret military team established to fight terrorism. Its existence is known only by a select few. Members are recruited from the best of the best.

**Colonel Wilson**—Brian's boss. He's the leader of the SDDU, reporting straight to the Homeland Security Secretary.

# Chapter One

*Soon.*

*Don't act strange. Don't draw attention. Don't even look alive.*

Brian hid his shaking hands under his arms. He had spent the last four years waiting for a chance to escape, but now that the opportunity was here it overwhelmed him. He took a slow breath. He was in better shape than he'd been at any of his previous attempts. Which still didn't guarantee that he could break out of his prison and make the two-week trek out of the Malaysian jungle.

"We'll be back in three days, four at the most," Jamil, the guerilla group's leader, said to his younger brother on the other side of the clearing, the tension obvious between the two men even from a distance.

The steadily pattering rain drowned out the younger man's reply. The mesh of banana leaves

Brian had woven among the top bars of the tiger cage leaked here and there, but the makeshift roof kept the worst of the weather off him. He watched his captors from the corner of his eye, keeping his head turned toward the trees. He didn't want them to know he was paying attention.

"Haven't you wasted enough time trying to convince everyone Hamid is wrong?" Omar raised his voice and could be heard now even over the rain. "We've become like old women, talking around campfires. Bullets win wars, not talk." He spat the words. "We can start by sending this one's head—" he jerked his thumb toward Brian "—to the city."

Jamil lifted a placating hand. There was a presence to the older man, a careful dignity that the others lacked. "We are freedom fighters, not terrorists."

And that's where he was wrong, Brian thought. Jamil and a couple of the older men in camp might have started out as freedom fighters, but Omar and his young friends were in this for entirely different reasons. They liked the outlaw power of bending to no government, taking what they wanted when they came across someone weaker.

Jamil nodded to his men and disappeared into the jungle with them. Brian stared straight ahead, not looking at the remaining fighters, but aware of each and every one. The small guerilla group consisted of about three dozen men. Eight had gone for supplies two days ago. Jamil was taking six to talk alliance with a larger group on the other side of the mountain.

For the next few days, the camp would be as thin as ever, and tomorrow night Ahmad would be on guard duty. Ahmad would let him go to the bathroom without pistol-whipping him first for the bother, or standing behind him the whole time with a rifle barrel pressed between his shoulder blades.

*Just a little longer. Just another day.* Brian closed his eyes. He needed some sleep, to have as much energy as possible when the time came. The familiar noises of the jungle filled the night, the chorus of frogs interrupted now and then by the shrill cry of a bird, the buzz and chirp of a million insects filling in the occasional silence.

His mind drifted, but something prickled at the edges of his consciousness. Something was missing. The camp was quiet. Unnaturally so. No human voices joined that of the jungle. He opened his eyes.

Omar still stood on the same spot, but a dozen of his men were gathered around him. Now what? He watched as some kind of silent communication passed between them and the men melted into the jungle one by one.

Minutes passed, then came the sounds of gunfire from the distance. Some of Jamil's men jumped up and ran into the forest. Brian swore under his breath. If Omar managed to wrest leadership of the group, he was finished.

A good hour went by before the last gun fell silent, and not long after that, the first fighters returned to camp. Jamil's men were not among them.

Brian swallowed his desperation and tried to catch Ahmad's eye. If he could get the younger man to come over, let him out of the cage… But Ahmad was busy at the other end of the clearing, joining the celebration that had begun.

It didn't take much before half the camp was drunk and the other half well on their way. Brian looked up at the darkening sky. They hadn't come for him yet, but he knew Omar would get to it sooner or later. Whether or not to keep their prisoner alive had been one of the main disagreements between the brothers. Omar would want to reassert his new authority by making a point.

*He had to go. Now.*

"Ahmad," he called out on a low voice when the man walked near him.

The young fighter turned to see what he wanted, but then stopped, his attention drawn to a commotion at the edge of the clearing. The group that had gone off for supplies was returning.

Damn it. Not that, too.

So much for taking advantage of a sparse camp. What the hell were they doing back? The trip to the nearest kampongs, the few villages that were this high up the mountain, usually took five or six days.

And then he saw the hunched figure they were shoving in front of them.

Another prisoner.

He leaned forward to get a better look at the young man. No, not a kid—it was a woman. Definitely a woman.

She was pushed close enough to the low fire that burned under a hatch-roofed shelter, so he could see her clearly now. Her hands were bound behind her, her mouth gagged. The light of the flames glinted off blondish hair.

Jamil hadn't been keen on the practice of exchanging hostages for money. On the odd occasion when Omar's men brought back some easy target they couldn't resist, they were sent upriver to a larger guerilla group whose leader, Hamid, was an expert in this kind of business. There had been talk of a job he had recently pulled, how they were expecting the batch of hostages to bring in over a million ringgits a head.

The woman turned for a moment, and the fire lit her face enough so that he could see her eyes. They were filled with stark terror, so vivid he could feel it in his own chest.

She stirred something in him, bringing back memories, making him remember why he had joined the Special Designation Defense Unit in the first place. It used to be his job to stop this kind of thing from happening, to get to the bad guys before they got to the civilians. But he had failed.

Where the hell had Ahmad gone? Now was the time to slip away, while everyone was busy with the new prisoner.

One of the men tied the woman to a palm tree. They probably would make her write a letter to her loved ones in the morning. Then in a week or two, the money would arrive and someone would walk her to the nearest village. At least, that's how Hamid ran his deals.

He glimpsed Ahmad at last. The man had strode back to the fire and was now taking his turn from the bottle, satisfying his curiosity about the prisoner. He was too far to call to without drawing attention.

The fighters were getting louder, and Omar was busy writing on loose sheets of paper on his knee, looking up now and then when his men toasted him. Then he rolled up the papers, tied them with a piece of string and handed them to Ahmad.

This was it. Brian got to his feet and crouched—the tiger cage did not allow him to stand to his full height. He called to the young fighter as the man walked by the cage. "I need to get out for a minute."

"I'll tell one of the guards."

The two men on guard duty were at the fire with the rest, having abandoned their posts to check out the new prisoner. Jamil wouldn't have tolerated that. Omar didn't seem to notice.

"It won't take long. The others…" He let his voice trail off.

The others would beat him for the fun of it. And they were drunk enough so they might not know when to stop. Ahmad understood and stepped to the nearby post for the handcuffs, threw them into the cage. Brian slipped on the rusty metal pieces and clinked them together, hoping it sounded enough like the click that locked them. And it must have, because the door opened to let him out.

He walked in front, dragging his right foot, exaggerating the limp. He wanted anyone who watched to think he couldn't run even if his life depended on it. And it did.

He stepped a couple of feet deeper into the jungle than was necessary, made sure they were behind thick enough vegetation. He fumbled with his rope belt, let his pants drop, then spun with full force and brought his fists to Ahmad's temple. The man folded without a sound.

Brian grabbed the gun even before he pulled up his pants. "Sorry, buddy."

He pocketed Ahmad's knife, took the rolled up sheets of paper. They would come in handy once he got far enough that he could risk starting a fire. He listened, but no shouts rang out from camp, no sign that his actions were heard or seen, just the coarse jesting of the men about the woman. As he turned to leave, he heard Omar join in. That didn't bode well for her.

A true leader knew how to rein in his men, but Omar had never been good at delayed gratification. He was too smart to intentionally kill her, but not smart enough to realize that if he let his men go at her, she probably wouldn't survive the night, and they would lose out on the ransom money.

Brian gripped the gun. He should be running right now. He should be a hundred feet away.

Ahmad groaned.

Two hundred.

He couldn't go back for her. What if she didn't speak English? She would probably fight him. He didn't look any different from the guerillas—even his clothing was the same, his original uniform having rotted off him in the jungle's humid air years ago.

She could get both of them killed. And even if he managed to get her away from camp, she would slow him down. What the hell could she know about jungle survival? She would probably keel over from the first bug that bit her. And no way to get her away unseen, either. The attention of every man in the camp was focused on her, and would probably stay on her for some time—an unexpected gift he should be taking advantage of.

And yet, he could not forget the look in her eyes. *Damn.*

He pulled the man's hat off and shoved it into his mouth, tied Ahmad's hands behind his back with his belt. With a last glance at him, Brian crouched and rushed left, moving silently over the mossy ground as he circled the camp.

SHE WAS GOING to suffocate.

Audrey Benedict tried desperately to draw enough air into her burning lungs, but her mouth was taped shut, and her nose was plugged from crying.

She didn't understand a word the men around the campfire were saying, but she had no trouble interpreting their savage expressions. She had a good idea what they had in store for her. She looked up to the stars and prayed, for herself and for her sister—for someone to get to Nicky in time, now that she had failed.

She took one jerky, hard breath after another, desperate to clear her airway. An urgent shout rang across the clearing. She scanned the darkness beyond the fire, struggling against the ropes that bound her hands. The guerillas were grabbing for their guns, rushing toward a young fighter who had staggered out of the forest. Some of them ran into the jungle behind him.

Were they under attack? Dear God, let it be a rescue team and not another group of bandits.

She felt a sharp tug on her rope before it went slack, then she was yanked back through the bushes with force. She scrambled to see who or what was behind her.

If she weren't gagged, she would have screamed.

As it was, she couldn't open her mouth, and the wildman of the jungle who had her didn't leave her time to faint. He grabbed her wrist tight enough to cut off circulation and pulled her after him with frightening speed, flying through the blind night without a sound. She, on the other hand, got caught on every branch.

Her right hand was still tied to her feet, loose enough to allow movement, but not so she could reach her face. He had her other hand and wouldn't let it go, though she pulled until she thought her skin would rip off.

She was dizzy from lack of air, her ears popping. Stop! She screamed, but it came to no more than an unintelligible sound in her throat. She threw her full weight to the ground, bent head to hand, ripped the tape off her mouth.

She gulped the night air, her surroundings coming back into focus slowly. The rifle hanging from the man's shoulder knocked against her elbow as he snatched the tape from her before she could toss it. He put a finger to his lips, barely visible under a fright of a beard that came to the middle of his chest. Okay, she was supposed to be quiet. She got that.

The man pulled her up, then forward again relentlessly, and she chose to believe he was trying to help her. She preferred it to thinking she was being kidnapped again. But even if that was the case, he was only one man. She was still better off than a few minutes ago.

A creek crossed their path and he dragged her into it, moving fast from stone to stone, going downstream in the middle. The canopy was thinner here, some moonlight filtering through. She followed his movements as closely as she could, trying to stay out of the water as much as possible. She'd read about the parasites.

*"Bolehkah tolong saya?"* She whispered one of the few sentences she knew in Malay. *Can you help me?*

A look of surprise crossed his face before he nodded and put his fingers over her lips. She flinched away from his dirty hand and split fingernails. He didn't seem to notice her distaste and moved on, hauling her behind him.

After a few hundred yards, they reached a bend where thick vines hung into the water from the branches above. He stopped and cut off her dangling ropes, tucked them into his shirt, then turned his back to her.

"Get on," he said in English.

She hesitated a moment, but when he gave an impatient grunt, she put her arms around his neck, keeping her face from the filthy dreadlocks that streamed halfway down his back.

He bent his knees and reached under her legs with his hands, wrapped them around his waist, then let them go to reach for the vine. The rifle scraped against her side. Could she get it away from him? The sudden possibility of freedom sent blood rushing through her head. Then common sense put in an appearance and prevailed. Even with a gun, her chance of making it out of the jungle alone was uncomfortably close to zero. For one, she had no idea which way to walk.

The decision was taken from her as they were moving up, higher and higher. She didn't dare let go of him now to grab for the rifle. He was going way too fast for as dark as it was.

*Freaking Tarzan.* Either that or the missing link. But he spoke English and he hadn't hurt her yet. She hung on to that for hope.

Sweet heavens but he stunk.

The higher he climbed, the tighter she gripped, until he growled again, and she remembered herself and loosened her arms. If she cut off his air, they'd both fall to their death.

They reached a limb at last, and he waited until she climbed on, guiding her with one hand. Then he leaped after her, with considerably more speed and grace than she had moved. He clamped onto her wrist again—not as tight this time—and pulled her behind him as they made their way from branch to slippery branch, tree to tree. Then they stopped, and she could hear men running through the jungle below.

Her knees shook. At least it was too dark to see the ground so she could pretend they weren't all that high up. The tree canopy was one solid mass beneath them, with a fifteen-to-twenty foot gap above, then another layer of canopy that blocked out most of the sky. After a few minutes, the man next to her grabbed her and pulled her forward again.

"Where are we going?"

He ignored her and she didn't have the wherewithal to demand an answer, needing to keep her full concentration on her feet so she wouldn't fall.

A good hour must have passed before they began to descend. He waited and listened before lowering her to the ground and jumping after her.

The first thing she saw was the mouth of a cave in front of them. Their flight from the guerillas apparently had a destination.

It would have been nice if that destination was a village from where she could have contacted the authorities for help, instead of a cave in the middle of the wilderness, but still, at least they would be out of the rain for a while. And maybe in the morning she could convince the wildman to lead her out of the jungle.

"Come on." He pulled her forward.

She followed him into the pitch-black cave with some misgivings. Was he a hermit? Was he even sane? Her eyes adjusted to the darkness slowly. The place was about the size of her living room back home. He led her to the back and helped her climb the rock face.

"Is this where you live?"

"Hurry." He pointed with his head, and she spotted the ledge a good fifteen feet above. She slipped, but before she had the chance to fall, he propped her up and came after her.

The rock was covered with something soft and slippery that stunk bad enough to make her gag, the space she reached no more than a three-feet gap between the ledge and the ceiling. But it would keep them sheltered from view.

What little moonlight lit the cave didn't reach the back of the crevice where they lay side-by-side, their arms touching. When he moved away, she wanted to move after him until they touched again, needing that human contact, the knowledge that she wasn't alone in the darkness—but she didn't dare. She had no idea what to expect of him.

"Who are you?" she whispered, risking getting him mad at her for talking.

"Brian."

A normal, ordinary name, familiar. And he did speak English. She relaxed a little. "Are you American?"

"Montana."

Her lungs expanded. She tried to picture a cowboy inside the wildman but she failed. "I'm from New York. Audrey Benedict. What are you doing here?"

"The guerillas caught me a couple of years ago."

And then she remembered the large cage and something in it she hadn't been able to see because it had been too far from the fire. She'd had enough to worry about at the time to pay much attention to it. Had that been him? The horror of being kept in a cage like an animal, year in, year out, constricted her throat. God, what had they done to him? No wonder he looked barely human.

Was that what would have awaited her if he hadn't broken them out? Her insides trembled, slightly at first, then more violently. Then he found her hand in the darkness and squeezed it. In warning. She heard voices below. There were people in the cave.

She shook harder, saw light flicker above. The guerillas had a flashlight. Panic gripped her, pushing her muscles to bolt, but there was nowhere to go. An arm slid over her middle as Brian pulled her to him and held her tight in the darkness, probably only to restrain her from doing something stupid, but she didn't care. She burrowed into the comfort of the contact, curling against him like a child.

The night thundered outside, the rain coming in a downpour now, drowning out the sounds of the jungle. After a while, the men talked less and less, eventually falling silent, the flashlight no longer searching the walls. Had they decided to wait out the night?

She lay absolutely still, barely daring to breathe. Her limbs were going numb, but she didn't dare move. Passage of time was impossible to judge.

After what she thought might have been a couple of hours, the rain let up. A strange noise was filling the air. The men were talking again. She was pretty sure they were swearing. Had they found something? The odd din grew. Birds. The flapping of wings. But not quite chirping. The alien sound came closer.

Something brushed against her leg. Brian cradled her head, his lips close enough to her ear to touch it.

His voice was barely a whisper when he spoke. "Bats."

She jerked against him, but he held her tight. Something swooshed so close she could feel the wind of the wings on her skin. A claw scraped against her scalp.

Her mouth was muffled against Brian's chest before she had a chance to scream.

They were in a bat cave!

And guerillas hunted them below with machine guns.

Things were about as bad as they could get. Then she felt something soft splash on her forehead, and finally figured out what the spongy, rank dirt was below them. They were lying in bat droppings.

She gagged, but pressed her lips together, not daring to make a sound. She buried her face against the chest of the man next to her, who smelled only marginally better than their surroundings, and held on for dear life.

*Don't move. The bats won't kill you, but the men below will. Don't panic.* She repeated the thought over and over, hypnotizing herself to remain still and silent.

A good hour passed before all the bats were in and settled, and the cave was quiet once again.

"Are the men gone?" she whispered, her nerves as shaky as her limbs.

"They left when the bats started to come home." His chest rose and fell against her cheek. "Damn."

"What?" God, don't let it be more bad news.

"I wanted to get out before the bats got in. If we disturb them now, they'll start swarming and alert everyone around."

"We'll have to stay until they go hunting again?" She didn't have it in her. She couldn't handle it.

"We'll wait a while then see what we can do."

He must have known she was at the end of her rope, because he didn't make her wait long. "Move little by little, a fraction of an inch at a time," he said, and showed her what he meant.

She slid across the slippery rockface in increments, trying not to think of what she was sliding in. A bat screeched and flapped its wings above. Her heart pounded in her throat, sweat beading on her forehead as she waited.

Brian held still, too. Neither of them dared as much as breathe too hard. The night hunters settled back to sleep above.

More and more light filled the cave now, the sun coming up. Brian tugged on her arm. She kept her gaze on her feet, away from the bats, as she crept after him.

A half an hour passed before they made it off the ledge, but after that the going was easier and faster. Brian signaled her to stay back as he went to check out the cave's entrance.

He limped. She hadn't noticed that last night in the dark. He had seemed to move through the jungle with skill and confidence.

He was gone only a few minutes then stuck his head back in and motioned for her to follow. Thank God, it had been dark when he'd broken her out. He was even scarier in the daylight. If she'd seen him like this she might not have gone with him.

Filthy clothes hung on a surprisingly muscular body, his hair and beard matted like the fur of a wild animal—with plenty of gray in it. She figured him around fifty. There was a hardness to him, an uncivilized ferocity around his silvery blue eyes that startled her with their intensity. Under any other circumstance, she would have run screaming from the man.

As it was, she followed him deeper into the jungle, brushing bat droppings from her clothes. Who was she to turn up her nose at his appearance? In all likelihood, she didn't look much better.

He moved at a steady pace until they found the creek again. The rain stopped, a small comfort she appreciated. It'd been days since she'd been dry. Her wet clothes chafed her skin with every step she took; her feet felt like they were boiling inside the high-top leather.

He set down the rifle and took off his boots before wading into the water. "You should clean up," he said, fumbling with his mismatched shirt buttons.

"Is it safe?"

"We have a few minutes."

She shook her head and pointed at the creek.

"Fast-moving water is all right. The leeches and the other stuff that'll get you in trouble like stagnant pools. Stand on a stone. Don't drink."

The man didn't have a slow bone in his body. His clothes dropped with much greater speed than she'd been prepared for. He turned from her, but gave no other concession to privacy.

He was all bone and muscle under the dark skin that was a living memorial to the most deprived abuse—a horrifying array of scars visible through the dirt. His hair covered his wide shoulders. He reached for the rag tied around his waist and loosened it.

She looked away.

He probably was used to lack of privacy.

She set her sweaty feet free from the tyranny of the leather boots, and waded downstream. Lord, the cool stream felt good. She bent to wash her hands, then scooped up a handful of water and threw it on her face. If she found a deeper spot somewhere, she could attempt a quick full-body dip. No such luck. A quick scan proved the creek to be evenly shallow.

"Don't go far," Brian called after her. "There are some large predators out there, a bunch of poisonous stuff, too."

He was right. Her guide had been good about pointing out the hazards of the jungle—tigers and snakes on the top of his list. But her brain had been shook up since, her world turned upside down. She relieved herself, watching the bushes, then moved back closer to him.

They were in the middle of the Malaysian jungle, hunted by bloodthirsty guerillas—among other animals. And her sister was— No, she couldn't afford to think about Nicky now—couldn't, or she would fall apart.

She could do this. One step at a time. To save Nicky, she had to keep herself alive. Right now, all she had to focus on was cleaning up. It would help if predators didn't smell her from a mile.

"We can't stay long," he said without turning around. "We're too close to camp."

Audrey pulled her shirt over her head. Undressing in front of a stranger was the least of her worries.

# Chapter Two

Brian squeezed the water out of his "underwear," the back piece of an old shirt that had replaced his fallen-apart boxers two years back. He tied the patch of fabric in place before moving on to the rest of his laundry—didn't want the woman to think he was completely uncivilized.

He didn't dare wash his clothes too hard. The pants and shirt were threadbare enough already. The humid air of the jungle was hard on fabric. He sloshed the two pitiful pieces in the clear water and watched for fish, but gave that up after a few minutes. The creek was too shallow and rapid.

Audrey was splashing behind him.

"Try to keep your clothes and body clean. The smallest injury can get infected in the jungle, even bug bites." He was speaking from experience.

He put his wet pants and shirt back on and sat on

a flat rock that got some dappled sunlight from above. There were a few spots over the middle of the creek where the treetops didn't touch.

Then he turned his head and forgot the trees and the sunshine.

Audrey squatted by the edge of the water with her back to him, her wet blond hair streaming past her shoulder blades. She looked like one of the detailed fantasies he had used to pass time with while locked up in the cage. Pearls of water ran down her slim back—creamy skin, delicate curve of the spine—to her round bottom. A groan rumbled up his throat. She might not have looked real, but his body's response certainly was.

He wanted her then and there, on the wet moss—rough and furious. He wanted to empty himself into her. Hot arousal washed through him as he watched her slight movements. He felt his eyes narrow and his nostrils flare, the animal-like need taking him over for a moment, urgent and uncivilized. Then he remembered her face as she had stood by the fire, surrounded by the guerillas.

He got up and strode out of the creek, ashamed that his reaction to her hadn't been any better than theirs. Had they kept him in a cage long enough that he had turned into something that belonged there?

"What are you doing in Malaysia?" He scanned

the surrounding trees for food to keep himself busy, and spotted a banana tree. He climbed it while waiting for her response, ignoring the hard-on that made shimmying up the tree more than uncomfortable.

She didn't respond. *Interesting.*

There were plenty of Western tourists in Malaysia, as well as businesspeople. Then there were the crooks who came to the country to make money in the illegal gun trade or drug trafficking. She sure didn't look like she belonged to that group. Of course, appearances could be misleading.

Still, no matter who she was, she didn't deserve what Omar's men would have done to her.

He reached the top but didn't cut off the whole bunch of bananas. Instead, he broke off enough from here and there for them to eat and tucked them in to his shirt. He didn't want to be slowed down by carrying a load, and he didn't want to leave any telltale signs behind. He cut off a pair of leaves, too, and let them fall to the ground.

Audrey waited for him under the tree with her clothes safely back on, clean but soaking wet, hiding nothing. He wiped his forehead with the back of his hand. Damn, it was hot for this early in the morning.

"I'm on an adoption trip with my sister," she said, folding her arms in front of her.

From the way her moss-green eyes glistened as

she spoke, he figured the sister wasn't back at the Kuala Lumpur Grand Hotel, soaking in a hot tub. Since she wasn't here with Audrey, it was safe to assume she'd been killed when the guerillas had attacked them.

Unsure what to say, he offered her a banana and slung Ahmad's AK-47 over his shoulder. It had to be hard to lose a sibling. He could only imagine the special closeness between two people who shared the same blood. He'd never had that with anyone.

"I was adopted," he said.

She looked up from peeling, her eyes luminous in the sunshine.

Damn. Where the hell had that come from? It wasn't something he shared. He looked down, embarrassed at having said something so personal.

His gaze settled on her footwear. And seeing a problem he could fix, the next second he was back in professional soldier mode again. "Give me your boots."

She only hesitated a second before she sat to unlace them. When she handed him the first, he shoved his knife inside and made a couple of small holes in the leather, close to the sole, then repeated the procedure with the other one.

"What's that for?"

"So that moisture can get out. Whether we make

it or not will depend on how fast and how far we can walk. Always take care of your feet."

She nodded and put the boots back on.

He picked up a banana leaf, cut and twisted it until it resembled a very primitive wide-brimmed hat, then put it on her head. "It'll keep the creepy crawlers from falling into your shirt neck from above," he said, and made one for himself.

"I used to have a hat. It fell off in the boat. Thank you."

So she had come up the river. He'd pretty much figured that. Boat travel was the easiest way to get around in these parts. Which was exactly why he couldn't steal a canoe and paddle out. The river would be the first place where Omar's men would look for them, and there would be no place to hide on the water. As hard as it was going to be, they had no choice but to walk out. And they better get to it. "Come on. We'll eat as we go."

She fell in step behind him as he moved forward, listening for anything unusual in the cacophony of birdcalls. He could make out the sound of a couple of monkeys arguing in the distance, but nothing suspicious caught his attention.

"Are we going to a village?"

"To the river." Most villages in the vicinity were controlled by the guerillas. "It's called the Baram."

The night before, he had run off to the opposite direction, knowing he couldn't cross it in the dark with the woman in tow. "We have to circle back to it, get over to the other side and follow it to Miri."

"Can't we cross later? Shouldn't we be moving away from the guerillas?"

She was thinking and not following him blindly. Good. It showed presence of mind. They were going to need that. "We'll come out above the camp. They'll be watching the river below. That's the way out. The sooner we cross, the better. The farther down we get, the wider the Baram becomes."

She accepted that without argument. He liked that, too. She was independent enough to think for herself if needed, but smart enough to accept his authority. The strength of the team they forged would play a big part in their survival. So far, she was okay.

A fine mist started to drizzle from above, nothing that would slow them down, just enough to get them wet. There were more caves ahead, a good ten miles from here. If they reached them by noon, they could rest there, maybe light a fire to dry their clothes.

She finished eating and held out the peel. "What do I do with this?"

She knew now not to leave a trail. He grunted in approval as he took the peel from her, then handed her another banana. Maybe they stood a slim chance of making it out of here after all. He felt a twinge of guilt at having had considered leaving her behind with Omar. She hadn't turned out as bad as he had expected. But she would have to get better still.

When the last piece of fruit was gone, he stopped and buried their leavings, then held out the AK-47. "You know how to use this?"

She shook her head.

"Not much to it. Just aim and squeeze the trigger." He waited until she took the gun, tested its weight, held it to her shoulder. She looked unsure of herself, but at least she was giving it a try. He nodded to her with encouragement when she handed the rifle back, then turned and continued walking. "In case something happens to me," he said, "keep east by the sun."

Better to be prepared for every eventuality.

He had learned that lesson well as a marine, then again when he'd entered special training after being recruited into the SDDU, Special Designation Defense Unit, America's secret weapon against terrorism. SDDU soldiers were expected to be the best of the best, and damn, it had stroked his ego to have been chosen. They had better weapons and more freedom to use them than anyone, and didn't have to report to Congress or any military chain of command, but went straight to the Homeland Security Secretary.

Hell, Congress and all those generals didn't even know the SDDU existed. The unit had been created to deal with problems that couldn't be addressed in the open. To effectively fight terrorists who broke every rule, the U.S. needed a team that didn't have any rules tying their hands, either. And that was the SDDU.

It really burned him that he had gotten taken out on his first mission. And the fact that he would never now pass the physical to get back in got under his skin even more.

"Keep your eyes and ears open. If we come across trouble, drop and roll to cover."

Brian pushed forward, ignoring the pain in his bad leg. The old injury made a big difference. Not just the limp, but how weak the muscles were. It had been a while since he'd walked any farther than the bushes to relieve himself.

He had exercised over the years with the guerillas, done more push-ups and sit-ups than any ten men in a lifetime, but it was hard to exercise his legs in a cage that didn't allow him to stand up. He hated the weakness, the knowledge that he was outnumbered and outgunned. And if that wasn't bad enough, he had the woman depending on him now, raising the stakes of failure.

Damn. Things hadn't exactly turned out as he had expected. She ended up being more capable than he had thought, and he less so. It ticked him off and so did the sudden doubts that assailed him. Had he done the right thing by dragging her into the jungle? He had thought he could protect her, but what if he couldn't?

What the hell made him think she was better off with him? Maybe Omar would have reined in his men. Her letter would be on its way to her family by now. Sure as hell, he could offer her no guarantees.

"Thank you for bringing me with you," she said from behind at the exact worst moment.

He turned back to her. Didn't she realize they were in just as much danger now, if not more, than in the guerilla camp?

"You can thank me later. If we make it out of the jungle alive."


HAMID WENT THROUGH the plans, thinking of the men he had chosen, reevaluating them one by one. He trusted them as much as he trusted anyone. The first phase of his plan looked good to go, but phase two bothered him.

His men had taken too many hostages. Americans, too, which could spell trouble. Westerners didn't understand this part of the world, weren't willing to play by its rules. He had made a fortune and financed a veritable army by picking up a Japanese or Russian businessman now and then, demanding silence and ransom from their families.

This time, it might be different. Just the scale of the kidnapping guaranteed that the government and media would get wind of it. He hoped to hell they didn't choose to interfere. A smooth transaction was in everyone's best interest.

He shuffled the papers and cursed Muhammad, the captain responsible for this mess. Muhammad was greedy, both for money and power. He bore watching.

The steel door opened and one of his men came in. "A messenger came from Omar."

*From Omar.* It had happened then. He nodded his approval to let the messenger in, only slightly surprised, with a faint regret for the death of Jamil, who had been a friend in the old days. So the younger brother took the camp. It wasn't altogether unexpected.

Omar was another man he wouldn't want to turn his back to. In fact, Muhammad reminded him of Omar a lot.

The messenger looked unsure of himself as he conveyed his leader's greetings.

Hamid waved away the formalities. "How are things with my friend, Omar?"

"Jamil had an accident."

He expressed his regrets, having no illusions about what had happened. Most likely, the *accident* had been a bullet in the back. Omar had been coveting his brother's position for years.

Hamid leaned back in his chair, considering how this would effect his plans. He had been trying to get Jamil to join the operation, but Jamil had dragged his heels, disliking making war on civilians. Omar had no compunctions, which would make things easier. But could a man who would kill his own blood be trusted?

He watched the messenger closely. "All is well in camp?"

The man looked down. "We had a hostage that escaped."

Hamid lifted an eyebrow. Omar wasted no time going after money, did he? "The jungle will take care of him." He shrugged.

"It was a woman. That soldier prisoner broke out and took her with him."

He sat up straight, interested now, knowing well of Jamil's foreign soldier, the man he had insisted on keeping against advice. It was a running joke in the camps, how Jamil got stuck with him, wanting to make a point to his younger brother on who made the decisions.

That man could make it out of the jungle. That man could bring the army back with him. "When?"

"Yesterday."

"Omar has everyone out looking?"

The messenger nodded, looking more nervous now than when he had arrived.

"Did anything else happen?"

"He—the prisoner—got some notes Omar sent you about Jamil…."

"And?"

"He pledged his help with the attacks."

He stood up so fast he knocked the chair over. Swore. Damn the incompetent son of a bitch. He would not have his operation compromised now, not when everything was ready to go.

"Anything that would give us away?"

"That's all he told me," the man rushed to say.

He called out, and two fighters rushed in.

"Jamil's prisoner escaped yesterday. Send as many men as you can. Have Muhammad take them." This once, his captain was welcome to go overboard.

COME ON. COME BACK.

Audrey sat by the cave's entrance, the AK-47 laid across her legs as she stared into the jungle. She had no idea what time it was. Her watch, along with her jewelry, was the first thing the guerillas had taken after they had captured her.

Brian hadn't been gone more than a half hour, an hour at tops, but it felt like ten. She had plenty of time to worry about a whole list of worst-case scenarios.

Like what would she do if a tiger decided to pay her a visit, or the guerillas found her, or something happened to Brian and he didn't come back.

She rubbed her eyes. God, she was driving herself nuts. Brian would be back soon. Everything was going to be fine.

He had gone off to see if he could scare up some meat. They needed protein for strength, couldn't survive on fruit, he'd said. He'd promised to build a fire when he came back. She decided to focus on that. Her clothes were no longer soaking wet, but still damp enough to be uncomfortable.

He would be back for her. She had to believe that. She listened to the birdcalls above, watched for the burst of color that flashed between the branches now and then.

Was Nicky out there somewhere looking up at the trees, same as her? Dear God, let her be unharmed.

Something rustled in the undergrowth to the left. Her muscles tensed, her heart in her throat in an instant. She tried to see beyond the profusion of green fronds, but couldn't make out anything. She gripped the gun and drew farther back into the cave.

More noise, then a branch snapping. She held her breath. Brian? She didn't dare call out. Then she saw the fronds move. Something was definitely there, coming toward her.

A young fighter stepped into the clearing, scanning the area, rifle at the ready.

Her blood raced so fast it made her dizzy. She held her breath, hoping he couldn't see her in the darkness of the cave.

But he did, and smiled when their eyes met.

He called back, a single word, but no response came from behind him, which gave her hope. Maybe he had wandered out of hearing distance from the others.

She scampered back toward the deeper reaches of the cave, gripping her own gun in her sweaty palms, although she didn't dare shoot. She had never shot anything. Her chances of hitting him were one in a million.

If she started shooting he would shoot back, with considerably more skill than she had. And a gunshot, too, could alert the rest of his group to their whereabouts. She would only use the rifle if she had no other choice, and only if she was sure she would hit him.

As young as he was, she was no match for him. Escape and evade, the term she'd heard Brian use popped into her head. Panic propelled her forward as she turned to run, seeing less and less the farther in she got. Her boots slammed against stone, the sound echoing in the cave, mixing with the slap of her pursuer's steps.

Brian had said there were lime caves in these mountains that went on for miles underground. If this one had a fraction of that space— If she could evade this man until Brian came back— She rushed into a dark corridor, gasped the musty air, fear sending her lungs into overdrive.

Blindly she ran forward, her hands stretched in front of her in the darkness, hoping the path was straight. It wasn't. She smacked into the stone wall and dropped the gun, bent to search for it but felt nothing other than small rocks, cold and sharp under her fingertips. It had to be here. She swept the ground, frantic.

The man was close enough for her to hear his breathing, smell his sweat. Forget the gun. Her hand on the wall, she moved ahead, hoping for a fork in the road, or a crevice she could flatten herself into while he went by.

She hadn't walked a few steps when she was brought hard to the ground. The pain in the side of her skull was blinding. Her head spun for a moment as she struggled against the weight that pinned her down. She clawed at him, felt his fingers close around one wrist first, then the other as he swore in the darkness.

"No. Please." She tried to catch her breath.

He pulled her to her feet and dragged her toward

the light. She kicked and missed. He shook her and dragged her on, threw her to the ground once they were back in the larger cavern that received enough sunlight to see.

He asked something she couldn't understand. She shook her head as she sat up, then noticed the knife in his belt and lunged for it.

He outmaneuvered her with ease, but ended up falling on her, pressing her back into the sharp rocks.

Shouldn't have done that. Shouldn't have gone for his weapon. She had really pissed him off. The sight of his anger-reddened face paralyzed her limbs. Then his features changed as he brought up a hand to cup her breast.

"Stop." She struggled against him with new desperation.

He reached between them and ripped her pants. A scream pushed its way up her throat but she swallowed it back. His people were probably closer than Brian. She didn't want them to find her. There was a slim chance she might be able to fight off this one, but if the rest came, she was finished.

She felt around with shaking hands for a suitable rock on the ground. Nothing but dirt and gravel. Figured. At least a half-dozen rocks dug against her ribs. She tried to twist aside, but the man on top of her wouldn't allow her the movement.

*Expect the worse. Expect that you're going to get hurt.* The words of some self-defense expert from a TV show a couple of years ago floated back to her. She had to keep a clear head, resist the panic, look for an opportunity.

The man on top of her was stronger than she, and it wasn't even so much his extra bulk of muscles, but that he knew how to fight. She could do nothing to stop him.

Accepting the inevitable brought a strange sense of control. When he violated her body, there would be a moment of advantage. She would wait for that moment and try again for his knife. She would not allow him to take her back to camp. That was the most important thing. No matter what else he did, he must not keep her from her mission. Not when her sister's life depended on her.

She steeled herself, but instead of the pain she expected, the man's head snapped back and he fell from her. Brian slit the attacker's throat with one smooth move from ear to ear and shoved the lifeless body to the side.

"Are you all right?" He turned to her.

She stared at the gushing blood and threw up the bananas.

When Brian stepped forward, she backed away in horror. He towered over her, his hands bloody. *It was okay. He was okay.* He was the guy who had saved her, she told herself, but her brain had trouble catching up.

He stood for a moment, looking at her, then went to squat next to the man and search the body. She looked away, gagging anew at the sight of the blood that was now pooling on the ground.

"We have to get moving," he said a minute later.

She nodded and stood, held her pants together with one hand as she walked toward the opening of the cave.

"Where is the other gun?" Brian left the man and was coming toward her with the new rifle and the extra knife.

She flinched away. "Back in the corridor. I dropped it." Her voice trembled. "It's too dark to see in there."

He looked her over, then went back to the fallen man, took his belt and held it out for her. She couldn't bring herself to touch it. Brian nodded and gave her the rope that held up his own pants. When she didn't move, he helped her tie her khakis in place, touching her as little as possible. She was shaking by the time he was done.

"There are a half-dozen guerillas a quarter mile downhill. Stay behind me and stay quiet," he said as he stepped out of the cave.

## Chapter Three

His knee was killing him. Brian looked up, but could not see the sun from the thick canopy above. Still, it had to be close to the end of the day. The animals were beginning to make their evening sounds, and light had dimmed a little in the last half hour or so. Night fell fast in the jungle, and they hadn't found shelter yet. The hillside was supposed to be riddled with caves. Just not when you were looking for one.

"We'll stop here," he said.

At least the rain had quit for now. He leaned his gun against a tree trunk and scanned the ground for some dry leaves and twigs. But, of course, everything was wet and so were they. The air was cooling off fast. Their soaked-through clothing would be cold and uncomfortable during the night, if he didn't manage to make a fire.

He was used to this state of miserable affairs, but she wasn't. If she got sick and weak it would slow them down, and that was something they couldn't afford. And there was the matter of food, too. While he would have been fine with eating the meat raw, he doubted she felt the same. "Look for anything you think might burn."

"Won't a fire give us away?"

"Nobody walks in the jungle at night unless they absolutely have to. The chance of injury is too high, too easy to fall into something, getting bitten by things you can't see." He didn't mention the night predators, didn't want to make her too nervous to sleep. "My guess is Omar and his band will hole up somewhere for the night and start out fresh in the morning, hoping they'll come across our trail."

He reached for the paper in his shirt pocket. Soaking wet. Figured. A few minutes passed before he found a handful of dry leaves under a bush. He crumbled the leaves into a small pile, set a chunk of dry bark on top of them. From his shirt, he got some of the rope Audrey had been tied up with. That was wet, too, but it didn't matter for his purposes. He peeled off a quarter-inch strand and made a small bow with a green stick. Then he found a dry one, sharpened one end and placed it in the middle of the bark next to the tinder and began moving it with the bow, as fast as he could, putting on the pressure.

He saw Audrey shiver from the corner of his eye. It would have been good if he could have brought the shirt from the man he'd taken out at the cave, but he had to leave it behind. The last thing you wanted in the jungle was to smell like blood. She probably wouldn't have put it on anyway.

"Can I do anything?"

"No," he said at first, then changed his mind and instructed her on how to make a sleeping platform. Better for both of them if she pulled her own weight. If anything happened to him, her life would be easier if she'd learned a few skills. He worked on making the fire while he explained what needed to be done.

An hour went by, maybe two, before he caught the faint scent of smoke—he had lost his once keen sense of time while in the cage. He blew gently on the leaves until he saw the first ember glow in the night that had fallen around them. He gave it more air then fed the small fire. There. They would be fine.

Audrey brought him a handful of dry twigs.

He took the wood with a nod. "Are you all right?"

She hadn't said a word since they had left the cave. He had let her be, not wanting to push.

"Fine."

The fire had grown enough so he could see her face now. Her expression was somber, but the shock and revulsion he'd seen at the cave were gone. She had been scared out of her wits. The man he had been four years ago could have comforted her. Now he had no idea what to say, what to do.

He was no good for her. Hell, he was probably no good for anyone. For anything.

The question he had tried to avoid wouldn't go away. How was he supposed to go back to normal civilian life?

Because he definitely couldn't go back to his job at the SDDU. Not with his bad leg. That position was history. Trouble was, he didn't know how to do anything else.

For a moment back in the cave, she had looked at him as if he was as much of a monster as the man he had pulled off her. She was probably right. But by God, he wanted it to be different.

"I had to do that," he said quietly. "You're safe with me."

"I know." She lifted her gaze to him. "I should have handled it better. You did it for my sake."

Her acceptance loosened some of the tight darkness inside him. The light of the flames bathed her face in a warm glow as she looked straight into his eyes without a trace of fear or loathing.

"I was trying to reach his knife. I think if I did, I might have done the same."

"Sometimes you don't have a choice."

She nodded. "You saved my life twice. Thank you."

She reached out and put a hand on his, briefly, warm and soft. He jerked away on reflex, not used to human touch that didn't hurt, then swore as he burned the back of his wrist in the fire.

Startled, she pulled away.

Damn. "Which one of you was going to adopt?" he asked—the first question that came to his mind.

"Me."

He took a slow breath as he untied the small bundle that hung from his shoulder. "How come your husband didn't come with you?"

"I don't have a husband."

He opened the sack he'd woven from strips of palm leaves to carry the squirrel-like animal he had killed earlier.

"One of those independent women?"

"One of those women whose husband couldn't take the stress of infertility treatments and left her for a simpler relationship," she said quietly.

"Sounds like a real jerk." She was still young, though. He figured her for thirty, if that, with all kinds of possibilities still ahead of her.

She didn't respond.

"Sorry. It's none of my business."

"It's okay. And Josh is okay, too. I mean—I guess, some things just aren't meant to be." Sadness laced her voice.

Why the hell had he brought up this topic? Damn, he sucked at the pep-talk thing. Better focus on something he knew how to do.

He skewered their dinner—had already skinned and gutted the squirrel when he caught it—and held their meal above the flames. There was pitifully little meat on the bones, hardly enough for one person, let alone two, but it was better than nothing. They would manage.

She combed her fingers through her damp hair and moved closer to the fire. "How long have you been here?"

"Four years." The words burned his throat.

She looked up at him wide-eyed. "Have you ever tried to escape before?"

Hell, yes. That's how he had known about the caves. But they had caught him each time. He had been too impatient, trying to make a break for it before he had his strength back.

He shrugged. "For the first year, I couldn't walk. Then I got malaria and was too weak to get away. I did try, mind you. Then they stuck me in a damn cage."

"Why didn't they ransom you?"

"They didn't know who to ask for money. I wouldn't tell them who I was. And they thought I might have some useful information."

Then by the time they figured out he wouldn't talk, the disagreement over his fate had been too public of a quarrel. Jamil couldn't shoot him at that point without making it seem like he was bending to his younger brother's will. And they couldn't let him go, either. He had seen too much. Sometimes he wondered if Jamil was simply waiting for him to give up the fight and die.

Audrey was looking at him in bewilderment. "Why would they think you had any information that concerned them?"

"It's a long story."

"Are you some kind of a spy or something?" she asked after a while, staring at him with suspicion.

"Military."

"Why didn't they come to rescue you?"

"They don't know I'm alive."

His team had been spread out in the jungle, looking for a group of Muslim extremists who had crossed the border from Indonesia to purchase explosives. He had found a cache of TNT in an underground bunker, called in the location. Unfortunately, the Malaysian military had chosen that day to crack down on some bothersome guerillas and had dropped a couple of bombs over the forest where they'd thought the guerillas had been hiding. One of the bombs had hit the bunker.

The force of the explosion had thrown him clear, which was the only reason he had survived—with his skin torn off his side, his leg broken in several places and a severe concussion. Jamil and his men had found him, taken him with them. He remembered little of those first weeks. They'd recognized him as a soldier and had questioned him when he'd recovered. When he wouldn't speak, Omar had rebroken his leg.

"Do you have a family back in Montana?"

He turned the meat over the fire. "My parents have passed away. They adopted me when they were older." And marriage had never been in the cards for him. It didn't mesh with his job. "Do you have any other siblings?"

"Just Nicky."

"It must have been hard losing her."

A look of determination crossed her face. "I'm going to find her and get her back."

"She's alive? Why didn't Omar's men bring her back to camp?"

"A little over a week ago, we were supposed to go on a four-day tour to Gunung Mulu National Park. I had to stay behind at the last minute. The judge was asking for more documentation for the adoption and

I was meeting with the lawyer I hired here, so Nicky went alone. Not alone, I mean. A whole group went with a guide." She looked down at her hands. "They were attacked by guerillas and twelve tourists were taken hostage. The demand is a million dollars per person."

She had to be kidding. "You came to the jungle to rescue her?"

"I came to pay the ransom." She reached under her shirt and pulled out a crumpled, wet piece of paper. "It's a bank account I opened a couple of days ago."

He glanced at the smudged printout that showed a cool million as account total.

"The Malaysian government is negotiating with the guerillas and told the family members to stay put, but I couldn't do it. These things never end well. The military will attack, half the hostages won't make it. I've seen it on TV before…. No government will ever admit that they don't have everything under control."

"So you grabbed a million from your savings and ran off into the jungle? How were you planning on finding them? Does the government know where they are?"

She shook her head. "They're still gathering intelligence. My brother-in-law wired the money."

"Why isn't he here?"

"He's coming. I just— I didn't want to wait. I

hired a local guide who said he could take me to a village frequented by the guerillas."

"There are dozens of guerilla groups scattered over the island."

"I figured they could point me in the right direction."

"And what were you going to do when you got to the ones who have your sister?"

"Show them the account to prove that the money is here in the country, have one of the men come with me and Nicky to the nearest bank. I would have had the money wired there and given him the cash. He walks out with the money, I walk out with Nicky."

All right, there was a slim chance it could have worked, if she made it as far as the right guerilla camp, but trusting her fate to the first group of bandits she had come across had been a mistake. "There's no honor among thieves."

She gave him a don't-I-know-it look. "The guide led me to a village high up the hills and disappeared by morning. Then the fighters came and took me with them. They had me bound and gagged, I couldn't even talk to them."

"I used to have some connections," he said, surprising himself. "When we get to the nearest town, Miri, I'll see what I can do about your sister." He had a pretty good idea where the hostages were.

"How far is Miri?"

"A good week of walking if we don't run into any trouble."

He saw her pale in the firelight.

"I don't have a week. The ransom deadline is in four days."

Damn. He clamped his jaw together, fighting the inevitable.

She pulled her knees up and wrapped her arms around them, her eyes wide with desperation. "What if I allowed myself to be recaptured? I could show the fighters the bank statement and tell them they would get a reward if they took me to the group who has the hostages. Maybe you could follow us to make sure nothing bad happened," she added, barely disguised hope all over her heart-shaped face.

"That's not how it works, Audrey. These people don't engage in dialogue." He wanted to make her understand. "It would be like it was back at the cave."

She went still and after a moment, nodded.

"They might shoot you on sight because you made them chase you around. Or they might do worse. And if you told them about the money, they would take you to the bank to get it without going anywhere near your sister."

She stayed silent for a while. "You're right," she said, her eyes glistening. "I failed."

He hated the misery on her face. She'd come here

to adopt a child, and her sister had come to help. It wasn't fair.

Then again, what in life was?

He watched her struggle with her tears and something twisted inside him, an emotion he barely recognized shook loose—compassion. He opened his mouth. This was a bad idea. He drew in a lungful of jungle air, a mixture of the musty smell of decomposing leaves and the light scent of orchids. "We'll get your sister back."

In an instant, her eyes filled with so much hope and trust, he had to look away. Sure as hell, he didn't deserve anyone looking at him that way.

He had to be insane. The captivity had done it to him, and the beatings. Somewhere along the line he had lost his mind. Because if he wasn't one hundred percent stir-crazy, he wouldn't have committed himself to overtaking a guerilla camp alone.

No, not alone. Alone would have been a step up from what he was planning to do. He was going to try to pull off a major operation with a civilian in tow.

FINE, MISTY RAIN dampened her hair, but had not yet soaked her clothes.

"You know, the travel agent was right. She said Malaysia had two seasons, wet and very wet." Audrey licked her fingers, still hungry, but at least not starving. Their dinner had been reduced to a tiny pile of bones next to the dying fire.

She was about to fall over with exhaustion. The last time she'd slept she'd barely gotten a few fitful minutes on the bottom of the boat, gagged and bound, on her way to the guerilla camp. The desperation she had felt then slammed back into her anew. She couldn't shake a sense of dread, a premonition that getting Nicky back would be far more difficult than she had first imagined.

"Give me your pants."

*Excuse me?* She looked at Brian across the fire.

He picked up a thighbone from the pile, put it on a rock and smashed it with a smaller chunk of stone. "I'm gonna fix the rip." He chose a long, thin sliver of bone and worked it with his knife, drilling a hole in one end.

A needle. She stood and tugged at the rope. Having to use it to hold up her pants had been a pain. If she tied it loose, her clothes kept escaping; if she tied it tight, it cut into her abdomen. She fumbled. The fibers had swollen from moisture.

"Hang on."

He came around the fire to help and got on his knees in front of her, his dreadlocks sticking out in every which direction. She sucked in her stomach to give him room to work.

The wildman of the jungle was helping her take off her clothes. Her life had crossed over from the insane to the bizarre.

The rope loosened, and he returned to his spot without looking at her. He seemed to know instinctually what she needed and when—food, protection, privacy—and gave it without thought. She sat back down, took off her boots and pulled the bottom of her pants from her socks where they'd been secured to keep the bugs out.

"Here we go." He peeled a thin string from the rope and licked the end to smooth down the fibers.

She took off the pants and tucked her shirt around her legs. It came to midthigh. She glanced at Brian across the fire. "Hopefully, the bugs won't do too much damage. They can't eat me in just a few minutes, right?"

His hands shook as he tried to thread the needle, the movement slight at first, then growing more pronounced. The muscles in his face tightened with each attempt. She had noticed the shaking before, a trembling that came to his fingers and passed after a while. His nerves were shot. That he'd survived at all was in itself a miracle.

"Let me do that." She held out her hand.

He hesitated for a moment, his eyes burning like silver flames of an unearthly fire, then dropped the

needle and thread into her palm. She wanted to say
something to lighten his mood, but what did you say
to comfort a man whose life had been stolen away?
What could she possibly say that would make the
past four years okay? She focused on the needle and
went to work.

He didn't stay idle, either. When she glanced up,
he was rubbing two chunks of hard sandstone against
each other. He didn't stop until he got a flat surface
on one. He waited until the mist wet it, picked up the
smaller of his two knives and worked the blade over
the rock with smooth movements, away from him,
clockwise first then anticlockwise. The sound sent
shivers down her spine, reminding her of old horror
movies.

Maybe it was the darkness that seemed to have
swallowed them that turned her thoughts so morbid.
The night was a solid black wall starting a few feet
from their campfire, surrounding them. The calls of
wild animals, like that of angry invisible ghosts, startled her from time to time, made her draw closer to
the flames.

She had been able to appreciate the beauty of the
jungle when she had first seen it on the peninsula
shortly after their arrival. It had seemed a living,
breathing marvel. Now she found it threatening.

Brian examined the knife at the light of the flames,

then took his shirt off. As scary as his appearance was in general, his body was beautiful, despite the scars. And she appreciated the strength in it that had saved her life.

He grabbed his beard with his left hand and began to hack away with the right, tufts of hair falling at his feet. Once he was down to the last inch or so, he gathered some water from the palm leaves next to him, wet the stubble thoroughly, then shaved.

She put down the needle, grabbed the larger knife from the ground and cut off the extra thread, then put her pants and boots back on. There was nothing else to do but watch his progress. His hands had steadied. And thank God for that. She wasn't sure she would have been brave enough to offer her help with shaving, not with that deadly looking blade.

The fire was down to embers when he moved on to his hair. There hadn't been enough dry material to keep the flames going, but whatever they'd managed was enough. They had a hot meal in their stomachs and were warmed up a little. If nothing else, it lifted her spirits, which was probably one of the most important things. If she could keep her mind from sinking into despair and giving up, the battle would be half-won.

Brian cut the hair on the side methodically and progressed to the back, his movements turning awkward.

"Let me help." She rose and went to him. "Turn around."

She knelt behind him and worked fast, cutting as much by feel as sight. He tossed what had remained of the ropes that had once bound her into the fire, but the fibers were damp and gave but a few more minutes of light, producing plenty of smoke in the process. Then the last ember blinked out and they were shrouded in darkness. "Here's the knife." She held it out to where she'd last seen his hand.

"You keep it," he said.

She tightened her fingers on the handle, unsure where to put the small weapon.

He didn't move.

What was he waiting for?

She should probably brush the hair off his back. She shifted, reluctant to touch him. And how stupid was that? He had saved her life twice, had just given her a knife that was sharp enough to shave with. He wasn't about to throw her to the ground, for heaven's sake. She reached out with her left hand and brushed the clippings off, quick, businesslike. It was strange to touch him like this, feeling without seeing, the long ridges of his scars pressing against her fingertips. For someone as underfed as he was, he retained an amazing amount of muscle.

She snatched away her hand and stood in one motion, stepping back.

"Thank you," he said, his voice deep and thick.

She could hear him put on his shirt and move over to the raised platform she had built while he'd started their short-lived fire. He had instructed her on how to make a frame, how to stack on top the two dozen or so fallen branches he'd asked her to gather. She hoped the vines would hold and they wouldn't tumble to the ground in the middle of the night, although, they weren't high up—no more than a foot or so—just enough to keep the bugs and rats and snakes off them.

She stepped after him and felt for the edge of the platform, big enough for the two of them to sleep on without touching.

"Good haircut," he said, "by the feel of it."

"I wasn't taking a big risk. Anything had to be an improvement."

"It was that bad, huh?" There was a rare lightness to his voice.

"Scary."

"You don't strike me as the type who scares easily."

*Shows what you know.* She was scared of the jungle. She was scared for Nicky. She was even a little scared of him. First time in bed with a wildman, and all.

"What do you do at home when you're not dashing off to rescue people?"

"I work at a drug and alcohol rehab clinic." She had resigned her director of admissions position just before leaving for Malaysia, and took a cut in pay and title so she'd have more time to spend with her baby when they got back. And she was scared about that, too. If, after all the dreaming and hoping, she wouldn't turn out to be a good mother.

"So the urge to rescue runs deep in the blood."

Was he teasing her? The deadpan comment seemed so out of character, she was unsure how to respond.

"I had a boyfriend in high school who died of a drug overdose. I didn't even know he was using. He was class valedictorian. I got involved in every anti-drug support program after that. Things just progressed from there, I suppose."

She fidgeted on the bed.

"Know of a good twelve-step program for recovering washed-out POWs?" His voice was hard again, not a trace of lightness left in it.

She wanted desperately to say something that would help him, something that went beyond the usual you're-in-control-of-your-future platitude. In a sense, he was similar to the men and women she dealt with at work every day. Their lives were robbed from them by the substances they abused, just as the guerillas had stolen years from Brian. And yet in many other ways, he was profoundly different.

"Good night," he said, closing the conversation before she could form a response.

She was up long after his breathing evened, startled by a call or shriek of some wild animal every time she began to doze off. Small noises came from above, insects and God knows what else dropping on the palm leaf roof Brian had thrown together after he had coaxed the fire to life.

Her mind was restless, going to Nicky over and over again, wondering how she was doing, if her sister was still alive. Her clothes were damp and she was cold, wishing back the cave where they'd spent the previous night. Amazing what a difference dry clothes made.

Brian mumbled something.

"What?"

He spoke again, in another language. She could hear him kicking at the leaves that she'd piled onto the bamboo platform for comfort. Maybe he was having a nightmare. He probably had enough bad memories to fill a lifetime of scary dreams. She had only spent a day with the guerillas. He had been their prisoner for four years. She couldn't begin to comprehend what he had gone through.

The thought brought a slew of uncomfortable questions. What right did she have to ask him to go back? He had already suffered more than most people she knew did in a lifetime. He needed rest and sufficient food, and medical care for his bad leg.

She was prepared to risk everything to save her sister, even her life. But she had no right to ask him to do the same.

He kicked again, wildly, and must have hit one of the supports because the shelter rattled. She reached out and her fingers brushed against his face, registering how cold his wet skin was a split second before his hand closed around her wrist—tight enough to hurt.

Fear slammed into her. They couldn't see each other. He could snap her neck before he woke enough to remember her. "Brian?" She scrambled away from him as far as she could.

He eased his grip and a second later let her go.

"Sorry," he said after a while, his voice raspy from sleep.

"You had a bad dream." She rubbed her wrist, staying back.

Silence followed her words.

"Look," she said after a few minutes. "You don't have to come with me. If you could just take me close enough so I can get to them without getting lost." That would be enough. She would show the bank statement, and after that things should resolve quickly.

"I wouldn't hurt you," he said over his shoulder, misunderstanding her. "I said you could trust me."

"It's not that I don't. I do. But don't you think you've had enough? I'm grateful that you saved my life. But it's not your job to watch over me. You don't owe me anything." She said the words awfully bravely, even though she didn't feel very brave at the moment.

"We'll get your sister."

She wanted to protest and pretend that she wasn't melting in relief, but she couldn't bring herself to do it. She did need him, want him with her. He was offering. She wasn't stupid enough to fight him on this.

A steady drizzle came from above, some of it dripping through the makeshift roof. She pulled in her neck and wrapped her arms around herself. Under her brand-new shirt, she had on a cotton T-shirt and a thin cotton tanktop with a built-in bra under that—three layers of clothing and she was still shivering. Brian's shirt was torn in a couple of places, worn thin with use.

She scooted closer to him until she was touching his back.

He pulled away.

## Chapter Four

Brian stared into the forest that glistened in the rising dawn, and planned their route. They'd cross the Baram and go upriver on land instead of on the water. He didn't want to run into anyone who used the river. Omar wouldn't be looking for them in that direction, but he didn't want to be seen by anyone at all. News of strangers in the jungle had a way of spreading.

At least they didn't have to worry about food—fruit shouldn't be hard to find this time of the year. And he could hunt, too, although only if they came across easy prey—he couldn't afford to waste time.

He listened as unseen animals called to each other in the distance. The jungle didn't scare him. It was merely an obstacle they had to overcome.

Audrey's warm body pressed against his back—drawing him into a territory a hell of a lot more dangerous than the wild forest.

Her proximity was comforting and arousing at the same time. She'd rolled against him in her sleep at one point during the night, and he hadn't been able to find the strength to move away again.

The first substantial nonmalicious human contact he'd had in years. It left him weak in the knees. Damn, he was a sap. Pitiful. He had spent the night fighting the urge to turn to her, unable to sleep since she'd woken him.

He didn't know what he wanted from her—not all of him, anyway. His body had no doubts, but he tried to force his mind to run along more civilized lines. He wasn't sure what was right, what was realistic.

She was his responsibility, but she was all his fantasies come true, too. And she had earned his respect in the past twenty-four hours they'd spent together.

She was loyal, ready to give her life for family and brave, if a little misguided. Coming to look for the guerillas had been a less than well-thought-out plan, but he could understand her desperation.

He felt her stir then pull away, and rolled onto his back. He got lost looking at her mussed hair and sleep-heavy eyes.

"What?"

"You look beautiful." He hadn't meant to say that. The words came out choppy, like a rusty reflex. It had been a while since he'd last paid a compliment to a woman.

A rueful smile tugged up her tempting lips. "Thanks. But I'm going to have to take into consideration that you haven't been surrounded by women lately." She hesitated for a moment, then added, "You're not half as scary without the beard."

That was a start. She was obviously warming up to him. It was the first attempt she'd made at a joke since they'd met.

"We better get going before the rain starts again." He slid off the platform and stood, for a second just enjoying the luxury of being able to stand tall whenever he wanted.

Something else was standing tall, too. Just a morning thing. She didn't control his body. Right.

"We'll get breakfast where we find it. You can go to the bathroom over there." He nodded to a wide-trunked palm to his left. "I'll be behind those trees. Keep your knife handy."

He picked up her semidry socks and boots and handed them to her, then got his own.

When they were both back, he bent a large, slightly cone-shaped leaf that was filled with rainwater, so she could wash her hands and face, and another so she could drink.

She had a slim, long neck—plenty of landing

space for a platoon of kisses. He watched her swallow until he was getting hot and bothered again and decided it was best not to look.

After she was done and he had his fill as well, he broke off the leaf, dried it on his pants and folded it into a pouch. He collected his hair from the ground and packed it in, tying the leaf-bag to his belt with a piece of vine when he was done. "Tinder," he said before making another pouch and filling that one with ashes. He looped the rope around his shoulder, tucked away the needle. They started out as soon as he was done.

"Shouldn't we cover up all this?" She glanced back toward their makeshift camp.

He liked it that she was always thinking. It had been a long time since anyone had his back.

"We're far enough now. We shouldn't have to worry about Omar's men." Not that they were safe from the guerillas altogether. Different groups controlled the various areas of the mountain. But enough of the locals from the villages came into the jungle for hunting trips so that leftovers of a small camp wouldn't raise any suspicions if a couple of fighters came across it.

They moved at a good pace, as good as his bad leg allowed. The pain in his muscles, not used to exertion, was nothing compared to the pain in his bones. For as long as he could remember, the one thing he was always able to count on was the strength of his own body. He struggled to deal with this new handicap.

After about three hours of walking, he was forced to accept that they would have to stop to rest.

The rain hadn't started up again yet. That was good. But they hadn't come across any edible fruits all morning, and he was getting hungry. Audrey probably felt the same.

"We'll stop here to eat," he said, and laid his gun against a tree before lowering himself to a fallen log.

She sat next to him with a puzzled expression.

*She wasn't going to go for this. Not in a million years.* But he didn't have the strength or the time to go off on a hunt. And considering what had happened when he'd left her alone the last time, it was probably a good idea to stick as close to her as possible.

He gave Audrey a reassuring smile, reached for a thick, broken-off branch that lay next to them and lifted it, revealing a scampering jumble of grubs. He picked them quickly, as many as he could before the rest disappeared under the decomposing leaves.

"They have more nutrition in them per pound than vegetables," he said, holding his palm out between them, wishing he could have done better for her.

She stared at the wriggling mess, reached out a tentative hand and pinched a fat white one between her thumb and forefinger, lifted it to her mouth and swallowed it whole, then cleared her throat.

His jaw went slack from surprise.

"You've missed a couple of reality shows since you've been gone." She grinned. "People eat stuff like this on TV now almost every night to win prizes." She went for another grub and sent it after the first.

THE BUGS FREAKED HER OUT, but she wasn't about to show it.

If he could put up with it, and the pain that must have been just about crippling him all morning, then she sure wasn't going to whine. She had seen how he walked, how his limp had gotten more and more pronounced through the morning, the muscles in his face growing tighter and tighter. He was doing this for her, for Nicky, whom he'd never even met. She wasn't going to make his job harder by being difficult. She wasn't going to fuss over a couple of bugs.

The next one had a little dirt on it. Audrey blew off the leaf dust before she put the thing into her mouth. The grub wriggled all the way down but stopped once it reached her stomach.

He waited until she had her fill before he took any, as he had with the meat the night before and the bananas before that. She made sure she didn't take more than her share. With this latest course, it wasn't too difficult.

"Do you think we'll get there in time?" She watched him as he ate methodically, obviously not thinking of the food.

"It'll be close, but if all goes well, yes."

He looked remarkably different without the caveman do, and much younger. With the dreadlocks gone, a lot of the grays disappeared in the short, light brown mess she'd made of his hair. He was nowhere near fifty as she'd thought before—around his midthirties perhaps. He had great lips. Her attention lingered on the strong masculine line of his jaw. The skin that had been until now hidden behind the bushy beard was a shade lighter than the rest, giving the odd impression that he was wearing a mask.

And maybe he was. He had told her very little about himself. She opened her mouth to ask, but changed her mind. If he didn't want to talk about his past, she could respect that. He was helping her save Nicky. That was all she needed to know.

He examined the vegetation around them, got up, broke an eight-inch twig off a tree, brought it over and snapped it in half, offering one of the pieces to her.

"Toothbrush," he said, and started to chew at the end of his.

She followed his example. The bark was bitter but the inner fibers had a mild spicy taste.

"It's good to keep everything as clean as you can." He chucked his stick after a couple of minutes.

They rinsed their mouths, drank and moved on. When the sun reached its highest point in the sky and she noticed he was limping too hard again, she asked if they could stop to rest.

"Right over there." He pointed, and she followed him to a tree with yellow, podlike fruit hanging from it. "I've been hoping we would come across something to eat."

He grabbed a long stick and beat them down, and she picked them up.

"Looks like starfruit." Only smaller. She'd seen those in the grocery store but never had one.

"It is." He sat next to her on the ground and watched her as she took a tentative bite.

"Sweet." With just a hint of sourness in the juicy flesh. She gobbled the rest of the fruit, then grew embarrassed when she realized he was smiling at her fervor.

"Better than the grubs?" The starfruit juice glistened on his lips. A few drops ran down his chin, and he wiped them off with the back of his hand.

She swallowed. "Anything has to be better than grubs."

His mouth tugged up at one corner. "You'd be surprised."

She was about to ask him what he meant, but he tensed and put a finger to his lips.

What? She strained her ears but didn't hear a thing.

He motioned to her to stand and follow him as he examined the trees around them, selecting one that had branches starting low to the ground. He stepped up quickly and pulled her after him, higher and higher, until they could no longer see the ground from the leaves.

He lay on his stomach on the jumble of branches and she did the same, hanging on for dear life. He was watching something, then she spotted the opening in the foliage that gave them a view of what was going on below. A guerilla fighter passed under them, heading straight for the fruit on the ground. He picked up a couple, calling out to others who appeared soon. They gathered the starfruits and took potshots at the ones that remained on the tree.

She was holding on to the branches so tightly she was getting a muscle cramp in her arm, but she didn't dare move. Her blood pounded loudly enough in her ears to drown out half the voices below. She waited, as still as she could. Then a small movement caught her eye a few feet up the branch she was laying on. A spider. Not just any spider, this was the prototype, the mother and father of all spiders, as big as her palm with fingers outstretched. And it was coming toward her.

She had quarter-inch goose bumps, every hair on her body standing on end. She clenched her teeth and watched the beast move closer and closer. It would reach her face first. If she let go of the branch to try to shoo it away, she would fall.

She blew at it gently as it got within a few feet and stopped. It didn't seem to notice. She blew harder.

The fighters were still talking down below. Never a better time to take a break, for heaven's sake. The beast meandered forward a few inches as if trying to figure out what she was.

Eating grubs was one thing, but if Gargantua came another spidy step closer, she was going to get seriously freaked out. No way could she take it if the spider crawled on her face. She needed to think of something else. No matter what happened, she couldn't make a sound, couldn't let go of the branch.

Then she saw Brian's arm come into her field of vision and she looked up just in time to see him scoop up the beast. He placed it gently on a cross branch a good distance from her, and gave it a gentle shove in the opposite direction. Gargantua obeyed.

She was weak from relief, a wet noodle draped over the branch. She owed him. She owed him big.

Then finally the guerillas moved on. Brian waited a couple of minutes before starting to climb down, helping her descend after him. The job required patience, since her knees were still shaking. Her heartbeat was as labored as a marathon runner's.

He slid to the lowest branch with ease. As difficult as walking seemed for him, up in the canopy he moved like the lord of the jungle, having enough upper body strength to spare, allowing him to pull himself up, or lower himself from branch to branch with ease.

He held his hands out, and she thumped down next to him, right in the circle of his arms. She put one hand on his shoulder to steady herself, aware the instant they touched of the muscles beneath her palm, his darkening gaze on her face, his lips a few inches from hers. His eyes really were extraordinary. Fire leapt in them, but she didn't pull away.

She kissed him.

BRIAN FROZE.

Her soft, warm lips pressed against his and short-circuited his brain, sending an electric charge through his body that had sparks buzzing over the surface of his skin. He wanted more, he wanted all of her, with an urgency that stole his breath, but he also recognized the kiss for what it was—a gesture of gratitude and relief. And he would have had to be the worst kind of bastard to take advantage of it.

He pulled back and saw surprise flicker in her eyes before he looked away. Surprise at her own spontaneous gesture, or at his reaction? It didn't matter. He wasn't going there. He couldn't.

He stepped aside and turned, scanning the forest, forcing his brain to focus on finding a path. "We better go."

"I'm sorry." Her voice was small and edged with embarrassment. "I don't know what that was."

He glanced back at her, the touch of pink on her cheeks affecting him as much as the kiss had. "Fun," he said, and made his lips stretch into a semblance of a nonchalant smile he would have given her had they met four years ago. "It's just not a good idea."

"No. No, of course not." She busied herself with brushing off her clothes.

He liked the way she moved. Even in the smallest tasks she managed to seem efficient and purposeful. He couldn't help but remember the long, slim limbs that had mesmerized him when she'd washed herself in the creek. His body responded enthusiastically to the memory.

To punctuate another corporeal need, his stomach growled, reminding him how little they had eaten. She had to be hungry, too. "We should be able to find some more food if we keep our eyes open. If not sooner, then when we reach the river."

She nodded, her features taking on an expression of steeled determination. She was obviously way out of her comfort zone, but no one could ever tell that by looking at her. Her clothes were soiled with dirt, and marred by a couple of small tears left behind by the thorny vines. But she had zeroed in on their goal and didn't waste time with complaining about things that couldn't be changed.

He had to stop keeping a running list of the things he liked about her. Hell, it was pretty much everything. Liking her and doing something about it were two different things, however. "Ready to move out?"

"Absolutely." She regained her composure enough to flash him a cautious smile.

He really liked the way her eyes crinkled when she smiled.

HAMID LISTENED to his men report back, finishing his rice. No sign of the two that ran away. Where the hell were they?

If it were just the woman, he wouldn't have thought twice about it. But the man bothered him. Jamil's prisoner was a survivor. He had made it through malaria, beatings, years in that damn cage where Jamil had kept him like a pet. He could be halfway to Miri by now. No, maybe not halfway, the woman would slow him down.

They hadn't gone on the river. Omar's men were watching day and night. That was good at least. The jungle would slow them even further, give him more time to act.

He set the bowl down and got up, walked to the crate in the corner. The bombs were ready. They were as powerful as he could make them. But they were no longer safe here. If the man made it out, he could give the army Omar's location. And if Omar was captured, he might give their plan up to save himself.

He called for his men, looked at the two that entered. Good. They were part of the old guard. "You two and your brothers—" he nodded to the taller one "—will take the crate now."

"To the city?"

He nodded. It was too early, not what they'd planned, but at times like this, flexibility was the key.

"Is Muhammad coming?" the man asked.

"No." Especially not Muhammad. He had caused enough trouble already by bringing western hostages to camp. "You will go quietly. Keep a low profile. Don't stop at any camps. Take enough food. Don't even stop to hunt."

"Of course."

"You stay with the bombs and wait for me."

He would have to go. That part of the plan would have to change, too. Muhammad was too much of a man of impulse, he saw that now. Omar could have gotten the job done, he was eager enough to prove himself to volunteer for any mission. But if something went wrong, would Omar be willing to sacrifice himself for their cause?

Jamil would have, if he could have been talked into it, but too late to think about that now. Jamil was dead.

Hamid ran his fingers across the top of the crate. He would go. And when the time came, he would do whatever was necessary. First the bombs, to scare out of the country the foreign dogs who supported the current government and its malpractices. Then he would unite all the guerilla groups in the hills—he was making good progress with that—and go head-to-head with the military.

And then his country would finally be free.


THEY WALKED IN SILENCE, picking their way over fallen logs and through leafy bunches of vines that were hanging from the canopy, blocking their way.

"This way," Brian said, wincing at the stab of pain that flashed through his knee every time he put his weight on his bad leg.

The ground was waterlogged, extensive buttress root systems tripping them up, blocking their way.

"Look for game trails," he told Audrey. "It's the easiest going, as long as you remember to get off them at dusk. You don't want to run into any night predators."

"Have you ever come across a tiger?"

He glanced back. "The native tribes believe if you speak the word out loud one will appear."

"Oh." She looked around and stepped up until she was right behind him.

He hadn't planned on telling that story to anyone. Wasn't even sure what had really happened. But what the hell. What else did they have to talk about?

"Once," he said, keeping a steady pace. "I think. I could have been hallucinating. I was fighting malaria at the time."

"Was it after you were captured?"

He nodded. "I was pretty much out of it. The fever was so bad Jamil's men didn't even tie me up. I remember coming to in the middle of the night and deciding to escape. I made it about six feet before I collapsed behind some bushes and passed out."

"Were you attacked?"

"It was the strangest thing." He stopped to look at her. "I remember coming around, feeling a hot breath on my face—boy, did it stink. Think dog breath a hundred times over. I looked up into the face of this enormous beast. I thought, this was it, I was finished.

And it licked my forehead a couple of times then walked away."

She stared at him, her green eyes round. "It licked you?"

"I'll never forget it. He had a big tongue, rough. Maybe he liked the salt in the sweat." He shrugged.

"Maybe he was tasting you and decided there was something wrong with you and you might make him sick."

"Could be, although predators usually pick the sick and weak of the herd."

"True."

They moved on, and he held a bunch of vines out of the way to let her pass through, brushed off a giant beetle that had fallen on her shoulder before she noticed it.

"Did the tiger get any of the guerillas?"

He shook his head. "They found me in the morning. Never figured it out that I was trying to escape. They thought I went to relieve myself and passed out."

"They didn't keep you in the cage back then?"

"The first year they caught me, we spent on the trails, moving from one makeshift camp to another. Then we came across the place you saw, an abandoned poacher hideaway. It came with a handful of sheds and a tiger cage. Jamil took a liking to it."

"Jamil?"

"The leader before Omar. Omar was the one writing by the fire—short guy with the broken nose."

They walked on in silence for a while. She was probably thinking about the guerillas.

He was thinking about her lips on his.

She was a shock to the system, no doubt about it. He should have felt relieved that she wasn't scared of him, despite his appearance, but all things considered maybe it would have been safer for her if she were.

He would never consciously take advantage of her and their situation, but too much civilization had melted off him over the years, and even he wasn't sure what kind of man had walked out of that cage. He wasn't sure if he knew himself, if he could trust himself. At one point in his life he'd had principles, he had lived by a code. But while in captivity, all that had been replaced by a single objective: survival, for which he would have done absolutely anything.

He fought his way through some bushes and helped her. "We must be nearing the river. The closer we get, the more undergrowth there is."

As bad as visibility was in the jungle—no more than fifty yards—here they could barely see six feet around them. The tall plants gave a feeling of claustrophobia, putting him on edge, on alert for what might jump out at them.

Thankfully, they didn't have to fight the overgrown vegetation long. He spotted a winding trail a few minutes later.

"Deer and wild pigs." He examined the tracks, a jumble of hoofprints pressed into the soft soil.

They still had to duck under vines that hung from the branches above, but the going was a hell of a lot easier.

"How far is the river?" She kept close, careful not to fall more than a few steps behind.

"Just ahead, can you hear it?"

"No."

"Listen for the fishing birds."

They moved forward at a good pace, the soil growing soggier underfoot as they progressed. With all the rain, the river probably had been flooding a lot lately. High water would make crossing more difficult. On the other hand, dangerous waters meant less river travel, less chance of somebody seeing them.

"This probably will be the most difficult part. Once we get to the other side, things will be easier." He tried to give her something to look forward to.

Crossing a river was risky under the best of circumstances. Walking into floodwaters was sheer insanity.

They came around a bend in the trail and the water was in front of them, rolling slowly, brown with the mud it had washed down from the mountains. He watched drifting wood to gauge the river's speed, looked for white water that would indicate rocks beneath the surface. He picked out a spot on the other side that looked like a good target for landing, considering the current and the thick jumble of plants that covered the bank.

"I didn't realize the river would be this wide," she said behind him.

"It's the rainy season." He turned around and found her watching the water, her face reflecting her doubts. He didn't blame her. Nobody with a smidgen of survival instinct would want to go anywhere near that river.

He hunted around until he found a fallen branch, as thick as his wrist and about six feet long, then looked some more and picked up another, about the same. He stripped off side shoots with his knife, then dropped the two poles at Audrey's feet.

"Shouldn't we look for a better spot to cross?" She eyed the rolling water.

If only they had that luxury.

"Can't afford to waste the time. And we might not find any." He tossed her the rifle then picked a tree with a multitude of vines hanging from its branches and walked to it. "Better get to work," he called back over his shoulder. "Keep your eyes open."

They were on a well-traveled game trail used by

animals to get to the river. A prime hunting location for predators. He wanted to be gone from the spot before nightfall. As rare as tigers were these days, it was always better to err on the side of caution.

He climbed the tree, using the vines for leverage, and cut one thick stem after the other. They had to hurry, and not only so they wouldn't become supper for the local wildlife. They had to cross the river while they still had full daylight to guide them. Waiting until morning was out of the question.

Time was tight.

They couldn't afford to waste any of it if they were to save the hostages.

## Chapter Five

Sweat dripped from his eyebrows. Brian wiped his forehead with his shirtsleeve without missing a beat.

Cutting the vines took serious effort, their woodsy fibers hard to sever with a simple knife. A good axe or a hatchet could have done the job in a third of the time. And the more he cut, the duller the blade got from the rough work. He sized up the pile Audrey had carefully uncoiled and stretched on the ground. Should be enough. He climbed down, careful where he stepped.

"Hang on to this." He picked up a good length of vine and handed one end to her, pulled hard on the other to test it.

Now was the time to make sure there were no rotted sections, or areas where insects and rodents might have weakened the plant. They did the same to the next and the next until they were done, having to throw aside only two.

He sat by the pile and got to work. Audrey settled next to him, her thigh brushing against his when she leaned forward.

Being around her was like swimming in a tank full of electric eels. She zapped his senses, shorted his concentration with every move.

"Can I help?" Her luminous green eyes sparkled in the dappled light.

*Go someplace where I can't see you, and take temptation with you.*

No, that wasn't fair. It wasn't her fault that he had a hard time keeping his mind and hands off her. He focused on the work in front of them, pushed back the tide of primal urges rising in his blood.

"Like this." He held the ends of two vines together, made a loop and tied them in a secure knot.

She tried with another one and managed pretty well. He tested her knot. It held.

When all the vines were connected, he rechecked every single knot one more time. Then he tied one end of the line around a tree, the other around his waist, grabbed his pole and waded into the water. The river was about a hundred feet wide; he had more than enough "rope" the get him to the other side.

"Feed the line to me little by little. Hold tight if I slip." He walked farther into the murky water, using the pole to probe for holes in the river bottom in front of him.

The silt was soft and slippery. It sucked his boots in, making the crossing difficult.

"When I'm across, untie the line from the tree and tie it around your waist. Use the pole for support," he called back, then turned his attention to crossing.

He moved forward as fast as he could, not only because it was never a good idea to linger in water—too many nasty parasites that could make your life miserable for a long time—but because he hated to leave Audrey unprotected. The sooner they were both on the same side again, the better.

The water was all right, a few degrees colder than the air. In a few steps he was in to his waist, then his chest and his shoulders. Then the pole no longer reached bottom in front of him. He pushed away from the mud that was sucking his boots in, and began to swim, feeling the line pull tight, then loosen as Audrey gave him some slack.

The closer he got to the middle, the stronger the current grew. He let go of the pole and put everything he had into swimming, careful with the debris the river carried. In what seemed an eternity later, his feet touched semisolid ground again, and he was able to walk, losing his footing a couple of times, but making his way forward steadily.

Without the pole, the going was slower. He had to feel out where he was stepping before putting his weight on his foot. He couldn't afford to slip into a hole and break a leg.

But he reached shore soon enough, his clothes a soggy, muddy mess. He fought the plants that reached into the water and found a spot where he could climb the bank, and untied the line while he was catching his breath. Once he secured it to a tree, he waved to Audrey to follow.

The tight set of her mouth betrayed her nerves. Nothing but determination in her movements, though. She pushed herself to complete the task at hand, as always.

He pulled the line with each step she took forward, more nervous watching her than when he was in the water himself. She was doing well, keeping her head up, using the pole. Then she was swimming. He pulled the line, helping her. She drifted downriver, but the line held and kept her safe.

He only took his eyes off her to look for signs of danger every once in a while, keeping his ears on guard for the sound of approaching boats. They were lucky, it looked like she would make it. She was almost at the point where he figured her feet would start touching bottom again soon.

Then a log in the water upriver caught his attention, and he swore, pulling harder on the vine.

"Swim to shore," he yelled, not caring now who might hear him. She was in more immediate danger from the log than from anyone. If her line got tangled, she'd be trapped. "Go with the current! On your back. Forty-five degrees to shore. Swim backwards." It was the safest position for someone carried away by floodwaters.

He gave her back the whole length of the vine rope, and she understood, stopped fighting to reach shore where he was and let the current take her downriver, just trying to get across enough so the log would float by behind her. She almost cleared it. The log hit the line ten feet or so in front of her. He could see the patched length of vine tangle in the roots as the dead tree bobbed in the water, rolling in the current.

He pulled on the line, desperate. Maybe he could drag her in log and all. *Come on, baby.* But the vine rope didn't budge. He let it go. If it snapped, he would lose her.

Audrey was swimming for the log, probably hoping to hang on to it until they figured out what to do next.

"Keep away from it!"

It would be too easy to get tangled in the line and the roots. The log could roll and push her under. She heard him and stopped, paddling in place, waiting for him to save her.

He wasn't sure he could.

He rushed forward, blood drumming in his ears. Not many things scared him anymore, but watching her struggle at the end of the rope left him petrified.

He had to come up with something. Now.

She had a knife, but if she cut herself loose, without the line the water would carry her downriver. The current was too strong for her to make it to shore without help. If she stayed where she was, her strength would run out sooner or later and she would drown.

He scaled the nearest tree, slashed at the vines, made another line and ran through the forest. He had to reach her before her line snapped.

He was tying knots as he went, having a line less than half the size of the original ready by the time he reached the spot on the bank that was close enough, yet a little above her. That way he could let the current carry him instead of fighting it. He tied himself out and dived in, not bothering with a pole, swimming for her with everything he had. She swam toward him, both of them careful to avoid the log.

His lungs choked with the water he swallowed, but he reached her. "Hang on tight." He cut the vine that held her trapped.

The current grabbed on to the extra weight and pushed them both under for a second. They came up spluttering. He kicked with his feet to stay afloat, grabbed onto the rope, one hand over the other again and again, struggling to pull them in.

The progress was slow, swimming in the strong current with her hanging on to his neck damn near impossible. They spent as much time underwater as above it. But then his feet touched the muddy bottom, and soon hers did, too.

For a moment they clung to each other, standing together against the rage of the river that swirled around them. He barely caught his breath when he heard the spluttering sound of a motor then the next second spotted the boat that came from upriver.

*Damn.*

He pointed it out to Audrey, took a deep breath, and when he saw her do the same, pulled her under with him. He headed for an overhang of bushes by the bank, going by feel, the water so murky there was no point in opening his eyes. He held her hand tight, came up when he felt the branches with his other hand, pulled her farther in.

"Omar's men?" Audrey whispered against his ear.

Overhanging leaves hid them from view, but they could see the river through the small gaps between branches.

"Poachers."

The boat stopped and the six men inside looked over the tied-out log. One of them killed the motor, scanned both banks. Brian strained to hear what they were saying, but couldn't. Then they tensed, reached for their weapons.

He grabbed his knife under the water, knowing there was little he could do if they spotted his hiding spot. They had guns. Even if he threw the knife well and took one out, the other five would shoot Audrey and him into sieves.

But the men weren't looking at him. Soon they all turned their attention upriver. And then he could hear it, too, the sounds of a motor once again.

The boat that came around the bend was smaller than the poachers', but the four guerillas were better armed, holding semiautomatics instead of hunting rifles. The two groups watched each other warily, neither of them saying a word to the other.

For a moment, the tension was palpable in the air, every man gripping his gun. Then the guerillas floated by. Their small boat carried some kind of a crate, covered with tarp. The men were positioned two in the front, two in the back. He watched them carefully, but didn't recognize any.

The poachers waited a good ten minutes before they followed.

When they were out of sight, Brian waded from under the bushes and, once he made sure it was safe, he signaled to Audrey to follow. They made their way to shore—not an easy task. There was no game trail on this side, the vegetation thick to the point of impenetrable, as the plants fought for light.

He was careful to select the thinnest spot, to bend the branches instead of breaking them, to trample as little as possible. Even when he got past that first barrier, he made a point to walk on moss that would spring back up fast, or on stones, instead of in mud that would leave tracks—in case the guerillas came back later to investigate. Audrey followed his example without having to be told.

Once he was sure they couldn't be seen from the river, he stopped. "Check yourself over." He turned from her. "Let me know if you need help." He ran the odd scene on the river through his mind again. It didn't add up. His instincts bristled.

"I'm glad they didn't get into a fight," Audrey said behind him.

He peeled off his clothes and squeezed the water out, draped them over branches, careful not to put anything on the ground.

"That's just it. The poachers had a better boat and it was loaded. But the guerillas had better weapons. I thought they would attack." His legs and torso were all right, but he had a couple of leeches on each arm, five fatties on his shoulders where they had sneaked under his collar.

Judging by the squeak that came from behind him, they had gotten Audrey, too.

"Help," she said.

He turned and found her staring at two big ones just below the spot where her collarbones met. She still had her underwear on, and the soggy cotton tanktop that hid nothing.

"Don't pull," he said. "Their jaws can get ripped. Anything that stays under your skin ups your chances for an infection." A lighter or some salt would have helped, but they didn't have either. "If you can stand them for another minute or two, they'll get full and fall off on their own. It's the safest."

"Oh, gross."

"So tell me about your sister," he said as one of his *friends* dropped to the ground. He kicked it away with his boot, then looked around for food. A profusion of palm trees grew around the river, but it looked like the wildlife had already gotten to them.

"She's great. She's younger than me, very pretty, very wild. And she is brilliant, working on her Ph.D. in mathematics. If she wasn't my sister, I could really learn to hate her," she joked. "We missed spending time together and she decided to come with me for moral support. She's a teacher so she has the summer off anyway. Trev is always up to his neck in work. They got married last year. Actually, she met

Trev at my wedding." The last words were said on a tone slightly different from the rest.

He shook the water out of his boots, scraped off the river mud. "Do you miss your ex?"

She gave him a small, wry smile. "No. I still see him from time to time. Trev and he are close friends." She thought for a moment. "I miss the idea of true love, that it's supposed to last forever through thick and thin. I mean, I know now that the whole thing is just a fantasy. A couple is just two people, and people change, and sometimes they change in different directions. I guess I miss the innocence of believing that happily-ever-after is possible. My parents are divorced. I always swore that would never happen to me. I hate failing."

He could understand that sentiment. Brian shook out his pants and put them back on. "My father used to say romance was invented by greeting card companies and Hollywood to sell merchandise."

Pain was real, as was violence, the old man had said, and the struggle for survival. There were hormones and pheromones, and good old-fashioned primal sexual instinct, but that was all. Everything else was just stuff people deluded themselves into believing.

His parents had cared for each other and that made for a decent marriage and a fine home for him. But whatever their marriage had been before his father had gone off to war, it was certainly no passionate love affair after. The war had changed him, he used to say. It had changed both of them.

"Here we go."

Her leeches fell off almost at the same time as most of his, and she skipped to step away from them. She reached for the spot on her skin, but he stopped her. "Let it bleed for a while. The blood will cleanse the wound. It'll stop on its own."

He nudged the last leech on his shoulder, and when it let go, he put on his shirt, just as Audrey finished buttoning hers.

"Aren't you worried about blood loss?" She looked at him.

"A handful of leeches don't take enough to be concerned over."

"They're still nasty." Her voice was thick with revulsion.

"We better get going. We have to find a place to camp before nightfall. Tomorrow's gonna be a rough day. But if we keep a good pace, we'll be at Hamid's camp by tomorrow night."

She nodded and followed him without complaints. They walked upriver, at enough distance from the muddy bank to avoid leaving tracks and keep out of the dense undergrowth that grew there. He cut back to the water only twice, to remove the two vine ropes from the palms and toss them into the river.

Something about those guerillas didn't sit right with him. They might yet come back to look for the poachers. He didn't want them to find his and Audrey's tracks instead.

FIRE MADE all the difference. The smoke repelled the bugs, the heat kept the chill of the night at bay. Audrey picked the last of the meat off the fish bones. Compared to the bitter roots they had existed on all day, the meal seemed like an extravagant treat. Thanks to Brian.

He sat across from her, engrossed in making more hooks from bone. His clothes were drying on the bushes, side by side with hers. Since it wasn't raining for once, they were aiming for a dry night with dry clothes and some sleep in comfort. Their boots hung upside down, speared on three-foot-tall sticks to keep them off the ground and away from bugs. Brian had sprinkled the perimeter of their small camp with ashes to keep crawling insects away. Ants hated ashes, apparently, as did a number of their other bugsy friends.

If you had to be stuck in the jungle, this was the man to do it with. Audrey stood to stretch her legs, her eyes straying to his shoulders, the way the firelight played on the muscles that flexed when he put pressure on his knife. His hands were steady. She only remembered seeing them shake a couple of times today. Amazing what two days of freedom did to the man.

He was transforming slowly, in front of her eyes. He was moving better, his legs getting accustomed to walking. Even his gestures and the way he carried himself were changing. She could have sworn he had grown taller, although it was probably an illusion. He was walking straighter, his body growing used to being free from the confines of the cage.

"How old are you?" she asked, then regretted it. The question would probably make him think of the years he'd lost. "You don't have to answer. Never mind."

"What's today?"

She left the hotel a week ago. "The seventh. August," she added.

He raised his gaze to her, his expression inscrutable. "I turned thirty-one last month."

She stared at him. "I'll be thirty-one this fall."

They were the same age. It drove home the horror he must have been living in the past couple of years. When she had first seen him, she had thought him old enough to be her father. Even now— She would have definitely not guessed him to be thirty-one.

It wasn't his body—that looked powerful, ageless. She let her gaze slide over the wide shoulders again and the well-muscled arms, the flat stomach, then glanced away when she got to his underwear—if it could be called that—the handmade piece was little more than a loincloth.

The illusion of age came from the ever-present shadow on his face, and in his brilliant blue eyes. Eyes that said they'd seen too much.

She'd glimpsed eyes like that before at the clinic, seen the men and women who had tried to escape their memories by hiding behind drugs or alcohol. Half the people she'd admitted had had some history of severe trauma, physical or sexual abuse, rape, war. A handful of veterans were in residence at any given time.

Brian fed the fire.

Where would his past take him? He had such a strength, not just of his body, but a steel core inside.

He met her gaze, and she looked away.

She shook their clothes out, turned them on the branches to bring the wet sides closer to the fire. A wad of crumpled papers fell out of his pocket. "What's this?"

"Probably Omar's shopping list. It got wet before I had a chance to read it. I can read words here and there. None of it makes any sense. I kept them to use as tinder, but they never had a chance to dry out."

"Do you speak Malay?"

He nodded. "I picked up some over the years."

She flipped through the pages, her gaze settling on what looked like numbers. She pulled closer to the

fire. If she looked at it from just the right angle...
"There's a date here."

"Yeah?" Brian went back to carving, not looking too excited.

"August ten."

"Maybe he was asking Hamid to a meeting, although—" He set the hook aside and reached for the papers.

"What?"

"The guerillas don't exactly schedule like businessmen. It's always *in a few days,* or *after the monsoon.* They have a different sense of time here in the jungle. Giving or taking a day doesn't matter much. Hell, most of the time they probably don't even know what day it is."

"What's KL?" She scrutinized the paper over his shoulder.

"Where?"

She pointed.

"Damn."

"What?"

"I thought it was a blotch. KL is what the locals call Kuala Lumpur, the capital. Nobody but tourists say the full name."

He riffled through the pages. Silence stretched to a minute, then two.

"Are you thinking what I'm thinking?"

He turned to look at her. "The crate in the boat."

She nodded.

"Maybe the guerillas didn't shoot at the poachers because they couldn't risk return fire."

"Makes sense if the crate was full of explosives."

"Or maybe they were just in a hurry to get somewhere."

She tilted her head. "Kuala Lumpur, August tenth?"

He came to his feet and put on his pants. "When we get to Hamid's camp, we'll radio it in. "

"Do you think they're planning an attack?"

"A couple of days ago, I would have said no. Going after civilians wasn't Jamil's M.O. and Hamid wouldn't have done something this major without his support. But now…" He shrugged. "Omar is just hotheaded and bloodthirsty enough. He wants to make a name for himself. He wants to bring the fight to the next level. He probably has some kind of an agreement with Hamid. It makes sense." He stared into the fire, his expression pensive.

"This is major, isn't it?"

He nodded. "There've been changes. Talk. I don't know—a feeling around camp. Too much coming and going. I knew something was up, but I thought it was just Omar, trying to figure out a way to get himself to the top. If we are right and there's an attack planned in KL, it could be just the opening act. Omar and Hamid are both in on it. What if the others are, too? What if this is the beginning of a major offensive?"

"We have to let someone know."

"We can't be still in the jungle when it happens, that's for sure. I have a feeling the Royal Malaysian Air Force will retaliate by bombing the hell out of this patch of the island."

She checked her clothes, found them dry and put them on, except for the socks. Brian had warned her to let her feet breathe at night.

It said something about the man that he took care to explain the smallest things to help her avoid discomfort. He had been giving her a crash course on jungle survival as they'd walked, giving her his vote of confidence that she would remember and could handle things. Instead of treating her like a clueless burden, he related to her as an equal—a teammate. She appreciated that.

"So what do we do now?" she asked.

"Get as much sleep as we can, then start out at first light. Hamid probably has a satellite phone or radio. We'll call in what we know."

# Chapter Six

The rain had started toward dawn and forgot to stop. Although they kept close to the river, there was no point trying to get a fish for lunch—lighting a fire was out of the question. They ate grubs and whatever fruit they could find as they walked, boots sticking in the mud.

Starting midafternoon they started to check the water's edge more and more often, fighting the dense vegetation to get to it. Then they came across the spot they were looking for—a narrow area where the bushes had been cleared. Brian looked over the two motorboats pulled up on shore.

He watched the trail from the cover of the bushes, and when he was certain it was deserted, turned back to Audrey, who squatted behind him.

"I have to go check out the camp while there's still daylight to see."

She rose, ready to follow him wherever he would lead her. Her blind trust in him was gratifying and frightening at the same time. What the hell was he supposed to do with her? She'd be in danger if she came with him and she'd be in danger if he left her here alone. There was no safe spot for an untrained civilian in the jungle.

"What's wrong?" She blinked away the raindrops that clung to her eyelashes, squinting, puzzled at his hesitation.

She looked like a drowned mouse. She looked gorgeous. He'd had beautiful women at one time in his life, although his relationships had tended to be as brief as they were few and far between. One girl had accused him of missing the bonding gene. She had been right. He barely remembered her, other than that she'd been fun-loving and easy.

"I can't believe we're finally here. We're going to get Nicky back today."

He nodded. There was nothing easy about Audrey Benedict.

He motioned to her to stick to him as he followed the trail at a distance from the forest.

Unlike Omar's camp, Hamid's was much bigger than just a clearing in the jungle. Shacks spread up the hillside, with a large steel-frame building dominating the landscape, a gray satellite dish on top outlined against the green background. He could see all manner of industrial equipment, rusting, overrun by vines, in the process of being reclaimed by the jungle.

"An abandoned mine," he whispered to Audrey, keeping behind the bushes as he eyed the structures. There was nobody outside, and he couldn't blame them, the rain was coming down pretty hard. He could see shadows moving in several windows. They were watching.

He tensed when the door of one of the sheds opened, but the man who came out sprinted to another building without looking their way.

"Come on." He kept low as he moved ahead, circling the camp. They had to get the layout before night fell.

"How many of them do you think there are?" Audrey kept close behind.

With everyone inside, it was hard to tell. The rain complicated things. From the size of the dozen or so huts, he figured about fifty men. Of course, half the huts might be empty or, on the other hand, there might be many more guerillas, hiding from the weather in some mine shaft. There could be an army underground, the mine could probably hold hundreds. But he didn't think so.

Hamid's men had visited Jamil from time to time. His impression was that their group was larger than the one that held him captive, but not by much.

"Four, maybe five dozen." He gave her his best bet, seeing no sense in sugarcoating things. Better for her to know what they were facing, better to be prepared for it.

"Do you think the hostages…" She looked at him, her voice rough with worry.

"I'm sure they're still alive. Hamid is a professional at this kind of thing. They're probably in little danger until the deadline is up tomorrow."

Even after that, the man wouldn't kill all of them. Just one or two to show everyone he was serious, then he would probably set another deadline for the rest. Brian judged the distance between the buildings, tried to see if there was a way to get into the big one without having to use the front door that was most likely guarded.

He had a feeling that's where the hostages were. Somewhere down the mine, not the most ideal location for a rescue operation—like going to fight a bear in his cave. Getting trapped would be all too easy, and Hamid's men would have the home advantage. They knew every tunnel, while he would be fighting blind.

And alone. No way was he going to take Audrey in there with him.

He moved on, memorizing the terrain, careful to note distances, the position of the huts. There was very little activity. If the men moved around more he could have gotten a better handle on their number, but everyone seemed content to stick out the miserable weather inside.

Dusk came on them fast.

"Let's go while we can still see." He backed away, not wanting to waste time with fumbling around in the dark.

Hamid and his men were in for the night. Time to start putting his plans in action. They went back to the river, using the trail this time, listening for anything suspicious.

"Help me with this," he said when they got to the spot they'd found earlier. He heaved against one of the motorboats, pushing it into the water.

"Where are we going?" Audrey gave it her best effort as always, and the boat slipped into the river with ease.

"Just down a little. Get in." He helped her, then pushed out the boat even farther before pulling himself over the side. He grabbed the pole lying in the bottom and used it to give the vessel direction.

"I want the boats somewhere where we can get to them quickly, somewhere they wouldn't be looking for them when they come after us." He didn't turn the motor on, but let the river carry them. "What does your sister look like?"

"She's my height, short blond hair, skinny. She works out like a banshee. You're not going to have to worry about her keeping up unless she's injured."

The last couple of words came out shaky.

"She's fine. Hamid treats his hostages well. To him they're merchandise. He'd want to keep them in sellable condition."

She didn't respond to that, and her silence got to him more than if she had thrown a crying fit. There were words, he was sure of it, that someone who knew them could have spoken to comfort her. But it wasn't him. It filled him with an impotent anger he recognized as useless, so he forced his mind back to the hillside, to the camp, planning his route and course of action.

When they got a good two hundred feet from the trail, he jumped out and pulled the boat to shore, pushing it up on the slick mud into the cover of the overhanging vines and bushes. They scratched the hell out of his hands, but he ignored the pain, a minor irritation compared to his leg that was torturing him at full throttle.

Darkness fell by the time they were done. Getting back into the water without being able to see what debris was coming at him would be a reckless move, but he didn't have a choice. He had to get the second boat. Even if, God forbid, not all of the hostages were able to make it this far, he couldn't leave that one for the guerillas to follow in.

"Stay here. I'll bring over the other boat." He handed Audrey the rifle. "You keep this."

He hated to leave her alone, remembering well what had happened the last time she'd been left with the gun to fend for herself. And she was probably remembering, too.

"Nobody goes outside in weather like this, especially not at night," he tried to reassure her.

He couldn't see her face, but could see enough of her silhouette to know she was straightening her spine. He smiled into the darkness. *That's my girl.*

"Be careful," she said.

He reached out, but stopped short of caressing her face, waved a lame farewell instead and turned into the woods. Rain pelted him from above, his progress slower than he would have liked on the muddy, slippery ground.

He thought of Audrey behind him and the hostages ahead, the lives that depended on him. How the hell did that happen? He wasn't sure if he was up for the task. He was a broken man, and not just his bad leg. He was way out of practice. It was too much responsibility, more than he was prepared for. Still, quitting wasn't in his nature. He had to try.

He reached the boat, pushed it into the water

and floated down the swollen river with a fair
speed. The darkness was complete, he was going
by feel. Then he heard the most fake birdcall he'd
ever heard in his life. And a minute later he heard
it again. He grabbed the pole and pushed the boat
toward the sound, letting Audrey guide him to a
safe landing.

"You're a regular nightingale. Any other hidden
talents?" He jumped out, and she was right there,
helping.

"I can wiggle my ears." She pulled on the boat.

The woman wasn't afraid of work, that was for
sure. Come to think of it, she wasn't afraid of much.

"Did you run into any trouble?" she asked.

"Not yet. But I have a feeling I'll be coming across
some soon." He tied the second boat to a nearby palm
tree, next to the first. He wasted no time, but climbed
the palm and hacked off a good pile of leaves.

"I want you to stay here," he said after he skidded
down. "Cover the boats so they don't fill up with
rain." He could have turned them over, but he wanted
them to be ready to jump in, had a feeling they would
be leaving in a hurry. "Keep the gun. Don't be afraid
to use it."

This time when he reached out, he did touch her,
drew his crooked index finger over her wet cheek. "If
I'm not back by daybreak, get into one of the boats

and go downriver. Let the current float you, don't turn on the motor unless someone notices you and they give chase. Keep down. Make every bullet count."

"You need it more." She pushed the rifle toward him.

"It's not up for discussion," he said, and heard her long draw of breath.

"Okay."

She was smart enough to know that fighting over this would waste precious time.

"Do you want the bank statement?"

A second passed before he remembered what she was talking about. "Audrey, I'm not going there to negotiate."

He was bringing back all the hostages, or as many as he could, and he meant to push Hamid for an explanation of Omar's message. Although he had a date, Kuala Lumpur was a major metropolis. To prevent an attack, the government would need an exact location. Damn, it was a tall order—a tough operation he wasn't sure he was fit to attempt. But he was going to do it anyway.

The job was in his blood, trained into him—complete the rescue, save the weak. He had no fear for himself, no hesitation on that score, and he was glad to discover that here was at last some deep part of him that the guerillas didn't manage to take away, couldn't beat out. It was a fragment he recognized, something he could maybe build on to regain the rest.

She reached out a hand in the darkness and put it over his that somehow had come to cradle her face. "Be careful," she said again, with tremors in her voice this time.

That got to him. She was scared, and there was little he could do to protect her. He couldn't be in two places at the same time. He should have been able to offer some reassurance and comfort, but saying "you'll be fine" just didn't seem enough.

He stepped forward and enfolded her in his arms awkwardly, the gun between them. "I'll be back for you," he said, surprised at his own reluctance to move away.

She leaned her forehead against his chin. "I know."

It would have been the most natural thing to press his lips against the crown of her hair, but he couldn't do it. Instead, he walked away.

His mind was full of her, every cell of his brain, all his senses. His nose was full of her wet scent, her last words still ringing in his ears. God, he was pitiful. Thinking about her instead of what he was about to do was a surefire way of getting them both killed.

The mission. He refocused his mind, alert once

again as he moved forward in the jungle. He could barely see a foot or two in front of him, any noise an enemy might have made was drowned out by the rain. He was deaf and blind, in enemy territory, without as much as a gun. But he wasn't unarmed. He'd been a soldier an awful long time. He had his instincts.

He kept close enough to the river to let the sound of the water guide him, then once he reached the trail that led to camp, he followed that. He moved off it just before he reached the hillside camp, creeping forward slowly. Not that he was too concerned about running into anybody, but he was concerned about taking a wrong step and rolling down into a ravine, sinking into a rabbit hole and breaking a leg.

He reached camp after a couple of minutes. Lights shone in the windows, except for one shack. He kept in the shadows and stole closer to that one. He peeked in through the cracks in the wall, not wanting to put himself in line with the window. Just because the light wasn't on, it didn't mean nobody was in there.

But he lucked out. He could see the outlines of two people inside, both lying down. They were silent and unmoving. Good. He crept to the door, tried it. Unlocked. Which meant the two weren't hostages. He opened the door a fraction of an inch at a time then ducked inside, waited until his eyes further adjusted to the darkness.

He put his hand over the mouth of the first guerilla, his knife to his throat. The man woke with a start and grabbed for his wrist. Definitely not a hostage then, his hands hadn't been tied. Brian slit the man's throat and moved on to the other one.

When he was done, he tucked the man's handgun into his waistband, threw the two rifles over his shoulder. He pocketed the box of matches from the table on the way out.

He moved on to the next shack, looked inside. Four men there, playing cards, their guns within easy reach. He could have picked them off with a rifle, but didn't yet want to alert the whole camp to his presence. He waited, ducked deeper into the shadows when the door of another hut opened, then moved forward, keeping an eye on the fighter outlined by the hut's light. The man fumbled with his pants.

Damn. The guy was just taking a piss. He had hoped the fighter was on his way to another hut. But with the door open behind him, Brian couldn't take him out. He would have been in plain sight of everyone inside. Then someone in the hut swore, complaining about the rain blowing in, and the door slammed shut.

He was there in seconds. He held the man so he

wouldn't make a noise when he fell, dragged the body into the bushes in the back.

He risked a peek through the window that was partially obscured by vines. Two people remained inside. He could handle that. He left the rifles outside, put on the dead man's hat and shirt, stepped into the hut with his head down, one hand clutching the front of the blood-soaked shirtfront. The men came to their feet at once and stepped toward him, talking over each other. Both hands moving simultaneously, he cut the one on the right, and had his fingers wound around the throat of the one on the left. A minute passed before the guy stopped kicking.

Brian blew out the light, not wanting anyone to see the three dead bodies on the floor should they walk by outside. He discarded the bloody shirt, grabbed whatever weapons he could find, then moved on to the next hut.

Empty. He filled his pockets from the crate of hand grenades he found. He moved from hut to hut and did his job methodically. Search and destroy. The fighters that came at him ceased to be people. They were enemy combatants.

He pushed on until everything that he could do in silence had been done, then dumped his loot of weapons into the bushes, keeping one rifle and one handgun. Only four of the huts had guerillas in them now, each having more men inside than he could have handled without breaking the silence—nineteen altogether. He would worry about them on the way out.

Time to find the hostages.

He moved toward the main building that at one point must have been the entrance to the mine. There were a number of abandoned mines on Borneo; the island used to be rich in both tin and gold. He'd been in three of them within the first days his team had been dropped into the jungle—before he'd gotten blown up and captured.

Brian reached the corner of the tattered building and crawled under the raised floor, on his back in the mud, ignoring the insects that crawled over him, hoping none of them was fatally poisonous, praying he wasn't crawling into a nest of snakes. He pushed forward slowly, inch by inch, giving whatever lived under there time to get out of his way.

He could see the space above through the cracks in the bamboo floor. Six men—two sleeping, the rest talking. They were complaining about the weather. There were plenty of weapons in sight, each man's rifle within easy reach. He scanned the room, his attention settling on the table, on the pot of rice and pile of bones. His stomach growled, and he tensed, but nobody seemed to have heard him. He turned his head, spotted an opening that looked like it led to a tunnel at the back of the building. There we go. The way to get into the mine.

He crawled from under the building with the same careful deliberation as when he'd gotten in, brushed the bugs off and crept to the hut with the most guerillas in it. The five men were still up, arguing, cleaning weapons. Brian pulled the ring from one of the grenades and shoved it under the raised floor, dashed toward the bushes by the main building.

The explosion shook the hillside and brought plenty of men running, those who were still alive in the other huts and the six from the main building. He ducked inside, noted the large case of explosives by the door, hid behind a bed as he heard boots on stone—more men running up from the mine. He counted eight of them. When they were gone, he grabbed a flashlight and entered the shaft.

The floor was steep. He ran, putting his weight on the front of his feet to make as little noise as possible. Then he heard sounds ahead, nearing, and he ducked into a side passage and let another group of men pass. He didn't want to get into a gunfight yet, didn't want to alert those who guarded the hostages that he was coming. How many guerillas were still down there? Where were the tourists?

Finding them quickly was key. He had to get them up to the surface before the men in the camp above realized he was down here. He didn't like the explosives they had. It would be too easy to collapse the main tunnel and trap everyone below, buried alive.

He rushed forward and came to a door, solid metal. For a moment he considered a grenade to throw off the men on the other side, give him a chance to take a couple out before they got their bearings. But he still didn't know where the hostages were. He couldn't risk harming them. They could be hidden somewhere deep in the myriad tunnels, or they could be just on the other side of this door. The latter would be nice. He didn't have much time to look for them.

He kicked the door open, rifle raised in front of him.

And found himself face-to-face with Hamid and twenty of his men, armed to the teeth.

THE RAIN WAS COMING DOWN pretty hard, the river was rising. Audrey couldn't see it, but she'd had to move back three times now when the water reached her feet.

Had Brian made it to the camp yet? She strained her ears for the sound of gunfire, but couldn't hear anything. It seemed impossible that he would succeed. She'd seen the camp. The force he would meet would be overwhelming. She shouldn't have dragged him into this. She had sent him into sure death.

He had insisted on helping her. What pushed him forward? What made him override the instinct of self-preservation in the interest of others? She wondered if he regretted ever having met her. If it wasn't for her, he would have been halfway out of the jungle by now.

And then it occurred to her that they hadn't simply "met." He had saved her, choosing to risk his own freedom, his own life. He had made the decision selflessly, expecting nothing in return.

Despite his battered appearance, there was a strength in the man as she had never seen before. Tremendous courage, and yet vulnerability, too. And as little as they knew each other, she felt herself respond to him.

She kept her hands on the ropes that held the boats. One of the lines moved, grew taut. The water was high enough to lift that boat. The rope held, but she worried.

She planted her boots firmly in the muddy ground and pulled, managed to make some progress, felt as the bottom of the boat scraped into the mud, but no matter how much she struggled, she couldn't get it out of the water. The second she relaxed her arms, the water took the boat again, and when it did, the side banged against a rock a few feet ahead of her. *Bang.* She yanked at the rope, but the river had the boat now. *Bang. Bang. Bang.*

She waded into the water, wanting to put herself between the boat and the rock, to at least keep it quiet, keep from being discovered. She grabbed the

side of the other boat for support, and felt it wobble.
The water was taking this one, too.

*Bang. Bang. Bang.*

She couldn't let both boats slip into the water. She
wasn't sure how long the ropes would hold, how
long the palm tree would make it once the river was
high enough and the current and debris started to
push against the trunk. She took off her rifle and
threw it inside, grabbed the hull and pulled with everything she had, made some progress, infuriatingly
slow, but the boat did slide forward, inch by miserable inch.

*Bang. Bang. Bang.*

She pulled until her shoulders ached, until she
was breathing hard, sweat mixing with rain on her
face. But she got the boat to higher ground, untied
its rope from the palm tree and tied it up again to a
tree a couple of yards farther into the woods.

She waded into the water for the other boat, got
in up to her chest before she reached it and realized
she could do little. She had to untie it, let it move past
the rock and tie it up again. Pulling it out of the water
at this stage was beyond her strength.

Using the rope to guide her, she made her way
back to the palm tree, fighting against the might of
the river that tried to take her with it. Nothing else
mattered now but the next step, the next few inches

to grab onto the rope. She lost track of time, concentrating on her footing, making her aching arms work harder than she'd ever thought they could.

She reached the palm and found it standing in water now, the rope just below the surface. She tore at the swollen fibers but couldn't untie it.

*Bang. Bang. Bang.*

She had to do something. They were too close to camp. The rain dampened sound, but the clanging of the aluminum boat against the rock was just loud enough so she couldn't be sure how far it would be heard.

She wrapped her left arm around the rope, grabbed on, then with her right arm pulled her knife and sawed through the knot. The next instant the current caught the boat and it lurched forward, pulling her into the water. She fell face first, went under.

Freed finally, the boat was dragging her out into the deep water. It would drag her on, drown her, if she weren't careful. She came up sputtering but refused to let go. She had lost her knife and hung on to the rope with both hands now. But her strength was no match for the raging river.

She went under again, came up, coughing up water, struggling for air. She had only one choice, one thing to do if she wanted to live. She had to let go of the boat.

Tears stung her eyes as she relaxed her fingers and felt the rope slip from her. She struggled to reach shore, got knocked under by a jumble of branches rushing downriver, but she got back up again. Nicky was out there somewhere, and Brian. And they needed her, counted on her. She had to make it.

She'd lost her hat. Rain pelted her hard from above. She could see little to begin with, the water running into her eyes making things worse. She could make out land, just barely, only because the sky was a miniscule fraction darker above it then above the river.

*Swim.*

*One hand in front of the other.*

Her boots were pulling her down, but she kicked wildly, refusing to give up. She had to make it. It wasn't just her life at stake. Others counted on her.

She went under, fought her way up again, coughed up the nasty tasting water. *Kick. Left arm. Right arm. Breathe.*

She wasn't making any progress, nothing but exhaustion to show for her efforts. Then she remembered Brian's words when they'd crossed the river before, and she flipped on her back, swam for shore at an angle.

She was shaking with fatigue by the time she reached shore and collapsed onto the muddy bank, letting the rain wash over her face.

She had lost the boat. Their way to safety.

It was one thing for Brian and her to try to walk out of the jungle. Taking a dozen hostages with them on foot, some of whom might be sick or injured, was another matter. How on earth would they find food for so many people? They had barely found enough by scavenging as they went, to feed the two of them.

An explosion shook the air, coming from the direction of the hillside camp. Brian was out there, fighting guerillas, and she had his gun. Even if by some miracle he succeeded and brought the hostages with him here to their meeting point, one boat would not carry them all. Half of them would be trapped between the river and the pursuing guerillas.

She had to go and warn him.

Her teeth were chattering, her wet clothes pasted to her body, chilling her in the night air. Or was she getting some kind of fever? Didn't matter, couldn't worry about that now. The shakes probably came from the shock of having nearly drowned.

Audrey pulled herself up and dragged her exhausted body forward, feeling around in the dark. She had to find the remaining boat and the gun, and then she had to find Brian.

## Chapter Seven

Brian ignored the rifles pointed at him and kept his on Hamid. "Give me the hostages. You're not going to get the money anyway. You took too many this time, foreigners. The government has gotten involved."

He scanned the room, if the place could be called that, walls carved from rock, the crates that stood in for furniture, his eyes hesitating briefly on the only other exit.

"The government doesn't know its head from its ass." The leader seemed calmer than his men, his words slow, deliberate. He had a handgun tucked into his waistband, but he hadn't reached for it. An elaborate tattoo decorated his arm—a leaping tiger with a crown on its head.

"The army has you surrounded." If there ever was a time to bluff, this was it.

The man paused, his small brown eyes watching Brian sharply. "Why aren't they here?"

"I'm here. I'm the negotiator." And the recon team, the main force, and the backup.

"An American?" Hamid said the words with derision and made a dismissing motion with his hand.

But as relaxed as he seemed, tension was thick in the air. Brian looked at the men, making eye contact with one after the other, trying to determine which ones were scared, which ones were angry, if any of them might get nervous enough to shoot without waiting for an order from the boss.

When he turned back to Hamid, he made sure his voice was calm and even. "You kidnapped some Americans. Our governments are working together. Let the tourists go, they don't matter to you. Why die for them? Stay alive to fight for your cause."

Silence followed his words, the sounds of gunfire barely filtering down to where they were. Hamid's men were probably firing blindly into the jungle, but their panicked incompetence played right into Brian's hands, making it sound as if a good-sized battle raged above.

Hamid tapped his fingers on his gun belt. "What's in it for me?"

Brian relaxed a little. Good. The man was willing to negotiate. "They'll treat you like a political prisoner instead of a criminal."

The man laughed. "One prison is the same as the other. If I let the tourists go free, I go free, too."

Brian shook his head, determined to play out his ruse. "Not gonna happen." If he offered something that was too good to believe, Hamid would become suspicious. They stared at each other for a while before he spoke again. "The army came up the river by boat. No place to land a helicopter around here."

"So?"

"They'll have to take you back to the river. It's the middle of the night. If you run into the jungle, they will never find you."

The man thought on that for a while. "Why are you telling me this?"

"I don't care what happens to you. I get the American hostages home alive, my government will be happy with me, I get a promotion, the wife will be happy. End of story."

Hamid watched him closely. "I could give you a promotion."

Yeah, he probably could. He probably had money stashed away to finance his projects. "No can do, man. I'm the negotiator. I came down here, I have to come up with hostages."

"You don't look like a negotiator." Hamid glanced at his worn clothes.

"I got pulled off another job. Didn't have time to

go home and change." He smiled at the man. "It's not your regular nine-to-five type of work. You should understand."

Hamid waited, looked him over again, shook his head. "I don't believe you."

It would have been too easy, Brian thought a split second before the guerilla leader nodded to his men, and all hell broke loose.

Brian ducked behind a metal desk, clipped Hamid in the shoulder on the way. The man went down. Brian let some bullets fly then took cover again. A couple of the men were helping Hamid escape, the rest were shooting back. But Brian was the better shot. He had the room under control in five minutes.

He kicked in the door in the back of the room, grabbed a flashlight, ran down the mineshaft. The hostages were a good three-hundred feet in, tied arms and legs, six Westerners, four Japanese, two Indian and an Orang Ulu man—a local tribesman Brian figured must have been their tour guide. Brian cut the ropes off him then handed him the knife to free the rest while he looked around, hoping to find another way to exit the mine. Nothing. The other end of the shaft was closed in.

"Which one of you is Nicky?" he asked when he stepped back to the hostages.

A petite blond stood up by the wall. He ran the

flashlight over her face. She was Audrey's sister all right, same eyes, same determined set of the mouth.

"Your sister loves you very much," he told her, then helped the last person shrug off his ropes. "Let's go, people."

They followed him into the large room where he had fought with Hamid's men. Some of the women sobbed at the sight of the bodies that littered the floor. He didn't have time to worry about them.

"Everyone who knows how to shoot a gun, grab one," he said and riffled through the desk, stuffed handfuls of papers into his shirt before moving on.

He went ahead to check out the main building, but found it empty. Not for long. Soon Hamid's men would figure out there was no army shooting back from the forest and they would come back for him.

Except someone *was* shooting back. He stilled. Through the window, he caught a glimpse of a flash of gunfire that came from the bushes, directed toward camp. What the hell?

*Audrey.*

It had to be her. What the hell was she thinking?

She was no coward, and he liked that about her, but she had to learn to obey orders from a team leader when she was in a team operation. And he was the team leader here, damn it.

"Let's go. Keep down, get away from this building as fast as you can, too much explosives in here. Go to the right, into the jungle, and wait for me." He turned to the Orang Ulu man. "You take care of them. Don't leave."

"No, sir."

"What can I do?" One of the American men stepped forward, rifle in hand. He didn't seem happy that Brian had given lead to a mere native.

"You follow him." Brian jerked his head toward the tribesman. "Keep quiet, make sure everyone stays together. Your life depends on it."

"I'll take care of them. Don't worry about it. Those sons of bitches out there have it coming—"

"Your job is not to get revenge on the guerillas. You just focus on staying alive. Got it?" He waited until the man reluctantly nodded.

He scanned the rest of the group, noted who took weapons and who didn't. "Don't shoot unless you're shot at. Otherwise you'll just draw attention to yourselves," he told them, and hoped to hell they were paying attention.

The night and the rain made for poor visibility, working in their favor. Brian killed the light then stepped outside. Using up the hand grenades in his pocket, he covered for the hostages until they disappeared into the trees. Then he headed for Audrey. Damn it. He'd told her to stay put. Now he had to get her and scatter the remaining guerillas before he could come back to use the radio.

He crouched and just began to cut across the clearing when a group of men came around the side of the building, guns blazing. He threw himself on his stomach and did the best he could, but was nowhere near cover. Bullets slammed into the ground around him. Hard to shoot back without risking hitting the building—he was too close. If the explosives blew, he had a better than good chance he would blow with them.

He crawled backward, using careful aim. Then someone from behind him sprayed the men with bullets, and the next second he was blinded and deafened by a ground-shaking explosion.

He felt a pair of hands on his ankles, somebody pulling him toward the jungle. The gunfire had stopped.

"Audrey?" He twisted onto his back.

She let go of his legs and reached for his hands to help him up. "Are you okay?"

He nodded.

"Did you find Nicky?"

"She's waiting for us in the forest with the rest." He grabbed her and dragged her into the woods, into the cover of one of the larger trees, then leaning against the trunk crushed her to him, holding her for a long moment, feeling her heart beat against his chest. She was unharmed. Alive. "What the hell are you doing here?"

She lifted her head, hesitated before responding. "The river took one of the boats."

AUDREY CRINGED. She should have done more, fought harder against the river. Their lives depended on their ability to get away. But under the considerable guilt, a current of joy spread through her veins, and hope. Nicky was alive and free.

"The other one?" Brian asked as he moved forward carefully.

What? Oh, the other boat. "I pulled it to higher ground. The water is rising fast." She kept close behind him.

"Must be raining even harder up the mountain."

"Did you radio for help?"

He didn't say anything for a while. "You blew up the radio."

Oh, God. First the boat and now the radio.

He swore under his breath.

She waited for him to yell at her, to tell her she had practically sentenced them all to death. But instead, he stopped, raising his hands to signal for her to do the same.

She listened, but couldn't hear anything over the rain.

"Don't shoot," he called out.

The next second bullets flew into the trees a few feet to their left.

He pushed her down, flattened her into the mud, half-covering her with his body. The forest fell silent. "Don't shoot," he said again, his voice clipped with anger.

There was some scuffle ahead, people talking.

"Nicky," she said, hope making her voice thick.

And she could see a shadow separate from a tree, and heard her name called and she was on her feet, rushing forward into her sister's arms, the rain washing away her tears as fast as they formed. "Nicky."

"How did you get here?"

"Are you all right?" They spoke at the same time.

"Did they hurt you?" she asked, holding her breath until Nicky shook her head.

Brian was right there. "We have to move out."

And she could see the rest of the people now, the darker shapes in the dark of the jungle, coming forward one after the other.

"What the hell did you think you were doing?" Brian was chewing out one of them.

"Hey." The man stood his ground, not bothering to keep his voice down. "You sent us into the jungle. We didn't know if you were coming back or not. I have the right to defend myself, same as everybody."

Brian was silent. Ominously so. He was close

enough so she could feel the anger radiate from his body. Audrey detangled herself from her sister and stepped between the two men. "We have to get going."

"He could have killed you," Brian said.

She'd never heard his voice so tight. "I'm fine. Everyone is fine."

He stepped away. "Follow me closely, watch where you step, it's slippery. Make as little noise as possible. There are still plenty of guerillas out there," he told the group, then turned and started out.

Nicky came up behind her and took her hand. Audrey squeezed it, as they followed him.

"Who is he?" her sister asked close to her ear.

"Some kind of special forces," she whispered back. "He saved my life, Nicky. He saved all of us."

"He's scary."

She smiled. She'd had the same first impression of him. It seemed a lifetime ago. She shook her head in the darkness. "He is a hero."

"Where's Trev?"

"He sent the money. He's probably in the country by now. I didn't wait for him. I was so scared, Nicky," her voice broke off.

"I'm glad you came. Your guy is more help in this situation than mine would be, anyhow."

My guy? she thought, but for once, she didn't

mind being teased by her little sister. Over the last week or so, she had regretted every time she'd yelled at her when they were growing up for stealing her clothes or makeup, every time she'd been mean to her, made fun of her. God, it was good to have her back again.

The rain was easing off. It stopped completely by the time they reached the water. The moon was out over the river, giving some visibility at last.

Brian was going for the boat. The water had lifted it while she'd been gone, but the rope had held.

One of the men came forward. "Where is the rest of the rescue team?"

She recognized his voice. He was the same guy who'd sparred with Brian before.

"This is it." Brian wrapped the rope around his arm and pulled the boat in, fought with the current. A couple of the other men went to help him.

"You gotta be kidding me. Is that the only boat?" The troublemaker was working up his righteous anger.

"Yep." Brian heaved.

"We won't all fit. I demand that my wife and I get on." He raised his rifle without pointing it at Brian, but making his meaning clear. "If anyone should stay behind it's you. Our taxes pay your salary."

She moved forward, knowing what was coming,

but too late. The next second, the man was on his back in the mud, the rifle in Brian's hands.

"Take it easy, buddy." One of the men who was helping with the boat came over and spoke to the one on the ground. "He saved our lives. We need to thank him, shut up and do what he says."

The guy sat up, looking taken down a peg or two. He had wanted to take leadership of the group, probably. And he knew he wouldn't now. The rest wouldn't follow.

"Listen to me, all of you," Brian said. "There is a fair chance that we can all make it out of here, but it's not going to be easy. You are going to have to pull together. If you don't, you'll end up your own worst enemy. Two rules to remember—don't fight each other, don't fight the jungle."

He stepped back to the boat, tightened the rope.

Audrey moved over to him. "What are we going to do?"

He shook his head, and for the first time she saw something close to defeat in his eyes. And it scared her, more than anything had scared her so far.

"Not much until morning. Nobody can navigate this river in the dark. I was thinking about putting the weakest in the boat at first light. The rest of us can make it on foot." He shook his head.

"What's wrong with that plan?"

"Those who are too weak to walk, would be too weak to handle the boat the way the river is now. And it's dangerous. Guerillas use the river. There are rapids. They would need me with them."

"Then go."

"The people in the forest need me, too. And even if I go with the boat, we'll have to stop to rest, to eat. We're not going to make it to civilization before August tenth."

Oh, God, there was still that. Some kind of attack, possibly thousands of lives at stake. She had for a while forgotten about it in the joy of having Nicky with her, safe.

"You should go alone, that would be fastest." Resolve filled her, as the idea blossomed in her mind. "We'll stay and you'll send help. You taught me enough so I should be able to keep everyone alive for a couple of days. We have weapons. You can help us get to a cave then leave."

She wished she felt a tenth of the self-confidence that she forced into her words. "Or you could take the strongest of the men with you," she added when she thought of the perils of the river.

He looked at her as if she'd just given him a million dollars, kissed her on the lips, just like that, in front of everyone, and strode to the group of hostages, but not to the biggest and tallest men. He went to the shortest one.

"How far is your tribe?"

"A day's walk down the hillside," the man responded in a lilting accent.

"How big is it?"

"About fifty men."

"Friendly with the guerillas?"

The man spat on the ground.

"Would they protect these people until I send help?"

"They don't have much, but they would share. It's the way of the jungle. We have fine witch doctor."

"Will you take them there?"

"I owe you my life. I do what you tell me."

Brian hesitated for a moment, then nodded. "Listen up," he addressed the others as the first light of dawn crept across the sky above them. "Your guide will take you to his village. It's one day of walking, everybody can manage that. I'm going down the river and will send help as soon as I can."

The man who had given him trouble lurched forward. "You're taking the boat and leaving us behind?"

But he couldn't rile Brian. He was perfectly calm now. "Which would you rather do? Walk for a day led by a man who grew up in the jungle and knows more than any of us about surviving in it? Or spend five days on a river that's flooding out of control and is controlled by guerillas, a plain target in a small boat where anyone with a gun can pick you off from shore?"

The man made some noise, but backed down.

"When do we leave?" another one asked.

"Now. If you run into the official Malaysian rescue team, or anyone at all with a radio, you have to let the authorities know that there is a credible terrorist threat for Kuala Lumpur for the tenth of August. Given where you spent the last week or so, they're going to believe you."

Another man stepped forward and shook Brian's hand, and then more came with their thanks and handshakes, wishing him speed down the river, some asking him to send word to family if he got the chance. Audrey wanted to move forward to do the same, but Nicky was hanging on to her hand just as tight as she could.

"Is this a good idea?"

"There just isn't an alternative." She hugged her, still getting used to them being together, that Nicky was alive, unharmed.

"When did you get to be so tough?" Nicky asked when they pulled away. "I thought I was the family daredevil."

"Oh yeah, and look where going on a jungle tour got you."

"When we get home I'll be sticking to kiddy parks with stroller trails."

"Exactly. Don't make me have to come after you

again. You'll be an aunt soon. You're going to have to act responsible and dignified."

"Oh, man, you're kidding."

God, it was good to joke like that again. It made things feel a hell of a lot more normal, which they were still not. But the banter at least took some of the fright out of the night.

Brian sought her out at the end. "You'll be all right. I'll have the army up here in no time."

"You must take someone with you. You need someone to watch your back." The sudden worry about him going alone seemed ridiculous. If anyone knew what they were doing it was him. He had a vast knowledge of jungle survival. And still, she hated to see him go.

"I doubt any of the men would want to leave their wives." He ran his hand down her arm in a gesture of farewell. "And they wouldn't be much help anyway. They don't know anything about the jungle. I'd be watching out for them."

"Take me then," she said, and pulled away from Nicky. "You can't go alone. I know the jungle. You taught me. You'll need help with the boat."

"Audrey, no." Nicky pulled her back. "This is crazy."

She turned and gave her sister a fierce hug. "He saved my life, and yours. I can't let him go alone."

Nicky hugged her tighter, but after a while nodded against her shoulder and let her go. She glanced from her to Brian. "Why do I think I'm missing something here? You two are not—"

"I'll be fine." Audrey cut her off.

"Take care of yourself," Nicky said with a bittersweet smile. "Take care of each other."

"Will do. And you, too."

"A walk in the park." Nicky picked up the rifle Brian had taken from the man with the big mouth, slung it over her shoulder and gave Audrey an if-you-can-do-it-so-can-I look, that was way too familiar.

She shook her head as she hugged her one more time, then she turned to Brian. "I'm ready."

"You are not coming," he said, his voice hard, his face serious.

## Chapter Eight

How had this happened? Brian gripped the pole tight and, ignoring the rain, pushed a large chunk of drift-wood away from the boat, looking ahead, while Audrey scanned the river and the jungle for dangers behind them.

She was one determined woman. But to be truth-ful, he'd rather have her watch his back than anyone else. She was tough, had learned over the last cou-ple of days not to be squeamish, and pulled her own weight. And he knew her at least a little, more so than any of the men among the hostages. She had earned his trust.

They were on the way back. He felt lighter with the first half of their mission done. The hostages were reasonably safe. They had a good guide and good weapons.

"Do you think they'll reach the village safely?"

Audrey asked, her mind obviously running along the same lines as his.

"They should be fine. Hamid's men are probably nursing their injuries, holed up somewhere. If they think the army is in this part of the jungle, they are probably trying to hide."

"What does he want anyway? Him and Omar and the rest?"

He shrugged. "What do opposition forces always want? A change in government."

"To overthrow the monarchy?"

"Not quite. From what I heard over the years, Hamid figures himself to be some kind of a tragically overlooked heir to the throne. You should see the tattoo on his arm, a leaping tiger from wrist to elbow with a crown on his head."

"Kidnapping people—there's a real prince."

"He's raising money for a coup. And if he scares some foreigners out of the country at the same time, that's fine with him, too. He's a religious extremist."

"And Omar?"

"I don't think he much believes in their cause, and he doesn't follow any religion, that's for sure. He likes fighting. He wants power and since he doesn't have any under this government, he figures he might have better luck with the next, especially if he helps to bring it about."

He pushed some debris away from the boat, a bunch of branches and the bloated body of a young wild pig tangled up between them. He registered a moment of regret that the meat was too far gone to eat.

"They're halfway there," she said, and he knew she was thinking about Nicky.

"I can't believe you left your sister for me."

"I'm a known masochist. A glutton for punishment," she said in a dry voice.

"I thought maybe some kind of jungle fever addled your reasoning."

She turned a little, one perfect eyebrow cocked. "Ever considered you might be able to get more from a girl by sweet-talking than by calling her a lunatic?"

And his breath caught, as if someone had dropped a boulder on his chest. Because their conversation was so normal, so lighthearted, so not something he'd expected. It was almost as if she were flirting with him, sounding as if she wouldn't have minded at all if he tried to sweet-talk her.

God almighty. Did he still know how to sweet-talk? He felt like he just came across a field of landmines. And acting appropriately, he backed away.

"Your sister will be fine." He slid from the seat and sat on the bottom of the boat, ignoring the few inches of water. "Pull your head in. We're close to camp."

Audrey ducked down beneath the branches that

covered the boat on the side and on top, making it look like a tangled mass of a tree trunk broken off by the storm, floating downriver. They were in the middle of the water, letting the current carry them.

"Do you think they're watching the river?" She breathed the words.

"Not for us at this stage. We've been gone too long. But for flooding maybe. Omar's camp is not that far from here."

"But if the guerillas who ran off into the jungle last night got here before us—" she whispered.

"The boat is going a lot faster than anyone can in the jungle. Some will come to Omar without a doubt, but by the time they get here, we'll be far downriver."

He held his head up enough to see through the branches, keeping an eye out for driftwood, listening for anything suspicious, be it man-made noise or the sound of rapids ahead. He kept as low as he could. Their disguise was good enough to fool someone who happened to catch a glimpse of them from the corner of his eye, but would not stand up to closer scrutiny.

They cleared the area where Omar's men would have been if they were out there, but were slowed down shortly after that, coming to a stretch where the river widened out. The surface was littered with debris the water had washed down from the mountains.

Audrey directed the boat, while he used his pole to keep anything large from crashing into them—hard work for both of them. Night approached by the time they fought their way through the rough spot.

They pulled the boat to shore, up on higher ground as far in as they could, and turned it upside down to keep the rain from filling it, covered it with fallen leaves and branches.

"It's not bad from afar." Audrey stood back when they were done. "As long as nobody comes too close."

"There's less than an hour left before nightfall. Let's hope our luck holds." He moved forward.

"I'm starving," she blurted out. "Sorry, didn't mean to complain. Nothing you can do about it."

While their progress on the river was much faster than it would have been on land, it had disadvantages. Not being able to forage for food was one of them. He searched the trees above for any sign of fruit as they went. "We'll find something."

No time to fish now. He had to find a place to spend the night, light a fire, build a shelter. All that before darkness fell. But luck was with them for once—they came across a rock formation not a hundred feet from the river. There was a large indentation in the rock, not quite a cave, but a ledge that would protect them from the elements.

"Up there." He pointed, and helped Audrey climb.

Looked like they weren't the first to discover the place. Ashes blackened the rock floor farther in, left-overs of a long-ago fire. There were piles of leaves the wind had blown into the back of the crevice, a couple of chunks of deadwood left behind by who-ever had that fire. Enough to start one now.

"Here." He handed Audrey the waterproof matches he'd grabbed at the guerilla camp, then pulled the papers from his shirt. "Try to dry these."

He hadn't had a chance to look at them yet, didn't want to get them any wetter than he had to.

"I'm gonna look for some food." He stepped back out into the rain that had turned into a downpour.

He didn't bother to look for grubs, there was no sense searching the muddy ground. He walked back toward the river and looked for palm trees, came across a patch of wild berries and settled for that, picked his shirt full of the small semi-soft fruit. They'd had a poor diet so far, one that they couldn't make it on in the long term, but sufficient to get them through the next couple of days.

He spotted something high up a tree, thought it might be fruit, climbed and found it to be orchids, a multitude of them, and on a whim, he filled the rest of the room in his shirt with blossoms.

AUDREY LAID the mess of soaked papers near the fire next to her clothes, close enough to dry fast, but not so close that they'd burn. She anchored them with a stone to make sure a gust of wind didn't blow them into harm's way.

"Anything useful on them?" Brian climbed up and sat next to her, dripped on the floor. He took off his hat and wiped the water off his face, brushed his hair back.

"Too soggy. Didn't think I could pull them all apart without tearing them. Probably better to wait until they dry."

He looked over the ones that were readable. Blueprints one after the other, but no writing on them, no identification of what building they belonged to. Only one of the sheets was different. It contained some kind of a scribbled list.

"Embassies." Brian picked up that one. "That's something. If we get to KL in time, this might be enough of a clue to head off tragedy." He set the sheet down and placed a stone on top carefully, before turning back to her.

She eyed his bulging shirtfront with hope. "Find anything?"

He looked embarrassed for a second, reluctant.

"What?"

He reached inside and scooped a giant handful of white-pink blossoms, then hesitantly laid them at her bare feet.

"Oh, my God, these are beautiful." She glanced up at him. "Are they edible?"

He laughed, the first real laugh she'd heard from him, and it reached to her heart. He scooped out another handful, then another. The light of the fire danced on the petals, a soft scent filling their small shelter.

"They are for you," he said. "For coming with me."

She stared at him, speechless, the gesture so sweet and unexpected she didn't know for a moment how to react. "Thank you," she said, and although she wanted to reach out to him, she didn't. He hadn't reacted well to that in the past.

But there was something in the orchid-scented air between them that hadn't been there before. It made her feel self-conscious of the fact that she wore nothing but her underwear and tanktop, even though it had not been the first time she'd taken off her clothes to dry, nor was it the least amount of clothes he'd seen her in.

"These are to eat." He brought forth handfuls of berries next, and she fell on them shamelessly.

When his shirt was empty, he took it off and laid it by the fire to dry, putting his pants next to it. She kept her gaze averted as she ate. There was a newfound awareness between them, she didn't know what to do with. At some point he had transformed from wild man to simply a man she was interested in. It was absolutely crazy. They knew nothing about each other.

"Where did you grow up?"

"Ladder, a very small town. My father worked for the post office. My mother was a homemaker."

She deleted the cowboy image she'd been trying to put together. It never quite gelled anyway. "You never told me your full name."

He held her gaze, his masculine lips stretching into a wry smile. "Old habits die hard. I don't suppose it matters now. Brian Welkins."

He'd been on some secret jungle mission before he'd gotten captured. She didn't ask more about that. But she did want to know more about him. She knew his parents were gone and that he'd been their only child, adopted.

"Are you married?" she asked as it suddenly occurred to her, her heart beating harder as she waited for his response.

"Come on now, you've known me long enough to know that no woman would be crazy enough to have me." He was joking, but there was a sour tone to his words.

"You're not missing much. Marriage isn't all it's cracked up to be."

"Can't say I've ever been tempted to give it a try."

She stirred the fire with a stick. If they could keep it going for a while longer, they would have dry clothes for sleeping.

"My parents got divorced when I was in high school. I was so mad at them. I wanted a real family again. I got married way too early, for all the wrong reasons. Even if we didn't have all that stress from not being able to have a baby, I doubt we would have lasted. We just would have floundered longer."

Silence stretched between them.

"The bugs got you." He reached out to trace a finger over the row of red bumps on her arm.

The blinding lust that hit her out of nowhere froze her limbs for a moment, knocked the air out of her lungs. He misunderstood her reaction and pulled away.

"It's okay," she said, then felt embarrassed.

*It's okay?* What was she, an idiot?

His blue gaze fastened on her face. "I don't want you to be afraid of me. I would never hurt you."

"I'm not afraid." She ran her own finger over the tingling line his left behind. "I just don't always know what to expect."

He nodded and gave her a rueful smile. "Me neither." He looked away. "I'm not like other people. I've been away too long. I want to be just a man, but I don't know if I can do it."

There was a tug in the vicinity of her heart. "You are everything any man could ever hope to be. You're a hero," she said when she recovered.

"I'm damaged. And I want things I cannot have."

From the way he was looking at her, she understood what he wanted, and her blood lurched into a sprint through her veins.

*What do I want?* She looked away and her gaze fell on the orchids at her feet. *Him.* She wanted him, scars and all.

He stretched out on his back, his hands folded behind his head, his eyes closed. She scooted over and lay next to him on her side, watched the rise and fall of his chest in the light of the fire. Even undernourished, he was the most physically perfect man she had known. The scars that marred his skin could not detect from the strength of his body, the beauty of the muscles that carried her up the trees and pulled her out of the river.

She touched a fingertip to a raised bump. "The bugs got you, too." Her finger glided on to the next and the one beyond that, zigzagging over his ribcage.

He placed a hand over hers, pressed her palm against his skin. His heartbeat raced as fast as hers did. She looked up and found his eyes open, his gaze heated. And then she was scared. Not of him, but of her own reaction. Because she wanted him, a stranger, more than she had ever wanted another man before, more than she had wanted her husband.

She looked away, only to be confronted with the proof of his desire under the stretching loincloth.

"Brian…" Her voice tripped.

"Let me touch you." He waited, giving her time to say no.

Instead, she closed her eyes.

She expected an intimate caress, his fingers circling her breasts, or outlining her aching nipples. But it was the back of his hand on her cheek that she felt. And when his fingers did come to play on her skin, he drew with them the line of her jaw, her eyes, her lips. He followed the curve of her neck, hesitated at the hollow spot there and replaced his fingers with his lips and tasted her. And when he pulled away, she opened her eyes and looked into his.

"You're seducing me," she said, feeling as if the heat of the fire had moved deep inside her.

"I would love that more than anything." His sexy lips stretched into a semblance of a smile. "If I still knew how."

"Hey." She grinned at him. "I might not be as experienced as the average teenager, but I still know when I'm being seduced."

He dipped his head to the valley between her breasts, until she could feel his hot breath through the thin material of the tanktop. "I'll let you be the judge of things then," he said.

He pressed his lips to her body, dragged them over her breast until his mouth was over a nipple, then he sucked it through the tanktop. She grew damp between her legs in response and arched her back, shameless, wanting all he was willing to give.

His fingers moved over her stomach and gripped her hips and he ground himself into her. The shock of it, the electricity that zinged through her, brought her to the edge. It was too much, too soon. She wasn't used to it. Her body didn't work at these speeds.

He pulled back and scooped up the flowers, held them above her then let them slip through his fingers one by one, raining white-pink blossoms over her body. He kept one, feathered the soft petals over her lips, her neck, across the narrow strip of skin that showed between her tanktop and panties, then moved lower and caressed the soles of her feet, drawing curlicues with the orchid up her inner thighs.

When he got where he was headed, he brushed the flower over her underwear a couple of times before tucking it into the band. She trembled as he pressed his hot palm against her.

In a circular motion he pushed and massaged, while he bent over and fastened his lips on her nipple, her clothes still between them. He changed the rhythm then, to slower strokes, up and down, then circular again, the heel of his palm against her opening, his fingers against her swollen nub of pleasure.

As he had pulled her up hillsides, and rocks and

trees to save her life, he pulled her now to the sky, higher and higher. And then his teeth closed over her nipple and she tumbled.

The first thing she could hear was her own harsh breathing, her body still contracting. She looked at his badly cut hair, his head resting between her breasts, her mind swimming in confusion as her body was still swimming in bliss. How could he so fast? What he had done to her? Was it even possible?

She still had her clothes on, he'd never even gotten as far as her naked skin, let alone having any part of him inside her. Sweet heavens. The man and the way her body had responded to him took her by surprise. He singed her, turned her inside out. She loved every second of it. Audrey reached for him and ran her fingers through his hair, caressed his back.

He pulled up and turned her with her back to him, locked her tight into his arms. His lips were pressed hot against her shoulder, but he didn't move them, didn't move anything, although she could feel his hard length against her bottom. There was a thrill in knowing that she affected him this way.

"Go to sleep," he whispered into her ear, brushing his warm lips over her lobe.

"Brian?" She tried to turn and found herself gently restrained. "You don't have to— I mean, I want to. I want you."

Lord, it sounded pitiful and shameless. Her body hadn't even fully calmed down yet, but she did want him, again, still. How could he not know that? Or was there more to it?

He had broken through all her defenses with amazing speed and ease. And now she realized he wasn't about to let her come anywhere near his. The mask was still firmly in place. Was he hiding from her, or from himself?

He pressed his lips to her skin again, then repeated, "Go to sleep."

And from the strain in his voice she understood what it cost him to rein in his own passion.

"Let me touch you, then."

He drew a deep breath. "Maybe another time."

"Tomorrow we might not be alive. You need me as much as I need you."

"I don't want you to give yourself to me because I need you. Not to escape from reality, not for pity."

"Pity has nothing to do with it." The fierce denial tumbled from her lips. She tried to turn again, frustrated by the arms that wouldn't let her. "It's not fair. It's not fair to either of us."

She could feel his heartbeat against her back, slow and measured. Hers, on the other hand, was still scrambling. His heat enveloped her, comforted her, and it made her mad that he wouldn't let her give the same comfort to him. "What reason would you accept? What do you want?"

He touched his forehead against the back of her head and stayed silent for so long, she didn't think he would respond at all.

"I don't know," he whispered, his voice raspy and full of emotion. "I no longer even know who I am."

THE ARMY was in the jungle.

Hamid leaned his back against the rough stone of the cave, trying to think through the throbbing pain in his shoulder. At least it was cool in here, although far from quiet. His men in the back made plenty of noise, arguing about the attack the night before and taking care of their injuries, cursing the Royal Malaysian troops.

For a moment back at the tin mine, he had been certain the negotiator was bluffing. But no, his own men came across a village messenger this morning. There were soldiers not ten miles to the east of here.

They could be the ones who had attacked his camp, returning now with the hostages. He should have been notified when they'd first entered the jungle. Anger pulsed through him. Where had the village watchers been then? An example would have to be made. But not yet. He had other things to take care of first.

"I have an important job for you," he told the man across the fire from him.

"Anything," Omar responded.

A spark flew from the fire and landed by his feet, going out quickly on the cold stone.

"You must gather your men and what's left of mine and attack the army. We must slow them down, cause a distraction." Enough of a distraction for him to slip unseen down the river. He had to get to a doctor—there was one near Miri he trusted, one who had helped him in the past. Then he had to get to KL in time.

The fire popped, its flames not substantial enough to light the whole cave, but enough to show the greed on Omar's face. He missed Jamil, even if they hadn't always agreed on everything.

"I will defeat this army unit, I will take their big guns, I will unite the camps. And when you give the signal from KL, I'll be ready." The younger man punctuated his words by bringing his fist down on his knee.

Hamid sat straight, wanting to press his palm against the pain in his shoulder, but resisting. It would not be smart to show any sign of weakness in front of Omar.

"You are instrumental to the success of our cause," he said, and watched the calculating look in the other man's eyes.

He would have to be taken care of before he became a problem. But not yet. He still had usefulness left in him. And things were bad enough so they couldn't be picky.

He would let Omar handle the army unit. If the young hothead won, it would be a victory for them all. If he lost, and something happened to him…one less problem to worry about.

The camps were more or less united, and once he succeeded in KL, the stragglers would accept his leadership. But he had problems aplenty in other areas. Having the hostages escape had dealt a blow to phase two of his plan. He had counted on the ransom money for more weapons, had a couple of surface-to-air missiles on order. He needed them to effectively fight the Royal Air Force. He needed a decisive military victory.

"Stop by Ali's camp once you cross the river," he said, on second thought. "He will join you if you tell him I sent you."

"I don't need Ali."

"You misunderstand me, friend. It is Ali who needs you. I fear your brother was trying to convince him that a major offensive was not necessary. It would be good for him to see the army, to realize they were already in the forest. It would help him understand that the war has already started, whether he wanted it or not."

He needed Ali's calm reason to temper Omar's blind courage. They both would hate working with the other, but they would make a stronger team than either one fighting alone.

Allah willing, his line would be restored to the throne soon, the country put into the service of the one true god instead of foreign business interests. It had been bad enough when the Chinese skimmed off profits, and most businesses were owned by them, while the Malay people worked the land, peasants and servants in their own country. But at least the Chinese who lived on the peninsula had kept the profits invested in the country. They kept to themselves and respected Muslim law even if they didn't practice it.

The Western influx of businesses was changing the face of the country, however, and the government welcomed the Europeans and Americans, who looked at the natives as barbarians to be exploited. In its mindless quest for modernization, the government failed to protect the culture of the country and its citizens. Young Malay people worked in sweatshops under conditions little better than slavery, making products they would never be able to afford to buy, for business owners who took the profits and distributed them to their shareholders back in the west.

His country was under occupation, not by a foreign army, but by foreign businessmen. And to make things worse, it was the country's very own government who held it down, allowing it to be raped.

He was fighting in a righteous war. And he couldn't lose. If he lived to see victory, he would be king. If he fell, he'd be a martyr for his cause, and his brother would be forced to give up his misguided acceptance of the status quo. Yes, his brother would be forced to avenge him, to take up his weapons.

Either way, the true line of succession would be restored soon. The KL attack would start a tide that could not be turned back.

## Chapter Nine

Brian listened to the night, feeling every breath Audrey took, every heartbeat. She might not have thought that was enough for him, but in the past few years there had been plenty of times when he had thought he would never have another moment like this.

She had seen where he'd been, what he'd become, and yet she accepted him. He was stunned and humbled at once. He wanted to get up, rush out into the rain and dance, twirl her around, or bang his chest and shout into the night like Tarzan in triumph. Since she was sleeping, she probably wouldn't have appreciated either display of joy.

He stared into the darkness, trying to get his mind around all that had happened in the last couple of days, all the ways his life had changed. He sure hadn't foreseen this when he'd planned his escape.

He was laying amidst flower petals, with a beautiful woman in his arms.

It wasn't the first time—he had once known how to woo. But it was the most significant, the one he would never forget. And not because of the extraordinary circumstances, but because of the extraordinary woman.

He relaxed his arms, realizing suddenly how tense his muscles were. Something prickled his instincts, and he turned his attention to the outside world. He lifted his head and listened, but couldn't hear much over the rain. Their fire had gone out long ago. He reached for their clothes, finally dry.

"Audrey," he whispered to her. "Wake up. We have to get dressed."

She came awake at once. "What's wrong?"

He wasn't sure. There was now a slight tremor in the rock beneath them. Something popped in the distance, then again and again. Not gunfire. He yanked on his pants and shirt, his boots, found the papers and tucked them away. "Where are the matches?"

"In my pocket."

The sounds were getting louder. A rumble, like logs rolling. Had the river risen this high? Couldn't be. Not overnight. And then it clicked.

"Mudslide!" He grabbed her and they half slid, half fell off the rock. "This way. Away from the river."

The natural slope of the land would give the mud

direction. He didn't want to get caught in its path. He couldn't see it, could barely see a foot in front of his nose, but he knew the monster behind him. He'd seen it kill before in Haiti. He'd been part of the marine rescue crew that had retrieved the bodies. Mudslides were ferocious killers.

They ran, giving everything to it, but it soon became apparent they couldn't outrun the force of nature. Not in the dark, not with his bad knee. He searched for the biggest tree around, and prayed they were out of the main flow.

"Grab on." He latched on to a handful of vines and climbed up the tree with Audrey on his back.

"Is it safe up here?" she asked when they were sitting in the V of a branch.

"Safer than down there. Unless the mud takes the tree."

And as if to underscore his words, the monster reached them, shaking their precarious haven. He could hear trees falling all around, but theirs held. And then a thunderous crack rent the air and their branch shook as if a giant whacked his axe into the tree.

"What was that?"

"Probably a log hitting us." The mud rolled everything in its path with it.

"Will it knock down the tree?"

"Not a log, no."

"But?"

"A rolling boulder could. We should be out of the main flow though." He put his arm around her to make sure she didn't fall should the tree get hit again and shake harder.

She clung to him. He was aware of every point where they touched. Her soft body seemed to melt into his. He ran his hand down her back in a gesture of comfort, and found himself comforted by her nearness.

The rain was still coming down pretty hard, the few minutes they had actually spent in dry clothes nothing but a distant memory. When she shivered, he held her tighter, offering her some of his own body heat. "It'll be better when the sun comes up."

"It's fine," she said. "We're going to make it. We're both too stubborn to die."

He grinned into the darkness, his arms woven around her. They waited for sunrise like that, sleep impossible under the circumstances.

The devastation around them became apparent as soon as the first light of dawn appeared on the sky. That they could see the sky, was a telltale sign in itself. The thick canopy was gone; the trees razed where the main flow had been, thinned considerably on the edge. Their tree was one of the few still standing. The mud covered everything below.

"How deep do you think it is?"

He looked at the trees that had survived the night. "A couple of feet."

"Can we walk in it?"

He nodded. "But it would take us too long to fight our way to dry ground. And it's still raining. The mud might start moving again." He stepped over to another branch so he could see all around.

"Are we trapped?"

He grabbed a thick vine, tested it with his weight. "Ready to go?"

She was staring at him wide-eyed. "You can't be serious."

"You wrap it around one foot like this, hang on tight, and push away with the other. I'll be right there to catch you." He swung as hard as he could, sailed through the air, latching on to a branch on the next standing tree. "Come on, there's nothing to it." He threw the vine back.

She hesitated.

"I'm going to catch you. You have to trust me," he called out to her.

But his heart lurched into his throat when she did kick away and flew for a few precarious moments in the air, until he finally grabbed on to her and crushed her to him.

She looked up at him with a smile. "It wasn't too bad."

A couple of seconds passed before every nerve ending in his body got the message that she was here, safe in his arms, and he could let her go.

"Glad you feel that way," he said, "because we're going to have to do this again."

The second swing took them clear of the mud that now cut them off from the river.

"We can't get to the boat, can we?"

"Even if we could make it over there, I doubt we would find it."

"So we'll walk?"

"For now." They didn't have another option. "Walking would get us out of the jungle eventually, but it won't get us to civilization in time to warn Kuala Lumpur of the attack."

"We have to get back to the water."

"As soon as we can."

He started out, following the edge of the mudslide toward the river, and they walked all morning until they finally reached the Baram around noontime. It was tamer than he'd expected.

"The mud might have dammed it up somewhere above us. I wouldn't want to be on the water when that dam breaks," he said. Not that that was a worry at this stage. They no longer had a boat.

"Look over there." Audrey pointed to a fallen log down the bank.

The vegetation had been flattened by water that had overflowed the river basin not long ago, debris littering the muddy bank. He scanned the thick chunk of wood that had caught her attention.

Not just a log. He scrutinized the pointed end as he walked toward it. A canoe. The water must have lifted it somewhere upriver and dumped it down here. He ran, praying it wasn't broken, that half of it wasn't missing but was just buried in the mud. He was digging around it by the time Audrey caught up with him.

"Give me a hand. Pull here."

They heaved it toward the water and he flipped it over, scooped out the mud that still remained inside. As far as canoes went, it was a rather primitive one, cut with an axe from one piece of wood. And no paddles, he felt around in the mud, coming up empty-handed.

He grabbed a flat, straight piece of driftwood—better than nothing—then with Audrey's help pushed the canoe in the water. It didn't sink. *So far, so good.*

"Get in."

When she did, he handed her the rifles then pushed the canoe out far enough so the current would catch and carry it. But before he could climb up next to her, the canoe caught on something and rolled, taking her under.

She didn't come up.

He could see nothing in the murky water, tried to

feel around with one hand while holding the canoe with the other. He couldn't let the water take that. They needed it. Had Audrey hit her head? Had she gotten tangled in something?

He plunged under, searched desperately while struggling to keep the canoe in place. Oh, hell. He let go and clawed the opaque water with both hands, mad panic gripping him. How long had she been under? Less than a minute, it couldn't have been a full minute yet, although it felt like a lifetime.

Then his fingers brushed against cloth and he grabbed on, pulled her up. She was limp in his arms. He shook her and when he did, she sputtered and opened her eyes, pressed a hand against the reddish bump on her forehead.

"Can you stand?"

She nodded, coughing hard, and steadied herself.

The rifles. No time to look for them now. He threw himself into the water and went after the canoe. Damn, the current was strong. He caught the thing at last, afloat still with the air trapped under it. He struggled to turn it over and managed somehow, holding it in place with one hand, bailing water out with the other. There was no way he could drag it the fifty feet up to where she stood.

And she must have understood it, because she began walking, then swimming toward him. And after an eternity she reached him at last, and he heaved her into the canoe and got in after her.

"You're okay," he said instead of asking, not to reassure her, but because he needed to hear it, then went back to scooping water.

She pitched in, her hands shaky. They didn't stop until they were down to the last couple of finger's width in the bottom. The rain was easing off, the sun making a half-hearted effort to break through the clouds.

"How bad are you hurt?"

She tried to smile, but failed miserably. "Nicky used to get me worse while playing tennis."

"Runaway ball?"

"Runaway racket." She coughed. "We used to play doubles. She's like a windmill. A serious hazard on the court." The words were said with obvious love.

He brushed her wet hair out of her face. They'd both lost their hats—the least of his worries at the moment.

"I have a hard time picturing you in an ordinary life, playing tennis. I've only seen you as part of the jungle. An Amazon."

She laughed, but it turned into a coughing fit. He didn't dare reach out and pull her to him, for fear that they would upset the canoe's balance again.

"What are we going to do?" she asked when she could talk.

"We're fine for now."

The water carried them straight down the middle, but sooner or later he would need something to steer them away from drifting logs and other hazards. The river floated enough broken branches to make a pole or even another makeshift paddle, he just had to wait until they got close enough to one to grab it.

Audrey coughed the last of the water out of her lungs. "Phew. That was nasty. I'm not doing that again."

The thought that he could have lost her squeezed his lungs until he was breathing as hard as she was.

"You keep saving my life." Her jungle-green eyes looked at him, endless wells of trust.

He leaned forward carefully, cupped her face, and with his thumbs brushed off the drops of water that clung to her eyelashes. "Maybe it's *you* who is saving *my* life," he said, and kissed her.

And got lost in the softness of her lips. He had denied himself this the night before, and he had been right to do so. Because now that he reached the gates of heaven, there was no going back.

The meeting of their lips was like kissing for the first time—tentative, excitement mixing with a sense of awe. His hands moved to her shoulders to gather her closer, and she pressed against him. Then the canoe rocked and it brought him back to reason fast and hard.

He straightened and looked around, pushed away the jumble of driftwood that had bumped into them, keeping a sturdy stick that looked long enough to be of some help. Only when their path was clear did he turn his attention back to her, painfully aware that the slightest distraction, the smallest error in judgment could cost both of them their lives. What the hell had he been thinking?

*That he wanted her more than he had ever wanted anything.*

But he couldn't have her. Not under these circumstances, perhaps not ever.

"Keep your eye on the back, I'll watch the front. Same as we did with the boat."

And as they soon came to a spot where a tributary came into the river, making navigation even harder, that was the last piece of conversation they had for the rest of the day, other than quick directions thrown at each other.

When night fell they pulled the canoe out of the water and dragged it with them inland, not wanting to lose it. It was smaller and lighter than the boat.

He made their shelter far enough in the forest so that even if the water rose it wouldn't reach them—a makeshift platform, and two poles at each end that held the canoe upside down above them like a roof. They dined on a handful of crunchy roots he'd dug up by the riverbank. Then, unable to light a fire without smoking themselves out, they snuggled together for sleep.

A part of him, the selfish part, wished they would never find their way out of the jungle.

She lay facing him, his arms around her. The rain that had started up again drowned out everything but the sound of their breathing. She brought her hand up to his face.

"You are…" She took a deep breath. "You are not like anyone I've ever known."

He wasn't, although he would have given anything to be just an average man, someone who could have hoped for a future that included the woman in his arms. The darkness that surrounded them seeped into his heart.

"Are you telling me that I'm rough around the edges?" He tried to make light of it, and wished he could see her face, read her thoughts in her eyes. He could barely make out the shape of her head.

"Complex," she said. "On the one hand, you can kill a man without blinking an eye, which scares the crap out of me." She hesitated. "On the other hand, you are thoughtful, and gentle, and protective, and I have never felt as safe as I do when I'm with you."

His heart beat a slow thumping rhythm.

He saw himself differently. He was like the jungle—too overgrown, impossible to clear. His past was a tangle of vines that bound him.

She stretched up to put her lips against his.

Their soft comfort caught him by surprise. And he took them, because his throat suddenly tight, speech was beyond his ability. He felt as if in a fantasy, as if kissing a dream.

He brushed his lips across hers tentatively, knowing it would be better to leave things at that, but he couldn't. He covered her mouth with kisses from corner to corner, outlining the soft arches that drove him mad during the day. Then he kissed her face, wanting to drink her beauty until it replaced the darkness inside him. He pressed his lips against each eyelid in turn, grateful and humbled that she saw beyond appearances and somehow managed to glimpse the last vestiges of the man he had once been.

When he was done covering her with kisses, he returned to her mouth again. She parted her lips for him, and his heart melted. She tasted mildly spicy, like the roots they had eaten for dinner, intoxicating. He deepened the kiss, lost in the moment, lost in the sweetness of her.

"Audrey," he whispered her name when they came up briefly for air.

She slid her hands under his shirt, and desire

washed through his body, the sensation so hot and hard it took his breath away all over again. A mudslide couldn't have buried him so completely.

He didn't dare move while she unbuttoned his shirt, fearing he would scare her away, still expecting her to change her mind, to stop. It would have been probably the sanest thing to do.

But she didn't, not even when her fingers glided over his scars.

He reached for the bottom of her shirt, hesitant, but she helped him, and with the T-shirt and tanktop as well. And then her bare skin was against his, a sensation so overwhelming that for a moment he didn't move, just held on to her, memorizing it. The gentle curve of her breasts pressed against him, and when she shifted and her nipples dragged across his skin, a groan rumbled up his throat.

He waited for the mad, animal-like need that he had feared he would not be able to control, but instead he found another emotion surge from deep inside, one that didn't have to do as much with the primal act of sex as with this one specific woman.

His body had needs, yes, and they'd gone long unsatisfied, but he didn't just want to take her body. He needed more than release. He wanted to make love to her. He lifted his lips from hers and buried his head in the crook of her neck for a long moment, soaking up the exquisite sensation of their bodies touching.

His hands sought her soft skin, the curves he wanted to get lost in forever. He drank from her lips again, and unwrapped the rest of her as carefully as a child unwraps a most treasured present.

"You're beautiful," he said, and heard her chuckle in response.

"That compliment loses some of its effectiveness in the pitch-dark night."

"I have you memorized. And I don't need light to know the beauty in here." He put his palm over her heart.

She pressed her lips to his in response. The kiss was slow but thorough. When she tugged on his pants, he turned to make it easier, but resisted to help, to rush. The feel of her hands on him, there, sent fire coursing through his veins.

They finally had nothing between them, and he gently turned her on her back and tasted her at his leisure, her lips, the hollow of her neck, her breasts. He skimmed his fingers over her flat belly, drawing circles around her belly button, playing games over the curve of her hip.

He wanted to discover every inch of her, taste every patch of skin, make it his if only for a night.

He moved lower and tangled his fingers in the

silky curls between her thighs, drew a fingertip over the parting line slowly, inch by inch, from one end to the other, then made the trail back up again.

"Oh," she said, breathless, when he slipped into her. Her breasts pushed into his chest as she arched against him.

The way she responded to his touch was a wonder. She opened to him, gave herself to him freely and with abandon.

Nearly blind with need, he moved deeper inside, with one finger first, then two, and felt her respond, but then she reached for his wrist and pulled his hand away.

He obeyed, his ears ringing with the harshness of his breathing, willing his heated desire to calm, even as his body screamed for her. He wouldn't push her. If this was as far as she was willing to go, so be it. If it killed him, this was it.

But instead of pulling away, she pressed the palm of her other hand to his hardness and folded her fingers around him. "I want all of you."

Her words seared across his skin, sending every drop of blood he had into the part she was holding.

He pushed against her, pumped his hip—he couldn't help it now. She brought her hands to the small of his back, parted her legs and lifted her knees. He ran his fingers across her inner thighs. When she moaned with impatience, he moved over her, slipped one hand under her firm buttocks and lifted her for his entry.

"Are you sure?" He could barely croak the words out.

"Yes!" She leaned up and bit his shoulder, slipped her hands over his buttocks. "Trust me, I'm not going to get pregnant. And otherwise, I'm as healthy as a woman can get. I've been tested to oblivion during the fertility treatments."

He had been, too, he wanted to reassure her. Regular checkups for the members of the SDDU were mandatory and exhausting. Then she did some wicked little movement with her hips, rendering him unable to speak, managing no more than a reassuring grunt.

Her opening was moist and tight, and for a moment he simply rested against it, trying to catch his breath—a futile effort. He outlined her perineum with his dewy tip. She responded by squeezing her long slim fingers into his buttocks. *Oh, man.*

He pushed in a slow inch, then backed out, moved forward again. Her glorious body stretched to allow him in.

"Brian…" Like a prayer, she whispered his name.

*Next time we make love I want to see your face,* the thought burned through his mind, rushing to his lips. But since they both knew there wouldn't be a next time, he kept his mouth shut and lost himself in her.

The world fell away as he pumped in and out and, answering his rhythm, she moved beneath him. He dipped to taste her mouth, plundering her at the same time below and above, then moved to her breasts and ravaged them one after the other, his control slipping now.

He wanted to consume her, as she was consuming him, burning him up with need.

He wanted to race to heaven with her, and at the same time, he struggled desperately to hold back, to make it last forever.

He felt her body grip him even tighter, squeeze him with quick contractions, milking him wave after wave. There was no holding back then. He poured into her with so much force, it felt like he was pouring his soul out.

Bliss. Floating. Eternity.

Neither of them could move or talk for some time.

Then in some hazy recess of his mind a thought arose that he must be crushing her, so he flipped them over, sprawling her on top.

They stayed like that forever.

"That was hot," she said next to his ear, still gasping for air.

He grinned weakly into the night. "If it wasn't raining, we would have started a forest fire."

She giggled. An honest-to-goodness giggle. And it made something leap deep inside his heart.

He held her closer, tighter.

"What?"

"Nothing. I wish I could see you. I want to make sure you're real, not just a trick from some jungle spirit."

She took his hand and put it over her madly beating heart. "It's real," she said.

He kissed her, feeling her heart in the palm of his hand, and refused to think of that other reality that waited for them outside the jungle.

HER BONES were made of rubber, and just the memory of last night was enough to set her body tingling. Audrey stirred, opened her eyes and found Brian still sleeping. The rise and fall of his chest was slow and even. She spread her fingers on the middle of his chest where her hand rested, skimming the hard muscles beneath her fingertips.

He had made love to her with such gentleness, such reverence. He had been right. It did feel unreal. If they weren't still naked, entangled in each other, she would have thought it a dream. She burrowed into him, emotion choking her all of a sudden.

Last night had been the most beautiful night of her

life. They'd had no champagne, no candles, no choc-
olate, not even a real bed—nothing normally associated with romance and seduction.

But none of it mattered, the magic had come from
between them.

She let her gaze glide over the awakening forest,
drinking in the peaceful beauty of it. Frogs were
singing a serenade. The rain had stopped, she realized just as Brian's arm tightened around her. She
glanced up at him. He was awake after all, but was
keeping his eyes at a slit.

"Somebody's watching us," he whispered, his lips
barely moving.

Fear replaced her good mood in an instant, and she
turned into him more to hide her nakedness. The
guerillas had caught up with them. For a moment she
panicked, then from somewhere deep welled up newfound strength and resolve.

Screw them. She was ready to fight. For herself
and Brian, for what they had found last night. Nobody was going to take that away from her.

"Is your knife within reach?" He slid his hand off
her, maneuvering closer to his own weapon.

"I lost it when I lost the boat."

She heard something move in the bushes ahead to
the left, lifted a little so if Brian had to jump up, he
could get his arm from under her neck with ease.

But instead, he suddenly relaxed, letting his head fall back with a strangled laugh.

"What?"

"Look." He nodded toward the forest, and a second later a large orangutan sashayed out into the open.

He stopped and looked them over with interest, his orange fur wet and matted. The open perusal on his face was nearly human. She felt embarrassed by her nakedness.

*Oh dear.* She looked for her pants—out of reach.

Brian got up and pulled on his clothes. She stayed where she was, staring at the animal, too scared to move. It was pretty big, as tall as four feet, showing some nasty teeth as it curled its black lips.

"Is it dangerous?"

"Nah. Harmless things."

The orangutan lumbered closer, fingered the platform she was lying on, poked her naked belly. She forced herself to stay still, not wanting to provoke it. She was a city girl. She didn't know how to deal with wild animals. Her only exposure to the animal kingdom had been a couple of goldfish back in grade school.

"Brian?" she squeaked.

He looked up from buttoning his shirt, stepped closer. "Hands off, buddy, the lady is mine."

Her breath caught in her chest, and she recognized at that moment he realized what he had said, because he snatched his gaze from her and pretended to pay attention to his buttons again.

She worked up enough courage and grabbed her own semidry clothing, shrugged into it piece by piece, careful to keep a few feet between herself and the orangutan. "What does he want?"

"Who knows." Brian reached his hand toward the animal. "He's just probably curious."

The next second, without warning, the orangutan rushed up the nearest tree, startling her into a small scream. He disappeared from sight as quick as he had appeared.

"What was that about?" she asked, and heard gunfire in the distance just as the last word was out.

"We have to go." Brian jumped to the canoe.

She made quick work of dressing and went to help him. It wasn't easy. She kept slipping in the mud. Dammit. She scraped the back of her hand, but ignored the burn.

The guns sounded closer and closer.

Then the canoe was free, and they carried it toward the river, making slow progress between the trees.

Brian dropped the front finally. "We'd be sitting ducks on the water," he said, his face mirroring his frustration.

"Can we hide until they pass?" She set down the

back end and jumped when a succession of shots banged through the air somewhere nearby.

Whoever was shooting, she didn't think they were shooting at Brian and her. They were too far still. But they weren't poachers, either. She had shot a semi-automatic rifle when she'd gone after Brian to Hamid's camp, and that's what the shots sounded like now, coming fast together.

He looked at her, back at the canoe, hesitated for a moment, then grabbed her hand and lurched forward.

"Run!"

## Chapter Ten

They scampered through the forest, careful to make as little noise as possible, ducking under vines, zigzagging around obstacles. Audrey was gasping the humid air when they stopped a few minutes later. But at least they had managed to put some distance between them and the gunfire that seemed to come from every direction.

"Sounds like a major offensive." Brian scoured the woods.

A loud boom of some serious weapon punctuated his last word, coming from the east.

She jumped closer to him. "What was that?"

The tight set of his shoulders relaxed, and he flashed an unexpected grin at her. "The army."

"How do you know?" She held her soaring hope in check. Could it be so simple? Could rescue be just around the corner?

"That was a rocket launcher, not your standard guerilla ammo. It's too cumbersome to carry around in the jungle and not much use with the limited visibility the trees impose. Let's go."

"Do you think they came for the hostages?" She hurried to keep up with him as he moved forward, even passed him after a while, eager to spot their saviors. "We've done it, haven't we? They will protect us and send word of the KL attack."

"With some luck. We have to be very careful, though." And as if to punctuate his words, he grabbed her and pulled her back, shoved her behind him.

She gasped at his uncharacteristic roughness. "You don't have to—" Then she saw something move on the branch that a second ago had been inches from her face.

A snake.

"Don't move." Brian stood perfectly still, as the snake stared at them and lifted its head, ready to strike.

Her blood thundered in her ear. How on earth had she missed that? It was at least five feet, although hard to tell exactly since its length was draped, and in some sections coiled, around the gnarly branch.

"Is it poisonous?" She barely breathed the words.

"Move back slowly."

She couldn't. She was as paralyzed as if she'd

been bitten. All she could think of was Joey, her aunt's German shepherd that had gotten into a fight with a rattler during one of the summers she had spent with her aunt in Texas, and the painful death the poor dog had died, despite all intervention.

"Don't look at the snake. Look at your feet." Brian's voice was full of patience.

It reached her on some level. She had to move. He was in front of her and couldn't pull back until she did. He had put himself into harm's way for her once again. She took a deep, shuddering breath and pushed one foot back, then the other.

"You're doing fine, keep going."

The sound of gunfire filled the air again. They were so close. The army was here. They were as good as saved, and could tell them where the hostages were. Nicky could be back in Kuala Lumpur by tonight, and she with her, and Brian. She pushed away the panic that gripped her limbs and did as Brian had asked.

"I'm petrified of snakes," she said after they had gotten far enough to move normally and resumed their trek. She was watching every branch now, every spot she set her feet, instead of blindly following Brian, getting lost in her thoughts as she had earlier.

"They didn't seem to bother you before." He glanced back.

"Before?"

"When we passed them." He turned his attention to the woods again, led the way around a patch of giant root buttresses.

The muscles in her legs went weak. She pulled her neck in, feeling all of a sudden that the trees above them were full of nasty things just waiting to drop on her shoulders. She tugged the new leaf-hat he'd made her earlier firmly into place. Snakes. She hadn't seen them before. She'd been too busy thinking about Nicky, and surviving to the next day. She had been focused on Brian.

"It might not have been poisonous," he said over his shoulder. "I don't remember seeing that kind before. There must be a hundred species of snakes on Borneo, I doubt anyone but the local tribes know all of them."

Great. That information made her feel so much better. There were things she simply didn't need to know. She shivered in the heat, her skin covered in goose bumps from thinking about a hundred different snakes.

The gunfight ebbed, then started up again. The closer they got, the slower they went.

"You better stay here," Brian said after a couple of hundred feet. "This is going to be tricky."

"No," she said without thinking, as the panic she

had just conquered, slammed into her midsection again. "I don't want to stay alone."

He looked at her for a long moment then drew her in for a tight hug. "I hate the thought of leaving you behind, but they might shoot at me. Hell, they probably will. Things could get dangerous."

"What isn't?"

She lifted her face to him, and realized that more than she was scared of snakes and other jungle perils, more than she was scared of being left alone, she was scared for him. What if something happened to him and she wasn't there to help? "We're a team. I'm coming."

He watched her for a long moment, brushed his lips against her forehead suddenly, then let her go. "Okay. But only because I don't think it's safe to leave you tied to a tree. Stay behind me at all times."

She smiled at him and filled her lungs.

They crept from cover to cover, bush to bush. Then the vegetation thickened as they came to the edge of a swollen creek. The army was on the other side. She couldn't see them, but the gunfire was close enough for her to want to stay flattened to the ground.

Then after a while, the guns fell silent.

"I'm going to try to make contact," he said, and

led her to a large rock boulder. "You wait for me. I'm not going far."

She began to protest, but he silenced her with a look. "This part is not negotiable."

"Don't take any chances."

He looked at her with humor in his startling blue eyes. "I think it's a little too late for that."

He dropped to his stomach and crawled to the trees on the side of the creek. From her vantage point she could see both him and the other side. Then the leaves began to move over there. The army was coming. She could see the first soldier hack through the jumble of vines.

More came, scanning the jungle, their guns in front of them, ready.

Brian stripped off his shirt, stuck it out on a stick, a makeshift "white flag" that was dirty brown. "Americans," he yelled the single word at the same time, but it was no use.

They started shooting as soon as the first syllable was out. And they did a thorough job of it. She didn't have to be told to run. Brian pointed south, scrambling toward her, and she sprinted, pushed by a strong sense of self-preservation.

"Not too trigger-happy, are they?" she said when they were far enough so they could stop to catch their breath.

"They're in the middle of a fight. They're gonna shoot at everything that moves. Can't say I blame them. Still, I had to give it a try."

She was drowning in disappointment. It didn't work. Their best hope for survival was a bust.

"What are we going to do?" Without the canoe their mission was doomed, and they definitely couldn't go back that way to retrieve it. "Maybe if I went to them. They wouldn't shoot at a woman, would they?"

"Don't even think about it. We'll wait until nightfall, then I'll sneak into their camp and disarm a guard. I'll explain what's going on, so he can call off the rest. Then they can radio in what we have on KL and call in help to pick up your sister and the others."

It sounded feasible, not that she felt comfortable with it, but it had been a while since she had felt comfortable with anything. Brian had proven to her over and over again that he was capable, that he knew what he was doing. She had to trust him. And she did. "Sounds like a plan. What do we do in the meanwhile?"

"Find food and shelter. But if they move on, we're going to have to follow them." He took off his belt and jumped to the ground, ripped off his shirtsleeve, rolled it up.

"What are you doing?" Then she saw the dark patch on his pants. "You're shot!"

She dropped to her knees next to him, pressed the rolled-up cloth to the wound while he tied the belt in place to keep the pressure on.

"It's your good leg." Her gaze flew to his. God, it was so unfair.

"Just a flesh wound. Nothing serious." He smiled at her. "If all goes well, tomorrow morning they'll be airlifting us out."

She had to believe that. Because no way could Brian make it out of the jungle like this. And neither would she without him.

"Come on." He grabbed her hand and stood with her. "We have a lunch date with some grubs."

She wiped his blood on her pants and went with him, food being the last thing on her mind for once. He was injured. Reality was still sinking in. His injury changed everything. They no longer had the option of walking away from the army and trying to make it out of the jungle on their own. He needed help, and he needed it fast.

He grabbed a fallen branch to help him support his weight as he walked, and she watched his more pronounced limp. "Do you think this is going to work?"

"We'll make it work."

"What if the army…" She couldn't bring herself to finish the sentence, but her doubts echoed in her head. What if they couldn't make contact? What if the army attacked them thinking they were the enemy?

"If they get me before I can talk to them, I want you to find the river and follow it out of the jungle. Once you get down far enough there'll be some villages. Somebody will have a cell phone or a radio." His voice was thick. He didn't turn around to look at her.

"It's not going to happen," she rushed to say, wishing she had kept her fears to herself.

"I hope not, but it could. If there's one group trained as well in jungle warfare as mine, it's the Royal Malaysian Army. It's not gonna be easy to sneak up on them."

"But if I went to them? I'm a woman. I look foreign." She wished he would consider that as an option.

"They'd be shooting at you long before they saw you. They're at high alert, in the middle of an offensive. I shouldn't have tried to approach them at the creek. It was a mistake. If you end up on your own and meet up with soldiers, don't move toward them unless you have a large enough open area where you can come at them from far away. Walk with your hands high in the air, or down on your knees with your hands linked behind your head. Whatever you do, don't surprise them."

He stopped by a fallen log and lifted it, holding it with both hands.

She was trying to form an argument, but the foot-long centipede he'd uncovered stopped her thoughts. A long moment passed before she realized he was probably waiting for her to pick it up. "I'll chew off my own arm before I'm eating that."

But his attention wasn't on what was under the log.

He shook his head, nodded toward the woods, then slowly lowered the chunk of deadwood. What? She listened and heard the soft noise. A small deer, no bigger than a hare, stumbled from the bushes. It stared at them, drummed on the ground with its feet that were literally the length and thickness of a pencil, then darted to the right.

Brian lunged and threw himself at the animal, but he'd been too far, his legs not having enough power for the move. He missed by a foot, and the deer took off into the woods with dazzling speed.

"Damn." He groaned as he got up.

"Are you hurt?" She was at his side the next second, supporting him. Stupid question. Of course he was hurt. Fresh blood seeped through his pants. "Don't do that again."

He pulled away, as if he was embarrassed, and shrugged. "We need to eat."

"Was it a fawn? It was tiny. I can't believe how fast it ran." Although its head, legs and coloring were that of a deer, its body was rounder, strangely formed.

He found his stick and leaned on it. "A mouse deer," he said. "That's as big as they get. It would have made a fine dinner."

She'd only had venison once before and didn't particularly take to it, but the idea of real food, meat, made saliva gather in her mouth. Her stomach growled. She kicked up some leaf mold and found a half-dozen beetle-like bugs, with alternating brilliant red and blue stripes. "How about these?"

"Probably not a good bet. Bright color is usually a warning sign that they're poisonous."

She watched the bugs burrow into the dirt as she stood. She wasn't all that disappointed. "Maybe we'll come across some fruit."

But they didn't. It took another half an hour before they found a handful of grubs that were good to eat. And since the skies opened again by then, they washed down their lunch with some rainwater. When they were done, Brian helped her up a tree and wove some leaves together over them—not a terribly effective shelter, but the best they could do under the circumstances.

He sat in the V where the branch met the trunk, with his arms around her. Her back soaked up his heat, and she let her head fall onto his shoulder. His leg was elevated on a cross branch.

"How is it?"

"I'm glad this happened now and not before. We're almost out of here."

He took off the belt and checked his injury. It was no longer bleeding. His blood had clotted, the make-shift bandage stuck in the wound. He tore off his other sleeve and ripped it into a long strip, tied it around what was already there. "This should keep the dirt out."

She put her hands over his, wanting to hold on to him.

"Tonight I'll make contact. We'll be out of here in the morning," he said, as if sensing the despair that fought to take her over.

He was injured, dangerously so—even a minor wound could get infected enough to become a life threatening problem in the jungle. And yet he thought not of himself, but how to set her at ease. His strength had a way of strengthening her, as if they shared some invisible link.

"So tell me about this kid of yours," he said in a transparent attempt to take her mind off their problems.

And she did, to distract him from his. "Her name is Mei. Her mother is Chinese-Malaysian and she's too young to keep her. She's so beautiful, Brian."

Tears gathered in her eyes as she thought of the small picture the agency had sent her, the one Omar's men had taken along with everything else that had been in her pockets.

"How old is she?"

"Three months." She smiled through her tears. She had not specified age or sex when contacting the adoption agency, but was overjoyed as soon as they told her they'd found her a baby girl.

"You'll be a good mother." He pressed his lips against her neck, and their warmth seemed to spread through her whole body. "You don't scare easily."

She smiled and touched her cheek against his, rough with the beginnings of another beard. They hadn't had a fire the night before to shave by, and during the day he never wasted time with it. She didn't mind.

"Did you scare your adoptive parents?"

He groaned. "Don't remind me. God, the torture I put them through."

She tried to picture him as a mischievous, carefree little boy and the picture that blossomed in her mind softened her heart.

"I was trouble with a capital T," he said.

"Probably not more than any other young boy."

"I was definitely a restless spirit."

She could hear the smile in his voice. "But they loved you anyway."

"Yeah, they did. I owe them a lot."

His words were full of so much love and tenderness toward those people, it made her heart skip a beat, wanting to be so good a mother that Mei would feel that way about her someday. She was beginning to see Brian in a different light from her first wild-man-of-the-jungle impression. There were layers and layers to the man, a complexity that went beyond his identity as a prisoner or soldier.

The sudden upswell of emotion that constricted her throat left her bewildered. "Why don't you sleep," she said. "I'll keep watch. You need to store your energy for tonight."

He kissed her temple without saying anything, but after a while, she could feel his even breathing. She felt absurdly safe in the cocoon of his arms. It was ridiculous. They were in the wilds of the jungle, in the middle of an armed confrontation, both sides of which would just as soon shoot them as look at them.

She stared into the rain, listened for the sound of gunfire, but couldn't hear any.

It made her nervous. What if the army was moving on? Should she wake Brian? Not yet. He needed rest. She would wait a few minutes. They might start fighting again and she would know then what their location was. Even if they moved, that many people would leave a wide enough trail to follow. She would let Brian be. Give him a chance to regain his strength.

She relaxed against him, and he mumbled something in his sleep. She squeezed her eyes shut. *Dear God. If only one of us can make it out of here alive, let it be him.*

He would have made it if it hadn't been for her and the madcap rescue of her sister. After what he had suffered in this jungle, she couldn't stand the thought of him dying here. She couldn't stand the thought of anything happening to him, period.

BRIAN INCHED FORWARD in the darkness. It had taken them an hour to find the soldiers, creeping toward where he'd last heard gunfire. He glanced back at the bushes that hid Audrey. Her instructions were to not to move a muscle until he came for her. She hadn't protested this time, a good thing since he didn't have the energy to fight her.

He stole forward, cursing the pain in his legs. But he didn't mind that as much as he minded the fact that his injuries slowed him down. He had missed that deer earlier. What if it had been a bullet he'd been ducking from? He crawled another few feet. Where the hell were the guards? He was nearly in the camp.

He could see men sleeping on the ground in a haphazard pattern, but there was no fire and nobody watching. A trap? They couldn't have possibly known that he was coming. Were they baiting the guerillas? There was barely enough light to see the lumps of soldiers, no way to tell if they were grabbing their guns, watching from under hooded eyelids as he did. Then he was close enough to one of them to see the unnatural pose he was lying in.

Dead.

A cold feeling spread through Brian's stomach. He crawled over, alert to any noise or movement, and reached out, even though he could see now that the man's eyes stared blindly into the night. No pulse. His fingers came away sticky with blood. Damn. He'd been killed a while ago. And so had the rest of them. They wouldn't have simply gone to sleep with a bloody corpse in their midst, inviting predators. The lack of guards made sense now. There was no one alive for guard duty.

The guerillas had won the skirmish.

Brian swore under his breath. How many other army units were in the jungle? He didn't think the twenty or so men scattered around him was all. From the ruckus that had gone on all day long, he figured a larger force.

Where were the rest camping? He came to his knees, ready to go back to Audrey and break the bad news, hating to have to dash her hopes. But there was no sense in trying to do more right now, too dark to see. When the sun came up they could search the bodies for anything useful, then go and find the rest of the army. Then when night fell again, he would try the same approach.

A branch snapped in the woods to his right.

He threw himself to the ground, next to the dead body, and went still.

Where the hell was the man's gun? He scanned the ground as a small group of guerillas walked out of the forest. Damn. Too late now. The rifle was probably under the soldier, and he couldn't move him without drawing attention.

His first thought was Audrey, hoping that she would stay down and stay quiet. He'd left her far enough behind. Unless the men began to really spread out, she should be fine.

But the guerillas didn't show any inclination to separate from each other. They walked through the carnage, lifting rifles, clipping hand grenades off the belts of the fallen. Why hadn't they made camp for the night? He watched, his eyes only slits. Maybe they had a camp somewhere nearby and were heading back to it. Darkness had just fallen.

A few tense minutes passed, then it seemed they were finally moving off.

In Audrey's direction.

His pulse quickened. A hundred feet and they would be right on top of her.

Brian grabbed a hand grenade from the body next to him, but he couldn't throw it into the group. They were too close to Audrey now, he couldn't risk hitting her with shrapnel. He judged the distance, aimed to throw it short. He still might wound a couple and it would certainly get their attention.

He pulled the ring and tossed the grenade, then took off running in the opposite direction, just as the explosion shook the night.

They came after him with a vengeance. He dashed through the forest, ignoring the pain that throbbed through his legs and made him trip a few times.

*Go. Go. Go.*

He couldn't outrun them, but he hoped he could lead them away from Audrey enough so they wouldn't bother going back that way.

She would make it out. He had to believe that beyond anything else, because that was the only thing that kept him going.

He ducked behind a tree and leaned against it to catch his breath, and could hear them gaining on him. He darted forward. Just a little more. Just a little more.

Then they must have spotted him, because bullets began to fly.

Damn, he hated to leave her alone. He scanned the ground for somewhere to hide. If he weren't injured he could have gotten far enough ahead to lose them. He ducked behind a tree again and drew his knife. He wasn't about to let them just pick him off as if they were on a deer hunt. He owed it to himself to go out fighting.

When his ears told him they were right on him, he jumped out and threw himself on the closest man, buried the blade in his chest, then before the rest could react he was on his feet, ready to face the next.

He lunged for the guy, but a loud crack split his skull. It seemed literally. He felt like he was falling, but not just the short distance to the ground. His last thought was Audrey, that if she followed his advice and fled for the river, there was still hope for her.

People were talking around him, but it was all a ringing noise in his ears. When darkness came, more complete than even the jungle could produce, he didn't fight it. He had done what he could.

# Chapter Eleven

Something had gone wrong. There wasn't supposed to be a fight.

Audrey crept forward from her hiding place, listening for anything suspicious, hoping she would hear Brian calling to her. She had waited all night in the bushes for him to return for her. Instead, there'd been an explosion, then gunfire that moved off into the distance.

The only logical explanation she could come up with was that the soldiers had discovered Brian before he managed to make contact and they had pursued him. Not a large group, judging from the sound of their guns. She hadn't dared move all night, fearing they'd left some men behind, not wanting to break the promise she'd given Brian about staying put and staying safe. But the sun was coming up now, and she needed to find out what had happened.

She moved in a crouch, careful where she put her feet, watching for small branches on the ground that would snap under her weight. If she did make noise, she stopped and waited several seconds like she had learned from Brian.

The overnight downpour had stopped at dawn, but now and then a fat splatter of water still landed on her hat or shoulders, making its way down from the leaves above. It startled her each time, but she kept quiet and focused on the woods ahead of her.

She heard no voices, no movement, no man-made noise of any kind. It filled her with unease. She was sure she was close enough and the soldiers would be awake by now. Surely there were at least a few left behind to guard their camp.

And then she could see them on the ground through the leaves, and they were obviously dead. All of them.

Had Brian done this? Confusion swept through her. No, he couldn't have. He didn't have a gun. But then what had happened?

She hesitated, unsure of what to do. The sun was up. Brian had said if he hadn't returned by daylight she was to make her way to the river on her own. And yet she couldn't make herself walk away.

Watching for the slightest sign of danger, she came out into the open. Whatever she decided to do, her chances of survival would be better if she had a weapon. Strangely, the first couple of men she looked over, didn't have their rifles anywhere near.

Then she did see a gun, a pistol next to a body a little farther off. She walked among the dead and picked it up, tucked it into her belt. A few broken branches caught her eye. Somebody, a bunch of people, had rushed through this way. Had they been pursuing Brian?

Did she dare attempt to follow the track? Could she follow it? She knew nothing about tracking beyond the obvious. Right now she had a fair idea in which direction the river was and it wasn't far away. But if she ran off blindly, got turned around, lost her way…

Brian was in trouble. If the tables were turned he'd be on his way by now to save her, instead of sitting around weighing his options.

There was an extra clip of bullets on the man's belt and she reached for it, even though she had no idea how to put them in the gun. But by God, she would figure it out.

A slight sound reached her ear and she froze, almost dismissed it when it came again. Something was moving in the bushes on the other side of the field of bodies—something big.

She flattened herself to the ground behind a trio of basketball-size rocks, hoping those and some overhanging vines camouflaged her enough. She saw a flash of yellow.

The tiger came out into the open and looked among the bodies, meandering, sniffing. He didn't seem to be in any hurry. Audrey held her breath as the animal moved in her direction.

*Stay still. Stay still.* She repeated the words in her head, although they were unnecessary, her limbs truly and completely frozen with fear.

The tiger stopped a good thirty feet from her and let out a rumbling, coughing sound that scared her witless and squeezed her insides until she thought she would wet her pants. Then the animal locked his tremendous jaw over the shoulder of the man in front of him and dragged the body into the forest.

She began to shake, her stomach revolting at the sight of the soldier's disappearing feet. She could hear the noise of the body being dragged on the ground for a while. Some time passed before she could get up, move. She took a few steps into the opposite direction, then leaned against a tree and threw up water, the only thing that had been in her stomach.

Survival instinct gave her strength and pushed her forward. She clawed her way through some vines, then saw another body a short way ahead. This one was dressed differently than the soldiers. She walked closer and paled when she recognized him.

He was one of the guerillas who had captured her in the village at the beginning of her journey.

And the dead soldiers made sense all of a sudden. The guerillas had won the fight with the army. They were the ones who gave chase to Brian.

She tipped the body over with the toe of her boot, saw the familiar knife sticking out of the man's chest. Brian had gotten one of them. She pulled the knife, looked up to where she could barely make out a track in front of her and started forward again.

She'd gone no more than a hundred feet when she spotted a pair of boots sticking out of the bushes, similar enough to Brian's to make her heart lurch. She moved closer to investigate, her hands shaking from relief when she pulled the branches aside and looked into the face of a stranger. He was a soldier, apart from the others. Had he run when it became obvious that they were losing the fight? Her gaze caught on the top of a backpack that peeked from under the body.

He was covered in blood, his whole chin missing, taken off by a bullet probably. She heaved again, but there was nothing in her stomach to bring up. She didn't want to touch him.

*Brian would.*

He would leave no resource behind that might save their lives. Who knew what was in the bag— food, a map, matches. She took a deep breath and rolled the body, tried to pull off the backpack, but the man's arms had stiffened into an angle that made it impossible for her to work the straps. She pulled her knife and cut them.

She dragged the backpack away from the body before she opened it, pushed aside the clothes on top and gasped at the sight of a compact radio unit. There was something else too, a smaller electronic device that looked like one of those handheld organizers. She pushed the red button and some kind of a picture came up with numbers. Not just any numbers, she realized after a moment—coordinates. She had a GPS unit, Global Positioning System, that showed exactly where she was.

She knew her location and had the means to call for help. She sank to the ground as tears of relief filled her eyes. But the feeling of optimism didn't last long. Nothing but static came through the radio when she turned it on, no matter which way she twisted the dial.

Brian would know what to do with it. He could be even now lying somewhere in the woods, wounded. She turned off both units, threw them into the backpack and got up, started out again.

She didn't have to go far before she came across the spot where the men had camped for the night. She had not found Brian's body so far. But she knew his pursuers wouldn't have rested unless they had caught him. Which meant, he was most likely once again a prisoner. God knew what they were doing to him. She pushed on.

She didn't stop again until she had to relieve herself. She was weak with hunger, but at least no longer cold. Although her clothes were still damp, the temperature had risen enough to be comfortable. She opened the backpack and turned on the radio, turned the dial slowly, from one end of the spectrum to the other.

Then finally she found something, a man talking rapidly in another language.

"Hello." She grabbed the speaker. "I need help," she said, and realized there was probably a button somewhere she needed to push to transmit. She found a rubbery spot on the side of the receiver and pushed that in. "I need help," she repeated, her heart in her throat.

Silence.

Oh, she probably had to let go of the button. She did so, and the response came after a few seconds.

"Identify yourself. Out."

"I'm an American. I'm lost in the jungle. My partner was taken by guerillas."

A longer period of silence this time.

"How did you get this radio? Out."

"I found a group of dead soldiers a while back. They're a few miles from the river." She fished the

GPS out, turned it on and read the displayed numbers to the man.

"Stay where you are. I'm sending a man to get you. Out."

She thought of Brian, that he might be injured, what Omar's men might be doing to him. "I'm going to follow the guerillas. I'll let you know where I am again in an hour."

To her surprise, the man didn't protest or forbid her. "Let us know as soon as you spot them. Don't try to approach them. We'll be there as fast as we can. Out."

She thanked him and turned off the radio and the GPS, wanting to save the batteries and not wanting the static from the radio to alert anyone to her approach.

Despite the shade the trees provided, the rising heat got to her more and more as the day wore on. Walking in the jungle was drastically different without Brian. It was much scarier and savage, and she had no one to distract her from it.

The sound of a single shot made her duck into the bushes before her brain registered that it came from far enough away not to pose an immediate threat. At least it confirmed that she was still going in the right direction. The tracks she'd been following had crossed an old animal trail a while back and since that point she no longer had broken plants to guide her.

She hoped the guerillas had followed the trail, instead of having simply crossed it and covering their tracks.

When she saw a body slumped against a tree up ahead, she kept walking toward it, thinking it was another casualty, then his hand twitched, and she realized the young guerilla was sleeping, probably on guard duty.

She stepped off the trail, behind a tree, and waited. Nothing. She peeked out. It didn't look like he'd moved. She crept forward in the woods, keeping the trail in sight, glancing back frequently at the man.

She didn't have to go far before she heard noises up ahead. She radioed in her GPS location, not daring to raise her voice above a whisper, then shut off the radio. Bugs be damned, she got into the thickest of the brush for optimum coverage, moving forward one slow step at a time. Her progress was excruciating, not only because the dense vegetation held her back, but because she waited after each step to make sure she wasn't discovered.

The closer she got to them the slower she went, until inch by inch she finally reached the edge of a clearing and, laying under a shiny-leaved bush, she was able to see the men. There were a lot of them. She counted about a hundred. Were the various groups uniting?

Then someone she recognized stepped into the clearing, and her heart tripped. Omar.

She watched as he talked to a couple of the men, then walked around. She inched forward another foot to see where he was going. And then she saw Brian.

Oh, God. The emotions that washed through her at the sight were strong enough to take her breath away. What had they done to him? He was hanging by his tied hands from a tree, his feet barely touching the ground. His pants on one leg were completely soaked in blood, and his face was bloody, too, on the right side. She watched helplessly, with fury screaming inside, as Omar walked over to him and smashed the butt of his rifle against Brian's ribs.

He didn't cry out. Instead, he lifted his head an inch or two and looked right at her.

Could he see her? She scooted back. If Brian could spot her, then so could the others. Not that anyone was looking hard. The men were eating and talking, lounging around camp as if they didn't have a care in the world. No doubt they thought there was safety in their number.

Omar hit Brian over and over, then stopped to talk to him. She wished she could hear what he said as he played with the rifle. There was such a look of madness in his face.

He was going to kill Brian, she realized, and grabbed her pistol, closing one eye and concentrating on her aim. She pulled back what she thought was the safety and steadied her hand. There was a better-than-good chance that she was going to miss, but even if all she managed to do was cause a distraction, it could give Brian enough time to break free.

But just as she put her finger on the trigger, a hand came over her mouth, another pulled the pistol from her, the weight of a man pressing her to the ground.

Her first instinct was to struggle, but her brain kicked in on time and she held still. If a guerilla discovered her, he wouldn't have held her mouth. He wouldn't have cared if she made noise.

The army?

She glanced back at the clearing to see if they'd noticed anything and her blood froze. Omar had turned the rifle around and was resting the barrel against Brian's temple. He was still talking to him.

The man half on top of her tugged her back, and she moved with him. He let go of her mouth, and she could turn at last to look at him. A soldier. It *was* the army. They were finally here.

"Are you the American?" he asked when they were at a safe distance.

"You have to save that man," she said, and saw the rest of the soldiers.

The man gave them a signal and they moved ahead without a sound.

"You stay here. I've got many questions for you when I get back," he said, and went after them.

Brian was tied up, immobile and defenseless in the middle of a shootout. And she was going to sit here and wait? *Unlikely.*

Audrey rushed back toward the camp, circling it, hoping to reach the other side and Brian in time. She didn't have to be careful about noise now, the sound of gunfire was deafening in the air. Didn't have to worry about wild animals, either. The ruckus was sure to scare them far away from the place. She ran as fast as she could.

Omar came out of the bushes at a dead run, looking backward, barreling right into her, sending them both sprawling to the ground. She grunted, the air knocked out of her lungs by the impact, struggled to get up and get away from him. But he made it to his feet first and had his knife pulled from his belt the next second.

"Move." He dragged her up with the blade to her throat and yanked her forward, deeper into the jungle.

"No. Wait." She fought him, her hands on the arm that held the knife, but he was the stronger one between the two of them. "You can go faster without me. You don't need me."

But then as he sunk to his knee, she realized he was injured. Blood gushed from his side above the right hip. And still, he kept a good strong grip on her.

He probably knew he wasn't going to get far and wanted to use her as a shield when the army caught up with him. It wasn't the army that reached them first.

"Let her go." Brian stepped out from behind a tree. He had to be weak with blood loss, too, but he showed no sign of it.

His eyes were as cold as the blade Omar held against her throat, and the predatory flow with which he moved, closer and closer, more menacing than the tiger had been. She felt Omar shift behind her.

"Come one step closer and she's dead," he said.

"She gets as much as nicked and I'll tear you apart from limb to limb." Brian's gaze was fixed on the man, his voice so deadly, it made her shiver despite the heat.

She'd seen him in rough-soldier mode before, but she'd never seen him like this. He was tightly controlled, yet there was a glint of madness in his gaze, a ferocious darkness.

The blade pressed against her skin. She didn't dare move when Omar tightened his hold on her. He was breathing hard and sweating, not nearly as confident now that Brian wasn't tied up and helpless before him.

Brian advanced on them, the sight as paralyzing as that of the tiger had been. And Omar must have felt the same, because he didn't move, didn't cut her as he had threatened, even as he repeated, "Stop. Don't come any closer." His words had little strength now, they were underlined with fear.

Then the next thing she knew, Brian lunged at them, flying through the air as he attacked. She was knocked aside, and rolled away. By the time she looked back, the two men were locked in a deadly battle. Omar still had the knife but Brian was gripping his wrist, as they wrestled for control.

Brian came to be on bottom somehow, holding Omar off, trying to shove away the sharp blade aimed at his throat. And then he did, twisting the knife and letting his arms go lax. Omar's weight, suddenly released, pushed the blade through his own heart.

He died with a groan of disbelief torn from his throat, his eyes rounded as if in surprise.

Brian shoved the man off without another look at him and rushed to her. "Are you hurt?"

He looked her over, then when she shook her head, unable to speak, he crushed her to him.

"How is your leg?" she asked finally when the wave of emotions in her began to settle.

"Barely bleeding."

She examined the wound at his temple that didn't seem as bad up close as she had thought when she'd first seen it, a lot less damage than the blood suggested.

"A bullet got too close." He lifted his fingers to the

spot she was looking at. "Head wounds bleed like a bastard."

"Hang on." She walked over to Omar, ripped the flask off his belt and went back to Brian to wash the side of his face.

She used the corner of her shirt, and when she was done with his skin, she rubbed the dried blood out of his hair. He could have used a stitch or two, but probably he'd be all right without it.

Guns were still going off here and there, but the battle seemed to be nearing the end.

He ran a light finger over his temple. "When I saw you under that bush— Didn't I tell you to head for the river?"

"If I didn't follow you, I couldn't have given the army your coordinates. I found a radio." She smiled at the stunned look he gave her.

"You brought the army?"

Her smile widened into a grin.

"I should go help them," he said after a moment, but didn't move.

She burrowed against him, soaked up his strength, and gave thanks for the miracle that they were both alive. "Stay."

And he did.

He gave a strangled laugh and held her closer. "I've changed more than I realized," he said when she lifted her head and threw him a questioning look. "A couple of years ago, nothing and no one could have kept me from rushing back into the fray. Now, all I want to do is sit here and never let you go."

She told herself not to read too much into that even as her heart leaped. They'd been through a lot together. She was the first woman he'd seen in four years, for heaven's sake. A certain amount of attachment was natural and would probably wear off fast once he returned to the real world. She couldn't fall for him. Not now.

She was going to become a mother in a few days, that's what she needed to focus on. She couldn't get entangled in a relationship that had started out of mutual need under extreme conditions. Not even if she could have sworn she was losing her heart to the man. She would get over it. They both would.

She pulled away just as the soldier she'd talked to earlier came walking from the direction of the fight, a couple of men behind him. He stopped by Omar's body, then looked at them. "So who the hell are you?"

"Audrey Benedict. My sister is Nicky Brown, one of the tourists kidnapped by the guerillas."

"Brian Smith," Brian said, and smiled when the man drew up an eyebrow. "I'm a personal protection specialist hired by Miss Benedict."

She tried not to act surprised at his new last name

and the rest of his words, but wasn't sure she altogether managed.

"What do you know about the hostages?"

"They escaped the guerillas two days ago and headed for an Orang Ulu village. I can give you a fair approximate location."

The man nodded. "We'll pick them up." He turned to her. "You mentioned something about an attack in KL?"

She pulled the papers from her pocket and handed them to the man.

He looked through them. "Looks like you've been swimming."

"I have. But they were bad even before that. We were able to make out Kuala Lumpur and the date August tenth. This part here—" she stepped next to him and found the right sheet "—used to be a list of embassies."

"Call it in," he said to one of his men before turning back to her. "And you came by this how?"

"We were both captured by Omar. He wrote this to another guerilla leader, and we took it with us when we escaped," Brian said, pointing to one set of papers. "These I found at Hamid's camp where the hostages were." He indicated the rest.

"Right. We'll talk some more about this." He motioned to four of his soldiers and said something in

Malay before switching back to English. "There's a new logging road about two miles east of here with enough space for the chopper to land. I'm giving you an escort there and sending you to KL for further questioning."

"And you'll send someone for the hostages?"

He nodded. "If you're cleared in KL, you'll be having dinner with your sister tonight."

She wasn't sure whether to laugh or cry. Nicky would be safe soon, the whole nightmare over. They'd be together again. But she was pretty sure that as soon as they got to Kuala Lumpur, Brian would be gone. And as much as she knew that was for the best, she wasn't ready for it yet, reluctant to see him go.

There were still things unsaid between them. She could not possibly put her gratitude into words, and there were other feelings that were perhaps best left unsaid. She looked at him, hoping for a gesture, something to tell her what to do.

He smiled. "It's over."

She blinked hard, hating the words.

## Chapter Twelve

He wasn't ready. He didn't know what to say.

Brian stood in front of the door of the hotel room, overwhelmed with sensory experiences. The hustle and bustle of the streets, the sheer size of the hospital where Audrey and he had been treated, even the clothes he wore, felt alien. Everything was too much, too loud, too new, too complicated.

He had spent the night watching television in his hospital room—the doctors had kept him overnight, but let Audrey go—and what he'd seen left him bewildered. He would have a lot to learn, a lot to catch up with. He didn't know anything, it seemed. No, not true. He knew one thing. He knew what he wanted.

Audrey.

He wanted her unequivocally, forever. He had enough time to think to know that he was in love with her.

And he loved her enough to want what was best for her. He was pretty sure it wasn't him.

He had no job, no money, nowhere to live. She deserved better. She deserved a carefree man who laughed a lot, not one who had years worth of dark memories to weigh him down. She deserved to sleep next to someone who wouldn't wake her up with his nightmares in the middle of the night.

And yet he was here. Not only to thank her for paying for his bill at the hospital and leaving him cash at the front desk. He wanted to see her one last time. He needed to see that she was okay. Then he would walk away.

He knocked even though he had a keycard. Audrey had left it in the envelope with the money.

She opened the door and stared at him for a moment. Blinked. "Brian…"

God, she looked beautiful. She had her long hair down, the light gleaming off the golden strands that framed her face. She wore a pink figure-hugging sheath dress that made his mouth go dry. She was a different person. The grungy teammate who had fought her way through the jungle with him and ate grubs from the palm of his hand was gone. In her place, he found a dazzling woman, every inch a lady. Someone who took his breath away, but a woman he didn't recognize.

Her expression looked as stunned as he felt.

He glanced down at the pants and shirt he wore, and conscious of his yuppie haircut, ran his fingers through his hair. He hadn't meant to spend more of her money than it took to get to the hotel, but he had trouble with the doorman letting him in, taking him for a panhandler.

"You're so different…" The words rushed from her, before she caught herself.

And at last he looked past her clothes and found her eyes. Even they weren't the same. She had makeup on.

Something moved behind her and he had her pushed aside, his body positioned to protect her, acting on instinct before he knew what he was doing.

The two men who came out of the kitchen area of the suite looked at him with suspicion.

"Audrey?" The taller of the two came forward.

"It's okay, Josh. This is Brian Smith, the man I told you about."

So this was the ex-husband. Brian extended his hand, not liking the way Josh seemed to measure him up. The man's handshake was firm, perhaps firmer than necessary, maybe a message he wanted to send. Brian resisted the urge to squeeze back hard, and pulled away before crossing the border of polite.

"My brother-in-law, Trevor," Audrey introduced the other guy, moving by him, making his head swirl with the flowery scent of her soap.

"I wanted to thank you for what you've done. I talked to Nicky this morning. They ended up taking the hostages to Miri yesterday to get checked out. It was the nearest hospital. But they'll be all here by tonight. She asked me to convey her gratitude if I see you before she does."

Good to know some of the hostages, at least, felt that way. He'd caught coverage of that, too, the guy who had wanted to fight him for the boat, giving an interview about the reckless and irresponsible nature of the rescue, and the disrespect and lack of cooperation of the man who had come for them—a "hot-headed maverick," he'd said, "who took unnecessary chances with the lives of the hostages."

"You do this kind of thing often?" Josh was still checking him out.

"As often as necessary. I work in personal security," he said, sticking to the story he'd invented the day before.

"Audrey is lucky to have found you," Trevor interjected.

He glanced at her from the corner of his eye. She looked flustered. "Is everything all right?"

"Sure," she said, but didn't look at him.

"She'll be fine now that we're here," Josh said, and stepped between them.

"I suppose you came for your fee." The brother-in-law offered him a beer out of the minibar.

Saliva gathered in his mouth. There had been times in the past couple of years when he would have given his soul for a cold beer. Now he waved it off. He wouldn't be here long enough to finish it.

"I'll be taking care of everything, of course." Trevor put the beer down and reached for his checkbook.

"It's all taken care of," he said. The suite felt small all of a sudden, and for a crazy moment he wished they were still back in the jungle.

"If you prefer cash we can get it by this afternoon and bring it over to your hotel," Josh said, putting his patrician nose where it didn't belong. "Where is it that you're staying?"

He didn't know yet. His first thought upon release had been to see Audrey. "No further payment is necessary."

He would get the money Colonel Wilson was sending to him at the embassy, crash in an airport hotel for the night, then leave on the first flight in the morning. He didn't belong here with these people. They belonged with each other.

"Mind if I use your phone?" he asked Audrey, then when she nodded, he called down and asked for reception to get him a cab to the embassy and call up when it was here. All he needed were a few minutes to say goodbye.

But Josh interrupted his call with, "The embassy is closed today. They all are. Some kind of credible terrorist threat or something."

Of course. August 10. He glanced at Audrey. How much had she told the men?

"We already tried to call earlier, to ask for their help. I missed my court date for the adoption hearing," she said.

Great. He had wanted to give the money back that she'd left for him at the hospital, but it seemed he would need to spend more of it. He hated it, and hated even more the uncertainty of the future. More of the same waited for him back home. He'd probably been declared dead long ago, his apartment rerented, the money in his bank account God only knew where. What was the law for people who died without beneficiaries? The government probably had his savings by now.

"I will be—" He started to tell her that he would pay her back at the earliest opportunity, but Josh put his hand on the small of Audrey's back, and jealousy as hot and sharp as lightning nearly tore him in two. He wanted to kill the man, rip him apart. He had to leave. Now.

Audrey was safe with two men who obviously felt protective of her, one of whom was probably in love with her. They'd had their misunderstandings, but her ex obviously realized now what he had lost. And Josh was the kind of man she should have in her life. Brian clenched his jaw. What the hell did he have to offer?

He glanced at the clock on the wall without registering the time. "I'm late," he said. "I better get going." And with a nod to all three of them he walked out the door, not allowing as much as a goodbye look at her, not a handshake, nothing. If they touched, his heart might have shattered.

He put on numbness like he would have a uniform and, closing the door behind him, he walked away.

She deserves a normal life. He repeated it over and over to himself on the way down to the lobby, avoiding to look at his alien reflection in the mirrored walls of the elevator. He looked like a gentleman tourist instead of a soldier.

The unreasonable fury, the violent anger he felt toward Josh scared him. He wanted to kill the man for touching Audrey, for having a right to be in her hotel room.

He was no better than a wounded beast out for blood.

And that was exactly why he needed to protect Audrey from himself. Except—he thought—the emotions that nearly overwhelmed him weren't altogether unreasonable. He was a man, watching another guy take the woman he loved.

"She deserves a normal life," he murmured to himself. Josh was the right choice for her.

And then it hit him that he'd never given her that. Didn't she deserve a *choice?*

If he truly was a soldier, why wasn't he fighting for her instead of retreating?

HAMID WALKED TOWARD the elevator as the light came on. The door opened. There was one man in there, staring straight ahead. *The negotiator.*

Hamid turned to a guest room, presenting his back to the man, and knocked. He heard the elevator door close just as the door in front of him opened.

"Yes?" An older woman looked at him, her pencil-thin eyebrows drawn to midforehead as she took in his hotel uniform.

"You requested help with opening the extra bed, Madam?"

She looked baffled. "No. Certainly not."

"I apologize. I must have the wrong room number." He smiled cordially and walked away.

He didn't go back to the elevators to push the call button; he went to the stairs. That man could be staying at the hotel—an extreme case of bad luck—or he could be here for him.

Hamid ran over in his mind what he'd seen in the lobby. No extra security, no sign that his plans had been discovered, that somebody was setting a trap. Still, he had to be careful. He took the stairs two at a time to the twenty-third floor where his men were setting up the second bomb in a linen supply closet.

AUDREY STOOD in the middle of the room, feeling as if a typhoon had swept through her soul. Josh and Trevor were talking, but she couldn't focus her mind on a single word. *Brian was gone.* Tears burned her eyes, threatening to spill. *Think about something else. Anything.*

"Are we still going downstairs to eat?" She said the first thing that came to her mind, although she couldn't have cared less about food at the moment, wasn't sure if she could swallow a bite.

*Breathe in, breathe out.*

"I was going to tell you just before that guy came in. Funny that he stopped by, isn't it?" Josh watched her. "With him having been already paid and all. I hope he didn't form some unnatural attachment to you." He shook his head. "Anyway, the restaurant, even the ballroom, are closed to the public today. There's some huge reception going on. The German ambassador finished off his term and he's going back home, and the other diplomats and whatnot are giving a big send-off party. But there are plenty of great places in the city." He smiled and took her hand.

She barely registered his words. "Would you guys mind if we ordered in? I don't really feel up to going out."

"Sure."

"Of course."

The tears were coming. She backed away. It wasn't as if she was embarrassed to cry in front of them, it was that she didn't want to have to explain why she was crying when everything was finally back to being good as far as they were concerned. Nicky would be here soon.

"You order, I'll grab some ice." She picked the ice bucket off the counter and turned as the first tear spilled.

"I can get it." Josh was right behind her.

"I don't mind," she said. "I need to stretch my legs." And then she was out the door, relieved when he didn't follow.

She leaned against the wall and let out a big shivering breath. Brian was gone.

She had expected it, of course, but still it seemed too sudden. She hadn't anticipated how hard it would hit her. She had thought maybe— What? That he would ask for her phone number? That when their lives settled back at home, they could— She couldn't even finish the sentence. It seemed ridiculous now.

He left. Like that. What they had shared meant nothing to him. God, it meant the world to her. She had been what? Swift release after years of forced abstinence?

Tears washed down her face and she hiccupped. She wiped her eyes with the back of her hand. She'd always been a messy crier. The elevator dinged. Someone was coming to their floor. She headed for the staircase, not wanting to be seen like this.

She set the ice bucket down and leaned against the railing, took a couple of calming breaths that didn't help at all. The sound of footsteps came from above. Someone was coming down the stairs. Wasn't there any place she could get some privacy?

She looked up and saw a waiter. What was he doing in the staircase? He greeted her politely and she nodded to him. Then her gaze fell to his right arm, left bare by the short-sleeved white uniform shirt. A giant crowned tiger lunged on his tattooed skin.

Hamid?

They were here. The ambassador's gala. It all made sense in a flash.

She gripped the railing and must have emitted some noise, because the man looked back at her. She made for the door, but he was already there, pulling a handgun from the back of his waistband.

A month ago, she would have screamed, and if her legs weren't shaking too hard for the job, she would have tried to run. But the jungle had changed her. She rushed the man instead, bent her waist and slammed into his midsection, pushing him against the door. He dropped the gun, probably more from surprise than the force of her attack, and they both dove for it, reaching it at the same time.

She did scream then, putting her full lung capacity to good use. "Help!"

But it was too late, he was gaining the upper hand fast, rolling her under him, bending her arm until the barrel was pointing at her head.

Blood stained the white shirt on his shoulder. There was murder in his eyes.

"Brian!" she screamed again, on instinct before she realized it was no use, he was already gone.

And then like an apparition, he was there, lifting Hamid off her and throwing him down the stairs. The man rolled but came up quick at the landing. He still had the gun and aimed it at Brian.

"If you shoot, it will echo enough in this staircase for everyone to hear. You'll never make it down without being caught," she said, desperate to distract him enough for Brian to make some kind of a move.

Hamid kept the gun on him. "The people of this country would rise up to support me if I were caught. They want what I want, to be rid of the foreign dogs and their support for the false king." He spat. "When I win, there'll be celebrations on the streets."

She backed away, giving Brian room to maneuver. "If you do this, there'll be chaos and fear. Foreign investors will pull out, jobs will be lost, your people will suffer," she argued to keep his attention.

Hamid sneered at her. "Pain is necessary for growth."

"There are Malaysians in this hotel, guests and employees, as many as foreigners."

"They die as heroes." He braced the gun with both hands.

This was it. She snapped her head around, looked up as if she'd heard someone coming down the stairs above them. By the time she looked back, Brian was flying through the air, lunging at the man. Her ploy had worked. She'd distracted him long enough.

She rushed after Brian, but by the time she reached them they were tangled together, growling with effort to gain control of the weapon. Help. She needed to get help. She turned to rush back to the suite. Hamid heaved against Brian and smacked his bad knee to the railing. His hand slipped on the gun.

No time to go anywhere. He needed help now. When he turned, she threw herself on Hamid's head, thinking to cut off his air, or at the least, obstruct his vision. He bit her stomach. The sharp pain distracted her for a moment.

"Get away from here." Brian was pushing against her with his shoulder.

But she twisted finally and gained some leverage,

smashed her elbow into Hamid's face with all her strength. She heard his nose break and thought she might be sick. She drew a deep breath, struck again. "That's for my sister."

And then she heard Brian laugh, and she turned to him just as he got up, holding the gun. Hamid wasn't moving.

"I love it when you talk tough," he said, and pulled her to him. "I can't believe you beat him unconscious."

She did? She glanced at Hamid, then back at Brian, horrified at first, then relieved. "I did. I'm not a violent person, but he just pushed me over the edge."

"You don't have to explain it to me, honey." He brushed his lips against hers. "Are you okay?" he asked even as he was stepping away from her to tie up Hamid with his belt and throw him over his shoulder.

"You came back."

"I love you. I'm going to want to talk to you about that when this is over." He started up the stairs, but when she followed, too stunned to respond, he shook his head. "I'm going to dump him out in the hallway so he doesn't block the stairs."

"All the ambassadors are downstairs," she blurted, as the thought cut through the rest of the confused jumble in her head.

"Where was he coming from?" Brian opened the door, took Hamid out, then came back in a split second.

"Upstairs."

"I want you to start walking down. Go as fast as you can. When you reach the lobby, pull the fire alarm." He handed her the pistol. "If you see anyone you recognize from our little vacation in the woods, shoot first, ask questions later."

Her brain was still on *"I love you."* Then he started up the stairs and it snapped her back to the here and now.

"Shouldn't we sound the alarm right away?"

He shook his head. "As soon as we do, people will flood the stairs. I need a couple of minutes to see if I can find the rest of the men, or at least one of them, and get a location on that bomb. If it's already set, there might not be enough time to get the hotel evacuated. Our best bet is to find the damn thing so I can disarm it."

"You can do that?"

"Trust me," he said.

And she did. "I should tell Trevor and Josh."

"There's no time for explanations, Audrey. Would you rather try to save two or everyone?"

She nodded and opened her mouth to tell him she loved him, too, but he was already gone. She flew down the stairs, taking them two and three at a time. They had a hotel full of people to save. And they were just the team to do it.

WHERE WAS HE? Audrey scanned the crowd behind the police line. She'd spotted Trevor and Josh on the other side of the square filled with hundreds of hotel guests, but she couldn't see Brian anywhere.

Josh was making his way over to her. Great.

"Thank God." He put his arms around her when he reached her.

She pulled away.

"Look," he said. "I didn't just come here as Trev's friend. I came because of you, too."

"Josh, I—"

"I missed you," he interrupted her. "I thought about this. You don't have to adopt. We can find an egg donor who'd be willing to be a surrogate mother. The baby would still be mine."

"It's not going to work."

"Why not? I'm willing to overlook—"

"I'm in love with another man."

The look on his face was priceless. Clearly, this was not something he had ever considered.

She left him and pushed through the sea of people to the front, from where she could see the hotel's main door. They'd been out here for an hour. The bomb-sniffing dogs were inside, going from floor to floor, the bomb squad robot waiting on the sidewalk for his turn once the bomb was found.

She had told everything she knew to the police at least four times, and they'd finally let her go. And now she had nothing else to do but obsess over the man she loved.

Then she saw him coming through the front doors, and yelled his name. He stopped, scanned the crowd, spotted her when she waved.

"Got a job?" She pointed to the security tag on his shirt when he came over.

He drew up an eyebrow. "I found it. This way I don't have to stop every five seconds, explaining to someone what I'm doing here."

All right, so he wasn't a strictly go-by-the-rules type of person. She kind of liked that about him.

He pulled her through the police line and nobody questioned them. She threw herself into his arms, not caring about the horde of reporters and TV cameras trained on the building and at them.

"Come here." He pulled her toward a side entrance, one that led to the restaurant. He flashed his badge to the officer at the door and they were let in without questions. He locked the door behind them.

"What happened?"

"We got the bombs. There were two of them—both disarmed now. They already took out Hamid and his men through the back. They're taking the bombs next and then as soon as the staircase is cleaned they're going to let people back in."

"Cleaned?"

He moved closer, his blue eyes reflecting her face. She had gotten lost in those eyes and she wanted to stay lost forever.

"They have to get the bloodstains off the walls," he said, and for a moment she had to think what he was talking about.

"Was it bad?" She looked him over for injury, but couldn't find anything obvious.

"A couple of guys. I had to stop them." His voice was deep and breathless, as if he found it hard to talk.

Her gaze slid from his masculine lips to his wide shoulders. *Okay now, get a grip.* The man was coming from a fight. This was not the time to jump him.

She stepped back and bumped into a palm tree, glanced around. The restaurant had been transformed into a jungle theme for the ambassador's gala, complete with hundreds of potted palms, orchids blooming on every table and even an artificial stream.

For a moment she had a flashback to the days they'd spent together, what they'd gone through. She had a deeper connection to this man than any other she had known before. And he loved her. The joy of his declaration slammed into her all over again. They'd made it, the danger was over, and he loved her.

"Audrey—" he started to say something, but seemed to change his mind, and instead he kissed her hard on the mouth.

The meeting of their lips was like a switch being thrown—from sanity to insanity in half a second flat. She felt carried away on a mad river that rushed forth wildly, uncontrollable. Reason slipped beyond their reach, and they rode the rolling waters, hanging on to each other.

There were no degrees to the kiss. No tentative brushing of the lips first, no playful nibbles, no slow opening. He took everything at once with a fevered meeting of the tongues.

His hands cupped her face as he drank her, then moved lower, running over her body as thoroughly as if he were taking inventory. And then he reached the bottom of her dress and pulled it above her waist, grounded his hardness into her, bringing moisture to the V of her legs.

Her breath caught at the sudden onslaught of sensations, and she let her head fall against the palm tree, her hands pressed against the solid muscles of his chest. But then she didn't want even that little distance between them and moved her hands to his back, then to his tapered waist, to his firm buttocks. And she pulled him closer still.

He groaned into her mouth, and she felt a tug on her underwear, then it was gone, replaced by his warm hands that caressed her hips and went lower. Her eyes flew open, and as she stared at the crowd outside the restaurant window, she let out a squeal. "Brian!"

He turned his head to see what startled her, looked back, his eyes hooded with passion. "It's mirrored glass. They can't see in."

But reason was gaining a toehold. "What if security comes?"

This was madness. How had they gotten here so fast? How had he cut through all her defenses? She was a mature, reasonable, conservative woman. What happened to making love behind closed doors in a bed?

He nibbled her earlobe as he slipped a finger inside her. "Everybody is on the twenty-third floor. They'll be there for at least another hour."

Pleasure pinged through her and grew, rolling, gathering into an irresistible mass that made her quiver. She reached for his belt and despite her shaking fingers, made pretty quick work of it, pushed his pants and boxers down at the same time, gasped when he sprang free against her belly.

"Look who is happy to see me." She caressed his

silky hardness, enjoying the way his eyes darkened, thrilled at the way her touch affected him.

He leaned into her, but the potted palm tree behind her wobbled, too unsteady to hold their combined weight. He lifted her up, her legs wrapped around him, her damp center pressed against his hardness.

Holding her with one hand, he cleared a table with the other and lay her down, holding her legs in place. Then he was inside her with one steady thrust, and took her over and over until she drowned in the pleasure of it and screamed his name.

But he wasn't done with her yet. He was a powerful man and put every bit of that power into use, pleasuring her body, marking every dazed cell of hers as his. It was too much. She couldn't.

Her body felt like a live wire. What he did to her seemed unreal, impossible. But she felt tension build deep inside her once again, and when he finally poured his hot seed into her, his body shuddering, a deep groan torn from his chest, she sank into yet another wave of pleasure.

He didn't pull out, but instead lifted her and moved back, sat on the floor with her still on his lap, leaning his back against a giant potted palm, resting his forehead against hers.

Then after a while, when their breathing evened, he looked up and smiled.

"What?"

"You have orchid blossoms in your hair."

"I've gone native." She smiled back at him.

He nodded. "You certainly have."

Then his expression grew more serious. "Audrey, this is not why I came back...." He fell silent as if looking for the right words.

"I'm glad just the same that we got around to it." She grinned.

"You know, when I got you away from Omar's camp, I thought I was rescuing you, but I think at the end, you ended up rescuing me."

Her heart flipped over from the way he was looking at her. "We rescued each other."

He brushed his lips against hers, then pulled back. "You take away my reason. I tried to fight it. I'm not a hundred percent convinced this is the right thing for you. But I love you like mad, there's no help for it. It's like malaria. Once it gets into the blood, there's no getting it out." He glanced away, then back at her again. "I need to ask you a question."

She nodded.

"Who is Josh to you?" His face was as serious as she'd ever seen it.

"My ex-husband," she responded, unsure what that had to do with anything.

He put his hand over her heart. "Who is he here?"

It took less than a second to come up with a response. "Nobody."

He hugged her so fiercely, she could scarcely breathe.

"You've been worrying about that?" He had to be kidding.

"I'm a man with no family, no job, no home— very little to recommend me, really. But I'm a hard worker and I'm scared of little. I would work like hell to make a good life for us if you agreed to share yours with me. I know there are a hundred men out there who'd be better for you, could offer you more, but nobody on this earth could love you more than I. Can you give me a chance?"

She blinked the tears back from her eyes. "Yes," she said, and threw her arms around him. "If you can give *us* a chance. I have a daughter. We come as a package deal."

His reply came slowly. "It's almost too good to believe. I would love nothing more. I never pictured— but I might never again be the man I once was." He pulled back and searched her eyes. "My father, after the war he was different. He could never find his way back. I don't know if I can."

She smoothed the furrow from his forehead. "I fell in love with the man you are now."

His beautiful blue eyes sparkled with emotion. "Can you say that again?"

"I love you, Brian Welkins."

He held her tight, and she felt him harden inside her.

She grinned. Was he for real? "Making up for time lost, are we?"

"I'm all uncivilized. See what you'll have to put up with?"

"I like uncivilized," she said and rotated her hips. "I think I developed a taste for the wild and untamed."

He grinned, sudden relief flooding his face, followed by a look of mischief, and pushed in deeper. "Prepare for jungle heat."

*Epilogue*

He couldn't wait to get there and hold that little baby in his hands. Brian picked up the suitcases. Wow. What had she packed, iron ore? Then he heard a faint clinking—jars of baby food.

"Are you sure you're ready for this?"

He smiled at Audrey and Mei. "More than sure."

"You're not going to feel outnumbered? Some men would say three women in one house are too many."

"They don't know my girls." He winked at her. "You can never have too much love. I can't wait to see our new baby."

"I'm crazy about you," Audrey said.

As always, the simple declaration took his breath away. To have her, Mei and another baby soon was such an unexpected and humbling blessing.

"You have the adoption papers?"

"Right here." He patted his left inner pocket.

"It will be perfect, you know, them being so close in age." Audrey grabbed the diaper bag.

"They'll be like you and Nicky." He grinned. "We'll have to give them some little brothers to keep them on their toes." He was looking forward to having a large family.

"We have to stop by Nicky's. I forgot to drop off the key so she can come and water the orchids." She grabbed the dropping pacifier with the reflexes of a seasoned soldier, and pushed it back between Mei's rosy lips before the baby even missed it. "Business is taken care of?"

God, he loved them. He nodded. "Some old buddies of mine are going to take over while we're gone."

The business he'd built in the past year was thriving, offering survival-type team-building retreats to major corporations. He enjoyed his small company, founded with the $500,000 reward from the Malaysian government that had been the bounty on Omar's head. They had Hamid in custody, too. And since Brian had been instrumental in the guerilla leader's capture, he was going to get yet another reward. But even without it, his business brought in more than enough.

The work made him feel useful, providing him with enough that was familiar so that he felt comfortable stretching and trying new angles. He'd been a soldier once, then a prisoner, reduced to the level of a wild animal. But neither of those things defined him now.

Mei spit the pacifier half-across the room and reached her chubby little hands toward him. "Da-da," she said.

And he smiled, because that's exactly what he was. Father to the sweetest little girl, husband to the most exceptional woman. The past didn't matter. He was what he made of himself with his new family.

"Let's go then." Audrey took a last glance at the house. "We better not miss the plane."

"It's kind of fitting that we'll celebrate our first wedding anniversary in KL."

"Very." She gave him a quick kiss, then winked. "Hope we'll get a chance to sneak into the jungle."

"Count on it, wife." He recaptured her lips and deepened the kiss.